The Diaries
of Giacomo Meyerbeer

Frontispiece. Portrait of Meyerbeer standing. Steel engraving by D. J. Pound, after a photograph by Mayall, part of "The Drawing Room Portrait Gallery of Eminent Personages" (London, 1855).

The Diaries
of Giacomo Meyerbeer

Volume 3
The Years of Celebrity
1850–1856

Translated, Edited,
and Annotated
by Robert Ignatius Letellier

Madison • Teaneck
Fairleigh Dickinson University Press
London: Associated University Presses

Associated University Presses
440 Forsgate Drive
Cranbury, NJ 08512

Associated University Presses
16 Barter Street
London WC1A 2AH, England

Associated University Presses
P.O. Box 338, Port Credit
Mississauga, Ontario
Canada L5G 4L8

The paper used in this publication meets the requiremts
of the American National Standard for Permanence of Paper
for Printed Library Materials Z39.48-1984.

Library of Congress Cataloging-in-Publication Data

Meyerbeer, Giacomo, 1791–1864.
    [Diaries. English]
    The diaries of Giacomo Meyerbeer / translated, edited, and
annotated by Robert Ignatius Letellier.
      p. cm.
    Translation of the untitled and unpublished German diaries.
    Includes index.
    Contents : v. 1. 1791–1839
    1. Meyerbeer, Giacomo, 1791–1864—Diaries. 2. Composers—France-
-Diaries. I. Le Tellier, Robert Ignatius. II. Title.
    ISBN 0-8386-3789-2 (vol. 1; alk. paper)
    ISBN 0-8386-3843-0 (vol. 2; alk. paper)
    ISBN 0-8386-3844-9 (vol. 3; alk. paper)
    ML410.M61A3   2002
    782.1'092—dc21   98-52129
    [b]   CIP
                                           MN

PRINTED IN THE UNITED STATES OF AMERICA

Contents

List of Illustrations

List of Musical Examples

Introduction

THE HERITAGE OF THE 1840S

The worldwide successes of *Robert le Diable* (1831) and *Les Huguenots* (1836) had established Meyerbeer as the leading opera composer of his day. During the following decade, he built on this achievement in different ways. The time was ripe for return to his Prussian homeland, where King Friedrich Wilhelm IV had appointed him royal *Generalmusikdirektor* in Berlin (11 June 1842), a position that carried immense prestige but consumed valuable time and exposed the composer to irksome intrigues. The second half of the decade, introduced by *Ein Feldlager in Schlesien* (7 December 1844), the festival opera written for the opening of the newly rebuilt Berlin Court Opera, and the incidental music for Michael Beer's *Struensee* (19 September 1846), initiated a new period of creativity that was to culminate in the completion and production of *Le Prophète* on 16 April 1849, a huge triumph and the high point of Meyerbeer's artistic career.

THE CONSOLIDATION OF SUCCESS

The 1850s represent a unique period for Meyerbeer, perhaps the zenith of his career. Nothing illustrates this more than the success of *Le Prophète*, the fortunes of which were to dominate the next four years of the composer's life. The deeply serious theme of this opera, its dark musical *tinta*, the moving human situations of the tragic story, and the powerful, vivid music seized the imagination, as did the unusual depiction of the mother-son relationship. There were also plenty of opportunities for sensation and display—and some musical numbers, such as the Coronation March and the Skaters' Ballet, as well as the two alto arias for the fascinating character of Fidès, became extremely popular.

The year 1850 can be chronicled in relation to the triumphal progress of *Le Prophète*. Meyerbeer returned to Berlin after the heady days of the première and reprise of this his third *grand opéra* in Paris, and went first to Dresden and then to Vienna to supervise the first performances in both capitals (30 January 1850 and 28 February 1850, respectively). Scenes of rapturous acclaim greeted the

11

composer in both cities: he was called onto the stage, showered with flowers, and in Vienna crowned with the laurels of victory by the muses in a ceremony, the ultimate symbolic accolade of his artistic achievement. These events were consolidated by the first Berlin production (28 April 1850), where he was again presented with laurels, and the resumption of the performances in Paris (7 October 1850, with Marietta Alboni in the role of Fidès for the first time).

By the end of the year Meyerbeer could record that the opera had been given in some forty theaters across the world. The progress continued: by 5 May 1851 Pauline Viardot-Garcia could tell the composer that she had sung Fidès one hundred times; by 14 July 1851 it had attained its one-hundredth performance at the Paris Opéra; on 17 March 1852 it was in St. Petersburg; on 26 December 1852 it reached Italy, and was given for the first time in Florence; and by 25 November 1853 in New York. It was the favorite work of state occasions and royal galas, chosen to celebrate Louis Napoleon's election as president (9 January 1852), as a command performance for the visiting queen of Spain (30 September 1853), and to welcome the king of the Belgians to Berlin (9 May 1853).

Meyerbeer was indeed at the acme of his success: not only was he now commander of the Legion of Honor (4 May 1849), but the University of Jena conferred an honorary degree of doctor of music (14 July 1850), and further decorations followed from the monarchs of Saxony (1850), Austria (1851) and Bavaria (1853). King Friedrich Wilhelm IV ordered his portrait to be painted by Begas for his gallery of famous Prussian contemporaries (1851), and Queen Victoria sent him a carefully chosen gift as a mark of her and Prince Albert's personal esteem and admiration (1852).

LIFE IN BERLIN

The composer himself lived very quietly. The early 1850s saw him firmly established in his home city, and after the renewed conquest of Paris, Dresden, Vienna, and Berlin, he entered a period of calm, reflecting his even greater international prestige. He remained for the most part of each year in Berlin, deeply involved in the rich artistic life of the city. He would work in the mornings, receive and pay calls in the afternoon, and attend the theater or concerts in the evening.

The evocation of Berlin in the pages of Meyerbeer's diaries enables one to grasp the breadth of its diverse intellectual attractions. Regular performances by the Singakademie and the Domchor reveal a fine choral tradition and show the extent to which the Bach revival had taken hold (Meyerbeer participated in the centenary of Bach's death, commemorated on 30 July 1850). The symphony-soirées, developing from the quartet and then concert evenings established by Karl Möser in 1813, were another recurrent feature, and throw much light on the repertoire in mid-nineteenth century Germany, with Beethoven, Mozart, and

Mendelssohn already firm concert favorites. Meyerbeer's constant attendance at the opera shows the vitality of the Berlin houses, with the Court Opera and Italian Opera providing a characteristic and varied repertoire. As in Paris, he frequented the playhouse constantly, and the account of his visits to the Schauspielhaus and the Friedrich-Wilhelmstätisches-Theater conjures up a world even more remote than his theatrical annals of the French capital.

THE COURT COMPOSER

While Meyerbeer had long given up his direction of the Royal Opera, he could not escape the official aspects of musical life in the capital. His appointment to the senate of the Berlin Academy of Arts (14 August 1851), his membership in the royal order Pour le Mérite, and his close association with the monarch and other members of the royal family meant that he was constantly expected to attend meetings, write reports on musical matters, and supervise the regular concerts held at court by command of the music-loving king. These concerts form a constant point of reference in these years, and provide an intimate perspective on the social and aesthetic tastes prevailing in contemporary high society. Meyerbeer's choice of repertoire, the artists he selected to perform the programs, and the pleasure this afforded to Friedrich Wilhelm IV and to Prince and Princess Wilhelm of Prussia is a remarkable and informative record.

MUSIC FOR OFFICIAL OCCASIONS

Involvement in these diverse aspects of the intellectual and social life of Berlin had important consequences for Meyerbeer's creativity as a composer. Every year saw the arrival of a new work, usually written at the command of the king to mark some national event or circumstance in the life of the royal family. In 1850 Meyerbeer composed his second *Fackeltanz* for the wedding of Princess Charlotte with Crown Prince Georg of Saxe-Meiningen; in 1851 he wrote a special chorus, *Fredericus Magnus,* for interpolation into *Ein Feldlager in Schlesien,* as well as the *Ode an Rauch* to celebrate the unveiling of the sculptor's famous monument to Frederick the Great; in 1852 it was the cantata *Maria und ihr Genius,* written out of friendship for Prince Carl of Prussia, on the occasion of his silver wedding; in 1853 came the third *Fackeltanz,* this time for the wedding of Princess Anna with Prince Friedrich of Hesse. The most significant of these commissions was his eight-part setting of Psalm 91, written at the request of the king for performance by the Domchor, a piece that was to become Meyerbeer's most famous religious composition.

The Royal Friend

Meyerbeer's friendship with the Prussian royal family is perhaps the most striking feature of his life in Berlin. The intimacy and affection shown him by King
Friedrich Wilhelm IV is remarkable evidence of the principles of openness evinced
by this genuinely idealistic monarch. The revolutionary events of 1848 had frightened the king, and his subsequent decline into increasing ill health and mental
trauma would see the inexorable rise of antiliberal and nationalistic influences
during the regency and monarchy of his younger brother, Wilhelm. But the genuine freedom and tolerance of these days when "a Jewish banker who happened to
compose music" (to use Richard Wagner's notorious phrase) could be a cherished
figure at court is illuminating, and a salutary antidote to the sad rise of anti-
Semitism and xenophobia so characteristic of later nineteenth-century Germany.

Much the same attitude prevailed in France, where Meyerbeer was held in
particular affection by the Emperor Napoleon III and the Empress Eugénie. They
were devoted to his music, and held him in great personal affection. Only imperial intervention secured permission for the première of *L'Étoile du Nord* (with
its glorification of Peter the Great) in the face of France's growing political crisis
with Russia. Meyerbeer was invited to many court events, and even included in
the guest list of the imperial *villeggiatura* at Fontainebleau (8 November 1853).

In Paris, and especially in Berlin, Meyerbeer attained the fullness of his social and professional success. One cannot over-emphasize the significance of this
for him, both as musician and as emancipated Jew.

The Realization of a Lifelong Dream

If *Le Prophète* brought Meyerbeer renown as a definitive statement of his perception of *grand opéra* as an art form, the early years of the 1850s saw the slow but
steady realization of another aspect of the composer's operatic vision. Even in
his youth, on his first visit to Paris, he had expressed the wish to create an *opéra
comique*. On 31 December 1815 he had referred to "the special dream of my life:
writing something for the Théâtre Feydeau." *Opéra comique* represented the other
vital branch of the venerable French operatic tradition, which had become bifur-
cated with such rich consequences since the famous *guerre des buffons* in the
mid-eighteenth century. This division had seen the triumph of the "natural" simplicity of Rousseau's *Le Devin du village* (1752) over the stiff pathos of the *tragédie
lyrique* embodied in the grand mythological-classical works of Lully and Rameau.

Meyerbeer's move toward the comic mode had been initiated by the composition of *Ein Feldlager in Schlesien*, which, in spite of its serious patriotic purpose, has all the characteristics of the lighter genre (folk elements, smaller forms
and simpler structures, a basically cheerful and optimistic worldview). It was

Meyerbeer's intention from the beginning to reshape this *Singspiel* for the international stage in terms of the traditions of *opéra comique*, and work on the process began with Scribe on 20 June 1849, soon after the successful production of *Le Prophète*. Indeed, the composer's appetite for life was never keener. Far from being drained by the tortuous processes of creating, rehearsing, and mounting the première of the dark and complex Anabaptist tragedy, he was already living in the very different mental world of his next work. Composition of the new opera, begun on 1 August 1849, trailed off during the flurry of activity surrounding the Dresden-Vienna-Berlin productions of *Le Prophète*, but on 11 June 1850 he started composing again, and was involved in some way or another with work on the opera for the next five years.

The years 1849–53 record the various stages of the composition of *L'Étoile du Nord*, and give an extraordinary insight into Meyerbeer's working methods. Scrupulously studying the text, writing it out, and mulling over it, he would compose pieces, often while traveling, preferring to test them out later on the piano; sometimes he was happy with an idea or a piece, but on other occasions he ruthlessly jettisoned drafts and composed several versions of a phrase or the piece in question. Periods of great productivity were followed by fallow months when the pressures of family and social commitments hampered the flow of creativity. Reflective process was essential to the dramatic aspects of his operatic composition, reminding one of Schiller's aesthetic distinction between the "sentimental" or analytic artist who reflects, reduces, and reconstructs, and the "naïve" or more intuitively spontaneous creator who reproduces impressions of the outside world unreflectively, unmodified by his own interpretation of it (see Schiller's aesthetic discourse *Über naive und sentimentalische Dichtung*, 1795–96).

The usual lengthy process of rehearsing the new *opéra comique* began in September 1853, and in spite of political sensitivities surrounding the outbreak of the Crimean War, the première of *L'Étoile du Nord* on 16 February 1854 was another high point in the composer's life. In this score he moved to a new stage in his artistic development: despite a lightness of touch, a melodic fecundity, and a strong sense of humor, the musical language of this work was altogether unusual, showing a strong penchant for the ironic and for extremities, even exaggerations, of harmony, rhythm, and orchestration, with an inventive and exploratory handling of form. Although immensely successful, it is in its own way a challenging, specialized, almost mannerist work that never captured the heart of the public in the same way that the human drama and musical prodigality of *Les Huguenots* have always done.

The passion to involve himself ever more deeply in the world of *opéra comique* was still strong in Meyerbeer, and on 13 May 1854 he began enthusiastic work on the libretto and music of another opera of this kind, *Le Pardon de Ploërmel*, better known to the world as *Dinorah*. This new work, with a libretto by Barbier and Carré based on a Breton pastoral theme, was to absorb his creative attention for the next five years; indeed, it became an irresistibly sweet compulsion, leading to the neglect of work on his cherished project of *L'Africaine* and even endangering the working relationship with his bemused and celebrated principal collaborator, the formidable Eugène Scribe (see 8 and 10 October 1855).

While never ultimately attaining the enduring popularity of the *grands opéras*, over the next few years *L'Étoile du Nord* nonetheless repeated the international triumph of *Le Prophète*, adding further renown to the composer's already vast international reputation. As with *Le Prophète*, Meyerbeer himself supervised the first performances all over Europe, and his detailed accounts of the rehearsals and premières in Stuttgart (27 September 1854), Dresden (9 February 1855), London (19 July 1855), and Vienna (29 December 1855) relive the triumphant progress of *Le Prophète*.

THE RETURN TO ITALY

Immediately after his extended stay in Vienna (28 October 1855 to 6 January 1856), Meyerbeer left for Italy on his most significant visit since his youthful years of apprenticeship (1816–26). The first four months of 1856 were spent there (10 January to 25 April): based in Venice, he traveled throughout northern and central Italy, attending every possible performance of opera, ballet, and drama, noting in minute detail his reactions to a host of artists, especially singers, of varying standards and qualities, and in the process painting a vivid canvas of musical life in the remoter theaters of the period. It is a fascinating chronicle, and alerts the reader to the existence and achievements of many half-forgotten figures (like Rota, Mazzucato, Pedrotti, Carrer, Apolloni, De Ferrari, and many impresarios and singers active in Venice, Padua, Verona, Siena, Florence, Parma, Brescia, Genoa, and Milan).

The awe and enthusiasm that greeted him everywhere on his return to Italy after so many decades, the number of old friends he saw again, and the general rapture of the experience mark a unique period in his life, and the fulfillment of all the dreams of his youth when Italy had initially beckoned him as into a garden of delights. The delight was now fully his own.

ET IN ARCADIA EGO

The way of life is such, of course, that no joy is ever left unqualified. These extraordinary years in Meyerbeer's life are no exception to this. The dizzy height of his triumph in the months after the première of *Le Prophète* was clouded by the death on 27 March 1850 of his beloved brother Wilhelm Beer. The experience was a devastating blow to Meyerbeer and all his interests, both social and artistic;

this was intensified by the sad demise of his sister-in-law Betty, the forgotten wife of his tragic brother Heinrich, later in the same year (7 September 1850).

From then on the grim reaping of death was to become a gradually increasing ostinato in Meyerbeer's life. The composer Lortzing, a purveyor of joy and happiness if there ever was one, was next (21 January 1851), to be followed by Spontini, one of Meyerbeer's great predecessors in the evolution of French *grand opéra* (24 January 1851). They were succeeded by others whom he had known well, or who had played some important role in his life, like Caroline von Weber (23 February 1852), Gouin's wife (29 March 1852), the famous author Ludwig Tieck (28 April 1853), the influential Parisian journalist Armand Bertin (12 January 1854), the librettist Gaetano Rossi (25 January 1855), the writer, councillor, and man of the theater Karl Winkler (24 September 1856), and the kindly Berlin journalist Siegfried Josephy (22 October 1856).

But worst of all was the passing of Meyerbeer's beloved mother, Amalia Beer. The rehearsals and triumphant première of *L'Étoile du Nord* were overshadowed by the onset of Amalia's final illness, and the supreme sorrow of her death on 26 June 1854. This was the ultimate reminder of the sadness and transience of life in the midst of its diversities and occasional joys. Meyerbeer was never to feel the pain of parting so acutely again, and the thinness of his diary entries at this time reveal the depletion of his emotional energies.

INTIMATIONS OF MORTALITY AND THE SEARCH FOR REPOSE

After the exertions of *Le Prophète*, Meyerbeer had withdrawn to the mountains of Austria in August–September 1849. Visits to the health resorts, so often undertaken as recuperative trips, palliatives for his chronic alimentary problems, had often served as moments of repose and stimulus for his creative process. With the increasing challenges to his health and energy, and with the growing burdens of sorrow, these visits became more regular. The little Belgian resort town of Spa that Meyerbeer had visited many years before, where in 1830 he had completed *Robert le Diable*, now acquired a new meaning. The composer returned to Spa every year during the summer from 1850 to 1856, with the exception of 1853, when he went to Dieppe instead. (He needed to be near Paris in the weeks leading to the rehearsals of *L'Étoile du Nord*.)

In the charm and friendliness of Spa, deep in the woods of the Belgian Ardennes, where during the season elements of Parisian society reconvened in miniature, Meyerbeer found much peace and consolation. The beauty of nature, the waters of the famous springs, and the kindness of many friends and admirers were a therapy for him. These times were treasured moments in the composer's busy life, a sort of idyllic retreat as he became older.

Certainly his experience of an unexpected and devastating collapse of health during his sojourn in Boulogne (4 September–5 October 1852) as the result of a cholera infection, as well as the chronic indisposition of his wife Minna and his daughter Caecilie, were reminders to him of the fragility of well-being and the tenuousness of life itself.

Meyerbeer's progressively weakening constitution and the loss of so many loved ones, culminating in the death of his trusted confidant Louis Gouin on 13 October 1856, were intimations of his own mortality, and add an undertow of sorrow to this brilliant period of attainment and success, the crown of a glittering career, a life lived for music.

Abbreviations Used in This Volume:

BT = *Giacomo Meyerbeer: Briefwechsel und Tagebücher* (Berlin: De Gruyter, 1960 [vols. 1 and 2] and 1970, ed. Heinz Becker; 1975 [vol. 3] and 1985 [vol. 4], ed. Heinz and Gudrun Becker; 1998 [vol. 5], ed. Sabine Henze-Döhring, with the collaboration of Hans Moeller.

Clément & Larousse = Félix Clément and Pierre Larousse, *Dictionnaire des Opéras (Dictionnaire Lyrique): contenant l'analyse et la nomenclature de tous les opéras, opéras-comiques, opérettes et drames lyriques représentés en France et à l'étranger depuis l'origine de ces genres d'ouvrages jusqu'à nos jours. Revu et mis à jour par Arthur Pougin,* 2 vols. (1905; reprint, New York: Da Capo, 1969).

DGM = *The Diaries of Giacomo Meyerbeer,* vol. 1, *1791–1839: The Early Years, Italy and the Parisian Triumphs,* translated, edited, and annotated by Robert Ignatius Letellier (Madison, N.J.: Fairleigh Dickinson University Press, 1999).

Loewenberg = Alfred Loewenberg, *Annals of Opera, 1597–1940, Compiled from Original Sources by Alfred Loewenberg, with an Introduction by Edward J. Dent,* 2d ed., revised and corrected (New York: Rowman & Littlefield, 1970).

Richel = Veronica C. Richel, *The German Stage, 1767–1890: A Directory of Playwrights and Plays,* Bibliographies and Indexes in the Performing Arts, 7 (New York, Westport, and London: Greenwood Press, 1988).

Wicks = Charles Beaumont Wicks, *The Parisian Stage: Alphabetical Indexes of Plays and Author: Part 3 (1831–1850)* and *Part 4 (1851–1875),* University of Alabama Studies, 14 (Tuscaloosa: University of Alabama Press, 1961, 1967).

The Diaries
of Giacomo Meyerbeer

1850

Tuesday 1 January. May God be with me! May Heaven bless this new year. May it be a year of fruitfulness, of peace and of prosperity; may it be a year of peace and unity for all mankind; may the world be freed of cholera.[1] May heaven bless my beloved mother, my dear wife, Minna, my three lovely children, Blanca, Caecilie, and Cornelie, my brother Wilhelm and his family, and me myself. Amen.

I had to work until midnight last night, in order to complete all my preparations for departure. At eight o'clock this morning I left for Brussels by rail, where I arrived only at seven o'clock in the evening. On the journey I met the well-known M. de Persigny (adjutant to the president, Louis Napoleon, and now ambassador in Berlin)[2] and M. de Lacour (French ambassador in Vienna),[3] whose acquaintance I have only made just now. The whole landscape from Paris to Brussels was covered in snow. I wrote to Gouin about the litany in act 3 of *Les Huguenots*,[4] Rossini etc. The change of air has had a beneficial effect on my cough.

Wednesday 2 January. Left at 7:30 in the morning by steam train for Cologne, where I arrived only at seven o'clock in the evening. Since I wanted to stay in Deutz in order to be nearer the train in the morning, I needed to cross the Rhine, but the bridge had been carried away by the severe winter weather, and I had to negotiate the river by steamer.

Thursday 3 January. Left early at 7:30 by steam train for Hanover, where I arrived at 7:30 in the evening. During the journey today I worked on the duet between Prascovia and Catherine.[5]

Friday 4 January. The train, which should leave Hanover at ten o'clock, could only depart at 11:15 on account of the delayed arrival of the Cologne train that links up with it. We thus reached Potsdam only at 9:30 in the evening, where I stayed overnight so as not to arrive in Berlin on a Friday. During the course of the day I worked on Catherine's couplets (act 1) with, it seems to me, considerable success.[6]

21

Saturday 5 January. Arrived in Berlin, where, thank God, I found my whole family in good health, with the exception of my brother Wilhelm, whose state of health is unfortunately very disturbing. Letters from Herr von Lüttichau and Kaskel.

Sunday 6 January. Called on Herr v. Küstner, von Humboldt, Spieker, and Bennewitz, all of whom, with exception of the first, were not at home. Letter from Dr. Bacher.

Monday 7 January. Wrote letters to Dr. Bacher, to Breitkopf & Härtel, and to Brandus, enclosing my song for four voices, "Der Wandrer und die Geister an Beethovens Grabe."[7] Preparations for departure to Dresden. Letters from Gouin, the contrabassist Müller from Darmstadt.[8] At three o'clock left for Dresden by train. Arrived there at nine o'clock in the evening. On the way I composed more of Catherine's couplets.

Tuesday 8 January. Called on the intendant of the theater, Herr von Lüttichau, and Karl Kaskel. In the afternoon I studied part of the role of Fidès with the singer Michalesi. In the theater heard Flotow's *Martha;* the bass Dall'Aste was very good.[9]

Wednesday 9 January. Rehearsed with Tichatschek, then with Demoiselle Michalesi. In the afternoon rehearsed the three Anabaptist roles. In the evening worked on the revision of the German text of *Le Prophète.*[10]

Thursday 10 January. Held a piano rehearsal with the chorus. As I walked into the rehearsal hall, the chorus received me with a song of welcome. Worked on the revision of the German text. In the theater: Cherubini's *Der Wasserträger* [*Les Deux Journées*]. I wrote to Gouin.

Friday 11 January. Piano rehearsal with the singers, and in addition went through the role of Fidès with Michalesi. Letter from the *Oberstkämmerer,* Count Lanckoronski, in Vienna,[11] informing me that the Latin texts and several other expressions in *Le Prophète* will have to be changed by the censor.[12] Letter from Dr. Bacher. Dined at Kaskel's.

Saturday 12 January. Before the rehearsal I had a conference with Hofrat Winkler about the necessary changes in the text; then I rehearsed with the choirboys and afterward held a rehearsal with the singers. Dined with Herr von Lüttichau. In the evening I was at a benefit concert where I heard the cantata *Das Paradies und die Peri*[13] by Robert Schumann. The composer himself conducted his own work,[14] so that on this occasion I saw, for the first time, the face of the man who, as a critic, has persecuted me for the last twelve years with deadly enmity.[15]

Sunday 13 January. Rehearsal with Tichatschek, Demoiselle Michalesi, and Demoiselle Schwarzbach,[16] in which I tried the three singers in their duets and trios. Dined with Aunt Jette. In the theater: Kotzebue's *Menschenhass und Reue*,[17] very well acted by Madame Bayer and Herr Emil Devrient.[18]

Monday 14 January. Piano rehearsal with the singers of *Les Huguenots*. In the evening studied the role of Fidès with Michalesi, and the *mise en scène* of act 1 with the stage manager. Wrote a long letter to Dr. Bacher. Letter from Berlioz.

Tuesday 15 January. Visit from the music critic Dr. Schladebach*. Visit from the concertmaster Lipinski* and Kapellmeister Reissiger; the latter, in fact, visits me every day. Piano rehearsal of *Les Huguenots*. To Herr von Lüttichau. Called on Concertmaster Lipinski. I wrote to Berlioz and to Wilhelm. Letters from Gouin, J. P. Schmidt.

Wednesday 16 January. Rehearsal in which I united the singers with the chorus for the first time. Afterward I called on Hofrätin Winkler and Madame Eduard Ebers.[19] In the theater: Bellini's *Die Familien Capuleti und Montecchi*. Demoiselle Michalesi, with a wide-ranging voice and lovely mezzo-soprano timbre, sang Romeo really well; Madame Palm-Spazer was also very good as Julia.

Thursday 17 January. Letter from Léon de Wailly. Four-hour *mise en scène* rehearsal of acts 1 and 2. In the evening practiced the duets with Demoiselles Michalesi and Schwarzbach. I feel the onset of a cold.

Friday 18 January. First orchestral rehearsal. Dinner at Karl Kaskel's, where I made the acquaintance of the Austrian ambassador, Count Kufstein,[20] and the French ambassador, d'Andrée. Glittering ball at the Noble Casino.[21]

Saturday 19 January. Second orchestral rehearsal. Dined at the Austrian ambassador's. Evening party at Eduard Devrient's, where I made the acquaintance of the artists Bendemann[22] and Hübner.[23]

Sunday 20 January. Rehearsal of the *mise en scène* of act 3. Dined at Hofrat Winkler's. Soirée at the old Madame Kaskel's,[24] where I met Berthold Auerbach* again.[25]

Monday 21 January. *Mise en scène* rehearsal. Separate rehearsal with the organ. In the evening, when the theater performances were over, rehearsed the dancers in the Skaters' Quadrille. In the theater: again heard Flotow's opera *Martha*.

Tuesday 22 January. Orchestral rehearsal with the *mise en scène*. Dined at the

French ambassador, Andrée's. To the theater for *Nathan der Weise*[26] in celebration of Lessing's* birthday.

Wednesday 23 January. Mise en scène rehearsal of act 4. Called on Gutzkow*, but did not find him at home.

Thursday 24 January. Mise en scène rehearsal of acts 4 and 5. Wrote to Dr. Bacher. Dined with my cousin, Sophie von Brandenstein.[27] In the evening continued the revision of the German text with Hofrat Winkler.

Friday 25 January. Orchestral rehearsal with the *mise en scène.* Finished the revision of the text with Hofrat Winkler. Went through the role of Fidès with Michalesi for the last time. Wrote to Burguis concerning Küstner and Wieprecht.

Saturday 26 January. Wrote to Gouin. Orchestral rehearsal with *mise en scène.* Visit from Gutzkow and Berthold Auerbach. After the theater, rehearsed the sunrise [in act 3].

Sunday 27 January. Today was merely a *répétition d'accord,* which I did not attend. Called on the Kapellmeisterin Weber. Visit from Gutzkow. News from the director Wurda, that *Le Prophète* was given on the twenty-fourth in Hamburg, and was received with great applause. In the theater *Dorf und Stadt*, after Auerbach's *Novelle*,[28] by Madame Birch-Pfeiffer,[29] was excellently acted.

Monday 28 January. For the first time a general rehearsal of all five acts: it lasted five hours. Prince Albert*, the heir presumptive, who was present, summoned me to his box in order to express his approval. Called on Geheimrat Dr. Carus, the music critic Schladebach, the splendid actress Bayer. After the theater rehearsed (with piano) the sunrise in act 3 in its relation to the music. Letters from Kapellmeister Proch, Dr. Bacher.

Tuesday 29 January. For the second and last time a dress rehearsal of all the acts, which went very well. Herr von Lüttichau presented me, on behalf of the king of Saxony, the Knight's Cross of the Order of Merit, with a very flatteringly composed diploma.[30] Dined at Herr von Lüttichau's, where I made the acquaintance of the Oberstkämmerer Herr von Czechau.[31] Soirée at Berthold Auerbach's, where he read his drama *Andreas Hofer*.[32]

Wednesday 30 January. In the evening to the first performance of *Le Prophète*. The public called me out after acts 2, 3, 4, and 5, twice in fact after act 4. At the end I was showered with flowers and garlands. The king summoned me to his box after act 4 to express his satisfaction. After the performance a deputation from the orchestra brought me a laurel wreath. The singers were also repeatedly called out. I nevertheless felt that the public's reception of the individual musical pieces was lukewarm, and this could not have been otherwise: the singers and the chorus were, on the one hand, exhausted, because yesterday, and the day before yesterday, there had been two dress rehearsals with the performance today following immediately—without even a day of rest. Then, on the other hand, out of the desire to do everything correctly, they were unduly anxious and self-conscious, and all of them, with the exception of Michalesi, sang untidily. This was particularly true of Tichatschek in the role of the Prophet. Michalesi, on the other hand, was marvelous and carried all the rest.

Thursday 31 January. Because I have agreed to conduct the rehearsals of *Le Prophète* in Vienna, I left this morning at eleven o'clock by express post for Teplitz, since the railway via Breslau has become impassable because of heavy snowfalls. I arrived in Teplitz at 7:30 in the evening.

February 1850

Friday 1 February. I took a private express coach to Prague for myself, which in all cost me twenty-five to thirty gulden. I set off early at 7:30 and was in Prague by six o'clock in the evening. I went to the theater within half an hour of arriving in order to acquaint myself with the auditorium. They were performing *Unverhofft*, a comedy by Nestroy.[33] The director of the theater, Hoffmann,[34] and the director of the Conservatoire, Kittel,[35] recognized me and accompanied me home.

Saturday 2 February. I left by train for Vienna at 5:30 this morning, and we arrived there at 9:30 in the evening. The cold has mellowed into a thaw.

Sunday 3 February. Visit from Dr. Bacher. Conference with the intendant of the Court Theater, Herr von Holbein, and the kapellmeister, Proch. In the evening I studied part of the role of the Prophet with the tenor Ander. In the Kärntnertor-Theater: Verdi's *Hernani* in German; I heard only a few scenes of it.

Monday 4 February. Piano rehearsal with the Prophet (Ander), the three Anabaptists (Draxler, Kreutzer,[36] Hölzel[37]), and Oberthal (Staudigl). Called on Demoiselle Zerr. In the evening I played all the choruses to the chorus master, and then rehearsed the duets with Madame Lagrange and Demoiselle Zerr. Visit from Castelli.

Tuesday 5 February. Rehearsal with the chorus. In the evening rehearsed with Lagrange. Called on Saphir, Hofrat Dingelstädt, and his wife. News from Benedict that *Le Prophète* was given on 25 January in Marseilles with great success.

Wednesday 6 February. Piano rehearsal with the principal and secondary roles. In the evening practiced with Lagrange and Ander. Called on the lord chamberlain, Count Lanckoronski, who is negotiating with me about the changes that the present censor has demanded in *Le Prophète*. They are harmless; the most important is that the "Domine, salvum fac regem" must be sung in German instead of in Latin. Went to see Count Moritz Dietrichstein, who has already called on me twice.

Thursday 7 February. Piano rehearsal with all the soloists and the chorus together. In the Burgtheater, the first performance of Bauernfeld's historical drama in four acts, *Franz von Sickingen*.[38] It was very well acted, and Bauernfeld was called out three times, but opinions over the success of the play are nonetheless divided. Soirée at Saphir's. Letter from Gutzkow, who sent me an article he had written about me in the *Leipziger Zeitung*.[39] Letter from the theater director Wurda in Hamburg: news that the fourth performance of *Le Prophète* took place there to a capacity house.

Friday 8 February. Held no rehearsal, since the theater was booked for the rehearsals of Hoven's opera[40] and a ballet. Letters from Gouin and Küstner. I see in the *Journal des débats* and in a letter from Julius [Beer] that *Le Prophète* was given on 29 January in Amsterdam with great success by the German Society there. Had a long discussion with the stage manager, Just,[41] about the *mise en scène*. Dined at the Prussian ambassador, Count Bernsdorf's.[42] In the Kärntnertor-Theater: Verdi's *Macbeth*. Staudigl and Madame Hasselt-Barth[43] sang the principal roles very beautifully.

Saturday 9 February. For several days now I have had a cold, with weakness of the limbs, headache, increased coughing. First *mise en scène* rehearsal of the first two acts. A deputation from a charitable association has requested me to conduct their benefit concert, but I had to decline on account of the continuing rehearsals of *Le Prophète*. Visited Dessauer and Tichy.[44]

Sunday 10 February. Today is my beloved mother's birthday. May God preserve her. Today there was no rehearsal. Conference with Kapellmeister Proch concerning several musical details. Called on Frau von Holbein and Dessauer. Wrote to Karl Kaskel. Letters from Kapellmeister Dorn, from Kaskel. News from Minna that *Robert* was performed at the Italian Opera in the Königstadt in Berlin to great applause: Signora Fiorentini[45] sang Alice.

Monday 11 February. First orchestral rehearsal of acts 1 and 2. Even this undoubtedly excellent orchestra required four hours in order to decipher act 2, the easiest in *Le Prophète*. When I appeared, Kapellmeister Proch introduced me to the orchestra, which received me with a threefold *salve* of applause and a fanfare of drums and trumpets. I responded with more or less the following words: "Gentle-men. It has always been one of my cherished musical wishes to study an opera with the outstanding orchestra of the Kärntnertor-Theater, whose classic achieve-ments I have so often admired. I am deeply happy that this honor is extended to me today, and I entrust myself to your good will, your indulgence, and your pa-tience." In the afternoon I wrote to Küstner and Burguis. In the evening I prac-ticed Zacharias's *couplets* in act 3 with Draxler, and then heard Donizetti's *Maria di Rohan* in the Kärntnertor-Theater. Staudigl, who actually has little of his lower register left and is good only in baritone parts, did very well in this opera. Letter from Gouin: the forty-fifth performance of *Le Prophète* in Paris (receipts 9,198 fr.).

Tuesday 12 February. I felt so unwell that I was obliged to miss the orchestral rehearsal in the morning and the *mise en scène* practice in the evening so that I could take to my bed and sweat it out. I have consulted a homeopathic physician, Dr. Fleischmann.[46] Visit from Hofrat Deinhardstein.

Wednesday 13 February. I am improving only slowly, but nonetheless presided at an orchestral rehearsal of act 3 in the evening. Kapellmeister Proch had actually rehearsed this act with the orchestra yesterday. Letters from Kapellmeister Sobolewski* and the writer Gottschall* from Königsberg. Visit from Geheimrat Jüngken from Berlin.

Thursday 14 February. My indisposition does not improve. *Mise en scène* rehearsal of act 3 of *Le Prophète*. In the evening I took the tenor Ander through some of his role, then went to the Kärtnertor-Theater for Rossini's *Der Barbier von Seville*. Madame Lagrange sang Rosina—to great enthusiasm. Visit from Count Moritz Dietrichstein.

Friday 15 February. My indisposition continues. I went with the Kapellmeister Proch to the physharmonicum-builder Deutschmann[47] to inspect an organ for *Le Prophète*. Rehearsal with the orchestra and *mise en scène* of the first three acts. In the evening I practiced the two duets and trio with Demoiselle Zerr, Madame Lagrange, and Herr Ander, and then in the Kärntnertor-Theater heard a couple of acts of Verdi's *Macbeth*. After the theater I called on Baroness Pereira.[48]

Saturday 16 February. Stage rehearsal of act 4; we completed only one-half of the act. Visit from [Mme.] Hasselt-Barth. In the Kärntnertor-Theater: *Laura*, a big ballet based on the story of Cinderella,[49] music by Kapellmeister Reuling.[50] Letters from Gouin, Küstner, Kaskel. Wrote to Kaskel (eighteen thalers for Schladebach).[51]

Sunday 17 February. Conference with the ballet master Golinelli,[52] the stage manager, Just, and the chorus master, Weinkopf,[53] about the *mise en scène*. I called on Bauernfeld, Grillparzer, Heinrich von Wertheimstein. I answered Küstner's letter. Visit from the singer Lutzer (now Hofrätin Dingelstedt), formerly so famous, who sang several things for me. In the Kärntnertor-Theater: Verdi's *Hernani*. After the theater I wrote to Brandus.

Monday 18 February. My state of health is improving. Rehearsal of act 4 with orchestra and singers. In the evening I practiced act 5 at the piano with Demoiselle Zerr, Madame Lagrange, and Herr Ander. Letter from the singer Frank in Dessau.

Tuesday 19 February. Stage rehearsal of act 4. Visit from Hofrat Dingelstedt. I answered Gutzkow's letter.

Wednesday 20 February. Orchestral rehearsal of act 5. In the afternoon rehearsed the first cavatina with Demoiselle Zerr. To the Kärntnertor-Theater for Rossini's *Wilhelm Tell*. Demoiselle Krall,[54] a promising beginner, was Mathilde. Herr Wurda, director of the Hamburg Theater, called on me in my box.

Thursday 21 February. *Mise en scène* rehearsal of acts 4 and 5. In the afternoon rehearsed with the organist, and took Zerr through her cavatina. Stayed at home in the evening to arrange the score for my conducting.

Friday 22 February. Orchestral rehearsal with *mise en scène* of acts 3, 4, and 5; it lasted from 10 until 2:30. Called on Kuranda, but did not find him at home. Letters from Burguis and Blanca that have made me very anxious for my dear brother Wilhelm. I stayed at home in the evening to arrange the score for my conducting.

Saturday 23 February. First orchestral rehearsal of all five acts with *mise en scène*. I conducted today for the first time. The rehearsal lasted six hours and went badly. To the Kärntnertor-Theater for Donizetti's *Linda di Chamounix*. Madame Wildauer sang Linda very well indeed.

Sunday 24 February. No rehearsal. Visit from Kapellmeister Proch. Visit from the singer Stöckl-Heinefetter, whose vocal depth is well suited to Fidès.[55] Called on Saphir and the Baden ambassador, Baron Andlaw. Dined at Dr. Bacher's. In the evening arranged the score for conducting.

Monday 25 February. This cold still lingers on. Second rehearsal of all five acts. The orchestra is still not giving its best and appears to accustom itself to my beat only with difficulty. In the evening prepared the score for conducting.

Tuesday 26 February. Dress rehearsal of *Le Prophète*, which I conducted. Holbein made the mistake of allowing access to the public, so it was as full as at a first performance. The reception was cool beyond all expectation: neither the singers nor I were called out, and there was hardly any applause.

Wednesday 27 February. Called on Frankl, Deinhartstein, Liebenberg, Prince Esterházy. In the evening visits from Hofrat Dingelstedt and Tichy, afterward a stage rehearsal of the sun. Letters from Winkler, Küstner, the regimental band-master Urban[56] in Hamburg.

Thursday 28 February. Extended morning rehearsal with the organ, the chorus, and the orchestra lasting until 2, which was rather late considering that the first performance of *Le Prophète* was due to begin at six o'clock. The desire for tickets has been insatiable for weeks; up to 100 gulden have been paid for a single economy seat. As early as 9 o'clock in the morning, people began queuing outside the theater; by twelve o'clock such a large crowd had gathered in the square in front of the Kärntner Gate (where the theater is located) that soldiers were called in to control the situation. At 6 o'clock the performance began. I conducted; on my entry into the orchestra, I was received with loud and prolonged applause. I was called out twice after act 2, twice after act 3, three or four times after act 4; and after act 5 I lost count of the curtain calls. As I came out for the last time, an actress appeared as the muse Polyhymnia[57] and crowned me with a laurel wreath. This very beautiful garland was later fixed in a lovely frame presented by the administration of the Imperial and Royal Court Theaters[58] (the inscription reads: "To the great composer on the day of the first performance of his *Prophet*"). On the orchestral side, the performance was very good, on the choral side unsurpassable. Ander sang the Prophet superbly; he is now incontestably Germany's first tenor. Likewise, Demoiselle Zerr was quite outstanding as Berthe, and made something really impressive of this ungrateful role, especially in the act 5 trio, and in a way that Castellan has never been able to do in Paris. On the other hand, Madame Lagrange had little appeal as Fidès, even though she sang the role well; her voice is toneless, she pronounces German badly, and is no actress. The numbers that provoked furore this evening were: Berthe's Cavatina and the Chorus of Revolt in act 1, the quartet in act 2, the Women's Duet, the march, the organ scene and the finale as a whole in act 4, the aria, the duet and the trio in act 5. It appears, with God's help, to have been a very great success.[59]

Heard through Count Dingelstedt that *Struensee* was performed in Stuttgart a year ago with success.

March 1850

Friday 1 March. I began to make the necessary calls that I had had to neglect during the rehearsals. I received a visit from the *Oberstkämmerer*, Count Lanckoronski. *Der Wandrer*, which appeared today, and the evening paper, *Wiener*

Zeitung, carried very good reports about the production of *Le Prophète*.[60] Big soirée at Louis Pereira's, where French comedies and *tableaux vivants* were performed by distinguished dilettantes.

Saturday 2 March. Farewell visits. I sent Kapellmeister Proch a gold watch-and-chain worth 125 gulden: he attended to all the musical concerns and details during the rehearsals. I bade farewell to the theater staff.

Sunday 3 March. Second performance of *Le Prophète*, to an equally crowded house, which went just as excellently as the first, and was applauded by the public just as enthusiastically. Lagrange, the only one whose performance found any opposition, seemed to appeal more today and was called out after the act 2 arioso. All other curtain calls were as on the first night. Proch conducted. Initially the public did not know that I was in the theater, but the rumor spread during act 3, and I was called out twice after acts 3, 4, and 5, respectively. Visited the minister of the interior, [Alexander] Bach. The overture to *Struensee* was performed in today's Gesellschaftskonzert—and will be also be played in the Philharmonic Concert which will take place in eight days' time. The "Mailied" and "Mère grand" have also been performed in several concerts since my arrival.

Monday 4 March. Preparations for departure. I had to sit for a sculptor who wants to make a statuette of me, and had to listen to Demoiselle Therese Schwarz sing the role of Fidès; she did not please me. At 7:30 in the evening, I left by the train that travels to Berlin via Breslau. All the Viennese newspapers and journals are favorably disposed toward *Le Prophète*; only *Die Reichszeitung* is carping, but decently so,[61] while the *Punch* has not yet reported anything.[62]

Tuesday 5 March. We traveled through the night and arrived in the morning at 9:45 (one and a quarter hours later than usual) at the Prussian border post of Oderberg, where the Prussian customs inspection takes place and the carriages are changed. We journeyed so slowly that by the time we reached Cosel, the train that travels from there to Breslau had already left, and we had to stay in this dump for four hours until the second train came: we arrived in Breslau at 9:30 at night instead of four o'clock in the afternoon. During this delay in Cosel I made the acquaintance of several of my traveling companions: a privy councilor from Frankfurt, a young Belgian (who appears to have traveled through the whole of Europe), and an old Polish woman and her daughter from Gleichwitz near Pilchowitz (who appears to know Hännchen Styrum very well).[63]

Wednesday 6 March. At 8:15 in the morning departed by train for Berlin and arrived there in the evening at 7:30. May God bless the return to my native city.[64] I found my dearest mother, my dear wife Minna, and my three beloved children

well, praise God, but my poor brother Wilhelm much worse than I had anticipated. May God the Almighty be merciful and kind to him.

Thursday 7 March. My dear brother Wilhelm recognized me when I stood at his
bedside, but delirium soon reasserted itself. In order to determine whether I should
give the role of Berthe to Köster or to Tuczek, I went to the theater, where various pieces were performed. I heard Madame Köster and the bass Salomon* in the
act 3 duet from *Les Huguenots;* both pleased me very much.

Friday 8 March. To Herr von Humboldt, Herr von Küstner, Wilhelm. Conference
with Kapellmeister Dorn about the rehearsals of *Le Prophète* in Berlin. Letter
from Gouin with news of the fiftieth performance of *Le Prophète* in Paris (receipts 9,870 fr.). Wrote to Gouin. Spent the evening with Wilhelm.

Saturday 9 March. Wilhelm's condition is somewhat better today (thanks be to
God). The king invited me to dinner in Charlottenburg; both he and the queen
were extremely friendly and obliging to me. I learnt through the queen that *Le
Prophète* has been produced in Schwerin. In the Opera House I heard the first
two acts of my *Ein Feldlager in Schlesien.* The performance was lame, the applause very sparse. The military music and a number of choruses in this opera
had been much reduced. Jenny Lind sang my "Mère grand" with Tuczek in her
concert today.

Sunday 10 March. I wanted to hold the first rehearsal of *Le Prophète* today, but
Bötticher was hoarse, and it did not take place. Called on [Felix] Eberty,[65] the earl
of Westmorland, Spieker. Wrote to Dr. Bacher.

Monday 11 March. First piano rehearsal of *Le Prophète.* After supper, to the English ambassador, the earl of Westmorland's, where Jenny Lind sang *Lieder.*

Tuesday 12 March. No rehearsal, since they were giving the *Mulatto.*[66] Called on
Count Redern, Rellstab, Küstner. Played through the rest of the choruses with the
chorus master, Elssler.

Wednesday 13 March. Second piano rehearsal. Called on Count Redern. Moving
letter from my old friend and librettist, Gaetano Rossi, in Verona; I had sent him
200 fr. from Vienna.[67] Through the earl of Westmorland, I found out that *Les Huguenots* was produced in St. Petersburg for the first time, at the Italian Opera (as
Die Guelfen und Ghibellinen) with much success. Mario and Grisi sang the principal roles.[68] Letters from Brandus and Härtel.

Thursday 14 March. Third piano rehearsal. In today's *Reform* is a small, negative article from Vienna directed against *Le Prophète*.[69] Conference with Herr von Küstner concerning the engagement of Ander. In her concert today, Jenny Lind again sang "Mère grand" and the Flute Piece from the *Feldlager*.

Friday 15 March. Fourth piano rehearsal. Called on Bote & Bock. Yesterday I studied the role of Fidès with Marx, who will be singing it only during the rehearsals. Visit from the music dealer Dr. Härtel from Leipzig.

Sunday 16 March. No rehearsals on account of the elections to the First Chamber. I used this opportunity to go to Madame Köster, and studied the role of Berthe with her. Called on the French ambassador, M. de Persigny. Letter from Karl Kaskel in Dresden: the performances of *Le Prophète* there, which had been interrupted by the illness of Madame Michalesi, were resumed the day before yesterday. Visit from Professor Rungenhagen.

Sunday 17 March. Fifth piano rehearsal. Letter from Gouin: fifty-third performance of *Le Prophète* (receipts 6,841 fr.). This sharp reduction in the takings can be ascribed to the consternation prevailing in Paris because of the election of three socialist representatives.[70] *Les Huguenots* was recently produced in Reval for the first time, under the title *Raoul und Valentine*, with great success (so I read in the *Theaterchronik*).

Monday 18 March. Called on Count Redern. Private rehearsal with Köster. In the evening a piano rehearsal.

Tuesday 19 March. No rehearsal on account of the production of *Fidelio*.[71] I therefore practiced only with Marx, and played the dances[72] to the ballet master, Hoguet. Letter from Cornet about the performance of *Le Prophète* in Hamburg.[73] Farewell visit to Jenny Lind, who sang me Taubert's "Echo."[74]

Wednesday 20 March. Piano rehearsal with the singers. Called on Henri Blaze and Schlesinger. Letter from Kaskel, who, on behalf of Geheimrat Carus in Dresden, sent me a philosophical discourse by the latter on *Le Prophète*.[75]

Thursday 21 March. Coughed slightly, but feel that I have caught a bad cold. Piano rehearsal.

Friday 22 March. Piano rehearsal. Wrote to Breitkopf & Härtel. Letter from Winkler in Dresden.

Saturday 23 March. Rehearsed with the chorus, then with the singers.

Sunday 24 March. No rehearsal. Called on Henri Blaze and Spieker.

Monday 25 March. Rehearsed with the singers and chorus united for the first time. Wrote to Carus and Kaskel.

Tuesday 26 March. First correction rehearsal (without singing) with all the string instruments.[76] For several days now I have been going to Wilhelm three times a day, before and after rehearsals and in the evenings. Unfortunately, the illness will not take a positive turn, and his strength is being drained daily by the fever. Visited the intendant [von Küstner] to find out whether one could, with probity, rehearse on Maundy Thursday. Letters from Gouin, Dr. Bacher, Kapellmeister Krebs*, and Wilhelm Speyer, who reported to me on the ninth performance of *Le Prophète* in Frankfurt and its brilliant success. Wrote to Gouin that Madame Viardot must come to Berlin.

Wednesday 27 March. Second correction rehearsal with the string players. I was suddenly called from the rehearsal, since my poor brother Wilhelm's health had dramatically deteriorated. At 5:30 he was taken from us: the playfellow of my youth, the confidant of all my thoughts, the helpful, concerned friend who was fanatically devoted to my artistic activity and my musical fame. His death is an irreplaceable loss to me in every aspect of life, in every matter of the heart. May God grant him eternal peace, eternal blessedness, and may God help my poor eighty-three-year-old mother, who now buries her third son, to bear this terrible blow.

Thursday 28 to Saturday 30 March. Spent almost the whole time with my poor mother to comfort her, and to help her with the preparations for the burial of my beloved brother.

Sunday 31 March. The funeral of my beloved brother, which was marked by a great manifestation of sympathy for the deceased: representatives of the arts, science, the civil authorities, and the magistracy, as well as the ministers Brandenburg,[77] Rabe,[78] and Ladenberg,[79] all were present. Over one hundred carriages followed the procession. The king sent his personal equipage as escort; he had already, the evening before, written my mother a letter of condolence in his own hand. The preacher Auerbach[80] read the oration over the coffin before it was carried out of the death-chamber. The funeral indicated just how much the deceased, in spite of so much hostility, had been esteemed and honored by his fellow citizens. Stayed with Mother all day.

April 1850

Monday 1 April. Wrote a letter of thanks, ostensibly to Humboldt, but actually for the king. Rehearsed acts 1 and 2 with the wind instruments and corrected the parts. Wrote to the music director Klingenberg in Görlitz.

Tuesday 2 April. Rehearsed act 3 and half of act 4 with the wind instruments and made corrections. The princess of Prussia conveyed through Countess Haacke her condolences to me on the death of my brother.

Wednesday 3 April. Rehearsed the second half of act 4 and act 5. Visit from Maurice Schlesinger from Paris. Conference with Herr von Küstner at the stage manager Stawinsky's.

Thursday 4 April. No rehearsal, since Patschke was not ready with the amendments of the errors that had been discovered during the correction rehearsals. Wrote to Kapellmeister Krebs in Hamburg, to Munk in Paris.

Friday 5 April. Madame Viardot has arrived. To Herr von Küstner. First orchestral rehearsal with the singers acts 1 and 2, and then the ballet in act 3. Letter from Gouin: fifty-ninth performance in Paris of *Le Prophète* (10,577 fr. receipts), the last performance before the departure of Madame Viardot.

Saturday 6 April. Letters to Henri Blaze and Schlesinger. The music director Klingenberg from Görlitz introduced to me a singing pupil, Fischer, who has a pleasant high soprano voice, even though it is not strong. *Le Prophète* was given a few days ago in Darmstadt.[81] Because of the orchestral rehearsal of *Robert*, there was no practice of *Le Prophète*.

Sunday 7 April. Conferred with Madame Viardot about the arrangement of the German text. Went through the roles in the first four acts. Conference with the music director Wieprecht about the stage music in *Le Prophète*. To the Church of the Jewish Reform, where prayers were read for my deceased brother Wilhelm. Called on Holtei, who is presently in Berlin. Because of the production of *Robert*, there was no rehearsal of *Le Prophète*. On 2 April, *Le Prophète* was given in Antwerp with great success.

Monday 8 April. Orchestral rehearsal of act 3 and the first half of act 4. I was invited to a soirée at Prince Karl's.

Tuesday 9 April. Exploratory piano rehearsal with Madame Viardot, Herr Tichatschek, and the other singers. In the evening to a Court Concert in Charlottenburg, which I had to lead (from the piano). Demoiselle Niessen and Herr Tichatschek sang, the latter including, among other things, my "Mailied." Herr Viereck (violoncellist) and Herr Studemund (pianist) from Schwerin also played.[82]

Wednesday 10 April. Third orchestral rehearsal of the second half of act 4 and all of act 5. Dined with the minister of foreign affairs, Schleinitz.[83]

Thursday 11 April. Fourth orchestral rehearsal of acts 1, 2, and 3 together. In the afternoon an organ rehearsal. Today *Le Prophète* will be performed for the first time in Düsseldorf.

Friday 12 April. Fifth orchestral rehearsal of acts 4 and 5. In the evening, a piano rehearsal of *Les Huguenots*. In Paris, reprise of *Les Huguenots* (191st performance) with Roger, Madame Laborde, Demoiselle Julienne, Levasseur (receipts 8,290 fr.).

Saturday 13 April. Orchestral rehearsal of *Les Huguenots*. Madame Viardot sang Valentine, Mademoiselle Trietsch from Hamburg the Page,[84] and Tichatschek Raoul. In the evening I went to the Königstädter-Theater, where the Italian Opera performed my *Robert* for the last time this season. Pardini (Robert)[85] and Madame Fiorentini (Alice) have wonderful voices, and Madame Penco (Isabella)[86] and Labocetta (Raimbaud)[87] also sing very well. Yet this performance did not satisfy me at all. The music does not suit Italian singers, it seems to me.

Sunday 14 April. Today there was no rehearsal. Conference with the stage manager, Stawinsky, about the *mise en scène*. News of the second performance of the revival of *Les Huguenots* in Paris: this was the 192d performance (receipts 4,939 fr.). The reprise did not attract as much interest as one might have expected. Demoiselle Julienne appears to have sung Valentine very badly. In the Opera House: *Les Huguenots* with Madame Viardot and Tichatschek. The theater was packed, even though a seat in the first row cost two thalers. The public, however, was very cold. The presentation, musically and scenically, went very well.

Monday 15 April. First *mise en scène* rehearsal (acts 1 and 2) took place this evening. Called on Lady Westmorland.

Tuesday 16 April. Second *mise en scène* rehearsal: repeated acts 1 and 2 and tried the first half of act 3. Called on Minister Ladenberg. Today *Le Prophète* was given in Cologne for the first time. The opera has also been given in the Italian Opera in Lisbon with success.

Wednesday 17 April. *Mise en scène* rehearsal of act 3 prior to the Court Concert.

Thursday 18 April. Orchestral rehearsal with the *mise en scène* of acts 1, 2, and 3. Court Concert at Charlottenburg, where Mesdames Viardot and Niessen sang a psalm for two voices by Marcello *(Come la cerva anela)*[88] that pleased the king very much.

Friday 19 April. *Mise en scène* rehearsal of the second half of act 4.

Saturday 20 April. Mise en scène rehearsal of acts 4 and 5.

Sunday 21 April. No rehearsal. In the theater: *Les Huguenots* again at the highest prices and with Madame Viardot and Herr Tichatschek; very full, but not as much as the first time.

Monday 22 April. Conference with the intendant and Madame Viardot. In the evening in the theater a rehearsal of acts 4 and 5 for the first time with orchestra and *mise en scène*.

Tuesday 23 April. Orchestral rehearsal with *mise en scène* of acts 1, 2, and 3. I conducted for the first time. The orchestra received me with a fanfare and great applause.

Wednesday 24 April. Orchestral and *mise en scène* rehearsal of acts 4 and 5. Since Madame Viardot was unwell, Demoiselle Marx sang her part and was applauded by the orchestra.

Thursday 25 April. Dress rehearsal of all five acts. Brandus arrived here from Paris.

Friday 26 April. Dress rehearsal (the last I directed from the orchestra), to which so many spectators came that the house was crowded. I saw to it that every member of the orchestra received two tickets. The performance was outstanding, but the reception on the part of the audience extremely cold. Only at the end of act 4 did they come to life and call for me. Ganz presented me with a laurel garland on behalf of the orchestra. Only Köster (Berthe) was given lively applause in the act 5 trio. Letter from Doktorin Mundt in which she expresses the wish for reconciliation.[89]

Saturday 27 April. Spent the whole day apportioning tickets and attending to all the thousands of things that precede a first night.

Sunday 28 April. First performance of *Le Prophète*.

From here until 3 June I did not maintain my diary, but have only indicated in summary the most noteworthy things to have happened to me.

I conducted the first and second performances of *Le Prophète*; I was called out after acts 3, 4, and 5, as were the singers. The opera was given eleven times in the space of a month, to packed houses and at unusually high prices (two thalers in the balcony or first dress circle). Nevertheless, public reaction to the work was very divided. It occasioned many unfavorable judgments, that is to say, the greater number of critics were against rather than for the work. During the second performance the king summoned me to his box after act 3 to express his satisfaction to me. Ninety-one members of the Royal Orchestra[90] (which consists of eighty-four actual members) had a silver laurel garland made with an inscription, stating that the orchestra dedicated and presented this to Generalmusikdirektor Meyerbeer as a sign of their respect. One day I was fetched by a deputation of the *Kapelle* and led into the concert hall of the Schauspielhaus where I found the ninety-one members of the orchestra in festal costume. I was received with a fanfare. Kapellmeister Dorn read a speech to me, to which I briefly replied, and the laurel garland was handed over to me. Kapellmeister Taubert, who absented himself from this demonstration, ensured that all sorts of unkind remarks about this speech appeared in the papers. I invited the members of the orchestra collectively to dine with me; but since there were too many of them for one dinner, I gave three.[91]

After the departure of Viardot, who did not receive the enthusiastic appreciation in the role of Fidès that her glorious achievement warranted, Demoiselle Johanna Wagner from the Hamburg Theater performed the role twice, to the most extraordinarily enthusiastic reception. This, too, was really a beautiful performance. Her lovely, full voice, particularly in its depth, and her attractive, youthful figure exerted a dramatic effect on the Berliners.

Les Huguenots was performed three times by Viardot and Tichatschek during their sojourn here.

The wife of the writer Mundt (she likewise is an authoress; she writes under the name of Mühlbach), who together with her husband has written the most vehement articles against me for years, sent a letter to me on the occasion of the dress rehearsal of *Le Prophète*, in which she expressed the wish for reconciliation. I called on them.[92]

For the wedding of the daughter of Prince Albrecht of Prussia with the crown prince of Meiningen[93] I again composed, by command of the king, a *Fackeltanz* for brass instrument, which was performed at the marriage in Charlottenburg.[94] The same evening began with a Court Concert with orchestra, which I conducted, and which also featured the overture to *Struensee*.

On 30 May my beloved wife Minna left for Ischl with my children.

Since Kapellmeister Dorn very much wished to be presented to the king, I arranged that some of his songs should be sung at a Court Concert and that he himself should accompany them.

Le Prophète was given with great success at Brunswick.

Robert has done very well at the Covent Garden Theater in London with Grisi, Castellan, and Messrs. Mario, Tamberlik*, and Formes*.

Les Huguenots has been given for the first time in Stettin and Bamberg with great success.

In May the singer Alboni made her début at the Grand Opéra in Paris in *Le Prophète* with extraordinary success. With her as Fidès, *Le Prophète* has generated colossal takings.

Rellstab read me his libretto *Ascaldus*.

June 1850

Tuesday 4 June. I called on the Swedish singer Demoiselle Ebeling.[95] I heard *Don Juan,* in which Johanna Wagner sang Donna Anna to great enthusiasm; she was called out after both her arias.

Wednesday 5 June. Renewed resolutions to a more regular musical activity. Wrote a letter of recommendation to Liszt for the blind pianist Krug*. Letter to Küstner with my opinion (which he requested) about the singing ability of the daughter of the mayor of Görlitz, Fischer. Conference with Geheimrat Schönlein about my state of health. Called on Professor Dehn and on Schlesinger. I visited the new Friedrich-Wilhelmstädtisches-Theater[96] for the first time, and saw Nesmüller's *Die Zillerthaler*[97] in the Vaudeville. Demoiselle Auguste Schulz is the best singing member of the troupe.[98] Letters from Brandus and Camillo Gritti in Venice.[99]

Thursday 6 June. To Herr von Küstner about the rehearsals for Ander. Studied the role of Fidès with Madame Berend-Brand from the Stadttheater in Frankfurt-am-Main.[100] Dined at Count Redern's. In the theater: C. M. von Weber's *Oberon.* Demoiselle Wagner sang Rezia as guest role. Letters from Ziegesar, intendant of the Weimar Theater,[101] and from Karl Kaskel. Wrote to Ziegesar.

Friday 7 June. To Schönlein; conferred with him about my cure. Wrote to Dr. Bacher in Vienna.

Saturday 8 June. Answered the composer Draschke*, who had made me the rather droll offer of being in some way helpful to me in my compositions. Dined at Prince Karl's. Then went on to the earl of Westmorland, who had likewise invited me to dinner.

Sunday 9 June. Called on Wieprecht and the singer Ander from Vienna, then immediately went on to Teichmann, Schönlein, Madame Zimmermann,[102] Madame Dielitz,[103] the composer Emilie Mayer,[104] etc. I was, therefore, hindered from resuming composition on the new opera [*L'Étoile du Nord*], which I had resolved to do today. In the Opera House I heard *Don Juan.* Madame Berend-Brand sang Donna Anna: a powerful, sweet-sounding soprano voice, also a wide-ranging, passable agility, but, on the whole, far below Johanna Wagner.

Monday 10 June. Because of my physical discomfort, I was unable to work all day. Rehearsed *Le Prophète* with the singer Ander, which, however, did not work well because of the absence of Madame Köster and Herr Bötticher. Dined with the intendant-general, Herr von Küstner.

Tuesday 11 June. In the early morning I began (for the first time in a long while) to busy myself again with the composition of the new opera, except that the subject had become so remote to me after the six-month break that I could not remember the pieces I had composed last year. It will take several sessions to pull together the scattered threads. In the evening from 9 to 10 busy with the new opera.

Wednesday 12 June. Orchestral rehearsal of *Le Prophète* for the tenor Ander. In the Schauspielhaus: *Deborah*, a folk play by Mosenthal.[105]

Thursday 13 June. Studied the role of Fidès with Madame Berend-Brand. Twelfth presentation of *Der Prophet*: crowded house; Demoiselle Wagner the Fidès as her last guest role. She won great applause, was often called out, and finally showered with flowers and garlands. Ander from Vienna, the Prophet as his first guest role, pleased very much in act 2, less in the following.

Friday 14 June. Visits from Emil Naumann* and [Johanna] Wagner, from the singer Ebeling, the tenor Moriani,[106] and Julius Weiss. Dined with the Austrian ambassador, Herr von Prokesch-Osten.

Saturday 15 June. Piano and orchestral rehearsals of *Le Prophète* for Madame Berend-Brand, who will sing the role of Fidès (very badly, it seems to me).[107] In the afternoon, in the Garnisonkirche, heard the rehearsal of the first part of Mendelssohn's oratorio *Elijah*, which I still hardly know; then to a *soirée musicale* at the singing teacher Mme. Zimmermann's, where her pupils performed several church compositions by the young composer [Theodor] de Witt. Letter from Dr. Bacher.

Sunday 16 June. Matinée musicale given by Mantius with three of his pupils. One of them, Demoiselle Kellberg, sang Fidès's arioso from *Le Prophète*, and not badly at all.[108] Called on Lady Westmorland. Thirteenth performance of *Der Prophet*: still full, but less than usual. Ander sang the Prophet even better than the first time, and received greater applause. Madame Berend-Brand as Fidès was very bad.

Monday 17 June. The resolution to regular daily musical activity went unfulfilled once again, and I hereby renew it. May God help me eventually to put it into practice. To Count Redern, to Herr von Küstner. Attended the performance of Mendelssohn's oratorio *Elijah* in the Garnisonkirche. In the evening, at Mother's, wrote out the text of the new opera. Wrote to Major Blesson,[109] to Josephy[110] together with twenty-five thalers for the widow of Conradin Kreutzer,[111] to the theater agent Michaelson.

Tuesday 18 June. Worked for an hour on Catherine'e couplets (act 1). In the evening in the Opera House there was a performance, the proceeds of which were destined for the erection of a national soldiers' memorial. They gave the Festival March and Folk Song *Borussia* by Spontini,[112] the second act of my opera *Ein Feldlager in Schlesien,* and the "Lied von der Majestät" by Taubert.[113] Today I once more kept to my resolutions very imperfectly.

Wednesday 19 June. Cold rubdown, followed by a one-hour walk. Called on the Swedish singer Ebeling with Rellstab, and then introduced her to Lady Westmorland. Wrote to Count Waldersee, who wants my *Fackeltanz* for the son of the prince of Prussia.[114] In the Opera House: Flotow's *Martha;* Herr Ander was Lionel, Madame Berend-Brand Martha.

Thursday 20 June. Wrote to Kullak on Minna's behalf.[115] In the Schauspielhaus: *Die kluge Königin, oder Mulier taceat in Ecclesia,* comedy by Raupach.[116]

Friday 21 June. In Paris the seventy-first performance of *Le Prophète* (twelfth presentation with Alboni): receipts 9,966 fr. More than one hundred people from Angers came by railway train to attend the performance. In the evening worked on the piano version of the *Fackeltanz.* The fourteenth [Berlin] performance of *Der Prophet* took place today to a crowded house, but with a much colder reception than usual, since Berend-Brand apparently sang and acted very badly. I was not in the theater.

Saturday 22 June. My friend Dr. Bacher arrived here from Vienna. I gave a dinner to which I invited Prof. Rungenhagen, Prof. Dehn, Flodoard Geyer, the preacher Geyer, the kapellmeisters Lortzing and Dorn, Dr. Wenzel, Hofrat Teichmann, Stawinsky, Ander, Zschiesche, Wieprecht, Elssler, Julius Weiss, Prof. Bötticher.

Sunday 23 June. Completed the piano version of the *Fackeltanz.* In the evening I took leave of Dr. Bacher, who travels to Paris tomorrow.

Monday 24 June. Hoarseness and a headache caused me such discomfort that I could not work all day. I consulted Schönlein. Reprise of *Le Prophète* in London at the Italian Theater, Covent Garden (on 20 June), which has again been successful, apparently.

Tuesday 25 June. Dined with Geheimrat Dr. Jüngken. Wrote to Professor B. L. O. Wolff in Jena, who has informed me that the University of Jena has elected me doctor of philosophy.

Wednesday 26 June. In the Opera House: Beethoven's *Fidelio.* Herr Ander was Florestan and Madame Köster Fidelio, both very good.

Thursday 27 June. To Intendant-General von Küstner to tell him that Marx should not sing the role of Fidès. In the Friedrich Wilhelmstädtisches-Theater: *Ein Marqueur bei Kroll,* farce in one act (after the French);[117] *Die Kunst, geliebt zu werden* (after the *Philtre champanois*), comedy in one act, music by Gumbert;[118] *Eine Berliner Grisette* (after the French), farce with singing in one act, music by Lortzing.[119] All three pieces were acted briskly and vivaciously. Herr L'Arronge,[120] Herr Weirauch,[121] and Herr Ascher[122] are all very good comedians, Herr Marchion a very pleasant tenor for this type of comic acting,[123] and Demoiselle Auguste Schulz a charming exponent of the lively and sentimental genre,[124] both as singer and actress.[125]

Friday 28 June. To Spieker, Dehn, and Schlesinger. Wrote to Dr. Kullak and the Lieutenant Count von Waldersee; I sent the latter the piano score of my new *Fackeltanz* for the son of the prince of Prussia. In the Opera House, in celebration of the recovery of the king[126] and for charitable reasons, there was a performance of various scenes by the tenors Ditt, Reer,[127] and Ander.

Saturday 29 June. Wrote out the text of the [new] opera. In the Schauspielhaus: Shakespeare's *Der Komödie der Irrungen,*[128] a play about the confusion of names.

Sunday 30 June. To Count Redern. A certain Demoiselle Wertheim asked me to hear her sing; she has a dainty, full-sounding head voice.[129] In the Opera House: Spohr's *Jessonda.* Herr Ander sang for the last time. Worked on the canon in act 1.

July 1850

Monday 1 July. To Count Redern. Wrote to Lady Westmorland in London and sent her the *Fackeltanz.* Sent Count Redern my opinion about the composer Fuller's request. Visit from the singers Medola[130] and Schütz-Oldosi.[131] Visit from Herrn Hans von Bülow*[132] and Adolf Mosson.[133] Worked generally on the first act of the new opera. To the singer Ebeling.

Tuesday 2 July. In the morning worked on the canon in act 1. In the Opera House *Yelva,* drama by Scribe[134] with melodramatic music by Reissiger.[135] An article against me in *L'Indépendance belge* of 30 June agitated me so much that in the evening I was not able to compose; I wrote to Gouin about it.[136]

Wednesday 3 July. Visit from Rellstab, from the ballet master Horscheldt.[137] The whole morning went by without my being able get down to composing. Spent the afternoon with my mother. Visited the chief of police, von Hinkeldey.[138]

Thursday 4 July. To Geheimer Kabinetsrat Illaire to get him to intervene with the king on behalf of the young composer de Witt.[139] Farewell visit to Rellstab; I returned his libretto *Ascaldus,* which he had wanted me to set. However, because of the many other libretti I have taken on, I am no longer able to consider it.

Friday 5 July. Visit from the composer de Witt and the sister of Marx. Weakness of the limbs and a headache have made any work impossible.

Saturday 6 July. Called on Lowther, the secretary at the English Embassy.[140]

Sunday 7 July. Worked a little today on the canon. Visit from the music director Seiffert of the military orphanage at Potsdam.[141] In the Opera House: the ballet *Thea oder die Blumenfee,* music by Pugni.[142]

Monday 8 July. Visit from Demoiselle Ebeling. Dined with the earl of Westmorland; the reigning duke of Parma[143] was also there and was very friendly. The cold rubdowns tire me so much that I feel sleepy all day and therefore cannot get down to work.

Tuesday 9 July. Called on the French ambassador, M. de Persigny, Herr and Madame Decker,[144] the Belgian ambassador Nothomb. In the evening worked a little on the canon.

Wednesday 10 July. I was invited by the king to dine at Sans Souci. The king and the queen were extraordinarily kind and friendly toward me, as was the prince of Prussia, who told me that in London he heard only *my* operas. My neighbor at table was General Radowitz.[145] Since the king wishes to have a Court Concert on either Friday or Saturday, I went to the Opera House to attend to the necessary arrangements.

Thursday 11 July. Devoted the whole morning to preparations for the Court Concert scheduled for Saturday. Dined with the French ambassador, M. de Persigny.

Friday 12 July. Rehearsed the Court Concert at Demoiselle Ebeling's. Called on Baron Gall, intendant of the Württemberg Court Theater in Stuttgart. I wrote to Gouin, and then to Dr. Bacher. Letter from Brandus. To the Friedrich-Wilhelmstädtisches-Theater with Jülchen von Haber[146] and Bertha Arndt to see Beckmann and his wife[147] in the guest roles: they performed *Die Reise nach Spanien,* a farce by Hermann (after Théophile Gautier)[148] and *Der Kürmärker und die Picarde,* a vaudeville by Louis Schneider.[149]

Saturday 13 July. Rehearsal with chorus, orchestra, and singers of the Court Concert. We practiced, among other things, the Children's Chorus from *Le Prophète* and, since there is no organ for the concert, we used the orchestral arrangement that I provided for this purpose in the supplement to the full score. It worked rather well.

Sunday 14 July. Letter from the dean of the University of Jena, Professor Snell,[150] in which he officially informs me of my election (entirely unsolicited) to a doctorate of philosophy and the liberal arts, and forwards the diploma to me. Dined with Anton Gubitz[151] at Mother's. Letters from Vienna—from Spina and [Johanna] Wagner's father informing me of the great success of the reprise of *Le Prophète* there.[152]

Monday 15 July. To Minister Schleinitz. Conference with my doctor, Geheimrat Schönlein. Letters from Gouin and the music publisher Senff*, editor of the musical paper *Signale* in Leipzig.

Tuesday 16 July. Called on Spohr, whom I did not find at home.

Wednesday 17 July. Visited Spohr. Wrote two letters to Kabinetsrat Illaire, with my opinions about the recent performances of de Witt and Lescinsky. In Kroll's open-air summer theater: Gustav Schmidt's* comic opera *Prinz Eugen der edle Ritter*. The music is fluent and pleasant and has good comic declamation, but absolutely no invention.[153]

Thursday 18 July. Sent off my written opinion, requested by Minister Ladenberg, of Tschirch's* prize composition. I hosted a dinner: my guests were Kapellmeister Louis Spohr, the painter Kaulbach,[154] the Austrian ambassador Prokesch von Osten, the French ambassador de Persigny, the English ambassador Lord Westmorland, the Belgian ambassador Count Nothomb, Alexander von Humboldt, Geheimer Kabinetsrat Illaire, the minister of foreign affairs von Schleinitz, the minister of religious affairs von Ladenberg, Herr von Olfers, Professor Rungenhagen, Lowther, M. de Jaucourt.[155] In the Opera House: the ballet *Thea die Blumenfee*, music by Pugni.

Friday 19 July. *Matinée musicale* at Spohr's, where he performed several of his own lovely compositions, particularly a string quartet in E-flat major,[156] which, on account of its beauty and elegance and the splendid control of the part writing, is of outstanding worth. Yesterday I confided to Humboldt how unpleasant it has been for me to learn, in conversation with Count Redern, that the latter has proposed to the king that a souvenir (i.e., a gold snuffbox) should be presented to me, since none of the works the king has commanded of me (*Feldlager, Struensee,* etc.) has as yet been accorded any distinction or reward. I feel myself honored enough to carry out the commands of the king without any remuneration; should, however, the king wish to grant me some sort of recognition, then this could only be an order, or a more prestigious musical position, if it is to be at all appropriate to my personal circumstances. Already today the excellent Humboldt wrote to me that he had consulted with the Geheimer Kabinetsrat Illaire, and that the order-in-cabinet, which had already been prepared together with the snuffbox, would not be sent to me. Called on Crelinger.[157]

Saturday 20 July. I traveled to Potsdam to thank Herr von Humboldt for his intervention. At 3 Count Redern arranged a performance of the Domchor in honor of Spohr. They sang, among other things, Lotti's* *Crucifixus* (six voices)—and very beautifully.

Sunday 21 July. Today Madame Birch-Pfeiffer dined with Mother. Wrote to Gouin together with a letter ostensibly for him, but really for Nestor Roqueplan.

Monday 22 July. Studied the role of Berthe with the singer Molendo from Cassel, who has a very pretty soprano voice. Worked a little on the canon. In the Schauspielhaus: the first performance of *Im Walde*, a pastoral play by Charlotte Birch-Pfeiffer;[158] it was well received, but without much enthusiasm. The play has several very workable situations; the material is taken from the *Mare au Diable* by George Sand.[159] It could perhaps provide material for a sentimental rustic *opéra comique* for the Théâtre Feydeau.

Tuesday 23 July. Wrote out virtually the whole canon. In the Friedrich-Wilhelmstädtisches-Theater saw Beckmann in Benedix's* *Der Vetter*.[160] To Birch-Pfeiffer together with a vocal score of *Le Prophète*. The Italian opera troupe of Havana has performed *Les Huguenots* in New York with great success (according to *La Gazette musicale*).[161]

Wednesday 24 July. Studied the role of Vielka with Ebeling. Began to write the vocal part of the canon into the full score.

Thursday 25 July. Worked on the instrumentation of the canon. Because of the weariness and sleepiness induced by the water cure, it has not been possible, even with the best will in the world, to continue working.

Friday 26 July. Visit from the secretary to the Neapolitan Embassy, Tschudi,[162] who on behalf of the duke of Parma asked me for an inscribed vocal score of *Le Prophète*. In both morning and evening I worked a little on the canon.

Saturday 27 July. Called on Geheimrat Johannes Schulze. Scored a little of the canon in the morning and evening.

Sunday 28 July. Letter from Humboldt that the king, in spite of my refusal to accept his gift of the golden snuffbox, has not abandoned the idea, and instead of giving me an order, or a really impressive musical post, now wishes to present me with his bust as reward for all the works I have composed for him. I answered Humboldt immediately. I went to the Friedrich-Wilhelmstädtisches-Theater where Beckmann and his wife are starring for the last time in the farce *Der Vater der Debütantin*[163] and in the rustic vaudeville *Das Versprechen hinter'm Herde,* which is in Austrian dialect.[164]

Monday 29 July. Wrote to Minna about Blanca's attraction to the Catholic faith. To Geheimrat Johannes Schulze to tell him that I will accept the post of curator of the Michael Beer Foundation. In the evening I worked a little on scoring the canon.

Tuesday 30 July. Called on Howard.[165] Visit from the singer Ebeling. Scored the canon for a while. In the afternoon to the Singakademie for a musical celebration in remembrance of the hundredth anniversary of J. S. Bach's death, and the fiftieth of Fasch's death. They performed a piece by Fasch ("Ich will dich, Ewiger, erheben"), then excerpts from J. S. Bach's Mass in B Minor, and finally J. S. Bach's church cantata *Gottes Zeit ist die allerbeste Zeit.*[166] This cantata is of the greatest beauty, simplicity, and sublimity of expression, independent of contrapuntal feats: it made the deepest impression on me. Then I visited the singer Johanna Wagner, who was passing through here after her guest appearances in Vienna. According to Hofrat Teichmann's official communication, the takings from the first fifteen performances of *Le Prophète* in Berlin amount to 21,062 thalers 24 silverlings.

Wednesday 31 July. Wrote in answer to Raymond, *k. k. Hofsekretär* in Vienna, who on behalf of the Oberstkämmerer Lanckoronski asked me whether I think Madame Berend-Brand could sing Fidès. I answered in the negative. Visit from Hofrat Teichmann. I wrote to the earl of Westmorland in London and to Geheimer Kabinetsrat Illaire.

August 1850

Thursday 1 August. The French troupe, led by Demoiselle Rachel*, gave their first performance here today: Alexandre Dumas's *Le Mari de la Veuve*[167] and Corneille's *Les Horaces.* Demoiselle Rachel played Camilla.[168] Letters from Gouin and Dr. Bacher.

Friday 2 August. Studied the role of Vielka for a while with Demoiselle Ebeling. To Schönlein. Wrote to Karl Kaskel.

Saturday 3 August. Wrote a letter to Professor K. Snell, dean of the faculty of philosophy in Jena, to thank him for the honorary degree of doctor of philosophy and the liberal arts from the University of Jena. Visit from Wieprecht. Letter from the son of the prince of Prussia in Bonn.[169] Wrote in reply. Wrote to Barthold Senff, music publisher and editor of the *Signale für die musikalische Welt* in Leipzig. He had wanted a manuscript of mine for publication. Visit from the comedy director Putlitz*, who wants a letter of recommendation for Paris. Visit from two young Belgian artists who brought me a testimonial from the famous violoncellist Servais*. French production in the Opera House: Racine's *Andromaque* (Madame Rachel was Hermione).[170]

Sunday 4 August. Called on Demoiselle Rachel. In the Opera House: C. M. von Weber's *Oberon*.

Monday 5 August. Wrote to Baron Ziegesar, intendant of the Weimar Theater, and at the wish of the young prince of Prussia sent him my new *Fackeltanz* for the hereditary grand duchess of Weimar, together with the Adam's *Le Toréador* and Wagner's *Tannhäuser;*[171] the grand duchess had sent the latter for my perusal.[172] Wrote letters of introduction to Scribe and Alexandre Dumas for Baron Putlitz. In the evening to the French production at the Opera House: Lebrun's *Marie Stuart*, a reworking of Schiller's play.[173] Mademoiselle Rachel played Mary Stuart.

Tuesday 6 August. I wrote to Rabbi Arnheim in Glogau,[174] to Holtei in Grötz, to Herr von Raymond in Vienna, to Dr. B. A. Lehmann in Burg. Visit from Rellstab. Heard Lortzing's *Zar und Zimmermann* in the Opera House.

Wednesday 7 August. Wrote to Gouin, to Taillandier in Paris (who wants to send me a libretto, *Jeanne d'Arc,* through E. Blanc),[175] to Spina in Vienna. I saw Flotow's *Martha* in Kroll's Summer Theater.

Thursday 8 August. To Schlesinger and to Ebeling.

Friday 9 August. A cold shower for the first time. Wrote to Doktorin Livia Frege in Leipzig and sent her my *Quarante Mélodies*.[176] Wrote to the Belgian customs inspector Monet in Henri Chapelle near Verviers; he used to be in Verviers, and was always so kind at the inspection of my effects whenever I passed through Belgium. He wished to have my autograph, and I sent him the song "Pauvre Louise"[177] with my letter. Wrote to Count Camillo Gritti in Venice, who had asked for the performing rights to *Le Prophète* in Italy. Wrote to Herr Heugers in Amiens and returned the manuscript of *Samson*. Through Elssler, I gave the chorus (the hired ones) a present of 120 thalers for their trouble and achievement in *Le Prophète*.

Saturday 10 August. [No entry.]

Sunday 11 August. In the Opera House I heard Conradin Kreutzer's *Das Nachtlager von Grenada:*[178] very melodious, prettily scored music, but with no trace of drama or characterization.

Monday 12 August. The recurrence of cholera in Berlin has been officially announced. In Kroll's Summer Theater: Lortzing's *Der Waffenschmied.*[179]

Tuesday 13 August. Letter from the composer [Siegfried] Salomon*.

Wednesday 14 August. In the theater a French production: Corneille's *Polyeucte* (Madame Rachel as Pauline),[180] Barthet's *comédie en 1 acte*, *Le Moineau de Lesbie* (Madame Rachel as Lesbie).[181] To Schönlein.

Thursday 15 August. Called on Dr. Julius Beer. Letter from Herr von Bockelberg, Prussian ambassador in Munich.[182]

Friday 16 August. Called on the Belgian ambassador Nothomb. Visit from the singer Demoiselle Ehrenbaum from Munich. Preparations for departure.

Sunday 17 August. Called on General Wrangel,[183] who wants a patriotic march with cavalry bugle calls from me. The singer Ebeling. To Minister Ladenberg. To Count Redern: announced my four-week absence.

Sunday 18 August. On account of my departure, today I omitted the water cure. At 6:30 in the morning I left by train for Hanover where I arrived at 5:45 in the evening. This train is two hours faster than the one that leaves at eleven o'clock.

Monday 19 August. Diarrhea; I therefore decided to remain in Hanover today and to stay in bed, in order to allay the cold. I started on Rousseau's* *Confessions,*[184] which until now I had never read. I composed a little of Peter's romance in act 3.[185] Read in a Hanoverian newspaper that in the summer theater there *Le Prophète* was performed for the seventh time.

Tuesday 20 August. The disposition to diarrhea and the stomach pains have not passed, and since cholera is prevalent around here, the greatest precautions are necessary. At 9:15 I left for Cologne by train where I arrived at 8:45 in the evening.

Wednesday 21 August. At ten o'clock in the morning I left by train for Verviers, and the trip took four hours. The railway goes on for another half hour to Pepinstère, and from there bad omnibuses take one on to Spa in another one and a half hours.[186] In Verviers I made the acquaintance of the general inspector of customs, Mercier; it was for the latter's daughter that the customs inspector Monet recently wrote to me, requesting a musical autograph, which I subsequently sent him. Herr Mercier was very pleased to meet me and fetched his wife and daughter. He will bring his daughter to Spa so that I can test her singing abilities. Began composing on the journey today and completed the *chanson* of the two *cantinières* in act 2,[187] and almost all of the romance in act 3.

Thursday 22 August. I stayed in bed all day to combat the heavy cold and diarrhea through sweating and fasting. I had Doctor Lesack call on me.[188] Visit from the director of the casino, Herr Davelouis,[189] whom I knew from an earlier trip, and who allowed me the use of his piano since there is nothing appropriate for hire. He has rendered me a very great service.

Friday 23 August. I arose around midday. Letters from Gouin, from Minna, from Dr. Bacher, from Madame Livia Frege in Leipzig, from the singer Engst in Vienna,[190] from Burguis. I wrote to Mother and answered Gouin and Dr. Bacher. In the evening a visit from Brandus from Paris, who is journeying to Brussels and made this detour to come and see me.

Saturday 24 August. Letter from Zimmerman in Dresden.

Sunday 25 August. Called on Étienne Arago, who came to see me just after my arrival in Spa.[191] In the evening partially wrote out the Chanson des Vivandières. The discomfort in my stomach makes me so feverish that I called for Doctor Lesack.

Monday 26 August. Visits from Étienne Arago and Davelouis. Letter from Brandus in Brussels. Played in the casino and won ten fr. In the evening wrote out some more of the Chanson for the two Vivandières in act 2.

Tuesday 27 August. Visit from Davelouis. Visit from Duchesne, who for some years now, during Berlioz's absences, has had charge of the *feuilleton lyrique* in *Le Journal des débats*.[192] I wrote "Marguerite du poète" in Duchesne's album.[193]

Wednesday 28 August. For the first time in a while I again had a cold rubdown. Visit from Dr. Bacher. Wrote to Brandus, enclosing a recommendation by Davelouis to Perrot, editor of *L'Indépendance belge*.[194] Letter from Dr. Sass.[195] Wrote to Demoiselle Rachel: recommendation for Dr. Bacher.

Thursday 29 August. Departure of Dr. Bacher. Worked on the third couplet of the Chanson. Quartet serenade for me by Servais, Léonard, and two other artists.

Friday 30 August. Letter from the journalist Kossak in Berlin, who formerly wrote so much against me, wanting a loan of 150 thalers, which I will not refuse. Visit from the president of the Chamber of Deputies in Brussels, Verhaegen,[196] who wanted to make my acquaintance. Visit from an old French lady, Lavernette, a relation of Lamartine, who brought me a French Paternoster of her own arrangement that she wants me to set to music. In the evening there was a lovely concert by the first among all violoncellists, Servais, the violinist Léonard, and his wife, born Mendès, cousin of Madame Viardot.[197] At the conclusion a bouquet of roses was thrown to Madame Léonard. However, instead of keeping them, she came over with the director of the orchestra and presented them to me, a gesture applauded by the public.

Saturday 31 August. Answered Dr. Sass's letter; he is presently in Brussels. Visit from Herr Gits,[198] who recently serenaded me with his choir. In the evening I finished writing out the *chanson*, polished it, and indicated the principal details of the instrumentation. Letters from Duchesne, Viardot, Gouin.

September 1850

Sunday 1 September. Letter from Dr. Bacher from Hanover. Letter from Burguis. I answered Kossak and sent him the requested loan of 150 talers. In the evening I began to write out Peter's romance in act 3.

Monday 2 September. I wrote to Burguis that I am prepared to return to Berlin immediately if this would comfort my mother a little at this time, when the serious illness of my sister-in-law Betty[199] must be distressing her so much. Second concert by the violoncellist Servais and the violinist Léonard. They are both excellent artists, especially Servais. Léonard's two violin pieces, *Souvenir de Grétry* and *Fantasie über Gott erhalte Franz den Kaiser,* are lovely compositions.

Tuesday 3 September. Wrote to Brandus in Brussels. In the evening I continued writing out Peter's act 3 romance.

Wednesday 4 September. Through Burguis I have had news of the grievous agony of my poor sister-in-law Betty. May Almighty God sustain her. In the evening wrote out Peter's act 3 romance and indicated the principal details of the instrumentation. Read more of Rousseau's *Confessions.* The work did not live up to my expectations. It is frequently improper, even indecent, and Rousseau's character appears in a bad light in many respects. There are certainly many beautiful poetic details; what pleased me most was the sojourn in the Charmattes with Madame de Warrens, and the scene where he picks cherries with the two young girls. I was also struck by his many mannerisms[200] and bad habits, some of which I share, although I, unfortunately, cannot compensate as Rousseau did with the spark of genius.

Thursday 5 September. My birthday. The resolutions that I have so often made and never kept, I renew again today. I want: (1) to compose something every day, or at least to improvise ideas at the piano; (2) to devote at least one day in the week to my correspondence; (3) to read some noble classic work every day, even if only a few pages; (4) to copy out some passages from good books. May God bless this new year of my life into which I am entering today. Visit from Brandus, who came here from Brussels. He has come to Brussels to see tomorrow's production of *Le Prophète*. In the evening went with Brandus to the theater: Léon Guillard's vaudeville *Le Bal du prisonnier*.[201]

Friday 6 September. Wrote to Burguis about my servant Karl Heger. Letter from [Albert] Wagner in Hamburg. In the evening I wrote the vocal line of the act 3 romance into the full score.

Saturday 7 September. Slept badly last night and had disturbing dreams. It really seems to me that during this course of mineral waters I cannot pursue my evening work, since when I do so I have a bad night.[202] I will therefore, unfortunately, have to give up any work for the fourteen days I still want to stay here. Today I received the sad news that my poor sister-in-law Betty died on the 5th, after the most distressing suffering. May God be merciful to her soul and grant her eternal peace, eternal blessedness. I wanted to score Peter's romance in the evening, but I was so physically exhausted that I kept on dropping off to sleep.

Sunday 8 September. Letters from Karl Kaskel, Dr. Sass, Burguis, Brandus. On the sixth *Le Prophète* was performed in Brussels. The reception was apparently rather cold, the performance not good. Madame Wiedmann was Fidès, Herr Octave the Prophet.[203] In the evening in the theater: Scribe's vaudeville *Louise, ou la réparation*[204] and Varin's *Le Cuisinier politique*.[205]

Monday 9 September. [No entry.]

Tuesday 10 September. Letter from Mr. Méquillet in Antwerp, who has invited me to the reprise of *Le Prophète* there.[206] Letter from Lavry (known as Winands)[207] reporting to me on the second performance of *Le Prophète* in Brussels, which appears to have fared better than the first. Letter from Heugers in Amiens. Walked with an Englishman, Rappart [?], who seems to be extraordinarily well versed in the musical scene all over Europe and speaks about music with much knowledge. Wolowsky, the brother-in-law of Léon Faucher and a member of the Assemblée Nationale,[208] and the son of the director of the bank in Paris, Count d'Argout, came to take their leave of me. In the evening finished scoring and revising the act 3 romance.

Wednesday 11 September. Visited the English couple, Herr and Madame Rappart. In the evening I did not work in order to see whether I could obviate the sleeplessness and bad dreams I have experienced of late. All I did was read the piano score of Ambroise Thomas's *Le Songe d'une nuit d'été*.[209]

Thursday 12 September. The night was better, even though I woke up intermittently. Visit from Jules Janin, who has just arrived,[210] and from the two directors of the big Théâtre de la Monnaie in Brussels, Hanssens and Vizentini,[211] who invited me, on behalf of all the artists of their theater, to attend a performance of *Le Prophète* in Brussels. They say it has been a great success in spite of reports to the contrary in the papers.

Friday 13 September. Letters from Saint-Georges, Burguis, Brandus. Report from Lagrange that *Le Prophète* has already had fifteen performances in Pest to crowded houses and great enthusiasm.[212]

Saturday 14 September. Called on Janin and Arago. Letter from the singer Grosser.[213] Wrote to Scribe in the evening.

Sunday 15 September. Wrote to Gouin. Visit from the chief inspector of customs in Verviers, Herr Mercier, who brought his daughter so that I could assess her singing.

Monday 16 September. Read *La Religieuse de Toulouse*, a novel by Jules Janin.[214] This is more and better than a novel; it is the history of the religious struggles in the reign of Louis XIV, and especially the chronicle of a women's religious institution, *Les Filles de l'Enfance*. It is written with great talent and erudition, is both learned and amusing, and has two completely new and highly dramatic situations that could be effectively employed in the theater. In the evening Demoiselle Vandermersch gave a *séance*[215] in which she displayed the feats of small trained songbirds that are really quite astonishing. After this to Alexandre Dumas's comedy *Amour et contreband, ou Le Cashemire vert*,[216] an insignificant work.

Tuesday 17 September. I wrote to Dr. Bacher. Letter from Gouin.

Wednesday 18 September. Wrote to Gouin. In the evening answered Dr. Friedrich Sass in Brussels, and at the same time enclosed a letter of recommendation for him to M. de Persigny in Paris.[217]

Thursday 19 September. Letter from Gouin. In the theater: Alfred de Musset's *Un Caprice*.[218]

Friday 20 September. Took leave of Jules Janin, who is returning to Paris. Letter from Dr. Bacher.

Saturday 21 September. Bought presents for my children. Letters from Gouin, Dr. Bacher.

Sunday 22 September. Farewell visit to Étienne Arago and Davelouis. Informed Minna that I am going to Paris, but have not yet told Mother.

Monday 23 September. Hoarseness and throat irritation. Decided to sacrifice the day and to stay here peacefully.

Tuesday 24 September. Wrote to Mother about my departure for Paris. At one o'clock I traveled by diligence to Pepinstère in one and a quarter hours, and from there by rail to Brussels in five hours.

Wednesday 25 September. At nine o'clock I set off by train to Paris. We arrived at six o'clock in the evening.

Thursday 26 September. My cold is severe, but the throat irritation has almost disappeared. In order to protect myself, I stayed at home almost the whole day. Visit from my faithful friend Gouin. Letter from Sass in Brussels. Answer from Persigny.

Friday 27 September. Called on Armand Bertin, Véron, Nestor Roqueplan. Visit from Brandus. Went to see Scribe. In the Grand Opéra: Lebrun's* one-act opera *Le Rossignol*.[219] In the Opéra Comique the two last acts of Thomas's *Le Songe d'une nuit d'été*. In the Grand Opéra Madame Laborde sang the principal role, in the Opéra Comique Madame Ugalde. I was so tired that I kept falling asleep, and so cannot allow myself any critical observations for today.

Saturday 28 September. Called on Karl Kaskel, Crémieux, Scudo, Brandus. In the Opéra Comique: *Giralda, ou La Nouvelle Psyche*, music by Adam, a delightful imbroglio, full of comic complications.[220] Adam's music, several trivial things notwithstanding, has many charming and witty pieces, and shows once more that, of all the French composers, he has the greatest talent for the actual *buffo* genre.

Sunday 29 September. Called on Édouard Monnais. Today for the first time since my indisposition, I slept again with the wet towel, and recommenced with the cold wrap and the cold rubdown. In the Opéra Comique: *Jeannot et Colin*, music by Nicolò [Isouard].[221] Demoiselle Lefèbre sang the role of Thérèse with a very pretty voice, much fluency, and very good style. Then came Boieldieu's *La Dame blanche*.

Monday 30 September. Long conference with Scribe about the *Feldlager* in London. In the Opéra Comique: *Giralda.* Mademoiselle Félix-Miolan* sings with extraordinary correctness, good style, and a lovely fluency, but she has hardly any voice, is cold, and is certainly no actress.

October 1850

Tuesday 1 October. Conference with Scribe about the *Feldlager* in London. *Représentation extraordinaire à l'Opéra*[222] in which Alboni sang the rondos from *La Sonnambula* and *La Cenerentola*, Cerrito and Saint-Léon danced in the ballet *La Vivandière*, music by Pugni, and the actors of the Théâtre Français performed Molière's *Les Femmes savantes.*[223]

Wednesday 2 October. Conference with the regisseur of the Opéra, Le Roi, to prevent *Le Prophète* from being given with Alboni, which Roqueplan wishes to do, and which I would regard as damaging since it will harm the *rentrée* of Madame Viardot. Visited Véron, Berlioz, Gouin. In the Grand Opéra: the ballet *Stella, ou Les Contrebandiers*, music by Pugni.[224]

Thursday 3 October. Conference with Scribe. Soirée at Frau von Kalergis.[225]

Friday 4 October. Called on Madame de Girardin, Fiorentino. Conference with Scribe. Visited the singer Mario, who urgently requested me to produce one of my new operas in London at Covent Garden in the coming spring.[226] In the Opéra Comique: *Le Songe d'une nuit d'été*, music by Thomas. Madame Ugalde sang the principal role very beautifully.

Saturday 5 October. Conference with Mario. Called on M. and Madame de Girardin. To Nestor Roqueplan, Madame Ungher-Sabatier, Brandus. Stayed at home in the evening in order to read through the libretto of *L'Étoile du Nord* again.[227]

Sunday 6 October. Called on Véron, Demoiselle Alboni, Gouin. Studied the role of Berthe with Mademoiselle Laborde. In the Opéra Comique: *Le Songe d'un nuit d'été.*

Monday 7 October. Called on Fiorentino, Berlioz, Gouin. In the evening in the Grand Opéra, attended the reprise of *Le Prophète* with Alboni, to a crowded house (receipts 10,759 fr.). Alboni as Fidès pleases the Parisians quite extraordinarily, much more so than Viardot; she has a very beautiful voice of exceptional range, and sings all the tender or sentimental parts of the role wonderfully well. But in the dramatic, energetic sections she does not approach Viardot, who completely surpasses her as an actress.

Tuesday 8 October. Bordogni came to me with his Berlin pupil, the tenor von Osten, who sang me a few things: a lovely, soft voice, but a *voix blanche*,[228] still awkward in expression and fluency, and destined always to be only a *mezzo carattere*.[229] Stayed at home in the evening in order to write down my observations about act 3 of the new opera for Scribe.

Wednesday 9 October. Called on Hequet, Buloz, Adam, Brandus, Gouin, and twice on Scribe, in order to confer with him about changes to the new opera. In the evening heard *Le Prophète* at the Opéra (75th performance; 9,964 fr. receipts); Alboni made a far greater impression on me today than on the day before yesterday.

Thursday 10 October. Conferred with Scribe about the new opera. Called on Jules Janin, Carafa, Auber. Visit from Benelli[230] and the agents of the Madrid Theater Directorate, who came personally to invite me to their city to conduct *Le Prophète*. In the evening I felt too unwell either to go to the theater or to work.

Friday 11 October. Wrote to Küstner and to Griepenkerl. Called on Gouin, Léon de Wailly, Duponchel, Madame Fiorentini. Conferred with Scribe about the new opera. Stayed at home in the evening, since I still felt unwell.

Saturday 12 October. Conferred with Scribe about *L'Africaine* and *Le Prisonnier du Caucase*.[231] I visited the famous singer Frezzolini, who sang for me; the voice, however, fell far below my expectations.[232] Visit from Lumley. I told him that under no circumstances could I give him the *Crociato* revised for this season, and that only at the end of this year could I determine whether or not I would be able to give him the *Feldlager* for London. Stayed at home in the evening.

Sunday 13 October. Attended the *distribution des prix*[233] in the Gymnase Musical, where Carafa is the director. Among the musical pieces played was the march from *Le Prophète*. In the Opéra Comique: *La Fée aux roses*, music by Halévy. Demoiselle Lefèbre sang the principal role.[234]

Monday 14 October. Léon de Wailly read me the plan for an opera that takes place in India: it did not appeal to me. Dictated letters for Princess Albrecht (hereditary princess of Meiningen),[235] who wants my *Fackeltanz*, and for Oettinger in Leipzig, who dedicated his novel *Rossini* to me a few years ago.[236] In the Grand Opéra the ballet *Stella*. Pugni's music is very pretty.

Tuesday 15 October. Called on Fanny Lewald*, Professor Stahr,[237] and Moritz Hartmann,[238] all of whom had visited me. Went to see the Russian prince Soltikoff, who had presented me with his book of Indian illustrations.[239] Visits from Buloz, the *littérateur* Taillandier and a certain Demoiselle Urlaub from Bremen, who wanted me to test her voice.[240] At Brandus's the violinist Loyet played a fantasy on themes from *Robert le Diable* and asked me to accept the dedication of the piece. In the evening to the Théâtre Français for the first performance of Scribe and Legouvé's *Les Contes de la Reine de Navarre,*[241] and also the theatrical début of Mademoiselle Madeleine Brohan.[242] Both the play and the debutante had a brilliant success.

Wednesday 16 October. Visit from Herr Naumbourg, cantor of the local synagogue, who asked me to compose a musical piece for their liturgical use.[243] Conference with Scribe about the new opera and the changes to *L'Africaine.* In the Opéra Comique: the first performance of *Le Paysan,* opera in one act with music by Poisot;[244] *L'Amant jaloux,* music by Grétry.[245] With George to Heine.[246] Visit to Dr. Koreff.

Thursday 17 October. Called on Armand Bertin. Visit from the singer Charton*: lovely voice, but already worn and no longer pure; good dramatic expression. The bass Lemaire has a really beautiful voice, but needs more coaching. To the Opéra Comique for act 1 of *Giralda.* Then to a soirée at the house of Madame Sabatier, the once-so-famous Ungher, where the young singer Lagrua from Dresden,[247] who has still not sung in the theater, sang Alice's first romance in *Robert le Diable*[248] with a lovely, full, wide-ranging soprano voice. She will be an excellent singer *pour le genre Falcon.*[249]

Friday 18 October. Visit from Dr. Bamberg. Called on the Prussian *chargé d'affaires,* Count Schulenburg,[250] (with my autograph[251] for the hereditary Princess Charlotte von Saxe-Meiningen). Called on Bonoldi.[252] Visit from Brandus. Heard *Le Prophète* at the Opéra (seventy-eighth performance with receipts of 8,912 fr.).

Saturday 19 October. Wrote to the student Aland on the island of Rügen. In the Théâtre du Vaudeville: Leuven's *La Maison du garde chasse;*[253] Bayard and Dumanoir's *Le Vicomte de Létorières.*[254] Demoiselle Déjazet played the title role (the young Vicomte) perfectly, and I was very much entertained by this deft little play.

Sunday 20 October. Called on Duponchel. Wrote to the music dealer Schuberth in Hamburg.[255]

Monday 21 October. Read Camoëns's* *Lusiads* in a French translation.[256] Called on Madame Viardot, Count Pillet-Will,[257] and Gouin. Visits from Henri Blaze, Kastner, Marschenko, the cantor of the synagogue Naumbourg. In the Grand Opéra: the ballet *Le Violon du Diable,* music by Pugni (with Mademoiselle Cerrito).

Tuesday 22 October. Called on Madame Viardot, Madame Marschenko. Concert of the Philharmonic Society, under the direction of Berlioz. The remarkable pieces were "Sara la baigneuse," a song for three alternating choruses by Berlioz,[258] the *Ouverture des Francs Juges* by Berlioz,[259] and several italian arias by the famous singer Frezzolini *(soprano acuto):*[260] she sings with great warmth, expression, and lovely style, but the voice is no longer fresh.

Wednesday 23 October. In the Opéra Comique: *Le Songe d'une nuit d'été.* In the Grand Opéra: the seventy-ninth performance of *Le Prophète* (with Alboni): receipts 9,963 fr.

Thursday 24 October. Today I promised Nestor Roqueplan to decide by the end of the year whether or not I will give him *L'Africaine.* Called on Countess Rossi, Gye. In the Opéra Comique: *Giralda.*

Friday 25 October. I took Madame Viardot to Madame Sabatier-Ungher's, where I made the acquaintance of the singer [Mme.] Fiorentini. The son of the piano tuner Kelly, and Chéri, violinist at the Opéra,[261] played me a duet on themes from *Le Prophète.* In the Théâtre des Variétés: *La Gamine,* vaudeville in one act by Deslandes.[262] A neat little play in the earlier genre of this type of theater, with a charcoal burner, a sack heaver, and a spoiled child, played outstandingly by Hoffmann, Lecler, and Demoiselle Virginie.[263] Then a new play, *L'Anneau de Salomon, légende,* by Henri Berthoud,[264] a bad piece even though something could have been made of the basic idea *donnée.*[265]

Saturday 26 October. Sore throat, so stayed at home all day. Visits from Gouin, Brandus, Sina, Sax, and Gye, the director of the Covent Garden Theatre.

Sunday 27 October. In the Théâtre Montansier: *La Plus Belle Nuit de la vie, vaudeville en 1 acte* by Carré and Barrière;[266] *Phénomène, vaudeville en 1 acte* by Varin and Biéville;[267] *Les Deux Aigles, vaudeville en 2 actes* by Bayard and Biéville[268] in which Achard appears.[269] All the plays were delightful and well acted.

Monday 28 October. Visit from Eberty, who has arrived here with Anna Eberty from Switzerland. Visit from the painter Michael, who has won the prize from the late, blessed Michael's foundation.[270] Dined at Count Pillet-Will's, where I made the acquaintance of the prince of Monlear[271] and the famous artist Robert Fleury.[272] In the Opéra heard a few acts of *Le Prophète* (eighty-first performance, with Alboni; receipts 8,467 fr.).

Tuesday 29 October. Visited Eberty. In the evening in the Théâtre de l'Ambigu-Comique *Marianne,* melodrama by Michael Masson and Anicet Bourgeois;[273] it contains many interesting situations, but also many improbabilities; in the end, though, it was better than many other melodramas. Saint-Ernest acted Bernard very well.

Wednesday 30 October. Went to see Roger. He does not want to perform in *Le Prophète* tomorrow, because he is appearing in *La Favorite* today, and does not want to sing such strenuous roles on successive nights; I nonetheless persuaded him to do it.[274] To Scribe. In the Grand Opéra: *La Favorite*. Alboni sang Leonore.

Thursday 31 October. To Scribe. Visited Gathy, to whom I gave the full score and poem of *Struensee*. In the Opéra Comique: *Les Deux Gentilhommes*, opera in one act, music by Cadaux.[275] Then to the last performance of Alboni in *Le Prophète*, which was full to overflowing and very brilliant (receipts 9,955 fr.).

November 1859

Friday 1 November. Last visit to Scribe. He promised me not to give *Les Sorcières* to any composer until I have brought *L'Étoile* to production.[276] Called on Véron, Madame Sabatier, Madame Viardot. Wrote to Paul Fouché.[277] Wrote in Madame Buloz's album.

Saturday 2 November. Farewell visit to Madame Viardot. In the Opéra Comique: Grétry's *L'Amant jaloux.*

Sunday 3 November. Preparations for my departure.

Monday 4 November. At eight o'clock I left for Brussels by rail *(train de grande vitesse),*[278] which has only first class) and arrived there at five o'clock. In Valenciennes two Englishwomen boarded my carriage, a mother and daughter, who recognized me from my portrait and were very happy to make my personal acquaintance. They told me that they have been traveling for nearly thirteen years through the whole of Europe for their own pleasure. The mother composes, the daughter plays the piano. In Brussels I had wanted to call on Julius [Beer], but since he had company, I did not want to present myself in traveling clothes. In the Théâtre du Vaudeville I saw the seven-year-old Montbland (who scored such success recently in the Théâtre Montansier in Paris,[279] in *La Fille bien gardée*, a vaudeville in one act by Labiche and Marc-Michel[280]) and Grassot,[281] also from the Théâtre Montansier, in *Un Oiseau de village*, a vaudeville in one act by Bayard and Vanderburch.[282] On the evening of my arrival in Brussels *Le Prophète* was performed, but I did not go.

Tuesday 5 November. Went to see Julius and his wife, and left at 11:30 by train for Cologne. In the carriage I began composing Prascovia'a aria with some success.[283]

In the Cologne newspaper, *Le Prophète* is announced in a new production; it has already been staged here—last year actually.

Wednesday 6 November. At 7:30 left Deutz by train for Hanover, where we did not arrive until nine o'clock in the evening: in Minden we had to wait a long time for the train coming from Berlin.

Thursday 7 November. At five o'clock I left Hanover by train. On the journey I worked on Prascovia's aria. At four o'clock in the afternoon I was in Berlin and found, thanks be to God, my precious mother, my beloved wife and my three lovely children—Blanca, Caecilie, and Cornelie—in the best of health. May God bless and protect us all.

Friday 8 November. Consulted Geheimrat Schönlein about my state of health. In the Opera House: Mozart's *Die Zauberflöte*. Herr Bertram made a mediocre guest appearance as Papageno.[284]

Saturday 9 November. Called on Count Redern. Because I had a headache today, I arose late and did little, but in the evening I worked fairly well at Prascovia'a aria. Wrote to Gouin, to Professor Giuseppe Rossi in Linz.[285]

Sunday 10 November. Letter from Gouin: eighty-third performance of *Le Prophète*, return of Madame Viardot (receipts 5,696 fr. 98 c.). Called on Count Redern and Herr von Küstner, whom I did not find at home. Wrote to Dr. Bacher. In the evening worked on Prascovia's aria.

[As the next entry explains, a letter case with the notebook containing the diary of 10–26 November was lost.]

Wednesday 27 November. Visit from the conductor [Hubert] Ries. Called on the Ministerin Frau von Ladenberg.[286] At the Symphony Soirée I heard a new symphony by Spohr, *Die Jahreszeiten*,[287] which aroused little interest. This evening my long letter case, containing my current diary, the account of my expenses, and my musical sketches, was incomprehensibly mislaid. It is extremely unpleasant for me to have lost these intimate things, and God knows into whose hands they may fall. There is consequently a small gap in my diary.

Thursday 28 November. The loss of the letter case agitated me so much that I had a bad night and consequently omitted the cure. Called on the intendant-general [von Küstner] to confer about Pfister's* studying *Le Prophète* with me.

Friday 29 November. Spent three hours scoring Prascovia's aria, and came within a few bars of completing it. Visit from Fanny Lewald. In the Friedrich-Wilhelmstädtisches-Theater: Lortzing's *Der Wildschütz*. The tenor Tappert sings with a really vibrant voice, even if it is not strong.[288]

Friday 30 November. Answered the singer Garrigues, who wrote to me from Coburg[289] that in the production of *Le Prophète* there they wish to replace the bass-clarinet part with a basset-horn, which would sound an octave higher. Went through act 2 of *Le Prophète* with Pfister for the first time. Finished scoring Prascovia's aria. In the evening began composing the women's duet in act 1.[290]

December 1850

Saturday 1 December. Called on Lord Westmorland. My friend Dr. Bacher from Vienna surprised me with a visit; he is on his way to Paris. Visit from Generalintendant von Küstner to regulate the rehearsals of *Le Prophète*. Matinée in the Opera House for the benefit of the wives and children of the departing Territorial Reserve:[291] Festive March and Song *Borussia* by Spontini, act 2 of Adam's ballet *La Jolie Fille de Gand*,[292] and act 2 of Flotow's new opera, *Sophie Catherina*.[293] Dined at Geheimrat Jüngken's, where I made the acquaintance of the Kommerzienrat Berend from Danzig and his daughter, Melitta Berend. Then I visited my mother, and subsequently went with Blanca to the Austrian ambassador, Herr von Prokesch's. I took his wife my *Quarante Mélodies*.[294]

Monday 2 December. I composed a little of the Women's Duet in act 1. I wrote a letter of recommendation for the singer Wertheim, who will soon commence in Berlin, for Bordogni in Paris. Studied the role of the Prophet with Pfister. Dr. Bacher and Kullak dined with me. Wrote to Gouin and Karl Kaskel, also to Dr. Bamberg in Paris.

Tuesday 3 December. Letter from Gouin about the 200th performance of *Les Huguenots* on 29 November with Madame Viardot: receipts 6,400 fr. 94 c. Letter from Kaskel in Dresden, who mentions that Lagrua, in her first theatrical debut as Alice in *Robert*, has been very successful. Visit from the director Fritze.[295] Called on Herr von Küstner in order to regulate the rehearsals of *Le Prophète*. Studied the role of the Prophet with Pfister. In the evening worked on the Women's Duet.

Wednesday 4 December. Piano rehearsal of *Der Prophet* with Pfister and the three Anabaptists, but Mantius did not come. Called on Madame Lagrange who, because of hoarseness, could not rehearse with Pfister. I had a severe headache and could not work in the evening. Today, for the first time this season, *Roberto il Diavolo* at the Italian Opera in the Königstadt (Castellan sang Alice).

Thursday 5 December. At eleven o'clock a piano rehearsal of *Der Prophet*, then visited Madame Lagrange, Lady Westmorland, and Mother. In the evening I wrote to Brandus and sent him my song "Liebesbote"[296] for his album. I answered Professor Bischoff* in Bonn, editor of *Die rheinische Musikzeitung*, who had sent me his essay on *Le Prophète* that appeared in this paper.[297]

Friday 6 December. Anonymous letter from Königsberg reproaching me for not answering the music director Sobolewski. At his wish, I went to Herr von Küstner to confer with him about the rehearsals of *Der Prophet*. In the evening visits from the Austrian ambassador von Prokesch and his wife, and the singer Demoiselle Kurt—all of which prevented me from working until 8:30, when I attended to the Women's Duet a little.

Saturday 7 December. Went through the role of the Prophet with Pfister. In the evening I did not work at all.

Sunday 8 December. Wrote in Kapellmeister Taubert's album. Paid five thalers toward the memorial for Kapellmeister Nicolai.[298] Went to the theater with my daughter Blanca: Beethoven's *Fidelio*, and the ballet *Paul und Virginie*, with music by Gährich.[299]

Monday 9 December. Worked a little on the Women's Duet. Called on Madame Castellan, Frau von Oven,[300] Geheimrätin Jüngken and my mother. Dined with the Belgian ambassador, Herr von Nothomb. Quartet-Soirée at Ries's, where I heard Mendelssohn's Quartet in E Minor.[301]

Tuesday 10 December. Visits from the music dealer Bock, Emil Naumann, and the singer Lewinstein. In the evening worked happily on the ensemble of the Women's Duet and completed this section.

Wednesday 11 December. To Herr von Küstner: conference about the rehearsals of *Der Prophet*. Congratulated the actress Madame Wolff on her seventieth birthday.[302] The son of the Viennese theater director Pokorny wants me to act as his guarantor, since the police apparently do not want to let him come here; this I cannot do, since I have never seen him except once with his father, and I furthermore know nothing about his official intentions.[303] Dinner with Prince Karl. In the evening with the children and Schönlein to Kroll, in order to see his Christmas exhibition *(Die Wendung des Gedankens)*.[304] Afterward worked a little on the Women's Duet.

Thursday 12 December. [Sent] four thalers and ten silverlings to the music publisher Schloss in Cologne[305] for the 1851 *abonnement*[306] to *Die rheinische*

Musikzeitung. Worked on the Women's Duet for two hours. After dining, I finished composing the Women's Duet and began to write out some of it.

Friday 13 December. Studied the role of the Prophet with Pfister. In the Opera House: Rossini's *Der Barbier von Seville*. Madame Lagrange starred as Rosina, and interpolated the Variations by [Pierre] Rode into the Singing Lesson.[307]

Saturday 14 December. Piano rehearsal of *Der Prophet* with Pfister, Madame Lagrange, Madame Köster, and the three Anabaptists. In the evening wrote out the Women's Duet for a little while. Letter from Dr. Bamberg.

Sunday 15 December. To Herr von Küstner about the rehearsals of *Der Prophet*. Wrote out some of the Women's Duet. In the Opera House: *Sophia Catherina*, opera by Flotow.

Monday 16 December. In the morning orchestral rehearsal of *Der Prophet*: the first three acts. In the evening rehearsal of acts 4 and 5. Then to a musical soirée at Kommerzienrat Berend's (he is from Danzig).

Tuesday 17 December. In the morning *mise en scène* rehearsal of all five acts [of *Le Prophète*]. Wrote to Gouin in the evening. Letter from Dr. Bacher.

Wednesday 18 December. First dress rehearsal of *Der Prophet,* which lasted from 10 until 3:30. Wrote out more of the Women's Duet.

Thursday 19 December. Wrote out more of the Women's Duet. Karl Kaskel, Stadtrat Hertel from Dresden,[308] Kapellmeister Dorn, and the music director Emil Naumann dined with me. In the evening wrote out more of the Women's Duet.

Friday 20 December. Wrote out some of the Women's Duet. Visit from the piano teacher and journalist Bloch (twenty thalers).[309] Dress rehearsal of *Der Prophet*. Then I attended a big evening reception at Lord Westmorland's.

Saturday 21 December. Big dinner at Count Redern's.

Sunday 22 December. *Der Prophet* was not given today on account of the illness of Mantius.[310] The music publisher Härtel from Leipzig called on me. In the evening finished writing out the duet.

Monday 23 December. Visited Mantius. Wrote down my opinion of Geissler's antiphonal for the Academy.[311] Began to write the vocal parts of the Women's Duet into the full score. In the evening to a sitting of the Academy of Arts.

Tuesday 24 December. Visited Mother and [Paul] Taglioni. In the evening wrote the vocal parts of the Women's Duet into the full score. Because of Caecilie's chickenpox, there were no Christmas decorations for the children.[312]

Wednesday 25 December. Letter from Brandus. Finished writing the vocal parts of the Women's Duet into the full score. To the Italian Opera for Donizetti's *Linda di Chamounix*: Madame Castellan sang Linda.

Thursday 26 December. Scored four sides of the Women's Duet, and again four sides in the evening. Visit from the singer Demoiselle Marx. Letter from Kaskel.

Friday 27 December. [Went] with the singer Marx to Geheimer Kabinetsrat Illaire, but we did not find him at home. Scored four sides of the Women's Duet, and in the evening another three sides, but I felt these to be rather weak.

Saturday 28 December. At Count Redern's request, compiled a written report on the music of Kammermusiker Schulz for Euripides' tragedy *Hippolytos*.[313] Sitting of the Academy of Arts. Called on Professor Wichmann, then scored three pages of the Women's Duet.

Sunday 29 December. Scored several pages of the Women's Duet. In the evening to the reprise of *Der Prophet* (sixteenth performance). Madame Lagrange was Fidès, but reactions to her were mixed, some even negative. Herr Pfister was applauded as the Prophet, which, in light of his amateurish[314] acting and singing abilities, one can only regard as a sort of encouragement. The chorus, especially the children's chorus, and the orchestra performed very well. In spite of the raised prices the house was crowded, but the applause very restrained.

Monday 30 December. The singer Pfister called to express his gratitude for the trouble I took with him in studying *Le Prophète*. Continued scoring the Women's Duet, and finished it in the evening. Letter from Julius in Brussels, with the news that the overture to *Struensee* was very well received at a concert there.

Tuesday 31 December. Called on Count Redern. To the clarinetist Schick[315] in order to ask his advice about a passage in the Women's Duet that seems difficult to me. Indicated to Pfister several corrections in his role. This evening we finally held the Christmas presentations for our children and acquaintances; this had been postponed for so long because of Caecilie's illness. In the morning I revised part of the orchestration of the Women's Duet, and this evening revised the rest. Then I visited my mother, so bringing the old year to an end. I am grateful to Almighty God for preserving my family and me in good health this year. Sadly, in the past months, I have had to mourn the loss of my beloved brother Wilhelm. *Le Prophète* has been produced in more than forty theaters this year and with much success[316] nearly everywhere, thanks be to God.

NOTES

1. Cholera is a highly dangerous and infectious disease, outbreaks of which occur especially in poor, populous regions of the world, like India and central China. The cholera bacterium, transmitted through infected food and water, causes a profuse, painless, watery diarrhea with consequent extreme dehydration, weakness, and often death. This disease, with its high fatality rate, first spread over the world from Asia in the 1820s when deadly waves of cholera swept out of Bengal. It manifested itself in Europe in 1831–32 and returned again in 1848, 1853, and 1865–66, with a concentration mainly in the poorer parts of towns. It spread through contaminated water supplies. The relatively small impact of the disease outside of working-class areas, the resistance of medical opinion to the idea that a disease could be communicated by an apparently clean water supply, and the occasional nature of the outbreaks prevented its incidence from creating a sustained pressure for sanitary reform. Only in 1883 did the bacteriologist Robert Koch (1843–1910) isolate the bacterium that causes the disease. That settled the debate once and for all. His discoveries contributed to the understanding and control of this and other diseases (like anthrax, typhoid, and tuberculosis), especially by preventative inoculation. See Arno Karlen, *Biography of a Germ* (London: Victor Gollancz, 2000).

2. Jean-Gilbert-Victor-Fialin, duc de Persigny (1808–72) was a prominent figure in the Second Empire. He became adjutant to Louis Napoléon in 1848, a deputy in the Legislative Assembly (1849), ambassador in Berlin (1850–51), minister of the interior (1852–54 and 1862–66), and ambassador in London (1855–61).

3. Edmond Delacour (1805–73) had French diplomatic postings in Vienna and Stockholm before becoming ambassador in Vienna (January 1851–March 1853).

4. *Les Huguenots*, no. 14b *Litanie* ("Vièrge Marie, soyez bénie").

5. *L'Étoile du Nord*, no. 8 *Duo de Catherine e Prascovia* ("Ah! Ah! quel dommage").

6. *L'Étoile du Nord*, no. 2 *Couplets de Catherine* ("Écoutez! écoutez! Poum! poum!").

7. *"Was schwebet durch die Räume" für Bass Solo und 3 Soprane* (text by Ferdinand Braun; French words by François de Maurice Bourges) (1845). No. 40 in the *Quarante Mélodies*.

8. The letter to Kapellmeister Müller concerned the preparations for the first performance of *Le Prophète* in Darmstadt (1 April 1850).

9. Francesco Maria Dalle Aste (1820–c. 1886) sang Zacharie in the first Dresden performance of *Le Prophète*. He had been trained by Joseph Staudigl in Vienna, where he worked at the Kärntnertor-Theater as first bass (1837–49). After a brief stint in Hamburg, he moved to Dresden in 1849, where he stayed until 1852. For fuller biographies of some of the lesser-known singers of the German provincial stages, see the entries in *BT*, 5.

10. The German translation of *Le Prophète* was by Ludwig Rellstab.

11. Karl, Graf von Lanckoronski-Brzezie (1799–1863) succeeded Moritz Graf von Dietrichstein in May 1849 as *Oberstkämmerer*, or lord chamberlain, at the imperial court in Vienna, a post he was to hold until his death. As director of the two Court Theaters he was also in charge of the imperial jewel collection, the scientific museums, the mint and antiquities museums, the amber collection, and the picture gallery (*BT*, 5:810).

12. In the aftermath of the political upheavals of 1848, the stringency of the reimposed Habsburg autocracy under the young Emperor Franz Joseph and his prime minister, Prince Felix Schwarzenberg, was at its height. Anything that could be construed as pertaining to Catholic ritual and its liturgical language, or anything that could be regarded as critical of monarchy as an institution, had to be modified or removed.

13. Robert Schumann, *Das Paradies und die Peri*, oratorio, op. 50 (text by Emil Flechsig & the composer after Thomas Moore's oriental tales in verse, *Lalla Rookh* [1817]; completed in 1843, first performed in Leipzig, 1847).

14. Robert Schumann lived from 1844 until late summer 1850 in Dresden as composer and conductor of the Gesangverein.

15. This means that Meyerbeer did not come face to face with Schumann, nor was he aware of his presence, at the Concordia in Vienna in December 1847.

16. The soprano Franziska Schwarzbach (1825–80) sang Berthe in the first Dresden performance of *Le Prophète*. She was trained at the Leipzig Conservatoire, and made her debut there as Marguerite de Valois in *Les Huguenots* (1846). In 1848 she became part of the ensemble at the Dresden Court Opera.

17. Kotzebue's famous five-act drama *Menschenhass und Reue* was written for private theatricals in Reval, and first publicly produced in Berlin at the Königliches Schauspielhaus (1789) [Richel 87]. It enjoyed a worldwide success for many decades, and was familiar in England under the title *The Stranger*. Its themes of remorse, repentance, and reconciliation, and its dramaturgical effects of coincidence and ruse, exercised a great literary influence.

18. Emil Devrient had worked as an actor in Dresden since 1844. He epitomized the so-called Weimar style of acting, which had been inaugurated by Goethe during his time as director of the Weimar Court Theater (1791–1817). Goethe's "Rule for Actors" suggested that they were to be models of decorum on stage, paying scrupulous attention to articulation, with constant grace and formality in stature and gesture. For Marie Bayer, see 25 January 1855.

19. Madame Ebers was the wife of a wealthy Dresden stockbroker.

20. Franz Seraphicus, Graf von Kuefstein (1794–1871), *k.k. Geheimer Rat und Kämmerer*, was extraordinary ambassador and minister at the Saxon Court in Dresden.

21. The Noble Casino was in the Hôtel de Pologne in the Schlossgasse.

22. Eduard Julius Friedrich Bendemann (1811–89) was a historical painter. He studied with his father-in-law, Julius Hübner, and with Wilhelm Schadow in Berlin. In 1838 he was appointed professor at the Academy in Dresden, and was active in the decoration of the throne room and ballrooms in the Dresden Castle.

23. Julius Hübner (1806–82), a historical and portrait painter, studied with Wilhelm Schadow in Berlin and Düsseldorf. In 1839 he obtained a position at the Academy in Dresden, eventually succeeding Julius Schnorr von Carolsfeld as director in 1871. In 1840 he created the curtain for the Dresden Court Theater, which had been rebuilt by Gottfried Semper.

24. This was Sara Kaskel (1774–1858), the wife of the Dresden banker Michael Kaskel and the mother of Carl Kaskel, one of Meyerbeer's closest friends.

25. Auerbach, relieved of the pressure of poverty by the success of his *Schwarzwälder Dorfgeschichten* (4 vols., 1843–53), which was popular with the public, had just moved to Dresden where he would live until 1859. Thereafter, he settled in Berlin for the rest of his life.

26. Lessing, *Nathan der Weise*, drama *(ein dramatisches Gedicht)* in five acts (first

published in 1779, first performed posthumously at the Theater an der Behrenstrasse, Berlin, 14 April 1783) [Richel 99]. In the person of the noble Jew, Nathan, the play promotes tolerance and the belief that true religion is not a question of dogma or faith, but of ethical behavior. The play expressed the best tendencies of the Age of Enlightenment.

27. In 1849 Sophie Ebers married a second time, to Adolf Freiherr von Brandenstein (1805–88).

28. Auerbach's combination of incipient realism with a romantic pastoral idealism, juxtaposing the simplicity of rural life with the complexities and insincerity of urban existence, set the fashion for peasant literature. *Dorf und Stadt* (1847) was based on his story *Die Frau Professorin* (1846), one of the twenty stories that make up the collection *Schwarzwälder Dorfgeschichten*.

29. *Dorf und Stadt*, drama in five acts (Berlin and Vienna, 1847) [Richel 17]. Birch-Pfeiffer specialized in adapting novels for the stage.

30. The king of Saxony was Friedrich Albert II*. The text of the diploma is reprinted in *BT*, 5:812.

31. Heinrich Anton von Zeschau (1789–1870), the Saxon statesman, was president of the Geheime Finanzcollegium (1831) and won considerable repute for his role in the reconstruction of Saxon industry. Although forced to retire in the aftermath of the 1848 disturbances, he found new employ as chancellor of the royal household (1849) (*BT*, 5:812).

32. Auerbach, *Andreas Hofer*, historical tragedy in 5 acts (published in Leipzig, 1850; first performed at the National Theater in Berlin, 22 February 1879).

33. Nestroy, *Unverhofft*, comedy in three acts, from a play by J.-F.-A. Bayard & Phillipe Dumanoir (Vienna, Theater an der Wien, 1845, published 1848) [Richel 111] .

34. This was Johann Hoffmann (1802–65), director of the Ständertheater in Prague (1845–52). He had been engaged as a singer in Berlin (1829–35), and was almost certainly known to Meyerbeer. In 1852 he assumed direction of the Frankfurt Theater, and in 1855 the Theater-in-der-Josephstadt in Vienna.

35. Johann Friedrich Kittl (1806–68) was director of the Prague Conservatoire from 1843 to 1865.

36. Heinrich Kreutzer (1817–1900) studied with Giuseppe Ciccimarra and made his début in Laibach (Ljubljana) (1836). He appeared in various Viennese theaters before being engaged as a principal tenor at the Kärntnertor-Theater (1849–56), where he enjoyed much success. He sang Jonas in the production of *Le Prophète*.

37. The bass-baritone Gustav Hölzel (1813–83) made his debut in Graz (1830) and appeared on many stages before being engaged at the Kärntnertor-Theater (1843). He sang the role of Mathisen in *Le Prophète*.

38. Bauernfeld, *Franz von Sickingen*, drama in four acts (first performed in Vienna and Frankfurt in 1850) [Richel 10].

39. This short article is reprinted in *BT*, 5:815.

40. This was *Ein Abenteuer Carls des Zweiten*, comic opera in one act by Johann Hoven (i.e., Johann Freiherr Vesque von Püttlingen) (freely adapted from the French by Saloman Hermann Ritter von Mosenthal; Vienna, Kärntnertor-Theater, 12 January 1850). The opera had only a few performances and was revived only once, in 1852.

41. The bass Karl Just (1808–61) made his debut at the Königstädter Theater in Berlin in Boieldieu's *La Dame blanche*, and in Vienna at the Vienna Court Opera (1831), where he remained until 1860; from 1848 he functioned as stage manager.

42. Albrecht Graf von Bernstorff (1809–73) was Prussian ambassador in Vienna from 1848 to 1851.

43. The Dutch soprano Anna Maria Wilhelmine Hasselt-Barth (1813–81) studied with Josef Fischer in Karlsruhe and Pietro Romani in Florence, and made her debut in Trieste (1831). After singing in Munich, she appeared at the Kärntnertor-Theater in 1839, where she sang with great success until 1850.

44. This is the Hungarian nobleman Tichy von Omlasz.

45. Claudia Fiorentini, the daughter of an Italian consul in Seville, made a guest appearance in the Italian Opera in Berlin. This dramatic soprano became a great favorite with the public, appearing at the Théâtre Italien in Paris in the winter of 1850, and at Her Majesty's Theatre in London in 1851.

46. Friedrich Wilhelm Karl Fleischmann (1799–1868) was, from 1836, the leader of the Gumpendorfer Spital, which had been founded in the wake of the cholera epidemic in Vienna (1831). In 1842 he helped to found the private union of Austrian homeopathic physicians, which became public in 1847.

47. Jacob Deutschmann (1795–1853) had further elaborated the physharmonicum (c. 1830) patented by Anton Haeckl in Vienna in 1823. The physharmonicum was a keyboard instrument with operative languets originally developed around 1820.

48. See 12 January 1847.

49. *Laura*, ballet in three acts (Vienna Kärntnertor-Theater, 3 November 1849), scenario based on the fairy tale *Cinderella*, with choreography by Golinelli*. This work was performed twice during Meyerbeer's stay in Vienna (10 and 16 February 1850).

50. Ludwig Wilhelm Reuling (1802–79) was a German conductor and composer. He studied with Rinck and Seyfried, and became a theater conductor in Vienna (1829–54), where he composed thirty-seven operas and operettas (esp. *Alfred der Grosse* [Kärntnertor-Theater, 1840]), as well as seventeen ballets. He also wrote overtures, chamber music, and songs.

51. This was Julius Schladebach* the physiologist and music critic who wrote an article on *Le Prophète* in the light of its Dresden performance (1850).

52. Giovanni Baptista Golinelli (1809–84) worked at the Vienna Court Opera as dancer and ballet master (1836–59). He choreographed the ballet for *Le Prophète*.

53. Franz Seraph Weinkopf (d. 1884) was chorus master at the Vienna Court Opera (1841–70).

54. Emilie Krall (1831–1914) studied with Karl Kunt before being engaged by the Kärntnertor-Theater, where she made her debut in Johannes Hager's opera *Jolanthe* (1848). She later worked at the Dresden Opera (1856–71).

55. Clara Stöckl-Heinefetter (1813–57) had already been engaged by the Kärntnertor-Theater (1830s, 1845–47), where she sang Alice. She lost her voice later in 1850.

56. Christian Urban (1775–1860).

57. Polyhymnia, the Muse of Song ("She of many hymns").

58. Tgb. *k. k. Hoftheater*.

59. *Le Prophète* enjoyed a brilliant career in Vienna during the nineteenth century. It was performed there 180 times, one of the last reprises being conducted by Gustav Mahler (1911). It was revived in May–June 1998 with Placido Domingo and Agnes Baltsa.

60. These reports are reprinted in *BT*, 5:826–27.

61. The article was apparently by the composer Joseph Dessauer, and is reprinted in *BT,* 5:821.

62. A positive discussion by the critic Saphir eventually appeared in *Der Humorist und Wiener Punch*. It came in three parts, divided between volumes 54, 55, and 56, and had been written two days after the first performance on 28 February. It is reprinted in *BT*, 5:822.

63. Meyerbeer's cousin, Johanna Franziska Victorine, Gräfin von Limburg-Stirum (née Ebers) (1808–78).

64. Nathan Haskell Dole gives a succinct account of the daily pattern of life Meyerbeer followed in his home city: "The year 1850 he spent in Berlin, working from early morning into the afternoon in his room overlooking the Thiergarten Park. After three o'clock he received calls, and usually spent the evening at the theatre or went to a concert" (see "Meyerbeer" in *The Lives of the Musicians*, 2 vols. [London and New York: Methuen and Co., 1903], 1:342).

65. Felix Eberty was Meyerbeer's maternal first cousin once removed.

66. *The Bondman*, opera in three acts by Balfe (Alfred Bunn, after Mélesville's *Le Chevalier de Saint-George*; London, Drury Lane, 11 December 1846). It was given in German as *Die Mulatte* (trans. J. C. Grünbaum; Berlin, 25 January 1850), and performed in Berlin six times between 25 January and 31 March 1850.

67. Meyerbeer sent Rossi a monthly allowance until his death on 25 January 1855. See the composer's letter to Amalia Beer of 29 October 1848 (*BT*, 4:451) and arrangements for the transmission of funds from Vienna on 2 March 1850 (*BT*, 5:167).

68. Mario's partnership with Grisi, which started in 1839, was one of the most successful in operatic history. Their personal relationship lasted until she died in 1869, but they were never able to marry. Their appearances in *Les Huguenots* were particularly sensational. See Elizabeth Forbes, *Mario and Grisi: A Biography* (London: Victor Gollancz, 1985), pp. 85–87.

69. *Deutsche Reform* 800 (14 March 1850): 431. The article is reprinted in *BT*, 5:830.

70. After the expulsion of the thirty-one Socialist and Radical deputies from the Assembly by the High Court of Versailles for their part in instigating the rebellion in June 1849, by-elections for the vacant seats were held on 11 and 12 March 1850. Three of the vacancies were in Paris. The shock outcome saw the seats return to the Socialists: Lazare Hippolyte Carnot, François Vidal, and René Vicomte de Flotte. The Left acclaimed it as a great victory. "On the Bourse, the funds immediately fell by 3 per cent. The police reported that the mood among the wealthy classes at Versailles was one of utter panic when the result of the Paris by-election was announced" (Jasper Ridley, *Napoleon III and Eugénie* [London: Constable, 1980], p. 266).

71. Beethoven's opera had first been produced in Berlin on 11 October 1815. With Weber's *Der Freischütz*, Mozart's *Don Giovanni,* and Mozart's *Die Zauberflöte*, it became one of the most popular works at the Court Opera (685 performances until 1937) (see Loewenberg, col. 590).

72. Tgb. *pas.*

73. Julius Cornet (orig. Michael Josef Anton Cornet) (1793–1860) was an opera singer before becoming impresario at the Hamburg Opera (1841–47), then regisseur at the Berlin Court Opera (1851–52), director of the Vienna Court Opera (1853–57), and finally director of the Viktoriatheater in Berlin (1857–60).

74. "Hier in Waldes grünen Hallen," the second of the four lieder, op. 74 (words by Rellstab), that Taubert dedicated to Jenny Lind.

75. "Meyerbeers *Le Prophète*," *Blätter für literarische Unterhaltung* 68/69 (1850).

76. Tgb. *Quartet.*

77. Friedrich Wilhelm Graf von Brandenburg (1792–1850) was the Prussian minister president.

78. Karl Julius Rudolf von Rabe (1805–83) was the head of the Prussian ministry of finance from 1849.

79. Adalbert von Ladenberg (1798–1855) was the Prussian minister of culture (1848–50).

80. Baruch Auerbach (1793–1864) was rabbi of the Berlin Jewish community and founder of their orphanage, the Moses Mendelssohn'sche Waisen-Erziehungs-Anstalt. Wilhelm Beer had been the curator since 1838.

81. The Darmstadt performance took place on 1 April 1850 with Mathilde Marlow as Fidès.

82. The cellist von Viereck was a member of the Schwerin nobility; August Studemend (1825–90) was eventually to found a piano school in Schwerin which was maintained by his descendants until 1995.

83. Alexander, Graf von Schleinitz (1807–85), entered the Prussian civil service in 1828, eventually becoming foreign minister in Brandenburg's cabinet. Schleinitz, who had liberal sympathies, retired in September 1850, but under Wilhelm I took up office again (1858–61).

84. Sophie Trietsch (1831–58) was engaged for Berlin in 1850, where her special success was as Ännchen in *Der Freischütz*. She had sung Berthe in the Hamburg production of *Le Prophète* at the beginning of the year.

85. Gaetano Pardini had made his debut at the Königstädter-Theater in 1847 and was to leave this house later in 1850. Meyerbeer commented positively on his voice on 22 September 1847.

86. Elena Rosina Penco (1823–94), an Italian soprano, was engaged to sing in Dresden in 1849 and subsequently at the Königstädter-Theater in Berlin. After appearing in Constantinople and on several Italian stages, she went to the Théâtre Italien in Paris (1855), where she remained, enjoying great success, until 1872. She also appeared occasionally at Covent Garden.

87. The Italian tenor and cellist Domenico Labocetta (1823–96) had made his debut at the Königstädter-Theater in 1846. He left Berlin in 1851 to pursue his singing career, which took him as far afield as America. He left the stage in 1877 to become professor of violoncello at the Conservatorio S. Pietro a Maiella in Naples. Meyerbeer first heard him on 7 April 1847, and on that occasion admired his voice.

88. Marcello, *Psalm 41 (Qual anelante cervo)* from the *Estro poetico-armonico; Parafrasi sopra i cinquanta primi Salmi* (Venice, 1724–26, in 8 vols.) for one, two, three, and four voices with *basso continuo* for organ or clavicembalo.

89. See the appendix to the diary entry for April 1850.

90. Tgb. *Kapelle*.

91. The names of the members of the Royal Orchestra are listed in *BT*, 5:841.

92. Luise Mühlbach (pseud. of Klara Mundt, née Müller). Her three-act comedy *Lady Ellen* (first performed Hamburg, 1844; Berlin, 1845) [Richel 109] enjoyed modest vogue. She held a salon in Berlin frequented by her writer colleagues, especially from the theater circles. See also 30 May 1847 and 4 July 1861.

93. Georg of Saxe-Meiningen (b. 1831, reg. 1866–1914) was the son of the anti-Prussian duke Bernhard II (1800–1882), who was forced to abdicate (20 September 1866) as a condition of peace after the Austrian defeat in the Austro-Prussian War.

94. *Fackeltanz* no. 2 in E-flat Major for military band, later arranged for orchestra by Wieprecht. It was composed for the wedding of Princess Charlotte of Prussia (1831–55) with the Crown Prince Georg of Saxe-Meiningen (1826–1914).

95. Mathilda Ebeling (1826–51) made her debut in Stockholm (1844) and first appeared in Berlin a year later. In 1848 she went to Paris to complete her studies with Viardot-Garcia, before returning to the Prussian capital as guest artist.

96. In May 1847 Friedrich Wilhelm Deichmann obtained a concession for the construction of a theater in the Friedrichstadt district of Berlin. The new stage was inaugurated on 17 May 1850, with Albert Lortzing as kapellmeister; Lortzing composed his *Fest-Ouverture* in E-flat major for the occasion. In 1883 it became known as the Deutsches Theater.

97. *Die Zillerthaler, Liederspiel* in one act by Joseph Ferdinand Nesmüller (1818–95) (text by the composer; Hamburg, 15 October 1849).

98. Auguste Sabine Schulz (1826–1903) was the principal artist of the ensemble assembled by the new Friedrich-Wilhelmstädtisches-Theater.

99. Camillo Vincente, Conte Gritti, the husband of the singer Esther Mombelli, had been the administrator of the Teatro La Fenice (1819–25), and continued to exercise influence in artistic circles in Venice.

100. Magdalena Behrendt-Brandt (1828–98), an Austrian mezzo-soprano, had sung Fidès in the first performance of *Le Prophète* in Frankfurt (25 February 1850).

101. Ferdinand Freiherr von Ziegesar (1812–54) became intendant of the Weimar Court Theater in 1847, a post he occupied until his death.

102. Emmy Zimmermann (c. 1789–1854) was a pupil of Garcia-Viardot, and worked as a soprano in Berlin, Dresden, Leipzig, and Hanover. She later established herself in Dresden as a singing teacher.

103. Emilie Dielitz was a Berlin singer who had studied with Bordogni. She toured Italy several times before taking a post at the Königstädter-Theater in Berlin (1848).

104. Emilie Mayer (1821–83) studied with Löwe in Stettin, and with Marx and Wieprecht in Berlin. In 1850 she debuted as a composer with a string quartet and symphony. Her works were widely played in German (Munich, Leipzig, Halle, Cologne) and other cities (Vienna, Lyons, Brussels, Budapest).

105. Mosenthal, *Deborah*, *Volksschauspiel* in four acts (first performed in Prague in 1847, then in Berlin and Dresden in 1849, and Vienna in 1864) [Richel 107]. The play enjoyed great popularity, including a long run in London.

106. Napoleone Moriani (1806–78) studied with Ruga, and made his debut in Pavia (1833). He sang with great success throughout Italy and in Vienna (1842), Prague and Dresden (1843), London (1844), and Paris (1845, 1849–50). His voice began to decline in 1844, and he retired in 1851. He was one of the most famous singers of his day, noted for the intensity of his acting and the simplicity of his singing. He was particularly renowned in roles by Donizetti, Bellini, and Mercadante. He created the tenor leads in *Maria di Rohan* and *Linda di Chamounix* in Vienna for Donizetti.

107. It was reported in the *Berlinische Nachrichten von Staats-und gelehrten Sachen* on 15 June 1850 that Meyerbeer was obliged to alter the part in several places because Behrendt-Brandt's *tessitura* was not sufficiently low (cf. *BT*, 5:850).

108. Louise Kellberg (b. 1826) was a member of the Berlin Court Opera from 1848 to 1850. Later she worked in Riga (1850–51), Prague, and Cologne (from 1853).

109. Johann Ludwig Urban Blesson (1790–1861) pursued a distinguished military career in the Napoleonic Wars, and then became a lecturer in a military academy. From the 1830s he wrote on military matters, editing the *Militärliteraturzeitung* and the *Zeitschrift für Kunst, Wissenschaft und Geschichte des Krieges*. He appears to have made some unidentified contribution to Rellstab's text for *Ein Feldlager in Schlesien* (cf. Meyerbeer's letter to him on 17 June 1850; *BT*, 5:226).

110. Siegfried Julius Josephy (1792–1856) was the owner of the Haude and Spenersche bookshop.

111. Conradin Kreutzer had died on 14 December 1849.

112. Spontini, *Volksgesang (Borussia)* (words by Alexander Duncker) for chorus and orchestra, and *Marcia trionfale* (in five parts with cantabile trio) (1818), written as a tribute to Prussia.

113. Taubert's *Lied von der Majestät* (words by Alexander Duncker) had first been performed on 15 October 1849 by Mantius.

114. Alfred, Graf von Waldersee (1832–1904), an infantry lieutenant, was adjutant to Prince Karl.

115. Kullak had just founded a conservatory in Berlin with Julius Stern and Bernhard Marx.

116. *Mulier taceat in ecclesia, oder Die kluge Königin*, tragicomedy (*historische Tragödie*) in three acts by Ernst Benjamin Raupach (1784–1852) (first performed in Berlin, 1833) [Richel 121].

117. *Ein Marqueur von Krolls*, farce in one act after the French of Labiche by Bernhard Anton Herrmann. Meyerbeer attended the first performance.

118. *Die Kunst, geliebt zu werden*, *Liederspiel* in one act after the French by Adolf Bahn (7 July 1847 at the Königliches Theater in Potsdam). The music was by the Berlin composer Ferdinand Gumbert (1818–96).

119. *Eine Berliner Grisette*, comedy after the French by Otto Stotz (the first performance had been a few days earlier, on 16 June 1850). Two of songs that Lortzing had composed for the incidental music were published by Schlesinger: "Lied vom unterdrückten Gefühl" and "Weissbielied."

120. Eberhard Theodor L'Arronge (orig. Aronsohn) (1812–78) worked at Halberstadt, Dessau, and Danzig before being contracted by the Königstädter-Theater (1846–51) and the Friedrich-Wilhelmstädtisches-Theater (from 1851).

121. August Wilhelm Weirauch (1818–83), actor and playwright.

122. Anton Ascher (1820–84) was the regisseur at the Friedrich-Wilhelmstädtisches-Theater.

123. Heinrich de Marchion (1816–90), the actor and tenor, made his debut in Lübeck (1833). He worked on several stages, including Hamburg, the Königstädter-Theater in Berlin (1835–36), the Carltheater in Vienna (1843), and in Hamburg again (1848–51). After innumerable guest appearances, he moved to Dresden (1858), where he remained a celebrated *buffo* tenor until his death.

124. Tgb. *Fach.*

125. See 5 June 1850.

126. On 22 May 1850 an attempt was made on the life of King Friedrich Wilhelm IV on the station of the Berlin-Potsdam railway. He suffered a gunshot wound on the lower arm.

127. Julius Reer (1817–84) had made his debut at the Königstädter-Theater in Berlin, and worked subsequently in Breslau, Dresden, and Hamburg (1841–75). He was a particular favorite of King Wilhelm Friedrich IV and was frequently guest artist in Berlin.

128. Shakespeare, *The Comedy of Errors* (first produced 1591–94?), and included in the First Folio (1623). Holtei's production was first performed in Berlin in 1849.

129. No biographical details are available on Wertheim. Meyerbeer thought highly enough of her voice to recommend her as a pupil to Bordogni later in the year (2 December 1850)

130. Actually Augusta Molendo (1827–1902), who was engaged in Cassel (1845–51).

131. Amalie Schütz-Oldosi (1804–52) had enjoyed a brilliant career as a soprano in

Italy, singing the works of Rossini, Donizetti, and Bellini. She retired from the stage in 1825, but sought to rekindle her career around 1850.

132. Hans von Bülow had just moved to Berlin, where he joined democratic groups.

133. Lieutenant Adolf Mosson was Minna Meyerbeer's brother, the composer's cousin and brother-in-law.

134. Scribe, *Yelva, ou L'Orpheline russe, vaudeville* in two acts (with Villeneuve and Desvergers; Paris, Théâtre de Madame Saqui [= Théâtre du Gymnase Dramatique], 18 March 1828) [Wicks 6087].

135. *Yelva, die Waise aus Russland, Melodram* in two acts after the French by Theodor Hell [= Karl Winkler] (Dresden Hoftheater, 21 November 1828). The first Berlin performance had been on 14 December 1849.

136. See *L'Indépendance belge* 20, no. 181 (1850), *édition du soir*. It is reprinted in *BT*, 5:856–57.

137. This was the Munich dancer August Horscheldt (1830–87) was made guest appearances at the Berlin Court Opera in 1850.

138. Karl Ludwig Friedrich von Hinckeldey (1805–56) had been president of police in Berlin since 14 November 1848, and was particularly concerned with police and charity organizations providing for the poor. Amalie Beer and the composer presumably met him in connection with this kind of work.

139. Meyerbeer's intervention led to the granting of a royal stipend that enabled the young De Witt, who was seriously ill with a lung disease, to travel to Rome. There he continued his studies and pursued research on old music in the libraries.

140. William Lowther was attaché at the British Embassy in Berlin (1842–51).

141. This is apparently an error of transcription on the part of Wilhelm Altmann. The name is actually Fr. Steffens (b. 1797), a music teacher and director of the music school of the Royal Military Orphanage in Potsdam (1848–57) (cf. *BT*, 5:857).

142. Pugni, *Théa, ou La Fée aux fleurs*, ballet in three acts (choreography Paul Taglioni; London, Her Majesty's Theater, 18 March 1847). The first Berlin performance was at the Court Opera on 9 November 1847.

143. After the defeat of the Italian independence movements in 1848–49, Ferdinando Carlo III of Bourbon headed a dictatorial government under the Austrian occupation; he was eventually assassinated in March 1854.

144. Rudolf Ludwig von Decker (1804–77), the owner of the Deckerschen Geheimen Ober-Hofbuchdruckerei, a publishing firm, and his wife, Pauline von Schätzel (1811–82), a celebrated singer until her marriage in 1832. She made her debut in Berlin in 1828, created the title role in Spontini's *Agnes von Hohenstaufen* (1829). She sang Alice in the first Berlin performance of *Robert le Diable* on 20 June 1832.

145. General Joseph Maria von Radowitz (1797–1853) was one of the conservative advisers of King Friedrich Wilhelm IV in proposing a new constitution for Prussian union, and was very briefly the successor of the liberal Graf von Schleinitz as foreign minister (27 September to 2 November 1850) before the failure of his political plans. He was a devoted admirer of old Italian church music and wrote several essays on music in the fifth volume of his *Gesammelten Schriften* (Berlin, 1852–53).

146. Meyerbeer's niece, Julie, the daughter of Wilhelm Beer. She became the wife of Samuel Arthur von Haber (1812–92), a banker, first in Karlsruhe and later in Paris.

147. Friedrich Beckmann (1803–66) and his wife, the soubrette Adele Muzzarelli (1816–85). Beckmann was the principal actor of the Königstädter Theater in Berlin (1824–44) before moving to Vienna, where he worked at the Burgtheater (1846–66). The couple

had been invited back as guests artists for the opening of the Friedrich-Wilhelmstädtisches-Theater, and stayed in Berlin until 28 July 1850.

148. Herrmann, *Die Reise nach Spanien*, farce in two acts after Gautier and Paul Siraudin's vaudeville *Le Voyage en Spagne* (Paris, Théâtre des Variétés, 8 September 1843). Bernhard Anton Hermann (1806–76) was a book dealer in Hamburg and Riga, and editor of the *Wandsbecker Boten* and the *Hamburger Courier*. He collaborated on several newspapers and translated 123 French plays into German.

149. Schneider, *Der Kürmärker und die Picarde*, comedy in one act (first performed in Berlin, 24 August 1842; Hamburg, 1845; in Dresden, 1847; and published 1859) [Richel 135]. The incidental music was by Hermann Schmidt.

150. Karl Snell (1806–86), a mathematician and physicist, had been a professor at the University of Jena since 1844, and was dean of the faculty of philosophy.

151. Anton Gubitz was editor of the *Monatsschrift für Dramatik, Theater, Musik* (Berlin, 1846–48) and the author of several historical dramas (*Kaiser Heinrich und seine Söhne, Sophonisbe, John der Ziegler* [Berlin, 1851]).

152. Carl Anton Spina (1827–1906) was a member, and then leader (1851), of the publishing house Anton Diabelli & Co. in Vienna. Albert Wagner (1799–1874), the brother of the composer Richard Wagner, was a singer who worked in Würzburg and Bernburg, and sometimes as a regisseur in Berlin.

153. Gustav Schmidt, *Prinz Eugen der edle Ritter*, opera in three acts (text by the composer and Alexander Rost, after a poem by Ferdinand Freiligrath; Frankfurt, Stadttheater, 26 August 1847).

154. Wilhelm von Kaulbach (1804–74) was director of the Academy of Art in Munich (1847). He was frequently in Berlin at this time, completing a cycle of paintings for the New Museum. He was a friend of Ignaz von Olfers, the director general of the Royal Museums in Berlin.

155. François, vicomte de Jaucourt (b. 1825), was attaché at the French Embassy in Berlin (1850).

156. Louis Spohr, String Quartet in E-flat Major, op. 58, no. 1?

157. Louis Crelinger was king's counsel on the Justice Commission in the Geheimes Ober-Tribunal of the Prussian Ministry of Justice.

158. Charlotte Birch-Pfeiffer, *Im Walde*, drama *(ländliches Charaktergemälde)* in four acts (Hamburg, Thalia Theater, 7 August 1850) [Richel 17]. Meyerbeer attended the first Berlin performance.

159. George Sand, *La Mare au diable* (1846), a novel of rustic life *(roman champêtre)* about a young widowed farmer, Germain, and a young servant girl, Marie, who in spite of their respective plans for marriage and work discover their love for each other during a nocturnal adventure near a lake reputed to be haunted.

160. Roderich Benedix, *Der Vetter*, comedy in three acts (first performance in Leipzig, 21 November 1846, and in Vienna, 1847) [Richel 14]. Benedix was the most popular German writer of comedy since Kotzebue.

161. The performance was on 24 June 1850. See *Revue et gazette musicale* 17, no. 29 (1850): 248, reprinted in *BT*, 5:860–61.

162. P. Baron von Tschudy de Flums was secretary at the Berlin legation of the Kingdom of the Two Sicilies.

163. *Der Vater der Debütantin, oder Doch durchgesetzt, Posse* in four acts by Bernhard Anton Herrmann, after Théaulon de Lambert and Bayard's *comédie-vaudeville, Le Père de la débutante* (Paris, Théâtre des Variétés, 28 October 1837).

164. *Das Versprechen hinterm Herd, eine Scene aus den österreichischen Alpen mit Nationalgesängen* by Alexander Baumann (Vienna, Burgtheater, 9 December 1848).

165. Sir Henry Francis Howard (1809–98) served at the British Embassy in Berlin, first as attaché (1832–46), then as secretary (1846–53).

166. J. S. Bach, *Gottes Zeit ist die allerbeste Zeit,* Cantata no. 106 (1711?) (known as the *Actus tragicus* or "Funeral Cantata").

167. Alexandre Dumas *(père), Le Marié de la Veuve,* prose *comédie* in one act (with Anicet Bourgeois & Eugène Durieu; Paris, Comédie Française, 4 April 1832) [Wicks 10997].

168. Typical of Corneille's "French classical tragedy," *Horace* (Paris, Palais-Cardinal, March 1640) deals with Livy's story of the patriot who saved the state and murdered his pacifist sister. Rachel had made her debut in this role at the Comédie Française on 12 July 1838.

169. Friedrich Wilhelm Nikolaus Karl, prince of Prussia (1831–88), son of Prince Wilhelm, became king of Prussia and emperor of Germany for ninety-nine days in March–June 1888 before dying of throat cancer. He had begun his studies at the University of Bonn in 1850, and wrote to thank Meyerbeer for the copy of the second *Fackeltanz* the composer had sent him (see 19 and 28 June 1850).

170. The theme of Racine's *Andromaque* (Paris, Louvre, 17 November 1667) was probably inspired by Vergil; it depicts the captive Andromache and the vacillations of her captor, Pyrrhus, torn between her and the proud Hermione, on whom depends the sanity of Orestes.

171. *Tannhäuser und der Sängerkrieg auf Wartburg, Handlung* in three acts by Richard Wagner (text by the composer, based on a Middle High German poem, the *Wartburgkrieg* [c.1250] and on the *Tannhäuserlied* [c. 1515]; Dresden, Court Opera, 19 October 1845). It was created by Johanna Wagner, Schröder-Devrient, Tichatschek, Mitterwurzer, and Dettmer, with the composer conducting, and very successful in Dresden (500 performances by 1913). After the 1849 production in Weimar, it began to spread throughout Germany (in 1853 and 1854 alone to fifteen new stages each year), and to every corner of the world (e.g., New York on 4 April 1859, the first Wagner opera in America; Buenos Aires, 1894; Johannesburg, 1905). Meyerbeer appears to have loved this work, consistently attending performances and noting nineteen contacts with the score in his diary.

172. Meyerbeer thus knew Wagner's opera, even though he had not heard it in performance.

173. *Marie Stuart, tragédie* by Pierre-Antoine Lebrun after Schiller (Paris, Théâtre-Français, 6 March 1820). Lebrun (1785–1873) specialized in neoclassical tragedies. He was a member of the Académie Française (1828), director of royal publishing (1830), and a member of the Senate (1853).

174. Heymann Arnheim (b. 1796) was a theologian and teacher (1827) at the Jewish Community School in Glogau. He became head teacher in 1840.

175. René-Gaspard-Ernest Taillandier (1817–79) was a literary historian. After a successful career in Paris, he moved to Strasbourg (1840) and then Montpellier (1843). In the same year he became a correspondent for the *Revue des deux mondes,* and later professor of literature at the Sorbonne (1863), and a member of the Académie Française (1873).

176. This collection of Meyerbeer's *Lieder, mélodies,* and *canzone* had just been published in Paris by Louis Brandus. Livia Frege specialized in song recitals (see 29 August 1849).

177. The manuscript of this unpublished song, "Le Lai de la pauvre Louise" (text by Sir Walter Scott), is kept in the Pierpoint Morgan Library in New York.

178. *Das Nachtlager in Grenada, romantische Oper* in two acts (K. J. Braun von Braunthal, after Friedrich Kind's drama; Vienna, Theater in der Josephstadt, 13 January 1834), Kreutzer's most famous and enduring work, also performed in Czech, Swedish, English, Croatian, Hungarian, Slovian, Flemish, and Lettish. It reached New York in 1862, and is still occasionally revived.

179. Albert Lortzing, *Der Waffenschmied, komische Oper* in three acts (text by the composer, after Friedrich Julius Wilhelm Ziegler's *Liebhaber und Nebenbuhler in einer Person* [1790]; Vienna, Theater an der Wien, 31 May 1846). One of Lortzing's great successes, a lightly romantic comedy turning on his favorite theme of an aristocrat disguised as a workman. It was performed in Czech, Swedish, Hungarian, and Croatian, and is still given in Germany.

180. Often regarded as Corneille's finest tragedy, *Polyeucte martyr* (Paris, 1641 or early 1642) deals with the social obligations of a martyr, caught between his aspiration to a glorious death and his duty to his faithful wife, Pauline.

181. Meyerbeer had seen Rachel in the same role in Paris on 13 October 1849.

182. Heinrich Friedrich Philipp von Bockelberg (1802–57), *Kammerherr* and *Legationsrat*, was extraordinary Prussian ambassador and authorized minister in Munich.

183. Friedrich Heinrich Ernst von Wrangel (1784–1877), Prussian general, later ennobled as a count.

184. *Les Confessions de Jean-Jacques Rousseau contenant le détail des événements de sa vie et de ses sentiments secrets dans toutes les situations où il s'est trouvé* (written 1765–70, published posthumously 1781 and 1788), a type of *autobiographie romancée* that is misleading on fact but revealing of the author's psychology. The work covers the period from his early life to 1766, when he left the island of Saint-Pierre. Rousseau claimed to present the self-portrait of a man "in all the truth of nature," describing all the incidents of his agitated life, his reactions to them, and his spiritual development. He concealed nothing, even those things which could have put him in a bad light, like his meanest actions and sexual abnormalities. It spite of his morbid sensibility, it is regarded as a work of sincere self-revelation. There are passages containing exquisite descriptions of scenery and domestic life.

185. *L'Étoile du Nord*, no. 15b *Romance de Pierre* ("O jours hereux de joie et de misère").

186. Meyerbeer's particular association with Spa was cemented by his many visits there during the 1850s. He visited Spa every year from 1850 to 1856, with the exception of 1853.

187. *L'Étoile du Nord*, no. 13b *Couplets des deux Vivandières* ("Sous les ramparts du vieux Kremlin").

188. Dr. Lambert Joseph Lezaack (1800–1869), also at some point the mayor of Spa, provided Meyerbeer with many friendly contacts.

189. Édouard Davelouis was director of the casino (which his father had managed since 1822) until its closure in 1872. He was among Meyerbeer's closest acquaintances in the resort.

190. Betty Engst (1832–55), an alto, trained in Prague and was engaged by the Vienna Court Opera (1849–53). There Fidès was one of her most successful roles.

191. The writer Étienne Arago had written innumerable comedies and vaudevilles during the 1840s, but lived in exile in Belgium after the collapse of the July Monarchy. Like Meyerbeer and Jules Janin, he became a famous figure in Spa.

192. This was the section of the paper dealing with musical criticism.

193. "La Marguerite du poète" (text by Henri Blaze de Bury) (1837). No. 32 of the *Quarante Mélodies*.

194. Henri-Édouard Perrot (1808–73), French journalist, settled in Brussels in 1831, was a correspondent for the *Journal des débats*, *Temps*, *National*, and *Quotidienne*, as well as various local papers. After working as a stenographer in the Senate, he became the editor and then director of the *Indépendance belge* (1843), which became one of the most important of Belgian liberal newspapers. In 1856 he sold his shares and worked in the political arena.

195. Dr. Friedrich Sass (1817–51) was a German journalist, an editor in Hamburg and Berlin (1841), and Paris correspondent of the Berlin *Nationalzeitung* and telegraphic communications (1848). He 1850 he was denounced as promoting Socialist journalism, and expelled by the French minister of the interior. He sought refuge first in London, then in Brussels, and petitioned the minister for permission to return to Paris.

196. Pierre Théodore Verhaegen (1796–1862), a lawyer and politician, after a long career as a deputy was elected to the presidency of the Belgian legislature by the liberal and Catholic parties (28 June 1848). He resigned his position in September 1852 because of disillusionment with growing reaction, and eventually retired from politics altogether in 1859.

197. Léonard had married the singer Maria Joaquina Petronella Paula Antonia Sitches de Mendi (1827–1914) in 1849. She was the niece of Manuel Garcia.

198. George Alexander Gits (b. 1822) was the director of the music school in Spa. He settled in London in 1865.

199. Rebekah ("Betty") was the widow of Heinrich Beer.

200. Tgb. *tics.*

201. Léon Guillard, *Le Bal du prisonnier, comédie-vaudeville* in one act (with A. Decourcelle & J. Barbier; Paris, Théâtre du Gymnase Dramatique, 27 October 1849) [Wicks 6757].

202. "The great celebrity enjoyed by Spa is due to its mineral springs. These resemble Pyrmont in Walbeck and Schwalbach in Nassau, being chalybeate, and containing carbonates of magnesia, soda, manganese, and sulphates of soda and potash, together with copious carbonic acid in unusual quantity. The waters are sparkling, and to the ordinary taste quite palatable and digestive. Formerly used only in the shape of a beverage, they are now largely employed for baths as well. They are efficacious in liver and nervous diseases and also in the case of dyspepsia" (*Guide to Belgium and Holland* [London, New York, and Melbourne: Ward, Locke & Co., c. 1900], p. 164).

203. The alto Mme. Widemann and the tenor Octave Benoît were part of the ensemble of the Théâtre de la Monnaie in Brussels in the 1850–51 season.

204. Scribe, *Louise, ou la réparation, comédie-vaudeville* in two acts (with Mélesville & Bayard; Paris, Théâtre de Madame Saqui [= Théâtre Gymnase Dramatique], 16 November 1829) [Wicks 4711].

205. Varin, *Le Cuisinier politique, comédie-vaudeville* in one act (with J. X. Boniface; Paris, Théâtre du Palais Royal, 4 November 1848) [Wicks 8161]. Varin was actually called Charles Victor Voirin (1798–1869).

206. Méquillet was a theatrical agent in Antwerp.

207. Charles-Adolphe-Joseph Lavry (1817–50) was a critic and secretary of the Société de Gens des Lettres Belge. He used the alias "Winands."

208. Actually Wolowsky. Louis-François-Michel-Raymond Wolowsky (1810–76) had to flee from Poland because of his part in the Revolution of 1830. He settled in Paris where

he became a professor at the Conservatoire des Arts et Métiers. Later he resumed politics, eventually entering the Assemblée Nationale in 1848.

209. Thomas, *Le Songe d'une nuit d'été, opéra comique* in three acts (J. B. Rosier & A. de Leuven, based not on Shakespeare's play, but on an episode from the poet's life, with Queen Elizabeth and Sir John Falstaff also appearing as characters; Paris, Opéra Comique, 20 April 1850). This work was very successful in France, and was regularly performed into the twentieth century (Paris, 1915; Lille, 1936; Brussels, 1937). It also enjoyed a respectable international career, reaching Mexico in 1879 and Glasgow in 1898.

210. Jules Janin, the novelist and noted literary critic of the *Journal des débats*, visited Spa every summer from 1845 to 1860, 1849 and 1857 excepted. See Albin Body, *Meyerbeer aux eaux de Spa* (Brussels: Veuve J. Rozez, 1885), p. 99.

211. The composer Charles Louis Hanssens* became principal conductor (1848) and then director of the Théâtre de la Monnaie in Brussels (1850–53). Auguste Vizentini (1811–91), an actor and theater director in Paris, became second director and regisseur at the Théâtre de la Monnaie (1850–52).

212. The first performance of *Le Prophète* in Pest was at the National Theater on 11 June 1850, in the Hungarian translation of Beni Egressy and J. Szerdahelyi (see Loewenberg, col. 874).

213. Henriette Grosser (b. 1818) worked as a member of the chorus and in secondary parts at the Berlin Court Opera before working in Königsberg and Prague. From 1850 she appeared as guest artist on several stages, including Dresden (1851–52).

214. Janin's novel had just appeared in Paris, published by Lévy Frères.

215. Fr. "session" or "sitting".

216. Alexandre Dumas *(père), Amour et contrebande, ou Le Cachemire vert, comédie-vaudeville* in one act (in collaboration with Eugène Nus; Paris, Théâtre du Gymnase Dramatique, 15 December 1849) [Wicks 7220].

217. Dr. Sass's application for permission to return to Paris had not been answered, and hence he turned to Meyerbeer for help. The latter wrote to the French ambassador in Berlin on Sass's behalf, but also to no avail. Sass was obliged to remain in Brussels working at the office of telegraphic communications until his premature death on 13 November 1851.

218. Alfred de Musset, *Un Caprice, comédie* in one act (Paris, Théâtre Français, 27 November 1847) [Wicks 7317].

219. *Le Rossignol, opéra* in one act by Louis Sébastien Lebrun (Charles Guillaume Étienne; Paris, Opéra, 23 April 1816). It was performed 227 times in Paris until 1852, and was the composer's most successful work.

220. Adam, *Giralda, ou La Nouvelle Psyche, opéra comique* in three acts (Scribe; Paris, Opéra Comique, 20 July 1850). This work was successful in Paris, and revived there as late as 1915. It was also given in German, Portuguese, Spanish, Russian, English, and Swedish throughout the nineteenth century (e.g., Boston, 1885; Mexico, 1893).

221. Isouard, *Jeannot et Colin, opéra comique* in three acts (C. G. Étienne; Paris, Opéra Comique, 17 October 1814). The work was revived in Paris in 1850 and 1857, but otherwise enjoyed only a limited career in German, Polish, and Danish, despite reaching New York in 1827.

222. Fr. "an extraordinary performance at the Opéra."

223. Molière, *Les Femmes savantes, comédie* (Paris, Palais-Royal, 11 March 1672).

224. Pugni, *Stella*, ballet in two acts (scenario and choreography by Arthur Saint-Léon; Paris, Opéra, 22 February 1850). This work was modestly successful, performed thirty-two times until 1852.

225. Maria Kalergis (1822–74), a pupil of Chopin, settled in Paris and established friendly relations with composers like Berlioz, Liszt, and, after 1860, Wagner and Cosima. She later married Sergei Sergejewich Count Muchanow.

226. Mario was considered Rubini's successor; he was "elegantly handsome, with a winning stage presence, and an extraordinarily sweet-toned voice" (John Warrack and Ewan West, *The Oxford Dictionary of Opera* [Oxford and New York: Oxford University Press, 1992], p. 443). He enjoyed some of the greatest successes of his career in Meyerbeer's operas. "*Le Prophète* of London had a vast advantage over that of Paris in the remarkable personal beauty of Signor Mario, whose appearance in his coronation robes reminded one of some Bishop-Saint in a picture by Van Eyck or Dürer . . . ," observed Henry Fothergill Chorley. Meyerbeer's operas were to be synonymous with the fortunes of Covent Garden in the nineteenth century. Chorley goes so far as to say that "[t]he production of *Le Prophète* may be said to have saved the new Italian Opera House, then notoriously floundering in embarrassments, with a company which was a republic, and, for the time, in a state of discontent amounting to anarchy" (*Thirty Years' Musical Recollections* [1862; reprint, London and New York: Alfred A. Knopf, 1926], pp. 264, 265).

227. This is the first mention of the definitive title of the new *opéra comique*.

228. Fr. "white voice."

229. See 12 September 1849.

230. Giovanni Battista Benelli (1773–1857) was a theater agent whose career as an impresario took him to Bologna, Paris (Théâtre Italien, 1816), and London (King's Theatre, 1823–24), then Italy and Paris again (from 1844).

231. This scenario was based on Alexander Pushkin's story *The Prisoner in the Caucasus* (written in 1820–21, published 1822); Scribe had already presented it to Meyerbeer on 27 November 1849. The composer did not take it on. The most famous operatic version of the story was written by César Cui (1883).

232. Erminia Frezzolini (1818–84) was singing in London during 1850, and was soon to join the company of the Théâtre Italien (1853–57). She had created Giselda (*I Lombardi*, 1843) and Giovanna (*Giovanna d'Arco*, 1845), for Verdi, and was famous for her pure, sweet tone, legato singing and purity of expression, as well as her beauty and dramatically affecting stage presence.

233. Fr. "prize giving."

234. The Parisian soprano Constance Caroline Lefèbvre (1828–1905) achieved great success in the *concours* (competition) of the Conservatoire in October 1849, and was immediately engaged by the Opéra Comique, where she sang roles in Auber's *La Part du Diable* and *La Sirène*. She was chosen by Meyerbeer to create the role of Prascovia in *L'Étoile du Nord* (1854).

235. Wilhelmine Frederike Luise Charlotte Marianne, princess of Saxe-Meiningen (1810–83), was a daughter of King Willem I of the Netherlands.

236. Eduard Maria Oettinger, *Rossini, komischer Roman* (Leipzig, 1845). The novel was translated into French as *Rossini: L'Homme et l'artiste* (Brussels, 1858) and into Italian (Venice, 1867).

237. Adolf Wilhelm Theodor Stahr (1805–76) was a literary historian and a writer. He was a teacher in Oldenburg before settling in Berlin (1852). During a trip to Italy (1845) he made the acquaintance of Fanny Lewald, whom he eventually married in 1855. His stay in Paris (1850) resulted in a two-volume book, *Zwei Monate in Paris* (Oldenburg, 1851).

238. Moritz Hartmann (1821–72), a writer, was forced to flee Austria and Germany in

the wake of the 1848 revolutions. He lived in exile in Switzerland and England before settling in Paris in 1850, where he became the correspondent of the *Kölnische Zeitung*.

239. Prince Aleksei Soltikov, *Voyages dans l'Inde pendant les années 1841–46* (Paris, 1848; with thirty-six lithographed plates). See 14 December 1849. Meyerbeer's pocket calendar for October 1850 also shows that he consulted Ferdinand Denis's book *Le Portugal: L'Univers, ou l'Histoire et description de tous les peuples, de leurs réligions, mœurs, coutumes, etc.* (Paris: Didot, 1846), suggesting renewed reading and research for the *Africaine* project. A memoir of the prince, who was a regular visitor to Paris, was recorded by Glinka: "In the early spring Prince Aleksey D. Soltykov arrived in Paris from Egypt. I had known him for a long time and had seen him often in 1853. We would go riding in the Bois de Boulogne so early in the season that there was scarcely anything green about, and later in the summer, we dined and otherwise passed the time together. He was an artist at heart and a diplomat (monstrously polite) in appearance" (Mikhail Ivanovich Glinka, *Memoirs*, trans. from the Russian by Richard B. Mudge [Norman: University of Oklahoma Press, 1963], p. 237).

240. Elisabeth Uhrlaub had written to Meyerbeer on 4 October 1850 with this request (see *BT*, 5:296).

241. Scribe & Legouvé, *Les Contes de la Reine de Navarre, ou La Revanche de Pavie*, prose *comédie* in five acts [Wicks 7988]. Gabriel-Jean-Baptiste-Ernest-Wilfrid Legouvé (1807–1903) first worked as a novelist (*Édith de Falsen*, 1840), then turned to the stage. Scribe invited him to collaborate on several projects, esp. the famous tragedy *Adrienne Lecouvreur* (1849) written for Rachel.

242. Madeleine Brohan (1833–1900) had become a student at the Conservatoire at the age of fifteen, and after only eighteen months of tuition won first prize. She was engaged by the Comédie Française, and after her triumphant début, witnessed by Meyerbeer, continued working there until 1881, with only a brief interlude in St. Petersburg.

243. Samuel Naumbourg (1817–80) worked as a cantor in Munich and Besançon before becoming principal cantor in the Great Synagogue of Paris. He edited the liturgical handbook *Chants religieux des Israélites* (Paris, 1847, 2 vols.). The 1863 edition contained contributions by Halévy and Meyerbeer (the choral prayer "Uvnukho yomar").

244. Poisot, *Le Paysan*, *opéra comique* in one act (words by Jules Édouard Alboize de Pujol). For Clément & Larousse, this little work contained "les qualités plus solides, de la verve mélodique, un sentiment vrai de la déclamation, une harmonie correcte et variée" [solid qualities, melodic verve, true declamatory sentiment, a correct and varied harmony] (2:853).

245. Grétry, *Les Fausses Apparences, ou L'Amant jaloux, comédie en trois actes, mêlée d'ariettes* (Thomas d'Hèle; Versailles, 20 November 1778; Paris, Comédie-Italienne, 23 December 1778). This work was widely performed throughout the late eighteenth century (in German, Polish, Danish, Swedish, Dutch), and was revived in Paris in 1850 and in the twentieth century (Liège, 1930, and Geneva, 1931).

246. George Beer was Meyerbeer's nephew, the son of Wilhelm Beer.

247. The singer Emma Lagrua (1831–65) was part of the ensemble of the Dresden Court Opera (1850–51), then worked at the Paris Opéra, where she created the role of Irène in Halévy's *Le Juif errant* (1852).

248. *Robert le Diable*, no. 3 ("Va! dit elle").

249. Fr. "in the style of Falcon." The famous Marie Cornélie Falcon* created Valentine in *Les Huguenots* and gave her name to a particular timbre of smoky, dramatic soprano voice.

250. Legationsrat Karl Ernst Gustav von der Schulenburg, Herr auf Priemern, Bretsch, und Drüsedau (1814–90), was first secretary at the Prussian Embassy in Paris.

251. This was the autograph of the *Fackeltanz* no. 2 in E-flat Major.

252. Meyerbeer had first met Francesco Bonoldi (1800–1873) in Italy in 1818, as a singer. He later became a singing teacher and honorary member of the Accademia di Santa Cecilia in Rome (1844).

253. Adolphe de Leuven, *La Maison du garde chasse, comédie-vaudeville* in one act (with L. Lhérie; Paris, Théâtre du Vaudeville, 5 May 1850) [Wicks 10826].

254. Bayard and Dumanoir, *Le Vicomte de Létorières, comédie-vaudeville* in three acts (Paris, Théâtre du Palais Royal 1 December 1841, with a revival at the Théâtre du Vaudeville, 16 October 1850) [Wicks 13917].

255. Julius Ferdinand Georg Schuberth (1804–75) founded bookshops, music shops, and publishing houses in Hamburg (1826), Leipzig (1832), and New York (1850).

256. *Os Lusíadas* (1572), the national epic of Portugal, concerning the voyage of Vasco da Gama to India. It was to have an important influence in the genesis of *L'Africaine*: generally, in the epic concept of the Portuguese voyages of exploration and colonization of the Indies; and specifically, in the image of Adamastor, the giant of the sea, imprisoned in the ocean around the Cape of Good Hope (canto 5; used in Nelusko's ballad in act 3 of the opera).

257. Comte Michel-Frédéric Pillet-Will (1781–1860), banker, economist, and amateur musician. He established cordial relations with many celebrated artists, particularly Rossini. Meyerbeer records meeting him on 9 January 1849.

258. Berlioz, *Sara la baigneuse* for chorus and orchestra (words by Victor Hugo), op. 11 (1834, rev. 1850).

259. Berlioz, Overture *Les Francs-juges*, op. 3 (1836).

260. It. "sharp (or high) soprano."

261. The violinist Victor Cizos, known as Chéri (1830–82), studied at the Paris Conservatoire, where he won first prize (1849), and was engaged by the Opéra. He studied composition with Adam, winning *grand prix* (1855). Later he became orchestra leader in various Parisian theaters (Variétés, Châtelet, Gymnase).

262. Paul Deslandes, *La Gamine du Faubourg, drame-vaudeville* in one act (Paris, Théâtre des Variétés, 22 April 1847) [Wicks 10548].

263. No biographical details are available for Hoffmann and Lecler. Déjazet also called herself Virginie.

264. Samuel Henri Berthoud, *L'Anneau de Salomon, légende* in one act (Paris, Théâtre des Variétés, 24 October 1854) [Wicks 6459].

265. Fr. "subject."

266. Pierre Michel Carré *(père)* and Théodore Barrière, *La Plus Belle Nuit de la vie*. Wicks [12388] describes this as a *folie-vaudeville* in one act, and lists the collaborators as Carré, Ch. Voirin Varin, A. Chapeau, and J.-Henri Tully (Paris, Théâtre du Gymnase Dramatique, 21 October 1831).

267. Varin and Biéville, *Phénomène, ou L'Enfant du mystére, vaudeville* in one act (with E. Desnoyers; Paris, Théâtre du Palais Royal, 26 October 1850) [Wicks 12273].

268. Bayard and Biéville, *Les Deux Aigles, comédie-vaudeville* in two acts (Bayard & E. Desnoyers [according to Wicks 8327]; Paris, Théâtre du Palais Royal, 17 October 1850).

269. Pierre Frédéric Achard (1808–56), a comedian.

270. In 1850 the artist Max (Mayer Isaac) Michael (1823–91) won a scholarship from the Michael Beer Foundation to study in Paris. He became a genre and portrait painter, and in 1875 professor at the Berlin Academy of Art.

271. He was actually Fürst Julius Max Thibaut von Montléard (1787–1865).

272. Joseph-Nicholas-Robert Fleury (1797–1890), a French historical artist and lithographer. In 1855 he became a teacher at the École des Arts in Paris, and eventually the director (1863).

273. Masson and Anicet Bourgeois, *Marianne*, *drame* in seven acts (Paris, Théâtre de l'Ambigu-Comique, 28 September 1850) [Wicks 11069].

274. It is interesting to compare this somewhat laconic observation with the reactions of Roger that have been have become part of the general body of received opinion. Charles Stuart cites from Roger's *Le Carnet d'un ténor* (Paris, 1880): "The tenor Roger who 'created' Jean in *Le Prophète* spoke of his [Meyerbeer's] 'egotistical, Machiavellian brain', his trick of saying the most biting things in the sweetest manner, his eyes full of tenderness, his lips pursed as if for a kiss" (see *The Decca Book of Opera* [London: Werner Laurie, 1956], p. 260).

275. Justin Cadaux, *Les Deux Gentilhommes*, *opéra comique* in one act (Planard; Paris, Opéra Comique, 17 August 1844). This small work obtained a measure of success because of its stylish music.

276. Scribe's libretto *Mosquita la sorcière*, written in collaboration with Vaëz, was nonetheless set by Dominique-François-Xavier Boisselot, and produced at the Théâtre Lyrique in 27 November 1851, two and a half years before the première of *L'Étoile du Nord*.

277. This was the librettist Paul-Henri Foucher.

278. Fr. "express train."

279. This was actually Céline Montaland (1843–91), who made her debut at the age of six. She had such great success in *La Fille bien gardée* that a series of special roles for children were written for her, and a series of tours brought her to the attention of a wide public. In 1860 she returned to Paris, where she continued her successful career in various theaters (the Porte-Saint-Martin, Gymnase, Palais-Royal, Odéon, and, from 1884, the Comédie-Française).

280. Labiche and Marc-Michel, *La Fille bien gardée*, *comédie-vaudeville* in one act (Paris, Théâtre de Palais Royal, 6 September 1850) [Wicks 9301].

281. The actor Paul-Louis-Auguste Grassot (1800–1860) made his debut in Paris at the Théâtre Montmartre (1825). After engagements in the provinces, he returned to Paris to work as a comedian at the Palais-Royal (1838–59).

282. Bayard and Vanderburch, *L'Oiseau de village*, *comédie-vaudeville* in one act (Paris, Théâtre du Palais Royal, 4 August 1849) [Wicks 11793].

283. *L'Étoile du Nord*, no. 9b *Couplets de Prascovia* ("La, la, la . . . En sa demeure"). Meyerbeer first worked on this piece on 26 November 1849.

284. Heinrich Bertram (1825–1903) was a baritone from the Stadttheater in Königsberg. This was his only guest appearance at the Berlin Court Opera.

285. This was the scholar Giuseppe (Joseph August) Rossi (1790–1863), who had been the professor of Italian at the University of Graz (1835) and then a teacher in the Italian school in Linz (1841). He was also correspondent for the *Wiener Theater Zeitung* (until 1859).

286. This was Albertine Ladenberg (née Weinbeck) (1805–84), the wife of the Prussian minister of state.

287. Spohr, Symphony no. 9 in B Minor *(Die Jahreszeiten)*, op. 143 (1850).

288. Tappert was engaged by the Stadttheater in Stettin, and alternated with the Stadttheater in Magdeburg.

289. Malwina Garrigues worked at the ducal Hoftheater in Coburg and Gotha from

1849 to 1853. She was later to become famous with her husband, Ludwig Schnorr von Carolsfeld, as the creators of the eponymous protagonists of Wagner's *Tristan und Isolde* (1865).

290. *L'Étoile du Nord*, no. 8 *Duo de Catherine et Prascovia* ("Ah! ah! quel dommage"), resumed for the first time since Meyerbeer's preparatory work on it (3 January 1850).

291. Tgb. *Landwehr*, the militia or yeomanry of men aged between thirty-five and forty-five.

292. Meyerbeer first saw *La Jolie Fille de Gand* in July 1842.

293. Flotow, *Sophia Catharina, oder Die Grossfürstin, grosse Oper* in four acts (Charlotte Birch-Pfeiffer; Berlin, Court Opera, 19 November 1850). It was given on several other German stages and in Swedish (1852), and revived in Berlin (1858).

294. This was Irene Gräfin von Prokesch.

295. Franz Fritze was a classical philologist. He was to translate the *Sämmltliche Tragödien des Sophokles* (Berlin: A. Förstner'schen Buchhandlung, 1852, with a foreword by Ludwig Tieck).

296. Meyerbeer's song "Confidence" (words by François de Maurice Bourges) was published in Paris by Brandus et Cie (1851).

297. Ludwig Bischoff's extensive article appeared in eight parts in the first volume of the *Rheinische Musik-Zeitung für Kunstfreunde und Künstler* (1850), numbers 2 (13 July), 3 (20 July), 5 (3 Aug.), 8 (24 Aug.), 12 (21 Sept.), 13 (28 Sept.), 16 (19 Oct.), 19 (9 Nov.). The article was a rebuttal of the negative and anti-Semitic opinions promoted by Eduard Krüger in the *Neue Zeitschrift für Musik* 49 (18 June 1850): 253–56. Citations from both articles are provided in *BT*, 5:886–87.

298. The monument was built under the auspices of the Berliner Tonkünstler-Verein and was unveiled in the cemetery at the Oranienburger Tor on 11 May 1851.

299. *Paul und Virginie*, ballet with music partly composed partly arranged by Wenzel Gährich, choreography by Michael-François Hoguet (Berlin, Court Opera, 13 March 1848).

300. Charlotte von Oven (née von Hagen) (1809–91) was an actress who came to Berlin in 1833 from Munich. Until her marriage in 1846 to the landed gentleman Alexander von Oven, she was a member of the ensemble of the Royal Theaters. Henze-Döhring speculates that she turned to Meyerbeer in connection with the separation from her husband, which was finalized in 1851 (cf. *BT*, 5:884).

301. Mendelssohn, String Quartet no. 4 in E Minor, op. 44, no. 2 (1837).

302. Amalie Wolff (née Malcomi) (1780–1851) was the wife of the dramatist Pius Alexander Wolff* (d. 1828). She was trained by Corona Schröter in Weimar, and was engaged, with her husband, by Count Brühl for the Royal Theaters in Berlin in 1815.

303. Alois Pokorny (1825–83) was the eldest son of Franz Pokorny, and after the latter's death in August 1850 succeeded him as owner and director of the Theater an der Wien. The enterprise was plagued by debt, and his unsuccessful management led to bankruptcy in 1862 (cf. *BT*, 5:887).

304. Ger. "A kaleidoscope of thoughts."

305. Michael Schloss (1832–91), a book and music publisher in Cologne.

306. Fr. "subscription."

307. Pierre-Jacques-Joseph Rode, *Variationen*, op. 10, properly for violin.

308. Theodor Julius Hertel (1807–80), city councilor and later mayor of Dresden.

309. This was perhaps Waldemar Bloch (1820–72).

310. Mantius was singing the role of Jonas.

311. Karl Bethmann Geissler (b. 1802), an organist, and later cantor and teacher in

Zschopau, was dedicated to the study of old music, and produced a book entitled *Das Antiphonien-Buch für die evangelisch-protestantische Kirche Deutschlands*. Meyerbeer's report is reprinted in *BT*, 5:887–88.

312. Meyerbeer's relaxed attitude to Christmas is an indication of his open, if not slightly syncretic, attitude to formal religious practice.

313. Adolph Schulz (b. 1817), a violist, was a *Kammermusikus* of the Royal Orchestra. Meyerbeer must have provided a positive recommendation, because Schulz's incidental music to Franz Fritze's metrical translation of Euripides' *Hippolytos* was produced in Berlin on 25 April 1851.

314. Tgb. *schülerhafte*.

315. Friedrich Schick (b.1794), a much admired clarinetist, was made a *Kammermusiker* of the Royal Orchestra in Berlin (1818) and staff oboist of the Emperor Alexander Regiment (1832–47). He was given the title of *Musikdirektor* in 1842.

316. Tgb. *Glück*.

1851

Wednesday 1 January. Unfortunately I have only partially kept to the resolutions made on my birthday on 5 September. I hereby renew them, that is to say: to compose something every day, even if it is only a phrase, to attend to my correspondence regularly, not to postpone anything concerning my affairs, but to keep everything *à jour* by regular diligence. I must also read an act of the new libretto every day so as to saturate myself with it. May Almighty God preserve in health and happiness my beloved mother, my precious wife Minna, and my three lovely children, Blanca, Caecilie, and Cornelie, in the year ahead. May he mercifully protect us all from illness and misfortune, and make us cheerful and contented. Amen, may it be so. I spent the whole morning making New Year's calls and sending New Year's cards. In the evening I heard the seventeenth performance of *Der Prophet.*

Thursday 2 January. After breakfast I took a walk, during which I experienced such headache and sudden weakness that I had to sleep for an hour, and could not work for the rest of the day. Dined at the earl of Westmorland's. In the evening to the Academy with the children, where we saw lantern slides of the classical masters; during the spectacle the Domchor performed several pieces *a capella*, and most beautifully. Some music by Orlando di Lasso* was particularly lovely.[1] Then went to view the Christmas exhibition at Gropius's.[2] Afterward, I went to see my mother. Today I did not keep to my work resolutions.

Friday 3 January. To Geheimer Kabinetsrat Illaire, to support a petition by the singer [Pauline] Marx: on being pensioned off, she feels she should be free to seek engagement elsewhere, in spite of the wording of her contract. Then to Marx herself. Afterward began to work on a new middle *tempo* in Danilowitz's aria that I had composed earlier.[3] In the afternoon visited my dear mother, who is not well. In the evening finished composing the middle *tempo* of Danilowitz's aria. Today I kept to my resolutions imperfectly.

Saturday 4 January. After breakfast worked further on the recasting of Danilowitz's aria. Visited my dear mother who, thank God, is much better. Afterward called on Herr von Humboldt. At 1:30 until 3, and from 5 until 6, worked on Danilowitz's aria. Then to the Königstädter-Theater for Cimarosa's *Il Matrimonio segreto*; Madame Castellan sang Carolina. This is a good production with rounded ensemble work. Fulfilled only the musical part of my resolutions, and then only passably. Letters from Henri Blaze de Bury in Paris, from Dr. Bacher in Paris, from Herr von Scherb in Vienna, who suggests that I write an opera on Napoleon.[4]

Sunday 5 January. Worked a little on Danilowitz's aria, but felt a heaviness in my head and a chill in my limbs, and had to give up the work. Dined with Mother. Spent a few moments in the eighteenth performance of *Der Prophet*. Trietsch had to double for Köster again. Mantius sang Jonas for the first time. The applause was lukewarm. Called on Herr von Ladenberg. After the theater I composed for a while.

Monday 6 January. [No entry.]

Tuesday 7 January. Flodoard Geyer and the sister of the singer Marx came to see me. Completed the composition of Danilowitz's aria and began writing it out.

Wednesday 8 January. Finished writing out Danilowitz's aria. To the symphony-soirée where, among other things, they performed an overture by Gade, *Im Hochland*.[5] Saw in the *Revue et gazette des théâtres* that the overture to *Struensee* had extraordinary success at a concert in Brussels.

Thursday 9 January. Devoted the whole morning to preparing for tomorrow's Court Concert and inviting the various artists. There should have been a performance of *Der Prophet* today, but on account of Pfister's sudden indisposition it was canceled. Dined at the earl of Westmorland's. Wrote a few pages of the vocal line of Danilowitz's aria into the full score. Letter from Gouin.

Friday 10 January. Letter from Karl Kaskel. Spent the whole morning rehearsing and preparing for the Court Concert. There was only enough time left to write a few pages of the vocal line of Danilowitz's aria into the full score. In the evening the Court Concert at Charlottenburg took place. The performers were the pianist Anton von Kontsky, a very brilliant player, the little Venetian violinist Maria Serato,[6] the little violinist Gross,[7] the tenor Mantius, and the singers Castellan and Lagrange (they sang, among other things, the act 1 duet from *Le Prophète*). The king was again very friendly and talkative. I stayed for *souper*.

Saturday 11 January. Before breakfast I scored three pages of Danilowitz's aria.

Soirée at Geheimrat von Jüngken's, where Madame Jüngken[8] and Fräulein Bork[9] sang the duettino from *Le Prophète* and "Mère grand." Answered the communication from Geheimrat Johann Schulze concerning the Michael Beer Foundation and sent a copy to Professor Herbig.[10]

Sunday 12 January. Called on the new French ambassador, Lefèbre,[11] and Prince Sultkowsky.[12] The day before yesterday, at the Court Concert, the minister of trade von der Heydt[13] asked me for a copy of my *Fackeltanz,* which I also played for him. As a consequence he invited me to a big dinner today. Scored three pages of Danilowitz's aria. Then to a big evening reception at the Belgian ambassador, Herr von Nothomb's.

Monday 13 January. Letter from Herr von Lüttichau in Dresden. Answered Herr von Lüttichau. Scored five pages of Danilowitz's aria. After lunch scored another two sides. To Kapellmeister Dorn's concert (I requested two tickets and sent him four friedrichs d'or for them). He performed three of his compositions: a symphony, four vocal quartets, and a very romantic *Requiem.*[14] Taken as a whole the compositions reveal a considerable technical training, great aptitude, and many points of interest in the handling of form, harmony, and instrumentation.

Tuesday 14 January. Scored two pages of the aria. Visit from Mantius, who wanted me to hear one of his singing pupils. With Lord Westmorland, called on Madame Castellan and Madame Lagrange.

Wednesday 15 January. Scored several pages of Danilowitz's aria. Visit from Herr Gye, director of the Italian Opera in Covent Garden, who wants *L'Africaine* for the next season in London. Called on Herr von Humboldt, but I did not find him at home. In the evening I finished scoring Danilowitz's aria.

Thursday 16 January. I worked for an hour, and generally tried to recall what I had earlier composed for the introduction. Visited Herr von Humboldt. In the evening worked on the introduction.

Friday 17 January. Worked on the introduction. Called on Madame Birch-Pfeiffer and the music dealer Schlesinger. Finished composing the introduction, from the beginning to Danilowitz's aria, and wrote it out. Letter from the music director Müller in Brunswick who wants the publishing rights to my *Fackeltanz,* since it is often played there, apparently.

Saturday 18 January. Even though I composed the drinking chorus in the introduction in Gastein, I nonetheless began to rework it afresh, since the earlier composition does not please me. I worked with good results today. I then went to the palace for the *Ordenfest* to which I had been invited. Today turned out to be a particularly glittering occasion, because it combined the 150th anniversary of the founding of the Prussian monarchy[15] with the dedication of the palace chapel, which the king has recently refurbished. The Domchor sang Emil Naumann's setting of Psalm 66 very beautifully,[16] a lovely choral song with words by the old poet Simon Dach,[17] Mendelssohn's very beautiful *Liturgie*,[18] and finally a *Te Deum* by Caldara.[19] At the reception, I sat between the librarian, Geheimrat Pertz,[20] and the statistician, Geheimrat Dieterici.[21] After supper the king and all the princes and princesses of Prussia conversed with me in the friendliest way. I then visited Mother and worked again with some success on the drinking song in the introduction.[22]

Sunday 19 January. Worked on the drinking chorus. Visited Rellstab, who is ill, then worked again. Dined with Mother; President von Zander[23] was also there. Nineteenth performance of *Der Prophet* in Berlin, with Lagrange and Pfister (for the first time at the usual prices). Since there was no seat for me (because the intendant had given away the two small personal boxes), I worked on the drinking song from seven until ten o'clock.

Monday 20 January. Even though I completed the drinking song yesterday evening, I began to alter it, stimulated as I was by writing out an earlier setting. I am now again satisfied with the piece. Farewell visit to Demoiselle Lagrange. Visited Mother. Demoiselle Marx (the singer), the composer Kroll, the composer Peter Cornelius,[24] and a young violinist recommended by Dehn, all came to see me. To the Friedrich-Wilhelmstädtisches-Theater with my daughter Blanca and Schönlein's children where we saw the most thrilling folk drama, *Bajazzo*, after the French melodramatist Adolphe Dennery.[25]

Tuesday 21 January. Called on Major Danckelmann (adjutant to Prince Albrecht): he played me his *Fackeltanz*.[26] Today I received the diploma of a member of the Philharmonic Society of St. Petersburg together with a very gracious communication.[27] Letters from Gouin, Kaskel, Bacher. Visit from the composer Karl Müller from Brunswick, who introduced his son to me. In the evening I wrote out the whole of the drinking song.

Wednesday 22 January. The stage manager of the Friedrich-Wilhelmstädtisches-Theater, Herr Ascher, came to ask me to speak to the king on behalf of the family of the worthy composer Lortzing (who died suddenly yesterday in his forty-seventh year).[28] Called on the Hessian ambassador, Count Görtz,[29] and on Herr von Haber.[30] In the evening continued working on the introduction. Attended a big dinner at Alexander Mendelssohn's.[31] Afterward to the Singakademie, where I heard a performance of Mendelssohn's oratorio *Paulus*.

Thursday 23 January. Wrote an attestation for Burguis. Letter from Kaskel. [Wrote] a letter of recommendation to Kaskel for the young violinist Maria Serato from Venice. In the theater heard the first two acts of Flotow's opera *Sophie Catherina.* Afterward worked for another hour on the introduction.

Friday 24 January. At nine o'clock attended the funeral of Lortzing. Schlesinger came to see me with the son of the famous singer Braham.[32] After lunch, conferred with Schlesinger about a concert to be given for the benefit of Lortzing's widow;[33] then called on Frau von Oven (Charlotte von Hagen) for the same purpose. Wrote to the widow of Kapellmeister Lortzing and sent her maintenance of ten friedrichs d'or.

Saturday 25 January. Visit from the editor Ascher about Lortzing's benefit. With Dr. Piper to Count Redern about the concert in aid of the building of Cologne Cathedral. To Schlesinger: conference about the concert for Lortzing. The young Peter Cornelius and his sister[34] called on me; she sang for me in a vibrant mezzo-soprano voice. Visit from the English singer Raffter,[35] who performed for me: she had been introduced to me by Regierungsrätin A. Bandemer. Worked on the introduction during what was left of the morning, and in the evening.

Sunday 26 January. The son of the conductor Müller from Brunswick played me a violin piece on themes from *Le Prophète.* Dehn was also present. Attended a big dinner at Geheimer Kabinetsrat Illaire's. In the Theater: Mozart's *So machen sie alle (Così fan tutte).* Then to a big soirée at the Belgian ambassador's. The whole day was lost for work.

Monday 27 January. To the general director of post Schmückert[36] about the affair of the *Revue des deux mondes.*[37] Worked a little on the introduction. I held a dinner: present were Flodoard Geyer and his brother, Prof. Rötscher, Josephy, L. Ganz, Emil Naumann, Gianpietro, Kapellmeister Orsini, Teichmann, Wieprecht, Dr. Lange, Kontsky, Köster. Afterward to Konsky's concert.

Tuesday 28 January. Worked diligently on the introduction. In the evening likewise worked for four hours, and finished composing the introduction. Letters from Wilhelm Wagner in Frankfurt[38] and Karl Kaskel.

Wednesday 29 January. At one o'clock I was invited to a morning reception at the princess of Prussia's, where the pianist Kontsky played. To the symphony-soirée, where I heard a *Frühlings-Symphonie* by Ehlert* and Mendelssohn's overture to *Athalie.* Then with my daughter Blanca to a ball at the Geheimer Kommissionsrat Carl's.[39]

Thursday 30 January. On the whole I did not feel well and could not work. Dined with the Austrian ambassador, Herr von Prokesch. In the evening began writing the vocal parts of the introduction into the full score.

Friday 31 January. To the funeral of Kapellmeister Möser.[40] Visit of condolence to the earl of Westmorland. Visited Count Redern. I was summoned to dinner at Charlottenburg by the king. In the evening I was invited to a ball at the Hanoverian ambassador, Herr von Kniephausen's,[41] but did not go and rather continued writing the vocal parts of the introduction into the full score.

February 1851

Saturday 1 February. Spent the whole morning on preparations for the Court Concert on Wednesday. Today at one o'clock in the morning, the colossal Kroll Etablissement in the Tiergarten burnt down completely. By God's grace, the wind did not blow in the direction of my mother's house, which otherwise would certainly have fallen victim to the flames. The prince of Prussia and Prince Karl visited Mother to express their relief.

Sunday 2 February. Spent the morning on preparations for the Court Concert. Dined with my mother; Alexander von Humboldt was also there.

Monday 3 February. Held an orchestral rehearsal of *Struensee*. The alto Cavilla[42] sang me an aria from *Le Prophète*. In the Italian Opera, Rossini's *L'Inganno felice*:[43] a good performance. The tenor Labocetta and the bass Bianchi di Mazoletti[44] were particularly good.

Tuesday 4 February. Before breakfast I scored two sides of the introduction. Big orchestral rehearsal for the Court Concert. Madame Cavilla, a contralto from Vienna who is going to perform Fidès here, sang the role to me. She has a strong, wide-ranging alto voice, but sings badly.

Wednesday 5 February. Dress rehearsal of *Struensee*, from 10 until 1:30. In the evening after the celebration of a great *cour*, the Court Concert took place in the White Hall of the palace before a gathering of more than a thousand people; Archduke Leopold of Austria, who had just arrived, was present.[45] I conducted the following pieces: (1) the overture to *Struensee*; (2) the Countess's aria from *Figaro* (Madame Castellan);[46] (3) the Mist Chorus from Méhul's *Uthal*; (4) March of the Caravan and Storm in the Desert from Félicien David's *Le Désert*; (5) the scherzo from Mendelssohn's *A Midsummer Night's Dream*; (6) aria and chorus from Gluck's *Iphigenie in Tauris* (Madame Köster);[47] (7) a piano piece (Kontsky); (8) the "Inflammatus" from Rossini's *Stabat Mater* (Madame Castellan).

Thursday 6 February. Wrote several sheets of the vocal parts of the introduction into the full score. In the evening attended the reprise of *Struensee* in the Schauspielhaus, which took place before a crowded house and was very well received. Then to a big soirée at the Austrian ambassador's, where I was introduced to Archduke Leopold (son of Archduke Reiner),[48] who is visiting Berlin.

Friday 7 February. Wrote the vocal parts of the introduction into the full score all morning, and then scored it in the evening. Afterwards to a big ball at Count Redern's. Letter from Gouin.

Saturday 8 February. Lost the whole day making and receiving visits. In the evening to a ball at Dr. Emil von Haber's; I attended for the sake of my daughter Blanca.

Sunday 9 February. Received visits all morning. At midday I was the guest of [Rittergutsbesitzer] Josephy in a gathering of the second Philharmonischer Verein (three hundred persons in all). The conductor Ganz proposed my health at table, and this was taken up with great enthusiasm.

Monday 10 February. Spent the whole morning with my mother to do the *honneurs* for the many visitors who called today on her eighty-fourth birthday. May God preserve my precious, beloved mother for many years and allow all to go well with her. Amen. Dinner was at midday with Mother. Then to a concert by the Sternscher Gesangsverein. They performed: (1) an eight-part psalm setting by Mendelssohn;[49] (2) Mendelssohn's Piano Concerto [no. 2] in D Minor[50] played by Franck; (3) Mozart's *Ave Verum*;[51] (4) "Quando corpus morietur" from Rossini's *Stabat Mater*;[52] (5) Mendelssohn's *Walpurgisnacht*.[53]

Tuesday 11 February. Called on Count Redern about a commemorative service for Spontini.[54] Maurice Schlesinger from Paris came to see me, as did Dehn, who read me a long report he has written for the king about his musical journeying through the Prussian provinces.[55] Visits from Gye and Julius Weiss. Dined at the earl of Westmorland's. In the evening wrote out two sheets of the vocal parts of the introduction into the full score.

Wednesday 12 February. Worked from 10 to 1 on changes to the introduction. With my daughter Blanca to a soirée at Madame Birch-Pfeiffer's, who read her new drama: *Magdala, oder Vater und Tochter*.[56] Letter from the theater director Martin in Dessau:[57] *Le Prophète* has been given there with great success, and I am invited to attend a performance.

Thursday 13 February. Gave Major W. Danckelmann my *Fackeltanz* for the hereditary princess of Meiningen; he had already asked for it twice through Count

Redern. In the evening worked from 7 until 10 on the orchestration of the drinking song in the introduction.

Friday 14 February. To Count Redern concerning the memorial performance for Spontini. From 12 until 3 scored the drinking song. With my daughter Blanca to the Opera House, where, for the benefit of Lortzing's dependents, his opera *Zar und Zimmermann* was given to a capacity audience.

Saturday 15 February. From 11 until 1 scored the drinking song. In the evening from 6 until 10 finished scoring the chorus and proceeded further with the introduction to the 6/8 G minor section ("La guerre"),[58] writing out the vocal parts and beginning the orchestration.

Sunday 16 February. Finished scoring the chorus and then attended a conference with the intendant-general, about calling Michalesi to make a guest appearance as Fidès, and to Schlesinger, about the concert for Lortzing's dependents. Dined with Hofrat Dr. Lehwess.[59] In the evening wrote out ten pages of the vocal parts of the introduction in the full score.

Monday 17 February. Letter from Taubert, who on behalf of the orchestra informs me that they will play in the concert arranged by Schlesinger and Kossak* for the dependents of Lortzing, which I am due to direct, but only on condition that I wish it. My [positive] answer. To this purpose I diligently studied the scores of Beethoven's *Die Ruinen von Athen* and Weber's *Precioza*, both of which I will conduct in this concert.[60] In the evening attended the Sternscher Gesangsverein, where the chorus wanted to study both of these concert pieces.

Tuesday 18 February. Wrote to Buloz. Answered Küstner concerning his request about the singer Csillak.[61] At one o'clock rehearsed the declamation in *Precioza* with Frau von Oven. In the evening wrote to Gouin and studied the scores of *Precioza* and *Die Ruinen von Athen*, from the point of view of conducting them in concert.

Wednesday 19 February. The whole morning was taken up with the orchestral rehearsal of *Precioza* and the two pieces from *Die Ruinen von Athen*. To Count Redern. Attended a big dinner at Consul Wagener's.

Thursday 20 February. Called on Frau von Oven and the young Westmorland.[62] In the evening was the concert for the benefit of Lortzing's family. In spite of the high price (two thalers) it was crowded. I conducted.

Friday 21 February. Answered Geheimrat Johann Schulze concerning the Michael Beer Foundation. In the evening scored the continuation of the introduction.

Saturday 22 February. During the night my precious wife Minna was taken ill with glandular swelling (parotitis). We consequently had to cancel all invitations to the ball that we intended giving tomorrow. To Herr von Humboldt; yesterday evening he informed me in writing that the king has commanded the general director of museums, Olfers, to have my portrait painted by the artist [Karl] Begas.[63] This will be for the collection of famous men in royal service that the king is preparing for the palace.[64] In the morning I scored the introduction for two and a half hours. In the afternoon to Count Redern, then in the evening from six-thirty until ten o'clock continued scoring the introduction.

Sunday 23 February. The conductor Franz Schubert* from Dresden came to see me. Continued scoring the introduction from 11 until 1, and again in the evening for another three hours. Today I completed the instrumentation and revised it. Letter from Roger in Paris. Letter from the music publisher Leibrock* in Brunswick, who also wants to publish the *Fackeltanz*.

Monday 24 February. Conference about the Lortzing affair with Kommerzienrat Praetorius.[65] In the evening to a soirée at Hofbuchhändler Alexander Duncker's.[66]

Tuesday 25 February. To Intendant-General von Küstner concerning Roger's guest appearance. Began scoring the canon in act 1, which has only been half completed. Big dinner at Mother's; Frau von Oven was also there. Worked on the instrumentation of the canon, then to a musical soirée at Kommerzienrat Berend's, where Demoiselle Melitta Berend and Demoiselle Kunde sang my nocturne "Mère grand" very beautifully.

Wednesday 26 February. Worked on the instrumentation of the canon. Wrote to Lumley, director of the Italian Opera in London: I cannot accept his invitation to come to London to give my *Feldlager*. To the countess of Westmorland to bid farewell.[67] To the symphony-soirée: heard a Symphony in C by Taubert.[68] To a big Court Ball at the palace, to which I and all the other knights of the order Pour le Mérite were invited. Letters from Gouin, from Dessauer.

Thursday 27 February. Introduced Madame Wartel to Herr Rellstab. Continued scoring the canon and completed it. Big dinner at the banker Rittergutsbesitzer Oppenfeld's.[69] In the evening I took up Catherine's *couplets* again, even though I had composed them earlier, in order to revise and partially recast them.

Friday 28 February. Devoted the whole morning to preparations for the small Court Concert that took place today in the Queen's Rooms. Castellan sang my romance "Rachel à Naphtali." The blind violinist Jettelbach and the pianist Kontsky played, and the Domchor performed several pieces.

Portrait of Meyerbeer by Karl Begas (1853), commissioned by King Friedrich Wilhelm IV of Prussia. The composer is wearing the insignia of the Ordre pour le Mérite and holding the manuscript of the Coronation March from *Le Prophète* (painted 22 Feb.– 8 June 1851). The original painting has been missing since World War II.

March 1851

Saturday 1 March. Awoke with a severe sore throat, headache, and aching limbs. I was unable to work.

Sunday 2 March. The indisposition continues: I could do nothing other than write letters to Roger and Gouin. Letter from Cambiasi* in Milan.

Monday 3 March to Tuesday 4 March. The cold, headache, and aching limbs are improving, but still persist. I have to stay at home all the time, but am not able to work, since my head is affected by the indoor air; I also cannot go to the Court Ball to which I have been invited this Tuesday. In the evening I began to write out Catherine's *couplets* in act 1. Visit from Dr. Lehmann who now lives in Glogau and reported to me on the great success of *Le Prophète* there.

Wednesday 5 March. My condition is improving, but the sore throat still lingers. Visits from the Dutch singer Weinthal,[70] Stahlknecht,[71] Burguis, and Dr. Kossak*, who wanted enlightenment on several details concerning the composition of *Struensee*. Studied the role of the Prophet with Pfister. Count Redern came to see me. In the afternoon accompanied Concertmaster Schubert in his violin piece for the soirée tomorrow, then finished writing out the *couplets*.

Thursday 6 March. Held a stage rehearsal with orchestra of *Der Prophet*, in which Demoiselle Johanna Wagner is starring as Fidès. Then a rehearsal of the concert that is taking place at Count Redern's. In the evening accompanied the said concert at the piano. The king and the entire court were present. Madame Köster and Demoiselle Wagner sang the duettino from act 1 of *Le Prophète*.

Friday 7 March. I caught cold again at the soirée last night. Wrote the vocal line of the *couplets* into the full score. Visit from Albert Wagner. In the evening to the (twentieth) performance of *Der Prophet,* which was so crowded that many people could not find a place. The king and the whole court, as well as the grand duke [Georg] of Mecklenburg-Strelitz, were present from the beginning to the end. Demoiselle Wagner sang Fidès. The public was fairly animated. Letters from Tichatschek and Geheimer Justizrat Gross in Dresden, who invited me to come on Monday to Hofrat Winkler's fiftieth anniversary of service in Dresden.

Sunday 8 March. Began scoring the *couplets*, and in the morning worked very successfully on this. In the evening to a musical soirée at Geheimrat Jüngken's, where Madame Jüngken and Herr Horkel[72] sang the duet from act 5 of *Le Prophète*.

Sunday 9 March. In the afternoon finished scoring the *couplets*. Took Madame

Köster my *Quarante Mélodies*. Answered the Swedish ambassador, Herr von Hochschild.[73] Congratulated Hofrat Winkler in Dresden on his fiftieth jubilee. Answered the theater directorship in Dresden.

Monday 10 March. Today I went to the artist Begas, who is going to paint my portrait by command of the king. There, for the first time in a long while, I was overcome by faintness, as has happened on occasion in Paris and Vienna just after I had eaten. In the evening to a big musical soirée at the banker, Herr Rubens's.[74] A big fire has badly damaged the House of Assembly (First Chamber).

Tuesday 11 March. Second sitting for the painter Begas. Letter from the singer Monari to tell me that *Les Huguenots* was given at the Italian Opera in Trieste with great success. To the theater for Adam's *Giralda*.

Wednesday 12 March. Third sitting for the painter Begas. To the Italian Opera for Donizetti's *Lucrezia Borgia*. Afterwards to a ball at Geheimrat Carl's.

Thursday 13 March. Fourth sitting for the painter Begas. Began reflecting on the duet for Catherine and Peter. In the evening to the Opera: *Robert der Teufel* for Madame Köster's benefit. The king came for half an hour.

Friday 14 March. In the evening there was a Court Concert in Charlottenburg, but without singing: only Kontsky played the piano and Schubert the violin. I accompanied the latter on the piano. Letter from Roger in Paris; I immediately sent it on to Herr von Küstner.

Saturday 15 March. Called on Madame Castellan. Answered Theodor de Witt's letter from Rome, and delivered it into Madame Zimmermann's safekeeping. Performance in the Schauspielhaus: *Der grosse Kurfurst* by Köster, the husband of the singer. An incidental march, which is used for the overture, and a song were composed by Taubert. The play has achieved moderate success.[75]

Sunday 16 March. Wrote a testimonial for the harpist Zabel.[76] [Sent] fifteen thalers support to Gustav Nicolai. Worked on the duet for Catherine and Peter. To Madame Wartel's concert at twelve o'clock: Madame Castellan sang "Rachel à Naphtali." Worked on the duet in the evening.

Monday 17 March. Bade farewell to Madame Castellan. Worked on the duet. Letter from Winkler in Dresden. The king sent me the present of a marble bust of himself with a marble plinth made by Rauch's master hand, and accompanied by a very gracious letter.

Tuesday 18 March. Fifth sitting for the painter Begas. Spent the evening at home, but worked only a little on the duet, since I felt chilled.

Wednesday 19 March. Called on Herr von Humboldt, Lady Westmorland, and the French ambassador, Lefèbre. Sixth sitting for the painter Begas. Dined with Lord Westmorland. In the evening worked on the duet; began writing out the first part. Letter from Ledsam in Birmingham who, on behalf of the committee of the big festival there, has invited me to compose an oratorio for 1852.[77]

Thursday 20 March. Seventh sitting for the painter Begas, which Lady Westmorland also attended. In the afternoon Rellstab came to see me.

Friday 21 March. Eighth sitting for the painter Begas. Visit from Rellstab, who had his singing pupil, Demoiselle Stubbe, perform for me.[78] In the evening worked on the *andante* of the duet, but only a little since I had a bad headache.

Saturday 22 March. In the afternoon heard Spohr's oratorio *Die letzten Dinge*[79] in the Matthaeus Church in the Tiergarten. The Dresden Theater has sent me 480 thalers from a benefit performance for the dependents of Lortzing.

Sunday 23 March. Charity concert in which the Domchor performed Palestrina's *Crux*,[80] Lotti's *Crucifixus*,[81] Fesca's *Paternoster*,[82] Mendelssohn's *Hymne*.[83] To the theater for Flotow's *Grossfürstin*. After the theater, worked on the *andante* of the duet with good results.

Monday 24 March. To Herr von Humboldt. Ninth sitting for the painter Begas. Worked on the duet for two hours.

Tuesday 25 March. Worked a little on the duet. I gave a big dinner to which I invited the Austrian ambassador, Herr von Prokesch; the English ambassador, Lord Westmorland, and his son; the secretary to the English legation, Howard; the French ambassador, Lefèbre; Herr von Humboldt; Spieker; Count Redern; the president of police, von Hinkeldey; Geheimer Kabinetsrat Illaire; the minister of trade, von der Heydt; Dr. Cornelius; Dr. Wagen;[84] Böck; Geheimrat Dieterici; Geheimrat Carl; Generalpostdirektor Schmückert; Herr von Haber; Marquis Lucchesini;[85] Konsul Wagener; and Begas. In the theater heard act 2 of Mozart's *Figaros Hochzeit*. Today Herr Burguis began taking dictation of my letters. Sent 100 thalers to be divided among the Christian and Jewish poor of Munich, as I do every year on the anniversary of my late, blessed brother Michael's death.

Wednesday 26 March. Tenth sitting for the painter Begas. Visits from the singer

Marra, from the singer Fischer,[86] from Concertmaster Ries, from Herr Weinthal, and from Count Redern, who confidentially informed me that Lieutenant von Hülsen is to become intendant of theaters.[87] In the Königstädter-Theater a group of fifteen Hungarian instrumentalists gave a concert of pieces by Hungarian composers, mostly on Hungarian themes, played with fire, sonority and an enthusiasm that quite invigorated me. They also performed the march from *Le Prophète* very beautifully.[88]

Thursday 27 March. A severe bout of diarrhea weakened me so much that I was unable to work. Visits from the young Cornelius and his sister, from Doctor Herczevi, the leader of the Hungarian Music Society,[89] and from the singer Pardini. In the evening wrote two letters to Gouin (one of them ostensibly so; actually for Buloz) and a letter to Brandus.

Friday 28 March. Returned the young Cornelius his music. Worked on the duet. In the Opera House: Nicolai's *Die lustigen Weiber von Windsor.*

Saturday 29 March. Worked on the duet. Called on Gutzkow and Eduard Devrient.

Sunday 30 March. Answered Countess Schlick in Prague; she has dedicated some songs to me, and sent them.[90] Attended a midday concert of the Hungarian Music Society. Dined with Dr. Hermann Jacobsohn.[91] Ball at Madame Kunde's.

Monday 31 March. I listened to the playing of the pianist Robert Goldbeck* from Brunswick; Count Redern sent him to me. Worked a little on the duet. In the evening I finished all but the smallest details of the duet. Letter from Gouin.

April 1851

Tuesday 1 April. Called on Gutzkow and his wife, and Marra, but found no one at home. Eleventh sitting for the painter Begas. Worked for an hour on writing out the duet. In the Friedrich-Wilhelmstädtisches-Theater heard act 1 of Donizetti's *Die Tochter des Regiments,* in which Madame Marra sang Marie. Her voice has only some *éclat* in the upper register; the middle has been completely wiped out. Then heard act 3 of *Robert der Teufel.* Herr Salomon sang Bertram today. The theater was not as full as usual for this opera.

Wednesday 2 April. Replied to the Philharmonic Society in St. Petersburg, through the Russian Embassy. [Wrote] to Herr Ledsam, president of the musical society in Birmingham. [Wrote] to Hermann Sillem in London.[92] The new intendant of theaters, Herr von Hülsen, called on me, but I was not at home. In the evening finished writing out the duet.

Thursday 3 April. To Count Redern. To Herr von Hülsen: this time *he* was not at home. Wrote two sheets of the vocal parts of the duet into the full score, and orchestrated one of them. Dined at Prince Karl's. To the commemorative service for the late, blessed Michael, conducted by the Jewish preacher Auerbach; unfortunately I came too late because the dinner at the prince's lasted too long. Visited Mother. Wrote six sides of the vocal parts of the duet into the full score. Then to a soirée at Countess Neal's.[93]

Friday 4 April. Scored three sides of the duet before breakfast, then later five pages. In the Opera: Donizetti's *Die Tochter des Regiments*. The new intendant of theaters, von Hülsen, introduced himself to me in the Opera House. After the theater, wrote eight pages of the vocal parts of the duet into the full score. Letter from Felix Kaskel in Dresden.

Saturday 5 April. Wrote the rest of the vocal parts of the duet into the full score. Scored seven sides of the duet. *Le Prophète* has been given in Mainz with much success (according to the *Theaterzeitung*), also in Stuttgart, Metz and Grenoble.

Sunday 6 April. Matinée musicale at the music teacher Ebeling's; his singing pupils sang some of his own compositions, both of them very bad. In the evening finished scoring the duet.

Monday 7 April. Twelfth sitting for the painter Begas. Called on the singer Mario. In the evening undertook a further revision of the duet.

Tuesday 8 April. The birthday of my beloved wife, Minna. May God grant her good and enduring health after such a long illness, and preserve the dearest one for me and for the children into a ripe old age. Amen. At midday I gathered our whole family in its widest sense, twenty-four people in all, for a dinner in her honor. Letter from Gouin. [Wrote] to Gouin, to the conductor Tschirch in Liegnitz,[94] to Kapellmeister Braneka in Vienna,[95] to Bordogni in Paris. In the evening read act 1 of Halévy's *La Dame de pique*.[96]

Wednesday 9 April. Worked on the first chorus of the act 1 finale. Attended a performance of Sebastian Bach's *Passion Music*[97] in the Singakademie. Afterwards worked a little on the first chorus of the act 1 finale.

Thursday 10 April. Unpacked my compositions and rearranged them. In the evening to the Opera House for Spontini's *Ferdinand Cortez*: Madame Köster sang Amazili for the first time.

Friday 11 April. Worked on the act 1 finale.

Saturday 12 April. Continued working on the act 1 finale. Soirée at my sister-in-law, Doris Beer's.[98]

Sunday 13 April. Walk in the open air during which several good ideas for the soldiers' chorus in the act 1 finale occurred to me. [Wrote] to Georg Müller in Brunswick, to Schucht* in Sondershausen. In the Opera House: *Der Prophet* (twenty-first performance). Madame Krebs-Michalesi sang Fidès, but elicited little response; the whole production was received rather coldly.

Monday 14 April. Dined with the king in Charlottenburg. In the evening worked a little on the finale.

Tuesday 15 April. Spent some time arranging my music and books. Wrote out only a little of the act 1 finale. In the evening attended the sitting of the Academy of Arts. Called on Kapellmeister Krebs.

Wednesday 16 April. Letter from Gouin. In Roger's benefit at the Grand Opéra in Paris they performed, among other things, act 4 of *Les Huguenots* and act 5 of *Robert*. *Le Prophète* has been performed in Danzig with only moderate success, according to the *Wiener Theaterzeitung*. In the evening wrote out a little of the act 1 finale.

Thursday 17 April. From 11 until 1 wrote out what I had composed of the act 1 finale. Visit from the vice-president of the Academy, Prof. Herbig, and Prof. Rungenhagen: they invited me to compose a cantata for the celebration that the Academy of Arts is arranging for Professor Rauch when his statue of Frederick the Great is exhibited. I declined however, because, as I explained to them, I am obliged to deliver my new comic opera in the near future. I nonetheless offered to compose the chorus of reception that will proceed the cantata. In addition the Academy has nominated me a member of the Festival Committee. In evening wrote out more of the finale.

Friday 18 April. [Wrote] to the bass Lindemann in Hamburg.[99] Finished the reordering of my books and music. From 11 until 1, then from 7 until 9, worked on the finale, but without satisfying results.

Saturday 19 April. The famous Norwegian violinist, Ole Bull*, came to see me. From 11:30 until 3 tried to work on the finale, but without success. Headache and a cold made it impossible for me, in the evening as well. Conference in the Academy with Herbig, Rungenhagen, and Professor Kopisch, who will write the chorus of reception for the Rauch celebration that I have promised to set to music. *Le Prophète* has been given in Toulouse with great success.

Sunday 20 April. From 12 until 2:30 worked on the finale. Today at last a happy inspiration came for the *stretta buffa* with three themes playing against each other: for so long it just would not develop as I had wished.[100] In the evening wrote to Gouin, worked a little on the finale.

Monday 21 April. Wrote out the finale, particularly the combination of the three themes in the vocal parts. I am presently suffering a great deal from headaches, which always last a few hours; I was hence obliged to stop working. Called on the French ambassador, Lefèbre. From 7:30 until 10:30 in the evening continued to write out the finale.

Tuesday 22 April. Letters from Roger in Paris, from the theater director Hoffmann in Prague. From 11:30 until 2 finished writing out the finale, up to the entry of the Hymn of Peace from my *Feldlager* with which the act will close. [Wrote] a letter recommending the violinist Levy to Brandus in Paris. In the evening a long sitting of the Festival Committee of the Academy of Arts for the Rauch celebration. On coming home, I began working on the chorus that I have to compose for this occasion.

Wednesday 23 April. Worked on the *Festgesang* for the Rauch celebration. However, my headache and cold soon forced me to stop. Dined with Eberty.

Thursday 24 April. Worked on the *Festgesang* for the Rauch celebration. Visit from the author of the festal song, Kopisch, in order to discuss with him several changes that I would like in his text. Visit from Geheimrat Dr. Schönlein, who prescribed a sea bath for me this summer; before starting this he wants me to begin drinking the curative Eger-Franzen waters here in Berlin. Visited Hofrat Teichmann. Worked for two hours on the *Festgesang*. Letter from Georg Müller in Brunswick.[101]

Friday 25 April. Attended the general rehearsal of the Greek tragedy *Hippolytus*, with music by Kammermusikus Schulze. Sitting of the musical section of the Festival Committee in order to choose a composer for the Rauch celebration cantata. Worked a little on the *Festgesang*. Dined at Count Redern's. [Wrote] to the composer F. Bonoldi in Paris.

Saturday 26 April. Because of headache I felt myself so badly disposed to work that I did very little with the *Festgesang*.

Sunday 27 April. In the morning hours, the most favorable for composing, I completed the *Festgesang* up to the coda. In the theater heard *Die Kirmes*, opera in one act by Taubert,[102] and the ballet *Das hübsche Mädchen von Genf*, music by Adam.

Monday 28 April. Called on Humboldt. The young Goldbeck again played me some of his compositions. In the evening worked on the *Festgesang*, but only a little because of the headache.

Tuesday 29 April. Headache and a heavy cold meant that I worked little in the course of the day, and then without success. Letter from Gouin. [Wrote] to Roger in Paris, to the music dealer Leibrock in Brunswick.

Wednesday 30 April. Visits from Count Redern, the concertmaster Jähns*, the theater director Roeder from Riga,[103] the theater agent Michaelson.[104] To Praetorius in order to assess the sum of contributions for Lortzing's family. Finished writing out the *Festgesang*.

May 1851

Thursday 1 May. Neglected the cure so as to enable myself to work systematically on the *Festgesang*. From 7 until 9 revised the piece (the vocal parts especially), and then scored two pages. Visit from the painter Herr Herrenburger, the husband of Tuczek.[105] From 12 until 2 wrote the vocal parts of the *Festgesang* into the full score. In the Friedrich-Wilhelmstädtisches-Theater: *Angela, Liederspiel* by Benedix (insignificant).[106]

Friday 2 May. Scored the *Festgesang* for a couple of hours in the morning and evening. The daughter of the tenor Julius Miller sang for me.[107]

Saturday 3 May. After breakfast worked on the instrumentation of the *Festgesang* until headache forced me to stop. Called on Countess Westmorland and Madame Zimmermann. From 8:30 until 10 scored one and a half pages. Letter from Gouin: the ninety-one performances of *Le Prophète* have brought in 732,218 fr. 93 c. From today the Parisian letters have begun arriving in the evening of the third day.

Sunday 4 May. In order to work more consistently on the scoring of the *Festgesang*, I neglected the cold rubdown and wrap-up and worked on it for two hours before breakfast (two pages). To a performance by Jähn's Gesangverein[108] with my little daughter Cornelie; afterward I took the child to the East Indian Museum, where there is an exhibition of many fearsome, warlike objects belonging to the wild inhabitants of the island of Borneo.[109] Heard the young eleven-year-old, Liepmanssohn from Landsberg, play the piano: insignificant. Wrote ostensibly to Cornet in Hamburg elaborating my opinions about his abilities as a theater director. Scored two pages.

Monday 5 May. To Count Redern. Otherwise I could work only a little in the morning and evening, since I was indisposed by headache and cramps. Letter from Madame Viardot in Paris, informing me that she has sung in *Le Prophète* for the 100th time.

Tuesday 6 May. To Rellstab. Worked for two hours on the *Festgesang* and finished scoring it. To Ladenburg. [Wrote] to Röth in Augsburg, and enclosed an autograph. In the evening to *Der Prophet* (twenty-fourth performance in Berlin). Demoiselle Wagner sang Fidès as her first role. Crowded house. Mother attended the theater again for the first time since Wilhelm's death.

Wednesday 7 May. To Begas to sit once more for my portrait [the thirteenth session]. To Rellstab about a new ending for the *Feldlager* for 31 May, when it will be performed to celebrate the unveiling of the statue of Frederick the Great. To Lady Westmorland. In the evening completed scoring and writing out the *Festgesang*.

Thursday 8 May. To Rellstab, who gave me the new song he has written to conclude the festival performance of the *Feldlager*.[110] Went to sit for Begas again [the fourteenth session]. In the evening to the theater: *Die Kirmes*, opera in 1 act by Taubert, and the ballet *Esmeralda*, music by Pugni. Gouin reports that in the month of April the Grand Opéra gave fourteen performances that brought in 73,284 fr. Of these four were of *Le Prophète*, with receipts of 33,958 fr.; the other ten works made only 39,326 fr. in all.

Friday 9 May. Before breakfast I completely revised the *Festgesang* and passed it on to the copyist, Patschka. I then started composing the new song for the *Feldlager*. Letter from Gaetano Rossi in Verona. To Geheimrat Kugler.[111]

Saturday 10 May. Worked on the song for the *Feldlager*. To the earl of Westmorland. To Generalintendant von Küstner. Completely wrote out the *Feldlager* song, but have not yet scored it. In the late evening attended a soirée at the Belgian ambassador's.

Sunday 11 May. Today my nephew Julius [Beer] and his wife [Regine] arrived in Berlin. Bade farewell to the countess of Westmorland. I want to return to my new opera again; because of the *Festgesang* and the *Feldlager* song, it has become a virtual stranger to me. In order to refresh my memory, I read through the big ensemble in act 2 very carefully, and in the evening began to work on it.[112]

Monday 12 May. Worked on the ensemble in act 2. Studied the role of Saldorf in my *Feldlager* with the singer Salomon. Visit from Johanna Wagner's father. In the evening began writing the vocal parts of the *Feldlager* song into the full score.

Tuesday 13 May. To Rungenhagen, with Kapellmeister Dorn, to discuss using the chorus of the Singakademie in the Rauch cantata. Finished scoring the *Feldlager* song.

Wednesday 14 May. Today my beloved wife Minna departed for Ischl with my three children. Dined with the French ambassador, Lefèbre.

Thursday 15 May. To Rellstab: played him the new *Feldlager* song. Conference with Generalintendant von Küstner about the rehearsals of the *Feldlager*. Conferred with Wieprecht on the same subject. Visits from the Swedish singer Ebeling and the wife of the tenor Julius Miller. From today on I will again dine with my mother every day. In the Königstädter-Theater: Nestroy's new comedy.[113]

Friday 16 May. To Herr von Küstner with the mother of the harpist, Zabel, to plead for his appointment. Dined with the English ambassador, the earl of Westmorland.

Saturday 17 May. To Rungenhagen concerning the rehearsals of my *Festgesang*. Went through the role of Vielka with Tuczek. In the Friedrich-Wilhelmstädtisches-Theater *Die Macht des Vorurteils*, drama in four acts: it treats of the relationship between Jews and Christians.[114] The actor Marr from Hamburg, who stars in it, is an excellent artist.[115] Letter from Lindpaintner in Stuttgart: in *one* week the following were performed: *Robert* (fiftieth performance), *Les Huguenots* (twenty-sixth performance), *Le Prophète* (sixth performance since 31 March).

Sunday 18 May. Worked on a new finale for the *Feldlager*, in case it cannot be performed with the new song: I adapted the earlier dream sequence, where the march in the overture is joined to "Heil dir im Siegerkranz," and added words to the march.

Monday 19 May. To Kopisch, to confer about the poem at the conclusion of the Rauch celebration. To Mantius, to play him the new song in the *Feldlager* that he is going to sing. To Rungenhagen and Grell to play them the *Festgesang* for the Rauch festivity, since they will be directing the choral rehearsals in the Singakademie. In the evening held a piano rehearsal of the *Feldlager*.

Tuesday 20 May. I wrote a new conclusion for the song in the *Feldlager*, and arranged the words of the closing chorus of the Rauch celebration to fit my music for the *Festhymne*. To Stawinsky to discuss the *tableaux* in the *Feldlager*. Letter from the Music Festival Committee in Lille, which has invited me to attend their performance of scenes from *Le Prophète*. Letter from Brandus. Held an orchestral rehearsal (without the vocal parts) of the *Festgesang* in the Singakademie.

The piece is very impressive, I think. Wrote to Professor Kopisch. Attended a commemorative service in the Singakademie for F. W. Steinmeyer;[116] they performed two pieces by Fasch: a *Requiem* and "Selig sind die Toten."[117] In the evening harmonized a new accompaniment for the conclusion "Heil dir im Siegerkranz."

Wednesday 21 May. Took leave to travel from Count Redern. Played the *Feldlager* song in its present form to Rellstab.

Thursday 22 May. [Wrote] to Richebé, president of the music festival in Lille, to Krespil the vice-president, to Brandus in Paris, to Lindpaintner in Stuttgart. Occupied with preparations for departure. At 12 left for Dresden, where we arrived only at 8 in the evening. Schlesinger and Herr von Puttkammer[118] were fellow travelers in the train. Visited Kaskel. Schlesinger brought me a very pleasant, flattering[119] article by Damcke* from the Petersburg newspaper entitled "Meyerbeer und sein Opern."

Friday 23 May. At 6:30 left by rail for Prague, where we arrived at two o'clock. On the way I worked on the quintet in act 2. I suffered all day from a cramping, diarrhetic condition that affected me badly, as did back and side pains. I suspect that these symptoms, which so often recur, are a sign of hemorrhoids. *Le Prophète* will be given in Prague tomorrow. Ditt will make his guest appearance as the Prophet.

Saturday 24 May. At five o'clock in the morning left Prague by train for Vienna, where we arrived at 7:45 in the evening.

Sunday 25 May. At nine o'clock in the morning I went to my beloved wife, Minna, who is staying at the Munsch Hotel with our children, to congratulate her on our silver wedding anniversary. I thought to surprise her, but she already knew, through Bertha Arndt, that I intended visiting her today. After lunch I called on Dessauer. With the children to the Burgtheater: *Der geheime Agent*, new comedy by Hackländer*, which is a refined, ingenious intrigue and very popular.[120]

Monday 26 May. Called on the *Oberstkämmerer,* Count von Lanckoronski, in order to thank him for his letter, forwarding the Franz Joseph Order; he was not at home. So I went on to his chancery director, Hofsekretär von Remont, then to Saphir, Dessauer, Count Moritz Dietrichstein, Herr von Holbein. To the rehearsal of Donizetti's *Maria di Rohan*, where I heard the tenor Fraschini. In the evening Rossini's *Il Barbiere di Siviglia*, an outstanding performance.

Tuesday 27 May. At 6:30 left for Prague by train. My little daughter Cornelie was the only one of my family who came to my room, at 5:30 in the morning, to bid me good-bye.[121] At 7:30 in the evening we arrived in Prague.

Wednesday 28 May. At 6:30 in the morning departed by railway train for Berlin, where we arrived at 8:30 at night. I found my beloved mother in good health, thank God.

Thursday 29 May. Held an orchestral rehearsal of the *Feldlager* in the early morning. In the afternoon rehearsed the chorus of the Singakademie in my *Scena* for the Rauch celebration.

Friday 30 May. Held a dress rehearsal of the *Feldlager*. In the Friedrich-Wilhelmstädtisches-Theater, the Opera Company of the Königsberg Theater in East Prussia gave Boïeldieu's *Die weisse Dame* surprisingly well; Demoiselle Fischer, the prima donna, has a pretty, wide-ranging voice. *Le Prophète* has been performed with success in Elbing,[122] I am reliably informed in a letter from Truhn*.

Saturday 31 May. Tremendous celebration for the unveiling of Rauch's monument of Frederick the Great. I watched the event from a window of the Academy, even though the king had ordered that Cornelius and I should be part of the academic deputation. In the evening, by royal command, a gala performance of my opera, *Ein Feldlager in Schlesien*, with admission by royal invitation only. After act 2, the king summoned Rauch and me to his box and expressed his satisfaction in the friendliest, kindliest manner. The performance itself passed by coldly and without interest.

June 1851

Sunday 1 June. To Count Redern and Herr von Humboldt. Wrote to Minna in Vienna. Started to work a little again on the quintet in act 2. Today the *Feldlager* was again performed, this time for the paying public.

Monday 2 June. Worked a little on the quintet in act 2. In the Academy there was a rehearsal, with orchestra and chorus, of my *Hymn* for the Rauch celebration. Visit from the Belgian painter, de Biefve.[123] Letter from Dr. Bacher in Dresden.

Tuesday 3 June. Arrival of Dr. Bacher and Brandus from Dresden. Dr. Bacher dined with my mother. In the evening I went with him to the theater, to a revival of Gluck's *Iphigenie in Aulis*. Demoiselle Johanna Wagner sang Klythemnestra very beautifully.

Wednesday 4 June. I felt rather feeble today, and consulted Schönlein about my indisposition. Visits from Bacher and Brandus.

Thursday 5 June to Friday 6 June. The influenza infection continues, and makes it impossible for me to work.

Saturday 7 June. My indisposition does not improve. [Wrote] to Minna in Ischl. I called on Herr von Humboldt. Held a general rehearsal of my *Rauch Ode* in the Singakademie.

Sunday 8 June. For the first time in a year, I have again unfortunately experienced an attack of convulsive coughing. To Begas, who again wanted me to sit for my portrait [the fifteenth session].

Monday 9 June. Today the academic celebration for Rauch took place in the Singakademie. I conducted the *Festhymne* myself. Since there was no applause throughout the whole ceremony, I do not know whether my music aroused any interest. The king summoned me to his box at the end of the celebration and said many obliging things about the *Hymn.* To the Friedrich-Wilhemstädtisches-Theater for Dittersdorf's *Der Doktor und Apotheker*,[124] performed by the Königsberger Opera Society.

Tuesday 10 June. Convulsive coughing. Called on the earl of Westmorland and Mother. Answered Truhn in Elbing (dictated to Burguis). Returned the lithograph to the copper engraver Müller in Dresden.[125] Dined with the earl of Westmorland, where I made the acquaintance of the wife of the new English ambassador, Lady Bloomfield.[126]

Wednesday 11 June. On the orders of the doctor, I stayed in bed all day. Visit from the famous Friedrich Schneider* from Dessau, who has come here to conduct his oratorio *Das Weltgericht.*[127]

Thursday 12 June. The famous pianist Döhler from St. Petersburg[128] and his wife, born Countess Scheremetief,[129] came to see me. Visits from an oboist from St. Petersburg, from Brandus, Albert Wagner, Wieprecht, Madame Arndt. I wrote to Minna and Gouin.

Friday 13 June. Visits from Tichatschek, Albert Wagner, Brandus, Bock, the singer Roger from Paris. Dictated letters to Burguis.

Saturday 14 June. No actual coughing fit in the course of the day.

Sunday 15 June. Continuous coughing. Visit from the singer Roger.

Monday 16 June. Coughed a great deal. Visits from Brandus, Schlesinger, my mother, and my nephew Julius, who played me an overture he has written. Invitation from the Philharmonic Society of St. Petersburg to attend their jubilee in March. Letter from Dr. Bacher in Vienna. [Wrote] to Dr. Bacher, to Sax concerning a problem Dr. Dehn has about a trumpet passage in a Bach keyboard concerto.[130]

Tuesday 17 June. Continued coughing. In the evening I began working a little for the first time since becoming ill, and began to write the trio ("Joyeuse orgie").[131]

Wednesday 18 June. The sore throat eased a little, but if I try to speak I start coughing. Stayed at home all day, but worked only a little on the trio. Visits from the earl of Westmorland and Roger and his wife.[132]

Thursday 19 June. Throat irritation. Today, at last, I was able to go out for an hour. Visits from Count Redern, Alexander von Humboldt, Brandus. Unfortunately, I hardly worked at all, only briefly in the evening for an hour.

Friday 20 June to Saturday 21 June. The cough and the sore throat are easing. I hardly worked at all. On Saturday I supervised a dress rehearsal of *Les Huguenots* with Roger and Demoiselle Wagner. Dr. Bacher is coming to Berlin to attend this performance of *Les Huguenots*.

Sunday 22 June. To the new intendant of theaters, von Hülsen, in order to persuade him that Tuczek should sing the role of Berthe in *Der Prophet*. With the kapellmeisters Taubert, Dorn, and Professor Rungenhagen presented *en deputation* an address from the musicians of Berlin to Lord Westmorland: they have collectively written to him on his departure from the city.[133] Dined at Mother's with Brandus and Dr. Bacher. Today Roger makes his Berlin début in *Les Huguenots*; Demoiselle Wagner sings Valentine; on account of my cough, however, I dared not go.

Monday 23 June. The cough and sore throat have significantly diminished. Read through and corrected the piano version of the *Ode an Rauch*, prepared by Brissler.[134] With Roger to Spieker, with Bacher to Westmorland, to Count Redern. Visits from Dr. Bacher, Brandus, Bock, Neithardt, Madame Arndt.

Tuesday 24 June. Attack of convulsive coughing. Rehearsed the duet in *Der Prophet* with the ladies Wagner and Tuczek. [Wrote] to Auber (with an enclosure from Herr von Humboldt): informed him of his nomination to the order Pour le Mérite.

Wednesday 25 June. Coughed a great deal. Presented Burguis with a silver sugar bowl and twelve teaspoons for his tea service. Worked on the trio for a little while and wrote it down. In the evening to *Les Huguenots* (second appearance of Roger, to a crowded house). The king summoned me to his box after act 2, said many flattering things about my music, and introduced me to the grand duke of Hesse-Darmstadt, who was present.[135]

Thursday 26 June. Before breakfast composed a little for the trio and wrote it out. To Roger, to Schlesinger. In the evening, held a rehearsal of *Der Prophet*.

Friday 27 June. Held a piano rehearsal of *Der Prophet*. To Brandus and Roger. In the afternoon drove with Mother, Regine and Julius to the health springs. In the evening, a soirée at the Austrian ambassador's, where Roger sang.

Saturday 28 June. Held a dress rehearsal of *Der Prophet*: Roger, Mademoiselle Wagner, Madame Tuczek. Attended a serenade in the evening arranged by the young Cornelius. Today I worked on the trio for one and a half hours before breakfast.

Sunday 29 June. Worked on the trio before breakfast. In the evening attended the performance of *Der Prophet*: Roger as the Prophet, Madame Tuczek, Demoiselle Wagner, to a packed house and unusually lively approval, an outstanding production.

Monday 30 June. During the day I hardly coughed at all. I traveled to Potsdam to wait on the grand duke of Hesse-Darmstadt, and to present him with a copy of my *Quarante Mélodies*. Went to see Roger. Big dinner at my mother's: Roger and Demoiselle Wagner were also present. Tomorrow Brandus travels back to Paris.

July 1851

Tuesday 1 July. New resolutions to regular diligence and activity. Gave my answer to the Philharmonic Society in St. Petersburg, through the Russian chargé d'affaires, Baron Budberg.[136] Began correcting the proofs of my *Ode an Rauch*. After lunch, to Geheimrat Schönlein, to consult with him about my state of health.[137] In spite of the fact that *Der Prophet* was playing at the Opera with Roger, I went to the Friedrich-Wilhelmstädtisches-Theater to hear Dittersdorf's comic opera *Hieronymus Knicker*.[138] Unfortunately, I did not work today. To Geheimrat Johann Schulze.

Wednesday 2 July. Worked on the trio before breakfast: wrote a new concluding *cabaletta*. Count Wielhorsky from St. Petersburg came to see me, as did Count Redern and several others.

Thursday 3 July. Worked for one and a half hours before breakfast on the trio. Visits from Kontsky, the singer Guthmann,[139] Madame Roger. Worked for another few hours on the trio. In the Friedrich-Wilhelmstädtisches-Theater, heard Dittersdorf's *Hieronymus Knicker* for the second time, with great enjoyment.

Friday 4 July. Before breakfast worked a little on the trio, but quite insignificantly, I think. Several visits to Roger etc. I was invited to dine with the king at Sans Souci, where there were many guests, the grand duke and the grand duchess of Hesse,[140] the duchess of Leuchtenberg (who is the daughter of the emperor of Russia),[141] etc. The king presented me to the duchess of Leuchtenberg and was in general very gracious to me. Then I went to the Opera, where Roger sang Georges Brown in Boieldieu's *Die weisse Dame* to great applause.

Saturday 5 July. Worked on the trio for a while before breakfast. At nine o'clock Herr von Hülsen notified me that the king wants a private performance of the music that Dorn and I wrote for the Rauch celebration.[142] I therefore went to Potsdam to ask the king if I should also have Roger and Kontsky participating in this concert; but once there, I learned from Herr von Hülsen that the king had postponed the concert. In the afternoon I consulted my doctor, Geheimrat Schönlein, who wants me to resume the water cure as of tomorrow. In the Viennese newspaper *Der Wanderer* I read today of my daughter Blanca's change of faith, despite the fact that this took place discreetly in a small village. God grant that this news will not reach the ears of my dear, good mother who, I fear, would be very angry about it.[143]

Sunday 6 July. Today I resumed the cold rubdowns, but without the wrap-up. Worked a little in the morning and evening on the trio. Dined at my mother's: Mesdames Tuczek and Birch-Pfeiffer were also there. I accompanied the latter home; her daughter declaimed several things to me.[144] Called on Roger, Count Redern, Herr von Prokesch. Received a handwritten letter from the king in which he commands the *Struensee* overture for the Court Concert the day after tomorrow.

Monday 7 July. Visit from Herr von Woltersdorff, director of the Königsberg Theater.

Thursday 8 July. Letter from the countess of Westmorland. Letter from Auber in Paris. Rehearsed the Court Concert all morning. The conductor Schlösser*, from Darmstadt, came to see me. Court Concert at the New Palace in Potsdam,[145] which

I conducted: (1) the overture *Struensee*; (2) the romance from the Donizetti's *La Favorite* sung by Roger;[146] (3) my *Ode an Rauch*; (4) Dorn's *Festkantate*; (5) romance from *Les Huguenots* ("Plus blanche que la blanche hermine") sung by Roger; (6) piano piece played by Kontsky. The king, all the members of the royal households, and Princess Marie (the duchess of Leuchtenberg)[147] said many friendly and obliging things to me.

Wednesday 9 July. Did hardly anything all morning. Visit from Count Dietrichstein. Dined in Glienecke with Prince Karl. To Herr von Humboldt about Auber.

Thursday 10 July. From 11 until 1:30 finished writing the trio. After lunch at Mother's, Madame Birch-Pfeiffer read out her new comedy in four acts, *Wie man Häuser baut*.[148] It is very dainty, and deals with personalities from the time of Frederick the Great's father.[149]

Friday 11 July. Visit from Kapellmeister Dorn. Called on Kapellmeister Schlösser from Darmstadt (and wrote something in his album). Began to score the trio, but only for a little while. Letters from Dr. Bacher in Vienna, from Brandus in Paris. Subscribed to Behr's Readers' Library for a month.[150] In the evening to the Schauspielhaus, where the Königsberg Opera Company gave a guest performance of Dittersdorf's *Der Doktor und Apotheker*. The *buffo* Düffke is very good indeed.[151]

Saturday 12 July. The music director Tschirch from Liegnitz and General Ogareff from St. Petersburg[152] came to visit me. Scored only a few pages of the trio. In the Schauspielhaus: Hebbel's *Judith:*[153] Madame Hebbel(-Engelhaus) made a guest appearance in the title role.[154]

Sunday 13 July. Visits from General Ogareff, adjutant to the emperor of Russia, and from Bock, who brought me a printed exemplar of my *Ode an Rauch*. Visited Count Dietrichstein, Geheimrat Johann Schulze, and Wieprecht. Scored a side of the trio in the morning, then three more sides in the evening.

Monday 14 July. Called on the Russian general Ogareff (wrote something in his album), Rauch (took him the *Ode* with a personal dedication), Kommerzienrat Praetorius (about the Lortzing committee), Schlesinger (text of *Struensee*). Scored three sides of the trio, and another three in the evening. Then bade farewell to Julius and his wife Regine, who are leaving Berlin tomorrow.

Tuesday 15 July. The twenty-first birthday of my beloved daughter Blanca: May God preserve and bless her. Scored several sides of the trio. Visit from Geheimrat Schulze who gave me the agreeable news that the senate of the Academy of Arts has proposed to the ministry that I be nominated to membership of the senate. In the evening I scored a few sides.

Wednesday 16 July. For the first time in a long while resumed the cold showers, under the personal supervision of Dr. Lieberkühn. Dined at Spieker's. Scored some of the trio. Visit from Rellstab and the singer Ebeling. Conference about the Lortzing Foundation with Kommerzienrat Praetorius. In the Schauspielhaus: Dittersdorf's *Hieronymus Knicker*, performed by the Königsberg Company.

Thursday 17 July. [Wrote] to the countess of Westmorland in London, enclosing the *Ode an Rauch* and the new song for the *Feldlager*. In the evening scored a little of the trio. Letter from Gouin: my *droits d'auteur* for Paris and the provinces for the month of June was 482 fr. 15 c. On the 14 July was the 100th performance in Paris of *Le Prophète*. The 100 performances of my opera have brought in 788,075 fr. 70 c., an average of 7,880 fr. for every performance.

Friday 18 July. The poet Hebbel from Vienna came to see me, as did Schlesinger from Paris. Called on Geheimrat Schulze. Dined with Prince Friedrich, the king's cousin.[155] Called on Count Bury.[156] In the evening I finished scoring the trio.

Saturday 19 July. From 9:45 until 11, worked on the revision of the trio, and completed this in the evening. [Wrote] to Gouin.

Sunday 20 July. The Viennese pianist Levy[157] from St. Petersburg came to see me. Began to compose the quintet. Dined with the sculptor Rauch. To the Opera House for Dittersdorf's *Der Doktor und Apotheker* by the Königsberg Company.

Monday 21 July. Called on Hebbel and Geheimrat Kugler. Read through the new opera libretto by Madame Birch-Pfeiffer, *La Réole*.[158] In Batavia, at the installation of the new governor, *Les Huguenots* was performed by the resident French troupe with great success.[159]

Tuesday 22 July. Visit from the singer Ebeling. After lunch I called on Madame Birch-Pfeiffer. In the evening read the memoranda by Taubert, Dorn, and Wieprecht on the reorganization of Möser's class at the Royal Opera House. The king has requested me to report on this.

Wednesday 23 July. [Wrote] to Dr. Bacher, to General Ogareff in Warsaw, enclosing the second *Fackeltanz*. Read through the memoranda on the Möser class once more. In the Schauspielhaus, attended von Himmel's *Fanchon* by the Königsberg Opera Company.

Thursday 24 July. To Geheimer Kabinetsrat Illaire to confer about my report on the Möser class. Visit from the singer Röder-Romani who sang for me.[160]

Friday 25 July. Kapellmeister Dorn came to see me, as did Madame Zimmermann, who wanted me to hear some of her singing pupils. Answered Cambiasi in Milan, enclosing some biographical notices. [Attended] Schenk's *Der Dorfbarbier* and Dittersdorf's *Hieronymus Knicker* by the Königsberg Opera Company.

Saturday 26 July. Spent the morning having the appropriate visas stamped in my passport by the French, English, and Belgian ambassadors. Visit from Rellstab, concerning a new text for my *Ode to Rauch*. Studied part of the role of Vielka with Demoiselle Ebeling. After lunch to Madame Birch-Pfeiffer to persuade her to give drama lessons to Demoiselle Ebeling.

Sunday 27 July. Called on Herr von Humboldt. Wrote to music director Truhn in Danzig (enclosing twenty thalers) and Kapellmeister Müller in Brunswick. In the evening worked on the quintet for the first time in several days.

Monday 28 July. Busy all day with preparations for departure.

Tuesday 29 July. [Wrote] to Gollmick in Frankfurt-am-Main, to Haslinger in Vienna. Letter from Dr. Bacher. At midday began my train journey to Spa. Arrived in Hanover at 10:30 at night.

Wednesday 30 July. The train for Cologne should leave at 10:15, but departed half an hour later. In Minden I met General Nostitz and his wife.[161] We arrived in Cologne at nine o'clock in the evening; wanted to visit Hiller and Professor Bischoff, but both were away.

Thursday 31 July. At ten o'clock left by train for Pepinstère; from there one travels by omnibus for one and a half hours to Spa. I arrived at four o'clock in the afternoon. I want to use the cold springs, as I did last year. In the evening the local choral society serenaded me by torchlight.

August 1851

Friday 1 August. I am again staying at the Hotel du Pays Bas, as I did last year, but this time on the second floor, where I am renting a room with alcove and lower bathroom at 4½ fr. daily. I felt such numbness in my head that I could not work all day. In the theater I attended the vaudeville *Croque Poule* by Rosier,[162] and then a performance by the little dwarf couple who call themselves "Le Prince et la Princesse Colibri."[163]

Saturday 2 August. Wrote to Brandus enclosing the title page of *Le Prophète*, with the casting, for Fétis. Exhaustion and a numbness in my head make work almost impossible. Studied English phrases.

Sunday 3 August. Tried to work on the quintet, but without success. Visited the Princess de Georgie and Countess Kralovsky, both of whom I had met in Baden. In the theater: *L'Avouvé et le Normand,* vaudeville by Vanderburch,[164] in which Joseph Kehn played the Norman;[165] he is an actor in the genre of Bosquier-Gavaudan,[166] with lots of *couleur,* fire, and a lovely voice. *Les Extases de Mr. Hochenez,* vaudeville by Varin, a very amusing farce.[167]

Monday 4 August. Letter from Dr. Bacher. Began to work seriously on the quintet: labored for two hours with little success. Visit from a singer, Madame Jessegre, who wanted me to hear her. Charity concert for the poor in which two society ladies performed, Madame Hédouin (the singer)[168] and Madame Jerrés (on the piano).

Tuesday 5 August. Letter from Brandus. Visit from Davelouis. Today I again feel nervous and agitated. I tried to work for a few hours on the quintet, but could not find the appropriately recollected mood for it.

Wednesday 6 August. Moritz Schlesinger came to see me.

Thursday 7 August. For the last six days I have been studying English phrases every day, in order to prepare myself for a somewhat special trip to England. The widow of Marshall Davoust accosted me in the street in order to make my acquaintance.[169] I still cannot find the right disposition for composition. In the theater: *Les Trois Péchés du Diable, vaudeville-féerie* by Varin and Lubize;[170] *Lord Herrilion en voyage,* vaudeville by Dartois and Biéville. Joseph Kehn [Kelm] played the Lord with great verve and *vis comica.*[171]

Friday 8 August. Worked on the quintet for a while without especial success. I wrote to Gouin.

Saturday 9 August. Walked with the old Princess Eckmühl (Marschallin Davoust). A Russian, Baron Medem (from Odessa), introduced himself to me on the promenade.

Sunday 10 August. [Wrote] to Gouin and to Sina in Paris (enclosing 100 fr. from me and 100 fr. from Minna: our contribution for a journey to a watering place). In the theater: *Bataille de dames* by Scribe and Legouvé.[172]

Monday 11 August. Letter from Kastner in Paris. For the first time in a long while, I worked with some success on the five-part ensemble in the quintet.

Tuesday 12 August. Finished composing *à peu près* the five-part ensemble in the quintet. While I was composing this, a peculiar passage, most definitely in two parts, occurred to me, which I wrote down in my notebook; perhaps I will be able to use it in the duet in act 3. Dined with Davelouis.

Wednesday 13 August. Burguis has written to tell me that Madame Valentin[173] and Marianne Mendelssohn[174] showed Mother the newspaper article about Blanca's conversion. I wrote to Mother. Letter from Busschop* in Bruges, who has sent me a fugue on four notes that he has composed.[175]

Thursday 14 August. Letter from the director of the Academy of Arts in Berlin, Professor Herbig, who gave me the very happy news that the king has approved the proposal to nominate me to the senate. I had feared that this proposal could have been rejected by the king on religious grounds. I wrote to Herr von Humboldt. In the theater: *Lampard le serpent, ou La Jeunesse de Grétry*, vaudeville by Théaulon,[176] and then another vaudeville, *Rossignol, ou Le Peintre colleur:*[177] two bad plays; Joseph Kehn [Kelm] acted in both.

Friday 15 August. Worked on the stretta of the quintet. In the evening I was in *en train* for composing, when I was frightened by a mouse that ran across my pianoforte.

Saturday 16 August. Began writing out the five-part ensemble of the quintet. Continued with this in the evening.

Sunday 17 August. Zimmermann from Paris came to see me on his journey through Belgium. In the theater: Siraudin's *Monsieur Lafleur*,[178] and *La Fée cocotte*, vaudeville by Mélesville[179] in which the eight-year-old Celine Montalan acted and danced charmingly.[180]

Monday 18 August. Finished writing out the ensemble of the quintet. In the evening worked on the stretta of the quintet, with reasonable success. Letter from the countess of Westmorland in London.

Tuesday 19 August. Letter from Moritz Schlesinger in Paris. I wrote a letter of recommendation for Zimmermann to Karl Kaskel. Worked on the stretta of the quintet, with good results. In the evening continued working, but without particular success.

Wednesday 20 August. I felt unwell, and passed the morning packing and making farewell visits. Bischofsheim from Brussels (Regine's uncle) called on me.[181]

Thursday 21 August. At one o'clock I left Spa for Pepinstère by omnibus. From there by rail to Brussels, where we arrived at six o'clock. To the Théâtre des Galéries Saint Hubert,[182] where the company of the big Théâtre de la Monnaie performed *Une Avonture de Scaramouche*, a comic opera by Ricci*. The music, which quite appealed to me sixteen years ago at La Scala in Milan, today struck me as unendurably dull.[183] Madame Cabel* who is very popular here, seems only average to me.[184]

Friday 22 August. Left Brussels at 8:30 by *train de grande vitesse*. Arrived in Paris at 5:30. So as not to be seen, I lodged in the Faubourg Saint-Germain in the Hôtel des Ministres.

Saturday 23 August. Since I have actually come here only to consult my dentist about my teeth, I want to pass the thirty-six hours of my stay incognito. I saw only my loyal friend Gouin and the tailor Boudgoust, from whom I ordered some suits.

Sunday 24 August. At eight o'clock in the morning left Paris by train. On the first platform I met Paul Taglioni from Berlin—so blowing my incognito. At 11:30 I arrived at Boulogne-sur-Mer, where I am going for a sea cure. Letter from Mehmel in St. Petersburg.[185]

Monday 25 August. Since I feel very uncomfortable and agitated, I did not begin bathing. Visits from Sina, Panofka. On the street I met [Benny] Goldschmidt from Paris.

Tuesday 26 August. Bathing in the sea so overheated[186] me that could hardly work, and only in the evening did I begin to write out a little of the quintet.

Wednesday 27 August. Wrote out the quintet for two hours. In the evening Dr. Bacher came to see me, so that I hardly worked at all.

Thursday 28 August. Before and after my sea bathe wrote out a little more of the quintet, also in the evening for a while.

Friday 29 August. Wrote out the quintet for an hour before and an hour after my sea bathe, and also in the evening. While improvising on the piano in the evening, I involuntarily began composing the trio in act 3,[187] even though I have not yet finished writing out the quintet. This season in London, Covent Garden has performed *Les Huguenots* eight times, *Le Prophète* seven times, and *Robert le Diable* six times.

Saturday 30 August. Before and after my sea bathe, I worked on the act 3 trio and wrote out the quintet. In the afternoon, I improvised on Catherine's romance in act 2. In the theater: *Bonsoir, Monsieur Pantalon, opéra comique* in one act by Grisar.[188] I was so tired that I slept through virtually the whole performance.

Sunday 31 August. After breakfast wrote out the trio for two hours. News from Berlin that Ebeling (from Stockholm), who made her début as Alice in *Robert* to great expectations, experienced a complete fiasco. I went to see Lablache as he passed through here. In the evening wrote out the trio for three hours. *Le Prophète* has been given with great success in Bordeaux, Bamberg, and Constantinople.

September to October 1851

Monday 1 September. Bad headache and *échauffement*[189] all day. In the evening wrote out the trio for two and a half hours.

Tuesday 2 September. I felt chilled all day and also extraordinarily exhausted. I could work on the quintet for only two and a half hours in the morning and not at all in the evening.

Wednesday 3 September. I lay on the sofa until lunch. By eight o'clock I had already taken to my bed.

From 4 September to 5 October

In the night of 3–4 September I was awakened by terrible stomach cramps, which were then followed by severe diarrhea and vomiting. It was, my physician Dr. Dunant maintains, a very fierce attack of sporadic cholera. The illness developed into an inflammation of the stomach and intestines. I was bedridden for more than three weeks, during which time I could take only lukewarm water mixed with a few drops of orange or red currant juice. Every attempt, even the strongest remedies, to purge me through the stomach was useless. When my strength returned a little, I traveled on Saturday, 4 October, to Paris, but since the train from Boulogne to Paris takes six hours, I needed two days because of my great weakness.

From 5 October to 21 October

In Paris I again lodged in the Hôtel des Ministres. I put myself under the care of the famous physician Dr. Andral.[190] Since I was suffering continually from head-aches, and dizziness particularly, any talking exhausted me. I therefore stayed in this distant *quartier* to avoid all visits. I paid Dr. Andral 240 fr. for four visits.

During this period in Paris I sent letters to Geheimrat Illaire about the Möser classes, to Weber's widow about the completion of the *Pintos*, to Herr von Engelhard[191] and the Kammermusiker Mehmel in St. Petersburg about the Glinka score that had been sent to me. I directed this score to Herr Budberg in Berlin, for forwarding to St. Petersberg.[192] Sent Lux's* letter to Dehn.

As far as theatrical experiences are concerned, I saw the following: in the Grand Opéra, *Le Prophète* with Alboni, Demoiselle Poinsot,[193] and Herr Gueymard; Auber's *L'Enfant prodigue*[194] and his *Zerline, ou La Corbeille d'oranges*[195] (with Alboni); in the Opéra Comique Donizetti's *La Fille du régiment* (with Madame Ugalde, Coulon),[196] Halévy's *La Fée aux roses*, Méhul's *Joseph*, Grisar's *Bonsoir, Monsieur Pantalon*; in the Italian Opera Donizetti's *Lucrezia Borgia* (with Madame Barbieri-Nini,[197] Graziani,[198] Fortini the baritone[199]).

I agreed to inform the director of the Opéra Comique, Émile Perrin, by the end of December whether I will be able to come to Paris around April to begin rehearsing my new opera; should my state of health not allow this, I will give the opera to him in October [1852]. I also promised to notify Lumley of the outcome of this arrangement with the Opéra Comique, and to keep Scribe abreast of developments.

Wednesday 22 October. Farewell visits. Scribe came to confer with me about the changes to *L'Africaine*.[200] Visits from Lumley, Roqueplan, Bunn, Balfe. [Wrote] to the music dealer Klemm in Leipzig, who wants to make a statuette of me for his collection of famous composers.[201] [Wrote] to Busschop in Bruges.

Thursday 23 October. Thank God that I have been so much restored to health that I am able to travel. At 12:45 I left Paris by rail; I was accompanied by Roqueplan, Brandus, Bacher, and Vivier as far as Valenciennes, where I spent the night.

Friday 24 October. Left Valenciennes at 9:30 by express train[202] for Brussels, where I arrived at 1:30. In the evening I went to Théâtre de la Monnaie for Donizetti's *Lucie di Lammermoor* in order to hear the daughter of the singer Duprez, who is currently enjoying a great reputation.[203] I wanted to judge whether she could possibly replace Ugalde in *L'Étoile du Nord*,[204] since the latter's voice has begun to decline badly. Demoiselle Duprez sings with great mastery, taste, and fluency, but she leaves me cold, and appears to be an insignificant actress. Since I was sitting at the back of my box and, moreover, since I do not actually know anyone in Brussels, I believed myself to be unobserved. How great, therefore, was my astonishment when, at the beginning of the act 3, instead of the music of *Lucia*, the orchestra and the *chœur* began playing the *Appel aux armes* from *Le Prophète*.

At the same moment the whole audience turned toward my box and began to applaud so furiously that I had to come forward and bow several times. When the piece had ended, the public began its jubilation anew, again directed toward my box, so that I had to appear and bow for several minutes.

Saturday 25 October. At 7:30 left Brussels by train for Cologne, where we arrived at five o'clock in the afternoon.

Sunday 26 October. I wrote to the conductor and present theater director in Brussels, Hanssens *(jeune),* to thank him for the improvised celebration that he arranged for me the evening before last in the Théâtre de la Monnaie. Then I wrote to Count Brandenburg of the Prussian Embassy in Paris, and sent him a receipt from the postmaster of Cologne for the dispatches that I had taken on his behalf; then to Gouin, that Brandus should inquire of Roger and Gustav Vaëz about Lockroy*, and should send me a frontispiece of the score of *Le Prophète* for Fétis. At four o'clock I left by train for Düsseldorf, where I had never been before. In the evening I went to the theater; they gave Mozart's *Die Zauberflöte.* None of the singers were above average, not one could have appeared in a big theater, and yet the performance was most tolerable and animated by a certain sense of ensemble. What heavenly music this *Zauberflöte,* what a wealth of melodies, what freshness, even after sixty years!

Monday 27 October. At nine o'clock I left Düsseldorf by rail. In order to conserve my still depleted energies, I went only as far as Minden. Wrote to Scribe about *L'Africaine,*[205] and to Gouin. Read through acts 2 and 3 of the new opera again.

Tuesday 28 October. Traveled by a local train of the Minden railway to Hanover. On the way I read through act 1 of the new opera again. At one o'clock by train to Brunswick, where I arrived at 3. In the evening wrote a part of the text of the new opera in a small notebook.

Wednesday 29 October. Left Brunswick at 9 in the morning by train. At three o'clock in the afternoon I arrived in Berlin, where my beloved daughters Blanca and Caecilie were waiting for me on the platform. At home I found my precious wife, Minna, and my youngest daughter, Cornelie, very well, thank God. I also found my beloved mother in good health, praise God. May God bless my return to my native city. Received from Rotterdam the diploma of an honorary member of the Society for the Propagation of Music in Holland.[206] Invitation from the Philharmonic Society of St. Petersburg to compose something for their jubilee and to conduct it myself in Russia.

Thursday 30 October. My physician, Geheimrat Schönlein, came and thoroughly

examined me. Visit from Teichmann, to whom I gave instructions for the intendant of theaters concerning Johanna Wagner. [Wrote] to Kabinetsrat Illaire: returned the reports by Taubert, Dorn, and Wieprecht concerning the Möser violin
classes. [Wrote] to Mlle. Babnigg in Breslau.[207]

Friday 31 October. Visits from the director of the Covent Garden Theatre, Gye,
from Dr. Bacher who arrived in Berlin last night, from the singer Wagner, who
wanted to confer about her engagements in Berlin and London. [Wrote] to the
Philharmonic Society in St. Petersburg, to the Rotterdam Society for the Propagation of Music in Holland.

November 1851

Saturday 1 November. I am still abstaining from daily work on the doctor's orders. Visit from Dr. Bacher. Wrote to Karl Kaskel, to Kapellmeister Braneck in
Vienna.[208]

Sunday 2 November. The day passed, like all the others, in useless inactivity, since
my physical weakness allows me to do no work.

Monday 3 November. Letter from the director of the Opéra Comique, Émile Perrin,
from Brandus, from Gouin: the 115th performance of *Le Prophète* took place in
Paris, the last appearance by Alboni (receipts 9172 fr. 95 c.).

Tuesday 4 November. [Wrote] to Fétis in Brussels, to the poet Rossi in Verona
(together with 200 fr.), to Gouin (together with 2400 fr.). Letter from Karl Kaskel.
Very friendly letter of welcome from the great and wonderful Alexander von
Humboldt.

Wednesday 5 November. The bad weather, which has made it impossible to go
out, paralyzes my digestion, which remains poor, and perpetuates the headache,
so that any activity is still impossible for me. Visits from Dr. Bacher, and from
the father of the singer Johanna Wagner, who asked me to examine her contracts
for Paris and London. In the evening I answered Herr von Humboldt's letter.

Thursday 6 November. Passed the day, as with all the others since my return, in
total inactivity.

Friday 7 November. Abdominal cramps. I had to remain lying on the sofa all day.

Saturday 8 November to Tuesday 11 November. Blennorrhea.[209] My headaches
continue to be so severe that I definitely cannot work. *Le Prophète* has been given

in Zürich with great success. In Detmold the new theater will open with *Le Prophète* this coming 15 January.

Wednesday 12 November. In the morning and afternoon walked Unter den Linden.[210] Two letters to Gouin, the second ostensibly so, actually for Roqueplan. Sent *Struensee* to Fétis.

Thursday 13 November. My state of health does not improve. Visit from Count Redern about the Court Concert on the 19th. In the Friedrich-Wilhelmstädtisches-Theater: Méhul's totally charming opera *Je toller, je besser (Une Folie).*[211]

Friday 14 November. To Count Redern about the Court Concert. Wrote to Johanna Wagner in Magdeburg about the Court Concert.

Saturday 15 November. My head is so sensitive that speaking to different people one after the other immediately causes me a headache. Visit from the conductor Wieprecht. Attended a sitting of the senate for the first time in my capacity as member of the senate of the Academy of Arts. In the evening to a concert of the Erkscher Männergesangverein, where only folk songs were performed, and very nicely too.[212] My neighbors were the banker Brüstlein[213] and Bettina von Arnim. The concert was held in the newly built hall that belongs to the Treubunde: a really beautiful place, especially the décor, though the acoustics are dampened. Visit from Herr von Küstner. *Struensee* was performed in the Schauspielhaus to a full house; it was also given once this summer during my absence. Letter from Dr. Bacher.

Sunday 16 November. Visit from the new intendant of theaters, Herr von Hülsen. At the wish of Count Redern, I read Sobolewsky's setting of Lord Byron's *Himmel und Erde* in order to report to the king on its suitability for the Court Concerts.[214] Letter from Fétis in Brussels.

Monday 17 November. Busy all day with preparations for the Court Concert that will take place on the nineteenth for the Queen's Name Day. Letter from Dr. Bacher.

Tuesday 18 November. The Court Concert has been postponed on account of the death of the king of Hanover.[215] Sternau from Cologne came to see me and discussed writing a linking declamatory text so that the *Struensee* music can be used in concert performances.[216]

Wednesday 19 November. Did absolutely nothing. In the evening to the Opera for the first performance of the opera *Castilda* by the reigning Duke Ernst II* of Saxe-Coburg-Gotha.[217] My headache was so severe that I had no appreciation of what I heard, and therefore can pass no judgment on the work. After act 3 I left the theater with my daughter Blanca.

Thursday 20 November. Visit from Rellstab, who brought me the poem "Das Vaterland." We gave a small ball today out of love for my daughter Blanca.

Friday 21 November. Today it is twenty years since the première of *Robert le Diable* in Paris, and today the 329th performance will take place there. To the Opera House for Boieldieu's *Johann von Paris* and *Persische Nationaltänze*, a dance *divertissement* by Paul Taglioni. These national dances are very piquant and most charmingly ingratiating.

Saturday 22 November. With my niece Anna Eberty to a quartet recital by the four Müller brothers from Brunswick: Haydn's Quartet in B-flat Major,[218] then a very lovely Quartet in D Minor by Franz Schubert (the famous composer of songs), which I heard for the first time.[219]

Sunday 23 November. Visit from the famous Belgian violoncellist Servais. Answered the director of the Court Theater in Darmstadt, Tescher,[220] who, on behalf of the grand duke, has invited me to a performance of *Le Prophète* there.

Monday 24 November. Called on Servais, Count Redern, and Schlesinger. I feel so weakened by diarrhea that I could not keep my resolution to begin work again on my new opera. I have furthermore been deeply demoralized by a communication from Burguis that Richard Wagner has vehemently attacked me in his new book on the future of opera.[221] I subsequently found a manuscript essay written by the hand of the same Richard Wagner (ten years ago), which he gave to me at that time for publication, and in which he praises me extravagantly; it is entitled "Über den Standpunkt der Musik Meyerbeers."[222]

Tuesday 25 November. Passed today uselessly, as has happened so often lately. Visit from the blind pianist Krug.

Wednesday 26 November. Again passed the day in inactivity. In the evening to the quartet recital of the Brothers Müller: Haydn's Quartet in C Major with the wonderful variations (in G) on "Gott erhalte Franz den Kaiser";[223] Quartet in C Minor by Litolff[224] (an English pianist), which contains many eccentric things but also has many interesting details and talented features; Beethoven's Quartet in E-flat Major.[225] Visit from Madame Dülken* from London, whose daughter plays the new instrument the concertina.[226]

Thursday 27 November. Visit from the blind pianist Krug; he played me a fantasy on *Le Prophète*. Geheimrätin Jähnigen[227] asked me for the final aria in *Ein Feldlager in Schlesien,* which I added for the new scene; she wants to have it sung in some *tableaux vivants* she is arranging. A Herr von Heeringen from America visited me to show me a new form of musical notation.[228] In the evening to a concert rehearsal where, for the first time, the finale of *Lorelei* was performed, the only piece from this opera that Mendelssohn completed; he wanted to write this opera for Jenny Lind in London, but died before he could.[229] In Königsberg, in East Prussia, Michael's *Struensee* has been performed with my music. The production does not appear to have been particularly distinguished.

Friday 28 November. Wrote letters but otherwise did nothing.

Saturday 29 November. In the Opera House: a concert for the Cologne Cathedral building fund. Included was a festive overture in C major by Beethoven that I had never heard before,[230] a splendid, interesting piece, a chorus by Gabrielli *(a capella),*[231] a song by Haydn,[232] a song by Taubert, sung collectively by the Domchor, the finale from Mendelssohn's opera *Lorelei,* Beethoven's Ninth Symphony with chorus. The orchestra was very good. Prof. Rötscher sent me *Judas Ischariot,* a drama by Demoiselle Elise Schmidt.[233] Kaskel has written to me urgently, on behalf of Caroline Weber, requesting an end to the *Pintos* affair.

Sunday 30 November. Congratulatory visit to Herbig, whose daughter is to marry a Herr von Arnim.[234] Called on Professor Rötscher.

December 1851

Monday 1 December. Letter from Scribe, together with the scenario of the first two acts of *L'Africaine.* Wrote to Karl Kaskel that I will come to Dresden either at the end of this or the following week to put the *Pintos* affair in order. In the evening, a sitting of the musical members of the Academy, where Herr von Heeringen explained his new method of notation.

Tuesday 2 December. Sent the Chorus of the Mothers from *Le Prophète*[235] and the sextet from the *Hymne an dem König* to Rellstab in order to have them incorporated into the new *Rauch Cantata.*

Wednesday 3 December. In the Opera House: Donizetti's *Lucrezia Borgia.* Demoiselle Wagner sang Lucrezia, the new tenor [Theodor] Formes* Gennaro.

Thursday 4 December. I called on Herr von Humboldt. Wrote an answer to Fétis in Brussels. A letter from Kaskel, who, on behalf of Kapellmeisterin Weber, requests the return of all the compositions of C. M. von Weber that she sent me six or eight years ago for use in the arrangement of Weber's *Pintos*; in the event of my having lost them, she wishes 1,000 thalers in compensation. In the evening to the Singakademie for a performance of Handel's oratorio *Judas Maccabaeus*.

Friday 5 December. To Count Redern. I spent the whole morning at home look-ing for Weber's music, which Weber's widow wants back; I was fortunate enough to find it all, including the score of *Silvana*. In the evening to the Friedrich-Wilhelm-städtisches-Theater, where they performed a comic dance scene, *Jesuiten-Polka*,[236] and then a vaudeville, *Guten Morgen, Herr Fischer*, after *Bonsoir, M. Pantalon*.[237]

Saturday 6 December. Letters from Truhn, from Kabinetsrat Illaire. [Wrote] to the Brothers Müller (Carl Müller) in Brunswick, to Kabinetsrat Illaire. Called on Herr von Humboldt. Visits from Landrat von Saldern[238] and Count Redern.

Sunday 7 December. To the concert by the five Tschirch brothers, who are all composers and perform their own works. Ernst Tschirch seems to me the only one who possesses a genuine talent.[239] Count Redern informs me that the Court Concert will definitely take place on Wednesday.

Monday 8 December. Letters from Gouin, from Bacher. To Count Redern about the Court Concert.

Tuesday 9 December. Count von Arnim came to see me,[240] as did the conductor Neithardt, the pianist Mme. Brzowska, and the singer Mme. Gadi.[241] Answered Glöggl in Vienna. In the Opera House: Bellini's *Die Montecchi und Capuleti*. Demoiselle Wagner was really excellent as Romeo.

Wednesday 10 December. Rehearsal of the Court Concert, which took place this evening in Charlottenburg and turned out very well. The four Müller brothers from Brunswick were included at my suggestion, and played two quartets by Haydn and Beethoven. The two young demoiselles Dülken respectively played the new instrument called the concertina (a perfected accordion) and the pianoforte very beautifully. Demoiselle Wagner sang the Furies' Scene from Gluck's *Orpheus* with chorus,[242] and the cavatina from Rossini's *Tancredi*.[243] The Domchor sang the lovely song "Heilige Nacht" by [Michael] Haydn[244] and Taubert's "Schlummerlied."[245] The violinist Mertens[246] and the pianist Brzowska also participated. The king was very gracious to me and conversed for a long time.

Thursday 11 December. For the first time since my illness began on 4 Septem-ber—in other words, after more than three months—I started working on my new opera again. I read through the finale, which has not yet been scored, and began to write the vocal parts into the full score. To the symphony-soirée for Beethoven's

Symphony no. 1 in C, the overtures *Die schöne Melusine* by Mendelssohn[247] and *Euryanthe* by Weber, and Mozart's Symphony [no. 41] in C with the final fugue.

Friday 12 December. The bad weather has such an exhausting effect on my nerves that I wrote only a few pages of the vocal parts of the act 1 finale into the full score. In the Friedrich-Wilhelmstädtisches-Theater: *Die Heimkehr aus dem Fremde*, comic opera by Felix Mendelssohn. Mendelssohn composed this operetta as a very young man to celebrate the silver wedding of his parents: refined, witty, piquant music, with happy, comic brush strokes in the orchestration; only the thematic invention is inferior.[248] Then *Ein Abenteuer Karls II* by Hoven (i.e., Vesque von Püttlingen).[249] Read Heine's *Romanzero* and his *Tanzpoem, Faust.*[250]

Saturday 13 December. Letters from Gouin, Bacher, from the directors of the Cologne Conservatoire. [Wrote] to Giuseppe Rossi in Linz, returning his Italian libretto manuscript. Read through my different *traités*[251] with Kapellmeisterin Weber. [Wrote] to Karl Kaskel in Dresden.

Sunday 14 December. Answered Glöggl in Vienna. To the Opera House for Spontini's *Olympia*. This was a good production; the *mise en scène* of the Triumphal Scene in act 3, formerly so notoriously heavy and un-Grecian both in costume and action, is now surprisingly new, splendid, and picturesque. The music, which I have not heard for perhaps fifteen years, impressed me less than I had anticipated from my earlier memories; with the exception of the very beautiful overture, a slow *tempo* in the act 1 finale, and the women's duet, I found a dryness of invention, a lack of themes, which significantly distinguishes this work from *La Vestale* and *Cortez*.

Monday 15 December. Wrote to the countess of Westmorland in Vienna. Had a copy of my piece "Der Wanderer und die Geister" copied for the Glögglische Institut in Vienna, revised the copy, and sent it, together with a letter to Demoiselle Glöggl, for delivery to her father. Wrote in the albums of Mertens, Bote & Bock, and Herr Teichmann.[252]

Tuesday 16 December. Letter from the composer and man of letters Eduard Doctor in Linz.[253] Improvised at home. Carefully read through Lord Byron's *Hebrew Melodies* for a second time, to see whether I should set them to music in English for England. In the Singakademie attended a rehearsal of Emil Naumann's *Mass*[254] and Taubert's *Vaterunser.*[255]

Wednesday 17 December. Answered the director of the Cologne Music Conservatory. [Wrote] to Gouin. Letter from Kaskel. [Wrote] to Fétis, to the composer Eduard Doctor in Linz.

Thursday 18 December. Letter from Scribe in Nice. Read through the plan of the first two acts of the revised *L'Africaine*; it does not please me very much. Read through Sobolewsky's cantata *Himmel und Erde* in order to prepare the requested report.

Friday 19 December. Letter to J. B. Schmidt. Letter from Truhn. [Wrote] to Truhn, to Kaskel. Attended the funeral service of the young Swedish singer Ebeling; the preacher Krummacher delivered a really lovely, liberally minded funeral oration.[256] Read more of Sobolewsky's cantata. Symphony-soirée: the overtures to *Leonore, Egmont, Coriolan,* and the Symphony no. 2 in B Major by Beethoven.

Saturday 20 December. Passed the day uselessly, unfortunately, as has been the case so often lately. News from Gouin of the début of Madame Tedesco in *Le Prophète.*[257] She appears to have succeeded without creating the sensation in this role that Viardot and Alboni have always generated. The unfavorable timing (the very days of the presidential election) meant that the production was poorly attended and cold.[258] Wrote to the composer and music critic Damcke in St. Petersburg.

Sunday 21 December. Letter to Dr. Bacher. Death of Professor Rungenhagen, director of the Singakademie. Musical gathering at the concertmaster Leopold Ganz's that featured the Beethoven string trios and the eleven-year-old violin virtuoso, Bernard.[259] In the theater: Cherubini's *Der Wasserträger.*

Monday 22 December. [No entry.]

Tuesday 23 December. To Count Redern, Schlesinger. Letter from Glöggl in Vienna, who, on behalf of his codirectors, is offering me the honorary directorship of the new Musical Institute for Choral Singing that he has just founded.

Wednesday 24 December. At 8:30 in the morning attended the commemorative service for Rungenhagen in the Singakademie, then his funeral.

Thursday 25 December. Answered Glöggl, declining. Visited Count Redern. To Tuczek.

Friday 26 December. Rehearsed the music for the Court Concert with the singer Mme. Gadi. Wrote to Scribe in Nice enclosing my observations on the plan for the first 2 acts of *L'Africaine* that he had sent me.[260]

Sunday 27 December. Rehearsed various pieces for the Court Concert with Herr von Osten and the violinist Köckert.[261] [Wrote] to Gouin enclosing a letter ostensibly for him, but really for Émile Perrin, director of the Opéra Comique.

Sunday 28 December. Letters from Dr. Bacher, from Glöggl, from the music director Sobolewsky in Königsberg: he wishes me to recommend him as music director of the Berlin Singakademie. Court Concert in Charlottenburg with the singer Gadi, the tenor von Osten, the violinist Köckert, the Dülken sisters. The king was extremely gracious to me and reproached me for not coming to tea, since I had awaited his arrival with the other artists in the antechamber.

Monday 29 December. [Wrote] to Dr. Bacher in Paris.

Tuesday 30 December. Letter from Sina. [Wrote] to Isidor von Mauritius in Zerbst, who has sent me her novella about *Le Prophète*.[262] Letter from Herr von Humboldt. With my niece, Jülchen von Haber, to the theater: first performance of Mendelssohn's opera *Die Heimkehr aus dem Fremde*, which had already been given in the Friedrich- Wilhelmstädtisches-Theater; *Das Herzvergessen*, comedy in one act by Putlitz,[263] and the ballet *Der Geburtstag* by Hoguet.[264]

Wednesday 31 December. Called on Count von Stollberg,[265] A. von Humboldt, Herr Budberg. [Wrote] a letter, ostensibly to Gouin, but actually for Roqueplan. Letters from Gouin, Scribe, Bacher. The old year is at an end. May God bless the new year. May it be a happy, blessed year for me and my family, as well as for the whole of mankind.

NOTES

1. This exhibition in the buildings of the Royal Academy was held under the auspices of the Verein Berliner Künstler "to establish a fund for the support of its needy members and their surviving dependents." The display of each of six paintings was accompanied by a choral piece: the program listed Guido Reni's *Annunciation* (with a piece by Eduard Grell), Rubens's *Adoration of the Shepherds* (Christoph Gottlieb Schröter), Johann Friedrich Overbeck's *Presentation of Christ in the Temple* (Otto Nicolai), Rubens's *Holy Family Returning from Egypt* (Giacomo Antonio Perti), Raphael's *Holy Family* (Bernhard Klein), and Raphael's *Transfiguration* (Nicolai). The whole was performed in darkness, with the voices coming from a mysterious distance. The piece by Roland de Lassus was probably a deviation from the printed program (cf. *BT*, 5:890).

2. Karl Wilhelm Gropius (1793–1870) was scene designer and painter at the Königliches Schauspielhaus until 1868. He became a member of the Academy of Arts (1822), and after completing his education had traveled widely. In Paris he had seen the diorama of Jacques Daguerre and Charles-Marie Boutons, and consequently established his own in Berlin (1827) where twenty-six pictures were exhibited until 1850. A permanent display of paintings, an art business, a press, and a Christmas bazaar were attached.

3. *L'Étoile du Nord*, see no. 2: *Andante* G-flat ("Amoureux vulgaires, Vos feux ordinaires").

4. Friedrich Edler von Scherb (b. 1830) was an officer and writer, a contributor to

the *Humoristische Blätter* and the *Neue Fliegende Blätter*, and author of a book on the Rothschilds (1892).

5. Gade, Overture *Im Hochland*, op. 7 (1844).

6. Maria Serato was eleven years old at the time, and had just appeared in Leipzig as part of a series of concerts given in several German cities.

7. Adolf Gross (b. 1841) had given concerts in Königsberg and Leipzig, playing a tiny violin. His first Berlin appearance had been at the Singakademie on 7 December 1850.

8. Marie Jüngken (née Seidler) (d. 1876) was the wife of the medical professor Johann Christian Jüngken.

9. Emilie Karoline Friederike von Borcke (1805–91) was a Berlin dilettante who had studied with Stürmer.

10. Friedrich Wilhelm Heinrich Herbig (1787–1861), a historical and genre painter, had been a member of the Academy of Arts since 1823. He became professor (1831), a member of the senate (1838), and eventually vice-director (1845).

11. Armand Eduard Lefèbvre (1800–1864) had succeeded Persigny as French ambassador in Berlin on 29 December 1850.

12. This was August Anton Fürst von Sulkowski (1820–82), hereditary member of the Prussian Upper House.

13. August von der Heydt (1801–74) as Prussian minister of trade, industry, and public works (1848–62) instituted many innovations and improvements in post, telegraphs, transport, and industry during his tenure in office.

14. The concert comprised Dorn's Symphony in E Major, the vocal quartets "Frühlingslied" and "Käferhochzeitstanz," and *Missa Pro Defunctis*.

15. Frederick Elector of Brandenburg became the first king of Prussia, crowned Friedrich I on 18 January 1701.

16. Naumann, *Psalmodie des 66. Psalms* ("Jauchzet Gott, alle Lande"), op. 10, no. 2.

17. Simon Dach (1605–59) was professor of poetry at the University of Königsberg, and then rector there (1656). Dach's chorale had been performed at the coronation of King Friedrich I in 1701, and was traditionally sung at celebrations of the Order, on this occasion presumably in Carl Loewe's arrangement (*BT*, 5:892).

18. Mendelssohn, *Die deutsche Liturgie* for eight-voice chorus, with sections "Kyrie," "Ehre," and "Heilig" (1846).

19. Caldara, *Te Deum laudamus, 8 Voci, con Strum'ti* (Vienna, 17 March 1724).

20. Georg Heinrich Pertz (1795–1876) was a historian and the editor of *Monumenta Germaniae historica* until 1874. He worked as royal archivist in Hanover (1823) and Brunswick-Lüneberg before becoming head royal librarian in Berlin (1842). He was later *Geheimer Oberregierungsrat* and a member of the Academy of Science.

21. Karl Friedrich Wilhelm Dieterici (1790–1859) was the director of the office of statistics in the Prussian ministry of the interior, as well as being a member of the Academy of Science and professor of the faculty of philosophy at the University of Berlin.

22. *L'Étoile du Nord*, no. 1e *Suite de l'Introduction* ("Eh bien et toi? Je bois à Czar Pierre première").

23. Christian Friedrich Gotthilf von Zander (1791–1868) was president of the Royal Prussian Tribunal.

24. Peter Cornelius had been a pupil of Dehn (1844–50), and would go to Weimar to study with Liszt in 1852.

25. Dennery, *Paillasse, drame* in five acts (with Marc-Fournier; Paris, Théâtre de la Gaîté, 9 November 1850) [Wicks 11914]; translated by M. F. Marr [Richel 103]; also translated into Italian as *Pagliaccio* (Milan, 1851).

26. Ernst Freiherr von Danckelmann (1805–55) was also an amateur composer and wrote a *Fackeltanz zur Vermählung der Prinzessin Charlotte von Preussen* for the occasion of the princess's betrothal on 18 June 1850.

27. See *BT*, 5:319–20 for the text of the letter.

28. Lortzing died on 21 January 1851. He had lived in poverty in Berlin, despite the popularity and frequent performances of his operas. His death came even as he was about to be dismissed from his humble post at the Friedrich-Wilhelmstädtisches-Theater.

29. This was Karl Heinrich Graf von Görtz-Wrisberg.

30. Emil von Haber (1807–81), son of the banker Salomon Freiherr von Haber of Karlsruhe, lived in Berlin as a private man of means.

31. Alexander Mendelssohn founded the banking firm Mendelssohn & Company together with his father Joseph in 1828. After the death of the latter in November 1848, he continued the business with his cousin Paul Mendelssohn-Bartholdy, the brother of the composer.

32. This was the baritone John Hamilton Braham (1818–62). He had made his debut in London (1843) and had just appeared in a concert in Leipzig (December 1850).

33. Rosina Regina Lortzing (née Ahles) (1800–1854), the mother of five children, was in a desperate financial situation after the premature death of her husband.

34. This was Auguste Cornelius (1826–91), a writer and translator.

35. Angelina Raffter was making a guest appearance at the Königstädter-Theater. From 1852 she worked as coloratura soprano and soubrette in Riga, then in Frankfurt-am-Main and Hamburg.

36. Geheimer Oberregierungsrat Gottlob Heinrich Schmückert (1790–1862) was director of the general post department of the Prussian ministry of trade, industry, and public works.

37. Meyerbeer's subscription had presumably been lost in the post.

38. This was Dr. Wilhelm Wagner, the editor of the Frankfurt-based *Didaskalia: Blätter für Geist, Gemüth und Publizität*.

39. Geheimer Kommerzienrat Heinrich Conrad Carl, the director of the Schwendy wool factory and chairman of the Berlin Merchants' Union (1846–58), was one of the most prominent figures in the industrial life of the city.

40. Karl Möser (b. 1774) had died on 27 January 1851. He was violinist and concert master of the Royal Orchestra in Berlin, and had famously arranged quartet evenings (from 1813 onwards) in which the works of Haydn, Mozart, and Beethoven were played. These were later expanded into the equally popular "symphony-soirées" given by the orchestra.

41. This was actually Karl Wilhelm Georg Graf zu Inn- und Knyphausen (1784–1860), who was the Hanoverian representative in both Berlin and Dresden.

42. Mme. Cavilla had just been engaged as alto in Bonn. In 1852 she went to Erfurt and then suddenly retired from the stage.

43. Rossini, *L'Inganno felice*, opera *(farsa per musica)* in one act (Giuseppe Maria Foppa; Venice, San Moisè, 8 January 1812). This was Rossini's first great success, performed all over the world in the 1820s (Rio de Janeiro, 1824; Santiago, 1830—the first opera to be performed in Chile). Revived in Berlin (1850) and Naples (1870).

44. Bianchi de Mazoletti was the bass at the Königstädter-Theater for the 1850–51 season; there he sang Bertram, among other roles.

45. Archduke Leopold of Austria (1823–98), son of Archduke Reiner, entered the army and became general in 1867.

46. Mozart, *Le Nozze di Figaro*, no. 22 ("E Susanna non vien!...Dove sono").

47. Gluck, *Iphigénie en Tauride*, no. 1 ("Grands dieux! soyez-nous secourables").

48. Rainer Joseph Johann Michael Franz Hieronymus, archduke of Austria (1783–1853), was the seventh son of Emperor Leopold II.

49. Mendelssohn, *Psalm 98* for eight-voice chorus, op. 91 (1843).

50. Mendelssohn, Piano Concerto no. 2 in D Minor, op. 40 (1837).

51. Mozart, *Ave verum corpus*, motet K. 618 (1791).

52. No. 9 from Rossini's *Stabat Mater*, oratorio for soprano, alto, tenor, and bass (Paris, 1832).

53. Mendelssohn, *Die erste Walpurgisnacht*, cantata for chorus and orchestra (words J. W. Goethe), op. 60 (1832). See 19 August 1844.

54. Spontini died in Maiolati on 24 January 1851.

55. In the spring and autumn of 1850 Dehn had visited many libraries in seminaries, castles, and schools across the whole Prussian state in order to secure scores, manuscripts, and publications through purchase or exchange for the Royal Library in Berlin. His report was dated 10 February 1851, and ran to sixty-three pages (cf. *BT*, 5:897).

56. Birch-Pfeiffer, *Magdala, oder Vater und Tochter*, drama in four acts (Berlin, Königliche Schauspiele, 29 March 1851) [Richel 17].

57. J. Martini was theater director in Halle, and then in Dessau (1849–53). In 1852 his Dessauer Schauspieler- und Operngesellschaft made a guest appearance at the Summer Theater in the Kroll Etablissement.

58. *L'Étoile du Nord*, no. 1e *Fin de l'Introduction* ("Vengeance").

59. Heinrich Lehwess (1796–1852), an esteemed physician, had practiced in Berlin since 1823.

60. Beethoven, Incidental Music to August von Kotzebue's *Festspiel, Die Ruinen von Athen*, op. 113 (Pest, Deutsches Theater, 9 February 1812). Weber, Incidental Music to Pius Alexander Wolff's *Schauspiel mit Gesang und Tanz, Precioza*, J. 279 (Berlin, Königliche Schauspiele, 14 March 1821).

61. Actually Rosa Csillag (orig. Goldstein) (1832–92), a Hungarian singer.

62. This was the Honorable Julian Henry Charles Fane (1827–70), the younger of the two surviving sons of five children of the earl and countess of Westmorland. Since 1845 he had been attaché at the British Embassy in Berlin. His diplomatic career continued as secretary in Vienna (1860) and Paris (1865–68). Like his father, he was talented littérateur and musician, and featured as a poet (*Poems*, 1852), a translator (*Poems by Heinrich Heine*, 1854) and, under the pseudonym Edward Trevor, collaborator with Bulwer Lytton on the poem *Tannhäuser, or the Battle of the Bards* (1861). In 1851 he won the Chancellor's Medal for English Poetry at Cambridge.

63. Karl Begas (1794–1854) trained and first worked in Paris. In 1821 he joined the court of King Friedrich Wilhelm III as resident artist, a role he continued with Friedrich Wilhelm IV, who engaged him to paint the portraits for a projected gallery of the members of the order Pour le Mérite (1842).

64. The collection was destined for the Hohenzollern Museum in Schloss Monbijou, Berlin. While all the other items in the collection have remained intact, the portraits of Mendelssohn and Meyerbeer have been missing since 1945. See H. Becker and G. Becker, *Giacomo Meyerbeer—Weltbürger der Musik* (Wiesbaden: Dr. Ludwig Reichertverlag, 1991), no. 189. Reproduction has only been possible through a surviving negative owned by the Stiftung Preussischer Schlösser und Gärten Berlin-Brandenburg.

65. Kommerzienrat Emil Friedrich Wilhelm Praetorius was the owner of the Berlin firm Koeppen & Schier and manager of the State Loan Office.

66. Alexander Friedrich Wilhelm Duncker (1813–97) was a book and art publisher in Berlin, who had taken over the business Duncker & Humboldt from his father in 1837. Meyerbeer had close association with him at Franzensbad in July 1847.

67. The Westmorlands were moving to Vienna, where the earl was taking up a new ambassadorial post (1851–54).

68. Taubert, Symphony in C Major, op. 80. It was published by Bote & Bock.

69. Georg Moritz Oppenfeld (1794–1859) was a landed gentleman in Pomerania and a banker, the part owner of M. Oppenheims Söhne.

70. Mme. Weinthal was a Dutch contralto. A pupil of Garcia, she appeared as guest artist at the Königstädter-Theater and in several concerts.

71. Adolph Stahlknecht (1813–87), a violinist, founded the Stahlknecht Quartet with his brother Julius (1817–92), the violinist Julius Rammelsberg, and the violist Eduard Ganz. Adolph had worked in the orchestra of the Königstädter-Theater before joining the Hofkapelle (1840). He was an admired musician and composer (of twenty-five string quartets). At Meyerbeer's instigation, he initiated the Berlin matinée musicale, where he introduced his own chamber music.

72. Horkel (b. 1830) had been a member of the Domchor since 1843.

73. Carl Freiherr von Hochschild (1785–1859) was the Swedish ambassador in Berlin from 1850 to 1854.

74. Benny Rubens was a Berlin money broker, owner of the firm Mertens & Rubens.

75. *Der grosse Kurfürst*, drama *(vaterländisches Schauspiel)* in five acts by Köster with incidental music by Taubert (Berlin, Königliche Schauspiel, 15 March 1851) [Richel 83]. The theme of the Great Elector Friedrich Wilhelm of Brandenburg was presumably part of the 150th celebration of the Prussian monarchy. The play was given five times in the season.

76. Albert Zabel was harpist in the orchestra of the Royal Opera from 1851 to 1854. Meyerbeer had known him since his youth. See 23 July 1845.

77. J. F. Ledsam was chairman of the Birmingham Festival Committee.

78. The soprano Stubbe was guest artist at the Stadttheater in Stettin in the 1850–51 season, and was to sing in the first concert of the Société Sainte-Cécile in Paris (1852).

79. Spohr, *Die letzten Dinge* (text by Johann Friedrich Rochlitz; Cassel, St. Martinskirche, Good Friday 25 March 1826); known in English as *The Last Judgment*.

80. Palestrina, motet "Crucem sanctam subit," no. 7 of the *Liber Primus Motettorum* (Rome, 1569).

81. Lotti, *Crucifixus*, motet for six voices (c. 1736). This was one of the most popular pieces of church music from the early eighteenth century, and was frequently performed in Berlin.

82. Fesca, *Vater unser für vier Solostimmen und Chor*, op. 18 (c. 1840). Alexander Ernst Fesca (1820–49) was a pupil of Rungenhagen.

83. Mendelssohn, "Lass o Herr" for alto, chorus, and orchestra, op. 96 (1843), also known in the arrangement "Hear my prayer" for soprano, chorus, and organ (1844).

84. This is actually Gustav Friedrich Waagen (1794–1868), a writer on art who had lived in Berlin since 1823, where he became director of the Art Gallery (1830).

85. Franz, Marquis von Lucchesini (1787–1867), was the royal chamberlain to Princess Marie of Prussia.

86. The bass August Fischer (1798–1868) studied in Vienna with Giuseppe Ciccimarra, and worked in Pest, Vienna, Darmstadt, and Paris before moving to the Königstädter-Theater in Berlin (1831). He was finally employed at the Königliche Schauspiele (1837), where

he sang smaller roles. His visit to Meyerbeer may well have been in connection with his retirement from the stage in 1851.

87.   Botho von Hülsen (1815–86), in addition to his military career, became intendant general of the Royal Theater on 1 June 1851, and was named *Kammerherr* at the same time. He held the post until his death, and proved himself an excellent administrator, whose artistic point of view was very similar to Meyerbeer's. He promoted new works of topical and international note (Verdi, Gounod, Bizet), while not neglecting the German repertoire. There is no substance to the allegation that he did little to promote Wagner (see Sieghard Döhring, "Nationalismus contra Internationalismus: Die Berliner Hofoper unter Küstner und von Hülsen," in *Apollini et Musis, 250 Jahre Opernhaus unter den Linden,* ed. Georg Quander [Frankfurt-am-Main, 1992], pp. 93–115, esp. pp. 108ff.).

88.   This was the Loczer Hungarian Music Society, which played the Rakoczy March, a mazurka by Kálozdy, and Hungarian national songs in their concert. In addition, they performed marches from *Ein Feldlager in Schlesien* and *Le Prophète* and the overture to *Guillaume Tell* (cf. *BT,* 5:902).

89.   The leader of the Loczer Hungarian Music Society was actually the kapellmeister Johann Kálozdy.

90.   Elise Gräfin Schlik zu Bassano und Weisskirchen (1790–1855) was a composer of songs, who held a series of highly regarded concerts in her houses at Teplitz and Prague. She dedicated to Meyerbeer her *Drei Lieder für Mezzosopran oder Bariton mit Pianofortebeg.,* op. 2 (Vienna: Verlag Glöggl, 1850).

91.   Dr. Hermann Jacobson was a Berlin businessman, joint owner of the firm Jacobson & Riess, a city councilor, and member of the Ältesten-Kollegium of the Berlin Merchants' Union.

92.   Hermann Sillem (1788–1849) had founded the London banking house Hermann Sillem & Co. with whom Meyerbeer was in frequent contact concerning his investments.

93.   Pauline Elisabeth Luise Wilhelmine Ferdinande Amalie Gräfin von Néale (1779–1869) had been lady-in-waiting to Princess Luise Radziwill, and was a close friend of Lady Westmorland.

94.   Liegnitz is now Legnica in Poland.

95.   Actually Johann de Deo Beranek (1813–75), the organist at the Augustiner- and Franziskanerkirche in Vienna (1846). He continued studies with Preyer and Sechter while also becoming organist at the Hofburgkapelle and in Schönbrunn, and a teacher at the Präparandie des k. k. Waisenhaus (1852). He was also active as a composer and critic (for the *Wiener Zeitung,* the *Wandrer, Die Presse*).

96.   Halévy, *La Dame de pique, opéra comique* in three acts (Scribe, based on Pushkin's novella [1834]; Paris, Opéra Comique, 28 December 1850). This work achieved only forty-seven performances, unjustly so, according to Clément & Larousse: "L'opéra . . . renferme des beautés musicales incontestables, et néanmois il n'a obtenu qu'un succès d'estime" [the opera contains incontestable musical beauties, and yet achieved only passing success] (1:291). Halévy dedicated the work "à mon ami le docteur Joseph Bacher de Vienne."

97.   Bach, *Passio secundum Matthaeum,* BWV 244 (Leipzig, Thomaskirche, Good Friday 1727).

98.   Doris was the widow of Wilhelm Beer.

99.   This is the singer Guilio Julius Edward Lindemann (1822–86), who was discovered by Wagner in Leipzig (1847) and subsequently sang in Dresden, Hamburg (1849–55), Munich (1856–62), and Cassel (1863–83). He had participated in the Hamburg premiere of *Le Prophète,* and sang in several operas by Meyerbeer and Wagner (*BT,* 5:905).

100. *L'Étoile du Nord*, no. 9c *Choeurs des soldats et Ensemble des soldats, des ménétriers et des jeunes filles (Pas redoublé)*.

101. This was actually Gustav Müller.

102. Taubert, *Die Kirmes*, comic opera in one act (Eduard Devrient; Berlin, Court Opera, 23 January 1832). This was Taubert's first and most successful opera, and would later be revived in Karlsruhe (1855) and again in Berlin (1889).

103. Ferdinand Röder (1808–80) was originally an actor. He became the theater director in various cities: Nuremberg (1849), London and Amsterdam, and Riga (1850–53). After an unsuccessful venture in Cologne and Bonn, he established a theatrical agency in Berlin (1856).

104. This was the theater agent Hermann Michaelson (1800–1874).

105. Johann Andreas Herrenburg (1824–1906) was a landscape and architectural painter. After several expeditions to Greece, Egypt, and the Middle East, he returned to Berlin (1848) and fulfilled several commissions for King Friedrich Wilhelm IV. He married the singer Leopoldine Tuczek in 1850.

106. Benedix, *Angela*, drama in one act (Vienna, Burgtheater, 14 June 1851) [Richel 12]. This Berlin performance antedates the premiere by six weeks.

107. Julius Miller (1774–1851) made his debut in Flensburg (1800), and, after appearing in Berlin, Königsberg, Amsterdam, Dresden, and Leipzig, eventually settled in Berlin. No biographical details are available concerning his daughter.

108. Jähns directed a choral union for spiritual and secular music from the 1840s until 1870. The approximately one hundred members used to practice in the hall of the Ministry of the Interior.

109. This was part of the ethnographical collection *(Ethnographische Abteilung)* of the New Museum, an exhibition of original artifacts, costumes, weapons, and models of the homes of the indigenous peoples of Central and South America, Africa, and Asia.

110. Rellstab's song, *Fredericus Magnus* "Für solchen König Blut und Leben."

111. Franz Theodor Kugler (1808–58) was an art historian and an honorary member of the senate of the Academy of Arts in Berlin (1842). Ladenburg entrusted him with restructuring of the Prussian artistic institutions (1849–50). He was also a writer and composer of songs.

112. *L'Étoile du Nord*, no. 13d *Quintette* ("Cesse cette badinage").

113. *Mein Freund*, farce in three acts by Nestroy with incidental music by Carl Franz Stenzl (Vienna, Carltheater, 4 April 1851).

114. Actually *Die Macht der Vorurteile*, drama in five acts (Elisabeth Sangalli; first performance in Frankfurt, 1848) [Richel 128].

115. Heinrich Marr (1797–1871) made his name playing the classical repertoire in Hanover, before moving to the Burgtheater in Vienna (1838–44), Leipzig (1844–48) and Hamburg (1849–52). Later he worked as regisseur in Weimar (1853–57) and then again in Hamburg (as *Oberregisseur*).

116. F. L. Steinmeyer was theologian and former member of the Singakademie.

117. Fasch's funeral motet "Seelig sind die Toten" was written on the death of Prince Louis of Prussia in 1797. This and his eight-part *Requiem* were both printed in the third edition of his *Werkausgabe,* prepared by the Singakademie (Berlin: Trautwein, 1839).

118. Geheime Oberregierungsrat von Puttkammer was an official in the Prussian Ministry of the Interior.

119. Tgb. *mitläufigen*.

120. The première of Hackländer's *Der geheime Agent* had been a few days before on 14 May 1851.

121. Meyerbeer wrote in loving appreciation to his little daughter Cornelie from Prague. The letter, translated by Mark Violette, is cited in Heinz and Gudrun Becker, *Giacomo Meyerbeer: A Life in Letters* (Portland, Ore.: Amadeus Press, 1989), p. 132.

122. Elbing is now Elblag in Poland.

123. This was the artist Edouard de Biefve (1808–82), who was trained in Brussels and Paris.

124. Dittersdorf, *Doktor und Apotheker*, opera in two acts (Johann Gottlieb Stephanie, based on a French play *L'Apothicaire de Murcia*; Vienna, Kärntnertor-Theater, 11 July 1786). This was Dittersdorf's most successful work, consistently revived on German stages up to the present. In its day there were performances in English, Danish, Russian, French, Swedish, Dutch, and Hungarian. It reached New York in 1875.

125. This was August Müller, part of the family of copper engravers living in Dresden (F. Müller at Rosengasse 11).

126. Lady Georgiana Bloomfield (née Liddell) (b. 1822) was the wife of John Arthur Douglas Lord Bloomfield (1802–79), the British extraordinary ambassador and plenipotentiary to Prussia and Anhalt-Dessau. He was accredited on 17 July 1851 and remained in Berlin until 1860. From 1861 to 1871 he was ambassador in Vienna.

127. Schneider, *Das Weltgericht* (text by Johann August Apel; first performed in Leipzig, Gewandhaus, 6 March 1820). This work made Schneider famous, and was one of the most performed oratorios of the nineteenth century.

128. The pianist and composer Theodor von Döhler (1814–56) studied with Czerny and Sechter and appeared as a child prodigy. He stayed in for some years in Naples and St. Petersburg, as well as making several concert tours, before settling in Florence in 1848.

129. Döhler married Countess Elizaveta Sergeevna Ceremetev (1818–90) in 1846 in St. Petersburg.

130. Meyerbeer's letter to Sax (Berlin, 16 June 1851) is cited in Becker, *Giacomo Meyerbeer: A Life in Letters*, p. 133.

131. *L'Étoile du Nord*, no. 12 *Trio* ("Eh bien! à ce joyeux repas").

132. Madame Roger accompanied her husband on all his tours.

133. The earl of Westmorland was leaving Berlin to take up his new duties as ambassador to Vienna.

134. Friedrich Ferdinand Brissler (1818–93), a pianist and music teacher at the Stern Conservatoire (1845), prepared piano scores of operas and symphonies for the firm Bote & Bock (1848).

135. Ludwig III (1806–77). From 1848 to 1877 he was regent of the Grand Duchy of Hesse.

136. Andreas Freiherr von Budberg was *Hofrat* and *Legationsrat* at the Russian Embassy in Berlin; from 29 December 1851 he became full plenipotentiary.

137. "He was invited to St. Petersburg by the Emperor of Russia to direct the music of 'Struensee' for the fifty-years' jubilee of the Philharmonic Society, but his failing health obliged him to decline. Berlioz and Spohr were also asked, but were unable to accept" (see Nathan Haskell Dole, "Meyerbeer," in *The Lives of the Musicians,* 2 vols. [London and New York: Methuen & Co., 1903], 1:342).

138. Dittersdorf, *Hieronymus Knicker*, opera in two acts (text by the composer; Vienna, Leopoldstadt, 7 July 1789). Originally written for the private theater of the prince bishop of Breslau, Count Schaffgotsch, in c. 1787, this was Dittersdorf's most popular opera after *Der Doktor und Apotheker*. It was given on every German stage until 1810, and was frequently revived in the nineteenth century.

139. This was Bertha Gutmann (b.1801), a concert singer educated in Vienna.

140. Mathilde Grand Duchess of Hesse-Darmstadt (1813–62) was a member of the royal house of Bavaria. She married Ludwig III in 1833.

141. Grand Duchess Maria Nikolayevna (1819–76), daughter of Tsar Nicholas I, and wife of Maximilian Eugen Joseph Napoleon, duke of Leuchtenberg, whom she married in 1839.

142. Dorn had written a cantata "Höhen des Ruhmes erklimmen ist mühevoll" for the Rauch celebration.

143. While Meyerbeer remained faithful to Judaism all his life and was a deeply religious man, he appeared to retain an openness to all forms of Christianity. His devotion to his daughter was unaffected by her baptism and conversion to Catholicism. Amalia Beer, on the other hand, was a devoutly orthodox Jewess.

144. Wilhelmine Birch (1836–1916) was an actress and novelist. In 1857 she married Herr von Hillern.

145. Tgb. *palais*, i.e., the Neue Palais in Potsdam.

146. This is the tenor romance "Un ange, une femme inconnue from act 1 of Donizetti's *La Favorite.*

147. Meyerbeer designates her *Grossfürstin*, an untranslatable combination of grand duchess and princess.

148. Birch-Pfeiffer, *Wie man Haüser baut*, drama *(lokales Zeitgemälde)* in four acts. It was first produced four months later (Berlin, Königliche Schauspiele, 23 October 1851) [Richel 18].

149. This was another play in celebration of the foundation of the Prussian monarchy.

150. The Berlin bookshop B. Behr's at 12 and 13 Oberwallstrasse specialized in foreign and travel literature, and had a French and English lending library attached to it.

151. Karl Düffke (1816–80) sang at the Friedrich-Wilhelmstädtisches-Theater until 1853, then at the Royal Theater, with much success. In 1860 he joined the Hoftheater in Hanover, where he worked for rest of his life.

152. This was the Russian general Nicolai Alexsandrovich Ogarev (1811–67).

153. Hebbel, *Judith*, tragedy in five acts (Berlin, Königliche Schauspiele 6 July 1840, Vienna, 1849) [Richel 60]. It describes, in biblical terms, the conflict between the individual striving for self-expression and a general social order, which the heroine succeeds in rejuvenating.

154. The actress Christine Hebbel (née Engelhausen; pseudonym Engelhaus) (1817–1910) made her début as a child in Brunswick, and was engaged in Hamburg (1833) before being contracted to the Burgtheater in Vienna (1840–79). Her guest appearances at the Königliche Schauspiele in 1851 saw her in roles not only by her husband, Hebbel (whom she had married in 1846), but also by Goethe (Iphigenie), Schiller (Maria Stuart), and Mosenthal (Deborah).

155. Friedrich Wilhelm Ludwig, prince of Prussia (1794–1863), a general in the Royal Prussian Cavalry.

156. This was Ange-Henri Blaze de Bury, who wrote several treatises on Germany and whose stories were often set in Germany, especially Weimar.

157. This was perhaps Sigmund Levi (1823–84), who cofounded the conservatory in Stuttgart in 1857.

158. Birch-Pfeiffer's libretto *La Réole* was eventually set to music by Gustav Schmidt (opera in three acts; Breslau, Stadttheater, 24 January 1864).

159. The performance of *Les Huguenots* in Batavia took place on 24 May 1851.

160. The Bohemian soprano Bertha Röder-Romani (b. 1829) worked as a member of her husband Ferdinand Romani's opera company in Amsterdam and London. She later appeared in Cologne and Riga (1850–52).

161. August Ludwig Ferdinand, Graf von Nostitz (1777–1866), served as a Prussian general until his retirement in 1848, when he became Prussian ambassador in Hanover (1850–59). Hc was married to Clara Luise Auguste Hatzfeld (1807–58).

162. See 20 November 1849.

163. The dwarf couple Colibri were called the smallest in the world, and appeared in theatrical presentations (pantomime and dance) all over Europe (London, Paris, Vienna and Berlin [Dec. 1851]). "Colibri" is the French for hummingbird.

164. Vanderburch, *Le Avoué et le Normand, ou Fin contre fin*, *comédie-vaudeville* in one act (Paris, Théâtre du Gymnase Dramatique, 8 June 1837) [Wicks 6701].

165. Meyerbeer means the actor and singer Joseph Kelm (1807–82), who made his debut at the Théâtre de la Renaissance in Paris (1839). After engagements in the provinces, he appeared at the Théâtre du Vaudeville (1848), and won particular popularity at the Folies Nouvelles as a comedian in the works of Hervé (1855–59).

166. The actor Jean-Fulchran-Sébastien Bosquier-Gavaudan (known as Bousquier) (1776–1843) worked in Paris from 1798, particularly at the Théâtre Montansier (i.e., Théâtre des Variétés) (1802–35) where he specialized in role types like the lover, the servant, and the comic. His particular talent was as a vaudeville singer. Between 1804 and 1810 he also wrote a series of *comédies, opéra féeries, comédies-vaudevilles,* and *vaudevilles.*

167. *Les Extases de M. Hochenez, comédie-vaudeville* in one act is by Marc-Michel, not Varin (Paris, Théâtre du Palais-Royal, 9 December 1850) (*BT*, 5:919).

168. Mme. Hédouin was the wife of the station master in Valenciennes.

169. Actually Louise-Aimée-Julie Davout (née Leclerc), princess of Eckmühl. She was the widow of Louis-Nicholas Davout, duc d'Auerstädt, prince d'Eckmühl (1770–1823). He was the French marshal who served successfully with Napoleon from the pro-Revolutionary revolt (1790) to the Hundred Days. Napoleon created him duke (1808), prince (1809), and minister of war (1815). He was entrusted with the repression of Hamburg in May 1813. Henriette Mendelssohn, an aunt of the composer, wrote of the ferocity of the marshal and the domestic tyranny exercised by his wife (*Die Familie Mendelssohn 1729 bis 1847: Nach Briefen und Tagebüchern,* ed. Sebastian Hensel [1879; reprint, Leipzig: Insel, 1995], p. 90).

170. Varin and Lubize, *Les Trois Péchés du Diable, vaudeville-féerie* in one act (Paris, Théâtre du Gymnase Dramatique, 14 September 1844) [Wicks 13752]. Lubize was the nom de plume of P. H. Martin.

171. Latin, "comic energy."

172. Scribe and Legouvé, *La Bataille de dames, ou Un Duel en amour*, prose *comédie* in three acts (Paris, Comédie-Française, 17 March 1851) [Wicks 14807]. This was one of Scribe's most successful plays.

173. This was probably the wife of Francesco Cosma Damian Valentini (b. 1789), a native of Rome who had lived in Berlin since 1813 as a teacher of Italian language and literature. He was appointed a professor (1825) and became director of the Italian Society he had founded (1836) (*BT*, 5:920).

174. Marianne Mendelssohn (née Seligmann) (1799–1880) had married Alexander Mendelssohn in 1821.

175. Busschop, *Fugue pour deux sopranos, ténor et basse, avec accompagnement d'orgue ou de piano* (*BT*, 5:920).

176. No details about this *vaudeville* by Marie-Emmanuel-Guillaume-Marguerite Théaulon de Lambert are available.

177. This is either *Le Rossignol, comédie-vaudeville* in one act (Vanderburch; Paris, Théâtre du Gymnase-Dramatique, 1 October 1837), or *Le Rossignol des salons, comédie-vaudeville* in one act (Déaddé & X. de Montépin; Paris, Théâtre de Porte-St-Martin, 19 May 1850) [Wicks 13004].

178. Paul Siraudin and R. Périn, *Monsieur Lafleur, comédie-vaudeville* in one act; Paris, Théâtre des Variétés, 13 December 1844) [Wicks 11468].

179. Mélesville and Xavier Boniface, *La Fée cocotte, comédie-vaudeville* in one act (Paris, Théâtre du Palais Royal, 14 May 1857) [Wicks 17143].

180. Meyerbeer had first seen Celine Montaland in Paris on 4 November 1850.

181. This was the banker Louis Raphaël Bischoffsheim (1800–1873), the father of Regine Bischoffsheim whom Meyerbeer's nephew Julius married in 1849. He came from Mainz and established a banking house in Amsterdam with branches in Antwerp (1827), London (1836), and Paris (1846). He moved to Paris in 1850, where he soon played an important role in the business and financial life of the city, becoming cofounder of the Compagnie des Chemins de Fer du Midi, the Société Générale, the Banque des Pays-Bas, and the Banque Franco-Egyptienne. The marriage of his nephew and the move of Julius and Regine to Paris meant that Meyerbeer had close contact with Bischoffsheim.

182. The Théâtre Royal des Galeries Saint Hubert was established in 1847 under the management of Auguste Nourrit*, and was originally intended for *opéra comique*. During the period 1850–52 a visiting Italian opera troupe performed its own repertoire.

183. Ricci, *Un'avventura di Scaramuccia, melodramma giocoso* (Felice Romani; Milan, La Scala, 8 March 1834). This was the most successful of Luigi Ricci's comic works written without his brother Frederico's collaboration, and came three years after his principal serious work, *Chiara di Rosembergh* (Milan, 1831).

184. Cabel was to create Dinorah for Meyerbeer in eight years' time.

185. Heinrich Mehmel (d. 1870) was a contrabassist in the orchestra of the Imperial Theater in St. Petersburg.

186. Tgb. *echauffierte*.

187. *L'Étoile du Nord*, no. 16 *Trio Danilowitz-Grischenko-Pierre* ("Mon devoir est s'apprendre à votre majesté").

188. Grisar, *Bonsoir, Monsieur Pantalon*, opera in one act (De Morvan & J. P. Lockroy [based on John Oxenford's farce *Twice Killed*]; Paris, Opéra Comique, 19 February 1851). This was the composer's most successful work, performed in Paris until 1874, and given elsewhere in Europe in English, Polish, Danish, Czech, Hungarian, and especially German (in J. C. Grünbaum's translation, revived in Zürich, 1907, and Hanover, 1911).

189. Fr. "Feverishness."

190. Gabriel Andral (1797–1876) was one of the most renowned doctors of the period. Since 1839 he had occupied the chair of general pathology and therapy as well as being a practitioner at the Charité in Paris. His publications *Clinique médicale* (5 vols., Paris, 1823–27, rpt. 1842–48) and the *Traité d'anatomie pathologique* (Paris, 1829) became standard works, while the *Essai d'hématologie pathologique* (Paris 1843), in which he investigated the role of blood analysis in diagnosis, was a pioneering work in medical history.

191. The astronomer Vasily Pavlovich Engelhardt (1828–1915) was an admirer of Glinka's music and a collector of his autographs.

192. Mehmel, of his own accord, had sent Meyerbeer a manuscript copy of Glinka's *A*

Life for the Tsar that belonged to Engelhardt. Meyerbeer's reluctance to examine this and the score of *Ruslan and Ludmilla* for fear of possible later unconscious plagiarism is discussed by Johannes Weber, *Meyerbeer* (Paris: Librairie Fischbacher, 1898), pp. 43–44. Such fears were not ungrounded; see the instance of unconscious plagiarism from Donizetti's *Don Sébastien* on 17 August 1852.

193. The soprano Poinsot was a pupil of Duprez. She made her début at the Opéra in 1851 as Rachel in *La Juive*, and in the same year she sang Alice in *Robert le Diable* and Berthe in *Le Prophète*.

194. Auber, *L'Enfant prodigue, grand opéra* in five acts (Scribe; Paris, Opéra, 6 December 1850). Auber's only opera on a biblical theme did not achieve great success; it was performed in Paris only forty-four times, and had only a modest career in English, Italian, and German. The last revival was in Florence (1875). Some of the music gained a certain currency in twentieth century when used by Frederick Ashton for his ballet *Les Rendez-vous* (1937).

195. Auber, *Zerline, ou La Corbeille d'oranges*, opera in three acts (Scribe; Paris, Opéra, 16 May 1851). Written especially as a vehicle for Marietta Alboni, this work was among the composer's least successful, given only fourteen times in Paris, with further performances only in Brussels and London.

196. The bass Joseph-Théodore Coulon (1822–74) specialized in the smaller, *comprimario* roles at the Opéra.

197. The soprano Marianna Barbieri-Nini (1818–87) was making her Parisian début in this performance at the Théâtre Italien. She had already achieved considerable success in Italy as a dramatic soprano in the operas of Verdi, for whom she created Lucrezia in *I due Foscari* (1844), Lady Macbeth (1847), and Gulnara in *Il Corsaro* (1848).

198. The tenor Lodovico Graziani (1820–85) is not to be confused with his illustrious brother, the baritone Francesco Graziani*. After his début in Bologna (1845), he became one of the leading Verdi tenors of the day. Although he lacked dramatic gifts, his clear and vibrant voice was ideal for Alfredo in *La Traviata* (the role he created in 1853), the Duke of Mantua, Manrico, and Riccardo. He was to sing Vasco da Gama in the Italian première of *L'Africaine* (Bologna, 4 November 1865).

199. Fortini was a member of the Théâtre Italien in the early 1850s.

200. Among other things, Meyerbeer proposed the Council Scene in the Lisbon admiralty that dominates act 1 of *L'Africaine*. Scribe included it in the reworking of the libretto that took place in the autumn/winter of 1851–52.

201. Bernhard Klemm was the owner of a musical instrument shop and lending institute, C. A. Klemm (founded by his father in 1821 in Leipzig). A miniature bust of Meyerbeer made of stearin was advertised in his catalog in 1852, and he presented the composer with a copy (cf. Meyerbeer's letter to him on 20 June 1852).

202. Tgb. *Spezial-Eisenbahnzug*.

203. Caroline Duprez (1832–75) had just made her début alongside her father in Donizetti's *La Favorite* (Rheims, 1851). She was engaged for the Théâtre-Italien (1850–51), and also appeared in London and Brussels as guest artist. From 1852 she was contracted to the Opéra Comique, where she stayed until 1856, and where she returned in 1863 after successful engagements at the Théâtre Lyrique (1858) and the Opéra (1860).

204. Caroline Duprez was indeed to create the role of Catherine for Meyerbeer in 1854.

205. Meyerbeer's letter to Scribe (Minden, 27 October 1851) is quoted in Becker, *Giacomo Meyerbeer: A Life in Letters*, pp. 134–36.

206. Dutch, *Rotterdamer Maatschappij tot Bevordering der Toonkunst*.

207. The soprano Emma Babnigg (1825–1904) sang at the Hofoper in Dresden (1843), at the Stadttheater in Hamburg, then at the Breslau Opera (1849–52, where she was particularly successful), and finally in Hanover (1852–53). After her marriage to Mampe (1855) she taught singing in Vienna. She sang Berthe at the first performance of *Le Prophète* in Breslau (20 November 1850).

208. This is actually Beranek. See 8 April 1850.

209. Ger. *Schleimhämoroiden*, a flux of intestinal mucus.

210. Unter den Linden is the grand avenue of Prussian Berlin named after the trees lining its route. The walnuts and limes were planted by the Great Elector Friedrich Wilhelm at the end of the Thirty Years' War in 1648 to flank a riding path that led toward the hunting grounds of Grunewald and the present day Tiergarten. "Two hundred years later, the master architect of neoclassical Berlin, Friedrich Karl Schinkel, made Unter den Linden the centerpiece of his new design for the city, with palaces, museums, embassies and government buildings flanking its 1.5 km extent." (See Andrew Gumbel, *Berlin,* Cadogan City Guides [London: Cadogan Books; Chester, Conn.: Globe Pequot Press, 1991], p. 57.)

211. Méhul, *Une Folie, opéra comique* in two acts (Jean-Nicolas Bouilly; Paris, Opéra Comique, 5 April 1802). This was the most successful of Méhul's comic works, and enjoyed particular popularity in Germany, where five different versions had great currency in the early nineteenth century. It was also widely given in Spanish, Swedish, Hungarian, Russian, Polish, and Dutch. A version by Kelly was performed on many American stages, and as far afield as Cape Town (1838). Méhul's original version was revived in Paris (1843, 1874), in Berlin (1851), in Königsberg (1874), and in Prague (1934).

212. The Erk Men's Choral Union was founded in 1843 by Ludwig Christian Erk (1807–83), who had been a music teacher at the Seminar für Stadtschulen in Berlin since 1835. He published a popular collection of folk songs for men's chorus (*Volksklänge* [Berlin, 1851]), and extended his union to incorporate mixed choirs (1852). The concert attended by Meyerbeer took place in the Förster Hall at 112 Friedrichstrasse, under the auspices of the Pestalozzistiftung (*BT,* 5:932).

213. Carl Gustav Brüstlein was the manager of Gebrüder Schickler (1821–59), one of the oldest banking houses in Berlin.

214. Lord Byron's mystery *Heaven and Earth* (1823) appeared in German in 1837. Meyerbeer's report must have read unfavorably, since there is no record of Sobolewsky's oratorio ever being performed at a Court Concert.

215. Ernst August*, king of Hanover and duke of Cumberland, died on 18 November 1851.

216. C. O. Sternau (actually Otto Inkermann) (1820–61) was a writer and book dealer from Cologne. In 1850 he had provided the Berlin publisher Schlesinger with a text linking the individual pieces of Weber's incidental music to *Precioza,* and now hoped to do the same for *Struensee.*

217. Ernst of Saxe-Coburg-Gotha, *Castilda, grosse romantische Oper mit Ballet* in four acts (M. Tenelli [Hofrat Johann Heinrich Millenet]; Gotha, Hoftheater, 13 March 1851). Duke Ernst's music was revised and scored by the court kapellmeister, Ernst Lampert. During the 1850s the work was performed in Vienna, Berlin, Brussels, Ghent, and London, with revivals in Gotha (1888), Darmstadt, and Leipzig (1892). The duke was a gifted composer who had been taught by Reissiger, among others.

218. Haydn, String Quartet in B-flat Major, op. 76, no. 4 (no. 78 from the 6 *Erdödy* string quartets, Hob.III:75–80) (1797).

219. Schubert, String Quartet no. 14 in D Minor (*Der Tod und das Mädchen*), D. 810 (1824).

220. Karl Tescher (1812–83) was a dancer and ballet master, and from June 1850 also director of the Court Theater and Music.

221. Richard Wagner's *Das Kunstwerk der Zukunft* had already appeared in Leipzig (Verlag Otto Wigand, 1850). In the same year, under the pseudonym "Freigedank," Wagner had also launched his notorious diatribe *Das Judenthum in der Musik* in the *Neue Zeitschrift für Musik* (3 and 6 September 1850) in which Meyerbeer and Mendelssohn were singled out for attack.

222. This essay was eventually printed in a small edition in Berlin by Leo Liepmannssohn (1886, eleven pages) and the original sold for 640 marks, after which it disappeared. Julius Kapp published the manuscript under the fictitious title *Über Meyerbeers "Hugenotten"* in *Richard Wagners Gesammelten Schriften und Briefe*, vol. 7 (Leipzig, n.d.). It is not mentioned by Ernest Newman in either *Wagner as Man and Artist* (New York, 1914) or *The Life of Richard Wagner* (New York, 1933–45), or in more modern works on Wagner like Robert Gutman, *Richard Wagner: The Man, His Mind, and his Music* (Harmondsworth, 1968). For further discussion, see *BT*, 5:929–30.

223. Haydn, String Quartet in C Major *(Kaiserquartet)*, op. 76, no. 3 (no. 77 from the 6 *Erdödy* string quartets, Hob.III:75–80) (1797).

224. Litolff, String Quartet in C Minor, op. 60.

225. Beethoven, String Quartet no. 10 in E-flat major *(Harp)*, op. 74 (1805–6).

226. Isabella Dulcken was thirteen at the time, and a virtuoso on the concertina. The duet-concertina was built by Charles Wheatstone, who patented it in 1844. This harmonica instrument allowed the right hand to play the melody and the left independently to provide the accompaniment. Isabella played a soprano concertina, and performed a piece by Giulio Regondi, *Souvenir aus der Oper Der Prophet;* Regondi and Richard Blagrove were the first teachers and composers for this instrument (cf. *BT* 5:935).

227. Geheimrat Jähnigen was general procurator in the Prussian Ministry of Justice and a member of the Council of State.

228. Ernst von Heeringen (1810–55) endeavored to institute a simplified form of musical notation. In Berlin he spoke to the Tonkünstler-Verein and the musical section of the Berlin Academy of Arts (1 December 1851), and further unsuccessfully tried to promote his reforms from Leipzig, writing in the *Neue Zeitschrift für Musik* during 1852.

229. Mendelssohn's opera fragment *Loreley* (text by Emanuel Geibel) was first performed in a concert in Leipzig on 27 March 1851.

230. Beethoven, Overture in C Major *Die Weihe des Hauses* (*The Consecration of the House*), op. 124 (1822).

231. This motet by Andrea Gabrielli was presumably one of the six-part settings from the collection *Psalmi Davidici* (1538).

232. This was the four-part Christmas song "Stille Nacht! Heilige Nacht!," no. 3 from Michael Haydn's collection *Drei Weihnachtslieder* (Berlin: T. Trautwein).

233. *Judas Ischariot*, a *dramatische Gedicht* (1848). Elise Schmidt (b. 1824) had been an actress (1838–49), and then emerged as a writer of stage works, stories, and reworkings of Greek dramas.

234. On 2 December 1851 Franziska Henriette Herbig married the Prussian *Junker*, Arthur Felix Karl Wilhelm von Arnim, Herr auf Gerswalde (1825–83)

235. The Chorus of Mothers was one of the pieces cut from the score of *Le Prophète* during rehearsals.

236. *Jesuiten-Polka*, a *komisches Tanzdivertissement* in one act by Richard Fricke with music by Richard Genée (Berlin, Friedrich-Wilhelmstädtisches-Theater, 5 December 1851).

237. *Guten Morgen, Herr Fischer, Vaudeville-Burleske* in one act from the French by Wilhelm Friedrich with incidental music by Eduard Stiegmann. First performed in Darmstadt, 1853 [Richel 42].

238. Landrat von Saldern was perhaps a member of the noble family Saldern-Plattenburg from Perleberg (West-Priegnitz) (see *BT,* 5:929).

239. The five Tschirch brothers were Karl Adolph (1815–75), a correspondent of the *Neue Zeitschrift für Musik* (1845–55) and later a pastor in Guben; Friedrich Wilhelm (1818–92), music director in Liegnitz; Ernst Leberecht (1819–54), a music teacher in Berlin; Heinrich Julius (1820–67), later music director and organist in Hirschberg; and Rudolf (1825–72), later royal music director in Berlin. The concert included the song *An mein Vaterland* (Julius), a spiritual cavatina (Adolph), a concert overture (Rudolf), excerpts from the opera *Frithjof* (Ernst), and the dramatic cantata *Der Sängerkampf* (Friedrich Wilhelm). It was Friedrich Wilhelm Tschirch*, not Ernst, who was to become more widely known as a composer.

240. This was the Prussian statesman Adolf Heinrich, Graf von Arnim (1803–68), who had been the minister of the interior (1842). The liberally minded Arnim had resigned in 1845, but became a member of the Second Chamber and then of the Upper House, or *Herrenhaus* (1854).

241. No biographical details exist for the Polish pianist Hedwige Brzowska and the Italian singer Giuseppina Gadi. Both appeared at a concert in the Singakademie (22 November 1851) and both were to assist at the Court Concert on 14 December 1851.

242. Gluck, *Orfeo e Euridice,* no. 22 *Scena* ("Deh! placatevi con me!").

243. Rossini, *Tancredi,* no. 7 *Scena e Cavatina* ("Oh patria!... Di tanti palpiti").

244. See 29 November 1851.

245. Taubert, "Schlummerlied" (text by Ludwig Tieck, the third of the *Vier Lieder für Tenöre und zwei Bässe,* op. 110.

246. Mertens was a Berlin pianist, composer, and violinist.

247. Mendelssohn, *Die schöne Melusine* concert overture for Grillparzer's play, op. 32 (1833).

248. *Die Heimkehr aus dem Fremde,* a *Liederspiel* (Karl Klingemann; Berlin, 26 December 1829 [privately], Leipzig, 10 April 1851 [publicly]). In this work Mendelssohn used all his mature style and special gifts of orchestration, but the musical forms again dominate the dramatic exigencies, as is typical of all his attempts at opera.

249. See 8 February 1850.

250. Heine's poem cycle *Romanzero* was published in Hamburg by Hoffmann & Campe in October 1851. It had reached its fourth edition by December. *Der Doctor Faust. Ein Tanzpoem. Nebst kuriosen Berichten über Teufel, Hexen und Dichtkunst* was published at the same time. These poems reveal the anguish and desolation of the poet's last years of illness. "When, however, in 1848, his health finally broke down; when he was fastened to his mattress grave, paralyzed, more than half blind, racked by agonies that only greater and greater quantities of opium could temporarily relieve—then Heine recognised the in-adequacy of a world view about which he had sneaking doubts the whole time. . . . In the poetry of Heine's last years the dream of a heaven built on earth is finally shattered. In *Romanzero* and *Gedichte 1853 und 1854* the reader is made to enter a world of suffering and humiliation—a world presided over by a capricious God. . . . The present has turned into a nightmare, the past into a torturing memory, the future into a vision of boredom or blank extinction" (Siegbert Prawer, *Heine: The Tragic Satirist* [Cambridge: Cambridge University Press, 1961], pp. 145, 284).

251. Fr. "contracts."

252. Perhaps this is Anton Tejchmann, a Polish composer whose songs were published by Bote & Bock.

253. This was the Austrian composer Ferdinand Eduard Doctor (b.1825).

254. Naumann, *Missa solemnis* for chorus and orchestra (1851).

255. Taubert, *Vater Unser, Psalm von Friedrich Gottlieb Klopstock*, for soli, chorus and orchestra, op. 87 (Berlin: T. Trautwein).

256. Friedrich Wilhelm Krummacher (1796–1868) was pastor at the Berlin Dreifaltigkeitskirche from 1847.

257. The Italian contralto Fortunata Tedesco (1826–1900) studied in the Milan Conservatoire, and made her début at La Scala (1844). She appeared in New York (1847–51) before being engaged by the Paris Opéra, where she sang Fidès (1851), Théodora in the première of Halévy's *Le Juif errant* (1852), and Venus in the notorious production of Wagner's *Tannhäuser* (1861).

258. The French constitution forbade the reelection of the president after the expiration of his four-year term. When Louis Napoleon realized that he could not obtain the three-fourths majority necessary for a revision of the constitution, he carried out a coup d'état on 2 December 1851. After defeating the Republicans in Paris on 4 December, he dissolved the Legislative Assembly, and decreed a new constitution that restored universal suffrage. A plebiscite approved the new constitution.

259. This was an eleven-year-old prodigy, Otto Bernhard, who played Charles de Bériot's first violin concerto.

260. Meyerbeer's observations are printed in *BT*, 5:479–82.

261. Adolph Köckert was a violinist from Prague who first performed in Berlin in the middle of November 1851.

262. Frau von Mauritius (who used the pseudonym Isidor von Mauritius) wrote novellas, many of them musical stories. Her *Gesammelte Schriften* appeared in eight volumes (1837–46).

263. Putlitz, *Das Herzvergessen*, *Lustspiel* in one act (first performed in Weimar, 1849, in Berlin, Königliche Schauspiele, 25 February 1850, and published 1853) [Richel 119].

264. *Der Geburtstag*, *divertissement* in one act (choreography by Hoguet; music by Carl Blum; Berlin, Court Opera, 29 March 1833).

265. Anton Graf zu Stollberg-Wernigerode (1785–1854), a lieutenant-general, was appointed a minister of the royal household and chamberlain (26 June 1851).

1852

Thursday 1 January. May God bless the beginning of the new year. May he grant my beloved family and me myself health, happiness, and prosperity. May he protect us from misfortune and illness. May he protect us from disgraceful or ignoble intentions and conduct, or desire for them. May he preserve the prosperity with which he has blessed us; may he favor me with genial musical inspirations, and help me to put them to good use. May he grant my daughter Blanca a good, worthy husband who will be faithful to her all life long. Amen, may it be so.

I personally entered my New Year's greetings at Prince Karl's and Prince Albrecht's, and visited Herr von Nothomb, Herr von Prokesch, and Herr Howard. I wrote to Scribe and returned the copy of the plan for the first two acts of *L'Africaine.* [Heard] Spontini's *Olympia.*

Only on one single occasion since my illness have I kept my resolution to work again on my new opera, and that was three or four weeks ago. In order to begin the new year well, I wrote at least a few pages of the vocal parts of the act 1 finale into the full score, so as not to begin my renewed activity tomorrow on a Friday. I have no more time today.

Friday 2 January. Visit from Rellstab, who read me the cantata *Germania* that he has written to music already composed by me: namely the *Ode an Rauch*, a sextet from the *Festhymne zur silbernen Hochzeit des Königs*, the Chorus of the Mothers from *Le Prophète* (on which I still have some composing to do), a bass aria, a big concluding chorus, and several recitatives. In the Schauspielhaus: *Das Gefängniss*, a comedy by Roderich Benedix, an entertaining intrigue.[1] Letter from Grüneisen in London.

Saturday 3 January. Passed the day uselessly.

Sunday 4 January. Wrote to Kaskel in Dresden, to Grüneisen in London, to Brandus in Paris, and sent him my contract with Delafield, together with Scribe's receipt for the sale of *Le Prophète* in London. Letter from Gouin. Visit from the vice-director of the Academy of Arts, Professor Herbig, who wanted to discuss the appointment of a teacher of composition for the pupils[2] of the Academy, in Rungenhagen's place; I proposed Grell. The two demoiselles Levy sang for me in order to have my opinion about their abilities. Visit from the violinist Köckert.

Monday 5 January. Today I was invited to dine with Prince Karl. However, in the morning, an invitation to luncheon at Potsdam arrived from the king. According to etiquette, therefore, I was obliged to decline Prince Karl. The king conversed much with me at table.

Tuesday 6 January. Visits from the music director Grell, from the writer Dr. Andreas Sommer with a young singer, Börner.[3] Kommerzienrat Praetorius came to ask me to conduct a concert for the benefit of firewood for the poor.

Wednesday 7 January. Dictated an answer to Glöggl in Vienna, who wants to publish "Der Wanderer und die Geister" and consequently would like the metronome markings. I pointed out that I had given the piece to Hofrat Schilling in Stuttgart for the Beethoven Album, and that only he could permit further printing. Perhaps I could give him another piece for publication in the future? I did, however, send him the metronome markings. Answered the music director Sobolewsky in Königsberg, who wants my recommendation for the directorship of the Singakademie. For the first time today I took Schönlein's stomach-strengthening medicine after lunch. Letter from Dr. Bacher. In the Opera House: *Fidelio* (with the *Leonore* Overture [no. 3] after act 1). Madame Köster sang the title role.

Thursday 8 January. Visit from the conductor Ganz about the charity concert. After a long interruption, at last worked again (for the second time) and orchestrated two pages of the act 1 finale of the new opera.

Friday 9 January. Visited Taglioni. Letter from Gouin: on 6 January the 119th performance of *Le Prophète* took place, by command of the president Louis Napoleon; tickets were given only to those invited by the president, namely the delegates who had come from the provinces for the presidential election. Wrote to Kaskel in Dresden. Scored the finale for one and a half hours. In the evening to the Singakademie: a commemorative service for the deceased director of the Academy, Rungenhagen.[4] They rendered most beautifully a spiritual song (more a chorale) by the deceased himself,[5] also his motet "Trauet um ein Hinterbliebenen," a chorus from Mendelssohn's *Paulus*, Fasch's "Selig sind die Toten," and then the whole of Mozart's *Requiem*. Madame Zimmermann came to see me.

Saturday 10 January. Edited a proposition that I want to present at today's sitting of the senate of the Academy: that Grell should be nominated to the vacant position on the senate caused by Rungenhagen's death, and also take over his academic teaching post. Visit from the conductor Ganz. Scored a few pages of the finale in the evening.

Sunday 11 January. Wrote out my proposition to the senate (about the election of Grell to Rungenhagen's position) as a memorandum and took it to Geheimrat Tölken,[6] so that it can be presented to the minister.[7] Visited Geheimrat Schulze. To the Friedrich-Wilhelmstädtisches-Theater for Adam's *Der Postillion von Longjumeau*. Madame Küchenmeister-Rudersdorf sang Madeleine, and Herr Tschekowski[8] Chaplou; both, while not excellent, were nonetheless very good, as was the whole production.

Monday 12 January. Dined with the Belgian ambassador, Nothomb. Called on Count Redern, who told me that there will be a Court Concert with orchestra on 22 January. Letter from Roger in Paris. Before going to bed, scored a page of the finale.

Tuesday 13 January. Visits from Herr Budberg, Humboldt. Through the Russian ambassador, Baron Budberg, I sent my *Ode an Rauch*, the *Hymne an dem König,* and the *Quarante Mélodies* to Damcke in St. Petersburg. Dined with General Wrangel. In the theater: Spontini's *Olympie*.

Wednesday 14 January. Called on Herr von Humboldt. Visit from the chamber musician Damm.[9] Symphony-soirée: Haydn's *Symphonie militaire*,[10] Cherubini's *Anacreon* overture,[11] Weber's *Jubel* overture,[12] Beethoven's *Eroica* Symphony.[13]

Thursday 15 January. Investigated music for the Court Concert.

Friday 16 January. Busied myself selecting the pieces for the Court Concert. Wrote to Roger. Dined with Count Redern. In the evening to Demoiselle Wagner about the items that she is to sing in the Court Concert.

Saturday 17 January. Constantly busy with the preparations for the Court Concert. To Count Redern, to Mesdames Köster and Herrenburger [Tuczek]. Dr. Bacher has arrived in Berlin. Letter from Gouin.

Sunday 18 January. Letter from Scribe in Nice, enclosing the thrice-altered plan of *L'Africaine*. Busy with preparations for the Court Concert. I was invited to the celebration of the order Pour le Mérite (as happened last year). At dinner, my neighbors were Alexander Duncker and Herr von Schack (the husband of Klara Gröditzberg).[14] In the evening I did not go to the *Feldlager* in order to prepare the music for the Court Concert. (The production was apparently crowded, but did not go well at all.) Dr. Bacher left in the morning.

Monday 19 January. To Count Redern. Orchestral rehearsal of the Court Concert from ten until two o'clock; in the evening practiced with the singers from six until nine. In the afternoon busy with several musical arrangements of the scores for this concert.

Tuesday 20 January. Rehearsed the singers for the Court Concert. Professor Herbig showed me a ministerial instruction, convening the musical section of the Academy, so that they can consider recommendations for a successor to Rungenhagen, with regard to both the senate and his teaching capacity. Since I, on behalf of the senate, had already sent a memorandum on this topic to the minister, proposing Grell, it is not obligatory for me.

Wednesday 21 January. In the morning, a big rehearsal of the Court Concert with orchestra and singers in the White Hall. In the evening this concert took place after the formalities,[15] beginning at 9:30 and ending at 11:30. The program: (1) the quartet from Mozart's *Idomeneo;*[16] (2) the big Scene in Tartarus and the duet (in G) from act 3 of Gluck's *Orpheus;*[17] (3) a piano piece by Herr Rosenhain;[18] (4) a trio for three sopranos by Curschmann; (5) the Children's Chorus and general ensemble from *Le Prophète*; (6) the seventeen-voice ensemble and act 1 finale from Rossini's *Count Ory;*[19] (7) the *Marcia alla turca* and Chorus of the Dervishes from *Die Ruinen von Athen;*[20] (8) a piano piece by Herr von Kontsky;[21] (9) the Hunt Overture from *La Chasse de jeune Henri* by Méhul. In the excerpt from *Le Prophète* I placed the children's chorus and the small orchestra (arranged to substitute the organ part) outside the concert hall, just in front of the doors of the chapel and out of sight of the audience, all to good effect. In the same way, just before the end of Méhul's Hunt Overture, I had twelve horns placed in the upper gallery of the hall, above the orchestra. Everything went superbly, both orchestra as well as chorus. The king, however, did not speak to me.

Thursday 22 January. Wrote to Kastner in Versailles: answer concerning the dedication of his work to the king. Called on Herr von Humboldt. I gave a dinner to which Johanna Wagner, the director of Covent Garden Theatre, Herr Gye, Alexander Duncker and his wife, Rosenhain, and Kullak were invited. Symphony-soirée: Mendelssohn's Symphony no. 4 in A Major; Beethoven's Symphony no. 8 in F Major; the overtures to Spohr's *Jessonda* and Spontini's *La Vestale*.

Friday 23 January. Wrote to Brandus, concerning the return of the Delafield contract. Wrote to Dehn, and sent the borrowed music back to the library.

Saturday 24 January. Wrote to Gouin, enclosing a letter ostensibly to him, but really for Roqueplan, stating that I cannot give *L'Africaine* next winter, but only in October 1854. Sitting of the senate of the Academy. I waited on the prince of

Prussia, whom I had not seen since his return from the Rhine. He received me very graciously, and said many obliging things to me about the last Court Concert, particularly singling out the Children's Chorus from *Le Prophète,* which was performed on that occasion. I returned the call of Count Dönhoff, but did not find him at home.[22] Dined at Prince Albrecht's: only a few people, and the company was not interesting. Then to a concert given by the Domchor: (1) Mendelssohn's setting of Psalm 2 ("Was toben die Heiden");[23] (2) Lotti's *Crucifixus*; (3) Durante's *Misericordias;*[24] (4) Haydn's motet *Du bist's, der Ruhe und Ehre gebärt,*[25] all *a capella.* Sextet for two violins, viola, violoncelli, and two concert horns[26] by Beethoven,[27] one of the immortal musician's weakest compositions; Quintet for piano, violin, alto, violoncello, and contrabass by Hummel:[28] greatly inferior to this composer's septet.[29]

Sunday 25 January. For the first time since my illness, dined with my beloved mother. Attended the Friedrich-Wilhelmstädtisches-Theater: Fioravanti's *Die Dorfsängerinnin* [*Le Cantatrici villane*]. Then to a *Polterabend*[30] given by the singer Johanna Wagner, in honor of her sister's marriage. Afterward to a big soirée at the Belgian ambassador, Herr Nothomb's. Letter from Kaskel in Dresden, that the Kapellmeisterin C. M. von Weber, who is mortally ill, wishes to prosecute me if I do not immediately pay the 2,000 thalers indemnity that I owe her, since I have not completed the *Pintos* by the agreed deadline. The lawyer's letter was attached. This unpleasant letter frightened away all sleep. I decided to travel to Dresden early on Tuesday to settle the matter myself.

Monday 26 January. Letter from Gouin. Wrote a letter ostensibly to Kaskel, but really for Kapellmeisterin von Weber. Visited Mother in order to receive her blessing for my journey. Drew up the receipt that Frau Weber will have to sign. Wrote to Rellstab.

Tuesday 27 January. At seven o'clock in the morning, I took the train to Dresden. My little daughter Cornelie was the only member of my family who woke up to wish me a safe journey (as she had already done in Vienna).[31] The child afforded me much joy by this gesture. At 12:30 the train arrived in Dresden. Visited my dear old aunt, Jette Ebers; unfortunately I found her unwell. Met with Max von Weber, son of Kapellmeisterin von Weber, and Karl Kaskel. I showed Herr von Weber the various contracts with his mother, where it is clear that I had already given 1,000 thalers, then for various periods of extension another 600 thalers, as well as 40 friedrichs d'or to Frau Birch-Pfeiffer for a new libretto for Weber's *Pintos.* In spite of these various outlays of money, Frau von Weber now wants the stipulated 2,000 thaler indemnity payment, since I have not completed the *Pintos* in the agreed period (which should have been the winter of 1850–51). It goes without saying that I paid the 2,000 thalers without objection; furthermore, I returned into Herr von Weber's hands the existing sketches of Weber's *Drei Pintos*, and indeed a second copy of these sketches made by the music director Jähns. Finally, I gave Herr von Weber a packet of other musical materials by Weber, which Frau von Weber had sent me several years ago to see whether I could use one of these pieces in the *Pintos*. I listed all of this in a detailed receipt for Frau von Weber and her son, Herr Max Maria von Weber, to sign.[32] So I am now completely finished with the unpleasant obligation of completing the *Pintos*, and because of it I have had to sacrifice the large sum of almost 4,000 thalers. I forgot to observe that the copy of Weber's sketches for the *Drei Pintos*, made by Jähns, was deposited in Kaskel's office sealed with both Herr von Weber's and my signets. I insisted on this, in case, at a later date, it should occur to some enemy to assert that I had used this material by Weber in my own compositions; these deposited sketches serve as my justification, and could be presented as proof to the contrary.

Wednesday 28 January. Another meeting with Herr von Weber: we parted on the friendliest terms. His mother could not receive me, however, since for the past few months she has been seriously ill. Visited Kaskel, Hofrat Winkler and Geheimrat von Lüttichau, the *chef des théâtres*. At 4:15 I left by rail for Berlin, where I arrived at nine o'clock in the evening and, praise God, found all my family well. I myself was rather unwell on the return journey. I found letters from Härtel in Leipzig, Karl Andrée in Bremen, Kapellmeister Müller in Brunswick, and Madame Ida Maetzner.[33]

Thursday 29 January. Letters from Brandus in Paris, from Bacher in Vienna. Extraordinary sitting of the senate of the Academy, in order to elect new members. Scored a few sides of the act 1 finale, but otherwise did nothing else today.

Friday 30 January. Letters from Gouin, from Brandus. Dr. Bacher writes from Vienna that, a few days ago, the sixtieth performance of the *Le Prophète* in the Kärntnertor-Theater took place to a capacity house. Wrote to Fräulein Cornelius. Visit from the Hungarian violinist Edmund Singer* (a Jew), who brought me letters of recommendation from the editor of the *Bremer Zeitung*, Dr. Karl Andrée, and from Breitkopf & Härtel. In the Opera House: Spontini's *Olympia*. Then to a soirée at Frau Doktorin Kunde's.[34]

Saturday 31 January. Letters from Dr. Bacher, from Glöggl in Vienna. Wrote to Scribe in Rome. Read the new plan of *L'Africaine* for the second time. In the evening I wrote to Gouin, and sent him a special second letter, so that he could show Nestor Roqueplan that I have received the complete scenario of *L'Africaine* from Scribe.

February 1852

Sunday 1 February. Wrote to Kapellmeister Gustav Müller in Brunswick, to d'Arod, *maître de chapelle honoraire du roi de Sardaigne à Lyon*,[35] to Dr. Bacher in Vienna. Gathering of the big Committee of the Singakademie, who chose five members from among themselves with the task of proposing three candidates for the post of director, in place of the late Rungenhagen. I was elected to one of these five places, with the biggest total of votes. In the evening in the Opera House I heard my opera *Ein Feldlager in Schlesien*: the production was good, and the house was very full, but there was very little sign of appreciation.

Monday 2 February. Letter from Damcke in St. Petersburg. Visit from the singer Marchesi,[36] who brought me letters of recommendation from Moscheles and Kaskel. In the Concert Hall: *Christus der Friedensbote*, an oratorio by Emil Naumann.

Tuesday 3 February. Letter from Dr. Bacher in Vienna. Visit from Baron Lauer,[37] Kapellmeister Dorn, the theater director Hoffmann from Prague, but I was not at home to receive any of them. During one and a half hours I scored three pages of the finale. Hardly worked at all.

Wednesday 4 February. Royal invitation to the Court Ball today. Wrote the vocal parts into the full score for one hour, and also scored some of the act 1 finale. The Italian bass Marchesi sang for me—a lovely voice, with fiery expression. Visit from Fräulein Armengard von Arnim.[38] Court Ball in the White Hall, which was very brilliant. The king spoke to me for a while.

Thursday 5 February. Visit from the Geheimer Kabinetsrat Illaire. Scored the finale for an hour. Wrote the vocal parts into the full score for two hours.

Friday 6 February. Visit from the music dealer Bock. Answered Professorin Ida Maetzner and Ministerin von Ladenburg. In the Opera House, the first performance of *Der Schöffe von Paris*, comic opera in two acts by Wohlbrück, music by Heinrich Dorn.[39] Then to a big soirée at Minister von der Heydt's. The king was also present and spoke to me; he repeated his wish that I should set the *Eumenides* of Aeschylus to music.[40]

Saturday 7 February. Letter from Dr. Bacher. To Count Redern. To Rellstab: gave him an honorarium of 200 thalers for his poem "Das Vaterland." Sitting of the senate. In the evening, wrote the vocal parts of the act 1 finale into the full score for an hour.

Sunday 8 February. Wrote to Liszt[41] and Kaskel. Visited Herr von Humboldt. In the Opera House: Dorn's *Der Schöffe von Paris*.

Monday 9 February. Wrote to Herr von Humboldt: invitation to Mother's birthday dinner. Studied the role of Raoul with [Theodor] Formes.

Tuesday 10 February. Letter, together with music, from Franz Otto.[42] Letter from Kaskel. I spent nearly the whole morning at my dear mother's, in order to help her receive the great number of visitors who came to congratulate her on her eighty-fifth birthday. At midday Mother gave a big dinner, and included Alexander von Humboldt among the guests.

Wednesday 11 February. Studied the role of Raoul with Formes. Scored the act 1 finale for one and a half hours.

Thursday 12 February. Visit from Stadtrat Dumont from Cologne: he brought me a letter from the Music Conservatory in Cologne, which is petitioning for state support. In the evening, revised the piano version of my first *Fackeltanz* for a publisher in Brunswick, J. P. Spehr.[43] Soirée at the Russian ambassador Herr Budberg's.

Friday 13 February. Today I revised the four-hand *Fackeltanz*, and sent it to Gustav Müller in Brunswick. Visited Mother: Johanna Wagner dined with her. Court Ball in the White Hall, which was very full and very brilliant.

Saturday 14 February. Letter from Kaskel enclosing an invitation from Dresden to Minister Beust's masked ball on 22 February.[44] To Count Redern, to confer with him about the twelve *tableaux vivants* that will take place on Friday at the palace, and for which I must study and arrange the music. Wrote to Gouin, together with an ostensible letter really for Lumley. The English chargé d'affaires, Howard, brought me an exceptionally lovely present from Queen Victoria of England: two pieces, groups modeled after antique sculpture, in the newly invented porcelain called *parian*.[45] This is apparently a response to my sending her the score of the *Ode an Rauch*.[46] After lunch to the painter, Professor Hensel, in order to explain the *sujets*[47] for the *tableaux vivants* that are to be presented, so that I can choose the appropriate music.

Sunday 15 February. Letters from Gouin, from Bacher. Busied myself searching for twelve pieces of music that will be appropriate for the twelve *tableaux vivants*. Marriage ceremony, then a big wedding reception at Madame Kunde's, whose daughter has married Lieutenant Baron von Rosenberg. Developed a sudden hoarseness.

Monday 16 February. I passed a bad night. Letter from Liszt. Visits from Howard, Truhn, the dancer Stullmüller,[48] Schlesinger (who wants the Flute Piece from the *Feldlager* for a concert on behalf of Glassbrenner), Kapellmeister Dorn. I called on Johanna Wagner concerning the Court Concert. Letter of thanks to the queen of England for the gift she sent. In the evening, visits from Count Redern and Herr Albert Wagner. On account of my indisposition, I did nothing.

Tuesday 17 February. Again slept very little. Wrote to Kaskel. Letter from the singer Salvatore Marchesi in Hamburg. Used the morning to peruse the scores that I will conduct at the Court Concert. I was invited to dine with the king. The king and queen spoke at length to me in the most friendly way.

Wednesday 18 February. Slept better. The sore throat and irritating cough have diminished. To the palace, in order to confer with Schadow, the palace architect,[49] about the position of the orchestra in relation to the painted scenes.

Thursday 19 February. Letters from Gouin, Kaskel. In the early morning, in the space of two hours, I scored my song "Mère grand" for tomorrow's music at court. Held a rehearsal with the orchestra and singers of all the pieces of music for the celebration. Then to the palace, to confer about the positioning of the orchestra with the arranger of the painted *tableaux*, Count Schaffgotsch.[50] The king has invited me to the *souper* and ball that will take place tomorrow after presentation of the *tableaux*. Dined with the Austrian ambassador, von Prokesch-Osten.

Friday 20 February. Held a big rehearsal in the palace in conjunction with the *tableaux vivants*. Wrote to Herr Bacher (47 Schützenstrasse) and returned his opera text *Otto der Schütz*. In the evening I conducted the music for the *tableaux vivants* at the Court Festival[51] in the palace, and then stayed on for the *souper* and ball, to which I had been invited by the king. Everything went very well.

Saturday 21 February. Wrote to Kaskel. To the concert given by the Domchor (choral pieces *a capella*, an octet by Prince Louis Ferdinand,[52] an octet by Mendelssohn[53]). Letter from the Cologne Music Conservatory, from Kapellmeister Proch in Vienna.

Sunday 22 February. I awoke, again plagued by aching limbs. To Geheimrat Johann Schulze, to wish him well on his nomination as counselor of the first class. Frau von Schulte from Hanover presented her niece, Fräulein Bock, to me so that I could test her singing voice. Fräulein Alwine Frommann dined with us. *Der Prophet* to a crowded house: Demoiselle Wagner and Madame Köster were outstanding. The whole performance went well; the king and the entire court were present.

Monday 23 February. Head cold with headache and such pressure in my head that I could hardly focus my eyes properly. Letter from Scribe in Rome. Wrote to Dr. Bacher in Vienna, Kapellmeister Schlösser in Darmstadt. Entered the vocal parts of the act 1 finale into the full score for two hours. Visit from Stadtrat Dumont from Cologne.

Tuesday 24 February. Today I was invited by the king to the Court Ball, but on account of my head cold could not go. Later, however, I decided to go after all: the occasion was very brilliant. *Le Prophète* has been given with great success in Lille.

Wednesday 25 February. Announcement that the widow of Carl Maria von Weber died on 23 February. Letter from Gouin. Wrote to the book dealer Schlodtmann in Bremen, who wants an autograph from me for a published autograph index.[54] Wrote ostensibly to Gouin, but really for Roqueplan: repeated that I cannot give *L'Africaine* in the coming winter. Visited the singer Salvatore Marchesi. Lua presented a young singing pupil, Fräulein Hirschberg, who sang for me. Visited the newly reopened Kroll Etablissement.[55]

Thursday 26 February. Wrote some of the vocal parts of the act 1 finale into the full score before breakfast. Letter from Kaskel. Symphony-soirée: Haydn's Symphony in E-flat,[56] Gade's overture *Nachklänge von Ossian*, Beethoven's Symphony no. 2 in D.

Friday 27 February. Before breakfast wrote two pages of vocal parts into the full score (act 1 finale). To Herr von Humboldt. To Rellstab: he returned 100 thalers of the 200 that I paid him for the cantata *Germania*, since he finds the amount too much. In the evening, finished writing the vocal parts of the act 1 finale into the full score. *Les Huguenots* has been given in English at the Drury Lane Theatre in London eight times, with success. Last year it was given in the small Surrey Theater.[57] Wrote to Kaskel.

Saturday 28 February. Before breakfast, reflected on the instrumentation of the Soldier's Chorus (in the act 1 finale) and scored one side of it. To Rellstab. Letter from the book dealer Schlodtmann in Bremen. To Geheimer Kabinetsrat Illaire, to pass on Truhn's petition.[58] The singer Johanna Wagner came to see me.

Sunday 29 February. Scored the Soldiers' Chorus for an hour before breakfast. Dictated a letter to Haslinger. Arranged everything for my departure (to Dresden, to hear Sontag sing). Scored for two hours before eating. After lunch visited Mother so that she could bless me before I travel. To the Opera House with my daughter Blanca, where we heard Weber's *Euryanthe*. Demoiselle Wagner was Eglantine.

In the theater I received a telegram from Kaskel that Sontag is not singing tomorrow.

March 1852

Monday 1 March. Scored the finale. In order to hear Sontag singing in Dresden, I set out at twelve o'clock by train, arriving there at 7:30.

Tuesday 2 March. Visited Kaskel and Sontag, who was not at home. To Herr von Lüttichau. In the theater: Donizetti's *Die Regimentstochter*. Sontag sang the title role, and interpolated the polka from the opera *Le tre nozze* by Alary.[59] Her singing was beautiful to the point of delight, and she also acted charmingly. The voice has gained in depth, has lost only a little from the top, and in general something of its tone. As a whole, however, it is still wonderful.

Wednesday 3 March. Called on Countess Rossi [Sontag], Kaskel, Max von Weber, Hofrat and Hofrätin Winkler. Letter from Bacher. In the theater: *Die Liebe Gaukeleien*, comedy by Boas.[60] It describes how Shakespeare came to write the comedy *What You Like;*[61] lovely verses, but hardly any action. Then *Gute Nacht, Herr Pantalon*, opera by Grisar. After the theater, to a big soirée at Count Schönburg's.[62]

Thursday 4 March. My dear daughter Cornelie's birthday. May God preserve my beloved child a hundred years, grant her a happy future, and make her good and courageous. Scored the finale for two hours. Called on Gutzkow, Count Galen (Prussian ambassador),[63] Marquis Leferrière (French ambassador).[64] Dined with my cousin Ebers. In the theater: Flotow's *Martha*. Madame Sontag was Martha, but was not nearly as excellent as in *Die Regimentstochter*. After the theater, I visited Sontag and agreed to write to her once Scribe has decided whether we can premiere the opera [*L'Étoile du Nord*] in London or not.

Friday 5 March. Scored two sides of the finale. Wrote to Dr. Bacher in Vienna. Called on Kapellmeister Krebs, the conductor Lipinski, Minister von Beust. Attended the rehearsal of Mendelssohn's "Ave Maria"[65] and the finale from the *Lorelei*. Visit from Kapellmeister Krebs. Called on Geheimrat Carus. In the evening, scored a little of the finale.

Saturday 6 March. At 6:30 in the morning set out for Berlin by rail. Arrived in Berlin at 12:30. I found letters from the following waiting for me: Madame Viardot in Danx Castle (Scotland), Gouin, Illaire, Oberstleutnant Frankenberg in Königsberg,[66] Goldtammer,[67] Kapellmeister Drouet* in Gotha, Marchesi in Amsterdam, Roger, Schlösser in Mannheim, Damcke in St. Petersburg. In the

Friedrich-Wilhelmstädtisches-Theater: *Die wanderenden Komödianten*, opera by Fiorovanti.[68]

Sunday 7 March. Unfortunately, did not work all day. In the evening to a concert by the Domchor. All the choral pieces were *a capella*: (1) a *Gloria* by Palestrina; (2) a motet by Gabrielli; (3) a *Pater Noster* by Bernhard Klein;[69] (4) *Psalm 43* by Mendelssohn;[70] (5) an eight-part *Crucifixus* by Lotti; (6) a nonet by Spohr;[71] (7) the quintet in E-flat major for piano, oboe, clarinet, horn, and bassoon by Mozart.[72]

Monday 8 March. Visit from the hotelier Wilkens from Stettin, who had his daughter, a pianist, play for me.[73] Sent Countess Rossi (Madame Sontag) in Dresden a present of the vocal score of *Robert*. Visits from Wieprecht and from Schlesinger from Paris.

Tuesday 9 March. Scored the finale. Wrote to Gouin, to Kapellmeister Drouet in Gotha. Coughed badly by night and day.

Wednesday 10 March. My dear daughter Caecilie's birthday: she is fifteen years old today. Scored a few pages. Court Concert by the Singakademie, to which I escorted Madame Arndt: *Des Heilands letzte Stunden*, oratorio by Spohr.[74]

Thursday 11 March. Letters from Dr. Bacher, Haslinger, Madame Küchenmeister. Scored a few pages. Visit from the harpist Krüger,[75] who brought me a letter of recommendation from Liszt. Called on Count Redern. At seven o'clock in the evening I was summoned to Princess Karl, who wanted to speak to me.

Friday 12 March. Sent Geheimrat von Köhne[76] the *Madrigal-Duet* by Abbate Clari.[77] Visit from the singer Madame Rudersdorf-Küchenmeister. Finished scoring the finale, thus completing it so far (I have not composed beyond the point where the theme from the *Feldlager* will come in).

Example 1. Theme from *Ein Feldlager in Schlesien*, used in *L'Étoile du Nord*

Wrote three pages for the album of the grand duchess of Mecklenburg and her daughter, at her request.[78] With the children to Dejean's *Cirque équestre,* where they play exceptionally fine music.[79]

Saturday 13 March. Professor Griepenkerl from Brunswick, Moritz Schlesinger and Frank from Paris,[80] and the harpist Thomas* from London all came to see me. I called on the singer Johanna Wagner. I partially revised the act 1 finale. Sitting in the senate of the Academy of Arts: Grell was introduced for the first time. To the evening sitting of the Committee of the Singakademie for the election of a new director in Rungenhagen's place. *Le Prophète* has been performed in Pressburg with great success. Letter from Herr von Hülsen.

Sunday 14 March. Completed the revision of the act 1 finale. Musical gathering at Bock's where, among others, the Hungarian violinist Singer (a Jew) played: he has a pithy, full, resonant tone, and is a very considerable artist. Then the English harpist Thomas performed excellently. Dined at my mother's with Begas, Madame Tuczek, and several other guests. In the evening wrote out the remainder of the text of the *Cantinière* into the small notebook.

Monday 15 March. Before breakfast spent an hour reading through the uncompleted ensemble in act 2; it was while composing this piece last summer in Boulogne that I fell ill. I continued with this for an hour after breakfast. Replied to Madame Viardot. Dined with Mother, where I also found Madame Birch-Pfeiffer. In the evening I attended a ball with my daughter Blanca at Geheimer Oberhofbuchdrucker Decker's.

Tuesday 16 March. Before and after breakfast, read through the ensemble in act 2, and reflected on its orchestration. After breakfast I began scoring the piece. Visit from Professor Griepenkerl. In the evening with my daughter Blanca to a ball at Geheime Rätin Gräfe's.[81] Letter from Brandus.

Wednesday 17 March. Scored two sides of the ensemble before breakfast. Introduced Professor Griepenkerl to Count Redern. Visits from the singer Demoiselle Wagner and Herr Kullak. The latter told me many interesting things about his stay in Weimar, where Liszt is gathering many musicians around him who subscribe to a new direction in music, which defines itself as freedom of musical thought, independent of any specific form: Richard Wagner is their ideal. In the evening scored several pages of the ensemble. My *droits d'auteur* in France for the month of February: 604 fr. 95 c.

Thursday 18 March. Before breakfast scored a side of the *Couplets des Vivandières*. Went with Professor Griepenkerl to Herr von Humboldt. Letter from Gouin. Wrote to Gouin. First hour of English tuition *à* twenty silver groschens with Herr Steil.[82] In the theater: Beethoven's *Fidelio*. Demoiselle Wagner sang Fidelio for the last time before her departure.

Friday 19 March. Scored one side of the *couplets* before breakfast. To Demoiselle Wagner. Conference in the Singakademie about the election of a new director.

Saturday 20 March. Before breakfast finished composing and writing out a small piano piece (in E-flat major); it is in my notebook.[83] Sitting of the senate of the Academy of Arts: I was chosen *à l'amabilité*[84] to arrange the division of the different subjects in composition taught to the pupils by Grell and August Wilhelm Bach. Concert by the Erksche Volkslieder-Gesangverein at Kroll's. They performed, among other things, Mendelssohn's overture *Ruy Blas*,[85] and Bernhard Klein's *Gesang der Geister über das Wasser.*[86]

Sunday 21 March. Scored a few pages of the *couplets* before and after breakfast. Letter from the composer Maschek from Temesvár in Banat.[87] Wrote to the composer Maschek. In the evening a religious service by the children of the Auerbach Orphanage in remembrance of my late, blessed brother Michael, on the eve of his anniversary.

Monday 22 March. Held a rehearsal of the Court Concert that the king has commanded for this evening in Charlottenburg. In the Jewish Cemetery, the Auerbach orphans held prayers for the repose of the soul of my late, blessed brother Michael, at his commemorative plaque. Mother and I attended the ceremony. At midday I was invited to lunch at Prince Karl's. In the evening I accompanied the Court Concert in Charlottenburg, and then stayed on to *souper*. The king spoke to me a great deal. The English harpist Thomas and the harpist Krüger from Stuttgart both played outstandingly. Formes and Tuczek sang songs, the latter my "Mailied."

Tuesday 23 March. Worked on the orchestration of the *couplets* before and after breakfast. Visit from the bass [Karl] Formes from St. Petersburg. Dinner with Count Redern. Soirée at the banker Rubens's, where Madame Schröder-Devrient sang.[88]

Wednesday 24 March. Before and after breakfast, and also in the evening, finished composing and revising the *couplets*, and continued scoring the ensemble. Visited Ratmeister Eberty, who is ill.[89] Letters from Kaskel, from Schladebach. After an interruption of six months, on account of the illness of Madame Krebs-Michalesi, *Le Prophète* has again been given in Dresden with great success.

Thursday 25 March. Scored two pages both before and after breakfast. Wrote to Countess Rossi in Hamburg: at her request, I will send her the duet (A major) from act 2 of *Robert*, with a view to her assuming the role of Isabelle. Letters from Gouin and Brandus.

Friday 26 March. Wrote a testimonial for the tenor Arnurius from the Court Theater in Schwerin.[90] Attended the commemorative service for my late, blessed brother Wilhelm at the cemetery. Finished scoring the five-part movement (G-flat major) in the ensemble. Called on Kammergerichtsrat Goldtammer. In the Opera: Flotow's *Sophia Catherina*.

Saturday 27 March. Scored and revised the ensemble for one hour before, two hours after breakfast, and in the evening for another few hours. Letter from Gouin.

Sunday 28 March. Scored and revised the ensemble for one hour before breakfast and for two hours after. Examination concert by the pupils of the music director August Wilhelm Bach. The Austrian pianist Ehrlich* brought me a letter of introduction from the poet Landesmann in Vienna; the pianist Dupont from Vervier also came to see me.[91] To Dr. Martin Runkel, who has written a cantata for the silver wedding of Prince Karl. Heard *Robert le Diable* in the Opera House. The house was very full; the production was, on the whole, good, not least because the best resources of singing and dancing were involved: Mesdames Köster and Herrenburger [Tuczek], Herrn Pfister and Formes (Raimbaud), the *danseuse* Forti in act 2, and Taglioni dancing the Abbess in act 3.[92]

Monday 29 March. For one hour before and for two hours after breakfast, arranged the vocal parts of the stretta of the finale. In the evening scored another three pages of the ensemble. Letters from the theater director Leo in Rostock,[93] and from Madame Célérier: news that the wife of my friend Gouin has died in Paris.

Tuesday 30 March. Wrote the vocal parts into the full score for one hour before breakfast, and afterward another three pages for two and a half hours, as well as scoring two pages, all from the ensemble. To Count Redern. Visit from the pianist Dupont. Wrote letters of condolence to both Gouin and Madame Célérier. I am commanded to arrange a Court Concert tomorrow at Charlottenburg.

Wednesday 31 March. Scored the ensemble for one and a half hours before breakfast. Busy all morning with preparations and rehearsals for the Court Concert. Invitation to tea and *souper* with the king in Charlottenburg. At the Court Concert this evening the Belgian pianist Dupont played (very beautifully), as well as the young violinist Biehrlich,[94] then Madame Köster and Formes sang songs and the duet from Spohr's *Jessonda*.[95] Letter from Fétis in Brussels: he has performed the overture and the first two entr'actes of my *Struensee* in the Conservatoire there, with much success.

April 1852

Thursday 1 April. For one and a half hours before breakfast, two hours afterward, and for one hour in the evening, finished scoring and revising the ensemble, i.e., up to the melodramatic conclusion, which I have not yet attended to. Called on Colonel White,[96] Charlotte von Hagen.[97] Second letter from Fétis.

Friday 2 April. At the request of Count Stollberg, read through the oratorio *Noah* by the Kammermusiker Damm,[98] in order to report on the feasibility of the composer receiving the desired royal support. Visit from Dupont. Wrote to Fétis in Brussels. In the Auerbach Orphanage: commemoration of the anniversary (according to the Jewish calendar) of my blessed brother Wilhelm.

Saturday 3 April. Headache and throat irritation, the symptoms of a chill, sent me to bed early yesterday. Today I felt somewhat better. I wrote the report, requested by Count Stollberg, on the musical abilities of the Kammermusiker Damm, and took it to him personally. Visits from the singer Mlle. Liebhardt from Vienna,[99] and from the pianists Ehrlich and Dupont. Sitting of the senate in the Academy of Arts. In the evening worked on the melodramatic start of the quintet, without especial success. Wrote to Count Redern, to Brandus. Letter from Countess Rossi (Henriette Sontag) in Hamburg.

Sunday 4 April. With Herr Dupont to the music dealer Bock. Sitting of the big Committee of the Singakademie, concerning the election of a new director: it was decided to postpone the election for seven months. Dined with Mother, who had also invited Emil Naumann. In the Opera House heard Spontini's *Die Vestalin*.

Monday 5 April. The coughing, the aching limbs, the generally chilled feeling, have increased. Wrote to Dr. Bacher. Kammermusiker Dam came to see me. With Dupont to Princess Karl, who asked me to bring him to her. I found, however, that I had mistaken the day, and that it should have been tomorrow. In the morning and evening, wrote down the melodramatic conclusion to the quintet.

Tuesday 6 April. I have a bad cold. Revised the melodramatic conclusion to the quintet. With Dupont to Princess Karl; just as he was about to begin playing the piano, the queen was announced, and we had to leave. Wrote to Gouin. I want to read through everything I had composed for the new opera [*L'Étoile du Nord*] before my illness, and subsequently have not examined. Today I read through the introduction (with which I am satisfied), and the canon (with which I am not particularly pleased). Letter from Albert Wagner in Hamburg. Wagner informs me that his daughter, Johanna, has given up her engagement with Lumley, and has signed a contract with Gye.

Wednesday 7 April. On Geheimrat Schönlein's orders, I stayed in bed until twelve o'clock in order to fight the cold more effectively. During these hours in bed I again read through all the pieces (ten by my count) that I have so far composed for the new opera. In the afternoon I read the vocal score of Felicien David's *La Perle du Brésil*.[100] Letters from Gouin, from Griepenkerl in Brunswick, from Valentin Grube in Regensberg (together with an opera text).

Thursday 8 April. Last night was much better, but I still stayed at home all day. In the evening I began composing the duet in act 3 act with great success.[101]

Friday 9 April. Answered Professor Griepenkerl. Wrote to Gouin, together with a letter ostensibly for him, but actually for Dr. Bacher. Visits from the pianist Grün from St. Petersburg, the music director of the Friedrich-Wilhelmstädtisches-Theater, Thomas,[102] and Demoiselle Olias from Dresden, who wanted to sing for me. Today I again stayed at home.

Saturday 10 April. Wrote to Countess Rossi in Hamburg. Letter from Kastner in Paris (with enclosures for the king, Humboldt, and the Academy). Visit from Dupont, Countess Pinto[103] (wants to be recommended for singing lessons), Kapellmeister Schindelmeisser from Wiesbaden[104] (who told me that this winter *Struensee*, with my music, was produced in the theater there), Emil Naumann. On account of the bad weather, I again stayed at home all day. In the morning I worked on the duet (act 3), in the evening worked on the trio.

Sunday 11 April. Easter. Worked for one hour before breakfast on the duet in act 3. Went to Mother, and then to the pianist Ehrlich from Vienna, who played me transcriptions of the overture to the *Feldlager* and of the Prayer of the Anabaptists from *Le Prophète*, with the most unbelievable virtuosity. Visit from the Belgian ambassador, Nothomb. Today was the first time in three days that I went out. However, I suspect that I have again caught cold on this outing. In the theater: Donizetti's *Die Tochter des Regiments*. Demoiselle Liebhardt from Vienna sang Marie as guest role.

Monday 12 April. Matinée musicale at Bock's, where the pianist Dupont played and Demoiselle Liebhardt sang, among other things, my song "Komm." In the evening worked on the duet in act 3, and began writing out some of the beginning.

Tuesday 13 April. Before breakfast worked on the stretta of the duet, with fluent inspiration. To Count Redern. Letters from Dr. Bacher in Hamburg, from Kapellmeister Drouet in Gotha. Wrote to Dr. Bacher, to Kapellmeister Drouet. In the evening worked on the duet.

Wednesday 14 April. Worked on the act 3 duet. To Count Redern. Letter from the music publisher Schloss in Cologne: he wants a song from me for an album he is publishing. In the Friedrich-Wilhelmstädtisches-Theater: Adam's *Der Postillion von Longjumeau.*

Thursday 15 April. Worked on the duet in act 3. Wrote to the music publisher Schloss, to Breitkopf & Härtel (recommendation for Ehrlich). Visit from Ehrlich. Today I had my twelfth English lesson. Concert in the Kroll Etablissement, at which, among other things, the overture to Richard Wagner's *Tannhäuser* was played. Letter from Gouin.

Friday 16 April. Wrote to Roger in Paris to see whether he could come to the Court Concerts during the visit of the empress of Russia to Berlin.[105] Worked on the duet in act 3 before and after breakfast. In the Opera House to a performance by the Italian singers from St. Petersburg, Tamburini, Madame Persiani, Herr Pozzolini (tenor), Rossi (buffo):[106] Donizetti's *L'Elisir d'amore.*

Saturday 17 April. Worked for one hour before breakfast on the duet in act 3. To Count Redern. Wrote to Marchesi in Frankfurt-am-Main, to see whether he can come to the Court Concerts in May. Letter from Schönfelder in Köslin.[107] Visit from the flautist Heinemeyer* in Hanover, who brought a letter of recommendation from Kapellmeister Georg Hellmesberger.[108] Visits from the clarinetist Baerman from München and the tenor Rademacher from Rostock, who sang me pieces from *Le Prophète*: a powerful, full voice, but the intonation is not always pure; the higher register is not attractive.[109] Returned the call of Bavarian Ambassador, Baron Malzen.[110] To Schlesinger. In the evening worked for two hours on the duet in act 3.

Sunday 18 April. Worked on the act 3 duet. Letters from Roger, from the music dealer Schloss. Visit from Dr. Bacher, who has come from Hamburg. In the Opera House: *Die Hugenotten* to a packed house and great enthusiasm. Formes sang Raoul for the first time, and very well, as did Madame Köster Valentine. Demoiselle Liebhardt, from Vienna, was very good as the Queen, but not excellent; Bost, the Marcel, was bad.[111]

Monday 19 April. Received several exemplars from the music dealer Spehr in Brunswick of my *Fackeltanz* no. 1, which they have published for piano in two- and four-hand arrangements. Letter from Gouin. For one hour before breakfast worked on the duet, which I have now finished composing. Dr. Bacher read me the plan he has prepared for the regeneration of the Vienna Opera.[112] Rehearsal with the Italian singers for Court Concert tomorrow. Visit from Madame Isaias and her daughter from Breslau; the latter wants to become a singer. To the Opera House for Donizetti's *Don Pasquale* by the St. Petersburg Italian Opera Society.

Tuesday 20 April. Attended the audition of the tenor Rademacher, at the wish of the intendant. To Dr. Bacher. For one hour before breakfast I began to write the vocal parts of the duet into the full score. Directed the Court Concert at Charlottenburg: the flautist Heinemeyer from Hanover and the pianist Ehrlich from Vienna performed, the latter the overture to the *Feldlager;* the singers of the Italian Society sang: (1) the trio from *L'Italiana in Algeri;*[113] (2) the duet "Là ci darem il mano" from *Don Juan;*[114] (3) the *buffo* duet from *Il Matrimonio segreto;*[115] and (4) the sextet from the [act 2] finale of *Lucia.*[116]

Wednesday 21 April. Wrote the vocal parts of the duet into the full score for one hour before breakfast. Visit from Dr. Felix Bamberg from Paris and from the director of the Kroll Orchestra, Engel.[117] To Herr von Humboldt. Delivered the letter and exemplars from Kastner today. Herr von Humboldt came to see me. Received a present of two crates of vegetables and fruit from Roger in Paris. In the evening, wrote the vocal parts of the duet into the full score. *Le Prophète* has been staged in Görlitz with great pomp.

Thursday 22 April. Worked for one hour before breakfast on planning the orchestration of the duet. Afterward did the same for another one and a half hours. Visit from the pianist Ehrlich. The music director of Kroll's Orchestra performed the overture and polonaise from *Struensee* in Kroll's Etablissement and invited me to attend the rehearsal, which I did. Worked for two hours on preparations for the scoring of the duet.

Friday 23 April. For one hour before breakfast wrote the vocal parts of the act 3 duet into the full score, and the same for two hours afterward. To Count Redern. Letters from Marchesi, from Körner [in Prenzlau], from Härtel in Leipzig. Wrote to Gouin.

Saturday 24 April. For one hour before breakfast, and for one hour afterwards, wrote the vocal parts of the duet into the full score. Telegram from Dr. Bacher in Vienna. Letters from Ruggieri and Roger in Paris.[118] Plenary sitting in the Academy; I presented Kastner's *Dance macabre.* In the evening finished writing the vocal parts of the duet into the full score.

Sunday 25 April. Telegram from Lumley in London, that the courts have ruled that Johanna Wagner must sing in his theater.[119] Began scoring the duet for one hour before breakfast. After breakfast scored another three sides. Concert by the young composer Julius Hopfe in which he performed symphonies and overtures of his own composition.[120] In the theater: Mozart's *Die Zauberflöte.*

Monday 26 April. Scored three pages of the duet for one and a half hours before breakfast, and two pages for one hour afterward. Visit from the music director Jähns. Visit from Dupont. To Schlesinger. Scored three pages in the evening. Report from Gouin on the first performance of Halévy's *Le Juif errant*.[121] *Droits d'auteur* for the month of March in France, 739 fr. Letter from Lumley. Wrote to Marchesi in Frankfurt-am-Main.

Tuesday 27 April. Scored the duet for one and a half hours before breakfast, and two more pages afterwards. Visit from the violoncellist Eichhorn from Karlsruhe[122] and from Ehrlich. Conference with the painter Hensel and Justizenrat Goldtammer about a cantata for the silver-wedding anniversary of Prince Karl. After lunch walked for three-quarters of an hour, during which I met Bettina von Arnim and spoke at length with her. Herr von Humboldt visited while I was out walking. In the evening scored the duet.

Wednesday 28 April. Scored the duet for one hour before, and one hour after, breakfast. Visit from the Parisian composer Adolphe Vogel. To Count Redern. To Alexander von Humboldt. Today, two years ago, *Der Prophet* was given for the first time in Berlin. It has had thirty-one performances since then. Letter from the composer Julius Hopfe. Letter of recommendation from Kaskel for the composer Vogel. Letter from Kossak about Sternau's poetic arrangement of *Struensee*. To the Opera House for the first performance of Taglioni's fantastical ballet in three acts, *Satanella, oder Die Metamorphosen*, music by Pugni.[123]

Thursday 29 April. Scored the duet before and after breakfast and completed it. Letter from Brandus. Letter from Moscheles in Leipzig. Visits from the French composer Vogel, the music director Engel (from Kroll), and the American pianist Hills.[124] While out walking, I met the famous sculptor David (d'Angers) from Paris, who is now exiled.[125] We spoke to each other for a long time. Visited Mother, who is rather unwell. In the evening revised the duet and completely finished it.

Friday 30 April. Letter from the princess of Prussia, who has recommended to me an opera composer (a dilettante), Herr Cüntzer. Letter from Émile Perrin, the director of the Opéra Comique in Paris. Letter from the Music Conservatoire in Cologne. Began composing the little cantata by Goldtammer for the silver wedding of Prince Karl [*Maria und ihr Genius*]. Wrote to Count Redern, to Marquis Lucchesini. Visits from Herr Cüntzer from Koblenz and the composer Vogel. Wrote to Gouin.

May 1852

Saturday 1 May. Before breakfast finished composing the strophes of Maria in the cantata for Prince Karl's silver wedding. Visits from Baerman and the American ambassador, Mr. Frey [Fay].[126] Wrote to Kossak. In the evening composed the strophes of the Genius in the cantata.

Sunday 2 May. Composed the strophes of the Genius for an hour before breakfast. *Matinée musicale* by music director Jähns, with his choral society. Dined with Mother, who had also invited Madame Birch-Pfeiffer. Wrote to Dr. Bacher in London. Letter from Gouin. In the Friedrich-Wilhelmstädtisches-Theater: the old opera *Zwei Worte, oder Eine Nacht im Walde*, music by Dalayrac,[127] then *Die Schwestern von Prag* by Wenzel Müller.[128]

Monday 3 May. Worked for an hour before breakfast (and in the evening) on the concluding strophe of the cantata. Wrote to Henri Vieuxtemps in St. Petersburg, to Gouin. The son of Kammermusiker Lawerenz[129] performed a fantasia on themes from *Le Prophète* on the *Waldhorn* for me.

Tuesday 4 May. Worked for one hour before breakfast on the closing strophe of the cantata. Wrote to Roger in Paris. Letters from Thomas, and the music director of the Friedrich-Wilhelmstädtisches-Theater. In the evening worked a little on the cantata.

Wednesday 5 May. Composed the first chorus of the cantata for one hour before breakfast. Paid a visit to Rellstab, who is ill. In the evening I finished composing the first chorus.

Thursday 6 May. Wrote out the first chorus of the cantata before breakfast. A young American pianist, Demoiselle Hills, played for me. In the evening worked on the cantata. Visit from Count Redern.

Friday 7 May. Worked on the cantata before and after breakfast. Count Redern came to see me. Letter from Gouin. To Kammergerichtsrat Goldtammer. To Professor Hensel. In the Opera House: Lortzing's *Der Wildschütz*.

Saturday 8 May. Today I finished composing and writing out the cantata *Maria und ihr Genius* for Prince Karl's twenty-fifth wedding anniversary (text by Goldtammer). Called on Hofrat Teichmann. Visit from Professor Hensel. *Soirée musicale* at Madame Zimmermann's.

Sunday 9 May. Meeting with Goldtammer and Hensel, in order to discuss the cover and the presentation of the cantata for the silver wedding of Prince Karl. Conference with Count Redern about possibly imminent Court Concerts. Dinner with the Turkish ambassador, Prince Caradja.[130] In the Friedrich-Wilhelmstädtisches-Theater: *Der Doppelflucht*, comic opera in three acts, music by the late ballet composer Hermann Schmidt: light and attractive music, but very flat and derivative.[131]

Monday 10 May. To Rellstab. Heard the singer Mathilde Graumann (now Marchesi)[132] singing at Count Redern's. Today passed by almost uselessly. Letter from Dr. Bacher. To Marchesi.

Tuesday 11 May. Two autographs for Professorin Jacobs.[133] Wrote a letter ostensibly to Gouin, but really for Émile Perrin. In Rostock my brother's tragedy *Struensee* has been given, with my music, and starring Hendrichs.[134]

Wednesday 12 May. Visit from the music director Commer, who presented me with his edition of all the Netherlandish composers.[135] Wrote to Kastner to inform him of his nomination as a knight of the First Order of the Eagle.[136] Wrote to Gouin. Letters from Gouin, Dr. Bacher, Madame Rudersdorff, Rellstab, from the musical writer Kraushaar in Cassel (enclosing his treatise *Der akkordliche Gegensatz*),[137] from the composer Tanwitz (together with his score *Die Eroberung von Konstantinopel*).[138]

Thursday 13 May. Letter from the poet Gaetano Rossi in Verona. To Geheimer Kabinetsrat Illaire, in order to back the dedication petition from Vieuxtemps, and requests for support from Patschke and Zimmermann. In the Opera House: Bellini's *Norma*. Madame Viala-Mittermayr,[139] from the Meiningen Theater, sang Norma: a broad but tired mezzo-soprano voice, no height, no depth, ordinary delivery, ordinary acting.

Friday 14 May. To the Belgian minister, Nothomb. Letter from Kapellmeister Marschner in Hanover. In the Friedrich-Wilhelmstädtisches-Theater: Mozart's *Der Schauspieldirektor*.[140] Herr Hassel, from the Frankfurt Theater, played the part of Schikaneder.[141]

Saturday 15 May. Began composing the trio. Sitting of the senate in the Academy: I checked the contents of the support fund for needy musicians, which is now my express responsibility. In the Friedrich-Wilhelmstädtisches-Theater: Lortzing's *Der Waffenschmied*. The tenor Benno Hirsch from Graz has a small but dainty voice and good enunciation.[142]

Sunday 16 May. Worked on the trio before breakfast. Visits from Count Redern and the composer Adolf Fischer.[143] Letter from Scribe in Venice: he informs me that he will be in Berlin around 25 May. Wrote to Kapellmeister Marschner in Hanover, to Madame Rudersdorf-Küchenmeister. Read through the plan of *Vasco*

[*L'Africaine*],[144] in order to write down my observations for Scribe. In the evening again read through the plan of *Vasco*.

Monday 17 May. Called on Hofmarschall von Lucchesini. Letter from Dr. Bacher in London. In the evening worked on the trio.

Tuesday 18 May. Letters from Gouin, from Madame Viala-Mittermayr, from Emil Naumann in Dresden. To Count Redern and Marquis Lucchesini. Worked on the trio in the morning with some success, also in the afternoon. In the evening to the ballet *Satanella*, music by Pugni.

Wednesday 19 May. Today, after an interruption of eight months, began the cold rubdowns again. May God bless this treatment. Answered the musical writer Kraushaar in Cassel. Wrote to the composer Tanwitz in Berlin, enclosing ten thalers support. Letter from Kastner in Versailles. To Count Redern and Marquis Lucchesini. Worked on the trio in the morning and the evening with good success. In the Garnisonkirche: *Elijah*, oratorio by Felix Mendelssohn.

Thursday 20 May. Today, ten years ago, *Die Hugenotten* was given in Berlin for the first time; I conducted. Before and after breakfast worked with good success on the trio. To Potsdam to Herr von Humboldt, in order to discuss Scribe's reception during his stay in Berlin. In the Opera House heard act 4 of *Der Prophet*. It was very full. Madame Viala-Mittermayr sang a mediocre Fidès, without any appeal. After the theater worked again on the trio with much success.

Friday 21 May. Letter from Illaire. Went to Marquis Lucchesini, Professor Hensel, and the copyist Patschke, concerning the performance of my cantata for the silver wedding of Prince Karl. Then to Madame Viala-Mittermayr, General Ogareff, and Herr von Stierle, adjutant to the emperor of Russia. Worked at my observations on the plan of *Vasco*. In the Opera: a gala performance for the emperor and empress of Russia where act 2 of my opera, *Ein Feldlager in Schlesien*, and the ballet *Thea*, music by Pugni, were given.

Saturday 22 May. Worked on the trio before breakfast. Rehearsed my cantata for Prince Karl with Mantius and Tuczek. Visit from the singer Mme. Bunke,[145] Justizenrat Goldtammer. Wrote to Vieuxtemps in St. Petersburg. To Hofrat Teichmann, and asked Hülsen for singers for the cantata for Prince Karl. Sitting of the senate in the Academy. Visits from the singer Mme. Viala-Mittermayr and Geheimrat Eisenbahndirektor Nörner.[146] I visited the writer Oettinger from Leipzig.

Sunday 23 May. Together with Mother, visited the grave of my late, blessed father on his birthday. Worked fairly diligently on the trio.

Monday 24 May. At the wish of the intendant-general, attended the audition of the tenor Young from Schwerin: lovely voice but, I believe, not strong enough for the opera house.[147] To Marquis Lucchesini. Rehearsal with Mantius, Tuczek and the Domchor of my cantata for the silver wedding of Prince Karl. Worked for two hours on the trio. Letter from Viardot. In the evening worked on the trio.

Tuesday 25 May. Worked for one hour on the trio. To Potsdam, where we members of the senate of the Academy presented Prince Karl the diploma of an honorary member of the Academy, on the occasion of the celebration of his silver wedding. Scribe arrived in Berlin, and I called on him. In the evening worked on the plan of *Vasco*.

Wednesday 26 May. With Tuczek, Mantius, and the Domchor to Glienecke, where, at ten o'clock, I conducted my cantata celebrating the silver wedding of Prince Karl. The emperor and the empress of Russia, the king and the queen, and many other crowned heads were present. The empress and the king spoke to me, but the emperor did not. Letters from the singer Marchesi, from Gouin (*droits d'auteur* in France for April, 499 fr.), from Dr. Bacher. In the evening I took Scribe and his wife to the theater for Spontini's *Olympia*.

Thursday 27 May. Worked all morning with Scribe on the plan of *Vasco*. In the evening I took him to the theater for Taglioni's ballet *Satanella*, music by Pugni. Then I escorted him to a masked ball at Kroll's Etablissement.

Friday 28 May. To the princess of Prussia at her command. She spoke with me about every conceivable thing, but never mentioned my cantata of the day before yesterday, even though she had been present at the performance. To Hofrat Teichmann about the engagement of Marchesi. Personally delivered invitations to the dinner I gave for Scribe today. Present were Herr von Prokesch-Osten, Count Redern, Marquis Lucchesini, Professor Rötscher, Herr and Madame Scribe, and his stepson.[148] In the evening worked on the trio.

Saturday 29 May. Wrote to Monsieur Viardot, Alexander Duncker. Today Scribe departed. In the evening worked a little on the trio.

Sunday 30 May. Woke up with severe and painful diarrhea, soon followed by stomach cramps, which I fear may develop into the terrible condition I experienced in Boulogne. Letter from Teichmann. Read the poem of *Lohengrin* by Richard Wagner and also part of the music.[149] Wrote to Gouin.

Monday 31 May. On the instructions of the doctor, I had to stay in bed until two

Eugène Scribe in middle age. Lithograph by Delannage.

o'clock in the afternoon. Then I worked for two hours on the trio. Letters from Dr. Bacher in London, Albert Wagner (father of the singer) in London.

June 1852

Tuesday 1 June. Things are a bit better. In the morning and after breakfast worked on the trio. Visit from the famous violinist Vieuxtemps from St. Petersburg. In the evening worked on the trio.

Wednesday 2 June. Today, unfortunately, I hardly did anything. Dinner with Prince Karl in Glienecke. In the Friedrich Wilhelmstädtisches-Theater: Dittersdorf's *Hieronymus Knicker*. In the theater spoke to Frau Bettina von Arnim and Frau von Guaita from Frankfurt-am-Main.[150] To Marquis Lucchesini in Potsdam. Letter from Marchesi.

Thursday 3 June. Letters from Gouin, Kastner, Illaire with the announcement of Kastner's Order. Wrote to the hereditary grand duke of Weimar,[151] and sent him my new cantata, which he has requested. Visit from the director of the Darmstadt Court Theater, Tescher, and later returned the call. Before lunch worked for two hours on the trio. In the evening worked on the trio.

Friday 4 June. Visit from Director Tescher from Darmstadt. From eleven until one o'clock worked on the trio. Wrote to Schlesinger, who wants to publish the new cantata. To the Opera for Lortzing's *Zar und Zimmermann:* Herr Kindermann, a very good baritone from Munich, sang the Tsar.[152]

Saturday 5 June. Letters from Gouin, Madame Viardot. Wrote to Kastner, Illaire, the music teacher Leder in Marianburg (together with a score). To Professor Hensel about regulating the shared expenses for the album for Prince Karl. From 12 until 2 worked on the trio. In the evening worked a little on the trio.

Sunday 6 June. Visit from the music director Neithardt: I gave him two louis d'or for himself and nineteen thalers for the Domchor as thanks for performing the cantata. Kapellmeister Dorn arranged for me to hear one of his pupils, the tenor Arnurius. Worked on the trio for two hours. Received a visit from Prince Georg (nephew of the king).[153] In the evening began scoring the trio (six pages).

Monday 7 June. To Count Redern, the painter Gerst (borrowed the sketches for the décor of *Les Huguenots*),[154] Herr von Humboldt. Scored three pages of the trio. Wrote to Dr. Bacher in London. Letter from Kapellmeister Sobolewsky in Königsberg, from Truhn (wanting a loan of fifty thalers), from Count Pillet-Will in Paris (dedicating music to me). Report to Count Redern on Sobolewsky's score *Heaven and Earth: A Mystery from Lord Byron.*

Tuesday 8 June. Wrote out the explanation of the *maquette* of the church décor for *Les Huguenots* for the French *décorateur.*[155] [Sent] the *maquette* of the church in *Les Huguenots* to Roqueplan. Wrote to Gouin, Sobolewsky, and Truhn (loan of twenty thalers). Visits from Kapellmeister Lindpaintner, Tharemba. Called on Prince Caradja, Lindpaintner, and Mother. In the evening scored seven pages of the trio. In Hamburg Hendrichs is performing my brother Michael's *Struensee,* with my music, in his benefit concerts.

Wednesday 9 June. In the morning and evening scored nine pages of the trio.

Thursday 10 June. Wrote to the poet Hermann Herz (returning an opera manuscript), to the music teacher Schönfeld in the Grand Duchy of Posen (returning a musical manuscript). Worked on the trio in the morning and evening, but not very much. Visited Mother and Herr von Humboldt.

Friday 11 June. Letters from Kastner, from Madame Zimmermann. Cabinet communication enclosing a petition from Madame Zimmermann for my assessment. Announcement of marriage between the composer Gounod* and Mademoiselle Zimmermann.[156] Rehearsed the small clarinet and piccolo parts of the Quick March from the *Feldlager* with Wieprecht, in order to ascertain the cause of the tonal impurity. Decided to have only the small F-clarinets (and no longer any G-clarinets), and further to have the first piccolo part playing an octave lower (as it is in fact written), but to leave the second piccolo part at the same height as before. Visit from the Viennese singer Mme. Czillak, who is singing Fidès there.[157] I hosted a dinner: the guests were Kapellmeister Lindpaintner, Dr. Lange, Julius Stern, Flodoard Geyer, Professor Herbig, Wieprecht, Hofrat Teichmann, Spieker, Stawinsky, Geheimrat Tölken, Music Director [August Wilhelm] Bach, Music Director Grell. Worked on the trio in the morning and evening.

Saturday 12 June. Wrote to Kastner and forwarded the Order decoration. Worked for one hour on the trio. Visit from Lindpaintner. With the latter to a sitting of the senate of the Academy. In the evening finished composing and scoring the trio in act 3.

Sunday 13 June. Wrote my opinion to Illaire about Madame Zimmermann's petition. Visited Herr von Humboldt and delivered Kastner's letter, but did not find him at home. Revised the trio. Letter from Gouin: I learned, to my great displeasure, that because of a mix-up of envelopes, the letter I had written to him had gone to Sobolewsky in Königsberg, and vice versa. Since there were many intimate things in the letter to Gouin (e.g., about my relationship with the *Charivari,* etc.) it is exceptionally unpleasant for me that this letter has fallen into Sobolewsky's hands. I wrote to Sobolewsky, sent the letter meant for him (returned by Gouin), and asked for the one inadvertently posted to him. In the Opera House: *Das Versprechen hinter dem Herde*, Alpine Scenes with Austrian melodies by Baumann.[158]

Monday 14 June. Tanwitz collected his oratorio *Die Eroberung von Konstantinopel*, which he had asked me to inspect. I gave him ten thalers. Letter from Lindpaintner and the painter E. Rabe.[159] Spent the whole morning partially revising my observations on the new plan of *L'Africaine*, and partially translating them into French. Letter from Dr. Bacher in London. Wrote to Gouin.

Tuesday 15 June. Finished writing my observations on *L'Africaine*, and sent them to Scribe through Gouin. Letter from Dr. Sachse, editor of *Die Hamburgische Theaterchronik*.[160] With Lindpaintner to Count Redern. Counted to ascertain how many pages of music paper are needed for the pieces in the *Feldlager*.

Wednesday 16 June. Wrote to Dr. Sachse. To the library, where I returned to Professor Dehn the works he had earlier supplied, and in exchange took out several books on India in order to research details for *Vasco*.[161] Dined with Princess Karl in Glienecke. In the evening read through the big book of copper engravings, *L'Inde française*.

Thursday 17 June. To Humboldt. Announcement to the king about my journey. To Count Redern about Sobolewsky. Wrote to the music director Damcke in St. Petersburg, Count Pillet-Will in Paris. To Count Redern. Visit from Kapellmeister Lindpaintner. Letter from Sobolewsky, who returned the missive meant for Gouin that I had mistakenly sent to him.

Friday 18 June. Wrote to the young Prince Caradja, son of the Turkish ambassador, together with an autograph.[162] Autograph and letter for Justizrat Strass.[163] To Professor Herbig, vice-director of the Academy, concerning my six-week journey to the watering places, and requesting leave from the sittings of the senate until 20 August.

Saturday 19 June. Preparations for departure. Wrote to Grube in Regensburg (returning an opera libretto). Wrote to Madame Walpurgis Hendrichs in Hamburg (also returning an opera libretto). Letters from Gouin, from Kastner. Wrote to Gouin.

Sunday 20 June. Called on the Russian composer Glinka.[164] Visit from Herr Brassier Saint-Simon, the Prussian ambassador in Stockholm,[165] who wants to introduce a Madame Norman, who will sing Fidès in Stockholm this coming winter.[166] Made corrections to the engraving of my cantata for the silver wedding of Prince Karl. Autograph for the German Album of the music director Klemm in Leipzig. *Le Prophète* has been given in Stettin and Nîmes to great enthusiasm. In the space of three weeks Hendrichs has played in *Struensee* four times in Hamburg. Wrote to Kapellmeister Sobolewsky in Königsberg, with an enclosure from Count Redern to me. Wrote to the book dealer Schlodtmann in Bremen, together with an autograph. Wrote to Behrends (he had sent me music for evaluation).[167] Sent 200 fr. support to Gaetano Rossi in Verona.

Monday 21 June. Finished the corrections to the cantata and sent them in. Preparations for departure. Letter from Dr. Bacher in London.

Tuesday 22 June. Left at twelve o'clock by train for Hanover, where we arrived at 9:30 in the evening.

Wednesday 23 June. Walked to the Pferdeturm: the new city areas of Hanover are very attractive. The new theater is most imposing from the outside (to a certain extent like the Teatro alla Scala in Milan). The region around Hanover, while not picturesque, is blooming and bright. Left at nine o'clock by rail for Cologne, where we arrived at nine in the evening.

Thursday 24 June. Received two letters from Gouin. Wrote down the observations that I have to make about Inkermann's poem for the music of *Struensee* (he calls himself Sternau). This poem describes the content of Michael's tragedy in the manner of Mosengeil's poem, which links together the music for Beethoven's *Egmont*.[168] Inkermann came at nine o'clock, and we had a long conversation on this topic. At 11:30 I caught the train from Cologne to Brussels, where I arrived at nine o'clock in the evening.

Friday 25 June. At 12:30 by railway *(train mixte)* to Paris, where we arrived at 10:45 by night. This train goes more slowly than the other two trains *de grande vitesse*, which leave respectively at eight o'clock in the morning and at six in the evening. It stops at more places, especially at Douai for an hour. Furthermore, one is inspected by the customs in Valenciennes, which is not the case with the express train. *Droits d'auteur* for May: 534 fr. These are the proceeds only for the provinces, since in May none of my operas was given in Paris. In Paris a letter was waiting from the hereditary grand duke of Weimar, at whose request I had sent my cantata for the silver wedding of Prince Karl.

Saturday 26 June. Visited my old friend Gouin. I moved into a wonderful *quartier* on the first floor of the Avenue Champs Élysées no. 26, at 250 fr. for fourteen days.

Sunday 27 June. Fetched the copper engravings of the Indian journey made by Prince Soltikoff from my residence.[169] I believe I have had a happy inspiration for the important refrain in the last finale of the new opera "Leb' ich? bin ich? träum' ich?" and immediately wrote down the whole melody.[170] Letter from Madame Viardot: she asks whether it is really true that I intend to give the role of the "Africaine" to Johanna Wagner and not to her. After lunch I polished the refrain. In the evening I began to work on the finale.

Monday 28 June. To Madame Viardot, who had already left, though; nevertheless, I found her husband's sister, Demoiselle Viardot. In the Opéra Comique: Grisar's *Le Carillonneur de Bruges*.[171] The new young contralto Demoiselle Wertheimber sang Beatrix.[172] I was so exhausted and sleepy that I heard hardly anything of the music. In the theater I received calls from the director of the Opéra Comique, Émile Perrin, Brandus, and Mlle. Wertheimber.

Tuesday 29 June. Letter from Dr. Bacher. Visit from Émile Perrin. Wrote to Rellstab. Visit from Brandus. Attended the Opéra Comique for *Galathée* by Victor Massé: fine, witty, piquant music.[173] Madame Ugalde was outstanding as Galathée, Demoiselle Wertheimber good in part as Pygmalion.

Wednesday 30 June. Called on Armand Bertin, Scribe, Brandus, Nestor Roqueplan. Visit from Scribe. I gave Scribe the lithographs from Prince Soltikoff's work on India. Letter from Dr. Bacher. In the Opéra: Halévy's *Le Juif errant.* Madame Tedesco and Demoiselle Lagrua sang the two women's roles.

July 1852

Thursday 1 July. Visit from Alexander Weill. Wrote to Dr. Bacher. In the Opéra Comique: Méhul's *L'Irato.*[174] The baritone Meillet still has a lovely voice.[175]

Friday 2 July. Émile Perrin and Ehrlich came to see me. To Gouin. In the Opéra saw *Vert-Vert,* ballet in three acts, music by Deldevez and Tolbecque.[176]

Saturday 3 July. Visit from the singer Masset. Visited Bischofsheim. Read through the score of Gomis's *Le Diable à Seville.*[177] In the Théâtre Français: *Ulysse, tragédie,* with choruses by Ponsard.[178] The music for the choruses and melodramas by Gounod: very interesting and clever music, which suggests that much is to be expected of him.

Sunday 4 July. Letter from Lemaire, theater director of Anvers [Antwerp]. Visit from the soprano Mme. Laborde, who sang me the role of Isabelle in *Robert.* Worked for several hours on the last finale, but unfortunately without success. In the evening, out of curiosity, and for the first time in my life, I visited two lowlife dance halls, La Chaumière and La Closerie de Lilla, both in the Boulevard Mont Parnasse, a peculiar world completely set apart.

Monday 5 July. Worked a little on the finale. In the Opéra: *Robert le Diable.* Depassio (Bertram) has a very beautiful, strong bass voice, but his singing is unpolished. Madame Laborde (Isabelle) is still good, as is Gueymard (Robert); Mademoiselle Poisot (Alice), mediocre. Letter from the wife of the composer Wolfram in Teplitz.

Tuesday 6 July. In the Théâtre Français, again attended the performance of *Ulysse.*

Wednesday 7 July. Wrote something in the album of Demoiselle Wertheimber. Visit from Herr Wertheimber. In the Grand Opéra heard Halévy's *Le Juif errant*, for the second time. The revival of *Le Prophète* in London at the Covent Garden Theatre, with Grisi as Fidès, has had great success.

Thursday 8 July. Called on Armand Bertin, Véron. Visit from Sax. In the Opéra Comique: Massé's *Galathée* and Méhul's *L'Irato*.

Friday 9 July. In the Opéra Comique: Auber's *Actéon* and Boieldieu's *Les Voitures versées*.[179]

Saturday 10 July. At ten minutes past eight o'clock I left by train for Brussels, where I arrived at five o'clock. The heat was frightful, and I was incapable of any work.

Sunday 11 July. Appalling heat. I visited Fétis and the composer Hanssens (the theater director). At one o'clock I left by train for Spa, where I arrived at 7:30. Letter from the singer Marchesi in Frankfurt-am-Main.

Monday 12 July. Called on Davelouis and Jules Janin. Again read Aeschylus's *Eumenides*, this time in the translation by Kopisch, which is more suitable for musical setting. The musicians of Spa serenaded me tonight by torchlight.

Tuesday 13 July. Jules Janin came to see me with the poet Ponsard. Letter from Geheimrat Illaire. In the evening worked inconsequentially on the finale.

Wednesday 14 July. Visit from the pianist Dupont, who has dedicated a piano piece to me. Letters from Gouin, Rellstab. Wrote to Gouin, to Karl Kaskel. Unpleasant article by Fiorentino in *Le Constitutionnel* about my stay in Paris.

Thursday 15 July. Birthday of my beloved daughter Blanca. On account of the great heat, I cannot make progress on the composition of the finale. Visited Jules Janin and the poet Ponsard. The latter read me fragments from his poem *Homer*.[180] In the evening worked on the finale.

Friday 16 July. Because of the great heat it was impossible for me to compose in the evening.

Saturday 17 July. Diarrhea. I worked on the finale in the morning, but not for very long.

Sunday 18 July. Stomach pains. Letter from the Société Bourgeois of Stavelot, inviting me to their musical festival. I replied immediately. Letter from the pianist Dupont in Liège. Letter from Gouin. In the evening revised the whole score of my new opera.

Monday 19 July. Stomach cramps. Dined with Davelouis, where I also found Ponsard and his friend Reybaud,[181] Jules Janin and his wife. Visit from Vermeulen, secretary of the Musical Academy of Rotterdam.[182] Vermeulen told me that the overture to *Struensee* has been played in concerts in Rotterdam, and that the German Opera Society of Amsterdam has performed *Der Prophet* with Mme. Romani.[183]

Tuesday 20 July. I felt too tense to work.

Wednesday 21 July. Attack of stomach cramps. Worked a little on the finale. Every type of work, even the lightest—particularly writing, though—is impossible for me at the moment. Letter from Gouin: *droits d'auteur* for the month of June, 376 fr.

Thursday 22 July. Letters from Henri Blaze, Dr. Bacher. Visits from Ponsard, Davelouis, Vermeulen.

Friday 23 July. Wrote to Gouin and Dr. Andral in Paris.

Saturday 24 July. Wrote to Gouin, to Henri Blaze de Bury, together with 500 fr. Letters from Brandus, Grüneisen. The poet Reybaud (Ponsard's friend), Dr. Joël from Vienna,[184] and Vermeulen all called on me.

Sunday 25 July. Hans van der Hoop from Rotterdam, vice-president of the Netherlands Society of Music, came to see me.[185] In the theater: *La Dame aux camélias*[186] by Alexandre Dumas *fils**.

Monday 26 July. Ear syringe. Pain in my left foot.

Tuesday 27 July. Wrote to Grüneisen, who has indirectly asked me for support, and sent him twenty-five pounds sterling. Visit from the English pianist and composer, Brinley Richards.[187]

Wednesday 28 July. I wrote to Baroness Willmar in Brussels,[188] who has recommended a musician, van Ghel, and sent me one of his compositions, a psalm setting, for my inspection; I find it clear and well organized. Worked a little on the new version of the Catherine's *couplets* in act 1, which I began on the way to Spa.

Thursday 29 July. Worked on the new version of the *couplets*, finished scoring it, and began writing it down.

Friday 30 July. Wrote to the lawyer Treite for Kastner, to Gouin for Perrin, to Dr. Bacher.

Sunday 31 July. Letter from Grüneisen in London. The headache is not severe, but my general nervous weakness is considerable: every time I go out I experience painful sensations in my head.

August 1852

Sunday 1 August. Visit from the violinist Léonard.

Monday 2 August. Began to work on my new version of the canon in act 1, since I am not pleased with the old one.

Tuesday 3 August. Worked with good results on the new version of the canon.[189] In the theater: *Mercadet*, a comedy by Balzac.[190]

Wednesday 4 August. In the morning finished composing and scoring the new canon, and revised it in the evening.

Thursday 5 August. Worked on the new version of Catherine's *couplets* in act 1. In the evening began writing out the vocal parts.

Friday 6 August. Letter from Gouin. Wrote to Gouin, to the music publisher Schloss in Cologne: promised a song for his album.

Saturday 7 August. In the evening wrote the vocal parts of the new version of Catherine's *couplets* into the full score.

Sunday 8 August. Scored the *couplets*.

Monday 9 August. [No entry.]

Tuesday 10 August. Wrote to Brandus in Paris, to Dr. Bacher in London. Scored the *couplets* in the morning and the evening.

Wednesday 11 August. Completed the instrumentation of the *couplets*. Visited Fétis. Letters from Gouin, Dr. Bacher, Gianpietro (Castellan).

Thursday 12 August. In the morning again began to work on the last finale, which I had put to one side in order to compose the new versions of the canon and the *couplets* in act 1.

Friday 13 August. Worked in the morning on the last finale.

Saturday 14 August. A restless night: constant headache and *échauffement.*[191] The doctor nonetheless allowed me to continue drinking the waters, but forbade me to do any work. This is a pity, since I was so much *en train* for the last finale. Letter from the music publisher Schloss in Cologne. In the evening worked a little on the act 1 finale.

Sunday 15 August. Letter from Scribe. In the morning and evening worked a little on the finale.

Monday 16 August. In the morning scored a little of the first *tempo* of the finale. Concert by the violinist Hubert Léonard and his wife de Mendi, a cousin of Madame Viardot.

Tuesday 17 August. Presented the *chef* of the Wind Band of Spa, Guillaume, with all the arrangements of my three French operas for military music, which have so far been published by Brandus.[192] In the morning finished scoring the first *tempo* of the finale. Today I heard the Wind Band play a potpourri of melodies from Donizetti's *Dom Sébastien* and, to my astonishment, heard in it a theme reminiscent of a passage from my new opera ("Près de toi, ma charmante"). I immediately composed a completely different melody for this passage, and believe it actually to be better than the earlier version.

Wednesday 18 August. In the morning I wrote down more of the finale. Letter from Gouin: in Paris the 127th performance of *Le Prophète* (receipts 9,502 fr.). The performance took place on the day after the big Napoleon Festival. Many strangers had come to Paris for this occasion, which accounts for the takings being so substantial.

Thursday 19 August. I wrote out the first *tempo* of the finale ("Wach' ich, träum' ich?") and wrote to Gouin.

Friday 20 August. Visited the singer Maray[193] and Fétis. In the morning scored the altered passage in the act 2 sextet ("Avec toi, ma charmante"). Letters from Wieprecht, Lux in Erfurt,[194] Bridgeman in London,[195] Bacher in London. Wrote to Dr. Bacher.

Saturday 21 August. The terrific, louring thunderclouds oppressed me so much that I could not continue composing.

Sunday 22 August. Finished scoring the *tempo agitato* of the finale ("Leb' ich, träum' ich?"). in the evening revised everything in the finale that I have so far orchestrated. Letter from Gouin: *droits d'auteur* for the month of July, 258 fr.

Monday 23 August. Wrote to Gouin, to Scribe. Letter from Kaskel. Visits from the English musician Ella, director of the Musical Union,[196] and from the Belgian singing teacher de Glimes.[197]

Tuesday 24 August. Worked on the act 3 finale in the morning and the evening.

Wednesday 25 August. Worked further on the act 3 finale in the morning. In the evening wrote the vocal parts of the finale into the full score.

Thursday 26 August. In the morning and evening finished composing and writing out the act 3 finale.

Friday 27 August. Letter from the composer Böhner from Gotha[198] and from his friend Lux in Erfurt. In the morning I scored a little of the act 3 finale. In the evening I invited several people to tea: Fétis, father and son, the musician Ella from London, Roper (an English dilettante), the violinist Léonard, the pianist Dupont, the father of the singer Maray.[199] The tea turned out to be something of a trial. The assembled musicians appeared to have such respect for Fétis, or to be so daunted by him, that no one said a word. Fortunately, *he* spoke nonstop, and since it was all about musical matters it was not without interest.

Saturday 28 August. In the morning and evening wrote the act 3 finale into the full score, and also began scoring it.

Sunday 29 August. Again during the morning and evening wrote the vocal parts of the act 3 finale into the full score, and continued scoring it.

Monday 30 August. Scored a little of the act 3 finale in the morning. In the evening to a concert, where the singer Mlle. Maray sang several arias (including "Grâce" from *Robert*); her voice is small, but sweet-sounding, and she has a lovely style, even if it is Italianate. The pianist Dupont and the young violinist Dupuis from Liège also participated.[200]

Tuesday 31 August. Letter from Bordeaux from someone whose name I cannot read, who offers me an opera text. In the morning scored a little of the act 3 finale, also in the evening, but very little.

September 1852

Wednesday 1 September. Letter from Dupont. In the morning and evening worked diligently on act 3 finale, both writing the vocal parts into the full score and continuing with the instrumentation.

Thursday 2 September. Letter from Scribe. Wrote to Gouin and Scribe. Scored the act 3 finale in the morning, and did the same in the evening.

Friday 3 September. Studied the role of Berthe in *Le Prophète* with Mlle. Maray, who will be singing it in St. Petersburg this winter. In the evening wrote to Gouin and Dr. Bacher. Scored a little of the act 3 finale.

Saturday 4 September. My health is improving, even though my stomach is constantly disturbed and works unpredictably. The headaches also continue. This evening, on the eve of my birthday, I finished scoring the act 3 finale. The newly composed pieces of the opera have now been completed. All that remains to be written is Catherine's coda in the act 1 finale (I am no longer satisfied with the present one), and then the arrangement of the six pieces from the *Feldlager* that will be integrated into the score.[201]

Sunday 5 September. My birthday. May God bless this new year of my life I am entering. May he preserve and protect and bless my beloved family and me myself, and may he direct our hearts and minds so that we follow his paths and deserve his blessing. I was busy all day with packing and making farewell visits. At Herr Davelouis's I made the acquaintance of Herr Perrot, the owner of the Belgian newspaper *L'Indépendance belge*, which is now so widely distributed.[202]

Monday 6 September. At nine o'clock I left by omnibus for Pepinstère, and from there went on to Brussels by rail. In the theater Madame Ugalde appeared as guest artist in Ambroise Thomas's *Le Songe d'une nuit d'été*.

Tuesday 7 September. At eight o'clock by train from Brussels to Amiens. From here by another train to Boulogne-sur-Mer: I am going because Scribe is there. I must discuss and work with him on the arrangement and translation of the six numbers from the *Feldlager* that are to be woven into the new comic opera.

Wednesday 8 September. Held a preliminary conference with Scribe about everything that we have to do together on *L'Étoile*. I have thought of a very striking, dramatic motive in order to integrate the Flute Piece more homogeneously with the rest of act 3. In the morning I wrote down all my general observations on the things that I still have to prepare for Scribe on the work. In the evening I made a *monstre*[203] of the Gypsy Roundelay. This took far more time than I had imagined, and I still had not finished it on going to bed.

Thursday 9 September. Finished the *monstre* of the Gypsy Roundelay for Scribe and took it to him.[204] Second conference with Scribe.

Friday 10 September. Yesterday evening and early this morning wrote down the *monstre* of the Flute Piece for Scribe.[205] Held a third conference with Scribe. Wrote to Gouin. In the evening worked at the scansion of the Hussar's Song for Scribe.[206]

Saturday 11 September. Finished the *monstre* of the Hussar's Song, and also that of the Grenadier's Song.[207] Fourth conference with Scribe: he brought me the French words of the Chorus of Pandurs[208] and the Gypsy Roundelay. Wrote to Herr von Humboldt on his birthday.

Sunday 12 September. The morning headaches have increased very much, and made it impossible for me to work before noon. Fifth conference with Scribe.

Monday 13 September. Letter from Sobolewsky. [Sixth] conference with Scribe. Fitted the new French words to the Gypsy Roundelay. Partially prepared the *monstre* of the *Arie des refrains* in the last finale.[209]

Tuesday 14 September. Finished the scansion of the *Arie des refrains*. In the evening partially completed the *monstre* of the trio of the Artilleryman, Hussar, and Grenadier.[210] [Seventh] conference with Scribe.

Wednesday 15 September. Completed the scansion of the trio before breakfast. [Eighth] conference with Scribe: adapted the scansion of the *Air du refrain*.

Thursday 16 September. A very severe head cold has affected me so much that I have not been able to work all day. Visit from Gye, director of Covent Garden Theatre in London; he came to Boulogne expressly to see me. Letters from Hédouin in Valenciennes, from Dr. Bacher in Paris. Wrote to Gouin.

Friday 17 September. I adapted the new words to the Flute Piece. Long [ninth] conference with Scribe.

Saturday 18 September. Before breakfast completely adapted and revised the new words for the Flute Piece. Worked out the scansion of the Quadruple Chorus.[211]

Long [tenth] conference with Scribe. In the evening positioned the new words of the Hussar's Song, and partially those of the Grenadier's Song.

Sunday 19 September. Before breakfast inserted the [new] words of the *Chanson du Grenadier* and wrote to Gouin. After breakfast worked out the scansion of the Battle Song.[212] Long [eleventh] conference with Scribe. In the evening busied myself with the adaptation of the words of the small *buffo* trio in act 2, which will not work without changes by Scribe.

Monday 20 September. Wrote down the translation of the Second Finale, with all possible details for Scribe. Long [twelfth] conference with Scribe. In the evening positioned the new words of the trio of the Hussar, Grenadier, and Artilleryman, which was all rather wearisome.

Tuesday 21 September. Before breakfast worked on a new *stretta* for the military *buffo* trio in act 2 with considerable success. Worked out the scansion of the sextet in the act 2 finale.[213] [Thirteenth] conference with Scribe. Worked out the scansion of the *Serment*[214] and of the stretta of the finale. Letter from the Regimental Kapellmeister Streck in Munich.

Wednesday 22 September. Before breakfast worked out the scansion of the first chorus of the finale. [Fourteenth] conference with Scribe. In the evening worked a little on the adaptation of the words of the Quadruple Chorus.

Thursday 23 September. Before and after breakfast worked on the adaptation of the words of the Quadruple Chorus. Scansion of the new conclusion to the act 1 finale as I intend it to be.[215] [Fifteenth] conference with Scribe. In the evening finished the adaptation of the words of the Quadruple Chorus. Made a copy of the *remarques générales* that I had set out for Scribe.

Friday 24 September. Before breakfast I suddenly thought of a new version of Prascovia's *couplets* (in the act 1 finale).[216] I felt impelled to finish the composition swiftly, to the end. [Sixteenth] conference with Scribe. Farewell visits to Scribe and to Blahetka.[217]

Saturday 25 September. Partially adapted the words of the act 2 finale before breakfast. Last [seventeenth] conference with Scribe in Boulogne. At 12:30 by train to Paris, where we arrived at seven o'clock.

Sunday 26 September. Unfortunately, passed the day uselessly. Visited Gouin. Brandus came to see me. Called on Perrin. Opéra Comique: *La Croix de Marie* by Aimé Maillart.[218]

Monday 27 September. My health is quite unexpectedly much better; heaven be thanked. Conference with Perrin, director of the Comic Opera. Opéra Comique: *Le Père Gaillard* by Reber.[219]

Tuesday 28 September. Called on Scribe, Véron, Fiorentino (1000 fr.), Julius [Beer], Haber, Roqueplan. Opéra Comique: *Le Père Gaillard* by Reber.

Wednesday 29 September. Called on Gouin, Berlioz, Julius. Wrote to the military kapellmeister Streck in Munich. Grand Opéra: *Le Juif errant* by Halévy.

Thursday 30 September. Worked for an hour before breakfast on adapting the words of the act 2 finale. Called on Armand Bertin, Girard, Vatry. Worked in the evening from 9 until 11: finished adapting the words of the act 2 finale and half the words of the Battle Song.

October 1852

Friday 1 October. Finished adapting the words of the Battle Song before breakfast. After breakfast read through the newly composed pieces, with an eye to the word changes that I want from Scribe. In my diary I will refer to this work of abridgment and the changes needed from Scribe as *Étoile*. After breakfast worked likewise for an hour. Grand Opéra: *Le Prophète.*

Saturday 2 October. To Brandus. Opéra Comique: *Le Père Gaillard.*

Sunday 3 October. Worked on the *monstres* of the new pieces of act 1 for Scribe. Visited Henri Blaze, Bischofsheim, Adam, Auber, Scudo, Ed. Monnais. Théâtre Lyrique: *Si j'étais roi* by Adam.[220] I felt such a pressure of the head that I dozed throughout and heard absolutely nothing of the opera.

Monday 4 October. Worked on the *monstres* for Scribe. In the Opéra *Robert le Diable* (335th performance, receipts 8,078 fr.), one of the better performances of the opera I have attended.

Tuesday 5 October. Unwell. Wrote to Lady Westmorland.[221] Letter from Madame Viardot.

Wednesday 6 October. I stayed at home the whole day and did not work at all.

Thursday 7 October. Worked on the *monstres* for Scribe for an hour before breakfast. After breakfast two hours of the same, finishing the whole work, which I revised in the evening.

Friday 8 October. Worked on the new version of Prascovia's *couplets* for an hour before breakfast. Wrote to Madame Viardot. Opéra Comique: *Les Porcherons* by Grisar.[222]

Saturday 9 October. Worked on the words for Reynolds in Prascovia's second couplet. Conference with Scribe. Opéra Comique: *La Fille du régiment* by Donizetti; *Les Voitures versées* by Boieldieu.

Sunday 10 October. Conference with Scribe. Opéra Comique: *Madelon* by Bazin,[223] *Galathée* by Massé.

Monday 11 October. My health improves. Conference with Scribe. Théâtre Lyrique: *Si j'étais roi* by Adam; a delightful *buffo* libretto. Adam's music contains many charming things, but is nonetheless not among his best compositions. Dr. Bacher came to see me.

Thursday 12 October. Letter from Breitkopf & Härtel. Visit from Zimmermann and his son-in-law Gounod. Sax let me hear his newly invented instruments. In the evening worked on the *Étoile*.

Wednesday 13 October. Conference with Scribe. Worked a little on adapting the words in the *Étoile*. In the Opéra heard the first two acts of Halévy's *Le Juif errant*.

Thursday 14 October. In the evening wrote out the new version of Prascovia's *couplets*.

Friday 15 October. Letters from Kaskel, Masset. Visited Véron. Opéra Comique: *La Fée aux roses* by Halévy.

Saturday 16 October. My health is restored. Investigated the Gates of Honor, and other preparations in the boulevards for the festive entry of Louis Napoleon to-day. I watched the procession itself at Bischofsheim's. In the evening I went to look at the illuminations all over Paris. Did no work.

Sunday 17 October. I was not ready for any work today. Variétés: *Le Mari de la dame des chœurs*, vaudeville by Bayard.[224] The comedian Arnal left me cold as usual, although the old comic was very good and also sang well. Wrote to the Marquis Martellini in Florence to say that Frezzolini is not to sing Fidès there.[225]

Monday 18 October. Scudo and Bacher dined with me. Stayed at home in the evening, but worked only a little.

Tuesday 19 October. Wrote to Lux, lottery receiver in Erfurt. To Scribe. As a member of the Comité de l'Association des Musiciennes I had to attend the public reading of Baron Trémont's will. The five different literary and artistic associations he has collectively remembered in his testament were invited, as well as many other charitable institutions. This will is a monument to philanthropy, the loftiness of the chronicler, and the administrative wisdom of the testator and is, moreover, wonderfully written. The reading itself exercised the most profoundly moving effect on all those present.[226] In the evening stayed at home, but hardly worked at all, since I felt so tired and tense.

Wednesday 20 October. To the rehearsal of Berlioz's *Requiem*,[227] which will be performed in memory of Baron Trémont on 22 October in St. Eustache, by 600 musicians. Opéra Comique: *Galathée* by Massé. Début of the bass Faure*, who sang the role of Pygmalion: a very brilliant first appearance. It is a pity he has so little depth.

Thursday 21 October. Letters from Madame Viardot, Countess Westmorland, Salvatore Marchesi. To my nephew Julius. To Gouin. Conference with Scribe. Visit from Lorini,[228] the *homme d'affaires* of the new impresario of the Italian Opera in Paris, Corti:[229] he wants the *Crociato*. In the evening worked without success on the conclusion of act 1.

Friday 22 October. Before breakfast I composed some of the conclusion to act 1, with good results. I attended the performance of Berlioz's *Requiem* in the Church of Saint Eustache. Even though it only partially corresponds to the concept of a true church style, is very unclear, without themes, and very idiosyncratic, it is nevertheless a highly remarkable work, rich in individual, grandiose beauties, with striking harmonic and instrumental effects. Visit from Auber. Before going to bed, composed a little of the conclusion to the act 1 finale.

Saturday 23 October. To Scribe. I had Berlioz, Hiller, Brandus, and Dr. Bacher with me for lunch.

Sunday 24 October. Letter from Herr von Humboldt. Worked before breakfast for one and a half hours on the conclusion to act 1 with good success. To Gouin. Visit from the pianist Wehle,[230] Dr. Bamberg, Simon.[231] Opéra Comique: *L'Ambassadrice* by Auber.

Monday 25 October. Worked for one and a half hours before breakfast on writing out the conclusion to act 1.

Tuesday 26 October. Worked for one and a half hours before breakfast on the conclusion to act 1. Attended the wedding of the young Brandus in the synagogue. Wrote to the music publisher Schloss in Cologne. Stayed at home in the evening, but I felt so tired and sluggish that I worked only inconsequentially on act 1.

Wednesday 27 October. Visit from Oliver Mason from Birmingham, who came to Paris expressly to invite me to compose an oratorio for the next Birmingham Festival, which will take place in three years' time. The pianist Wehle played me his fantasy on my song "Komm." In the evening scored the conclusion to act 1.

Thursday 28 October. The writer Duesberg asked for a loan of 100 fr., which I gave him. Visits from Émile Deschamps, Panofka, Oliver Mason. Unfortunately, the whole day was lost in this way. Grand Opéra: festive performance in honor of the return of the prince president from his journey. They gave one act of Auber's *Le Philtre*, two acts of different ballets, and a *Festival Cantata* by Massé, well thought out and written, but somewhat dry and without themes.[232]

Friday 29 October. Resolution to diligence. I have been in Paris almost a whole month, and still have not finished my new opera, which could have been possible, and, indeed, is necessary if I want to go *en répétition*[233] on 1 December. I therefore determined not to lose a minute more from now on, and yet it was only 1:30 before I got down to work. Letter from Madame Viardot. Worked for one and a half hours: began scoring the conclusion of act 1, and was then disturbed. In the evening, from 8 until 11, wrote the vocal parts of the conclusion to act 1 into the full score.

Saturday 30 October. I was able to start work only at 12:30, and worked until 3:30 scoring the conclusion to act 1, also in the evening. However, I felt so sleepy, that little was accomplished. Letters from Marquis Martellini in Florence, the music dealer Schloss in Cologne. Wrote to Madame Viardot.

Sunday 31 October. Scored a little of the conclusion of act 1, but was disturbed every now and then. Dined with my nephew Julius Beer. In the evening scored only a page. So far my resolution of the twenty-ninth, to work diligently every day, has not been put into practice. Letter from the impresario Ronzi of the Teatro della Pergola in Florence. *Le Prophète* has been produced in Hanover with gratifying success.[234]

November 1852

Monday 1 November. Began work at 10:45; scored the conclusion until 1:15. The composer Mereaux from Rouen[235] came to see me, and introduced his pupil Dotram [Dautresme*] to me: the latter wants to become my pupil. Visit from the manager of the new local Italian Opera, Corti and his *associé* Lorini, who want to produce my *Crociato*. Visit from my nephew George Beer, who has arrived from Amsterdam. I invited Tedesco, Le Roi, Leduc, and Gouin to lunch with me. At 3 again worked until 4:30; then Baron Taylor and Benelli came. After supper worked for another one and a half hours.

Tuesday 2 November. Worked from 11 until 1:30. Visit from Dr. Bacher. Letter from Marquis Lucchesini. Wrote to Professor Herbig. In the evening to the Grand Opéra for the dress rehearsal of Rossini's *Moses*.

Wednesday 3 November. Visit from Cornet, the new director of the Viennese Court Opera, from the theater director Morvan, from Brandus and Dr. Bacher. Today I completely finished composing, scoring, and revising the formal conclusion to act 1, from the moment when Catherine begins to sing on the ship to the fall of the curtain. Opéra Comique: *La Chanteuse voilée* by Victor Massé.[236]

Thursday 4 November. Morvan delivered to me his plan for an opera, *Le Dernier Jour de Pompei*. Siraudin described his plan for a short work for the Grand Opéra. Visits from Brandus, Leo, Viardot, Bacher, Cornet. With Leo to the Hôtel de Ville to look at the new murals by Lehmann, and to call on him there.[237] I had no time to write even a note today. Opéra Comique: the first performance of *Les Mystères d'Udolpho* by Scribe and Germaine Delavigne, music by Clapisson. The libretto is poor; the music contains much that is worthwhile, has obviously been written by the hand of a master, is well integrated, but lacks the vivifying breath of inspiration. The success is only mediocre.[238]

Friday 5 November. Conference with Scribe. Escorted the director Cornet to Madame Tedesco. Visits from the music publisher Schott from Mainz, and from Duponchel. From 1 until 4 virtually finished scoring the second version of Prascovia's *couplets* in the act 1 finale. At 4 studied the role of Valentine with Lagrua. In the Grand Opéra: the revival of *Moïse* by Rossini.[239]

Saturday 6 November. Visits from the violinist Cavillon and the artist Lemlein.[240] Worked from 10:30 until one o'clock, and in the evening from 8 until 11 on what I believe to be a happy change in Prascovia's aria.

Sunday 7 November. Visits from d'Ortigue and Madame Brandus. *Matinée musicale* by Ferdinand Hiller. Stayed at home in the evening, but had such a heaviness in my head that I could not work at all.

Monday 8 November. Worked a little on the change in Prascovia's aria. Wrote to the impresario Ronzi in Florence. Adam sent me two spare tickets to the Théâtre

Lyrique for this evening to hear his opera *La Poupée de Nuremberg*[241] and *Les Deux Voleurs*, opera in one act by Girard.[242]

Tuesday 9 November. Worked for three hours: completed the change to Prascovia's aria, scored and revised it. Visited Scribe. To Henri Blaze. In the evening read through the cantata and dramatic scene by Dautresme from Rouen. He will come tomorrow to hear my opinion on it.

Wednesday 10 November. Mereaux and Dautresme from Rouen came to me to hear my opinion of the latter's cantata; he wants to become my pupil. Visit from Seghers*, who would like to perform the overture to *Struensee* in his concerts.[243] I asked him to wait until Sternau's adaptation of the text is finished, when I will give the whole score to him. In the evening began a revision of act 1 of the new opera, before I give it to the copyist.

Thursday 11 November. Letter from Madame Rudersdorf-Küchenmeister, who asks my permission to give act 2 of *Robert* at her benefit in the Friedrich-Wilhelmstädt-isches-Theater. Wrote to Madame Rudersdorf in Berlin. Wrote to Count Redern: announced my indisposition; requested leave until the end of December; enclosed letters from Sobolewsky and Lux from Erfurt. Visit from Brandus. Studied the role of Valentine in *Les Huguenots* with Lagrua. Worked for two hours in the morning and two hours in the evening on the revision of act 1, and again made a change in Prascovia's *couplets*.

Friday 12 November. To Scribe. The writer Simon from Berlin came to see me: he wants data for my biography. Visits from Valentin de Lapelouze, and from Brandus. Opéra Comique: *Le Caïd* by Thomas. The *débutant* Faure was singing in it.

Saturday 13 November. Worked for two hours on the revision of the opera. Visits from Brandus and Cornet. Opéra Comique: *La Chanteuse voilée* by Massé. Afterwards worked for another two hours on the revision of the opera.

Sunday 14 November. To Brandus. In the morning worked only a little on the revision of the opera, and in the evening from 8:30 until 11:30. Dined with Célérier.

Monday 15 November. Letter from Émile Deschamps. Wrote to the directorate of the Gesellschaftskonzerte in Cologne. Completed the revision of the whole opera.

Tuesday 16 November. To Romieu.[244] To Armand Bertin. To Sax to hear his new instruments. Unfortunately, I could not get down to work at all today. Opening of the new Italian Opera: Rossini's *Otello*.

Wednesday 17 November. Visit from Brandus. The copyist who will write out the new opera came today for the first time. Down to work at 12:30. Today I began adapting, revising, and writing out those pieces from the *Feldlager* that are to be used in the new opera. Dined at Zimmermann's. *Droits d'auteur* for October, 498 fr. 90 c.

Thursday 18 November. Worked for two and a half hours, and again for two and a half hours in the evening.

Friday 19 November. Worked for two hours before breakfast. Called on Madame Benoit Fould, and on Henri Blaze. Visit from Stephen de la Madeleine. Worked for two hours. Invited Gouin to dinner. In the evening worked for three hours.

Saturday 20 November. Worked from 11 until 1:30. Called on Jules Janin and on Véron. Before supper worked for another hour. Visit from Dr. Wertheimer.[245] Worked for three hours in the evening.

Sunday 21 November. Called on Vitet and on Chaix d'Estanges.[246] Dautresme from Rouen came for the first time since his visit with Mereaux; looked through his compositions, and made my observations on them. Panofka showed me his singing method.[247] Could not work for even a minute all morning. Dined with my nephew Julius. Afterwards worked for two and a half hours.

Monday 22 November. Dined with Brandus, where I made the acquaintance of Jules Lecomte, the well-known correspondent of *L'Indépendance belge*.[248] Scribe came and discussed his ideas for a two-act opera for the Grand Opéra, *Trois Mois sous la neige*, which seems interesting to me.

Tuesday 23 November. Called Dr. Bacher. Théâtre de la Gaité: *La Bergère des Alpes*, melodrama in five acts by Dennery and Desnoyers: an interesting play.[249] An avalanche occurs in it, which took me back forty years to the opera *Der Bergsturz* by Weigl.[250] The collapse of the mountain was done better in that little opera, but the scenery is lovelier in the new play.

Wednesday 24 November. The dinner that I hosted today claimed all my time, and I composed only the new recitative that precedes the Hussar's Song.[251] The guests at my dinner were: Vicomte Paul Daru,[252] Benoit Fould, Armand Bertin and his brother Édouard, the lawyer Chaix d'Estanges, Vitet, Édouard Monnais, Gouin, Duponchel.

Thursday 25 November. Letters from Count Redern, from Marquis Martellini in Florence. To Carafa (with a score of *Le Prophète*), Blaze de Bury, Baroness Willmar, Nestor Roqueplan (with an album for Demoiselle Marquet).[253] Sat for the artist Lemlein, who wants to include my portrait in his big painting depicting the effects of music.[254] All this took up the whole morning. In the evening wrote the vocal parts of the Hussar's Song into the full score. In the Vaudeville: *La Dame aux camélias* by Dumas fils; Demoiselle Doche played the leading role.[255]

Friday 26 November. Finished writing the vocal parts of the Hussar's Song into the full score, and started on the Grenadier's Song. Worked for two hours on it. Went to see Dr. Bacher. Visit from Blanchard,[256] and from Dr. Bamberg. I hosted a dinner. The guests were: Romieu (*le directeur des Beaux Arts*), Véron, Roqueplan, Brindeau, Halévy, Auber, Adam, Thomas, Bouché. All in all the dinner cost me 400 fr., even though we were only ten persons.

Saturday 27 November. Worked for two and a half hours before breakfast, and one hour afterward. I made what I believe to be a happy change in the Grenadier's Song, and wrote some of the vocal part into the full score. Worked for an hour after lunch. Then to Gouin's box in the Vaudeville, for the first performance of *Les Paniers de la Comtesse*, vaudeville in one act by Léon Gozlan ([featuring] Mademoiselle Déjazet): nothing special.[257]

Sunday 28 November. Began working at 10:30 until 2. Between four and five o'clock I gave Dautresme instruction in composition, for the second time. In the Théâtre Lyrique: *La Perle du Brésil* by Félicien David: interesting music, especially from a purely tonal point of view, the lovely coloring worthy of the composer of *Du Désert*. On the other hand, the dramatic dimension of his talent is very small. The choruses work very well, the one for men's voices particularly.

Tuesday 29 November. Worked from 7 until 8:30. Scored the alteration in the Grenadier's Song, and finished entering the vocal part in the full score. Worked for another hour. In the evening worked for two and three-quarter hours. Began to write the vocal part of the Battle Song into the full score. *Le Prophète* has been performed in Stockholm with great success.

Wednesday 30 November. Worked from 10 until 1: wrote all the vocal parts of the Battle Song into the full score. Wrote to Madame Ungher-Sabatier in Florence; she would like to help the singers study their parts in *Le Prophète*. In the evening began to write the vocal parts of the Quadruple Chorus into the full score: worked for two and three-quarter hours.

December 1852

Wednesday 1 December. I worked from 7 until 9:45. Called on the Prussian ambassador, Count Hatzfeld, where I met the chief of police, Stieber, from Berlin.

At 2:30 began working again until 5. Visit from Brandus. In the evening in the Opéra: *Le Prophète*.

Thursday 2 December. Today the empire is proclaimed in Paris.[258] Worked for two hours before and one hour after lunch. In the Opéra Comique: *Le Chant de l'avenir*, cantata by Adam in celebration of Louis Napoleon's entry into Paris.[259]

Friday 3 December. Began work around 10:30: by 1 had completely written out and revised the vocal parts of the Quadruple Chorus. Visit from Polizeirat Stieber from Berlin. Dined with Berlioz.

Saturday 4 December. Conference with Scribe. Théâtre Lyrique: *La Perle du Brésil* by Félicien David.

Sunday 5 December. From 7 until 8:45 composed a new recitative to precede the act 2 finale.[260] Gave a lesson to Dautresme. After lunch worked for an hour.

Monday 6 December. Worked for two hours on the composition of Scribe's altered text of a part of the act 2 finale. Sat for the painter Lemlein, for my portrait in his *tableau, La Musique*. Visits from Baroness Willmar, and from Adolphe Sax, the famous maker of musical instruments. Worked for another hour on the finale. Dined with the Prussian ambassador, Hatzfeld, where I made the acquaintance of the Austrian ambassador, Baron von Hübner,[261] and the Russian ambassador, Herr von Kirleff.[262] Worked for another hour before going to bed.

Tuesday 7 December. Worked for only two hours before breakfast, and finished composing the new passages in the finale. In the Italian Opera: *Luisa Miller* by Verdi.[263] Desnoyer, from *Le Siècle*, was my neighbor. Visit from Sax.

Wednesday 8 December. Visit from the *Capitain des guides de l'empereur*, Piquemala, who is busy organizing the imperial military music, and wanted my advice. Worked for one hour before dining. Opéra Comique: *Madelon* by Bazin, *Le Domino noir* by Auber.

Thursday 9 December. Worked for one and three-quarter hours before breakfast. Visited Gouin, who is unwell.[264] To Dr. Bacher. To Théophile Gautier: arranged that he should translate the linking text of *Struensee* for the sum of 1,500 fr. The Belgian composer van Ghel, and then d'Ortigue, came to see me. Lent Dr. Bacher 2,000 fr. at his request, and through Gouin's mediation. In the Théâtre Italien: Verdi's *Luisa Miller*.

Friday 10 December. Letter from the father of the singer Johanna Wagner. Went to see Scribe. Worked for two hours. Visits from Leo, from the singer Mlle Cruvelli*, from Desnoyer, *rédacteur* of *Le Siècle* (with the singer Favelli from the Opéra Comique),[265] from the famous horn player Vivier. In the evening to the Opéra for *Les Huguenots*.

Saturday 11 December. Dined at Panseron's, where the organist Lefébure-Wély* was present, and performed very beautifully on a melodion with fifteen registers. Played in this way, the instrument offers marvelous effects.

Sunday 12 December. Worked for two hours in the morning and two and a half hours in the evening. Concert de la Société de Sainte Cécile in which, among other things, a *berceuse* from *Blanche de Provence* by Cherubini[266] and an *Ave Verum* by Gounod[267] were performed, two wonderful pieces.

Monday 13 December. Worked for two hours before breakfast. Went through the copies of the solo roles and choral parts of act 1 of the new opera with the copyist to verify that nothing has been missed. Called on Lord Westmorland. Gave a lesson in composition to Dautresme. Dined with Crémieux. Worked for another hour in the evening.

Tuesday 14 December. Worked for three hours. Again made a change in the act 2 finale, in order to clarify Pierre's role. Letter from Mac Dounel in Dublin,[268] who, on behalf of the Committee of the Industrial Exhibition in Dublin, invites me to provide a composition for the Hall of Industry in May 1853. Dined with Coste, where I made the acquaintance of Arsène Houssaye, director of the Théâtre Français,[269] and his wife. After table there was music making, and Demoiselle Claus, a very talented pianist from Prague, played.[270]

Wednesday 15 December. Neglected the rubdown in order to be able to work for one and three-quarter hours before breakfast. Letter from Marquis Martellini in Florence. Called on Girard, Gouin. Visits from Count Fontenilliat, French chargé d'affaires in Stockholm,[271] from Kapellmeister Chelard from Weimar, and from Leo. Worked for another two hours, and two and a half hours in the evening.

Thursday 16 December. Worked for three hours. Wrote to the opera Kapellmeister Romani in Florence. In the evening worked for three hours. Completed the act 2 finale, and started on the Flute Piece.

Friday 17 December. Neglected the cold rubdown in order to work for one and three-quarter hours before breakfast (on the Flute Piece). With the organist Lefébure-Wély to the inventor and manufacturer of the melodion, Alexandre*; another of his inventions can be used on any existing piano: it enables any note to be sustained for as long as desired without keeping the finger on the key.[272] Letter from Madame Ungher-Sabatier in Florence. Visit from the theater impresario Merelli. To the concert of the violinist Vieuxtemps: his new Violin Concerto in D Minor is a very pure, beautiful composition.[273] Afterward to the soirée that the *directeur général des musées,* Count Nieuwerkerke,[274] holds every Friday, and to which all painters, sculptors, musicians, etc., are invited. *Droits d'auteur* for the month of November: 336 fr. 40 c.

Saturday 18 December. Worked until breakfast. In the Italian Opera: *Norma* by Bellini. Demoiselle Cruvelli sang Norma.

Sunday 19 December. To Scribe. Worked for three hours. Visited my nephew Julius. Visited Bacher. I invited Berlioz, Léon Kreutzer, Baron Taylor, and Gouin to lunch with me. Afterward worked for another two hours and finished writing out the Flute Piece.

Monday 20 December. Revised the Flute Piece. Called on Fétis. Gave a lesson in composition to Dautresme. In the evening revised the final pieces of act 2.

Tuesday 21 December. Visit from the violinist Sivori. Opéra Comique: first performance of Auber's *Marco Spada.*[275] Début of Demoiselle Duprez.

Wednesday 22 December. Letter from the writer Karl Müller (Blau) from Pest: *Les Huguenots* has been performed in Pest in Hungarian to such extraordinary enthusiasm that there were ten performances in four weeks.[276] At Madame Wallet's (Scribe's natural daughter)[277] heard Beethoven's last quartets, played superbly by Chevillard, etc.[278] Read through the whole libretto of the *Étoile* again. I had Gentil and Gouin to dine with me. Then in the Opéra I heard acts 3 and 4 of Halévy's *Le Juif errant.*

Thursday 23 December. Read Sternau's (Inkermann's) linking text for the music of *Struensee.* Called on Germain Delavigne. Visit from Émile Perrin: we agreed that my new opera should be produced on 1 October in the coming year.

Friday 24 December. Letter from Georges Hainl*, conductor in Lyons. Visit from the Italian composer Concone*, who wanted me to hear his singing pupil, Demoiselle Martinelli. I visited Nestor Roqueplan. Dined at Countess d'Agoult's.

Saturday 25 December. Unfortunately did nothing, other than write to Count Redern concerning an extension of my leave until the end of January. Opéra Comique: *Marco Spada.* Letter from the poetess Chézy.

Sunday 26 December. Wrote to Albert Wagner. Gave Dautresme instruction in composition. Concert de Sainte Cécile: they played a symphony by Gade (A Minor) that contains several interesting movements.[279] Opéra Comique: *Le Caïd* by Thomas.

Monday 27 December. Letter from Émile Chevé*. To Scribe, Rebizzo, Gouin. To a concert by the pianist Haberbier.[280]

Tuesday 28 December. Called on the Tuscan ambassador, Prince Poniatowsky,[281] and gave him my *Quarante Mélodies* for the Marquis Martellini in Florence. Théâtre Lyrique: *La Perle du Brésil* by Félicien David.

Wednesday 29 December. Visit from Herr Valois, secretary to the delegations, who asked me, on behalf of the minister Persigny, to compose an occasional opera *(Charlemagne)* that would be given on 15 August in the Grand Opéra for the coronation of the Emperor Napoleon. In the Opéra the first performance of *Orfa*, a ballet in two acts on Nordic mythology, music by Adam.[282] *Le Prophète* has been given in Nuremberg and Hermannstadt (in Siebenbürgen).[283]

Thursday 30 December. Wrote to Mac Dounel in Dublin: declined the invitation to compose the cantata. Letter from Madame Ungher-Sabatier in Florence. At 2 began another revision of my new opera: (a) as composition; (b) in relation to the individuality of Demoiselle Duprez, in case I should give the role of Catherine to her; (c) synchronizing the word changes in the score with the libretto that I must submit to Scribe. Théâtre Italien: Verdi's *Luisa Miller*.

Friday 31 December. Wrote to Merelli in Vienna about the engagement of Ernesta Grisi. Visited Herr Valois and told him that I cannot undertake the composition of the occasional opera for the imperial coronation. In the space of two hours, I composed and wrote down the romance "Sentinelle" in act 2 of the new opera, which I regard as necessary for the role of Catherine in the event of Demoiselle Duprez singing it.[284] Dined with Véron. Then I went on to a soirée at Bischofsheim's. The old year is at an end. God bless the new year for all my loved ones and for me.

Notes

1. Benedix, *Der Gefängniss*, *Lustspiel* in four acts (Leipzig, Stadttheater, 24 April 1851; the first Berlin and Vienna performances had also been in 1851) [Richel 13].
2. Tgb. *élèven*.
3. Dr. Andreas Sommer (b. 1804), a theologian, worked briefly as a teacher at Christian Gottfried Nehrlich's singing school, and then as a private tutor in Berlin. Börner was a tenor who had sung in the Domchor since 1843.
4. Karl Friedrich Rungenhagen died on 21 December 1851.

5. Rungenhagen's motet *Trauet um die Trauernden* was written in 1827 for a commemorative service for Prince Ferdinand Radziwill.

6. Prof. Dr. Ernst Heinrich Tölken (1785–1869), professor of the history of art and mythology at the University of Berlin since 1823, was director of antiquities and the coin collection at the Royal Museum (1836–64) and secretary of the Berlin Academy of Arts.

7. This was Karl Otto von Raumer (1805–59), who had succeeded Ladenberg on 19 December 1850 as minister in the department of education and medical affairs.

8. He was actually Czechowski, a tenor from Schwerin newly engaged by the Friedrich-Wilhelmstädtisches-Theater. He was to work there for several years.

9. The composer and violinist Hermann Georg Dam (1815–58) had been a member of the Royal Orchestra since 1840. He composed the oratorio *Das Hallelujah der Schöpfung* in the same year; it was first performed at the Garnisonkirche, Potsdam, in 1847.

10. Haydn, Symphony no. 100 in G Major *(The Military)* (1793–94).

11. The overture to *Anacreon, opéra ballet* (1803), was a firm repertory piece in the nineteenth century.

12. Weber, *Jubel* overture, J.245 (1818).

13. Beethoven, Symphony no. 3 in E-flat major *(Eroica),* op. 55 (1803).

14. Kammerherr Arnold von Schack had married Auguste Maria Klara Benecke von Gröditzberg, the daughter of Wilhelm Christian Benecke von Gröditzberg, a Berlin banker and landed gentleman. See 1 May 1844.

15. Tgb. *cour.*

16. Mozart, *Idomeneo,* no. 25 Quartet ("Andrò ramingo e solo").

17. Gluck, *Orfeo e Euridice*: act 2—the Scene in Tatarus, a series of ballets, choruses, and solos (nos. 18–28); act 3—no. 39 Duet ("Vieni, appaga il tuo consorte").

18. Rosenhain played his *Nocturne* and *Le Carneval de Venise.*

19. Rossini, *Le Comte Ory,* nos. 16–18 ("Ciel! — Ô terreur, ô peine extrême").

20. Beethoven, *Die Ruinen von Athen,* incidental music to the play by Kotzebue, nos. 4 and 5.

21. Kontski played his *Themata aus der Oper "Macbeth" von Verdi.*

22. August Heinrich Hermann, Graf von Dönhoff (1797–1874), was a royal chamberlain, steward to the queen, and *Schlosshauptmann* of Königsberg.

23. Mendelssohn, *Der 2. Psalm* ("Warum toben die Heiden") for tenor, bass and double chorus, op. 78, no. 1 (1843).

24. Durante composed two versions of *Misericordias Domini,* both of which were published by Bote & Bock in the series *Musica sacra* (V, no. 9 and VII, no. 3).

25. Joseph Haydn, *Aus dem Danklied zu Gott* for soprano, alto, tenor, and bass (words by Christian Fürchgott Gellert), Hob.XXVc, no. 8.

26. Tgb. *konzertierende Hörner.*

27. Beethoven, Sextet in E-flat Major for two horns and strings, op. 81b (1794–95).

28. Hummel, Quintet in E-flat Major, op. 87 (1802).

29. Hummel, Septet in D Minor, op. 74 (c. 1816)

30. Ger. "eve-of-the-wedding party."

31. See 27 May 1851.

32. See *BT,* 5:952–53.

33. Ida Maetzner was a teacher in Berlin.

34. The Meyerbeer family were in close social contact with Frau Kunde and her daughters.

35. Prosper Sain d'Arod (b. 1814) was educated at the Conservatoire in Paris, won

the Prix de Rome (1841), and was active as a church composer and musician in Lyons. In 1852 he helped to found the École de musique réligieuse. He bore the title of "Honorary Kapellmeister to the King of Sardinia."

36. The baritone Salvatore Conte Marchesi* de Castrone was on a concert tour to Dresden, Hamburg, and Frankfurt-am-Main, and was to assist at two Court Concerts in May.

37. This is actually Generalmajor Adolph Reichsfreiherr von Lauer-Münchhofen (1796–1874), a musical dilettante who wrote theatrical works, songs, chamber works, and piano works. His visit to Meyerbeer was in connection with his *Requiem* dedicated to Prince Waldemar of Prussia. It was to have its première in the concert hall of the Schauspielhaus, and be performed by members of the Stern'sche Verein.

38. Actually Katharina Gisela Armgard von Arnim (1821–80), daughter of Bettina von Arnim. She married the diplomat Albert Graf Flemming in 1860.

39. Dorn, *Der Schöffe von Paris, komische Oper* in two acts (Wilhelm August Wohlbrück; Riga, Stadttheater, 27 September 1838). The work was not successful in Berlin, and had only four performances.

40. Meyerbeer never agreed to the king's request to set the choruses, something that Verdi fully understood: "I believe that Meyerbeer did exactly right, for in Aeschylus one is never sure whether characters are men or gods. The only true character in Aeschylus is Clytemnestra . . ." (*Conversations with Verdi*, ed. Marcello Conati [London: Victor Gollancz, 1984], p. 344).

41. Meyerbeer's letter to Liszt (Berlin, 8 February 1852) is cited in Becker, *Giacomo Meyerbeer: A Life in Letters*, pp. 139–40.

42. Franz Christian Otto was a pianist and composer; some of his piano works were published by Bote & Bock.

43. Johann Peter Spehr founded the music publishing firm of Spehr in Brunswick (1791). The business was sold to C. Weinholtz in 1860.

44. Friedrich Ferdinand Freiherr von Beust (1809–86) was a Saxon diplomat, and from 1849 a minister in the Saxon ministry of culture. He was later the ambassador to Austria (1866–71).

45. *Parian* (also known as "Paris porcelain" or "statue porcelain") was a type of porcelain invented and manufactured in England and used exclusively for figurines. It was unglazed and had a translucent, waxy gloss.

46. Queen Victoria and Prince Albert were devoted admirers of Meyerbeer's music, and her gift was acknowledgment of this and the extraordinary triumph of Meyerbeer's operas in the British capital. During 1851, the year of the Great Exhibition, visitors had flocked to London from all over the British Isles and abroad. The season at the Royal Italian Opera that had begun on 3 April continued until the end of August. "As in the preceding two years, the operas of Meyerbeer dominated the repertory; there were performances of *Les Huguenots* with Grisi and Mario, *Le Prophète* with Viardot and Mario, and *Robert le Diable* with Grisi and Tamberlik" (E. Forbes, *Mario and Grisi* [London: Victor Gollanz, 1985], p. 115).

47. Fr. "subjects," i.e., themes or topics.

48. The Austrian Anton Stullmüller (1805–71) was a noted dancer who spent his professional life as a soloist at the Berlin Court Opera (1833–52).

49. The architect and painter Hofbaurat Albert Dietrich Schadow (1797–1869) had worked since 1843 on the completion of the Berlin Palace. He became a member of the Berlin Academy of Arts in 1849.

50. Emanuel Gotthard Graf Schaffgotsch (1802–78) was a royal Prussian chamberlain and master of ceremonies, Princess Karl's chamberlain, and *Schlosshauptmann* of Breslau.

51. Tgb. *Hoffest.*

52. Louis Ferdinand*, prince of Prussia, *Ottetto* for piano, two violas, contrabass, clarinet, and two horns, op. 12.

53. Mendelssohn, Octet in E-flat, op. 20 (1825; rev. 1832).

54. The publisher Franz Schlodtmann edited the *Deutsches Stammbuch: Autographisches Album der Gegenwart*, 10 vols. (Bremen: Schlodtmann u.a. 1852). Meyerbeer provided a piano piece for the collection (dated Berlin, 20 June 1852), which appeared in vol.6. The manuscript is held in the library of the Benedictine abbey of Ettal (*BT*, 5:958).

55. The Kroll'sche Etablissement burned down on 1 February 1851, and was reopened on 24 February 1852 with a *bal masqué et paré*.

56. Possibly Haydn, Symphony no. 99 in E-flat Major (1793), but more likely Symphony no. 103 in E-flat Major *(The Drumroll)* (1795).

57. The Surrey Theatre was on Blackfriars Road and had been used as a playhouse since 1809.

58. Tgb. *Supplitz.*

59. *Le tre nozze, opera buffa* by Giulio Eugenio Abramo Alary (Antonio Berettoni; Paris, Théâtre Italien, 29 March 1851). The variations sung by Sontag were "Già della mente involasi." She and Lablache had also made a polka duet from this work famous.

60. Actually *Shakespeare, oder Gaukeleien der Liebe, Lustspiel* in three acts by Eduard Boas (Hamburg, Stadttheater, 24 February 1848; this was the first Dresden performance) [Richel 21].

61. I.e., Shakespeare's *As You Like It*, comedy in five acts (1599).

62. This was Karl Heinrich Alban Graf von Schönburg (1804–64).

63. Ferdinand Carl Hubert Graf von Galen (1803–81) had been Prussian ambassador at the Saxon court since 17 January 1850.

64. Actually Jean-Théophile-Anne, marquis de Ferrière-le Vayer (1812–64), who entered the French diplomatic service in 1836. After postings in Madrid, Brussels, Peking, Lisbon, St. Petersburg, and Hanover, he was appointed ambassador in Dresden.

65. Mendelssohn, no. 2 ("Ave Maria") from *Three Sacred Pieces* for tenor, chorus, and organ, op. 23 (1830).

66. Meyerbeer wrote to Lieutenant von Frankenberg between 29 April and 20 May 1851, asking for a reference concerning Demoiselle Glasow, who was seeking domestic employment in the Meyerbeer household.

67. Kammergerichtsrat Theodor Goldtammer (1801–72) studied law in Heidelberg and Berlin, and practiced as a lawyer in Breslau and Frankfurt-an-der-Oder before joining the ministry of justice in Berlin (1839). Apart from his writing on criminal law, he was the author of many poems (*Preussenlieder*, 1850), novellas, and plays.

68. Fioravanti, *I Virtuosi ambulanti, dramma giocoso* in two acts (Giuseppe Luigi Balocchi [Balloco], from Picard's *Les Comédiens ambulans* [1798]; Paris, Théâtre Italien, 26 September 1807). This was Fioravanti's second greatest success, and the first important Italian opera to be written expressly for the Théâtre Italien. It enjoyed a European currency until the 1830s, and was last revived in Berlin (26 February 1852).

69. Bernhard Joseph Klein, *Pater Noster* for two choruses, op. 18 (1827).

70. Mendelssohn, *Der 43. Psalm* ("Richte mich Gott") for double chorus and solo, op. 78, no. 2 (1843).

71. Spohr, Nonet in F Major for violin, viola, violoncello, contrabass, flute, oboe, clarinet, bassoon, and horn, op. 31 (1813).

72. Mozart, Horn Quintet in E-flat Major, K. 407 (1782).

73. Ferdinand Wilkens was the owner of the Hotel de Russie in Stettin. His daughter Karoline was a pianist who gave a series of public concerts in Stettin.

74. Spohr, *Des Heilands letzte Stunden*, oratorio (words Friedrich Rochlitz; Cassel, Martins-Kirche, Good Friday 1835); known in English as *Calvary* at the Norwich Festival, 1839.

75. Gottlieb Krüger (1825–95) was a harpist from Stuttgart.

76. Geheimrat Tuisko Hermann Adolph Köhne von Wranke-Deminski (1809–90) occupied the official positions of *Landschaftsdirektor* and *Provinzial-Feuersozietätsdirektor* in Berlin (see *BT*, 5:862).

77. Abbate Giovanni Carlo Maria Clari (1677–1754). The work referred to is perhaps the *Duetti e terzetti da camere*, op. 1 (Bologna, 1820).

78. Marie Wilhelmine Friederike Grand Duchess of Mecklenburg-Strelitz, born a princess of Hesse-Cassel (1796–1880), and her daughter Caroline Charlotte Mariane (1821–76).

79. The Berlin Circus was on Friedrichstrasse 141a. After closure for restoration, it opened again on 9 November 1851 with Cirque National de Paris, directed by Dejean, which specialized in virtuoso dressage by such riders as Baucher, Franconi, and Mme. Newsome.

80. Frank was the nephew of Louis Brandus, the son of Jacob and Johanna Frank.

81. Frau Graefe was the wife of Medizinalrat Eduard Adolph Graefe (1794–1859), a highly regarded surgeon who had settled in Berlin in 1825.

82. No biographical details are known of Mr. Style, Meyerbeer's English teacher at this time.

83. Tgb. *Gedankenbuch.*

84. Fr. "by friendly consensus."

85. Mendelssohn, *Ruy Blas*, overture to Victor Hugo's play, op. 95 (1839).

86. Klein, *Gesang der Geister über den Wassern* (words J. W. von Goethe), op. 42 (post.)

87. Vincent Maschek, a *Revisoratsbeampter* in Russberg, had won the place of teacher at the Musikschule des Musikvereins in Temesvár (1846). The music school was closed after the revolution of 1848–49, and was able to reopen for four years only in 1858. The region of Banat was long a center of German culture, and opera (especially Mozart) was given in the early nineteenth century (1831–33) by Theodore Müller's company under Ion Wachmann (1807–63).

88. The famous dramatic soprano Wilhelmine Schröder-Devrient had retired from the stage in Dresden (1847) at the age of forty-three. From 1850 she lived privately with her third husband, Herr von Bock.

89. This was Meyerbeer's nephew, the lawyer Felix Eberty (1812–84).

90. The tenor Fritz Arnurius (1828–75) worked at the Hoftheater in Schwerin.

91. Auguste Dupont (1827–90) was the professor of piano at the Brussels Conservatoire from 1850. During his 1852 visit to Berlin he gave concerts in the Schauspielhaus and in the Singakademie. Meyerbeer recommended him to Bote & Bock, who published his *Pluie de Mai, Étude de Trilles pour piano*, op. 2.

92. This was Marie Taglioni (1833–91), the daughter of Paul Taglioni and niece of her famous namesake. She made her début at Her Majesty's Theatre in London (1847),

and was then soloist at the Berlin Court Opera (1848–66) before marrying into the aristocratic house of Windischgrätz.

93. Carl Leo (d. 1855) was director and chief regisseur at the Stadttheater in Rostock.

94. Johanna Biehrlich was a young violinist from Jena. She also appeared at the Kroll'sche Lokale on 16 April 1852 with great success.

95. Spohr, *Jessonda*, no. 18 *Duett* ("Schönes Mädchen, wirst mich hassen").

96. This was Sir Michael White (1791–1868), who was promoted to colonel in 1846.

97. Von Hagen was the maiden name of the actress Charlotte von Oven.

98. There is no record of such a work; it is probably identical with *Die Sündfluth*, oratorio by Dam (words Ludwig Rellstab; Berlin, Garnisonkirche, 6 June 1849) (*BT*, 5:964).

99. The soprano Louise Liebhardt (1824–99) made her début at the Kärntnertor-Theater in Vienna (1845), where she specialized in coloratura roles, both comic and serious, until 1864, when she took up an equally successful appointment in London. During her guest appearance in Berlin, she sang roles by Donizetti, Lortzing, and Meyerbeer.

100. David, *La Perle du Brésil*, opera in three acts (J. J. Gabriel & S. Saint-Étienne; Paris, Théâtre Lyrique, 22 November 1851). This was David's first opera, and it enjoyed a modest career in Paris and Brussels, and was revived in Paris in 1883. It is remembered particularly for the famous coloratura aria "Charmant oiseau."

101. *L'Étoile du nord*, no. 18 *Duo de Prascovia et de Georges* ("Fusillé! Fusillé!")

102. Georg Thomas had succeeded Lortzing as music director of the Friedrich-Wilhelmstädtisches-Theater (1851). In 1854 he took up the same position in Drury Lane in London, and at the German Opera in Amsterdam.

103. Marie Therese Gräfin Pinto di Barri (née Simonis) (1828–1910) married Friedrich, son of the Prussian major Karl Friedrich Graf Pinto di Berri, whose family originated in Potsdam (*BT*, 5:953–54).

104. Louis Alexander Balthasar Schindelmeisser (1811–64) was trained as a conductor and composer in Leipzig and Berlin. He was kapellmeister in Berlin, Budapest, Frankfurt-am-Main, and Hamburg, went to Wiesbaden in 1851, and directed the first performance of *Le Prophète*. He moved on to Darmstadt in 1853.

105. Tsarina Alexandra Feodorovna, born Charlotte, princess of Prussia (1798–1860). She became the wife of Tsar Nicholas I of Russia from 1817 and was the favorite sister of King Friedrich Wilhelm IV.

106. The Italian bass Napoleone Rossi (1810–70) sang in Florence, Madrid, Milan (La Scala), and Paris (Théâtre Italien) (1833–42), where he was hailed as the successor to Lablache. He later pursued his career in London and St. Petersburg with great success, and was a favorite of the tsar.

107. Schönfelder was a music teacher from what is now Bojanowo, near Costyn in Posen.

108. The violinist Georg Hellmesberger (1830–52) was trained by his father Georg, a famous violinist and conductor at the Vienna Hofoper. From 1850 he was concert master at the Hofkapelle in Hanover.

109. The tenor Rademacher was working at the Stadttheater in Magdeburg at this time. Later he moved to Brünn, and then to Stockholm (1855).

110. Kammerherr Conrad Adolf Freiherr von Malsen (1792–1867) had been the Bavarian ambassador to Prussia since 1849.

111. The bass Eduard Bost (1813–79) (orig. Sattler) began his singing career in traveling companies before being engaged in Riga (1850) and then in Berlin (1851), where he remained for the rest of his life.

112. Dr. Bacher's devotion to music and his extraordinary abilities in organization and

restructuring were perceived by Berlioz, who commented on the task he had performed in revitalizing the Vienna Conservatoire: "A few years ago it was apparently in such decay that without the ingenuity and Herculean exertions of Dr. Bacher, who dedicated himself to saving it and putting it on its feet again, it would by now be defunct. Dr. Bacher is not a musician at all but one of those friends of music, of whom there are two or three comparable in Europe, who out of pure love of art will tackle and sometimes bring off the most formidable tasks, and who by the excellence of their judgment and taste acquire a real authority over men's minds, often achieving by their own efforts what sovereigns ought to do but don't. Energetic, persistent, determined, and generous beyond description, Dr. Bacher is music's staunchest champion in Vienna and the good angel of musicians" ("Travels in Germany II: Austria, Bohemia, Hungary," Second Letter (Vienna), from *The Memoirs of Hector Berlioz,* trans. David Cairns. [London: Panther Arts, 1970], p. 467).

113.   Rossini, *L'Italiana in Algeri,* no. 21 Trio ("Papataci! che mai sento"). Note that in the critical edition by Azio Corghi this is listed as no. 14 (Milan: Ricordi, 1982).

114.   Mozart, *Don Giovanni,* no. 7 Duet ("Là ci darem la mano").

115.   Cimarosa, *Il Matrimonio segreto,* no. 11 Duet ("Se fiato in corpo avete").

116.   Donizetti, *Lucia di Lammermoor,* no. 8 Sextet ("Chi mi frena in tal momento?").

117.   The Hungarian musician Josef Karl Engel (1821–88) was trained in Pest and worked as a violinist in the Theater an der Wien and the Carltheater before becoming the conductor of the concert orchestra at the Kroll'sche Etablissement (1851) and then the artistic director there (1852). He had great success, and married Auguste Kroll, the daughter of the founder of the Etablissement (7 June 1853). He could not compete with the Friedrich-Wilhelmstädtisches-Theater, and following the bankruptcy of Kroll, the Etablissement was forced to close on 1 April 1855.

118.   Roger had recommended Ruggieri to Meyerbeer in relation to the planned court festivities for the imminent visit of the empress of Russia. Henze-Döhring proposes two possible candidates: either Claude Fortuné Ruggieri, the famous fireworks specialist from Paris, author of *Éléments de Pyrotechnie* (Paris, 1802; second ed. 1810); or E. F. D. Ruggieri, an authority on court ceremonial and etiquette, eventual author of *Catalogue des livres rares et precieux composant la bibliothèque de E. F. D. Ruggieri, sacre de rois et des empereurs, entrées triomphales, marriages, tournois joutes, carrousels, fêtes populaires, et feux d'artice* (Paris: Labitte, 1873). See *BT,* 5:967.

119.   For Lumley's own account of the controversy with Johanna Wagner, see his *Reminiscences of the Opera* (London: Hurst & Blackett, 1864), pp. 330–38.

120.   Heinrich Julius Hopfe (b.1817) studied philosophy, and then music with Rungenhagen (1846), and became a music teacher and composer in Berlin. His works were performed at the Liebig'sche Concerts, and Meyerbeer heard his *Ouvertüre zu Shakespeares "Die lustigen Weiber von Windsor,"* the overture to his opera *Dolch und Harfe,* and his seventh (A minor) and eighth (G major) symphonies.

121.   Halévy, *Le Juif errant, grand opéra* in five acts (Scribe & Saint-Georges, based on the novel by Eugène Sue [1844–45]; Paris, Opéra, 23 April 1852). Even though this is one of the composer's most ambitious, powerful, and moving works, it held the stage for only two seasons, and was performed only forty-nine times. "On y retrouve à chaque page sa manière large et expressive, et des traces de sa profonde sensibilité" [one finds his broad and expressive style on every page, as well as traces of his profound sensibility] (Clément & Larousse, 1:625).

122.   The cello virtuoso Albrecht Eichhorn (1829–53) was actually from Coburg, where he was honored as a *herzoglicher Kammermusiker* before his early death.

123. Paul Taglioni was both scenarist and choreographer of *Satanella, phantastisches Ballet* in three acts. The ballet was based on Cazotte's *Le Diable amoureux*, and had appeared in an earlier form at Her Majesty's Theatre in London with Carlotta Grisi dancing (1850). The Berlin version supplemented Pugni's original score with new music by Peter Ludwig Hertel.

124. No biographical details are available for the American pianist, Miss Hills.

125. Arrests and deportations in the thousands had followed on Louis Napoleon's coup d'état of 2 December 1851. David* had undertaken extended trips to London and northern Germany, where he had attracted much attention with his busts of Goethe and, in Berlin, of Christian Rauch, Ludwig Tieck, and Alexander von Humboldt.

126. This was actually the secretary at the American legation, Theodore S. Fay.

127. Dalayrac, *Deux mots, ou Une Nuit dans la fôret*, opéra comique (Benoit-Joseph Marsollier des Vivetières; Paris Opéra Comique, 9 June 1806). This was Dalayrac's last big success, given in Paris until 1828, and revived there in 1862. It was performed in French, German, Russian, Swedish, Danish, Hungarian, Dutch, and English.

128. Meyerbeer first saw *Die Schwestern von Prag* on 20 June 1813. Wenzel Müller's once popular *komisches Singspiel* (Vienna, Theater in der Leopoldstadt, 11 March 1794) was by now only rarely performed.

129. F. Lawerenz played the *Waldhorn* in the orchestra of the Königstädter Theater (1824) before becoming a member of the Royal Orchestra.

130. Constantine Prince Caradja had been the Ottoman ambassador in Berlin since 12 January 1851.

131. Hermann Schmidt, *Der Doppelflucht, komische Oper mit Tanz* in three acts (freely adapted from the English; Berlin, Friedrich-Wilhelmstädtisches-Theater, 4 May 1852). Hermann Schmidt (1810–45) had lived and worked in Berlin.

132. The soprano Mathilde Graumann (1821–1913) married the baritone Count Marchesi de Castrone on 19 April 1852. The couple undertook many tours throughout Europe, frequently appearing together.

133. This is probably a reference to the wife of the Belgian painter Jakob Albert Michael Jacobs (1812–79) from Antwerp. In 1852 the Royal Museum in Berlin acquired his painting *Sonnenaufgang im Archipel*.

134. The actor Hermann Hendrichs (1809–71) worked in Frankfurt-am-Main, Hanover, and Hamburg prior to being engaged by the Berlin Court Theater (1844–68), where his chief roles were Faust, Egmont, Götz, Tell, and the Marquis of Posa.

135. Franz Aloys Theodor Commer (1813–87) was an organist in Cologne before studying with Rungenhagen and Marx in Berlin (1832). He was commissioned to arrange the library of the Royal Institute for Church Music, pursued historical researches, and edited various collections of old music (among them the *Collectio operum musicorum Batavorum saeculi XVI*, 12 vols, n.d.). He was made royal *Musikdirektor* (1844), a member of the Berlin Academy of Arts (1845), and repetiteur at the Theater School (1850). He founded (with Robert Eitner) the Gesellschaft für Musikforschung (1868).

136. Tgb. *Adlerorden*.

137. Otto Kraushaar (1812–66), a writer on music from Cassel, had studied with Moritz Hauptmann, whose ideas of the opposition of the major and minor modes he developed into a treatise entitled *Die accordliche Gegensätze und die Begründung der Scala* (1852), which appeared prior to Hauptmann's *Natur der Harmonik*.

138. This was the Berlin composer Julius Tanwitz. Meyerbeer was not able to examine his oratorio because of the pressures of time.

139. The German mezzo-soprano Antonia Viala-Mittermayr (1808–1900) studied with Fodor-Mainvilles in Paris and worked in Italy (Milan, Turin, Venice), then in Munich and Meiningen. During her guest appearances in Berlin she sang Fidès, as she had done in the first Munich performance of *Le Prophète* in 1850.

140. Mozart, *Der Schauspieldirektor, Komödie mit Musik* in one act (Johann Gottlieb Stephanie the younger; Vienna, Schönbrunn Orangerie, 7 February 1786). This was written for the small theater in the grounds of the imperial summer palace, and pokes gentle fun at the work of operatic professionals. Meyerbeer saw the arrangement by Louis Schneider (Berlin, 1845).

141. The *basso buffo* Samuel Friedrich Hassel (1798–1876) from Frankfurt scored great success in his guest appearance at the Friedrich-Wilhelmstädtisches-Theater.

142. After his engagement in Berlin, the tenor Benno Hirsch worked in Bremen and Riga (1857–58).

143. Adolph Gustav Fischer had trained at the Royal Berlin Institute for Church Music with Bach and Rungenhagen before becoming organist at the Johanniskirche in Moabit (1849), cantor and organist at the big Berlin Orphange (1851), and organist at the Hauptkirche in Frankfurt-an-der-Oder (1853).

144. This was the revised plan for *L'Africaine*. Meyerbeer had received the third draft from Scribe on 18 January 1851.

145. The singer Agnes Bunke Liebe (d. 1868) was a native of Breslau, where she made her début. She was later a member of the Dresden Court Opera (1850–58).

146. Nörner was an official of the Prussian railways.

147. The tenor Friedrich Young (1822–84) had studied with Kunt in Vienna, then worked in Pest and Frankfurt-an-der-Oder, before joining the company in Schwerin (1851–52). He returned to the National Theater in Pest, where he sang John of Leyden, in spite of Meyerbeer's doubts about the strength of his voice. From 1854 he worked at the Court Opera in Munich.

148. In 1842 Scribe had married the widowed Mme. Biollay. "Madame Scribe was known for her kindness and good works. She had two sons from her former marriage. . . . Scribe was a loving father, and the boys returned the sentiment" (Hélène Koon and Richard Switzer, *Eugène Scribe* [Boston: Twayne Publishers, 1980], p. 28). The Prussian atmosphere did not please Scribe: it seemed to him that in Paris the Opéra was built for the public, whereas in Berlin everything was centered on the court. He particularly resented that his working sessions with Meyerbeer were curtailed by the numerous obligations imposed on the composer by his official position. In fact, he disapproved of Meyerbeer's seeming lack of independence, remarking that his friend, so adulated in Paris, was hardly more than a "fort petit garçon à Berlin [et] le plus esclave des hommes de génie" [glorified servant in Berlin, and more a slave than a man of genius]. Auber, in a similar situation in France, had nonetheless "tenait bien autrement sa dignité d'homme de talent" [very differently, maintained his dignity as a man of talent] (see Jean-Claude Yon, *Eugène Scribe, la fortune et la liberté* [Saint-Genough: Nizet, 2000], pp. 276–77).

149. Wagner, *Lohengrin, romantische Oper* in three acts (text by the composer; Weimar, 28 August 1850). This, the apogee of German romantic opera, was written in 1846–48, and originally intended for Dresden, but rejected there. It was eventually produced in Weimar by Liszt, while Wagner was still a political refugee in Switzerland. The next productions were at Königsberg and Wiesbaden (1853), after which it spread throughout Germany and the world. It reached Vienna on 19 August 1858 (688 performances by 1936) and Berlin on 23 January 1859 (745 performances by 1935). It was the first of Wagner's operas to be

given in Italy (Bologna, 1 November 1871, conducted by Mariani). Meyerbeer appears to have admired the work deeply, and there are sixteen references to the score and various performances in his diaries.

150. Maria Magdalena Franziska Karoline von Guaita (née Brentano) (1788–61) was a relative of Bettina von Arnim, and the widow of the former mayor of Frankfurt-am-Main who died in 1851.

151. Karl Friedrich*, grand duke of Saxe-Weimar-Eisenach (1783–1853).

152. The baritone August Kindermann (1817–91) made his début at the Court Opera in Berlin (1837) and worked briefly in Leipzig before moving to the Court Opera in Munich (1846), where he pursued a highly successful career, winning especial renown as a Wagner singer. He retired in 1887.

153. This was Friedrich Wilhelm Georg, prince of Prussia (1826–1902), a son of Prince Friedrich Wilhelm Ludwig, the king's cousin. He pursued a military career, becoming a general of cavalry in 1866. He was also musically gifted, and wrote a series of dramatic poems under the pseudonym G. Conrad.

154. Johann Karl Jakob Gerst (1792–1854) was a scene painter at the Berlin Court Opera (1818–51). He was involved in creating the Berlin décor for several of Meyerbeer's operas: *Die Hugenotten* (1842, with Karl Gropius), *Ein Feldlager in Schlesien* (1844, with Gropius), and *Der Prophet* (with Gropius and Bruno Köhler).

155. Fr. "model for the scene-painter."

156. Gounod married Anna Zimmermann, the daughter of the French pianist Pierre Zimmermann, at the end of April 1852.

157. Actually Rosa Csillag; cf. 19 February 1851.

158. See 30 January 1847 and 28 July 1850.

159. Edmund Rabe (1815–1902) was an artist specializing in military subjects and lithographs, and a member of the Berlin Academy of the Arts since 1843.

160. Carl Albert Sachse (b. 1823) was a theatrical agent working in Hamburg. He sought to interest Meyerbeer in his publication and the composer duly took out a subscription.

161. In his appendix C, "Sources Consulted by Meyerbeer," J. H. Roberts, in *The Genesis of Meyerbeer's "L'Africaine"* (diss., University of California at Berkeley, 1977), pp. 189–93, provides a bibliography of the works consulted by Meyerbeer in his research of the background and *couleur* of his last opera, and particularly lists the books mentioned by the composer in his *Taschenkalender* for the second quarter of 1852. These include: Eugène Burnouf, *L'Inde française, ou Collection de dessins litographiés représentant les divinités, temples, costumes, physionomies, meubles, armes, et ustensiles, des peuples hindous qui habitent les possessions françaises de l'Inde et en général la côte de Coromandel et le Malabar,* 2 vols. (Paris: Charbrelie, 1827–35); F. Baltazard Solvyns, *Les Hindoûs,* 4 vols. (Paris: chez l'auteur, 1808–12); Johann Lucas Niecamp, *Kurtzgefasste Missions-Geschichte oder Historischer Auszug der evangelischen Missions-Berichte aus Ost-Indien; von dem Jahr 1705 bis zu Ende des Jahres 1736* (Halle: im Verlegung des Waysen-hauses, 1740); Lieut. Col. Mark Wilks, *Historical Sketches of the South of India, in an Attempt to Trace the History of Mysoor from the Origin of the Hindoo Government of That State to the Extinction of the Mohammedan Dynasty in 1779,* 3 vols. (London: Hurst, Rees & Orme, 1810–17); and Francis Buchanan, M.D., *A Journey from Madras through the Countries of Mysore, Canara, and Malabar,* 3 vols. (London: Cadell & Davies, 1807).

162. John Prince Caradja was the son of the Ottoman ambassador and also first secretary at the embassy. He was an amateur composer, and one of his marches was included by Bock in the collection *Königliche preussisiche Armee-Marsche* (vol. 2, no. 149). Meyerbeer

sent him an autograph consisting of the opening bars of the galop from *Le Prophète* which was auctioned at Christie's in 1993 (*BT*, 5:976).

163. Kreisjustizrat Dr. Strass was the legal adviser to the Friedrich-Wilhelmstädtisches-Theater.

164. Glinka himself left an account of the meeting: "The morning we checked into the Römischen Hotel, Meyerbeer came to see me and, among other things, said: 'Comment se fait-il, M. Glinka, que nous vous connaissons tout de réputation, mais nous ne connaissons pas vos œuvres?' [How is it, M. Glinka, that we know you only by reputation and not through your works?].

" 'Cela est très naturel,' I told him. 'Je n'ai pas *l'habitude de colporter* mes productions' [Oh, that is quite natural. You see, I am not in the habit of *peddling* my compositions].

"Incidentally, Meyerbeer was extremely affable and easy to get along with.

"S. Dehn showed me all the sights and I also spent many hours in the museum and at the zoological gardens. Dehn provided further diversions for me in the form of quartets and Moselle wine" (Glinka, *Memoirs* [Norman: University of Oklahoma Press, 1963], pp. 230–31).

165. Joseph Maria Anton, Graf von Brassier de Saint-Simon (1798–1872), had been Prussian ambassador in Stockholm since 1850.

166. This was actually Emma Normani, who sang Fidès in the first performance of *Le Prophète* in Stockholm on 8 November 1852.

167. The Berlin stockbroker Stadtrat F. W. Behrends was a dilettante composer who privately published some duets for soprano and alto with piano accompaniment.

168. The Meiningen theologian Friedrich Mosengeil (1773–1839) provided a linking text for Beethoven's incidental music (op. 84): *Beethovens Zwischenacte zu Göthe's Egmont; mit declamatorischer Begleitung von Friedrich Mosengeil* (Leipzig: Breitkopf & Härtel, 1811–12).

169. See 15 October 1850.

170. A letter from Rellstab of 11 June 1852 (*BT*, 5:615–16) provides seven variants for a passage intended as a refrain in the finale of *L'Étoile du Nord*. Meyerbeer chose the seventh of these ("Leb ich? — Bin ich? — Träum ich? — Wach ich?"), and once it had been translated into French, set it to music (19–22 August 1852). The passage was not used in the final form of the finale. See no. 19 *Final*, the G-major refrain "Ah! est-ce l'ombre fidèle . . . ai-je rêvé?"

171. Grisar, *Le Carillonneur de Bruges*, *opéra comique* in three acts (Saint-Georges; Paris, Opéra Comique, 20 February 1852). Given in Belgium, and revived in Antwerp (1897).

172. The French contralto Palmyre Wertheimber (1832–1917) was trained in the Conservatoire and made her début at the Opéra Comique in 1852, before being contracted by the Opéra, where she sang Fidès (1854). Later she worked at the Théâtre Lyrique, and again at the Opéra Comique (1860).

173. Massé, *Galathée*, *opéra comique* in two acts (J. Barbier & M. Carré; Paris, Opéra Comique, 14 April 1852). This was one of Massé's most successful works, performed in Paris throughout the nineteenth century and revived there in 1903 and 1915. It was also given in Danish, Spanish, German, Czech, Dutch, and English (Philadelphia and New York in 1886).

174. Méhul, *L'Irato, ou L'Emporté*, *comédie-parade* in one act (B. J. Marsollier des Vivetières; Paris, Opéra Comique, 17 February 1801). This work was very successful in

Paris, given there until 1833, and revived in 1852, 1868, 1899, and 1917. Its career in Europe was otherwise limited to the 1810s.

175. The French baritone Augustin-Alphonse-Edmond Meillet (1828–71) studied at the Paris Conservatoire, and made his début at the Opéra (1850). After appearing briefly at the Opéra Comique, he was contracted to the Théâtre Lyrique (1854), and later sang in the provinces (1861) and in Brussels (1863).

176. Deldevez and Tolbeque, *Vert-Vert, ballet-pantomime* in three acts (scenario A. de Leuven, choreography J. Mazilier & A. Saint-Léon; Paris, Opéra, 24 November 1851). This work was only modestly successful, and had only seventeen performances.

177. See 29 January 1831.

178. Ponsard, *Ulysse, tragédie* in three acts with prologue and epilogue (Paris, Théâtre Français, 18 June 1852) [Wicks 22162].

179. Boieldieu, *Les Voitures versées, ou Le Séducteur en voyage, opéra comique* in two acts (Vedel and Boieldieu, after E. Mercier-Dupaty, after a *vaudeville* [1806]; St. Petersburg, 26 April 1808). This was the most successful work of Boieldieu's Russian period, popular in Paris until 1836 and performed all over Europe. It was revived in Paris (1852, 1868, 1932) and on German stages (Berlin and Breslau, 1913, and Graz, 1918).

180. Actually it was Ponsard's *comédie L'Honneur et l'argent,* which would have its première at the Théâtre de l'Odéon on 11 March 1853. It was a great success in Paris and stayed in the repertoire of the Comédie Française until 1876.

181. The French critic and writer Louis-Marie-Roche Reybaud (1799–1879) specialized in cultural and political commentary. He was a member of the Académie des Sciences Morales et Politiques (1850). He also wrote a popular novel, *Jérôme Paturot à la recherche d'une position sociale* (Paris, 1843).

182. Adrianus Catharinus Gerardus Vermeulen (1798–1872) was a language teacher (1822) and then rector of the Gymnasium in Rotterdam, and secretary general of the Maatschappij tot Bevordering der Toonkunst, which he had cofounded. He was renowned internationally, and the recipient of many honors (member of the Accademia Santa Cecilia in Rome [1844], of the Prussian Academy of Arts [1855]).

183. This was actually Bertha Röder-Romani.

184. Dr. Felix Joël (1780–1856), a lawyer and the companion of Baron Rothschild (1820–50). He enjoyed financial independence, and was free to pursue his lifelong passion for theatrical affairs, in which he was an influential advisor.

185. The poet Adriaan van der Hoop (1827–62) was the vice-president of the Maatschappij tot Bevordering der Toonkunst.

186. Alexandre Dumas *(fils), La Dame aux camélias.* This celebrated piece had first appeared as a novel (1848); the five-act play had only recently been premièred in Paris (Théâtre du Vaudeville, 2 February 1852) [Wicks 16111]. Dumas's treatment of the familiar story of the love of the son of a respectable family for a courtesan has attained the status of a modern myth, especially after Verdi's operatic adaptation of it in *La Traviata* (1853).

187. Henry Brinley Richards* published an account of his interview with Meyerbeer in the *Musical World* 30, no. 33 (14 August 1852): 521: "My principal object in visiting Spa was to pay a visit to Meyerbeer, who is residing at the *Hôtel des Pays Bas.* He is, I regret to say, still suffering from ill-health. I was greatly pleased with his quiet, gentlemanly manner, and with his conversation. Fearful of fatiguing him by too long an interview, I made two attempts to rise, but he most kindly insisted on my remaining. We conversed upon all subjects. Of our friends in London he made many inquiries, and he was

particularly desirous of information as to the state of music, *chez nous*. He alluded in a very complimentary manner to Sterndale Bennet and Macfarren; and desired me to convey his remembrances to D—— and to G——. He added that he had not visited London in eighteen years, and that the last attempt to do so, a few years since, had been abandoned when he had reached Boulogne, in consequence of illness. He was of course rather desirous to know the result of Spohr's *Faust*, and of Grisi's success in the *Prophète*. Before my departure for Aix, he gave me a very cordial invitation to visit him at Berlin. Following the maxim of 'doing as the Romans do,' I hired a couple of horses and a guide, and rode up to the hills; for, as you know already, the country around Spa is well worthy a pilgrimage. The guide who accompanied me *à cheval*, gave me some interesting information as to Meyerbeer, and his mode of living there. He spoke of him with the utmost respect, and as a man remarkable for his charitable disposition. Every afternoon at six you may see Meyerbeer mounted on a donkey, gently jogging up the hills; and as his hours are known to the poor, they lie in wait for him, and very rarely fail to obtain some donation. *The* great fact at Spa now is, of course, the author of *Le Robert*. With my great admiration of his genius, I felt still the more pleased to hear him so highly spoken of for his virtues in other respects."

188. Christine Baronesse de Willmar (née de Rignée) (1810–68) was the wife of the diplomat General Jean Pierre Christine Baron de Willmar, the Belgian ambassador in Berlin (1840–45).

189. Meyerbeer had already reworked this canon (see 13 September 1849, 3 and 4 December 1849, 2, 7, 9, 17, 22–30 August 1850).

190. Balzac, *Mercadet le faiseur*, prose *comédie* in three acts (Balzac & Dennery; Paris, Théâtre du Gymnase Dramatique, 24 August 1851) [Wicks 19177]. It was actually an abbreviated version by Dennery of Balzac's five-act *Faiseur*. This highly influential play provided a prototype of the realist theater.

191. Fr. "overexcitement," perhaps "feverishness."

192. Thomas-Louis-Joseph Guillaume was the conductor of the resort band at Spa from 1849 until 1875. The arrangements for wind band were by Bernhard Mohr (1852).

193. The soprano Albina Maray (actually Albine Wodniansky Freiin von Wildenfeld) (b. 1832) sang in Vienna and St. Petersburg, and later made guest appearances in London.

194. Lux was a commissioner and lottery receiver in Erfurt. He wrote to Meyerbeer concerning the work of a friend, the composer Johann Ludwig Böhner from Gotha, who wished to dedicate his composition to King Friedrich Wilhelm IV.

195. John Vipon Bridgeman (1819–89) was for more than thirty years the editor of the *Musical World*, as well a librettist (for Balfe's *The Puritan's Daughter* [1861] and *The Armourer of Nantes* [1863]), and a translator (of Wagner's *Oper und Drama* and *Das Judenthum in der Musik*).

196. John Ella* wrote reviews and musical articles for the *Morning Post*, the *Musical World,* and the *Athenaeum*. He had discussed Meyerbeer in "Music in Paris in 1837", published in the *Musical World* (1838), and later in a *Personal Memoir of Meyerbeer* (London, 1868).

197. Jean-Baptiste-Jules de Glimes (b. 1814), a pupil of Fétis in Brussels, was singing teacher at the Brussels Conservatoire (1840), in London (1842), then again in Brussels.

198. The composer Johann Ludwig Böhner (1787–1860), a pupil of Belermann and Fischer in Erfurt, was a music teacher in Jena, and theater kapellmeister in Nuremberg (1811–14), and then Thüringen. He wrote an opera, a symphony, chamber music, and instrumental music.

199. Maray's father was Wodniansky Freiherr von Wildenfeld.

200. The Belgian violinist Jacques Dupuis (1830–70) was a teacher at the Liège Conservatoire (1850), as well as a composer of violin concertos and sonatas.

201. In fact, ten pieces from *Ein Feldlager in Schlesien* were reworked, but not all of them used: no. 6 *(Pandurenchor)*, no. 7 *(Zigeunerrunde)*, no. 9 *(Husarenlied)*, no. 10 *(Grenadierlied)*, no. 11 *(Terzett)*, no. 13 *(Quadrupel-Chor)*, no. 14 *(Kriegslied)*, no. 15 *(Schwur* from the finale to act 2), no. 16 *(Flötentrio)*, no. 19 *(Vision* from the finale to act 3). Later four other numbers were revised for inclusion in *L'Étoile du Nord*: the overture, the entr'acte, and ballet, which became no. 10a *(Entr'acte)*, no. 15 ("Ha, seht den Verräter") which became no. 14a ("O ciel"), and no. 15 (the *Dessauer-Marsch*) which became no. 14c *(La marche sacré et prière* "Dieu protecteur").

202. Henri-Édouard Perrot (1808–73) settled in Brussels and became correspondent for various newspapers *(Journal des débats, Temps, National)*, as well as writing for various local papers. For a short time he was a stenographer in the senate, an was the editor and finally director of the *Indépendance belge*. Under his direction it developed into one of Belgium's most important liberal newspapers. In 1865 he sold his rights of ownership to work in politics.

203. A *monstre* is a scansion or rhythmic model of an already extant musical motive or phrase to guide the librettist in the composition of the new text.

204. No. 7 *Zigeunerrunde* from the *Feldlager* became no. 6 *Scène et Ronde bohémienne de Catherine* in *L'Étoile du Nord*.

205. No. 16 *(Terzett)* in *Feldlager* became part of no. 19 (act 3 finale) in *L'Étoile du Nord*.

206. No. 9 *Husarenlied* became no. 10b *Récitatif et Chanson de la Cavallerie*.

207. No. 10 *Grenadierlied* became no. 10c *Récitatif et Chanson de l'Infanterie*.

208. No. 6 *Pandurenchor* became a Chorus of Cossacks, but was not eventually retained in *L'Étoile du Nord*. See 25 August 1853.

209. No. 19 *Vision* ("Weicht still zurück") became no. 19 *Finale* (the passage beginning "L'aurore succède").

210. No. 11 *Terzett* was not eventually used in *L'Étoile du Nord*.

211. No. 13 *Quadrupel Chor* was not eventually used in the French opera.

212. No. 14 *Kriegslied* became no. 11 *Chœur des conjurés*.

213. No. 15 *Schwur* became no. 13c *Sextour* ("De la part du général").

214. No. 14b *Serment* ("Dieu protecteur viens").

215. No. 9d *Prière et Barcarolle de Catherine* ("Veille sur eux").

216. No. 9b *Couplets de Prascovia* ("En sa demeure").

217. The Viennese journalist and poet Josef L. Blahetka lived with his daughter, the pianist and teacher Maria Leopoldine Blahetka, who had settled in Boulogne-sur-Mer in 1840.

218. Maillart, *La Croix de Marie*, *opérette* in one act (Lockroy & Dennery; Paris, Opéra Comique, 19 July 1852).

219. Reber, *Le Père Gaillard*, *opéra comique* in three acts (T. M. F. Sauvage; Paris, Opéra Comique, 7 September 1852). Although it was not successful, "la partition fut admirée des connoisseurs, en vue desquels M. Reber écrit sa musique" [the score was admired by the connoisseurs on account of the way in which Reber writes his music] (Clément & Larousse, 2:859).

220. Adam, *Si j'étais roi*, *opéra comique* in three acts (A. P. Dennery & J. Brésil; Paris, Théâtre Lyrique, 4 September 1852). This was one of Adam's most successful works, performed 176 times in Paris, given all over the world (New Orleans, 1858; Mexico, 1882),

and revived frequently into the twentieth century (Paris, 1934; Bucharest, 1936; Berlin, 1939); still famous for its overture.

221. The letter was one of condolence on the death of the duke of Wellington on 14 September 1852. Lady Westmorland was related to him through her father, William Wellesley-Pole, earl of Mornington.

222. Grisar, *Les Porcherons, opéra comique* in three acts (T. F. M. Sauvage & J. J. Gabriel; Paris Opéra Comique, 12 January 1850). It was also given in Belgium, and revived in Paris in 1865.

223. Bazin, *Madelon, opéra comique* in two acts (Thomas Sauvage; Paris, Opéra Comique, 26 March 1852).

224. *Le Mari de la dame des chœurs, vaudeville* in two acts (Bayard and F.-A. Duvert; Paris, Théâtre des Variétés, 12 December 1836) [Wicks 10992].

225. The first Italian performance of *Le Prophète* took place in the Teatro della Pergola on 26 December 1852 under the directorship of Luigi Ronzi, who had succeeded the late Alessandro Lanari, the initiator of the project. The role of Fidès was sung by Guilia Sanchioli. In writing to the Marchese Martellini del Falcone, grand chamberlain to the Tuscan court, Meyerbeer had pointed out that Frezzolini's voice lacked the darker timbre required for Fidès (see *BT*, 5:659). He had, moreover, been disappointed by the latter when he heard her on 12 October 1850.

226. Louis-Philippe-Joseph Girod de Vienney de Trémont (1779–1852) was a member of the Council of State (1809), and prefect of Aveyron (1810) and the Côté d'Or (1831).

227. Berlioz, *Grande Messe des Morts* for solo, chorus, and orchestra, op. 5 (Paris, Église Saint-Louis des Invalides, 5 December 1837). The work was performed in the context of a service of remembrance for the fallen General Charles, comte de Damrémont.

228. Achille Lorini had been an agent of the Agenzia Teatrale Europea founded by Alessandro Lanari, the impresario of the Teatro della Pergola in Florence (1848). Lanari's death on 7 October 1852 left Lorini free to work for Corti in Paris. In 1855 Lorini went to Argentina and Uruguay as impresario.

229. Alexandre Corti was the director of the Théâtre Italien from October 1852 until the end of 1853. During the Second Empire, the Italian Opera in Paris enjoyed an upswing in its fortunes, not least because of imperial patronage, especially that of the Empress Eugénie. The highly successful season was to open with Verdi's *Luisa Miller* on 6 December 1852.

230. The pianist Karl Wehle (1825–83), an employee of the banking house of Pillet-Will in Paris, studied with Thalberg in London, Moscheles in Leipzig, and Kullack in Berlin (1848). He appeared in public in Paris in 1854, and began a highly successful public career that took him around the world.

231. Eduard Simon (d. 1897) was the Paris correspondent of the Berlin *Nationalzeitung*.

232. Massé, *La France sauvée* (words by Philoxène Boyer).

233. Fr. "in rehearsal."

234. *Le Prophète* was first produced in Hanover on 11 October 1852.

235. The pianist and composer Jean-Amadée-Le Froid de Méreaux (1803–74) had worked in Rouen since 1836. He enjoyed a national reputation for his *Livres de grandes études* (1855), which was used in the Paris Conservatoire.

236. Massé, *La Chanteuse voilée, opéra comique* in one act (Scribe & De Leuven; Paris, Opéra Comique, 26 November 1850). This was Massé's first success, revived in Paris in 1863, and also given in German and Swedish.

237. Heinrich Lehmann was Leo's nephew by marriage. In 1852, within the space of

ten months, he painted fifty-six murals (containing 108 figures) for the banquet hall of the Hôtel de Ville, depicting the development of culture. They were destroyed during the Commune in 1871.

238. Clapisson, *Les Mystères d'Udolphe*, *opéra comique* in three acts (Scribe & G. Delavigne, after Ann Radcliffe's novel [1794]). It is not listed in Loewenberg, and even Clément & Larousse have not a word of commentary on it. The *Musical World* reported that "[t]he new opera of *Les Mystères d'Adolphe* [*sic*] does not, according to most of the Parisian papers, appear to have been a very great success, for the Opera Comique. The critics are particularly severe on Scribe's libretto" (30, no. 46 [13 November 1852]: 729). Two weeks later, however, it observed that "[t]he *Mystères d'Udolphe* . . . still continue[s] to attract" (30, no. 47 [20 November 1852]: 670).

239. This was the first revival of Rossini's *Moïse* since the première in 1827.

240. The French painter and lithographer Alexandre Laemlein (1813–71) lived in Paris from 1823. After training as a copper engraver, he specialized in portraiture at the Académie des Beaux-Arts (1829), as well as in the depiction of religious and allegorical scenes. He became professor at the École Speciale des Dessin (1855).

241. Adam, *La Poupée de Nuremberg*, *opéra comique* in one act (A. de Leuven & A. de Beauplan. after E. T. A. Hoffmann's story *Der Sandmann* [1817]; Paris, Opéra-National, 21 February 1852). It was performed ninety-eight times in Paris, and became one of Adam's most enduring works, popular in France and regularly revived up to the Second World War (Brno, 1936; Tel Aviv, 1938).

242. Girard, *Les Deux Voleurs*, *opéra comique* (A. de Leuven & L. Brunswick; Paris, Opéra Comique, 26 June 1841). "La musique n'offre rien de bien saillant" [the music has nothing striking to offer], according to Clément & Larousse (1:323).

243. Seghers founded the Société Sainte Cécile (1846) in Brussels, where his concerts of orchestral and choral works became famous.

244. Auguste Romieu (1800–1855) was the director of the Académie des Beaux-Arts.

245. See 7 September 1849.

246. Actually Gustave-Louis-Adolphe-Chaix d'Est-Ange (1800–1876), a famous Parisian lawyer.

247. This was Panofka's *Practical Singing Tutor* (London, 1852).

248. Jules Lecomte (also Leconte) (1814–64) was a writer who had lived in Paris since the 1830s. He founded the newspapers *Le Navigateur* (1834) and *La France maritime* (1834–37), and wrote novels of seafaring (*romans maritimes*). He also worked for several periodicals (correspondent for *L'Indépendance belge* [1846–56], *feuilleton* editor for *Le Siècle* [1855]), as well as being a playwright (e.g., the vaudeville *Les Eaux de Spa* [Paris, 1852]).

249. Dennery and Desnoyer, *La Bergère des Alpes*, prose *drame* in five acts (Paris, Théâtre de la Gaîté, 31 October 1852) [Wicks 14907].

250. See 12 March 1813.

251. *L'Étoile du Nord*, no. 10b *Récitatif* for Gritzenko ("Assez dansé").

252. Paul Henri Vicomte de Daru (1810–77) had a political career (1842–48) before becoming an industrialist and financier.

253. This was probably the dancer Louise Marquet.

254. This was to be Laemlein's big allegorical painting, *La Musique* (1853).

255. Meyerbeer first saw Mlle. Doche on 20 November 1849.

256. The critic Henri-Louis Blanchard was correspondent for the *Revue et gazette musicale* (1836–56).

257. Gozlan, *Les Paniers de la Comtesse, comédie-vaudeville* in one act [Wicks 20003]. Léon Gozlan (1806–66) was a playwright from Marseilles.

258. Following on the plebiscite of November 1852 and a resolution in the Senate concerning the restitution of the Empire, Louis Napoleon was confirmed as emperor. The Opéra consequently took on the title Académie Impériale de Musique.

259. Adam's cantata *La Fête des arts* (words by Joseph Méry) had first been performed at the Opéra Comique on 16 November 1852 with the soloists Ugalde, Lefèbvre, Wertheimber, and Battaille.

260. *Récitatif* for Gritzenko: "Que me commandez-vous maintenant, capitaine?"

261. Josef Alexander Freiherr von Hübner (1811–92) had been the Austrian ambassador in Paris since 14 October 1849.

262. Count Pavel Dmitrievich Kiselev (1788–72) had been the Russian ambassador in Paris since 9 May 1851.

263. Verdi, *Luisa Miller, melodramma tragico* in three acts (Salvatore Cammarano, after Schiller's drama *Kabale und Liebe* [1784]; Naples, San Carlo, 8 December 1849). This work rapidly spread all over the world, and retains a modest place in the repertory. It is interesting for its "domestic" theme, more intimate study of emotions, and the new flowing style that characterizes the last act.

264. This was the first sign of Gouin's mortal illness.

265. The Italian soprano Stefania Favelli worked in Vienna, Milan, Venice, and other cities before marrying Marchese Antonio Visconti Ajmi and retiring into private life in Milan. In Paris she sang the Countess in *Le Nozze di Figaro* at the Théâtre Italien.

266. *Blanche de Provence, ou La Cour des fées*, opera in three acts by Berton, Boieldieu, Cherubini, Kreutzer & Paer (Théaulon & Rancé; Paris, Opéra, 3 May 1821). This occasional work was composed to celebrate the posthumous birth of the son of the duc de Berri, the duc de Bordeaux. Cherubini's magnificent final chorus ("Dors, cher enfant, tendre fleur d'espérance") was the only piece to survive (Clément & Larousse, 1:158).

267. Gounod, *Ave Verum* for tenor solo and chorus.

268. This was Hercules Mac Dounnell (McDonnel?), the secretary of the Committee for the International Exhibition.

269. The French writer Arsènne Housset (known as Houssaye) (1815–96) had been a commissioner (1849) before becoming director of the Théâtre Français (1850–56).

270. Wilhelmine Clauss (b. 1834) had been giving recitals since 1849. During this season in Paris she gave three very successful concerts, playing music by Bach, Scarlatti, Beethoven, and Chopin.

271. Arthur Comte de Fontnilliat was the secretary at the French embassy in Stockholm (1851–54).

272. In order to avoid confrontation with the rival firm of harmonium builders, Debain, Alexandre called his instrument the *orgue-mélodium*.

273. Vieuxtemps, Violin Concerto no. 4 in D Minor, op. 31 (c. 1850).

274. The Dutch aristocrat Alfred Émilien Comte de Nieuwekerke (1811–92) became known as a sculptor in 1834 when he exhibited his equestrian *Guillaume le Taciturne*, and for his subsequent series of statues (*Napoléon* for Lyons). In 1849 he was appointed director general of the National Museum, and in 1852 intendant of the fine arts in the ministry of the imperial household.

275. Auber, *Marco Spada, opéra comique* in three acts (Scribe; Paris, Opéra Comique, 21 December 1852). By Auber's standards, this work achieved only a moderate success, with seventy-eight performances in Paris. It enjoyed a modest European career, and was

last given in Mannheim (1881), but never in London. It was revived as a ballet in 1857, with additional music taken from some of Auber's most popular scores.

276. *Les Huguenots* was first performed in Pest on 6 March 1839 (in German, translated by G. Ott). The Hungarian version was given on 6 November 1852 (translated by L. Nádaskay) (Loewenberg, col. 778).

277. Camille Wallet (née Grévedon) (c. 1825) married the auctioneer Charles Wallet in 1845.

278. The cellist Pierre-Alexandre-François Chevillard (b. 1811) founded a quartet with the violinists Jean-Pierre Maurin and Sabattier and the violist Mas, with the special intention of performing Beethoven's last seven quartets. Initially, after long rehearsals, they gave private performances for invited audiences. They then appeared in the Salle Pleyel, where they were much admired for the perfection of their interpretation and ensemble work. In 1855–56 they undertook an extended tour of many German cities. Chevillard became a professor of the Conservatoire in 1859.

279. Gade, Symphony no. 3 in A Minor, op. 15 (1847).

280. The pianist Ernst Haberbier (1813–69) from Königsberg gave some concerts in Paris, in which he played his arrangement of the overture to Rossini's *Guillaume Tell*.

281. Józef Michel Xawery Franciszek Jan Poniatowsky, prince of Monte Rotondo (1816–3), was a member of the Polish nobility. He studied music in Florence, sang as a tenor, and wrote ten operas (to Italian and French librettos, 1838–82). In 1848 he went to Paris, became the ambassador of the grand duke of Tuscany in Brussels (1849), and was made a senator by Napoleon III. After the fall of the Second Empire, he lived in England.

282. Adam, *Orfa*, ballet in two acts (scenario Henri Trianon, choreography Mazilier; Paris, Opéra, 20 December 1852). This was the fifth most popular of Adam's ballets, performed fifty-one times until 1860. The Nordic theme elicited some of Adam's most imaginative music.

283. Siebenbürgen was the mid-Danubian province of Banat, now divided between Serbia and western Romania.

284. The romance "Sentinelle" was not ultimately retained in the score.

1853

Saturday 1 January. God bless the new year. May it be a year full of blessings for the whole of mankind, but most especially for all my loved ones and for me myself. May God grant us health, prosperity in all our undertakings, peace of soul, and a cheerful spirit, and preserve the standard of living that he has given us in his mercy; may he grant my daughter Blanca a good husband who will make her happy, and whom she in turn will content. May he also grant a brilliant success to my new opera at its first appearance in Paris this year; may it be maintained for many years and spread all over the world. May he preserve my beloved mother for many years, and keep my precious wife, Minna, and my three dear children, Blanca, Caecilie, and Cornelie, well, happy, and cheerful. Amen, may it increase.

Busy all day with New Year visits. Dined with Roger. Letter from Madame Ungher-Sabatier in Florence: *Le Prophète* was given in the Teatro della Pergola for the opening of the carnival season on 26 December, with great success. Madame Sanchioli sang Fidès,[1] Octave John of Leyden.[2] Florence is the first city in Italy to give *Le Prophète*. The theater in Turin opened the carnival season with *Robert*.

Sunday 2 January. Called on Armand Bertin, Deligny,[3] Le Roi, Leduc. Had Gouin to dine with me. Opéra Comique: *Le Père Gaillard* by Reber.

Monday 3 January. Letter from Madame Ungher-Sabatier in Florence. Visit from De Leuven, who wants to write an opera text for me. Gymnase: *Un Fils de famille*, vaudeville in three acts by Bayard and Biéville:[4] a very fine play, outstandingly acted; a big *succès d'argent*.[5]

Tuesday 4 January. Letters from Pietro Romani, Ronzi and Martellini in Florence, who confirm the success of *Le Prophète* there. Letter from Vermeulen in Rotterdam. I hosted a dinner for fourteen people that cost me 480 fr. The guests were: Davison, Ryan, Bowlby (three editors of the *Times* and the *Musical World*), Berlioz, Fiorentino, Girard, Brandus, Gouin, Méry, Théophile Gautier, Coste, Bacher, Jules Lecomte. Bowes and Eugène Guinot were also invited but declined.

Wednesday 5 January. Scored Catherine's new romance in act 2. Wrote to Pietro Romani in Florence and enclosed an autograph: the song "Komm." Wrote to Madame Ungher in Florence. Porte-Saint-Martin: *La Faridondaine*, melodrama in five acts by Dupeuty and Bourget, with songs by Adam.[6] The singer Madame Herbert-Massy acted and sang the role of the Singer.

Thursday 6 January. Letter from Hofrat Teichmann. Wrote to Ronzi, impresario of the Teatro della Pergola in Florence, to Marquis Martellini in Florence. Finished orchestrating the new romance of Catherine in act 2 and worked on a new version of Peter's romance in act 3. Opéra Comique: Auber's *Marco Spada*.

Friday 7 January. Worked on the revision of the score, regulating it with the libretto. To Gouin. Visits from Dr. Bamberg and Brandus. In the evening worked on the revision of the score from 8 until 11.

Saturday 8 January. Letters from the impresario Merelli in Vienna, from Grüneisen. Wrote to Madame Viardot in St. Petersburg. Worked on the new romance for Peter in act 3, with good results. Big dinner in the Hôtel de Ville with the *préfet de la Seine*, Herr Berger.

Sunday 9 January. Finished writing out Peter's new romance in act 3, which seems to me to work well. Ball at Benoit Fould. Soirée at Catren d'Anvers. To the Théâtre Français: *Mademoiselle de la Seiglière*, comedy in four acts by Sandeau.[7]

Monday 10 January. Visit of condolence to Armand Bertin, whose wife died yesterday. Worked on the revision of the opera. Dined with Léon Kreutzer. To the concert by Gouvy*, who performed symphonies and overtures of his own composition.

Tuesday 11 January. Neglected the cold water cure in order to work on the revision of the opera. Attended the funeral of Madame Armand Bertin. Invited Davison and Brandus to dine at our *table d'hôte*. Italian Opera: the first two acts of Verdi's *Ernani*. Then to a big musical soirée at Crémieux's, in honor of his daughter's engagement.

Wednesday 12 January. Worked for two hours on the revision of the score. Called on Buloz, whom I found at home today. Wrote to Vermeulen in Rotterdam (enclosing the *Klopstock Lieder*). Worked for one hour on the revision of the score. To the concert of the superb violinist Sivori. He played the Concerto in B Minor *(La Campanella)* by Paganini.[8] Afterward worked on the score for another hour.

Thursday 13 January. After working for three hours I completed the revision of the score for Scribe. Called on Dr. Bacher. Dinner with Marquis Pastoret;[9] Scribe and Auber were also present. In the Théâtre Italien heard the last two acts of Verdi's *Ernani*. In Berlin the bass Formes has had great success, twice in *Les Huguenots* and twice in *Robert*. *Robert* has also been performed in Oran in Algeria.

Friday 14 January. Scored the new romance. Visit of condolence to Armand Bertin. Letter from Emil Naumann in Bonn. In the Grand Opéra: *La Xacarilla* by Marliani. Then the Concerto in D Minor by the violinist Vieuxtemps.[10] Later scored the romance for an hour.

Saturday 15 January. Finished scoring Pierre's romance in act 3. Opéra Comique: *Marco Spada*. *Droits d'auteur* for the month of December 1852: 552 fr.

Sunday 16 January. Read through the plan of *Vasco*, and my observations on it, because of a conference with Scribe on this subject. Scribe read out the first three acts, and then gave them to me. They seem very lovely, even though a first reading is not decisive for me. I stayed with him for three hours. My late, blessed brother's *Struensee*, with my music, has been performed in the Leipzig Theater. Théâtre Lyrique: *Le Roi d'Yvetot* by Adam.

Monday 17 January. Letter from Schott in Mainz. For the fourth time I altered the vocal phrase ("votre douce présence") in Prascovia's aria and wrote it out. Called on Count Hatzfeld. Visits from Dr. Bamberg and Brandus. Gave composition lessons to Dautresme. Big ball in the Hôtel de Ville given by the *préfet de la Seine*.

Tuesday 18 January. Letter from Madame Ungher in Florence. With Patania to Marquis Aguado, who wanted to take my portrait by photography; he is a dilettante in this field. Then Bowes asked me to visit the English family Benfield, who wished to make my acquaintance; they are a father and six children, every one of whom plays a different instrument, and all really very charming. Then I called on Bischofsheim. The whole day thus slipped by unprofitably. In the Italian Opera: Mozart's *Don Giovanni*. Mademoiselle Cruvelli was Donna Anna. Wrote to Vermeulen in Rotterdam, and sent him the *Hymne zur silbernen Hochzeit des Königs*, the *Sieben geistliche Gesänge* and the *Ode an Rauch*.

Wednesday 19 January. Carefully read through the plan of act 4 of the new *Africaine*, as well as the first three completed acts, several times, so as to make my observations for Scribe in our *entrevue* tomorrow. Opéra Comique: the first performance of *Le Miroir*, the first work of Gastinel*.[11]

Thursday 20 January. Again read through the plan of act 4, but I found Scribe dressed for going out when I arrived. Quartet recital by Chevillard, etc., in which only Beethoven's three last quartets are always played; today no. 14 with the fugue[12] and the glorious no. 12.[13] In the newly rebuilt Cirque d'Hiver, which holds 4,000 spectators, saw the equestrian artists Les Panderistes Espagñols, two Spaniards who accomplish the most unbelievable things in a dance with the *tambour de Basque*. If the method of handling this instrument could be taught to the dancers of the Opéra, it could be developed into a very original sailors' *divertissement* in act 3 of *Vasco. Hamlet* with the new *dénouement* by Alexandre Dumas[14] could make a lovely *opéra comique.*[15] Letter from Florence from the chorus of the Teatro della Pergola.

Friday 21 January. Conference with Scribe about act 4 of *Vasco da Gama.*

Saturday 22 January. For the fifth time composed the four-part passage in Prascovia's aria. Visit from Perrin, the director of the Opéra Comique. I was invited to the Court Ball at the Tuileries[16] and had dressed and traveled there: however, the line of waiting carriages was so long that after I had queued for three-quarters of an hour, I lost patience and returned home.

Sunday 23 January. In the Conservatoire Beethoven's Symphony no. 9 with chorus, and an *Incarnatus* for solo voice by Mozart with obbligato flute, oboe, and bassoon. Soirée with Hiller and Benoit Fould. Gave instruction in composition to Dautresme. *Le Prophète* has been given in Neisse in Silesia with success.

Monday 24 January. Visit from the violinist Bazzini from Florence. A sixth version of the four-part passage in Prascovia's aria suddenly occurred to me, and I believe that this will be the best one. Big ball at the minister of state, Achille Fould's.

Tuesday 25 January. Worked from 11:15 until 12:45: wrote down and finished scoring the fifth and sixth versions of the four-part passage in Prascovia's aria. Variétés: *Les Saltimbanques*, vaudeville in three acts by Dumanoir.[17]

Wednesday 26 January. Revised the new couplets for Catherine in act 2 and those of Pierre in act 3. Julius [Beer] came and showed me his new songs: progress is discernible. Théâtre du Palais Royal: *Yorit nom d'un chien, Madame Bertrand et Mademoiselle Raton,*[18] *Le Chapeau de paille,*[19] vaudevilles, all of them very amusing.

Thursday 27 January. Read through the first three acts of *Vasco* for the second time, and noted my observations for Scribe. Visited Dr. Bacher. Began a new revision of the score of the *Étoile*, regarding the length of the dialogue. Concert by

Ferdinand Hiller. He played, among other things, the French Suite by Sebastian Bach, a very beautiful work that I heard for the first time;[20] I perceived with amazement that Gluck had borrowed the lovely passage in the overture and in Agamemnon's aria in *Iphigénie en Aulide* entirely from this suite by Bach[21]

Example 2. Theme (Bach/Gluck) quoted from memory

Le Prophète has been given in Salzburg and Magdeburg.

Friday 28 January. Continued revising the score of the *Étoile* from 7:30 until 9, and finished act 1, which, by approximate reckoning, with the dialogue, seems to last one and three-quarter hours. Visits from the pianist Goldbeck and from Guillet. Returned Johanna Wagner's contract with the Opéra to Guillet. Dined with Scribe.

Saturday 29 January. Continued the revision of the *Étoile* before breakfast. Davison and Brandus came to dine with me. Italian Opera: *Luisa Miller*.

Sunday 30 January. Concluded the revision of the *Étoile*.

Monday 31 January Consulted Pleyel about a pianino. To the Ambigu-Comique: *La Case du Père Tom*, melodrama in five acts by Dennery and Dumanoir.[22]

February 1853

Tuesday 1 February. Wrote to Minister Fould concerning Munk. Began writing out the clauses of the *traité* with Perrin in order to confer with the *avoué* Gautier. To Scribe. To Janin. Visited the painter Henri Schäfer with Madame Janin, and saw his *atelier*.[23] Italian Opera: *Ernani* by Verdi.

Wednesday 2 February. Long conference with Scribe about many things that must still be added to and altered in the libretto of the *Étoile*. Farewell call on Véron. Wrote to Demoiselle Louise Rothschild, and to Dautresme. Finished writing out the *traité*. In the Grand Opéra: first performance of Verdi's *Luisa Miller* in French. Madame Bosio* made her début in the role of Luisa: she succeeded, as has the work on the whole.

Thursday 3 February. Conference with the lawyer Gautier about the *traité* with the Opéra Comique. Conferred with Scribe about the *Étoile;* today he gave acts 4 and 5 of the reworked *Africaine.* Took leave of Dr. Bacher. Opéra Comique: *Marco Spada* by Auber. However, I felt so unwell with a headache that I went home after act 2.

Friday 4 February. Yesterday Scribe gave me four verses by Jules Janin that are most suitable for album autographs. They read: *Dominus vobiscum! Dieu Vous conserve et Vous préserve de tout Album.* This I set to music for two voices in free imitation, and inscribed it immediately into the albums of Offenbach, Lefébure-Wely, and Bazzini. Wrote to Hiller. To Scribe. Attended to many things in connection with my departure. Opéra Comique: first performance of *Les Noces de Jeannette, opéra comique* with only two characters by Victor Massé, and utterly charming;[24] *Le Sourd, ou L'Auberge pleine* by Adam.[25] The late, blessed Michael's *Struensee*, with my music, has been performed in Freiburg in Baden, also in Leipzig.

Saturday 5 February. Spent the whole day preparing for my departure. To Scribe, who gave me gave me several of the requested changes to *Vasco,* while I, in turn, handed over to him his manuscript of the *Étoile.* I inserted markers in the understanding that he will send on the additional verses. To the lawyer Gautier.

Sunday 6 February. Left at 7:30 in the morning by rail to Brussels. Arrival at five o'clock in the afternoon. On the journey I read through the complete manuscript of *Vasco* for the second time. Wrote ostensibly to Gouin, but the letter is actually for Perrin. *Le Prophète* has been given in Hermannstadt in Siebenbürgen.

Monday 7 February. At 11:15 by train for Cologne where I arrived at seven o'clock. On the journey read through the complete manuscript of *Vasco* for the third time.

Tuesday 8 February. At 6:30 in the morning left for Berlin by train, where I arrived after 9 in the evening and, God be praised, found all my beloved family relatively well. On the journey read through the manuscript of *Vasco* for the fourth time. Letter from Alexander von Humboldt.

Wednesday 9 February. I have caught cold, and I was incapable of any work all day.

Thursday 10 February. Today is the birthday of my precious, beloved mother, who is eighty-six years old. How grateful I am to almighty God for preserving our darling so long. May he keep her on earth for many long years, in fullness of health and clarity of mind, and grant her joy to the end of her days. Amen. I spent the whole day with my mother. She gave a big dinner at which Geheimrat Schulze toasted her health in a very beautiful speech.

Friday 11 February. During the night I had a bad attack of convulsive coughing. Called on Count Redern. Visits from Alexander von Humboldt and Dr. Schönlein. Wrote to Gouin and Scribe. My cold unfortunately makes it virtually impossible to work. In any case, because of my superstition about Fridays, I did not want to begin my new activity in Berlin today. Wrote to the *Hofmarschall,* Count Keller, about announcing my arrival to the king.[26] Read through the music of Jullien's opera *Pietro il Grande,*[27] because I have heard that he borrowed substantially from my *Feldlager.*

Saturday 12 February. I felt so unwell all day that I could not work.

Sunday 13 February. Began work on *Vasco,* starting with Inez's romance "Adieu rive du Tage,"[28] which I started thinking about on the journey here from Paris. Soirée at Geheimer Rat Carl's. Letters from Sobolewsky in Königsberg, from Salvatore Marchesi in Brussels.

Monday 14 February. Letter from the music director Otto in Hamburg. Finished composing Inez's romance.

Tuesday 15 February. My health is improving, but unfortunately I did not work at all. Visits from Count Redern, Alexander von Humboldt, Kapellmeister Dorn, Demoiselle Johanna Wagner. *Le Prophète* has been given in Lemberg.

Wednesday 16 February. My health is much better, thank God. Visit from Count Redern. Finished composing and writing out Inez's romance in *Vasco.*

Thursday 17 February. To Count Redern about the Court Concert. Dined with the king in Charlottenburg. The king, as well as the queen, was again very friendly and kind to me. Scored a little of Inez's romance. With my daughter Blanca to a ball at Dr. Emil von Haber's.

Friday 18 February. Scored Inez's romance. To Count Redern about the Court Concert. Opera House: *Euryanthe* by C. M. von Weber. Letter from Madame Viardot in St. Petersburg.

Saturday 19 February. Finished scoring Inez's romance. No sooner had this been done than a completely different musical version of this romance occurred to me. Busy with the preparations for the Court Concert on Monday, and rehearsed with the violoncellist Cyprian Romberg.[29] In the evening to the choral concert by the Domchor, where, among other things, the glorious motet by Bach "Ich lasse dich nicht"[30] and Mendelssohn's *Psalm 42*[31] were performed. Then to a soirée at Geheimer Rat Jüngken's, where the pianist Marie Wieck* played. She will be assisting at the Court Concert. Delivered fifty-five thalers to Professor Herbig for the relief fund of the Academy of Arts: this is due on my attending a sitting of the senate for the eleventh time.

Sunday 20 February. Busy with preparations for the Court Concert. Wrote to Count Redern about this. For the same reason rehearsed with the violinist, Thérèse Milanollo. In the Opera: Auber's *Die Feensee* [*Le Lac des fées*].[32]

Monday 21 February. Worked for one hour before breakfast on the new version of Inez's romance, which now becomes a bolero.[33] The painter Phöbus Levin and the conductor Ries came to see me. Wrote to Herr von Humboldt: recommendation for the painter Levin.[34] Before lunch worked for another hour on the bolero. In the evening finished writing out the bolero.

Tuesday 22 February. Worked a little. In the evening I was summoned to Princess Karl, who wanted to talk to me.

Wednesday 23 February. New resolutions to diligence. I want to read the libretto of *Vasco* so often that I will know it by heart. Worked on the Vasco-Sélika Duet (act 2).[35] Read act 2 several times. In the Opera: *Cleopatra*, lyrical scene with chorus by Truhn.[36] Demoiselle Wagner sang Cleopatra. Then to *Der Wasserträger* [*Les Deux Journées*] by Cherubini. Afterwards I was invited to a big soirée by the Belgian ambassador, De Nothomb.

Thursday 24 February. For one hour before breakfast and for two hours after breakfast read through the first act and improvised on the *Scène du Conseil*.[37] Visits from Kapellmeisterin Lortzing, from the singer Formes, and from Salomon. Letter from Gouin. Worked in the afternoon from 5 until 6:30: generally improvised on *Vasco*. Quartet recital by the Brothers Müller.

Friday 25 February. Generally worked on *Vasco* for one hour before and one hour after breakfast, and one hour after lunch. Soirée at Anna Eberty's.

Saturday 26 February. Worked generally on the *Scène du Conseil* for one hour before breakfast. Several good ideas occurred to me. Worked in the same way after breakfast. Sitting of the senate in the Academy. Worked for one hour. In the Opera House: concert of the violinist Thérèse Milanollo.

Sunday 27 February. Worked for one hour before breakfast with good results and finished composing the chorus that begins the *Scène du Conseil*. Worked from 11 until 1. In the Opera House: *Die Vestalin* by Spontini.

Monday 28 February. Worked for one hour before breakfast on the *Scène du Conseil*. Wrote a letter of recommendation to M. de Bériot* for the violinist Louis Ries. In the afternoon to the Singakademie, where I cast my vote for Grell in the election of the director.

March 1853

Tuesday 1 March. Worked for one hour before breakfast on the *Scène du Conseil*. Visits from Müller from Brunswick, from Albert Wagner. In the evening to the Singakademie; attended the *dépouillement des votes:*[38] Grell becomes the new director with 140 votes to 17.

Wednesday 2 March. Worked for one hour before breakfast: happy inspiration for the Chorus of Slave Merchants.[39] Congratulated regisseur Stawinsky on his twenty-fifth professional anniversary, and presented him with ten bottles of champagne. Sitting of the musical section of the Academy. Visit from Viardot. With Rittergutsbesitzer Josephy to the concert of the Philharmonische Gesellschaft, which has nominated me one of their honorary members.

Thursday 3 March. Worked for one hour before breakfast on the Chorus of Female Slaves. Visit from the tenor Caggiati,[40] who brought me a letter of recommendation from our ambassador in Stockholm, Herr Brassier de Saint-Simon.[41] To Viardot. Worked on the Chorus of Female Slaves, but without success. Big dinner at the president of police, von Hinkeldey's. Musical soirée at the banker Rubens's: Robert Schumann's Piano Quintet in E-flat Major.[42] Letter from the composer Pietro Romani in Florence, with news that *Le Prophète* has already had twenty-seven performances at the Teatro della Pergola, to packed houses. Letter from the poetess Wilhelmine von Chézy in Geneva. Letter from the organist Leprévost in Montmartre.[43]

Friday 4 March. Worked in both the morning and afternoon, with good results, on the Chorus of Female Slaves, and completed it. Called on the pianist Otto Goldschmidt, husband of Jenny Lind. Soirée recital by the quartet of the Müller brothers: Haydn's Quartet in C Major with the variations on *Gott erhalte Franz den Kaiser*, Beethoven's Quartet [no. 5] in A Major,[44] Schubert's Quartet [no. 14] in D Minor,[45] all three works unrehearsed.

Saturday 5 March. Worked only a little in the morning. Dined with Mother; Viardot, Spieker, Begas, Justizrat Hellwig, Stadtgerichtsrat Nörner were present. In the evening hardly worked at all. Letters from Camille Pleyel, and Gouin.

Sunday 6 March. Wrote out the Slave Market Scene. Dined with the sculptor Wichmann.

Monsieur !   Berlin ce 27 février 53

Quoique bien des années se soient déjà passées depuis que j'ai
eu l'honneur de Vous voir pour la dernière fois, j'ose cependant
espérer que Vous m'aurez conservé cette bienveillance dont
Vous m'honoriez autrefois, & qui m'était bien chère. —
Dans cet espoir j'ose Vous présenter par cette ligne
Monsieur Ries, jeune Violoniste de Berlin, de beaucoup de
talent, qui se rend à Paris pour plusieurs mois, afin
d'y entendre & d'étudier les grands maîtres du Violon,
à la tête desquels Vous marchez victorieusement. Mr. Ries
aspire à l'honneur de Vous pouvoir le présenter à Vous,
& il serait au comble de ses vœux s'il pouvait avoir le
bonheur de Vous entendre, & si Vous voudriez Vous daigner
le entendre à son tour, & de l'honorer de Vos conseils.
Ce jeune homme par son caractère aimable, & par
son talent sérieux, serait digne d'une si haute faveur de
Votre part. Veuillez agréer Monsieur l'expression
des sentiments les plus distingués de
                      Votre

                        trèsdévoué
                        Meyerbeer

Meyerbeer's letter of recommendation for Louis Ries (27 February 1853)

Monday 7 March. For one hour before breakfast again took up the Scène du Conseil. From 11:30 worked on the *Scène du Conseil.* Visit from Count Redern: the king, he told me, very much wants me to compose an *a capella* setting of Psalm 91 for the Domchor. Big dinner at the minister of trade, von der Heydt's.

Tuesday 8 March. Worked for one hour before breakfast on the *Scène du Conseil.* Copied out the text of Psalm 91,[46] and started with studies preliminary to its composition.

Wednesday 9 March. Preliminary studies on Psalm 91 for one hour before breakfast. To Count Redern. Attended the obsequies of the famous geologist, Leopold von Buck, as member of a deputation from the Academy. Dined with Samuel von Haber. Soirée at the English ambassador, Lord Bloomfield's.

Thursday 10 March. Preliminary study of Psalm 91 and, at the same time, started on the composition of the same. *Matinée musicale* at Otto Goldschmidt's, the spouse of Jenny Lind. He played Mendelssohn's Trio [no. 1] in D Minor for piano, violin, and violoncello,[47] and the *andante* and finale of Beethoven's Piano Sonata [no. 1] in F Minor.[48] Johanna Wagner sang Schubert's "Ungeduld" and "Trock'ne Blumen."[49] Soirée at Geheimrat Illaire's, where there was also music making.

Friday 11 March. Composed some of the psalm. In the Opera House: *Cleopatra,* a monodrama by Truhn. *Robert le Diable* has been given with great success by the Italian Opera in Bucharest.[50]

Saturday 12 March. Composed some of the Psalm 91. Concert by the Domchor. Visit from the composer Kolb*; he brought me a letter of recommendation from Moscheles.

Sunday 13 March. Spent the whole morning working diligently at the psalm. Kroll's Theater: *Zampa* by Hérold.

Monday 14 March. Worked diligently for the whole morning on the composition of the psalm, and composed it completely up to the closing *fugetto.* Have not, however, written it out. Worked for two hours in the afternoon: began writing out the psalm.

Tuesday 15 March. Worked for one hour before breakfast on Psalm 91. Visit from the bass Formes. Worked from 11:45 until 2 on the psalm. To the Opera House for Bellini's *Die Familien Montecchi und Capuleti.* Demoiselle Wagner sang Romeo.

Wednesday 16 March. Worked for one hour before breakfast and one hour afterwards on Psalm 91. Letter from Deligny, on behalf of Roqueplan in Paris, concerning the engagement of Johanna Wagner. Busy all day with preparations and rehearsals for the Court Concert tomorrow, which also features the bass Formes. Worked in the evening on the psalm. Visit from Count Stollberg concerning the violinist Mertens.

Thursday 17 March. Worked for one hour before breakfast and two hours afterwards on the psalm. Rehearsal for the Court Concert, which was, however, canceled. In the evening worked on the psalm.

Friday 18 March. Worked for one hour before breakfast on the psalm, and likewise one hour afterwards. Visits from Bock and composer Kolb. At the wish of the Count Stollberg, wrote letters of recommendation for Mertens to Vieuxtemps and Brandus. Dined with Mother's, where I found Madame Birch-Pfeiffer, [Professor] Gubitz, etc. Worked on the psalm in the evening.

Saturday 19 March. Worked for one hour before, and one hour after, breakfast on the psalm. Visit from the bass Formes. Sitting of the senate in the Academy. Then worked for one hour on the psalm, which made sound progress today and which, as an imaginative concept, is approaching its conclusion.

Sunday 20 March. Worked on the psalm for one hour before breakfast. Wrote to Geheimer Kabinetsrat Illaire, and the Russian chamber musician Weitzmann*, about Dorn's jubilee. Worked for another hour. Sitting of the plenary committee of the Singakademie, concerning the election of a vice-director. Dined with Mother. Stayed at home in the evening, but did not work, since I felt unwell. *Droits d'auteur* for the month of February: 422 fr. 10 c.

Monday 21 March. I worked all morning on the psalm, which I have now completed in my mind. Letter from the minister of state, Achille Fould, concerning Munk.[51] Letter from Kapellmeister Sain-d'Arod in Lyon. Wrote to Kapellmeister Dorn: congratulations on his jubilee, together with six bottles of champagne. In the evening worked for two hours on the psalm: began writing it out.

Tuesday 22 March. Worked for one hour before breakfast on the psalm. Visit from the singer Hugo Hainan. Worked on the psalm from 10:30 until 2, and then in the evening for one and a half hours. *Le Prophète* has been given in St. Petersburg under the title *Die Belagerung von Gent* with great success, also in Lemberg.

Wednesday 23 March. Worked on the psalm for one hour before breakfast. Visit from the singer Schütky from Hamburg.[52] Worked on the psalm from eleven until two o'clock, then in the evening for three and a half hours. *Le Prophète* has been given in Riga and Liège.

Thursday 24 March Worked for a little before breakfast on the psalm. Visits from Professor Griepenkerl, and from Kapellmeister Dorn. Letters from Gouin, from Dr. Bacher in Paris. After breakfast, and also in the evening, worked on the psalm and wrote it out completely. Now all that remains is the revision which, in the main, with passages for eight voices, must be undertaken very carefully, and will take time. The Russian ambassador, Baron Budberg, sent me the *Journal de Petersbourg* in which Damcke has written a very enthusiastic account of the performances of *Le Prophète* in St. Petersburg. I further received, from an unknown hand in Florence, several reviews from the journal *Il Genio*, in which there is an outstanding reaction to the production of *Le Prophète* in Florence.

Good Friday 25 March. Worked on the revision of the psalm. Visit from the ballet master, Paul Taglioni. Wrote a letter ostensibly for Gouin, but actually for Roqueplan, that I will not have the *Afrikanerin* ready for the coming winter, but only in the autumn of 1854. Letter from Nouguier *(père)* in Paris[53]. In the evening to the Singakademie for Graun's *Der Tod Jesu*.

Saturday 26 March. Worked on the psalm for one hour before breakfast. Visit from the composer Lassen* from Brussels. Visit from Herr von Humboldt. Attended the liturgy in the Domkirche.[54] Worked a little more on the psalm.

Sunday 27 March. Worked on the psalm, and finished revising it. In the Opera House: *Indra* by Flotow.[55]

Monday 28 March. Worked on the fair copy of the score of the psalm (four hours).

Tuesday 29 March Worked on the fair copy of the score of the psalm (five hours).

Wednesday 30 March. Worked on the fair copy of the score of the psalm (six hours) and completed it.

Thursday 31 March. Made a last revision of the psalm. Handed the psalm over to Count Redern. Wrote to Pleyel and Gouin. Composed a small piano piece in 3/4 time, and wrote it down. In the Opera House: *Der Wildschütz* by Lortzing. Demoiselle Wagner sang the comic role of the Baroness very well.

April 1853

Friday 1 April. Through Gouin, sent Pleyel 925 fr. for the pianino. Visited Herr von Humboldt. Wrote to Brandus. In the Opera House: *Indra*. *Les Huguenots* has been given in Clermont-Ferrand for the first time.

Saturday 2 April. Today I again began composing *Vasco*; I resumed the *Scène du Conseil* where I had left off when I began the composition of the psalm. Visit from the music publisher Glöggl from Vienna, the Italian tenor Caggiati. Letters from Madame Birch-Pfeiffer, and from Gouin. Letter from the Marquise Martellini in Florence: the grand duke of Tuscany[56] has had *Le Prophète* performed in concert in his palace in Florence, including all the pieces that were omitted in the theater.

Sunday 3 April. I began to busy myself with the composition of Sélika's first cavatina.[57] *Matinée musicale* at the banker Herr Rubens's, where Kapellmeister Marschner from Hanover played a trio of his own composition. In the Königstädter-Theater: *Hunderttausend Taler*, a farce by Kalisch.[58]

Monday 4 April. Worked for one hour before breakfast on Sélika's cavatina. Letter from Madame Ungher in Florence.

Tuesday 5 April. Worked for one hour before breakfast on Sélika's cavatina. Letter from Dr. Bacher. Wrote to Gouin, and the minister A. Fould. Read through Patschke's copy of my psalm. In Kroll's Theater: *Die Ochsenmenuette*, opera in one act by Joseph Haydn,[59] and *Der Kalif von Bagdad* by Boieldieu.

Wednesday 6 April. Worked for one hour before breakfast on Sélika's cavatina. I delivered the copy of my psalm to Count Redern. I took my *Quarante Mélodies* and the aria from *Rinaldo* that I orchestrated to Madame Decker.[60] To Count Redern, to the music director Neithardt. Unfortunately, I did not compose at all. In Genoa, at a concert of the Società Filarmonica, the overture to the *Feldlager* was performed to great enthusiasm. Wrote to Dr. Bacher in Paris.

Thursday 7 April. Worked for one hour before breakfast on Sélika's cavatina. Wrote to Marquise Martellini in Florence. Letters from the poet Tauber in Vienna,[61] from Gouin. Wrote to Gouin.

Friday 8 April. My beloved Minna's birthday. Worked for one hour before breakfast on the cavatina and finished it. Visits from Caggiati and from the brother of the singer Cruvelli. Letters from Herr von Lüttichau and Dautresme in Paris. Wrote to Kapellmeister Sain-d'Arod in Lyons. In the Opera House: *Lucrezia Borgia* by Donizetti.

Saturday 9 April. Worked for an hour before breakfast writing out the cavatina.

Wrote to Herr von Lüttichau. Played my psalm to Music Director Neithardt, since he is to rehearse the singers. The soprano Mme. Howitz-Steinau, from Dresden, came to see me.[62] Letter from Gouin. In the Singakademie: Sebastian Bach's *Passion Music*. *Soirée musicale* at Count Redern's, where the tenor Caggiati sang.

Sunday 10 April. Sore throat, headache, throat irritation. Finished writing out Sélika's cavatina in the hour before breakfast. The writer, Dr. Sachse from Hamburg, came to see me. Started composing the new *Fackeltanz* [no. 3] for two hours.[63] Visit from Hofrat Teichmann. In the evening wrote to Gouin about the cuts requested in *Le Prophète*.

Monday 11 April. Letter from Music Director Emil Naumann in Bonn. Letter to Emil Naumann. In the evening began a new revision of the *Étoile*.

Tuesday 12 April. Worked for an hour before breakfast on the revision and improvement of the *Étoile*. Long letter to Gouin, in which I communicated the abridgments in *Les Huguenots* requested by the administration of the Opéra.[64] Wrote to Scribe enclosing the changes to the *Étoile*. In the afternoon to the Singakademie where I heard the rehearsal of Blumner's* oratorio *Columbus*.

Wednesday 13 April. Worked on the revision of the *Étoile* for one hour before breakfast. Wrote to the author Tauber in Vienna. Studied the role of Isabelle in *Robert le Diable* with the singer Howitz-Steinau. In the evening could not work on account of a persistent headache.

Thursday 14 April. Worked on the revision of the *Étoile* for one hour before breakfast and one hour after. To the Belgian ambassador, de Nothomb. To Haber, who is traveling to Paris. In the Friedrich-Wilhelmstädtisches-Theater: *Alles durch Magnetismus*, farce by Görner, music by Kriegmann.[65]

Friday 15 April. Worked for one hour before, and one hour after, breakfast on the revision of the *Étoile*. Letter from Dr. Bacher: recommends the singer Colson from the Théâtre Lyrique.[66] Letter from Brandus. Visits from Spieker, Kapellmeister Sobolewsky, Caggiati. Letter of recommendation to Grüneisen for Sobolewsky. In the Opera House: *Indra* by Flotow. Madame Howitz-Steinau sang Zigarette.

Saturday 16 April. Partially altered Pierre's romance for one hour before and after breakfast. Letter from Vermeulen from Amsterdam. Concert by Truhn in the Kroll Hall.

Sunday 17 April. Worked on and completed a second version of Catherine's aria in act 3 ("Est-ce l'ombre?"). I promised Madame Birch-Pfeiffer to do the work that the duke of Gotha has asked of me in October.[67] My brother's *Struensee*, with my music, has been given in Schwerin. In the theater: Auber's *Der Feensee*.

Monday 18 April. Letter from Mertens in Paris. Worked on adapting the new version of Catherine's aria in act 3 to its context in the finale. I was about to write out the piece, but then felt that the first version should be retained. Nonetheless, after breakfast began writing out this piece, and finished it at the first try. It comes up three times in the course of the finale.

Tuesday 19 April. Began to compose the *Fackeltanz*, which I am to write for the wedding of Princess Anna (daughter of Prince Karl) to the prince of Hesse. In the evening in Kroll's Theater: *Stradella* by Flotow. *Droits d'auteur* for March: 552 fr.

Wednesday 20 April. Worked on the *Fackeltanz*. Listened to the singer Mlle. Miller, niece of the banker Kirchhain.

Thursday 21 April. Composed the *Fackeltanz* for one hour before and two hours after breakfast. Answered the minister of state, Fould. Studied the role of Berthe in *Le Prophète* with the singer Howitz-Steinau. Big dinner for twenty-one people at Mother's. To Madame Birch-Pfeiffer, who had another letter from the duke of Gotha to show me.

Friday 22 April. Composed the *Fackeltanz* for an hour before breakfast. Visit from the singer Ellinger (of the Court Opera in Vienna). With Mother to Madame Crelinger, who celebrated her fortieth jubilee in the theater yesterday. Rehearsed pieces from *Le Prophète* at Johanna Wagner's, with her and Howitz-Steinau. Wrote to Gouin about Scudo.

Saturday 23 April. Composed the *Fackeltanz* for an hour before and after breakfast. Concert in the Singakademie: *Columbus*, cantata by Martin Blumner. Much originality in the handling, comprehension, harmony, and noble style; only melody is lacking, and the power of invention.

Sunday 24 April. Worked for one hour before breakfast on the *Fackeltanz*, virtually finishing the composition. Visit from the tenor Ellinger and his wife (a mezzo-soprano): they sang pieces from *Le Prophète* for me. In the evening attended a couple of acts of *Der Prophet* (fortieth performance, to a packed house), then wrote a letter to Gouin.

Monday 25 April. Wrote to the Comité des Auteurs et Compositeurs Dramatiques: I align myself with those composers who allow the use of their music gratis in vaudevilles. Wrote to Brandus. In the Opera House: *Die Makkabäer*, a new tragedy[68] by Otto Ludwig*.

Tuesday 26 April. Began to write out the *Fackeltanz*, which is almost completed. To Count Redern. In the afternoon, at 4:30, I suddenly heard that I had to direct the Court Concert in Charlottenburg. Johanna Wagner and Formes sang songs, and a mediocre pianist, Madame Schwehmer, likewise performed. I left at the commencement of *souper*.

Wednesday 27 April. Letter from Music Director Emil Naumann in Bonn, from Alex Duncker in Leipzig. Worked for three hours on writing out the *Fackeltanz*. Rehearsal with the Domchor of my Psalm 91. The outcome did not live up to my expectations. In particular, the passage in C major, from which I expected so much, just would not work. Big celebratory dinner in the English House in honor of Madame Crelinger's jubilee.

Thursday 28 April. Made some changes to my psalm, whereby the C major passage, which is apparently too high for the sopranos, can be sung in B-flat major. I immediately sent the changes to Neithardt for rehearsal. Dined with Mother. After lunch, Madame Birch-Pfeiffer read me the new opera libretto *(Santa Chiara)* that she has written for the duke of Gotha.

Friday 29 April. Wrote to Gouin, and sent him the abridgments requested for *Robert le Diable*.[69] Wrote to Brandus about Halévy in the Academy. To Birch-Pfeiffer, who read me her answer to the duke of Gotha, since it concerns me. In it I promise the duke to orchestrate his opera in three months, beginning in October and ending in January, or, should he feel able to do it, to correct his instrumentation, taking a month to do this, also beginning in October. Concert of the singer Kotzolt of the Domchor in which, among other things, *Der Rose Pilgerfahrt* by Robert Schumann was performed.[70]

Saturday 30 April. I composed a completely new passage for my psalm in place of the existing one in C major, which, in the recent rehearsal, was the only part that went badly and made no impression. Plenary sitting of the members of the Academy: all the nonresident composers I had proposed as members, and who had been accepted by the senate, were rejected by the full Academy. The exception was Hauptmann* in Leipzig. I believe all this was a cabal engineered by Dorn. Second rehearsal by the Domchor of my psalm, which went much better today and seemed more effective. Dined with Decker. Wrote to Brandus about Halévy. In the Opera House attended a performance of *Struensee*.

May 1853

Sunday 1 May. At nine o'clock to the funeral of the poet Tieck.[71] The preacher Sydow preached an outstanding, freethinking sermon at the graveside.[72] I wrote out the new C major passage of my psalm and revised it immediately. This took three hours. Then I played it to the music director Neithardt, who will rehearse it tomorrow with the Domchor. In the Friedrich-Wilhelmstädtisches-Theater: *Der Unsichtbare*, comic opera in one act by Eule;[73] *Der Menschenfeind und der Bauer*, farce in three acts after the French *Le Misanthrope et l'Auvergnat*.[74]

Monday 2 May. Visit from the music director Wieprecht. Read through the compositions by Ropiquet[75] (which have been addressed to the king), in order to provide Count Redern with a report about them. Letter from Brandus. Worked for two hours on writing out the *Fackeltanz*. Soirée at the Russian ambassador's.

Tuesday 3 May. To Rellstab. In the Singakademie, where several pieces by Bach and Fasch were rehearsed. Wrote out some of the *Fackeltanz*.

Wednesday 4 May. Wrote out the *Fackeltanz*, to within a few bars of completion. Third rehearsal with the Domchor of my new psalm: it went excellently; the altered C major passage works very well. Count Redern was present; he told me that the king has also commanded a *Fackeltanz* from Flotow, which I find personally hurtful. Letters from Brandus, from Halévy. In the Friedrich-Wilhelmstädtisches-Theater: *Der Doktor und Apotheker* by Dittersdorf.

Thursday 5 May. Visit from Herr von Humboldt. Rehearsal with Madame Zimmermann's singing pupils of my cantata *Maria und ihr Genius*. In evening began and completed the revision of the *Fackeltanz*.

Friday 6 May. Visit from the music director Render, from Brussels. To Count Redern. To Alexander von Humboldt about the election of a new knight of the order Pour le Mérite. To the concert of the violinist Singer.

Saturday 7 May. News from Count Redern that my psalm will be performed tomorrow in the Friedenskirche at Potsdam, by order of the king. Visit from the music director Neithardt; I gave him a present of five louis d'or in appreciation of the great trouble he has taken over the rehearsal of my psalm. Fourth rehearsal with the Domchor; Bock, to whose publishing house I have given the psalm, was also present.

Sunday 8 May. By royal command, my setting of Psalm 91 was performed this morning in Potsdam, at the service in the Friedrichskirche, in the presence of our king and the king of the Belgians;[76] all went outstandingly well. The king, however, did not send for me, as I had expected. In the evening to the Opera for *Indra* by Flotow. Letters from Gouin and from Gaetano Rossi in Verona. Wrote to Gouin about the *coupure*[77] in the act 4 finale of *Robert*. Letter from the reigning duke of Saxe-Gotha-Coburg, inviting me to visit him.

Monday 9 May. Visit from Regierungsrat Gaebler: I gave 3,000 thalers toward washing and bathing facilities for the poor. Visit from the music director Wieprecht: I played him the new *Fackeltanz*, which he will arrange for cavalry band. Visit from Brissler: I gave him my psalm so that he can make a piano version for the publisher Bote & Bock. In the Opera House today, by royal command, and in honor of the king of the Belgians, there was a gala performance of *Der Prophet*, to a crowded house. The performance was very good, but the reaction of the public cold.

Tuesday 10 May. Attended the reading of Dr. Gottschall's poem, *Zeno*.

Wednesday 11 May. In the evening again busied myself with the *Étoile*, and worked a little on Peter's romance.

Thursday 12 May. In the evening began to write out the revision of Pierre's romance. *Le Prophète* has been given in Temesvár to great enthusiasm.

Friday 13 May. Corrected the piano version of my psalm with Brissler. To Neithardt. Sent 200 fr. to Gaetano Rossi in Verona for his eightieth birthday. In the evening scored Pierre's partially revised romance.

Saturday 14 May. To Herr von Humboldt. Wrote a letter, ostensibly to Count Redern, but actually for the king, about the *Fackeltanz*.

Sunday 15 May. Worked for five hours on the piano score of the *Fackeltanz* that Bock will publish, and completed it up to the final 12/8 tempo.

Monday 16 May. With Wieprecht revised the arrangement of my *Fackeltanz* for military music, which he has made. To Count Redern. In the evening completed the piano score of my *Fackeltanz*.

Tuesday 17 May. Added the still missing parts for kettledrums, side drums, and triangle to the *Fackeltanz*.

Wednesday 18 May. Demoiselle Alwine Frommann dined with me. In the Opera

House: *Jessonda* by Spohr. Herr Rieger, a baritone with a very strong but brittle voice, sang Tristan.

Thursday 19 May. Rellstab sent me a new arrangement of the text of my *Ode an Rauch*, entitled *Hymne an Zeus*. Wrote to Rellstab, to Marquis Martellini, and to the grand duke of Tuscany. To Madame Birch-Pfeiffer, about my reply to the duke of Gotha. Visits from the famous dance composer Jullien from Paris, from the music dealer Bock, and from Brissler. Read through the new text by Rellstab for the *Ode an Rauch*. Endorsement of the urgent petition by Kammermusikus Schumann,[78] and attestation of the oratorio *Die Sündflut* for Kammermusikus Dorn.

Friday 20 May. Studied the score of *Struensee* with Jullien. To Schlesinger. To Rellstab. *Droits d'auteur* for the month of April: 397 fr. 25 c.

Saturday 21 May. Wrote to the music dealer Bayerhofer in Düsseldorf, and returned the three opera texts of Frau Kommerzienrätin Elbers. Wrote to Rellstab, and sent him an honorarium of six friedrichs d'or for his text *Hymne an Zeus*. With Jullien to Schlesinger about *Struensee*.

Sunday 22 May. Wrote to Emil Naumann in Bonn. Read through the English translation of my *Quarante Mélodies*, and examined the prosodic accentuation under the music with the English teacher Lloyd. In the Opera House: Mozart's *Figaros Hochzeit*. Herr Rieger made a guest appearance as Figaro.

Monday 23 May. Reached agreement with Bock about the publication of my three *Fackeltänze* and my psalm. Wrote to Tauber in Vienna (enclosing the music of my song "Liebesbote"). To Wieprecht, that he should order three small clarinets in F for *L'Étoile*. Second English lesson, in order to read and check the translation of my *Quarante Mélodies*. In the Schauspielhaus: *Struensee*, to a crowded house.

Tuesday 24 May. Third English lesson. Placed the metronome markings under the *tempi* of my psalm. To Professor Rötscher, about the critique of *Lady Tartuffe* by Mme. de Girardin.[79] Big rehearsal with the brass of my *Fackeltanz*.

Wednesday 25 May. To Herr von Humboldt. Metronome markings for the *Fackeltänze*. [Sent] the romance from *Les Huguenots* ("Parmi mes larmes") to Johanna Wagner. Continued with the English teacher. Presented six friedrichs d'or to Wieprecht for arranging the *Fackeltanz* for military music. Preparations for departure.

Thursday 26 May. To Count Redern, about the *Fackeltanz*. [Sent] the *Quarante*

Mélodies to Tuczek, and the scores of the first and second *Fackeltänze* and the piano version of the third to Bock.

Friday 27 May. Heinrich Brockhaus from Leipzig came to see me:[80] he asks permission for the local book dealer, A. Hofmann, to include my brother Michael's *Struensee* and *Paria* in a new edition of the German classics that he is preparing. I granted it on my mother's behalf. Wrote a letter, ostensibly to Herr von Humboldt, but actually for the king: even though my leave from 1 June to 1 December is contractual, I nonetheless request permission to travel.

Saturday 28 May. Letter from Breitkopf & Härtel. Answered that I have already allocated the publication of the comic opera [*L'Étoile du Nord*]. Conference with Wieprecht, about the relationship and nomenclature of the German brass instruments to those of Sax. To Count Redern. To Birch-Pfeiffer about the duke of Gotha: I cannot go to Gotha either now or later, and because of this, the duke wishes only that I should examine and correct the already completed orchestration. This I have agreed to, but still only in October. Letter from Gouin. Wrote to Gouin and to Émile Girardin. Gala performance by royal invitation to celebrate the wedding of Princess Anna. *Iphigenie in Tauris* by Gluck was performed. The king summoned me to his box to compliment me on the *Fackeltanz* and the psalm.

Sunday 29 May. Letters from Tito Ricordi* in Milan, from Tauber in Vienna. Visited the publisher Duncker, who celebrates his jubilee today. To Johanna Wagner.

Monday 30 May. The king has invited me to a ball this evening. Princess Anna, through Lucchesini, has sent me a lovely *épingle*[81] in gratitude for the *Fackeltanz*, which I composed for her Court Concert. Wrote to Dr. Bacher, to Ricordi in Milan, to Marquis Lucchesini, to the duke of Gotha. I had my beloved mother bless me before my journey.

Tuesday 31 May. Left early this morning at 7:30, by rail, for Cologne. May God allow me to attain the purpose of my journey: the production of my *Étoile* in Paris, under the most brilliant and fortunate circumstances. I was busy all day in the railway carriage with the correction of the plates of my psalm.

June 1853

Wednesday 1 June. At 8 by express train from Cologne to Brussels, where we arrived at 3:30. By the time we reached Verviers, I had finished the correction of the psalm, and immediately sent it to Burguis in Berlin for delivery to Bock.

Thursday 2 June. At eight o'clock by express train to Paris, where we arrived at five o'clock. My old friend Gouin came to me at once. In the Opéra Comique: *L'Épreuve villageoise* by Grétry[82] and *La Tonelli* by Ambroise Thomas.[83]

Friday 3 June. Visits from Brandus and Gouin. In the Opéra Comique: heard Grétry's *L'Épreuve villageoise* for the second time. This charming, melodious, witty music, so full of feeling, first performed in 1787,[84] nearly sixty-six years old, delighted me today even more than yesterday. Then they performed *Les Noces de Jeanette* by Massé: a lovely subject featuring only two characters, and ingenious, refined music, although a little *prétentieuse et tourmentée*.[85] Letter from Dautresme.

Saturday 4 June. In the Opéra Comique: *Les Mousquetaires de la Reine* by Halévy, for the début of the new tenor Puget.[86]

Sunday 5 June. Wrote to Scribe. Visited Henri Blaze. In the Opéra Comique I heard Ambroise Thomas's *La Tonelli*.

Monday 6 June. Letters from Marquis Martellini in Florence, and from Robert Griepenkerl in Brunswick. Began a new revision of the *Étoile*. Visit from Leduc. In the Opéra: a performance of *Robert le Diable* to a packed house; the chorus excepted, it went very well.

Tuesday 7 June. Letters from Scribe, and from Dr. Bacher. Worked on a few small changes to the duet of Catherine and Prascovia, and completed them, the instrumentation included. In the Opéra Comique: *L'Épreuve villageoise* by Grétry; *Galathée* by Victor Massé.

Wednesday 8 June. Called on Édouard Monnais, Armand Bertin, Véron. Worked on the *Étoile*. Opéra Comique: *Les Mousquetaires de la Reine* by Halévy.

Thursday 9 June. Letter from Emil Naumann in Bonn. Conference with Scribe concerning the casting of roles in *Étoile*. Visited Auber. Worked on the *Étoile*. Opéra Comique: *La Tonelli* by Ambroise Thomas.

Friday 10 June. To Gye, director of the Covent Garden Theatre in London, who visited me yesterday. Again read through the score of the *Étoile* completely. Visits from Fétis, Glinka, Felice Romani, Émile Chevé, Dr. Masson. Dined with Brandus; he had also invited Fétis.

Saturday 11 June. Visits from the violinist Mertens and from Dautresme. Called on Roqueplan, Scudo, Madame Tedesco. Worked on the *Étoile*. In the Opéra Comique: *L'Épreuve villageoise*. Afterward *Les Noces de Jeannette*.

Sunday 12 June. In the Church of St. Germain l'Auxrois heard an *a capella* Mass by Gounod, performed by the Orphéonists.[87] Then in the Conservatoire a dramatic exercise by the students:[88] *La Pie voleuse* [*La Gazza ladra*] by Rossini. Went to see Fiorentino. In the Opéra Comique: *La Fille du régiment* by Donizetti.

Monday 13 June. Called on Felice Romani, Brandus, Leduc. Visits from Duponchel, Weill. Worked on the *Étoile:* had a happy inspiration for another *tempo di mezzo* in Danilowitz's aria.[89] In the Opéra: *Le Prophète*, to a packed house.

Tuesday 14 June. Worked on the change in Danilowitz's aria, and completed it. Visit from Davis, the director of the French Theater in New Orleans. To the minister Fould, Persigny, and Léon Kreutzer. A monstrous article in *La France musicale*, a rejoinder to an attack on this paper in *La Gazette musicale*, in which, *par ricochets*,[90] I am criticized in the strongest way, agitated me so much that I fear evil consequences for my health. In the Vaudeville today I saw *Les Filles de marbre* by Barrière and Thibout.[91] This play is the big success of the day; it is entertaining, witty, and is outstandingly acted. *Droits d'auteur* for the month of May: 636 fr. 25 c.

Wednesday 15 June. Letter from the lawyer Bessel in Cologne: he offers me a libretto. The attorney von Carlowitz in Dresden has written, on behalf of a family in Schleswig-Holstein, to ask me for a musical contribution for their album. Sitting of the Commission de la Surveillance de l'Enseignement at the Conservatoire, from ten until four o'clock. In the Grand Opéra: *Moïse* by Rossini; I heard only the first act. Then to the Opéra Comique: *La Tonelli*.

Thursday 16 June. Visit from the minister of state, Fould, who asked my advice about the choice of a new director for the Opéra. Visited Nestor Roqueplan and Léon Kreutzer. Soirée at Henri Blaze de Bury's, where the famous poet of nature, the hairdresser Jasmin* from Agen, declaimed verses in the charming patois of Languedoc.

Friday 17 June. Wrote out the new *tempo di mezzo* in Danilowitz's aria for a while. To Gouin. Stayed at home, but worked very little because of a headache.

Saturday 18 June. Worked from 10:30 until 1:30 on the *Étoile*. Applied myself to the changes in the duet between Georges and Prascovia, without especial success. Then completed writing out the alterations in Danilowitz's aria. Called on Benoit Fould. Conference with Léon Kreutzer, who wanted personal information on several details for my biography, which he is writing for the *Musique contemporaine*. Dined with the minister of state, Achille Fould. Opéra Comique: the last two acts of *Les Mousquetaires de la Reine*.

Sunday 19 June. Visits from Gye, director of Covent Garden Theatre, from Herr and Madame Tedesco, Franco, Ferret (correspondent of *L'Émancipation*), Simon, Dautresme and his father. To Émile de Girardin, Perrin, Fiorentino, Roqueplan. Opéra Comique: *L'Épreuve villageoise*, and the last performance by Madame Ugalde in *La Tonelli*.

Monday 20 June. To Gouin. Visit from Sina, to whom I gave 200 fr. so that he can take his curative trip to Boulogne. Visit from Brandus. To Madame Tedesco: studied the role of Fidès with her. In the Opéra *Les Huguenots* (232d performance, receipts 6,015 fr.). Gueymard as Raoul was very good in acts 3 and 4. Madame Steller, making her début as Valentine, was average.

Tuesday 21 June. Visits from the director of the Opéra Comique, Émile Perrin, from Brandus, Dautresme, and Gouin. Dined with Benoit Fould.

Wednesday 22 June. Letter from Giaccone, impresario of the Royal Theater in Turin,[92] who has invited me there in February to conduct the last rehearsals and the first performance of *Le Prophète*. In the Opéra: *Le Juif errant*.

Thursday 23 June. Letter from Kapellmeister Romani in Florence. Worked from ten o'clock until twelve on the revision of the *Étoile*. Visits from the famous instrument maker, Adolphe Sax, and from the former director of the Opéra Comique, Basset, who wants me to mediate with Minister Fould in favor of his becoming director of the Opéra.[93] Visits from Dautresme, from the singer Mlle. Bertini, and from Édouard Monnais. In the evening continued on the revision of the *Étoile*.

Friday 24 June. Called on Janin and Romani. Continued with the revision of the *Étoile*. Dined at Bischofsheim's, where I made the acquaintance of Émile Augier*. In the Opéra: *Le Prophète* (144th performance, receipts 9,242 fr. 52 c.); Chapuis gave a very mediocre account of the role of the Prophet,[94] in place of the indisposed Gueymard.

Saturday 25 June. Sitting of the Education Commission in the Conservatoire. Finished the revision of the *Étoile*. I undertook this in order to establish how long the work (both music and dialogue) would last, and have unfortunately found that it is too long by half an hour. Conference with Maurice Bourges, who is to translate my psalm into Latin and French. In the Odéon: *L'Honneur et l'Argent*, *comédie* by Ponsard.[95] This play is enjoying an extraordinary success, and deserves it. The action might well be regarded as a little simplistic, but the characters and the dialogue are outstanding, and it is acted in the most masterly manner.

Sunday 26 June. Visit from the Cavaliere Lopez from Parma, intendant of the

Court Theater there, who wanted to confer with me about the forthcoming production of *Le Prophète* in Parma. A new revision of the *Étoile*, in order to confirm the length of the work. The purely musical section of act 1 lasted for an hour this time. Dined with Zimmermann in Auteil. Afterwards we all went round to Halévy's; he lives very close to Zimmermann.

Monday 27 June. Composed and wrote out a small piano piece for Felice Romani's album. Visit from the artist Herbig. To Romani, Adam, Roqueplan. Visit from the Cavaliere Lopez, about the production of *Le Prophète* in Parma. Answered the Brothers Giaccone, impresarios of the Royal Theater in Turin. In the Opéra Comique: Auber's *L'Ambassadrice*.

Tuesday 28 June. Visited Véron. Completed the second revision of the *Étoile*, to ascertain its length. Visits from Perrin, from Brandus. In the evening attended the Bal Mabille.

Wednesday 29 June. Called on the Russian composer Glinka.[96] To Roqueplan, together with the director of the Parma Theater, Cavaliere Lopez. Visits from the American singer May, and from the Dutch singer Bertini. Opéra Comique: Adam's *Le Sourd.*

Thursday 30 June. Revised the text of my *Canzonette* with Santo Mango.[97] In the evening read through the libretto of the *Étoile*, with an eye to possible cuts.

July 1853

Friday 1 July. Visit from Scribe. To Brandus, where I found Hiller. Worked on abridgments and sundry alterations to the *Étoile*. Composed a new first *tempo* (G minor) for the duet of Prascovia and Georges. Dined with Véron. In the evening once more read through the dialogue in acts 2 and 3, to check on performing time.

Saturday 2 July. Visits from Merelli, from Glinka. Finished composing and writing out the new G minor *tempo* in the duet between Prascovia and Georges, and also scored it.

Sunday 3 July. Conference with Scribe, about the *Étoile*. Worked a little on abridgments and changes in the introduction to act 1 and the act 3 duet. Completed this work in the evening.

Monday 4 July. Visit from the Kapellmeister Romani. Letter from Bowes (one of Gagliani's editors).[98] Letter from Edmond Roche.[99] To Brandus. Worked from 12:15

until 3:15: finished the changes and abridgments in the introduction and the scoring. In the evening, worked generally on the *Étoile*.

Tuesday 5 July. Letter to Giaccone, impresario of the Royal Theater in Turin. Wrote to Princess Anna of Hesse-Cassel (together with the *Fackeltanz*), to Count Redern (together with the psalm), to Marquis Lucchesini, and to the attorney Bessel in Cologne. In the evening worked on the *Étoile* from 9:45 until 11:45. Changes and abridgments in Prascovia's aria.

Wednesday 6 July. Worked on the *Étoile*. To Jules Lecomte. Opéra Comique: *L'Ombre d'argentine*, opera in one act by Montfort.[100] Afterward worked on the *Étoile* for one and a half hours.

Thursday 7 July. Visits from Cavaliere Lopez from Parma, from Sina, from Felice Romani. To Véron, who wanted to take notes for his memoirs, about my first arrival in Paris for the *Crociato* at the Italian Opera. Wrote to Professor Herbig: extended my leave until 15 October. Letter from Professor Naumann. Opéra Comique: Auber's *Haydée*.

Friday 8 July. Wrote to Emil Naumann: refused his request for Blanca's hand. Visited Count Hatzfeld. Made abridgments and consequent changes in the Gypsy Roundelay, and finished writing them out. After lunch worked for two hours on the *Étoile*: wrote out and scored the changes in the duet of Peter and Catherine.

Saturday 9 July. Visit from Perrin. Worked on the *Étoile*: made a change in the duet for Catherine and Prascovia. Dined at Benoit Fould's.

Sunday 10 July. Worked for four hours: scored the alterations, revised the act 1 finale once again, and wrote out virtually all the instrumentation of the Hussar's Song, and also two pages of the Grenadier's Song. Then I went on a *tournée*[101] to acquaint myself at last with the *guinguettes* of Paris, about which so much has been written: *La Grande Chaumière, Le Bal Montesquieu, Le Jardin de Paris* (previously the *Prado d'été*). The life in these *guinguettes*, especially in the area of *Le Jardin de Paris*, struck me as particularly fascinating.[102]

Monday 11 July. Composed a third version of the first *tempo* of the duet for Prascovia and Georges in act 3. Letters from Halévy, Dr. Bamberg, and Ludovic Picard. In the evening worked from 8:30 until 10:30, writing out the instrumentation of the Grenadier's Song.

Tuesday 12 July. I wrote a fourth version of the first *tempo* of the act 3 duet for

Prascovia and George, and also composed a small entr'acte to the third act.[103] Visits from Sax and Dautresme. In the evening wrote out the fourth version of the duet for George and Prascovia.

Wednesday 13 July. I felt unwell and did very little. Visit from the singer Charton-Demeur, who sang for me: she has a lovely voice and brilliant delivery. Visit from the singer Depassio. Opéra Comique: Boieldieu's *Les Voitures versées*, Auber's *Le Maçon*.

Thursday 14 July. To Roqueplan, Mr. Charton, Brandus. Visit from the singer Bertini. I could not work at all. Dined with Halévy at Auteuil.

Friday 15 July. For one and a half hours before breakfast scored the latest version of the first *tempo* of the act 3 duet. Visits from the singer Devries, Perrin, Brandus, Dr. Bamberg (a loan of 300 fr.). To the lawyer Gautier in the evening, about the contract with Perrin. Then finished writing out the instrumentation of the Grenadier's Song.

Saturday 16 July. Wrote out and scored a part of the melodramatic scene in act 1.[104] To Le Roi about the revival of *Les Huguenots*. In the evening began to write out the instrumentation of the *Kriegslied* (one sheet). On 11 July in London, Jullien's concert of the complete music for *Struensee:* it appears to have passed unnoticed.

Sunday 17 July. Letter from Marquis Lucchesini. To the attorney Gautier, concerning the contract with Perrin. Worked from 12:30 until 4: wrote down, scored and revised the entire melodrama in act 1. In the evening from 8:30 until 11 scored six pages of the *Kriegslied*.

Monday 18 July. *Droits d'auteur* for the month of June: 515 fr. 30 c. Long conference with the singer Octave [Benoit] about the cuts in *Le Prophète* for Turin and Parma. Long conference with Brandus about the contract for the Opéra Comique. Conference with the stage manager, director of the orchestra, and *chef de chant de l'opéra* about the cuts in *Les Huguenots*. In the evening arranged the abridgments in the first act of the *Étoile* for the copyist, and called on Gouin. I therefore could not work at all today on the *Étoile*.

Tuesday 19 July. Wrote out the instrumentation of the *Kriegslied* before breakfast. Visit from Dietsch. Spent nearly the whole morning explaining the abridgments to the copyist, and checking on whether he had done them properly. Looked for an appropriate abridgment in the big closing scene of act 3, and wrote out the modification.

Wednesday 20 July. Worked on the abridgments in the big ensemble in act 3: this is difficult to do without spoiling the piece. Visit from Director Quehl of the Ministry of Foreign Affairs in Berlin, who directs the whole official Prussian press: Dr. Bamberg introduced him to me. Conference with Brandus about the contract with Perrin. In the evening wrote out and scored the different abridgments in the act 3 ensemble.

Thursday 21 July. Visit from Abbé Goumard, *maître de chapelle* in the Church of St. Philippe du Roule, to whom I presented my psalm. Audition in the Opéra of the singer Madame Lafont from Marseilles. Conference with the lawyer Gautier concerning the contract with the Opéra Comique. In the evening worked a little more on the *Étoile.*

Friday 22 July. Letter from the Chevalier Lopez in Parma. Composed a fourth version of the passage in Prascovia's aria ("Croyant à mon..."), wrote it out, and scored it. Visits from the singer Demoiselle Klotz, from Herr Octave, and Dautresme. Wrote seven pages of the instrumentation of Quadruple Chorus into the full score. Dinner with Véron. In the Opéra Comique: acts 2 and 3 of Auber's *Haydée.*

Saturday 23 July. Letter from Count Redern. Wrote to Chevalier Lopez in Parma. Letter from Stawinsky. Wrote out several pages of the Quadruple Chorus. Conference with Perrin about the contract for my *opéra comique.* Dined with the Prussian ambassador, Count Hatzfeld. Opéra Comique: Monsigny's *Le Déserteur.*[105]

Sunday 24 July. Letter from Felice Romani. Visit from Madame Appiani and her daughter from Milan; the latter is a composer and wants to write an opera.[106] Gave lessons to Dautresme again, for the first time since my return to Paris. Finished writing out the instrumentation of the Quadruple Chorus in two hours. Afterward worked for one and a half hours on changes to Pierre's romance (act 3), and worked on a new orchestration of the second couplet. Dined at Dr. Bamberg's, where I found Quehl, the banker Hirschfeld, and other Germans; I also made the acquaintance of the famous writer Dr. Riesser from Hamburg.[107] To my unpleasant surprise the author Champein was also there: on account of his libeling of Madame Stoltz he had been obliged to flee, but now suddenly has reappeared in Paris.[108]

Monday 25 July. Worked for one and a half hours before breakfast on the newly conceived orchestration of the second couplet of Pierre's romance (act 3). Visit from the singer Delsarte.[109] To Gathy, to Gouin. Worked for another one and a half hours on scoring the second couplet. Completed this between 8:30 and 10.

Tuesday 26 July. Called on Fiorentino (see cash book), and Count Pillet-Will.

Began the writing the instrumentation of the act 2 finale into the full score. Shortened the finale somewhat.

Wednesday 27 July. Before breakfast worked on changes in the contract with the Opéra Comique. Visit from the singer Demoiselle Masson.[110] Worked a little on the instrumentation of the act 2 finale. Conference with the ballet master Mazilier* about the new *pas* in *Les Huguenots*. Conference with Sax and Brandus about the engagement of the singer Charton. In the Théâtre des Variétés: Favart's *Les Trois Sultanes*.[111]

Thursday 28 July. Visits from Leo, from Charton-Demeur, and Sax. In the evening worked for three hours on the new sequences, which the ballet master wants appended to the Gypsy Dance in *Les Huguenots*. I more or less completed them.

Friday 29 July. To Auber, to Le Roi, to Blanche, *sécretaire général du ministère d'état*: recommendation for Dietsch.[112] Letter from Emil Naumann. Finished composing and writing out the three new pieces for the ballet music in *Les Huguenots*. In the evening continued writing out the instrumentation of the act 2 finale (*Étoile*).

Saturday 30 July. Before breakfast wrote out the instrumentation of the act 2 finale for one and a half hours. To Berlioz and Vatry. In the evening worked for three hours on the instrumentation of the act 2 finale.

Sunday 31 July. Symptoms of a cold. For one and a half hours before breakfast scored the new sections of the ballet music. Called Berlioz, Véron, Brandus.

August 1853

Monday 1 August. My head was so numb that I could not work. To Sardou*, returning his manuscript of the libretto *Hamlet*. Played the ballet master Mazilier my new dance music for *Les Huguenots*. In the Opéra Comique: Auber's *Le Domino noir*.

Tuesday 2 August. Scored the ballet pieces for *Les Huguenots* (four and a half hours).

Wednesday 3 August. Finished scoring the five new pieces of ballet music for *Les Huguenots*. In the Opéra Comique: Ambroise Thomas's *Le Caïd*.

Thursday 4 August. Visit from the concertmaster Baerwald from Stockholm, cousin of the one I knew in Vienna.[113] By written invitation of the minister of state, Fould,

I today attended the rehearsal of *Les Huguenots* in the newly decorated opera house.

Friday 5 August. [No entry.]

Saturday 6 August. [No entry.]

Sunday 7 August. Wrote out the instrumentation of the act 2 finale [of *L'Étoile du Nord*]. Opéra Comique: Monsigny's *Le Déserteur*.

Monday 8 August. Wrote to Chevalier Lopez in Parma, enclosing the cavatina from the *Crociato*. In the Opéra: rehearsal of the trio in act 5 of *Les Huguenots*. In the evening wrote out the melodramatic scene in act 3[114] and sketched the entire conclusion of the opera [*L'Étoile du Nord*] in the full score.

Tuesday 9 August. My headache lasted the whole day and prevented me from working. Conference with Gautier, concerning the contract with the Opéra Comique.

Wednesday 10 August. The headache and stomach disorder continue. Wrote letters: otherwise did nothing.

Thursday 11 August. Visits from Davis, director of the theater in New Orleans, Émile Deschamps, Julius [Beer], Dehaes from Brussels,[115] with his daughter, who wants to enter the Conservatoire. Conference with Brandus and Perrin, where I signed the contract.[116] Opéra Comique: Monsigny's *Le Déserteur*.

Friday 12 August. Called on Louis Desnoyer, Théophile Gautier, Armand Bertin. Spent the whole day on packing and other preparations for departure to Dieppe, which the doctor has prescribed for the recuperation[117] of my cough. Delivered a copy of the *traité*, which Perrin must sign, to Brandus.

Saturday 13 August. Busy with preparations for departure. Conference with Perrin concerning the difficulties connected with the production of the *Étoile*: the Society of Authors now want to categorize it as a translation. Visit from Herr von Hülsen. In the evening completely wrote out the new entr'acte to act 3.[118]

Sunday 14 August. At nine o'clock left by railway train for Dieppe, where I arrived at two o'clock.

Monday 15 August. My nephew Julius and his wife arrived in Dieppe. Meeting with Vatel. In the evening scored three sides of the entr'acte to act 3.

Tuesday 16 August. Finished scoring the entr'acte.

Wednesday 17 August. In the evening began a new revision of the *Étoile*.

Thursday 18 August. In the morning and evening worked diligently on the revision of the *Étoile*. Made a good change (how the musicians tune their instruments in the [act 1] finale).

Friday 19 August. I appear to have caught cold from the brisk air. Continued with the revision of the *Étoile*.

Saturday 20 August. Worked in the morning and evening on the revision of the *Étoile*.

Sunday 21 August. Completed the revision of the *Étoile*. Visit from Brandus.

Monday 22 August. The idea occurred to me to integrate a solo for Gritzenko into the Cossack Chorus. This would provide Hermann Léon with a brilliant entry.[119] In the evening I finished composing this new solo, and wrote it out, to some extent.[120]

Tuesday 23 August. [No entry.]

Wednesday 24 August. Letter from Scribe. Letter from Brandus. Worked on the notes for Véron's memoirs.[121] Changed and improved the solo for Gritzenko.

Thursday 25 August. Abandoned the Cossack Chorus and the newly composed solo for Gritzenko, and in its place composed a fresh song for Gritzenko using the same words. The idea suddenly occurred to me this morning and pleases me (at least so far). Princess Mathilde (cousin of the emperor) sent me an invitation to hear music performed by Les Guides,[122] who were serenading her in her apartments, but I had already gone to bed.[123]

Friday 26 August. Letters from Brandus, Herr von Hülsen, Gouin, Lapelouze. Wrote to Brandus, Herr von Hülsen.

Saturday 27 August. Letter from Brandus. Finished writing out the new song for Gritzenko, and also made a copy of it to send to Paris so that the chorus parts can be written out immediately.

Sunday 28 August. Letter from Roger. In the evening there was a big *soirée musicale* at the emperor's, to which I was invited. The oboist, Henry, presented me to the emperor and the empress (at the express wish of the empress): both were exceptionally gracious and affectionate towards me.

Monday 29 August. Scored half of the new *chanson*.

Tuesday 30 August. Departed at 11:30 by train for Paris.

Wednesday 31 August. Colic spasms. I stayed in bed all day.

September 1853

Thursday 1 September. Conference with Scribe, concerning the possible objections by the Society of Authors to the *Étoile* as a translation. Opéra Comique: first performance of Halévy's *Le Nabab*, a success.[124]

Friday 2 September. To Brandus, to Gautier: conference about my contract. Visits from the famous tenor Tamberlick, from Tedesco, from Kapellmeister Baerwald, and from a young Swedish singer, Mlle. Michal, who has a very beautiful soprano voice.[125] Opéra Comique: Auber's *Marco Spada*.

Saturday 3 September. I began the cold-water rubdowns again. The director of the Opéra Comique, Émile Perrin, betook himself to the Commission des Auteurs et Compositeurs Dramatiques to explain to them that the newspaper reports, describing *L'Étoile du Nord* as simply a translation of *Le Camp de Silésie*, are a lie. Of the twenty pieces of music that make up the *L'Étoile du Nord*, only six are from *Le Camp de Silésie*. Everything else is new. The commission explained that it had never intended taking *démarche*[126] against the production of the opera, and decided that two of its members, Ferdinand Langlé[127] and Ambroise Thomas, should call on me to express the regret of the commission that I could ever have thought them capable of such an intention, and to convey to me their *sentiments de bonne confraternité et d'attachement*[128]. Call from Langlé and Aigoin,[129] the new *associé* of the directors of the Opéra: they did not find me in. Visit from the baritone Beaucé.[130] Scribe, who is president of the commission, came to tell me of the outcome. Conference with Gautier about the supplementary clauses to the *traité*.

Sunday 4 September. Strange letter from the theater agent Roux, giving me advice about how I should compose in future. I returned Langlé's call. Théâtre Lyrique: Adam's *Le Roi des Halles*.[131]

Monday 5 September. My birthday. May Almighty God bless my entry into this new year of my life. May he also bless my opera *L'Étoile du Nord*, granting it the special grace of recognition by the best of my contemporaries, the public, and the press; may it be brought to production this winter in Paris, with brilliant and enduring success. Théâtre Lyrique: Adolphe Vogel's *La Moissoneuse*.[132]

Tuesday 6 September. Conference with Gautier; read through the *traité* again. Visits from Roqueplan, Duprez with his daughter, and Simon. Almost finished scoring Gritzenko's new *chanson*. Visit from Marquise Martellini from Florence. Letter from Madame Charton-Demeur in Marseilles. Sent my Psalm 91 to Music Director Damcke in St. Petersburg.

Wednesday 7 September. Finished orchestrating Gritzenko's new *chanson*. At twelve o'clock met with Perrin at Brandus's, and we signed the *traité* for my *opéra comique*. With Scribe to the Opéra Comique, where he read the libretto of our new opera to the singers. They appeared to like most of it, but, I think, not the dénouement. Visit from the Swedish singer Michal. In the morning and evening wrote down reminiscences of my first sojourn in Paris, which Véron wants for his memoirs.

Thursday 8 September. Rehearsal of *Les Huguenots* in the Opéra, with the singers and chorus. In the evening *mise en scène* rehearsal of act 5 of *Les Huguenots*. Chorley* from London came to see me.[133]

Friday 9 September. For one hour before breakfast, and two hours afterward, played through act 1 of *L'Étoile du Nord* in order to prepare myself for the rehearsals. Called on Chorley, Gouin, Duprez and his family. Studied the role of Valentine in *Les Huguenots* with Mademoiselle Laborde. *Mise en scène* rehearsal of *Les Huguenots* in the evening at the Opéra.

Saturday 10 September. Revised and played through act 1 again for two hours. Perrin came to see me. In the Opéra: a general rehearsal of *Les Huguenots*. My partially new ballet music elicited no sign of enthusiasm, whereas, by contrast, the Bénédiction des Poignards, which was strengthened by a hundred choristers, created a tremendous impression, and I was called out by the musicians, to great applause.

Sunday 11 September. Very busy with the preparations for the first rehearsal of the comic opera, and the performance of *Les Huguenots*, both of which take place tomorrow. In the evening the dress rehearsal of *Les Huguenots*.

Monday 12 September. Read through act 3 of the *Étoile* several times, in order to write down the necessary observations for the copyist of the Opéra Comique. This copyist (Robin) arrived at ten o'clock: I gave him the full score of act 3, as well as the choral parts and full score of act 1, since the chorus master wants to begin the rehearsals of the *Étoile* today. I also began the singing rehearsals, insofar as I played through the roles, firstly of Demoiselle Duprez, and then of Demoiselle Lefèbre in act 1, and afterward sent them home with their scores. Letters from Madame Küchenmeister, Roger, George Sand, Appiani. Today the newly restored Opera House opened with *Les Huguenots* (233d performance, receipts 6,393 fr. 12 c.) in the presence of the emperor and empress. Up to act 4 the reception was rather cold. However, the Bénédiction des Poignards, with the reinforced chorus, exercised a tremendous effect, as did the subsequent duet in which Gueymard was very good.[134]

Tuesday 13 September. To Gouin. Sang Bataille his role in act 1.[135] I hosted a dinner *à 12 fr.* per person. The guests were Théophile Gautier, Chorley and Hullah* from London, Julius Benedict, Jules Lecomte, Berlioz, Gouin, Brandus, Édouard Monnais. In the Gymnase: the first performance of *Le Pressoir*, a pastoral genre picture by George Sand: a delightful play, acted superbly.[136] Madame Sand had sent me a stall ticket and a charming letter.

Wednesday 14 September. Played Duprez his daughter's role. In the Opéra: *Les Huguenots* (234th performance; receipts 9,873 fr. 71 c.).

Thursday 15 September. Rehearsal: Demoiselle Lefèbre and Demoiselle Duprez sang their roles in act 1 to me for the first time. Audition of the singer Michal from Stockholm in the Grand Opéra: a wonderfully beautiful voice. Opéra Comique: Halévy's *Le Nabab*.

Friday 16 September. The theater director Lumley from London came to see me. He came a second time in the evening. Studied Mocker's role in act 1 with him.[137] Changed several things in the chorus master's score. Visits from the singer Mlle. Bosio, and from Julius Benedict. Stayed at home in the evening without working because of a headache.

Saturday 17 September. Rehearsal with Bataille, with Demoiselle Duprez. To Perrin. Visit from the Swedish singer Demoiselle Michal.

Sunday 18 September. To Armand Bertin and Aigoin.

Monday 19 September. Rehearsal of the *Étoile* in my apartments. Dined with Benedict. In the evening to the Opéra for *Le Prophète* (145th performance; receipts 10,027 fr.).

Tuesday 20 September. Diarrhea. Stayed in bed all day.

Wednesday 21 September. I held a rehearsal of the *Étoile* in my apartments. Wrote to Gaetano Rossi in Verona, together with 300 fr. support. Letter from Hofrat Teichmann.

Thursday 22 September. Wrote to Herr von Hülsen. Rehearsal of the *Étoile*. In the evening composed a new recitative for the *Chanson du Grenadier*.

Friday 23 September. Rehearsal of the *Étoile*. In the evening to the Opéra Comique for Adam's *Le Toréador*; Donizetti's *La Fille du régiment*.

Sunday 24 September. For the first time held a rehearsal on the stage of the Opéra Comique. In the evening wrote down and scored Gritzenko's new recitative, as well as other small adjustments to the *Étoile*.

Sunday 25 September. Visits from the Danish composer Salomon, from the singer Octave, from the contralto Mademoiselle Wiedmann, from the journalists Simon and Jéré, and from a young man, Clerc de Nauvelle, whom Scribe has recommended: he wants to become a singer. Conference with Robin, copyist of the Opéra Comique. Played my [third] *Fackeltanz* to Sax and Mohr: they want to arrange it for Sax instruments.

Monday 26 September. Rehearsal of the *Étoile*. These rehearsals usually last three hours, and tire me so much, that afterwards I am no longer able to work. Wrote to Madame Charton-Demeur in Marseilles. Letter from the theater director Provini in Marseilles. The baritone Beaucé and the tenor Brignoli (the latter recommended by Fiorentino)[138] sang for me. In the Opéra: Donizetti's *Lucie de Lammermoor*.

Tuesday 27 September. Played the duet in act 3 for Madame Lefèbre and Jourdan.[139] The son of Ferdinand Langlé has asked me to compose a ballad in his new drama.[140] Visit from Émile Deschamps. In the evening worked on small *raccords*[141] in the *Étoile*.

Wednesday 28 September. Rehearsal of the *Étoile*. In the evening worked on connections in the *Étoile*.

Thursday 29 September. Played pieces from act 3 of the *Étoile* to Demoiselle Duprez, M. Bataille, Hermann Léon, and Mocker. Visit from the Danish composer Salomon.

Friday 30 September. Rehearsal of the *Étoile*. Visits from the poet Paul Faucher, Langlé, and my nephew Julius. In the Opéra: *Le Prophète* (146th performance; receipts 10,198 fr. 35 c.), which was given by command of Queen Christina of

Spain,[142] to a crowded house. Letter from the committee of the Karlsruhe Music Festival.

October 1853

Saturday 1 October. Rehearsal of the *Étoile*. Letter to Liszt in Karlsruhe. Wrote to the theater director Provini in Marseilles.

Sunday 2 October. Rehearsal of the *Étoile*: began act 3. Letter from Herr von Hülsen. Paul Faucher read me the plan of *Le Roi des aules (Erlkönig)*. In the evening lingered for a moment in *Robert le Diable*.

Monday 3 October. Letter from Kapellmeister Saint-d'Arod in Lyons. Rehearsal of the *Étoile*, for the first time with the chorus. Visits from Brandus and Madame Koreff. In the evening finished composing and writing out the ballad for the comedy *La Corde de pendu* by Langlé. Today saw the death of the great savant François Arrago*.

Tuesday 4 October. Rehearsal of acts 1 and 2 of the *Étoile*. Called on Buloz. Visit from the actor Brindeau of the Théâtre Français:[143] I played him the ballad that he is to sing in the comedy *La Corde de pendu*. Madame Laborde came to see me.

Wednesday 5 October. Called Armand Bertin. Attended the funeral of the great savant Arrago. Rehearsal of the *Étoile*.

Thursday 6 October. Rehearsal of the *Étoile*. Visit from Viardot. Wrote to Herr von Hülsen.

Friday 7 October. Visited Madame Viardot. Rehearsal of the *Étoile*. Studied my new ballad in the play *La Corde de pendu* with the actor Brindeau. Visit from Heinrich Schlesinger. In the evening wrote the vocal line of the ballad into the full score.

Saturday 8 October. Rehearsed the *Étoile*. In the Théâtre Lyrique: Adam's *Le Bijou perdu*.[144] Madame Cabel made her début in this opera: a very striking talent, especially for brilliant coloratura singing.

Sunday 9 October. No rehearsal of the *Étoile*. Finished scoring the ballad for the comedy *La Corde de pendu*.

Monday 10 October. Rehearsal of the *Étoile*.

Tuesday 11 October. Woke up with a sore throat, diarrhea, runny nose, and a headache.

I did not go to the rehearsal of the *Étoile*, and stayed in bed until four o'clock. Today I hosted a dinner (358 fr.) in the Café de Paris to which I invited ten people: Vicomte Paul Daru, Armand and Édouard Bertin, Reber, Berlioz, Cousin, Wihl, John Lemoine, Gouin.

Wednesday 12 October. Rehearsal, with the chorus, of the *Étoile*. In the evening examined the score and marked it with letters.

Thursday 13 October. Rehearsal of the *Étoile*. Visited Baron James Rothschild, who is here now, with Richard Wagner.[145] He was very embarrassed to see me for the third time without having called on me. A few hours later he came round. Visit from the theater director Woltersdorff from Königsberg. For the first time I witnessed the rites in a Portuguese synagogue, on the occasion of the induction of a new rabbi.[146] Made the acquaintance of the pianist Edouard Wolff* and his brother-in-law, Miot, owner of *Le Pays*.[147]

Friday 14 October. Rehearsal of the *Étoile*. Visited Liszt and the Princess Wittgenstein.[148] Worked for two hours on the revision of the score of the *Étoile*.

Sunday 15 October. Choral rehearsal of the *Étoile*. Called on Véron. Big dinner at the Prussian ambassador, von Hatzfeld's, in honor of our king's birthday. Afterward to the Grand Opéra, for the dress rehearsal of Limnander's new two-act opera *Le Maître chanteur*.[149]

Sunday 16 October. To Gautier to consult him about my *traité* with Perrin, who has began to raise problems about the costumes and the military music. Visit from Langlé. In the evening wrote a letter, ostensibly to Brandus, but actually for Perrin, and continued with the revision of the score of the *Étoile*.

Monday 17 October. To the Comédie Française: rehearsed my new ballad for Langlé's comedy, with Brindeau and the orchestra. The play is now called *Murillo*. Then a rehearsal of the *Étoile*. In the Opéra: first performance of Limnander's *Le Maître chanteur*.

Tuesday 18 October. Rehearsal of the *Étoile*. Visited Véron. In the Théâtre Français: *Murillo* (first performance), *comédie* by Aylic Langlé; music of the *ballade* by Meyerbeer.[150]

Wednesday 19 October. Rehearsal with Sax instruments of my [third] *Fackeltanz*, then a rehearsal of the *Étoile*. In the evening read and played through the trio and sextet in act 2.

Thursday 20 October. Rehearsal of the *Étoile*: tried the trio in act 2 for the first time. Opéra Comique: first performance of Cadaux's *Colette*.[151]

Friday 21 October. Rehearsal of the *Étoile*. In the evening played through and revised the sextet and Gritzenko's *couplets* (act 2).

Saturday 22 October. Altered a small phrase at the beginning of the sextet. Rehearsal of the *Étoile*: for the first time tried the sextet in act 2. Visited Madame Milland. (Milland and Mirker are two remarkably successful Jewish issuing-bankers who own *Le Constitutionnel du Pays* and *L'Entracte*.)

Sunday 23 October. Rehearsal of the *Étoile*. Visited Fétis and Cotterau.

Monday 24 October. Second rehearsal of my *Fackeltanz*; Fétis was also present. Rehearsal with the chorus of the *Étoile*. Dined at Count Pillet-Will's.

Tuesday 25 October. First *mise en scène* rehearsal of act 1 of the *Étoile*. Visits from Fétis and from Heugel*, to whom I have given the romance from *Murillo* for publication. I hosted a dinner today in my apartment for eleven people (cost, 300 fr.). The guests were: Véron, Auber, Halévy, Adam, Fiorentino, Édouard Monnais, Perrin, Gouin, Movel *(directeur du Conservatoire de Marseille),* Scribe.

Wednesday 26 October. The *Generaldirektor der Museen*, Olfers, from Berlin, the former singer Mme. Paulin from Berlin (now Madame Giacomelli), Heugel, and Grüneisen from London all came to see me. Second *mise en scène* rehearsal of act 1 of the *Étoile*. Called on Grüneisen. In the evening revision of the score of the *Étoile*.

Thursday 27 October. Letter from Sternau in Cologne. *Mise en scène* rehearsal of act 1. Heard act 1 of Halévy's *Le Nabab* in the Opéra Comique, then continued with the revision of the *Étoile*. Letter from the regisseur Moritz Ernst in Mainz: wants to give *Struensee* for a benefit.

Friday 28 October. Fourth *mise en scène* rehearsal. I did not participate so as to stay at home and work. Revision of the score of the *Étoile*, in order to make the second couplet of Gritzenko's *chanson* possible. In the evening likewise worked on the revision of the score.

Saturday 29 October. Letter from Maestro Romani, announcing the success of *Le Prophète* in Turin. Worked on the revision of the score. Rehearsed the act 1 finale with the chorus. In the evening spent a moment at Levasseur's benefit in the Opéra,[152] then continued working on the revision of the score.

Sunday 30 October. Worked on the revision of the score.

Monday 31 October. Rehearsal of act 2 of the *Étoile*.

November 1853

Tuesday 1 November. Fifth *mise en scène* rehearsal of act 1. Visit from Giacomelli.

Wednesday 2 November. Went through the *Chanson du Cosaque* (for Delaunay) with Garaudé.[153] Sixth *mise en scène* rehearsal of act 1, which, however, I did not attend, in order to work on the revision of act 1—which I worked at very diligently. At the organ-builder Alexandre's, I heard the newly invented piano made for Liszt: it has three keyboards of different registers, can prolong notes, etc.

Thursday 3 November. Rehearsal of act 2.

Friday 4 November. Seventh *mise en scène* rehearsal of act 1. In the evening lingered for a moment at *Robert le Diable,* where Boulo was singing Raimbaud and Madame Steller Alice.

Saturday 5 November. To the funeral of Germaine Delavigne's mother, where, quite of itself, the awkwardness between me and the composer Clapisson melted. Called on Scudo and Madame Zimmermann. Eighth *mise en scène* rehearsal of act 1. Worked a little on the revision of the score of the *Étoile*.

Sunday 6 November. Rehearsal of acts 2 and 3 of the *Étoile*. In the evening worked on the revision of the *Étoile*.

Monday 7 November. Revision of the stage music. For the first time, rehearsed the chorus and soloists in the *Étoile* together. Called on Véron. Dined at Count Pillet-Will's.

Tuesday 8 November. Revision of the stage music. Called on Véron. Ninth *mise en scène* rehearsal of act 1. Invitation from the Emperor Napoleon to join him for five days of his *villeggiatura* in Fontainebleau.[154]

Wednesday 9 November. Letter from the committee for the Weber Memorial in Eutin. Rehearsal of acts 2 and 3 of the *Étoile*. Worked for an hour before lunch and two hours in the evening on the revision of the stage music.

Thursday 10 November. Sitting of the Comité de Surveillance de l'Enseignement des Conservatoire, about the appointment of a professor of contrabass and oboe. Then the tenth *mise en scène* rehearsal of the *Étoile*.

Friday 11 November. Wrote to the duke of Bassano and to Scribe. Rehearsal of acts 2 and 3 of the *Étoile*. [Went] with Wolff to make the acquaintance of La Guéronnière.[155] In the evening completed the revision of the stage music and began the revision of act 3. Letter from Madame Ugalde in Nice.

Saturday 12 November to Wednesday 30 November. A redness, swelling, and pain appeared in the upper joint of my right arm. I had to carry my arm in a sling and was not allowed either to write or to play the piano. A big abscess developed, which fortunately diminished of its own. Letter from the duke of Saxe-Coburg-Gotha, who asks me to inspect and correct the revision of his new opera, *Santa Chiara*. On 28 November the king of Bavaria[156] established a new Order for Art and Science: my name was among the first on the list of those honored.

December 1853

Thursday 1 December. Visit from Émile Deschamps. Rehearsal of act 2 of the *Étoile* with the singers, then with the chorus. Conference with Scribe about the finale of act 2. In the evening worked on the version of the Chœur des Conjurés,[157] in which the military music will be replaced by the orchestra.

Friday 2 December. Audition with Sax of my [third] *Fackeltanz*. *Mise en scène* rehearsal, with the chorus and soloists, of acts 1 and 3. Played the military music of the act 2 finale of the *Étoile* to Sax and Mohr, and gave it to them to study. In the evening worked on the substitute for the military music in the Chœur des Conjurés.

Saturday 3 December. Third quartet rehearsal. First rehearsal of act 3. Visit from Simon. In the evening completed the changes in the instrumentation of the Chœur des Conjurés. Answered the duke of Saxe-Gotha.

Sunday 4 December. Feverish pulse. I stayed at home, and did not attend the rehearsal. Performance of my *Fackeltanz* in a concert *pour les incendies de la rue Bambourg:*[158] it was called for *da capo*.

Monday 5 December. I felt better, but stayed at home as a precaution. Dictated two letters to Dingelstedt. Scribe sent the changes to the act 2 finale, and I attended to them. Letter from the regisseur Ernst in Mainz. Wrote to Ernst.

Tuesday 6 December. On account of the terrible weather and my cough, which has unfortunately worsened, I stayed at home all day, and worked diligently on the changes to the act 2 finale.

Wednesday 7 December. Wrote to Dingelstedt in Munich about Shakespeare's *Sturm* [*The Tempest*], and to Cornet in Vienna. Finished composing the changes in the act 2 finale, and wrote the vocal parts into the full score.

Thursday 8 December. Letter from Professor Herbig. Wrote ostensibly to Dingelstedt, but actually for the king [Maximilian II]. First rehearsal of act 1 for the wind instruments only. In the evening worked on the instrumentation of the altered passages in the act 2 finale.

Friday 9 December. Scored the altered passages in the act 2 finale. First *mise en scène* rehearsal of act 2. Visit from the music dealer Schott, from Mainz. In the evening worked on the other changes in the act 2 finale that Scribe wants. Today my *Fackeltanz* was performed in the Grand Opéra for the benefit of the *caisse des pensions*,[159] but without the great enthusiasm it received in the Salle Sainte Cécile.

Saturday 10 December. Second rehearsal of act 1 with the wind instruments. Conference with Scribe about the changes in the act 2 finale. Visit from Carl Eckert.

Sunday 11 December. Completed and scored the various changes in the finale, and even revised the whole of it.

Monday 12 December. First rehearsal of act 3, with the wind instruments. In the evening worked on the new romance for the role of Prascovia in act 3, and finished writing it out.[160]

Tuesday 13 December. Worked on the orchestration of Prascovia's romance. *Mise en scène* rehearsal of act 1.

Wednesday 14 December. Letter from Dautresme in Elboeuf. Called on Armand Bertin. Finished scoring Prascovia's romance. *Mise en scène* rehearsal of act 2. In the evening composed a melodrama for the sextet, suggested by the *mise en scène*.

Thursday 15 December. *Mise en scène* rehearsal with the chorus and soloists of act 1. Conference with Sax and Mohr. In the evening scored the melodrama in the sextet.

Friday 16 December. Attended to a change in the duet for Prascovia and Catherine wanted by Scribe, and wrote it out. For the second time rehearsed act 3 and the act 1 finale, with the wind instruments alone, without singers. Perrin read me the comic opera *Psyche* by Barbier and Carré.[161] In the evening wrote out six pages of the entr'acte to act 2.[162]

Saturday 17 December. Mise en scène rehearsal of act 2. Dined with the painter Lehmann. In the evening to a soirée at Buloz's. *Le Prophète* has been given by the Italian Opera of New York.[163]

Sunday 18 December. Mise en scène rehearsal of act 2. Studied Cruvelli's role in *Les Huguenots* with her in the Opéra. In the evening arranged the orchestra in act 2, in case I should leave out the big band and retain the military music only for the small marches.

Monday 19 December. Letter from the poetess Chézy in Geneva. Letter from Kammermusikus Krämer in Coburg, on behalf of the duke. For two hours before the rehearsal, worked on the arrangement of the big *banda* in the finale, and completed this task. First quartet rehearsal of act 2, without singing. In the evening continued writing the act 2 entr'acte into the full score (one and a half hours).

Tuesday 20 December. Today the duke of Coburg's opera, *Santa Chiara*, arrived. Finished writing the entr'acte into the full score. Called on Véron and Madame Milland; took the latter the ballad. Visit from Heugel and [David Hermann] Engel*. In the evening attended to various changes that are needed in the score.

Wednesday 21 December. Made various changes, necessitated by the *mise en scène.* Played the finale to Bataille. Rehearsed the music of acts 2 and 3, chorus and soloists together. Called on Benedict. Théâtre Gymnase: *Diane de Lys*, drama by Alexandre Dumas,[164] the *grand succès du jour.*[165] Called on Véron.

Thursday 22 December. Rehearsal of the singers in act 2. Tried the Flute Piece with Mlle. Duprez and the two flautists on the stage. Worked on the alterations that still have to be attended to. Studied the role of Valentine with Demoiselle Cruvelli, for her début in the Opéra. In the Opéra Comique: Auber's *Marco Spada.*

Friday 23 December. Conference with Scribe. Second quartet rehearsal of act 2. Called on Halévy. Invited Davison and Berlioz to dinner at the Hôtel de Paris. Visit from Cornette.[166]

Saturday 24 December. Because of the indisposition of several singers, there was no rehearsal today. Wrote to the king of Bavaria. Called on M. Blanche, *chef du cabinet* of Minister Fould, and interceded for Dietsch and Cornette, who want to be nominated for the cross of the Legion of Honor. Dined with Buloz; Rémusat was also present. Wrote to Count Redern: requested an indefinite extension of my leave.

Sunday 25 December. No rehearsal on account of the indisposition of the singers. Made changes to the harp part in the act 3 finale. In the Théâtre Lyrique: Adam's *Le Bijou perdu.*

Monday 26 December. Rehearsal of the act 2 finale; *mise en scène* of act 1.

Tuesday 27 December. Rehearsal of the act 2 finale; then *mise en scène* of act 2. Called on Roqueplan. Théâtre Italien: Donizetti's *Lucia di Lammermoor. Droits d'auteur* for November: 332 fr.

Wednesday 28 December. Wrote to Sina, enclosing 100 fr. New Year's gift. With Madame Célérier to buy the *étrennes,*[167] which I want to give to my singers at the Opéra Comique. Called on Madame Milland. *Mise en scène* rehearsal of act 1 with the chorus and soloists. Rehearsed the act 4 duet in *Les Huguenots* with De-moiselle Cruvelli. Opéra Comique: Reber's one-act *Les Papillotes de Mr Benoist.*[168]

Thursday 29 December. In both the morning and evening began writing out the overture. First rehearsal with the wind instruments of act 2.

Friday 30 December. In the morning wrote out one side of the overture. Rehearsed the act 1 ensembles, chorus and soloists, as well as *mise en scène.* Then in the Grand Opéra, practiced the act 3 duet with Marcel in *Les Huguenots.* In the evening wrote out three and a half sides of the overture (in two and a half hours).

Saturday 31 December. Bought New Year's presents for the four lady vocalists in my comic opera—Mesdemoiselles Duprez, Lefèbre, Lemercier,[169] and Decroix[170]—and for Madame Jules Janin (altogether 950 fr.), as well as *bonbons* for the twenty-three women members of the chorus (140 fr.). Rehearsal, *mise en scène* with soloists and chorus, of the act 1 and 3 ensembles. Wrote out the overture for one and a quarter hours in the early morning, and did the same in the evening for two hours.

The old year is coming to an end. May God bless my loved ones and me as well; may the new year we are entering into tomorrow be happy, and bring much joy. Amen.

NOTES

1. The Italian mezzo-soprano Giulia Sanchioli (b. 1860), a native of Milan, was discovered by Pietro Romani in Rome, where she was singing Norma. She appeared on many Italian stages, in London and Barcelona. She sang Fidès in Florence (26 December 1852), Milan (31 December 1855), Genoa (17 May 1857), and Venice (22 January 1859).

2. Meyerbeer had first heard the tenor Octave Benoit on 26 September 1849 in Brussels; he made a fairly good impression on the composer.

3. The playwright and librettist Eugène Deligny (1816–81) was the author of many *comédies* and *vaudevilles,* as well as being the general secretary of the Paris Opéra (1846–54).

4. *Un Fils de famille, comédie-vaudeville* in three acts (Bayard & E. Desnoyers, according to Wicks [17403]; Paris, Théâtre du Gymnase Dramatique, 25 November 1852).

5. Fr. "financial success," i.e., a box-office success.

6. Dupeuty and Bourget, *La Faridondaine, drame* in five acts (with L. A. de Groot; Paris, Théâtre de la Porte-Saint-Martin, 30 December 1852) [Wicks 17092].

7. Sandeau, *Mademoiselle de la Seiglière,* prose *comédie* in four acts (with Régnier de la Brière; Paris, Théâtre Français, 4 November 1851) [Wicks 18715].

8. Paganini, Violin Concerto no. 2 in B Minor *(La Campanella),* op. 7 (1826).

9. Amédée-David, marquis de Pastoret (1791–1856), French politician and writer.

10. See 17 December 1852.

11. Gastinel, *Le Miroir, opéra comique* in one act (text by Bayard & Davrecourt), a "canevas fort léger" [very light sketch], according to Clément & Larousse (1:745).

12. Beethoven, String Quartet no. 14 in C-sharp Minor, op. 131 (1826).

13. Beethoven, String Quartet no. 12 in E-flat Major, op. 127 (1824).

14. Alexandre Dumas (*père*), *Hamlet, Prince de Danemark,* verse *drame* in five acts (with Paul Meurice, from the play by Shakespeare; Paris, Théâtre Historique, 15 December 1847) [Wicks 9829].

15. Jules Barbier & Michel Carré turned *Hamlet* into a *grand opéra* for Ambroise Thomas (9 March 1868).

16. Failing to obtain the hand of a princess of equal birth, Napoleon III married the Countess Eugénie de Montijo on 29 January 1853. The ball must be seen in the context of the celebrations surrounding this marriage. "Louis Napoleon in general's uniform, and Eugénie in a dress of white velvet *épinglé,* with a diamond crown on her head, entered the cathedral [Notre Dame] through the great door to the strains of the march from Meyerbeer's *Le Prophète,* preceded by all the great officers of state, and walked hand in hand up the aisle to the altar where they were married by the Archbishop of Paris. They returned safely to the Tuileries and appeared on the balcony. . . . In the evening, Paris was illuminated" (Jasper Ridley, *Napoleon and Eugénie* [London: Constable, 1979], p. 335).

17. *Les Saltimbanques.* Wicks [13082] lists only the *comédie-parade* in three acts by T.-M. Dumersan & Ch.-V. Varin; Paris, Théâtre des Variétés, 25 January 1838.

18. *Madame Bertrand et Mademoiselle Raton, comédie-vaudeville* in one act (Dumanoir & Lafargue; Paris, Théâtre du Palais Royal, 25 April 1851) [Wicks 18644].

19. Actually *Le Chapeau de paille d'Italie* (Marc-Michel & Labiche; Paris, Théâtre du Palais Royal, 14 August 1851) [Wicks 15482].

20. Johann Sebastien Bach, *Six French Suites,* BWV 812-817. These were composed

during Bach's Cöthen period (1717–23), and are called "French" because they carry on
the form established by Couperin, whose graceful manner of writing for the keyboard was
an influence on Bach. The music, infectious and seductive, is among the sprightliest Bach
wrote.

21.   Gluck, *Iphigénie en Aulide*, no. 1 *Ouverture,* no. 2a *Récitatif* ("Diane impitoyable")
and no. 2b *Air* ("Brillant auteur de la lumière").

22.   Dennery and Dumanoir, *La Case de l'Oncle Tom, drame* in eight acts (Paris,
Théâtre de l'Ambigu-Comique, 18 January 1853) [Wicks 15359].

23.   This was the studio of Ary Scheffer, the Dutch painter resident in Paris. His advice during the rehearsals of *Le Prophète* had a practical consequence on the staging of the
work, as remembered by Henry Chorley: ". . . Ary Scheffer—that most poetic of modern
religious artists, and passionately fond of music—watched its composition as though he
had been painting a picture" (*Thirty Years' Musical Recollections* [1862; reprint, London
and New York: Alfred A. Knopf, 1926], p. 264).

24.   Massé, *Les Noces de Jeannette, opéra comique* in one act (J. Barbier & M. Carré;
Paris, Opéra Comique, 4 February 1853). This was the composer's most successful work,
given in Paris 1,000 times by 10 May 1895, and performed all over the world.

25.   Adam, *Le Sourd, ou L'Auberge pleine, opéra comique* in three acts (F. Langlé &
A. de Leuven, after P. J. B. Choudard Desforges's comedy [1790]; Paris, Opéra Comique,
2 February 1853). It was also performed in Swedish, Spanish, German, Russian, and Norwegian, and revived in Paris on occasion (1893, 1934).

26.   Iwan Gustav Friedrich Alexander, Graf von Keller (1804–79), was court marshal
and intendant of the royal palaces.

27.   Jullien, *Pietro il Grande,* opera in three acts (S. M. Maggioni, translated from M.
D. Ryan's English text; London, Covent Garden, 17 August 1852). This was Jullien's only
opera, and a complete failure. Parts were played in a concert in New York on 22 September 1853.

28.   *L'Africaine*, no. 1b *Romance* ("Adieu mon beau rivage, adieu mon seul amour").

29.   This is the famous cellist Cyprian Romberg (1807–65).

30.   J. S. Bach, Motets BWV 225-231: no. 8 "Ich lasse dich nicht" (Additional Motet
Anhang 158).

31.   Mendelssohn, *Der 42. Psalm*, op. 42 (1837).

32.   Auber, *Le Lac des fées*, opera in five acts (Scribe & Mélesville; Paris, Opéra, 1
April 1839). This legendary fairy opera was not popular in Paris, where it was given only
thirty times. It was performed in England, Poland, and Bohemia, and most especially in
Germany (in J. C. Grünbaum's translation), where it was revived in Karlsruhe (1865) and
Stuttgart (1871).

33.   This bolero was omitted from the première by Fétis, and printed separately. See
Deuxième Partie de l'opéra L'Africaine (Paris: Brandus, 1865): no. 1 *Deuxième version
de la Romance.*

34.   Phoebus Levin (1836–78), a figure, portrait, and genre painter. A native of Berlin, he studied at the Academy under C. W. Wach, and regularly showed his work at their
exhibitions until 1868. He worked in Rome (1845–47) and in London (1855–78).

35.   *L'Africaine*, no. 6 *Récitative et Duo* ("Le maître a-t-il faim?").

36.   Clément & Larousse call Truhn's *Cleopatra* a *monodrame* (1:250).

37.   *L'Africaine*, no. 3 *Morceau d'Ensemble et Finale* ("Dieu que le monde révère").

38.   Fr. "counting of the votes."

39. The Chorus of Slave Merchants was later omitted from the revised scenario, and the music never completed.

40. Ettore Caggiati (b. 1817), Italian tenor.

41. The ambassador Brassier de Saint-Simon belonged to the noble Prussian family of landowners and military men.

42. Schumann, Quintet for Piano and Strings in E-flat Major, op. 44 (1842).

43. This was the organist Étienne-Alexandre Leprévost (1812–74).

44. Beethoven, String Quartet no. 5 in A Major, op. 18, no. 5 (1798/1800).

45. See 22 November 1851.

46. Psalm 91, "He who dwells in the shelter of the Most High" (RSV).

47. Mendelssohn, Piano Trio no. 1 in D Minor, op. 49 (1839).

48. Beethoven, Piano Sonata no. 1 in F Minor, op. 2, no. 1 (1793–95).

49. Schubert, "Ungeduld," and "Trock'ne Blume," no. 7 and no. 18 of the song cycle *Die schöne Müllerin* (words by Wilhelm Müller), D.795 (1823).

50. *Robert le Diable* was given at Bucharest on 15 January 1853 in Italian.

51. See 30 August 1849.

52. He was actually the bass Schutki. Prior to engagement in Hamburg, he worked in Vienna at the Theater an der Wien and is mentioned in correspondence between Meyerbeer and Dr. Bacher with regard to further performances of *Vielka* (e.g., 8 April 1847). The composer did appear to have a favorable impression of his abilities (see *BT*, 4:231, 268).

53. Louis Casimir Nouguier (1810–92) was a Parisian lawyer representing the interests of the publishers Escudier.

54. Meyerbeer's preparedness to attend the Easter liturgy in the principal church of Berlin is another indication of his openness to all forms of religious experience, and his positive, accepting attitude to Christianity.

55. Flotow, *Indra*. This was originally *L'Esclave de Camoëns*, *opéra comique* in one act (Saint-Georges; Paris, Opéra Comique [Favart], 1 December 1843), and later revised as *Indra, das Schlangenmädchen*, opera in three acts (G. zu Putlitz; Vienna, 18 December 1852) in which form it enjoyed modest popularity throughout the nineteenth century. It was given in Russian and Italian, with a series of German revivals between 1880 and 1910 (Coburg, 1901; Elberfeld, 1902) (cf. Loewenberg, col. 836).

56. Leopoldo II*, grand duke of Tuscany.

57. *L'Africaine*, no. 4c *Air du Sommeil* ("Sur mes genoux").

58. Kalisch, *Hunderttausend Taler*, farce in three acts (first performed in Hamburg, 1848) [Richel 78].

59. *Die Ochsenmenuette*, a *Singspiel* in one act by Ignaz Seyfried based on Haydn's music (G. E. von Hofmann; Vienna, Theater an der Wien, 13 December 1823). This *pasticcio* gave rise to an anecdote about Haydn composing an *Ox Minuet* for a butcher and receiving an ox as a gift in return. It was very successful on German stages up to the mid-nineteenth century, and even reached New York (1858).

60. See 9 July 1850.

61. The Viennese writer Joseph Samuel Tauber (1822–79) was a poet (*Gedichte*, Leipzig, 1847) and from 1853 the secretary of the journal *Der Wiener Lloyd*. Meyerbeer had met him in Berlin on 10 and 11 June 1847.

62. The German soprano Clementine Howitz-Steinau (1821–1914) worked principally in Hamburg (1849–51), Stuttgart, Dresden, and especially Karlsruhe (1853–64). She sang Berthe in the first Hamburg performance of *Le Prophète* (24 January 1850).

63. Meyerbeer's *Fackeltanz* no. 3 in C Minor (arranged for both military band and large orchestra by Wieprecht) was written for the wedding of Princess Anna of Prussia with Prince Friedrich of Hesse (see 28 May 1853).

64. By government order, officially promulgated on 5 May 1853, all performances at the Académie Impériale de Musique were to commence at 19:30 hours, and were to finish by midnight at the very latest. This necessitated cuts in many of the standard works of the repertoire.

65. Görner, *Alles durch Magnetismus.* Karl August Görner (1806–84) was a Berlin playwright, author of over twenty-five plays.

66. This was presumably the wife of the *ténor comique* Colson (1819–77). In September 1855 they both left Paris to perform in the French Theater in New Orleans.

67. Meyerbeer was asked to orchestrate the duke of Saxe-Coburg-Gotha's new opera, *Santa Chiara.*

68. Ludwig, *Die Makkabäer, Trauerspiel* in five acts, written in blank verse (first performed in Vienna, 1852; in Berlin, 1853; and published 1854) [Richel 102]. The subject is the Maccabean revolt against King Antiochus Eupator (167–161 B.C.). This work and *Der Erbförster* made Ludwig's name as a playwright.

69. In *Robert le Diable* the cuts proposed by Meyerbeer were: in act 2 the duet for Robert and Isabelle, and the *pas de cinq*; in act 4 the entr'acte, as well as parts of the duet and extended finale.

70. Schumann, *Der Rose Pilgerfahrt*, secular oratorio (words by Moritz Horn), op. 112 (1851).

71. Ludwig Tieck died on 28 April 1853.

72. Tgb. *freisinnig*, i.e. "broad-minded" or "enlightened."

73. *Der Unsichtbare, Singspiel* in one act by Carl David Eule (K. L. Costenoble; Hamburg, 7 July 1809). This work was successful in Germany, and performed into the 1830s. It was revived in Leipzig (17 January 1846), Berlin (6 February 1853), Dresden (11 July 1863), and Darmstadt (5 February 1869). Eule (1776–1827) composed five light German operas.

74. *Le Misanthrope et l'Auvergnat, comédie-vaudeville* in one act by Lubize, Labiche, and Siraudin (Paris, Théâtre Palais-Royal, 19 August 1852) [Wicks 19271].

75. N. Ropiquet (b. 1815) was a violinist in the orchestra of the Paris Opéra.

76. Léopold I*, king of the Belgians.

77. Fr. "cut."

78. This was T. Schumann, an oboist in the Royal Orchestra.

79. Girardin, *Lady Tartuffe*, prose *comédie* in five acts (Paris, Théâtre Français, 10 February 1853) [Wicks 18466].

80. Heinrich Rudolf Brockhaus (b. 1838), a publisher and book dealer.

81. Fr. "tiepin."

82. Grétry, *L'Épreuve villageoise, ou Théodore et Paulin*, *vaudeville* in two acts (P. J. B. Choudard Desforges; Versailles, 5 March 1784; Paris, Comédie-Italienne, 18 March 1784). Given in Paris until 1831, and frequently revived (in 1853, 1866, 1896, 1918), it reached New York in 1827, and was revived in Graz in 1897. For Clément & Larousse, this work "doit être considerée comme un chef d'œuvre" [should be considered a masterpiece] (1:395). The 1853 revival was reorchestrated by Auber.

83. Thomas, *La Tonelli*, *opéra comique* in two acts (T. Sauvage; Paris, Opéra Comique, 30 March 1853)."La partition de M. Thomas brille des qualitiés de sciences et de goût

qu'il déploie dans tous ses ouvrages" [Thomas's score displays the learning and taste that are in evidence on all his works] (Clément & Larousse, 2:1091).

84. The date was actually 1784.

85. Fr. "pompous and pernickety."

86. Henri Puget (b. 1813), a tenor engaged for the Opéra Comique by Perrin, where he had success in the role of Corilla in Halévy's *Le Nabab*. Halévy, writing to Scribe on 6 June 1853, observes that he "a de bien qualités, de la chaleur vraie, c'est un homme dont on peut tirer grand avantage" [he possesses fine qualities, real warmth, a man one could use to advantage] (see Halévy, *Lettres, réunies et annotées par Marthe Galland* [Heilbronn: Edition Lucie Galland, 1999], p. 110). He is not be confused with Jules Puget (1820–87), a tenor who sang in the provinces before being engaged by Carvalho for the Théâtre Lyrique (1864–87). He was known for the role of Pollione in the French translation of Bellini's *Norma*.

87. The *Orphéon* were choral societies sponsored by the government, which trained workers in the rudiments of music. See 28 May 1854.

88. Tgb. *Exercitium der éleven.*

89. It. "middle tempo," a free transitional section that occurs between the cantabile and cabaletta of an aria, duet, or ensemble.

90. Fr. "by implication."

91. Barrière and Thiboust, *Les Filles de marbre, drame* in five acts (Paris, Théâtre du Vaudeville, 17 May 1853) [Wicks 17387].

92. Vittorio Giaccone (b. 1810), trader and theater director.

93. Alexandre Basset (1796–1870) was the director of the Opéra Comique from 1845 to 1848. In May 1848 he was replaced by Perrin and Doux.

94. René Chapuis (b. 1828), a tenor engaged by the Opéra from February 1851 to 1855.

95. Ponsard, *L'Honneur et l'Argent, comédie* in five acts (Paris, Théâtre de l'Odéon, 11 March 1853) [Wicks 18031].

96. Glinka reports the visit like this: "Once, at the start of summer, when I returned from my morning stroll, I found Meyerbeer in our parlour with Don Pedro. Meyerbeer was talking of this and that with his usual amiability. When asked about the publication of my operas, I showed him some of the printed copies of *A Life for the Tsar* and *Ruslan* which I happened to have with me. The talk then turned to Gluck, and to my question 'Would his music be effective on the stage?' Meyerbeer replied that it was precisely on the stage and nowhere else that Gluck would become magnificent. He assured me that when I left he would pass the word to Berlin in good time and see what he could do about having Gluck's operas performed for me. At that time four of Gluck's operas were being produced: the two *Iphigénies*, *Armide*, and *Alcestis*. From Gluck we passed on to a discussion of other classical composers whereupon I expressed my views on art.

'Mais vous êtes très difficile,' [but you are very difficult] said Meyerbeer to me.

'J'en ai complètement le droit,' I replied. 'Je commence par mes propres œuvres, dont je suis rarement content' [I have the perfect right to be, because I start with my own works with which I am often not satisfied].

I never saw Meyerbeer again after this meeting. In the winter, or perhaps it was the early spring, he had the opera *Star of the North* put on at the Opéra Comique. I did not hear it, but I was indignant that he had treated Peter I very disrespectfully" (Glinka, *Memoirs* [Norman: University of Oklahoma Press, 1963], pp. 237–38).

97. This is the Italian text of the *Six canzonettes italiennes* (words by Pietro Metastasio) (1810), one of the works Meyerbeer composed while living in Darmstadt with the Abbé Vogler. F. N. dei Santo Mango was an Italian poet resident in Paris. In 1840 he had provided Meyerbeer with the words of the song "De miei giorni."

98. Actually John Antony Galignani (1796–1873), a newspaper publisher. From 1833, with his brother, William, he edited the paper *Galignani's Messenger* founded by their father (1814).

99. Edmond Roche (1828–61), French poet and musician.

100. Monfort, *L'Ombre d'argentine*, *opéra buffon* in one act (Bayard & Biéville; Paris, Opéra Comique, 28 April 1853).

101. Fr. "tour" or "walkabout."

102. *Guinguettes*: pleasure gardens, suburban places of refreshment (with music and dancing).

103. *L'Étoile du Nord*, no. 15a *Entr'acte* (*Allegretto scherzando*, G minor – G major, 4/4).

104. *L'Étoile du Nord*, nos. 3–4 *Scène* ("Catherine, chacun a son étoile").

105. Monsigny, *Le Déserteur*, *opéra comique* in three acts (J. M. Sedaine; Paris, Comédie-Italienne, 6 March 1769). This was Monsigny's most famous work, given all over Europe until the end of the eighteenth century, and also in America (New York, 1787; Boston, 1793; Philadelphia, 1798). It was performed in Paris until the end of the nineteenth century (revived in 1893 and 1911).

106. Giuseppina Appiani was the daughter of the prominent politician Antonio Strigelli. She had married a son of the neoclassical fresco and portrait painter and admirer of Napoleon, Andrea Appiani. Giuseppina Appiani was famed for her beauty, which she retained into her old age. Her daughter was Adele, to whom Donizetti dedicated an unpublished song, "Che cangi tempera mai più non spero" (see Herbert Weinstock, *Donizetti* [New York: Pantheon Books, 1963], p. 390).

107. Gabriel Riesser (1806–63), a Jewish writer and politician.

108. Marie-François-Stanislas Champein (1799–1871), French musician and journalist.

109. Delsarte (*jeune*) had been a second tenor at Adam's Opéra National (November 1847–March 1848).

110. See 9 January 1856 for detail on the mezzo-soprano Pauline Masson.

111. *Les Trois Sultanes, ou Soliman second*, verse *comédie* in three acts (Favart, arranged by J.-P.-Simon Lockroy; Paris, Théâtre des Variétés, 26 July 1853) [Wicks 22081].

112. Dietsch wished to be nominated for the Légion d'Honneur. See below 24 December 1853.

113. This was Johann Friedrich Berwald, not Franz Adolf Berwald. See 18 December 1846 and 26 January 1847.

114. *L'Étoile du Nord*, no. 19 *Suite et Fin du Final* ("Ma mère, tu l'avais prédit").

115. Perhaps this was the painter Oscar Dehaes (b. 1822)?

116. This contract, involving the composer, his publisher, and the administrator of the Opéra-Comique, was for *L'Étoile du Nord*.

117. Tgb. *Coupierung*.

118. This lighthearted interlude is widely known as no. 7 of the ballet suite *Les Patineurs* (arr. Constant Lambert, 16 February 1937).

119. The bass Hermann-Léon (orig. Léonard Hermann) (1814–58) was a native of Lyons, and a member of the Opéra Comique. He created the role of Gritzenko in *L'Étoile du Nord*.

120. *L'Étoile du Nord*, no. 5 *Scène et Chanson de Gritzenko* ("Enfants de l'Ukraine").

121. Having read the first two volumes of Véron's reminiscences, Meyerbeer wrote a letter acknowledging Véron's role in the origins of the *mise en scène* for *Robert le Diable*. This letter was eventually to appear in the third volume of the *Mémoires* (cf. 9 February 1854).

122. Les Guides: soldiers of an elite French cavalry corps of the eighteenth and nineteenth centuries. See 8 December 1852.

123. Princess Mathilde Bonaparte (1820–1902), daughter of Prince Jérome Bonaparte, had broken off affectionate relations with her cousin Louis Napoleon in 1837, and married Prince Anatoli Demidoff (1840). The latter, a philanthropist, renowned traveler and patron of the arts, had treated her very badly, going so far as to strike and insult her in public. This resulted in Tsar Nicholas I ordering him to live apart from her and pay her a handsome allowance. When elected president, Louis Napoleon nonetheless chose the divorced Mathilde to act as his hostess at all receptions and balls at the Élysée until his own marriage. Mathilde went on to become the muse of the Second Empire, and, despite all political vagaries, her salon remained a meeting place for the illustrious to the end of the nineteenth century.

124. Halévy, *Le Nabab*, *opéra comique* in three acts (Scribe & Saint-Georges; Paris, Opéra Comique, 1 September 1853). This work was not an enduring success, and achieved only thirty-eight performances. Clément & Larousse regard the plot as highly improbable, and observe that the composer "a sacrifié une partition assez riche en heureux motifs" [sacrificed a score abundant in fine themes] (2:766).

125. This was the soprano Louise Charlotte Helena Michal [Michaeli] (1830–75).

126. Fr. "steps" or "action."

127. This was the dramatist Joseph-Adolphe-Ferdinand Langlé (1798–1867).

128. Fr. "sentiments of warm fraternal attachment."

129. Marie-Charles-Louis Aigoin (b. 1817), a writer.

130. Beaucé sang at the Théâtre Lyrique (1855–58).

131. Adam, *Le Roi des Halles*, *opéra comique* in three acts (De Leuven & Brunswick; Paris, Théâtre Lyrique, 11 April 1853), one of the composer's less successful works, performed only thirty-nine times (1852–53).

132. Vogel, *La Moissoneuse*, *drame lyrique* in three acts (A. Bourgeois & M. Masson; Paris, Théâtre Lyrique, 3 September 1853). Clément & Larousse observe that this opera "n'a pas eu grand succès, mais . . . fait beaucoup d'honneur au musicien" [was not very successful, but does the composer great credit] (2:750).

133. Henry Fothergill Chorley had written enthusiastically on Meyerbeer as early as 1844 ("The Masterpiece of French Opera, *Les Huguenots*," in his *Music and Manners in France and Germany*). In 1849 he was present at some of the rehearsals of *Le Prophète*, as the guest of Pauline Viardot, and wrote at some length and with sympathetic but not uncritical perception of the composer's works (see "M. Meyerbeer's Operas: Characteristics" and "M. Meyerbeer's Operas: *Le Prophète*," in *Thirty Years' Musical Recollections*, pp. 223–29, 260–66).

134. This was a major revival of *Les Huguenots*, and it represented important aspects of the complex sociopolitical role the Théâtre de l'Opéra was perceived to play in the life of the nation. The new government regulations concerning performance times, the abridgments required in the classic repertory, and the simultaneous request for extra pieces of ballet music suggest new control and ulterior (political) motives. Jane Fulcher comments: "One may observe, then, the Opéra's tendency to aestheticize, to euphemize the grand

repertoire, to eviscerate it, to control its meaning through a strategy of substitutions and cuts. Such was already the case with the revival of *Les Huguenots* in 1853; critics noted the many deletions and the shifting emphasis towards *divertissements*" (*The Nation's Image: French Grand Opera as Politics and Politicized Art* [Cambridge: Cambridge University Press, 1987], p. 179). The new ballet sequence Meyerbeer was asked to provide bears this out, although it is interesting to note the spontaneous popular reaction to the incendiary Blessing of the Daggers, notwithstanding.

135. The bass Charles Amable Battaille* (1822–72) was the creator of the role of Peter the Great in *L'Étoile du Nord*.

136. George Sand, *Le Pressoir, drame* in three acts [Wicks 20734].

137. The tenor Toussaint-Eugène Mocker (1811–c. 1885), a pupil of Ponchard, made his début at the Opéra Comique (1830) and remained attached to this house for the rest of career. In 1861 he was appointed professor of *déclamation lyrique* at the Conservatoire. He created the role of Danilowitz in *L'Étoile du Nord*.

138. P. Brignoli was to sing at the Paris Opéra in 1854 and later at the Academy of Music in New York (in Verdi's *Il Trovatore* [2 May 1855], Pacini's *Saffo* [21 June 1858], Verdi's *I Vespri siciliani* [7 November 1859] and Rossini's *Mosè in Egitto* [7 May 1860]).

139. The tenor Pierre-Victor Jourdan (1823–79) created the role of Georges in *L'Étoile du Nord*.

140. Aylic [Allic] Langlé (1829–70), novelist and playwright, who used the pseudonym M. A. F. Langlois.

141. Fr. "connections."

142. This is Maria Cristina (1806–78), queen regent of Spain (1833–40 and 1843–54) for her daughter, Isabella II, until eventually forced into exile by revolution.

143. The actor Louis-Paul-Édouard Brindeau (1814–82) was at the Comédie-Française from 1842 to 1854, the height of his career.

144. Adam, *Le Bijou perdu, opéra comique* in three acts (A. de Leuven & P. A. A. Pittaud de Forges; Paris, Théâtre Lyrique, 6 October 1853). The work was popular in Paris, given 132 times between 1853 and 1862, and revived in 1873, 1896 and 1900. Outside France its career was modest (London, 1854; New Orleans, 1861).

145. Wagner was in Paris, with Liszt, Princess Wittgenstein, and members of her family, from 9 October to 29 October 1853, staying at Meyerbeer's usual residence, the Hôtel des Princes. See Ernest Newman, *The Life of Richard Wagner*, vol. 2, *1848–1860* (1933; reprint, Cambridge: Cambridge University Press, 1975), pp. 393–95.

146. This refers to the basic divisions in the medieval Jewish Diaspora. Meyerbeer, as member of the *ashkenazim* or Yiddish Jews of north and eastern Europe, would have been unfamiliar with the rituals of the *sephardim*, the Jews who settled in Spain and Portugal before the Inquisition, and who subsequently spread to England, Greece, North Africa and America.

147. Jules-François Miot (1809–83), a French politician.

148. Liszt and Wagner had attended a performance of *Robert le Diable* at the Opéra. For more on the Princess Wittgenstein, see 9 April 1855.

149. Limnander, *Le Maître chanteur*, opera in two acts (H. Trianon; Paris, Opéra, 17 October 1853). It was revived at the Opéra as *Maximilien* (1856), in Brussels (1874), and in Ghent (1876). Could the theme of this work have had some influence on Wagner's thinking, since he was in Paris at the time and no doubt saw it?

150. Langlé, *Murillo*, verse *comédie* in three acts. Wicks [19514] gives the Théâtre de la Gaîté as the venue.

151. Cadaux, *Colette* (the text of this *opéra comique* was by F. A. E. Planard).

152. This concert marked Levasseur's retirement, and included act 5 of *Robert le Diable*.

153. Edmund-Jules Delaunay-Ricquier (1826–99) was a singer at the Opéra Comique; Alexis Garaudé* was the theater *accompagnateur*.

154. It. "stay or retirement in the country" (from *villegiare*, to live at a villa in the country). Fontainebleau is about thirty-five miles southeast of Paris. The palace was built in the sixteenth century for François I by the architects Gilles de Breton, Philibert Delorme, and Serlio, and decorated by a group of Italian and French artists known as the Fontainebleau School, notably Il Rosso, Francesco Primaticcio, and Niccolò dell'Abbate.

155. Louis-Étienne-Arthur-Dubreuil-Hélion, vicomte de La Guéronnière (1816–75), French journalist and politician.

156. King Maximilian II (1811–64, reg. 1848–64), eldest son of Ludwig I, who had been obliged to abdicate in the Revolution of 1848 because of his reactionary measures and his relationship with the dancer-adventuress Lola Montez.

157. *L'Étoile du Nord*, no. 11, *Chœur des Conjurés* ("Assez d'opprobre, assez d'affronts").

158. Fr. "for those burnt [in the fire] in the rue Bambourg."

159. Fr. "pension fund."

160. *L'Étoile du Nord*, no. 17 *Couplets de Prascovia* ("Sur son bras m'appuyant").

161. The libretto *Psyche* was eventually set by Ambroise Thomas (26 January 1857).

162. *L'Étoile du Nord*, no. 10a *Valse*.

163. The first performance of *Le Prophète* in New York took place on 25 November 1853. It was to enjoy a prestigious career in this city, being revived there in 1872, 1884, 1892, 1898–99, 1900, 1902, 1918 and 1920 (with Caruso [in one of his most dramatic roles], Margarete Matzenauer, and Claudia Muzio), 1927 (with Martinelli, Matzenauer, and Corona), 1977 (with James McCracken, Marilyn Horne, and Renata Scotto) and 1979 (with Guy Chauvet and Marilyn Horne). The 1977 revival is discussed in the context of other modern stagings of Meyerbeer's operas by Andrew Porter in "Prophetic Strain [7 February 1977]," in *Music of Three Seasons: 1974–1977* (New York: Farrar Straus Giroux, 1978), pp. 499–507. For the 1979 revival, see Nancy Phelan, *Charles Mackerras: A Musician's Musician* (London: Victor Gollancz, 1987), pp. 196–97.

164. Alexandre Dumas *(père)*, *Diane de Lys*, prose *comédie* in five acts (Paris, Théâtre du Gymnase Dramatique, 15 November 1853) [Wicks 16485].

165. Fr. "the great success of the day."

166. Victor Cornette (b. 1795), musician.

167. Fr. "New Year's gifts."

168. Reber, *Les Papillotes de Monsieur Benoist*. This was the première (text Barbier & Carré); Clément & Larousse call it "un œuvre de goût, pleine de science et de sentiment" [a tasteful work, both learned and emotional] (2:833).

169. The soprano Marie-Charlotte Lemercier (died c. 1900) was a native of Blois and a member of the Opéra Comique where she created Nathalie, one of the *vivandières* in *L'Étoile du Nord*.

170. Marguerite-Jeanne-Camille Decroix (b. 1828) created the role of Ekimona, the second *vivandière*. She had earlier sung in Adam's Opéra National (1847–48).

1854

Sunday 1 January. God bless the new year. May he grant my new opera *L'Étoile du Nord* a brilliant and honorable success in Paris, and may it then spread farther to all the theaters of the world.

Monday 2 January. Second rehearsal for the wind instruments of act 2. Rehearsal of *Les Huguenots* with Demoiselle Cruvelli.

Tuesday 3 January. Mise en scène rehearsal with the soloists and chorus of the whole of act 1; it lasted (dialogue and music) for one hour and twenty-five minutes. Then rehearsed the last scene of act 3. Rehearsal with Sax of act 2, with the three military bands on the stage.

Wednesday 4 January. First complete orchestral rehearsal with soloists and chorus of act 1. It went well. The orchestra, which had played no role in the earlier partial rehearsals, applauded often. In the evening worked on the overture.

Thursday 5 January. Rehearsal to attended to details of Demoiselle Lefèbre's role. Then a piano rehearsal of *Les Huguenots* in the Grand Opéra, with Demoiselle Cruvelli. Today I hosted a dinner for seventeen members of the orchestra of the Opéra Comique. In the evening an orchestral rehearsal in the Grand Opéra of *Les Huguenots*, for Cruvelli. The orchestra received me with *applaudissement*,[1] while showing no appreciation of Cruvelli.

Friday 6 January. Wrote out more of the overture. *Mise en scène* rehearsal of act 2. Dined at Véron's. Opéra Comique: Massé's *Les Noces de Jeannette*.

Saturday 7 January. Unfortunately the sore throat and cough have returned. I stayed at home all day.

Sunday 8 January. Wrote out a little of the overture. In the evening held a rehearsal of *Les Huguenots* for Cruvelli in the Opéra.

Monday 9 January. Wrote out some of the overture. Second orchestral rehearsal in which the whole of act 3 was tried for the first time; it did not go well and was received coldly by the orchestra. In the evening finished writing out the overture and began revising it.

Tuesday 10 January. Finished revising the overture, and took it to Robin for copying. On account of the illness of Demoiselle Lefèbre, we could rehearse the act 3 finale with only the chorus, soloists, and the two flutes. Édouard Wolff and Cohen played me the [third] *Fackeltanz*, which Brandus has just brought out in an arrangement for four hands by Wolff. In the Théâtre Lyrique: Donizetti's *Elisabeth, ou Les Exiles en Sibérie.*[2]

Wednesday 11 January. On account of the continuing illness of Demoiselle Lefèbre, today there was a rehearsal of only the *mise en scène* of act 2, and of the act 3 finale. Today I hosted a second dinner for the orchestra, once more eighteen *couverts*. Grand Opéra: Donizetti's *Betly.*[3]

Thursday 12 January. The convulsive coughing has unfortunately increased. Because of the continuing illness of Demoiselle Lefèbre, there was no rehearsal today. Big dinner at the minister of state, Fould's. Today Armand Bertin died; he was a true, loving friend to me for twenty-five years.

Friday 13 January. Third orchestral rehearsal. Rehearsed acts 1 and 3, with the exception of Demoiselle Lefèbre's parts. She is still unwell. Called on Alexandre Dumas, but did not find him at home. Called on Demoiselle Cruvelli. Visit from Eckert. In the evening wrote down, and scored, several small pieces that have been necessitated by the *mise en scène* rehearsals.

Saturday 14 January. Worked for one and a quarter hours before breakfast on the additions and alterations to the act 1 finale. Letter to Birch-Pfeiffer, for the duke of Gotha, about an extension of the deadline for the revision of *Santa Chiara,* until 1 March. To Armand Bertin's funeral. Rehearsed the act 2 finale with the chorus. Called on Alexandre Dumas. In the evening worked on the revisions of the *Étoile.*

Sunday 15 January. Today there was no rehearsal. In the evening worked on *raccords*[4] and the revision of the *Étoile.*

Monday 16 January. Letters from the harpist Zabel, from Haslinger in Vienna.

Ensemble rehearsal of the chorus and soloists of the act 2 finale. In the evening in the Opéra: *Les Huguenots* (236th performance, receipts 7,166 fr. 68 c.): the début of Cruvelli as Valentine has been the talk of Paris.

Tuesday 17 January. Fourth orchestral rehearsal: tried the whole of act 2 for the first time. Called on Berlioz and Cruvelli. Even though I had visited Alexandre Dumas, and he received me very warmly, today I found a hostile article directed against me in his journal, *Le Mousquetaire*, which was signed by Léon Gatayer.

Wednesday 18 January. Wrote to Madame Birch-Pfeiffer, to Dr. Bacher. *Droits d'auteur* for the month of December: 428 fr. 60 c. *Mise en scène* rehearsal of the choruses of act 2. Romen read me the plan of a small comic opera. Called on Gouin and Nestor Roqueplan. In the evening worked on the revision of the *Étoile*.

Thursday 19 January. Finished revising act 2 of the *Étoile*. Fifth orchestral rehearsal: tried act 2 for the second time. To Édouard Bertin, to Scudo. In the evening began reading through the vocal score of the *Étoile*.

Friday 20 January. I continued working on the vocal score of the *Étoile* for Brandus. *Mise en scène* rehearsal with the two flutes of the act 3 finale, and then of the act 2 finale.

Saturday 21 January. Severe attack of convulsive coughing. Sixth orchestral rehearsal: act 1 romance and act 3 finale. Called on Berlioz. The third dinner that I hosted for twenty-two members of the orchestra. In the evening worked a little on the revision of the vocal score.

Sunday 22 January. Worked on the revision of the vocal score. Went through the role of Catherine in the *Étoile* with Demoiselle Lefèbre.

Monday 23 January. Seventh orchestral rehearsal: tried the act 2 finale several times, with the military band on stage and the ordinary orchestra, then the whole of act 2. In the evening altered details of the instrumentation.

Tuesday 24 January. Letter from Dr. Bacher in Vienna, who tells me that in a *concert spirituel* there the music of *Struensee* was performed with a linking text by Johann Gabriel Seidl.[5] Worked on the revision of the *Étoile*. *Mise en scène* rehearsal of acts 2 and 3. The opera is unfortunately far too long. In the evening began work on the cuts.

Wednesday 25 January. Worked a little on the cuts. Sixth orchestral rehearsal. Dined with the Prussian ambassador, Count Hatzfeld.

Thursday 26 January. Worked on the cuts. *Mise en scène* rehearsal. Visit from Gustav Robert, director of the Ministerial Lithographic Correspondence.

Friday 27 January. Wrote to Rellstab about the translation. Worked on the cuts.[6] Rehearsed the abridgments with the singers, then a *mise en scène* rehearsal of act 2.

Saturday 28 January. Letter from Leipzig from the composer and pianist Louis Lacombe.[7] Wrote to Dr. Bacher in Vienna. Worked on the cuts. Ninth orchestral rehearsal, then act 2 with *mise en scène* and the dialogue. Wrote to Scribe, Brandus, Monnais, and Robin.

Sunday 29 January. Letters from the duke of Gotha, from the singer Formes in Glasgow. Worked on the cuts. Visits from Perrin, from Madame Tedesco. Dined at Jules Janin's, where I made the acquaintance of the *procureur imperiale de la cour de la cessation*,[8] M. Rouland,[9] whom Perrin has chosen to arbitrate in our *traité* dispute. Conference with Scribe about the cuts.

Monday 30 January. Letter from Kaskel in Dresden. Wrote to Haslinger in Vienna. Today I did not attend the *mise en scène* rehearsal. Worked on the cuts and their instrumentation, as well as the arrangement of the military music for the first band, which I am omitting.

Tuesday 31 January. Tenth orchestral rehearsal. In the evening worked on revisions and alterations.

February 1854

Wednesday 1 February to Thursday 2 February. Because of a bladder infection, I stayed at home. Visit from M. Perrin.

Friday 3 February. Today I also had to stay indoors, on the doctor's orders. I used the day to make many alterations to the orchestration, necessitated by the weak voices of the singers. Visit from Perrin.

Saturday 4 February. Worked on changes in the instrumentation. Eleventh orchestral rehearsal. At nine o'clock in the evening received a telegram informing me that my mother is dangerously ill.[10]

Sunday 5 February. Worked on the changes in the instrumentation, in order to assist the very weak voices of the singers. *Mise en scène* rehearsal of the new dénouement, which has now been devised. The censor is making great difficulties about the libretto, because of the present political tension between France and

Russia.[11] In the evening composed the music for the new dénouement. Wrote out a series of remarks[12] for the leader of the orchestra, Tillmant*. At midnight a telegram: the doctors believe my mother to be in the gravest danger.

Monday 6 February. Scored the music composed for the dénouement. Called on Tillmant. Conferred with Édouard Monnais about announcements that pieces have been taken from the *Feldlager*, and about the letter to Véron (concerning the organ story in *Robert*).[13]

Tuesday 7 February. Spent all day in mortal anxiety, because for the last two days I have received neither telegram nor letter about the condition of my beloved mother. Today tried the overture for the first time.

Wednesday 8 February. Today, thank God, I received a very reassuring telegram, and also letters, concerning the condition of my beloved mother. Today, for the first time, the three acts were rehearsed, one after the other. Not counting the intervals, the opera lasted for three and a half hours.

Thursday 9 February. Worked on the instrumentation and abridgments. This evening the whole opera was rehearsed for the second time, with costumes and décor. Because of the difficulties that the libretto has encountered, in the light of the current tension with Russia, several high officials were present.[14] The opera did not go as well as yesterday, particularly on the orchestral side. The impression was only partially favorable. People complained a lot about length. Thank God that I have again received good letters about my beloved mother's health. Wrote a letter, ostensibly to Véron, but really for his memoirs, in which I refuted the rumor that I had to pay him for the organ that was used in *Robert*.[15]

Friday 10 February. Today is the eighty-seventh birthday of my dearly beloved mother. May God preserve the precious, venerable darling for many years, in strong health and untroubled spiritual fortitude. Conference with Scribe about the abridgments; I have already begun working on these.

Saturday 11 February. Worked on new abridgments, and a new march in place of the Dessauer. Long conference with Scribe and Perrin. Letter from Véron. Answered Véron. Letter from the Society of Austrian Friends of Music. Letter from the poetess Helmine von Chézy, who tells me about the performance of *Struensee* in her benefit concert.

Sunday 12 February. Worked on the abridgments.

Monday 13 February. In the morning and evening rehearsals of my opera. Conference with Perrin.

Tuesday 14 February. In the evening the dress rehearsal of my opera, in the presence of nearly all journalists and many other spectators.

Wednesday 15 February. Another small *répétition de raccord.*[16]

Thursday 16 February. Today, in the Opéra Comique, was the first performance of my three-act opera *L'Étoile du Nord.* Under God's almighty protection, and the blessing of my beloved mother (which she had already sent me in writing about three weeks ago), the performance was brilliant in the extreme.[17] Acts 1 and 2 aroused enthusiasm, act 3 rather less, even though it was nonetheless well-received. I was called out at the end. The emperor and the empress were present.[18]

Friday 17 February. Busy with visits and the distribution of tickets for the second performance. Conference with Scribe and Perrin.

Saturday 18 February. Second performance of *L'Étoile du Nord*, which was just as brilliant as the first.

Sunday 19 February. Made what seems to me a good and significant cut in the duet between Georges and Prascovia, but the director Perrin rejected it. Called on Madame de Cesena,[19] Scribe, and Favel, to whom I took the *Quarante Mélodies.*[20] Visit from Grüneisen and the music dealer Beale from London, who want to buy the *Étoile* for England. I received such a multitude of congratulatory letters and visits, as well as spoken and written requests for tickets to my new opera, that my head is bursting.

Monday 20 February to Tuesday 21 February. On account of so many activities, I have not been able to keep my diary. Demoiselle Duprez's hoarseness has meant that there could be no performance of *L'Étoile du Nord.*[21]

Wednesday 22 February. In the evening worked on the revision of the vocal score.

Thursday 23 February. Worked on the revision of the vocal score. Since Demoiselle Duprez's hoarseness continues, there was again no performance of *L'Étoile du Nord* today.

Friday 24 February. Worked on the revision of the vocal score. Dined with Perrin.

Saturday 25 February. Worked diligently on the vocal score during the day and in the evening.

Sunday 26 February to Monday 27 February. Worked on the vocal score and the *rectification*[22] of the libretto.

Tuesday 28 February. Big rehearsal of *L'Étoile du Nord,* which Perrin wants since, because of Duprez's hoarseness, the opera has not been performed for eleven days. Everyone, particularly the orchestra, was dissatisfied with this, especially because it is Mardi Gras today. I consequently rehearsed only four pieces. Worked on the vocal score.

March 1854

Wednesday 1 March. Called on Gye, director of the Covent Garden Theatre; Demoiselle Cruvelli; Guérin, theater director of Nantes; and Jules Lecomte. Demoiselle Duprez's hoarseness has at last ended, thank God, so that the third performance of *L'Étoile du Nord* could take place, superbly executed, to a crowded house. As of today I have made twenty-four tickets a performance available to the orchestra (two per person) until everyone has been to a performance. Letters from the theater in Frankfurt-am-Main and the Court Theater in Hanover; both want the *Étoile.*

Thursday 2 March. Conference with Scribe about the revision of the libretto. To Jules Lecomte, Madame Milland. Visits from Taglioni, Dr. Bacher, and Dr. Bamberg. In the evening worked on the vocal score.

Friday 3 March. Visit from Count Belmont who, on behalf of the duke of Saxe-Gotha who has arrived here, asks that I should call on him. Went to Édouard Bertin. In spite of the fact that Rossini's *Moses* had been announced in the Opéra, at the eleventh hour the emperor *par ordre* commanded *Les Huguenots,* and attended this performance with the duke of Gotha. Today's (fourth) performance of the *Étoile* was packed, the production outstanding, the approval and the three *da capo* calls all as in the earlier performances.

Saturday 4 March. Spent nearly all day reading through the libretto, the vocal score, and the full score of the opera *Santa Chiara* by the duke of Saxe-Gotha. I am invited to call on him tomorrow, and must deliver a report. Visit from Desolumier *(L'Europe artistique);* I gave him 500 fr., and half-promised to do the same every half year.[23] Wrote to Madame Tedesco in Lyons.

Sunday 5 March. To the duke of Gotha, as well as other visits (Léon Kreutzer, Milland, Véron, Eugène Borel).[24]

Monday 6 March. Worked on the vocal score. Fifth performance of the *Étoile*, to a packed house. The enthusiasm and the three *da capo* calls, all as in the earlier performances. Even though the performance was *par ordre* (by highest command), the emperor did not come, but the duke of Gotha did. During the interval he came on stage to compliment me.

Tuesday 7 March. Wrote to Benedict in London. Worked very diligently on the vocal score. Called on the duke of Gotha. In the Italian Opera: Bellini's *I Puritani*.

Wednesday 8 March. Worked on the vocal score. Conference with Provini, director of the theater at Marseilles, who wants to give *L'Étoile du Nord* as early as May. Visit from the composer Bergson, from Hamburg.[25] To Count Pillet-Will, who had me listen to Hermann[26] playing one of his [Pillet-Will's] violin compositions.[27] Dined at Princess Czartoryska's.

Thursday 9 March. Worked on the vocal score. Conference with Scribe about a new two-act opera for the Grand Opéra. Sixth performance of *L'Étoile du Nord*, to a packed house. Good production; the enthusiasm just as at the earlier performances.

Friday 10 March. Worked on the vocal score. To the Grand Opéra for Rossini's *Moïse*: Madame Bosio sang the soprano role very well; a new Italian tenor, Brignoli, was only average.[28]

Saturday 11 March. The duke of Saxe-Gotha came to Sax to hear his instruments; they played him my [third] *Fackeltanz*, which he liked. The seventh performance of *L'Étoile du Nord*, to a crowded house.

Sunday 12 March. Worked on the vocal score. In the Théâtre Lyrique: Gevaert's* *Georgette;*[29] the younger Boieldieu's *La Fille invisible*.[30]

Monday 13 March. In the Conservatoire: examination of the singing classes, which I had to attend as a member of the Commission des Surveillance de l'Enseignement. Dined at Count Pillet-Will's. Opéra Comique: Reber's *Les Papillotes de Monsieur Benoist*.

Tuesday 14 March. Today the individual pieces of the *Étoile* appeared in print. Received the contract of sale from Schlesinger for the publication of the *L'Étoile du Nord* in Germany (amounting to 8,000 fr.), and returned it to him signed. Théâtre Italien: Mozart's *Don Giovanni*.

Wednesday 15 March. Dined at Colonel Fleury's.[31] Examination in the Conservatoire.

Thursday 16 March. In the Italian Opera: *Don Giovanni;* Madame Frezzolini (Donna Anna), Madame Alboni (Zerline), Mario (Don Ottavio).

Friday 17 March. Big musical soirée at Duprez's, who has opened his newly built hall for singing courses.

Saturday 18 March. Called on D'Ortigue. In the Théâtre Lyrique: Clapisson's *La Promise*.[32] Mademoiselle Cabel sang the title role with great virtuosity and extraordinary verve. Unfortunate news that my beloved mother had to be bled again.

Sunday 19 March. Worked on the vocal score. Dined at Madame Fourtado's.[33] Letter from the music director Truhn in Berlin.

Monday 20 March. I hosted a dinner to which I invited Berlioz, Léon Kreutzer, Massart,[34] Baron Taylor, Kastner, Sax, D'Ortigue, Dr. Bacher, and Brandus.

Tuesday 21 March. Worked diligently on the vocal score.

Wednesday 22 March. Worked diligently on the vocal score. *Soirée musicale* at the minister of state Fould's.

Thursday 23 March. Wrote to Truhn in Berlin. Worked diligently on the vocal score. Called on Gustav Robert. With Formes to Roqueplan.

Friday 24 March. Worked diligently on the vocal score. Visit from Gustav Robert. To Provini: letter with permission for a performance of *L'Étoile du Nord* in Marseilles this season, under certain conditions. Wrote to Dessauer in Vienna for Géraldy, to Princess Poniatowsky for Bergson.

Saturday 25 March. Worked on the vocal score.

Sunday 26 March. Worked on the vocal score. Heard the singer [Mlle.] Carini.

Monday 27 March. Worked diligently on the vocal score. In the Grand Opéra: Spontini's *La Vestale*.

Tuesday 28 March. Worked diligently on the vocal score.

Wednesday 29 March. Worked very diligently on the vocal score.

Thursday 30 March. Worked on the vocal score.

Friday 31 March. Worked diligently on the vocal score. In the small Théâtre des Delassements Comiques: *Les Toiles du Nord*, a parody of my opera.[35] In the prologue to this play (a vaudeville), many flattering things were said about me.

April 1854

Saturday 1 April. Completed the vocal score up to the act 3 finale. Palianti read me the *mise en scène* of *L'Étoile du Nord*, which he is printing for the stage productions. Contributed 1,000 fr. to a subscription for the instrument-maker Sax who, because of debt, is threatened with the sale of his workshop. Wrote to Colonel Fleury on Sax's behalf. Letter from the singer Breiting in Darmstadt, who has asked for a loan of 1,000 fr.

Sunday 2 April. Letter from Ronzi, director of the Teatro della Pergola in Florence, who wants to give the *L'Étoile du Nord*. The headaches and convulsive coughing continue. Consequently I could work only a little on the vocal score. Dined with Scribe. I was further invited to a concert at the Prince de la Moskowa's, but because of my indisposition, I could not go.

Monday 3 April. Dinner (for twenty people), which I gave for the singers (both men and women) of the Opéra Comique who perform in my opera *L'Étoile du Nord*. In addition Perrin, Brandus, Édouard Monnais, and Camille Doucet were present. I had invited Véron but he declined.

Tuesday 4 April. Began correcting the printed vocal score.

Wednesday 5 April. Théâtre Français: *La Jolie fait peur, comédie en 1 acte* by Mme. de Girardin,[36] a very pretty play, superbly acted. Letter from Vesque von Püttlingen. Lumley, the director of Her Majesty's Theater in London, has offered to pay Brandus some 2,000 pounds sterling (which he owes him anyway) if he (Brandus) can arrange that, in the coming year, I will promise him (Lumley) *L'Étoile du Nord* for his theater instead of giving it to Covent Garden. In order to accord this great service to Brandus, I would like to commit myself to this course of action; but because Lumley is very unreliable, I would like to secure my interests by drawing up a contract. I worked at this contract all day, and also conferred with Gautier about it.

Thursday 6 April. Conference with Gautier about the contract with Lumley.

Friday 7 April. Passed the contract with Lumley over to Brandus, who traveled to London immediately with it. Visit from Herr Seager-Oswald, the director of a German and Italian opera company in London, who also wants the *L'Étoile du Nord* for this season, but I cannot give it to him because of my contract with Lumley. Charity concert in which the Princess Poniatowsky played Chopin's Concerto [no. 1] in E Minor[37] very beautifully. *Le Prophète* has been given in Avignon, and also in New York by the Italian Opera Company.

Saturday 8 April. Birthday of my beloved wife, Minna. Concert by the pianist Schulhoff.[38] Today I did not attend the *L'Étoile du Nord* (nineteenth performance). Even though Holy Week begins tomorrow, the receipts have dropped by only a few hundred francs, and exceed 6,000 fr.: 6,081 fr. in all.

Sunday 9 April. Called on Louis Desnoyer, and gave him the *morceaux détachés de l'Étoile du Nord*[39] for his daughter. In the evening spent a moment in Boieldieu's *La Dame blanche*. With Dr. Bacher to Frau von Guaita from Frankfurt-am-Main.[40]

Monday 10 April. To Fiorentino. Wrote to Vesque von Püttlinger in Vienna. In the morning to the Italian Opera for Rossini's *Stabat Mater*. Dined at Count Pillet-Will's.

Tuesday 11 April. Called on Fiorentino (see cash book). Took Madame Milland the *airs détachés de l'Étoile du Nord*, and bought a charity lottery ticket from her (*à* 100 fr.). Dinner given by Dr. Bacher; Alexandre Dumas was also there. Despite his nasty article against me in *Le Mousquetaire*, he was very friendly, and I, naturally, was not cross—which would have been *mauvaise compagnie*.[41] I was not at today's performance of the *L'Étoile du Nord*, where, despite the theatrically unfavorable period of Holy Week, the takings were even higher than before.

Wednesday 12 April. Worked diligently on the revision of the proofs of the vocal score, both in the morning and evening. Letter from the music dealer Schott, who is here in Paris from Cologne.

Thursday 13 April. Visit from Dautresme. To Schott.

Friday 14 April. Concert in the Salle Sainte Cécile, where the cantata *La Fuite en Egypte*[42] and the overture *Athalie* by Mendelssohn were played. In the afternoon to Count Pillet-Will's: Hermann and Rosenhain played several compositions by Count Pillet-Will.

Saturday 15 April. Consulted Dr. Andral, since the convulsive coughing shows no sign of diminishing. Visit from the music dealer Schott. Called on Mademoiselle Benedict from London, at Legouvé's. At his own wish, invited Alexandre Dumas and his son, with Dr. Bacher, to dinner. Called on Jules Janin. Today my *Fackeltanz* no. 3 was performed at the Opéra Comique in a *concert spirituel*. This was the fourth performance of this work in Paris.

Sunday 16 April. Called on Théophile Gautier and Leduc. Worked diligently on the correction of the vocal score.

Monday 17 April. Wrote to Gathy: sent him tickets for the *Étoile* and *Les Huguenots*, as well as 500 fr. In the evening I was invited to a ball in the Elysée Palace hosted by the emperor. The illumination of the garden, with its different *dessins*[43] and variously disposed plants and trees, was quite magical.

Tuesday 18 April. Visit from the composer Neukomm.

Wednesday 19 April. In the evening lingered a little at *Les Huguenots*. I heard the fourth act: Cruvelli and Gueymard were called out.

Thursday 20 April. Letter from Borachi, the new impresario of the Teatro alla Scala in Milan, who has invited me to oversee the staging there of *Le Prophète* in the spring of 1855. Letter from Fétis, who requests a loan of 2,000 fr. In the evening again attended a complete performance (the twenty-third) of the *Étoile*. It continues to sustain itself in capacity attendance, production, and audience enthusiasm.

Friday 21 April. Letter from the Musical Society of Rotterdam, who invite me to attend the twenty-fifth anniversary of their founding this coming July.

Saturday 22 April. Letter from Aloys Schmitt* in Frankfurt-am-Main. The receipts from the *L'Étoile du Nord* were among the highest to date—6,596 fr. 50 c., despite the *location à l'année*.[44]

Sunday 23 April. Visit from the *délégué*[45] of the music festival in Bordeaux: at his request I promised him the overture to *L'Étoile du Nord* for this festival. Sent Fétis the desired loan of 2,000 fr. Heard one act of *La Dame blanche* on account of the début of Demoiselle Rey, who turned out to be mediocre.[46]

Monday 24 April. Completed the corrections of the proofs of the vocal score. Called on Auber, who is ill. Sent the blind poetess Wilhelmine von Chézy in Geneva support of 100 fr. Opéra Comique: Thomas's *Le Songe d'une nuit d'été*.

Tuesday 25 April. In the Italian Opera: Bellini's *Beatrice di Tenda.* Madame Frezzolini sang Beatrice very beautifully.

Wednesday 26 April. In the evening worked on the pointing of Pierre's part for Faure.

Thursday 27 April. Worked on the pointing of Pierre's part for Faure. Visit from Perrin. Called on Madame Viardot, and presented her with the music of Catherine's role. Visit from Mason, director of the Birmingham Festival. Wrote to Romani, director of the Teatro della Pergola in Florence, answering his request for the *L'Étoile du Nord* for his theater. In the evening spent a short while at the *L'Étoile du Nord*, and then went to the Italian Opera, where they performed Mozart's *Don Giovanni.*

Friday 28 April. A deputation from the Birmingham Festival came to see me; they again invited me to compose an oratorio for this occasion. Called on Jules Janin. Visit from the singer Borchard, who has a lovely voice and good style. However, I fear that the role of Catherine lies too high for her, otherwise I would have acquired her for the Opéra Comique during Duprez's *congé.*[47] To Perrin about Demoiselle Borchard. In the Gymnase: Augier and Sandeau's *Le Gendre de Mr Porier:*[48] a very pretty play, very well acted.

Saturday 29 April. Finished the punctuation of Pierre's role for Faure.

Sunday 30 April. The Société des Auteurs et Compositeurs Dramatiques have elected me a member of the commission. I have already held this post once before.

May 1854

Monday 1 May. The cholera is increasing. Sent forty gulden to the writer Dangelmayer, at his request. Today the complete vocal score of *L'Étoile du Nord* was published by Brandus. Returned to Perrin the libretto *Les Saisons.*[49] Conferred with Édouard Monnais about the scenarios of *Judith* and *Luérons.*

Tuesday 2 May. Heard two acts of the *L'Étoile du Nord* (twenty-eighth performance). Conferred with Germain Delavigne about Scribe's scenario *Judith.*

Wednesday 3 May. Conferred with Scribe about the scenario of *Judith.* Gave the linking text of *Struensee* to Théophile Gautier for definitive translation. To Kalisch, Garfunkel, Gathy, Neukomm. In the evening *Le Prophète* in the Opéra. *Rentrée* of Madame Tedesco.

Thursday 4 May. Conference with Scribe about *Judith.* Visit from the composer Bergson, who spoke to me very favorably about a new singer at the Hamburg Theater, Demoiselle Mandl (from Temesvár in Siebenbürgen),[50] for the role of Catherine. Took the vocal score of *Étoile* to the Baroness Henri Blaze de Bury. In the evening attended the whole performance (the twenty-ninth) of *L'Étoile du Nord* (crowded house).

Friday 5 May. Dr. Wihl read me the tragedy *Susanne.*[51] Attended a sitting of the Commission des Auteurs et Compositeurs Dramatiques for the first time since my nomination. In the evening worked on the arrangement of the overture for *one* orchestra.[52] Letter from the Commission du Congrès Musicale in Bordeaux, who want the overture to *L'Étoile du Nord* for a charity concert. Letters from Dr. Bacher and Gaetano Rossi.

Saturday 6 May. Began the arrangement of the overture to the *Étoile* for a single orchestra. Dined with Jules Lecomte. Nadaud (who is enjoying a great vogue) sang some of his little songs, which are very pretty and refined, but as poetry rather than music.[53] Telegram from Cornet in Berlin.

Sunday 7 May. Worked on the arrangement of the overture for one orchestra. Answered Cornet by telegram. Visit from Schäler, correspondent of *Die Kreuzzeitung,* and from Dr. Wiehe. To a concert, where I heard a new type of harmonica. They played the "Grâce" aria from *Robert le Diable.* Also heard a quite extraordinary Belgian flautist, Reichert.[54] In the evening worked on the arrangement of the overture.

Monday 8 May. Letter from August Lewald in Stuttgart: wants the *Étoile* for performance in Stuttgart. Sent Lewald the *mise en scène* by Palianti and the libretto of *L'Étoile du Nord.* Wrote to Marquis Martellini, Romani. Called on Sax, Crémieux, and Éd. Monnais.

Tuesday 9 May. I have a bad cold, a real case of influenza.

Wednesday 10 May. My indisposition has much diminished, thank God. Gave Parent the overture, arranged for a single orchestra, for typesetting. Letter from the poetess Wilhelmine von Chézy. Visit from the husband of the singer Cabel. In the Théâtre Lyrique: Clapisson's *La Promise.*

Thursday 11 May. Conference with Scribe about the new opera *Judith.* Concert to raise funds for a monument to Balzac.[55] Madame Ugalde sang, and they gave *Le Sélam,* a symphony-cantata by Reyer.[56] To a big dinner given by the emperor in the Tuileries; the emperor and the empress conversed with me, and I made the acquaintance of the Marshals Vaillant[57] and Magnan.[58]

Friday 12 May. Director Cornet from Vienna came to see me. He is here in order to study the *mise en scène* of *L'Étoile du Nord*, which he wants to give in Vienna this autumn. Unpleasant letter from the music dealer Schloss in Cologne, relating to Heine.[59] Letter from Dingelstedt in Munich, who would like to give *L'Étoile du Nord* at the Industrial Exhibition there. In the Opéra heard an act of Halévy's *La Reine de Chypre*.

Saturday 13 May. Began working on the revision of the full score of *L'Étoile du Nord* for the printer. Visit from Cornet. Letters from Lewald in Stuttgart, and from Formes in London. Conference with Barbier about the poem for a new comic opera.[60] In the evening to *L'Étoile du Nord*: a good performance (the thirty-third).

Sunday 14 May. To Perrin concerning Faure. Visits from Leduc and Sax. Soirée at Perrin's.

Monday 15 May. Conference with Scribe about *Judith*. Visit from Malmene from Berlin, who has brought letters of introduction from the minister Manteuffel* and Count Redern. Wrote to Hofrat Dingelstedt in Munich, to Dr. Bacher in Vienna, to Ternisien of the magazine *Étoile du Nord*, who has sent me the present of a lovely table cloth because he has chosen *L'Étoile du Nord* as the escutcheon for a *magasin des nouveautés*.[61] In the Opéra Comique: Reber's *Les Papillotes de Monsieur Benoist* and Donizetti's *La Fille du régiment*.

Tuesday 16 May. Studied the role of Peter with Faure.

Wednesday 17 May. Visit from August Lewald, who has come on behalf of the Stuttgart Theater to see the *mise en scène* of *L'Étoile du Nord*, which will be produced in Stuttgart.

Thursday 18 May. Called on Berlioz.

Friday 19 May. Conference with Perrin.

Saturday 20 May. Conference with the poet Barbier about a new comic opera. In the Théâtre Lyrique: the first performance of Reyer's *Maître Wolfram*.[62]

Sunday 21 May. Letters from Cornet in Frankfurt-am-Main, from Count Festetitsch [Festetics], intendant of the Hungarian National Theater in Pest, who wants the score of *L'Étoile du Nord* for performance.[63] Visit from the writer Labat*, who was recommended to me by Scudo. He showed me his plan for a five-act libretto, *Ines de Castro*. Severe attack of coughing, influenza.

Monday 22 May. I still feel very unwell. Visit from the composer Gevaert with Sax.

Tuesday 23 May. Wrote down my observations on Scribe's plan for *Judith*. Wrote to Count Festetitsch: I promised to deliver him the score of the *Étoile* in November. Wrote to Prince de Rohan in London: refused, for my part, to accept the proffered title of a *vice-président* of the Société Industrielle. Called on Petit, *chef de la direction de la presse au ministère de l'interieur:*[64] a very important man, whose acquaintance I have made thanks to Gustav Robert, and who has proved very helpful to me. Dined with Théophile Gautier, where Bagani, the director of the Italian Opera, was also present. Visit from M. Tedesco. Called on Véron. Letters from Countess Westmorland, and from Madame Viardot.

Wednesday 24 May. Visit from Bergson. Farewell visits to the minister of state Fould, Jules Lecomte, and Madame Viardot. In the evening at the Opéra I heard a performance of the whole of *Le Prophète*.

Thursday 25 May. Visits from the journalist Albert Beckmann and from Raoul Allary, who makes wind instruments. He is an opponent of Sax, and came to me because he had heard that I had spoken to the emperor on Sax's behalf.[65] Heard two acts of *L'Étoile du Nord*, which was packed. The receipts were 6,121 fr.

Friday 26 May. To Scribe, to Schlesinger. Granted permission for the delivery of a score of the *Étoile* to the Court Theater in Stuttgart through Lewald.

Saturday 27 May. Visit from Seveste*, director of the Théâtre Lyrique. Barbier showed me his plan for a one-act comic opera, *Le Chercheur des trésors*. In the evening to *L'Étoile du Nord*.

Sunday 28 May. Concert of the Orphéonists, 1,400 singers, young women, boys and men, scholars and apprentices, under Gounod's direction: Ambroise Thomas's "La Vapeur," Adam's "Les Horloges," Halévy's "Les Forgerons." They are all very pretty, characteristic choruses.

Monday 29 May. To Perrin about *Le Chercheur des trésors*. To Roqueplan. Sent the vocal score of the *Étoile* to Lady Westmorland. Attended act 4 of *Le Prophète* in order hear Demoiselle Wertheimer.

Tuesday 30 May. To Blanche, *secretaire général*, about the singer Michal. To Auber about Malmene. In the Opéra heard Madame Donati, who is to sing the role of Isabelle: she has a really beautiful voice. In the evening drew up the contract with Brandus for the *vente*[66] of the score of *L'Étoile du Nord*.

Wednesday 31 May. To the attorney Gautier about the *traité* with Brandus. To the minister Fould, to intercede for the Théâtre Lyrique.[67] In the Opéra: the first performance of *Gemma*, ballet in four acts by Théophile Gautier, music by Comte Nicolò Gabrielli.[68]

June 1854

Thursday 1 June. To Gautier about the *traité* with Brandus. Visit from Langlé concerning the Théâtre Lyrique. Conference with Barbier about *Le Chercheur des trésors*. In the evening worked on the revision of the full score of the act 1 finale for the printer.

Friday 2 June. Letter from Guidi in Florence, the Italian publisher of the *Étoile*. Conference with Gautier about the *traité* with Brandus. Today I requested a *congé* of three months from the Commission des Auteurs et Compositeurs Dramatiques, which was granted.

Saturday 3 June. Drew up the contract for the Florentine *éditeur* Guidi, as well as a letter of permission for Brandus to sell vocal scores abroad. Called on Demoiselle Cruvelli. Sent Rossi in Verona a present of 200 fr. Signed the contract with Brandus.

Sunday 4 June. Conference with Scribe about *Judith*.

Monday 5 June. To Scribe, who gave me the first act of *Judith*. Letter from Dingelstedt in Munich. Letter from Count Festetitsch in Pest: promises not to give the opera before the Viennese production, but wishes to see the score as soon as possible. Wrote to Borachi in Milan, the impresario of the Teatro alla Scala, promising to accept his invitation to mount *Le Prophète*, if I have the time; recommended Viardot, Tedesco, Stoltz. Wrote to Count Festetitsch in Pest: permission for a production of the *Étoile*, but only in January. To Schlesinger: authorization to pass on the full score to Festetitsch, in accordance with his written application. In the evening at the Opéra Comique: the first performance of Massé's *La Fiancée du Diable*.[69]

Tuesday 6 June. At ten o'clock left by rail for Brussels. I read through the first tableau of *Judith*, which I want to read twice every day, to learn it by heart, so when the inspiration comes, I can begin composing right away.

Wednesday 7 June. At 10:45 by train to Cologne, where I arrived at 4:30. During the journey, I thought of and wrote down many musical ideas for the color[70] of the new opera *Judith*.

Thursday 8 June. Left at 6:30 in the morning by rail for Berlin, where I arrived in the evening at nine o'clock. Many letters from Gouin were awaiting me about the takings from my current opera performances.

Friday 9 June. [No entry.]

Saturday 10 June. Since I did not want to see my beloved mother for the first time on a *Friday*, I went to her only today. Thank God, I found her much better in mental clarity than I had expected. Called on Count Redern. Sitting of the senate in the Academy of Arts. Called on Professor Herbig. Consultation with Geheimrat Schönlein. Letters from Heine, Gouin, Brandus, and Marquis Martellini in Florence.

Sunday 11 June. In the night I was awakened to be told the terrible news that my dear mother had suffered another stroke.

Monday 12 June. [No entry.]

Tuesday 13 June. Worked on correcting the printed full score of the overture to *L'Étoile du Nord.*

Wednesday 14 June. Improvised rather vaguely on act 1 of *Judith*. Worked on the preparation of the full score for the printer. Letter from Kapellmeister Strauss in Karlsruhe.

Thursday 15 June. Letters from Viardot in London, from Palianti in Paris. The condition of my beloved mother has unfortunately again worsened.

Friday 16 June to Saturday 17 June. [No entry.]

Sunday 18 June. Wrote to Brandus with authorization for the sale of the *Étoile* in those countries where I have not already sold it to an *éditeur.*

Monday 19 June. To the intendant-general von Hülsen. Visits from Guglielmi and Schlesinger. Scribe sent act 2 of *Judith.*

Tuesday 20 June. In the Opera House: Nicolai's *Die lustigen Weiber von Windsor.* Madame Ney sang Frau Fluth.

Wednesday 21 June. To Herr von Humboldt. Carefully checked the German translation of the *Étoile* (the whole of act 1). *Le Prophète* has been given in Toulon and Avignon.

Thursday 22 June. In the morning and evening checked the German translation of the *Étoile.*

Friday 23 June. Called on Count Redern. To Herr von Humboldt. Completed checking the translations of the individual pieces from the *Étoile.* Conference with Grünbaum about changes in the translation.

Saturday 25 June. The king and the queen have asked for news of Mother's condition. *Droits d'auteur* for the month of May: 5,807 fr. (Grand Opéra 579 fr., Opéra Comique 5,228 fr.).

Monday 26 June. Sorrowful, inauspicious day. At noon my beloved mother's fearful, mortal agonies began and ended only two hours after midnight. What a terrible fourteen hours! What a mother I have lost!

Tuesday 27 June. Wrote to Scribe.

Wednesday 28 June. Letter from the music dealer Schloss in Cologne.

Thursday 29 June. [No entry.]

Friday 30 June. O bitter, harsh day! Today saw the funeral of my beloved mother.[71]

July 1854

Saturday 1 July. [No entry.]

Sunday 2 July. Worked on the preparation of the duet (act 3) for the printer. I also had to orchestrate the new middle section.

Monday 3 July. [No entry.]

Tuesday 4 July. Conference with Rellstab. Visit from Herr von Humboldt. To Count Redern. Departure of my beloved wife and children for the baths of Ischl.

Wednesday 5 July. Letter from Herr von Gall, intendant of the Stuttgart Theater: he invites me on behalf of the king to the production of the *Étoile.* Letters from Dr. Bacher, from Gustav Robert.

Thursday 6 July. [Letter] from Fürstenau in Dresden: wants my autograph for the Royal Library. Prepared the last finale for the printer, and sent it to Brandus. In the evening began correcting the first proofs[72] of the full score.

Amalia Beer, née Wulff, in old age. Contemporary engraving. (From A. Kohut,
Geschichte der Juden **[Berlin, 1898–99].)**

Friday 7 July. Letters from Cornet in Vienna, Borachi in Milan, Dautresme and
Franco Tedesco in Paris.

Saturday 8 July. [No entry.]

Sunday 9 July. [No entry.]

Monday 10 July. Scribe sent me act 3 of the new opera [*Judith*]. In the evening an extraordinary sitting of the musical members of the Senate, to examine the young violinist Bernard. Then I checked a little of the German translation of the *Étoile.*

Tuesday 11 July. Revised the German translation of the *Étoile.* Visit from the concertmaster Müller from Stockholm and his daughter, who has sung Fidès there. Lewald from Stuttgart came to see me: I promised to tell him by 1 September whether or not I will be able to come to Stuttgart. Wrote to Cornet in Vienna.

Wednesday 12 July. Completed the revision of the German translation of the *Étoile.*[73] Wrote to Eugène Borel in Marseilles.

Thursday 13 July. Wrote to Émile Deschamps, then to Gustav Robert, Maurice Schlesinger, Dautresme, Kaskel, Ungher-Sabatier, Dr. Bacher. Letters from Heinrich Heine, from the regisseur Seidl, enclosing an opera manuscript, from the countess of Westmorland. To Heinrich Schlesinger. Visit from Lewald.

Friday 14 July to Sunday 16 July. [No entries.]

Monday 17 July. Visits from Rellstab and Lewald.

Tuesday 18 July. [No entry.][74]

Wednesday 19 July. To Herr von Humboldt. Wrote to the king about indefinite leave.

Thursday 20 July. To Kabinetsrat Illaire.

Friday 21 July. Wrote to Cornet, to Dr. Bacher, enclosing Madame Ungher-Sabatier's letter for him. Letter from Rellstab.

Saturday 22 July. Preparations for departure.

Sunday 23 July. Left by rail at seven o'clock for Dresden, where I arrived at 12:30. After one and a half hours' rest, the train departed for Prague, where I arrived at nine o'clock in the evening.

Monday 24 July. Departed at 5:30 in the morning by train for Vienna, where we arrived at 7:30 in the evening. My friend Dr. Bacher was there to meet me. On the journey here, I composed the first romance of Manasses in *Judith.*

Tuesday 25 July. Visits from the director Cornet, and many other people from the opera theaters. I called on Obersten Direktor Lanckoronski, and the *Kanzleidirektor*, Regierungsrat Raymond. To the Kärntnertor-Theater: Thomas's *Der Traum einer Sommernacht*: Demoiselle Wildauer, Ander, Hölzel, Demoiselle Tietjens* (a lovely voice). Letter from Gounod; an order-in-cabinet from the king granting me indefinite leave.

Wednesday 26 July. The baritone Beck and Demoiselle Wildauer sang for me. Heard *Don Juan*.

Thursday 27 July. Heard Flotow's *Martha*. Called on the writer Zellner.

Friday 28 July. Visit from Count Moritz Dietrichstein. Heard *Lucrezia Borgia*.

Saturday 29 July. Wrote out the first romance of Manasses [in *Judith*], which I had composed on the journey. Leopoldstädter-Theater: *Eisenbahnheiraten*, a farce by Nestroy.[75]

Sunday 30 July. Early today, at seven o'clock, left by train for Prague, where I arrived at eight o'clock in the evening.

Monday 31 July. Left at seven o'clock by train for Berlin, where I arrived in the evening at nine o'clock. Letter from the theater director Ernst in Mainz.

August 1854

Tuesday 1 August. Preparations for my departure for Spa.

Wednesday 2 August. Left at 7:30 in the morning by rail for Cologne, where I arrived at ten o'clock in the evening. On route I met Frank, whom I had not seen in years.[76] Composed a second version of the Scene of the Levites before the Ark of the Covenant [in *Judith*].

Friday 3 August. At 9:30 left Cologne for Verviers, where we arrived at one o'clock. On the way I composed some of the duet in act 1. For twenty fr. I hired a carriage and two horses, which took me directly to Spa in one and a half hours.

Friday 4 August. Indisposition of abdomen and stomach.

Saturday 5 August. Called on Count Hatzfeld and Davelouis.

Sunday 6 August. Worked diligently in the morning and evening on correcting the proofs of the full score of *L'Étoile du Nord*. Dined with Davelouis, where I also found Jules Janin and his wife.

Monday 7 August. [No entry.]

Tuesday 8 August. Concert by Madame Bockholz-Falconi: she sang the arioso from *Le Prophète*. Then *Qui se ressemble, se gêne*, vaudeville in one act by Marc-Michel and Fontaine.[77]

Wednesday 9 August. [No entry.]

Thursday 10 August. Prepared the act 2 finale for the typesetter. Arranging this piece is very intricate, and has given me a lot to do.

Friday 11 August. Letter from Gollmick in Frankfurt-am-Main: he asks for a loan of 300 gulden. Concert by the famous Belgian flautist Reichert: extraordinary fluency, lovely alteration of tone; the tone, though, is harsh, without mellowness.

Saturday 12 August. Finished preparing the act 2 finale for the printer.

Sunday 13 August. Letters from the theater direction in Frankfurt (Mühling),[78] from Eugène Borel in Marseilles, from the painter Wehly in Munich. Further revision of the act 2 finale, which cost me extraordinary effort and much time. In the theater: Hérold's *Zampa*.

Monday 14 August. Letter from Daussoigne*, director of the Conservatoire at Liège. Visit from Dr. Bacher, who has been sent from Paris by Brandus with the very unpleasant news that he (Brandus) is bankrupt at the moment, has provisionally withdrawn from trade, and cannot honor the debts attendant on the publication of *L'Étoile du Nord;* he is due to pay these the day after tomorrow. Of the 40,500 fr. that constitute this debt, Brandus has only 15,000 fr. to pay: the rest has already been contributed by Beale in London (15,000 fr.), Schlesinger in Berlin (8,000 fr.), Guidi in Florence (2,500 fr.). Brandus has already cashed the sum of these, for which he, in the most indelicate manner, remains in debt to me. Since in French law the poet is entitled to a third of the selling price of the score, I have, through my ill-considered trust in Brandus, not only done myself out of my honorarium, but Scribe as well.[79]

Tuesday 15 August. Called on Madame Dülcken and her daughters, to apologize for not having come to their concert yesterday.

Wednesday 16 August. [No entry.]

Thursday 17 August. Letter from Madame Ungher-Sabatier. Visit from Vermeulen.

Friday 18 August. Wrote to Brandus about the affair of the payment, to Gollmick who, in a very ambiguous letter, has requested a loan of 300 gulden. I sent him this, as well as writing to him. I had already made him two smaller loans several years ago, a fact that did not prevent him[80] from writing against me later in *Die Frankfurter Oberpostamtszeitung.* He will no doubt do it again when he no longer needs me, but for heaven's sake, ingratitude is not going to harden my heart.[81]

Saturday 19 August. Two letters from Brandus. Wrote to Brandus, to Gouin. Visit from the pianist Rosa Kastner.

Sunday 20 August. [No entry.]

Monday 21 August. Letter of thanks from the senate of the University of Jena for the scientific instruments[82] that I presented to them when they nominated me doctor of fine arts four years ago.[83]

Tuesday 22 August. Did not work on the corrections in the evening, since I felt unwell.

Wednesday 23 August. Letter of thanks from Gollmick. Letter from August Lewald. Unpleasant article in *Die Kölner Zeitung,* which, without actually naming me, hints that I lost a lot of money in Brandus's bankruptcy. Theater: *Le Moulin à paroles,* vaudeville;[84] *La Fille de Dominique,* vaudeville;[85] Spanish Dance Company, Mademoiselle Petra Vargas.[86]

Thursday 24 August. [No entry.]

Friday 25 August. Wrote an autograph for Higgins (an Englishman). Concert of the singer [Mlle.] Lemaire: pitiful. The only interesting thing in the concert was an overture by Mendelssohn, entitled *An die Künste,* which I have always known as the overture *Ruy Blas.*[87]

Saturday 26 August. Wrote out the role of Pierre in the higher key (which I arranged for Faure) clearly, since it is to be printed in the full score as a supplement.

Sunday 27 August. Continued writing out the transposition of Pierre's role, and completed it. Visits from Fétis, from the prima donna of the local theater, Lemaire, who sang me the Ronde Bohémienne from *L'Étoile du Nord.*

Monday 28 August. Read through the libretto of the *opéra comique, Le Chercheur des trésors*, which Jules Barbier and Michel Carré sent me the day before yesterday.

Tuesday 29 August. Wrote to Lewald in Stuttgart: in the coming week I will indicate whether I can come to Stuttgart. Concert of the pianist Rosa Kastner, in which Demoiselle Bergano also sang.

Wednesday 30 August. Played the overture to *L'Étoile du Nord* for the music director Guillaume, and gave him the score. Gave Jules Janin *Le Chercheur des trésors* to peruse, after I had read it to him for the second time. Answered Rossi's letter from Verona and sent him 200 fr. support.

Thursday 31 August. Called on Janin: I had given him *Le Chercheur des trésors*, and he advised me against composing it, since he finds the text poor.

September 1854

Friday 1 September. Preparations for departure.

Saturday 2 September. Departure from Spa. At 9:30 I left by private coach (for twenty fr.) for Verviers. May God bless my setting forth, may he bless my cure, and grant me through it a strong, enduring health. Amen. In Verviers I took the train for Brussels. I intend going to Brussels to attend the debut of a new opera troupe and, consequently, to decide whether I can allow the director [Théodore] Letellier[88] the desired permission to mount[89] *L'Étoile du Nord*. However, there was a *relâche*[90] and instead I attended a small theater where I saw an intrigue, *Duchesse, ou échec et mal*.

Sunday 3 September. Wrote to Perrin about the reprise of the *Étoile*, to the *comité* of the Société des Auteurs et Compositeurs Dramatiques, requesting a three-month extension of my leave to 3 December. Théâtre de la Monnaie: Halévy's *Les Mousquetaires de la Reine*, all very mediocre.

Monday 4 September. Called on the conductor Hanssens, in order to discuss the casting of roles in *L'Étoile du Nord* for Brussels. At 10:45 left by train for Cologne.

Tuesday 5 September. My birthday. May God bless this new year of my life I am beginning. May he grant *L'Étoile du Nord* a brilliant and enduring world success. New resolution for my birthday: not to let any day go by without work and activity. At 6:30 in the morning started by train from Cologne to Berlin, where I arrived at 9:30 in the evening.

Wednesday 6 September. Letter from Gouin.

Thursday 7 September. Visit from Dr. Nimbs, theater director in Breslau.[91] Conference with Schlesinger. Wrote to Gounod, and ostensibly to Gouin, but actually for Brandus. Letters from Kaskel, from Emil Naumann.

Friday 8 September. Wrote to Madame Birch-Pfeiffer, to Kaskel, to Eugène Borel, to the poet Heinrich Meissner in Dessau, to Gouin, to Baron von Gall in Stuttgart, to August Lewald, to Herr von Humboldt to congratulate him on his birthday.

Saturday 9 September. Left at 9:15 in the morning by train for Stuttgart, where I am to direct the rehearsals of *L'Étoile du Nord.* This will be performed on 27 September for the birthday of King Wilhelm I*. In the evening, at 9:15, we arrived in Guntershausen.

Sunday 10 September. At 5:30 the train left for Frankfurt-am-Main, where we arrived at 10. I rested until 1:30, and then left by train for Stuttgart, where we arrived at 8:15 in the evening. God bless my entry, and grant a brilliant success to the impending production of *L'Étoile du Nord.*

Monday 11 September. Called on Baron von Gall, intendant of the theater, and the regisseur Dr. Lewald. Visit from Kapellmeister Kücken and Regisseur Lewald, from Kapellmeister Lindpaintner. Went through a part of their roles with Madame Marlow[92] (who will sing Catherine) and Herr Schütky (who will sing Tsar Peter).

Tuesday 12 September. Studied their roles with Demoiselle Grohmann (who will sing Prascovia) and Herr Jäger (who will sing Georges). Called on Hofrat Schilling. The intendant, Baron von Gall, came to see me. The king wished to make my acquaintance, and invited me to the palace: he was exceptionally friendly and kind to me. Afterward I studied the rest of their roles with Madame Marlow and Herr Schütky, then finally went to Kapellmeister Kücken for tea.

From 13 September to 1 October. Because during this whole period I was constantly busy with the rehearsals and other preparations for the production of *L'Étoile du Nord (Der Nordstern),* I had no time to keep my diary. The king overwhelmed me with graciousness and distinction; he had me to dine with him, personally showed me his splendid pleasure palace Wilhelma,[93] and invited me that evening to table—to a gala dinner in the Wilhelma, and a gala performance in the Court Theater. The crown prince,[94] the crown princess Olga (daughter of the Russian tsar),[95] Prince Peter of Oldenburg,[96] the queen of the Netherlands (one of the king's daughters),[97] Princess Marie[98] (who is married to Count Neipperg,[99] and likewise one of the king's daughters), together with the duke and duchess of

Weimar,[100] who were all in Stuttgart, all sought me out, and frequently invited me to their festivities. The orchestra, the chorus, and the singers, without exception, showed the greatest enthusiasm at rehearsals, and much devotion to me. The intendant, Baron von Gall, and Überregisseur Lewald have also behaved quite outstandingly. Only because of this general good will was it possible, in a period of less than six weeks, to rehearse and stage the opera in the prescribed time. Through Lewald's suggestion, I even made the acquaintance of the king's all-powerful mistress, Fräulein Stubenrauch,[101] and visited her twice. Kapellmeister Kücken, who had led the rehearsals until my arrival, and who will also conduct the performances after my departure, put himself to a lot of trouble and showed himself very sincere. Kapellmeister Lindpaintner, my acquaintance of forty years standing[102] (but whether my *friend* I do not know), also behaved kindly. The other musical and poetic dignitaries, the singing societies, musical unions, etc., took no notice of me. Among other interesting personalities, I met Hofrat Hackländer (the well-known writer); Überstallmeister Count Taubenheim; Weckerlin, cabinet secretary to the queen of the Netherlands; Baron Cotta, owner of *Die Allgemeine Augsberger Zeitung;* Baron Beaulieu, intendant of the Weimar Court Theater; Professor Ganter, theater critic of *Die Schwäbische-Merkur* (formerly my opponent and even now only partially well-disposed); Jay, critic of *Das Tageblatt;* Professor Zöllner, likewise a critic; Professor Seifert, critic of *Der Staatsanzeiger;* etc. The first performance, which I conducted myself, was on 27 September for the king's birthday: a gala performance, in a fully illuminated house, with the entire court and all royal officials in gala uniform. On such occasions the king is always applauded on his entry and then, according to etiquette, there is no more applause for the entire evening. This of course somewhat dampened the performance. The public nonetheless applauded on several occasions—after the overture, at the Gypsy Roundelay, and at the conclusion of each act. From the point of view of the orchestra and the chorus, the performance was outstanding. Schütky as Peter was very good, Marlow as Catherine excellent. At the conclusion of the performance, the king summoned me to his box in order to express his satisfaction.

The following day there was a big folk festival on the meadow at Cannstadt,[103] where the agricultural prizes for cattle rearing, fruit farming, and the like were presented, and a race was held. The people streamed in from all the districts of Württemberg; it is a unique, charming occasion. I was invited by the king to watch the whole proceedings from the royal grandstand.

On Friday 28 September the second performance of the *Nordstern* took place, which I again conducted to a capacity house. Today, when the public was allowed to applaud, I was received with enthusiasm on my entry into the orchestra, and called out after every act. After act 2, the crown prince summoned me to his box.

On Saturday 30 September, by royal command and at royal expense, the intendant, Baron Gall, gave a dinner for 400 people in my honor, to which notables in the arts, sciences, and the theater were invited. There was a long speech and poem of praise in my honor. On behalf of the king, the intendant presented me with the Commander's Cross of the Order of the Crown of Württemberg, a much esteemed decoration, which confers automatic membership in the Württemberg nobility.[104] The banquet was most cordial and animated; particularly attractive and fluent were the toasts proposed to the king of Prussia (as my sovereign) by Count Taubenheim, and the toast proposed to me by Baron Gall. In the evening I was invited to a big court *fête* by Princess Marie.

October 1854

Sunday 1 October to Saturday 7 October. In the late afternoon, at six o'clock, set out by rail for Paris. I slept at Bruchsal and traveled on Monday 2 October at 6:30 via Strasbourg to Paris, where I arrived at ten o'clock in the evening. Made various visits (inter alia to my friend Gouin in St. Germain). Preparations for the reprise of *L'Étoile du Nord.* Rehearsed the role of Prascovia with Demoiselle Rey. In the Opéra Comique: Hérold's *Le Pré aux clercs.* In the Grand Opéra: the *rentrée* of Cruvelli in *Les Huguenots*[105] (238th performance, receipts 8,696 fr. 40 c.). In the Théâtre Lyrique: the first performance of Gevaert's *Le Billet de Marguerite,*[106] a success. I composed a song for the album of the queen of the Netherlands, to her own words, which she expressly gave me. I sent it to her (on 6 October) through Baron Gall.

Sunday 8 October. Read through act 3 of *Judith* again, and then conferred with Scribe about it. Called on the poets Michel Carré and Jules Barbier, Demoiselle Cruvelli. Wrote a letter, ostensibly to Kaskel, but really for Lüttichau.

Monday 9 October. Visit from the singer Madame Ugalde, who sang for me. Rehearsal with Demoiselle Borchard, who must likewise learn the role of Prascovia. Wrote to Eugène Borel in Marseilles. Opéra Comique: Boulanger's* *Les Sabots de la Marquise.*[107]

Tuesday 10 October. Rehearsed in the Opéra Comique with Demoiselle Rey and Demoiselle Borchard. In the Italian Opera: Rossini's *Il Barbiere di Siviglia.*

Wednesday 11 October. Conference with Scribe about *Judith.* Rehearsal of the *Étoile.* Called on Berlioz, Théophile Gautier, Janin.

Thursday 12 October. Visit from Nyon, to whom I promised, in writing, my musical collaboration for *Le Journal des dames et demoiselles.*[108] Rehearsal of the *Étoile.* To the dress rehearsal of the new grand opera by Gounod, *La Nonne sanglante.*[109] My neighbor was Verdi, with whom I renewed my acquaintance.[110]

Friday 13 October. Mise en scène rehearsal of the whole of the *Étoile*. Letters from the opera director Hainl in Lyons, from Cornet in Vienna.

Sunday 14 October. Wrote to Cornet in Vienna: I will come at the end of November; he should fix the performance for 15 December. Went through the role of Prascovia with Demoiselle Rey. Madame Ugalde sang me the role of Catherine. Conference with Perrin. To Gouin, Brandus. Read through *Le Chercheur des trésors* once more.

Sunday 15 October. Auditioned Demoiselle Will, a contralto from Oldenburg. Conference with Perrin about *Le Chercheur des trésors*. Conferred with Barbier about *Le Chercheurs des trésors*. Dined with the Prussian ambassador, Count Hatzfeld, in honor of the king's birthday today.

Monday 16 October. Dress rehearsal for the reprise of *L'Étoile du Nord*, which went badly. Mademoiselle Rey, who sang Prascovia for the first time, was very poor. Letter from Scudo, who asks me for a loan of 3,000 fr.

Tuesday 17 October. Letter from the queen of the Netherlands, thanking me for the song, a setting of her own words, which I wrote in her album. Wrote down all the points where the chorus were not up to the mark at yesterday's rehearsal. Held a choral rehearsal. Kastner and Sax came to see me. Reprise of *L'Étoile du Nord* in the Opéra Comique, which went far better than I had dared to hope after the bad dress rehearsal. Only Demoiselle Rey was weak.

Wednesday 18 October. I feel I have caught cold. I had to stay in bed for the morning. Wrote to the orchestra director Hainl in Lyons that I cannot come; to Scudo, that I will grant the requested loan.

Thursday 19 October. Letters from Herr von Lüttichau and Karl Kaskel, from Hofrat Schilling, Dr. Bacher. Called on Fiorentino (1,000 fr.), Jules Lecomte (600 fr.). Heard one act of *L'Étoile du Nord*: it was again very full. Then to Berlioz's wedding soirée: today he married his mistress of long standing (Recio).[111]

Friday 20 October. Wrote to Kaskel, to Dr. Bacher. Lunch *(déjeuner)* at the minister of state Fould's. Sitting at the Hôtel de Ville of the Commission de Surveillance du Chant Populaire (the Orphéonists), to whose members I have been nominated by the *préfet de la Seine*. In the Grand Opéra: Gounod's *La Nonne sanglante*.

Saturday 21 October. To Petit, at the *Ministère de l'Interieur,* to confide my *griefs*[112] with the *rapport de la Commission del'Opéra* so that he can inform the emperor, through Moquard. Visit from Gye: I promised him *L'Étoile du Nord* for London, insofar as he is able to fulfill my conditions and convene all his singers. Spent a short time at *L'Étoile du Nord:* it was again very full.

Sunday 22 October. Visits from Alexander Weill, Buloz, and Perrin. Conference with Barbier, concerning my new opera *Le Chercheur des trésors.* Wrote to Davison. Invited Ella and Brandus to dine with me.

Monday 23 October. Telegram that, on account of the division of the estate, I am needed in Berlin, otherwise my coheirs will hold me responsible for the debts arising from it. Called on Kastner.

Tuesday 24 October. Wrote to Guidi in Florence, Marquis Martellini in Florence, Baron Gall, and Kapellmeister Lindpaintner.

Wednesday 25 October. Through the fault of my servant, I could leave by train only at ten o'clock in the morning.

Thursday 26 October. After traveling the whole night on the train, I arrived in Cologne at 5:30 in the morning, and left at 6:30 for Berlin, where I arrived in the evening at nine o'clock.

Friday 27 October. Attended the three conferences concerning my blessed mother's inheritance. Wrote to Barbier, and to Perrin on Bergson's behalf. In the Opera House *Die Niebelungen*, opera by Dorn; it contains much that is interesting and spirited, but is totally without originality.[113] Letters from Baron Gall, Kapellmeister Eckert in Vienna, the director Cornet, Cramolini (including a libretto).[114]

Saturday 28 October. Conference concerning the inheritance affair. To Kroll's, where the famous violinist Bazzini gave a concert.

Sunday 29 October. Wrote to Herr von Lüttichau in Dresden about the casting of roles in the *Étoile*.

Monday 30 October. Letter from Helmina von Chézy in Geneva. Conference concerning the inheritance matters. Started to write out a little of the duet for Judith and Manasses.

Tuesday 31 October. Called on Count Redern. Visit from Schlesinger. Wrote to Brandus: authorization to send the full score of the *Étoile* to Schlesinger. In the evening worked on the duet [in *Judith*] and wrote out some of it.

November 1854

Wednesday 1 November. Letters from Kaskel, from Dr. Bacher. Offered 100 gulden to Lewald to rework the dialogue in the *Étoile*. Letter from Herr von Lüttichau. In the evening worked for two and a half hours on the duet [in *Judith*].

Thursday 2 November. Worked on the duet, almost finishing and writing it out. In the Jerusalem Church: Handel's *Judas Maccabaeus*.

Friday 3 November. Worked without success on the conclusion of the duet. Sent 300 thalers for the victims of flooding in Silesia. Concert by the singer Madame Förster: mediocre.[115]

Saturday 4 November. Wrote to Herr Kaskel. Letters from Kapellmeister Lindpaintner in Stuttgart, and from Sina.

Sunday 5 November. Wrote to Herr von Lüttichau. Attended the experiments on telegraphy through music by Herr Sudre (called telephony);[116] he brought me letters of recommendation from Berlioz, Adam, and Lory. Dined at Count Redern's. To Hofmarschall Keller, in order to announce my arrival to the king. Heard acts 2, 3, and 4 of Dorn's *Die Niebelungen*.

Monday 6 November. Letters from Marquis Martellini in Florence, from Bataille in Paris. Wrote to Cramolini in Darmstadt and returned his opera libretto. Finished composing and writing out the duet in act 1 [of *Judith*]. Heard Demoiselle Hugot singing: she is the niece of Herr Sudre.[117] In the evening resolved the division of the matriarchal inheritance with my nephews and nieces.

Tuesday 7 November. To Schlesinger, to Vivier. Letters from Guidi in Florence, from Gouin, from Kaskel.

Wednesday 8 November. Dictated a letter to Cornet in Vienna, that I will give the score of the *Nordstern* only when [Mlle.] Wildauer has recovered. Letter from Hofrat Hackländer in Stuttgart. In the evening I was invited to a concert that the Hungarian composer Kéler Béla* gave in Kroll's Summer Garden. He performed his own composition, *Eine Nacht in den Karpathen*, in the style of Félicien David's *Le Désert*.

Thursday 9 November. Worked on the aria [from *Judith*]. In the evening to a commemorative celebration for Felix Mendelssohn, performed by the Sternscher Gesangverein.

Friday 10 November. Worked on the War Hymn of the Levites in act 1 of *Judith.* Visit from the writer Dr. Lindner, who has published a book on the first extant German opera.[118] *Droits d'auteur* for the month of October: 2,150 fr. In Kroll's Theater: *Der Engländer in der Klemme,* a vaudeville; *Signora Petipa, mein Name ist Meyer,* another vaudeville.[119] Madame Bremecker-Schäfer sang and danced in both pieces.

Saturday 11 November. Letter from the *Oberstkämmerer,* Count Lanckoronski, in Vienna. Traveled to Potsdam, to visit Herr von Humboldt. Worked on the War Hymn of the Levites. Musical soirée at Geheimrätin Reinhardt's.

Sunday 12 November. Worked on the War Hymn of the Levites. Visit from the two Hungarian flute virtuosi, the Brothers Doppler*, who played me several flute duets, with preeminent brilliance. Conference with Count Redern about the Court Concert. In the evening I was unwell and weak, apparently as a consequence of an upset stomach.

Monday 13 November. Letter from Henri Blaze. In the evening wrote to Count Lanckoronski.

Tuesday 14 November. Wrote to Gemmy Brandus: returned the contract of reclamation. Sent Sina in Paris 200 fr. In the evening I felt unwell and unable to work.

Wednesday 15 November. Letter from Lewald, together with the reworked dialogue in the *Étoile.* To Count Redern about the Court Concert. To the singer Sophie Förster for the same reason. To Frau Emil von Haber about Marx's marriage inquiries concerning Blanca. In the Opera: Gluck's *Orpheus.*

Thursday 16 November. Wrote to Dr. Bacher. Called on the wife of the pianist Moscheles.[120] Busy with preparations for the Court Concert. Friedrich-Wilhelm-städtisches-Theater: *Die Bummler von Berlin,* a local farce in four acts by Kalisch and Weirauch.[121]

Friday 17 November. To Bataille in Berlin. Letter from Cornet. Composed the aria of Osias in *Judith.*

Saturday 18 November. Composed part of act 1 of *Judith.* Busy with preparations for the Court Concert. Hosted a dinner to which we invited Madame Moscheles and her father [Herr Embden], Geheimrat Schulze, Geheimrat Langenbeck and his wife,[122] Justizrat Bennewitz and his children. Concert by the Domchor: a beautiful motet by Michael Bach,[123] and *Psalm 23* for male voices and piano by Schubert, really lovely.[124]

Sunday 19 November. Rehearsal of the Court Concert in my home: the violinist Bazzini, the flautists Doppler, [the singers] Madame Förster, Herr Formes, and Salomon. In the evening to Charlottenburg, where I accompanied all the pieces, as usual. The king and all the members of the royal household were very friendly to me.

Monday 20 November. Worked on act 1 of *Judith*. Visit from the writer Dr. Schucht from Sonderhausen. Letter from Herbert Reynoldson in London; he offers me 500 pounds sterling from the Drury Lane Theater if I will rehearse and conduct an English performance of *L'Étoile du Nord*.

Tuesday 21 November. Letters from the music director Schladebach in Dresden, and from Vivier in Hanover. Wrote to Vivier. Worked on the aria of Osias. Visits from Professor Griepenkerl, and from Alexander Duncker with a young singer. A concert in the Singakademie: Cherubini's *Requiem;*[125] a psalm by Blumner; Mendelssohn's *Lauda Sion*,[126] all with orchestra. The latter is a dry work that pleases me much less than Mendelssohn's other choral compositions.

Wednesday 22 November. *L'Étoile du Nord* has been given in Toulouse and Lyons, to great enthusiasm. Worked on *Judith* in the evening.

Thursday 23 November. Letter from Hofrat Schilling in Stuttgart. To Count Redern about the Court Concert. Worked on the aria of Osias. Visit from the singer Demoiselle Wagner. In the evening wrote letters to Lüttichau, Gouin, and Kaskel, and worked on act 1.

Friday 24 November. Wrote to Lewald in Stuttgart, together with 400 thalers for his new translation of the dialogue in the *Nordstern*. Wrote to Hofrat Hackländer in Stuttgart. Letters from Dautresme, and from Jules Barbier in Paris. Read through the altered manuscript of *Le Chercheur des trésors*.

Saturday 25 November. Letters from the *Oberstkammerherr* Lanckoronski in Vienna, from Brandus. Symphony-soirée: Symphony no. 4 in B-flat Major (Niels Gade), Symphony no. 8 in F Major (Beethoven), overture *Titus* (Mozart), overture *Jessonda* (Spohr).

Sunday 26 November. To Count Redern about the second Court Concert. Letter from Hartenfeld, director of the Literary and Artistic Bureau in Frankfurt-am-Main: he wants a musical contribution for an album. Wrote to Brandus: sent him the *traité* that I have signed. Wrote to the Commission des Auteurs et Compositeurs Dramatiques: extension of my leave until 15 February. In the evening studied the full scores of the pieces that I will conduct at the big Court Concert.

Monday 27 November. Letters from Gouin, Viardot, Kaskel. To the funeral of the painter Professor Begas. Rehearsed chorus and singers for the Court Concert. Wrote to old Gaetano Rossi in Verona, enclosing support of 200 fr.

Tuesday 28 November. Spent the whole morning rehearsing the orchestra for the big Court Concert tomorrow. Then a small rehearsal of today's small Court Concert. In the evening the Court Concert at Charlottenburg: Vivier (horn); Guglielmi (baritone) sang a church aria by Stradella, and my song "Komm": the ladies Wagner and Tuczek the duet (F major) by Kücken and my "Grossmutter." After the concert the king wanted to hear Vivier play Schubert's "Ständchen,"[127] but he did not have the music with him. As I do not know this music by heart, I did not want to undertake it. Prince Georg, however, improvised the accompaniment without the music, and it went tolerably. The king was very friendly to me, but the visiting king of Hanover ignored me.[128] I stayed to *souper*, against my better feelings, and told Count Redern that unless the court quartermaster-sergeant formally invites me, as on all other occasions, I will not do so again.

Wednesday 29 November. Festal entry of the princess of Dessau, bride of Prince Karl's son, Friedrich Karl. I neglected the rubdown, because Count Redern came to fetch me to the rehearsal of his two *Fackeltänze*. In one of these *Fackeltänze* he has used both the Dessauer and the Hohenfriedberger Marches, at the wish of the bridegroom. The restructuring of these 4/4 melodies into 3/4 presented great difficulties, which the count has overcome with great skill and success. Indeed, both *Fackeltänze* exercise a really attractive, celebratory effect. In the evening a big Court Concert, with orchestra, under my direction, as a congratulatory occasion for the royal family: Gluck's overture to *Iphigenie in Aulis*, Beethoven's Turkish March and Chorus of the Dervishes from *Die Ruinen von Athen*,[129] the Women's Duet with chorus from Rossini's *Graf Ory*,[130] the Consecration of the Banners from Rossini's *Die Belagerung von Korinth* (horn solo by Vivier and aria by Demoiselle Wagner).[131]

Thursday 30 November. Wrote to Oberstkämmerer Count Lanckoronski in Vienna, and to Viardot.

December 1854

Friday 1 December. To the princess of Prussia, who had requested me to come. To Herr von Humboldt. Wrote to Jules Barbier and Cornet.

Saturday 2 December. In order to hear the singers who will perform *L'Étoile du Nord* in Dresden, and to decide on the casting of roles, I set out for there this afternoon at two o'clock by rail, arriving at 8:30.

Sunday 3 December. Heard Marschner's *Der Templar und die Jüdin*: really lovely, talented, and often melodious music. A very good production.[132]

Monday 4 December. Visits from Kapellmeister Krebs, the baritone Mitterwurzer, Tichatschek, Winkler, and Jenny Lind-Goldschmidt.[133] Dined with His Excellency von Lüttichau. In the evening to the theater for *Die Waise von Lowood*, drama by Birch-Pfeiffer: a very impressive play.[134] Emil Devrient and Madame Singer were outstanding.

Tuesday 5 December. Conference in the theater with the scene painters and stage-hands. Called on Kaskel. Dined with my cousin, Sophie von Brandenstein. Gutzkow and Auerbach, who were present at the meal, proposed my health. The young singer Vestri, who has a lovely voice, sang for me. In the theater: Auber's *Der Maurer* [*Le Maçon*]. Letter from Count Schaffgotsch.

Wednesday 6 December. Wrote to Count Schaffgotsch. Called on the singer De-moiselle Ney. Then sang the role of Peter to Kapellmeister Krebs. Dined with the mother of my friend Karl Kaskel. Called on the writer Dr. Berthold Auerbach. In the theater: *Das Lorle*, vaudeville by Wages,[135] and *List und Pflegma*, vaudeville by Angely.[136] Visit from Schladebach.

Thursday 7 December. Farewell visits to Kapellmeister Krebs, Kaskel, Karl Banck, Geheimrat Lüttichau, and Gutzkow. Set out to return to Berlin at 4:15 by train; I arrived at nine o'clock in the evening. Letters from Brandus concerning Mirecourt,[137] from Gemmy Brandus, from the director of the Grand Opéra, Crosnier.[138]

Friday 8 December. Wrote to Brandus. Letter from the theater director Letellier in Brussels: *L'Étoile du Nord* has been very successful there. Letter from Ma-dame Bassi-Manna in Cremona.

Saturday 9 December. Letters from Lewald in Stuttgart, from Dr. Bacher. Letter of thanks from Rossi. Letter from the director Woltersdorff in Königsberg: he wants to produce the *Étoile* in May. A capella concert by the Domchor: Mendelssohn's *Motet*,[139] one of his most beautiful pieces; Stadler's* *Psalm 23* for solo voice;[140] Nicolai's *Psalm 32*, really lovely.[141]

Sunday 10 December. Wrote to Count Lanckoronski, and sent the score of the *Nordstern*. Gala performance of Weber's *Oberon*.

Monday 11 December. [No entry.]

Tuesday 12 December. Wrote to Cornet, Kaskel, to Crosnier, *directeur de l'Opéra,* that I will be coming to Paris in February. Generalintendant von Küstner, the book dealer Schaefer from Dresden, and the pianist von Bülow all came to see me.

Wednesday 13 December. Wrote to Münchheimer in Warsaw, to Herbert Reynold-son in London (I cannot give permission for the performance of the *Étoile* in Drury Lane). Letters from the pianist Sachs in Frankfurt-am-Main, and from Dr. Pyl in Greifswald.

Thursday 14 December. Wrote to Julius Sachs in Frankfurt-am-Main, returning his music. To Letellier, the theater director in Brussels. In the Singakademie: *Samson,* oratorio by Handel.

Friday 15 December. Worked a little in the evening.

Saturday 16 December. Visit from the pianist Herr von Bülow. Concert by the pianist Clara Schumann and the violinist Joachim*.

Sunday 17 December. To Count Redern about von Bülow. Called on Herr von Humboldt. Replied to the writer Gustav Nicolai, and sent him twenty-five thalers support. *Droits d'auteur* for the month of November: 3,541 fr. 70 c.

Monday 18 December. Letters from Gouin, Cornet, Scribe, Madame Stoltz. Anony-mous threatening letter concerning an unspecified injustice I am supposed to have done the singer Demoiselle Decroix. Letter from Truhn. In the evening wrote a long letter to Gouin (about the anonymous missive, and about Madame Ugalde); also wrote to Madame Stoltz.

Tuesday 19 December. Letter from Schladebach. Wrote to Schladebach. Visit from Herr von Bülow. Called on Roger, Dehn. In the Opera House: Donizetti's *Die Favoritin;* Demoiselle Wagner and Roger sang the principal roles outstandingly.

Wednesday 20 December. Letter from the widow of Spehr, which I immediately answered. Letter from Count Lanckoronski. Concert by Clara Schumann and Joachim.

Thursday 21 December. Letter to Count Lanckoronski. In the evening I was sum-moned to the Princess Karl, who spoke with me for one and a half hours.

Friday 22 December. Letter and power of attorney to the *agent des auteurs français*[142] in London, Bonard, so that he can protest against the production of the *Étoile* in London.[143] Wrote to Cornet in Vienna. In the Opera House: Boieldieu's *Die weisse Dame;* Roger sang Georges Brown.

Saturday 23 December. Letter from Lord Loftus, which I immediately answered.[144]

Sunday 24 December. Wrote to Davison in London, enclosing 100 pounds sterling. In the evening worked on the new polonaise for Tichatschek in *L'Étoile du Nord*.[145]

Monday 25 December. Wrote to Bonard. Finished writing down the polonaise, and added some words as pointers for the text, which has yet to be written. Michael's *Struensee*, with my music, has been performed with success in the Darmstadt Theater, and also in Danzig.

Tuesday 26 December. Conferences with Hofrat Teichmann and with Schlesinger.

Wednesday 27 December. Letter from Bonard. Wrote to Cornet and Count Lanckoronski. Gave new the polonaise to Grünbaum, so that he can fit words to it. In the Opera House: Dorn's *Die Niebelungen*.

Thursday 28 December. [No entry.]

Friday 29 December. Letter from Jules Barbier. In the early morning, then all evening, composed and completed a new *cantabile* (without words) for Tichatschek in act 3 of the *Étoile*.[146]

Saturday 30 December. Conference with Grünbaum about the words for the new *cantabile*. In the Schauspielhaus: *Der Fechter von Ravenna*. This tragedy by an anonymous author, which at present is arousing so much interest in Germany, has also elicited much enthusiasm here.[147] It does not appeal much to me, since one can find little sympathy with the characters, who, with the exception of Thusnelda, are ignoble.

Sunday 31 December. Letters from Bonard, Cornet, Dr. Bacher.

Notes

1. Fr. "applause."
2. Donizetti, *Elisabeth, ou La Fille du proscrit,* actually an adaptation of *Otto mesi in due ore, ossia Gli Esilati in Siberia,* opera in three acts (D. Gilardoni, from a melodrama by Pixérécourt, founded on a novel by S. Cottin [1806]; Naples, Teatro Nuovo, 13 May 1827), which enjoyed a modest success in Italian and German. The French version was translated by De Leuven & Brunswick, and the music arranged by U. Fontana (Paris, Théâtre Lyrique, 31 December 1853). While it had only thirty-five performances, it was more successful than the Italian original.

3. Donizetti, *Betly, ossia La Capanna svizzera, opera buffa* in one act (text by the composer, after Scribe's *Le Chalet* [1834] for Adam; Naples, Teatro Nuovo, 24 August 1836). It was popular throughout the nineteenth century. The French version was translated by Hippolyte Lucas, and the music arranged by Adam himself (Paris, Opéra, 27 December 1853).

4. Fr. "links."

5. Johann Gabriel Seidl (1804–75), Austrian journalist and poet. He was known for *Bifolien* (1836), *Gedichte in niederösterreichischer Mundart* (1844), and *Natur und Herz* (1853), and especially as the author of the words for "Gott erhalte Franz den Kaiser," which, with music by Haydn, became the Austrian imperial anthem.

6. Tgb. *coupuren.*

7. The pianist Louis (Brouillon) Lacombe (1818–84) had studied at the Paris Conservatoire with Zimmerman; after touring through France, Belgium, and Germany, and working with Czerny, Sechter, and Seyfried in Vienna, he settled in Paris (1839) and concentrated on composition. He wrote cantatas, operas, symphonies, chamber music, and instrumental music, as well as the essay *Philosophie et musique* (1895).

8. Fr. "imperial procurator at the court of suspension."

9. This was Gustave Rouland (1806–78), French lawyer and cabinet secretary.

10. Amalia Beer suffered the first of a series of fatal strokes. See 11–26 June 1854.

11. This refers to the growing tension that was leading inexorably to the Crimean War. Russia had demanded the right to protect the Orthodox subjects of the Ottoman sultan, and occupied the Danubian principalities on the Russo-Turkish border in July 1853. Britain believed that Russia, by occupation of these provinces, intended the destruction of Turkey and of British influence in the Mediterranean. There was further a dispute between Russia and France over the privileges of the Orthodox and Catholic Churches in the holy places in Palestine. Napoleon III welcomed the opportunity of war with Russia as a way of winning domestic support and of rearranging the map of Europe in France's interests. After the Russian Black Sea Fleet destroyed a Turkish squadron at Sinope, the British and French fleets entered the Black Sea (3 March 1854) to protect Turkish transports. Britain and France subsequently declared war on Russia (28 March 1854). The war lasted until the evacuation and occupation of Sebastopol (11 September 1855), and the threat by Austria to join the allies, forced Russia to accept preliminary peace terms (1 February 1856). The final settlement was worked out at the Congress of Paris (25 February–30 March 1856). A vivid and profusely illustrated history of this conflict is provided by Paul Kerr, Georgina Rye, Teresa Cherpas, Mick Gold, and Margaret Mulvihill, *The Crimean War* (London: Boxtree, 1997).

12. Tgb. *remarquen.*

13. Louis Véron's *Mémoires d'un bourgeois de Paris* had been appearing in six volumes in Brussels (Meline, 1853–56). Volume 3, containing the period of his memorable directorship of the Paris Opéra, was printed in Paris (Gabriel de Gonet, 1854).

14. "Owing to the outbreak of war with Russia, the censorship nearly forbade its presentation; but owing to the personal influence of Napoleon III, it was permitted after a few textual changes were made, such as eliminating the expression '*Vive la Russie*', and the changing of the word *tsar* to *ciel*" (Nathan Haskell Dole, "Meyerbeer," in *The Lives of the Musicians,* 2 vols. [London and New York: Methuen and Co., 1903], 1:342).

15. See 15 May, 30 September, and 23 October 1831. "You spared no expense with regard to the sets, costumes, and props. I recall these matters, insofar as it is still possible, only to confirm and acknowledge your steadfast and active contribution to the success of

Robert le Diable" (Meyerbeer to Louis Véron, Paris, 9 February 1854) (see Becker, *Giacomo Meyerbeer: A Life in Letters* [Portland, Ore.: Amadeus Press, 1989], p. 148).

16. Fr. "practice of the linking passages."

17. "For the first time in its history, the Opéra Comique opened its doors to a foreigner. Meyerbeer was allowed to write for that world-famous stage" (Dole, "Meyerbeer," 1:342). Meyerbeer's first *opéra comique*, the music of which has "unique density of texture" (David Charlton, *The Oxford History of Music,* vol. 9, *Romanticism: 1850–1890* [Oxford: Oxford University Press, 1990], p. 331), was performed 100 times at the Opéra Comique in its first year, and revived in Paris in 1855, 1867, 1878, 1885, and 1887 (a total of 406 performances). While this work never attained the vast popularity of the *grands opéras,* it was performed all over the world (New York, 1856 and 1876; Mexico, 1872; Madrid, 1877; Naples, 1879; Stockholm, 1881; Barcelona, 1882; Zürich, 1884; Liverpool, 1889; Buenos Aires, 1889), and was a particular favorite at Covent Garden, where it was given fifty-four times until 1890. Modern revivals have been in London, at the Camden Festival (25 February 1975), and in Ireland, at the Wexford Festival (October 1996).

18. The political implications of the event were considerable, and it is a sign of Meyerbeer's high standing with the Imperial couple that they attended the première at all. Louis Napoleon had just written to Tsar Nicholas I proposing that he should withdraw Russian troops from the Balkan principalities of Walachia-Moldavia. The British ambassador, Lord Cowley, "saw the letter as another sign that Louis Napoleon was weakening in his resolve to stand by the Turks. The British press criticized the letter as an act of appeasement, and noticed with some disquiet that on 16 February Louis Napoleon went with Eugènie to the Opéra-Comique to see Meyerbeer's *L'Étoile du Nord,* since Scribe's libretto told the story of how the hero of the opera, Peter the Great, defeated Charles XII and the Swedish invaders of Russia at Poltava in 1709. But in fact, Louis Napoleon's proposal in his letter to the Tsar was one which it was almost impossible for the Tsar to accept. . . . and any chance of Russia accepting the proposal was lost when Louis Napoleon's letter was published in *Le Moniteur* before he had received the Tsar's reply" (see Ridley, *Napoleon III and Eugénie* [London: Constable, 1979], p. 364).

19. This was presumably the wife of the journalist Amédée Barthélemy Gayet de Cesena (1810–89).

20. Perhaps the singer and teacher, Andrea Favel (later Lacombe), active in Paris from 1851 to 1877.

21. During the season 1853–54 *L'Étoile du Nord* was performed thirty-three times.

22. Fr. "corrections."

23. This was actually Laurent-Pierre-Charles Desolme (1817–77), journalist and dramatist, critic of *L'Europe artiste.* In October 1862 he was a contender for the license of the Théâtre Lyrique on the resignation of Charles Réty.

24. Eugène Borel (1802–66), a teacher from Marseilles.

25. Michael Bergson (1820–98) studied with Schneider in Dessau, and with Rungenhagen and Taubert in Paris. During the 1840s he lived in Paris and Italy, then in Vienna, Berlin, and Leipzig, before returning to Paris (1859). He took up a teaching post in Geneva (1863) before settling in London as a piano teacher. Apart from an opera (*Luisa di Monfort* [Florence, 1847]) and an operetta (*Qui va à chasse, perd sa place* [Paris, 1859]), he wrote piano music in imitation of Chopin.

26. The violinist Constant Hermann (also Hermant) (b. 1823) studied at the Paris Conservatoire (1836) (a pupil of Guérin and then of Habeneck, winning first prize in 1841),

and composition for three years with Leborne. His violin compositions include fantasies on themes from operas (like Thomas's *Songe d'une nuit d'été*, op. 11; and Clapisson's *Gibby le cornemeuse*, op. 12).

27. Count Pillet-Will "composa environ *cent solos* de violon avec accompaniment de piano" [composed about a hundred violin solos with piano accompaniment] (François Fétis, *Biographie universelle des musiciens et bibliographie générale da la musique,* 2d ed. [Paris: Librairie de Firmin Didot Frères, Fils et Cie., 1860–65], 7:58).

28. See 26 September 1853 for the first mention of Brignoli.

29. Gevaert, *Georgette, ou Le Moulin de Fontenoy, opéra comique* in one act (G. Vaëz; Paris, Théâtre Lyrique, 28 November 1853). The work had a run of forty-three performances until 1854.

30. Adrien Boieldieu, *La Fille invisible, opéra comique* in three acts (Saint-Georges & Dupin; 24 February 1854), was given only nineteen times.

31. This was presumably Major Fleury, actually Comte Émile Félix Fleury, who was aide-de-camp to Louis Napoleon.

32. Clapisson, *La Promise, opéra comique* in three acts (De Leuven & Brunswick; Paris, Théâtre Lyrique, 16 March 1854). It enjoyed sixty performances over two years.

33. This was Rose Furtado, wife of Élie, a member of the Parisian banking community. Meyerbeer first met him in October 1838, and a few days later introduced him to Amalia Beer (see *DGM,* 1:519). On 29 November 1847 Meyerbeer recorded a visit to Mme. Fourtado. By then she was presumably a widow; in a letter to his mother from Paris on 10 October 1848 the composer mentions that she had lost her only son, aged twenty-two years, who had drowned in the Ruhr (see *BT,* 4:448).

34. Lambert-Joseph Massart (b. 1811), professor of violin at the Paris Conservatoire, was a pupil of Rodolphe Kreutzer, and gave a concert at the Opéra at only eighteen (1829). He studied at the Paris Conservatoire until 1832, and became professor there in 1843, counting many famous violinists among his pupils (like Wieniawski). He composed a fantasy for the violin on a theme by Maria Malibran, and made transcriptions of Rossini's *Soirées musicales.*

35. *Les Toiles du Nord, parodie* in three acts (A. Monnier, A. Flan & A. Guénée; Paris, Théâtre des Délassements Comiques, 31 April 1854) [Wicks 21887].

36. Girardin, *La Jolie fait peur.* The première had been at the Théâtre Français on 25 February 1854 [Wicks 18365].

37. Chopin, Piano Concerto no. 1 in E Minor, op. 11 (1830).

38. The Bohemian composer Julius Schulhoff (1825–98) studied in Prague before moving to Paris, where he gave concerts under Chopin's patronage. He toured widely through Austria, England, Spain, and southern Russia before returning to Paris, where he established himself as a successful teacher and composer of salon pieces for the piano. After the Franco-Prussian War (1870), he settled in Dresden, then in Berlin.

39. Fr. "detached pieces," i.e., the separately printed and sold numbers of the opera.

40. For details of Frau Guaita, see 2 June 1852. She was the mother of the director of the Frankfurt Theater.

41. Fr. "bad form in company."

42. Berlioz, *La Fuite en Egypte,* part 2 of the *trilogie sacrée, L'Enfance du Christ,* op. 25 (1850–54).

43. Fr. "patterns," "designs."

44. Fr. "place in the year," i.e., in spite of the time of year.

45. Fr. "delegate."

46. The soprano Anaïs Rey was to sing her most significant part in September 1857: the title role in the French revival of Weber's *Euryanthe* at the Théâtre Français.

47. Fr. "leave."

48. Augier and Sandeau, *Le Gendre de Mr Porier*, prose *comédie* in four acts (Paris, Théâtre du Gymnase Dramatique, 8 April 1854) [Wicks 17680].

49. The libretto *Les Saisons* by Jules Barbier & Michel Carré was eventually set by Victor Massé (Paris, Opéra Comique, 22 December 1855).

50. Temesvár is now Timisoara in Banat, western Romania.

51. *Susanna und David*, drama in four acts by Karl Ludwig Werther (first performed in Berlin 1853, published 1855) [Richel 160].

52. The overture to *L'Étoile du Nord* has a *ripieno* part for stage military band.

53. Charles-Gustav Nadaud (1820–93) was a native of Roulaix, where he studied at the Collège Rollin and won prizes in Greek, Latin, and rhetoric. He then worked in his father's textile business. In 1848 he went to Paris and dedicated himself to poetry. The following year his first collection of lyrics appeared, which he set to music himself. From 1849 he published a series of *chansons*, salon operas, novels, stories, travelogues, and vocal *solfeggi*. On 15 August 1861 he was nominated a knight of the Legion of Honor. He later traveled to Italy (1866) and to Egypt, Greece, and Turkey to study the folk music (1883). In Roulaix he founded a musical society, Le Choral Nadaud. In the light of Meyerbeer's observations, it is interesting to read that Nadaud was judged a sensitive musician: in spite of his shortcomings and harmonic eccentricities, his compositions were "flüssig geschrieben und passt sich dem Text genau" [fluently written, with close attention to the text] (Hugo Riemann, *Musik in Geschichte und Gegenwart* [Cassel and Basel: Bärenreiter Verlag, 1949–51], 9:1243). Nadaud's songs with music appeared in *Le Ménestrel* and *L'Illustration* (1853–70) and in fourteen volumes (1861–70).

54. Matthieu-André Reichert (b. 1830), the Belgian flautist, was the son of a traveling musician, and played first in cafés and dance halls. He was discovered by M. Demeur, and became his pupil at the Brussels Conservatoire (1844), where he won first prize (1847). He gave concerts throughout Belgium and Holland, was engaged by Jullien, and toured more widely, even reaching Brazil (1863). He composed pieces for the flute characterized by novelty of form and technical difficulty. Fétis describes him as "l'un des virtuoses flûtistes les plus habile et les plus extraordinaire du dix-neuvième siècle" [one of the most skillful and extraordinary flautists of the nineteenth century] (*Biographie universelle des musiciens*, 7:212).

55. Honoré de Balzac died on 18 August 1850.

56. Reyer, *Le Sélam*, designated a *symphonie orientale*, but actually a four-act opera with text by Gautier (Paris, 5 April 1850).

57. General Jean-Baptiste-Philibert, comte Vaillant (1790–1872), had directed the French attack on Republican Rome (June 1849). He became a marshal of France and minister of war in the Second Empire, and played a prominent role in the war on Austria in Italy (1859).

58. General Bernard-Pierre Magnan (1791–1865), French soldier, who served at Waterloo (1815), in Spain (1823), and in Algeria (1830). He became general of a brigade (1839) and of a division (1845), suppressed the uprising in Lyons (1849), and took an active part in ensuring the success of Louis Napoleon's coup d'état (2 December 1851). He was a marshal of France (1852) and commander of the army in Paris (1859).

59. This was the music dealer Michael Schloss. Heine felt that Paolo Taglioni's bal-

let *Satanella* (music by Pugni) (1852), with its subject of a female devil, had been modeled on his *Tanzpoem Faust* (1851). Even though the topos of devil incarnated as a seductive woman had been used by Cazotte in *Biondetta* and by Lewis in *The Monk*, and Heine had been assured that there was not the slightest resemblance between the ballet and his poem, after the triumph of *Satanella* in Vienna (1853) the poet, always looking for new sources of financial support, asked that Meyerbeer try to secure him a percentage of the royalties accruing from the ballet. Even if it had been in Meyerbeer's capacity to do as Heine asked, the composer regarded the request as impudent and troublesome, as his confidential correspondence with Gouin shows. He did not take action on Heine's behalf, thereby only aggravating the poet's mischievous attitude toward him. See Heinz Becker, *Der Fall Heine-Meyerbeer: Neue Dokumente revidieren ein Geschichtsurteil* (Berlin: De Gruyter, 1958), pp. 113–17.

60. The outcome of these negotiations would be Meyerbeer's second *opéra comique*, *Le Pardon de Ploërmel* (*Dinorah*).

61. Fr. "drapery and fancy goods store."

62. Reyer, *Maître Wolfram*, *opéra comique* in one act (text by F. J. Méry). This was Reyer's first opera, performed only twenty-three times until 1857. It was later revived in Baden (1863), Brussels (1868), and Paris (1873 and 1902).

63. Count Léo Festetics von Tolna (1800–1884) was chief intendant of the Hungarian National Theater in Budapest. He was also active as a composer of Hungarian national melodies: Liszt wrote some piano variations on his "Pástor Lakodalmas" (Vienna, 1859).

64. Fr. "chief press officer at the Ministry of the Interior."

65. See 1 April 1854.

66. Fr. "sale."

67. On the death of Jules Seveste, the direction of the Theatre Lyrique was taken over by Émile Perrin (from 26 July 1854) who was subjected to several new onerous conditions by the ministry. Perrin was granted a privilege that was to run for three years, at the end of which the minister could withdraw it if the experiment had not proved successful (see T. J. Walsh, *Second Empire Opera: The Théâtre Lyrique Paris,* 1851–1870 [London: John Calder; New York: Riverrun Press, 1981], pp. 52–53).

68. The choreographer of *Gemma* was Fanny Cerrito herself; there were only seven performances.

69. Massé, *La Fiancée du Diable*, *opéra comique* in three acts (Scribe & Romand). The score made little impression, even though it does "renferme des morceaux intéressants" [include interesting pieces], according to Clément & Larousse (1:452).

70. Tgb. *Kolorit.*

71. At Amalia Beer's funeral Meyerbeer's setting of Psalm 91 "was sung as her requiem . . . mourned by the whole nation" (Dole, "Meyerbeer," 1:342).

72. Tgb. *épreuven.*

73. The German translation of *L'Étoile du Nord* was by Ludwig Rellstab (as *Der Nordstern*).

74. Meyerbeer wrote to Louis Brandus from Berlin on 18 July 1854 concerning the delay in publishing the score of *L'Étoile du Nord* (see Becker, *Giacomo Meyerbeer: A Life in Letters*, pp. 149–51).

75. Nestroy, *Eisenbahnheiraten, oder Wien Neustadt, Brünn* (from a play by J.-F.-A. Bayard & Victor Varin; Vienna, Theater an der Wien, 1844).

76. The pianist and composer Eduard Franck (1817–93) was a piano teacher at the Cologne Conservatory. In 1867 he moved to the Stern Conservatory in Berlin.

77. Marc-Michel and Fontaine, *Qui se ressemble, se gêne, comédie-vaudeville* in one act (with A. Peupin; Paris, Théâtre de la Gaîté, 21 May 1842) [Wicks 12693].

78. Julius Mühling (1795–1874) was a singer and actor before becoming theater director in Aachen (1830), Cologne, and Hamburg. From 1848 to 1852 he directed the Stadttheater in Frankfurt with Leonhardt Meck, eventually becoming the artistic director there (1852–55).

79. For discussion of this episode, see Reiner Zimmermann, *Giacomo Meyerbeer: Eine Biographie nach Dokumenten* (Berlin: Henschel Verlag, 1991), pp. 376–77.

80. Tgb. *ce qui ne l'a pas empêché.*

81. Meyerbeer's first dealings with Gollmick were in October–December 1840.

82. Tgb. *physikalische Instrumente.*

83. Meyerbeer had presented the University of Jena with a mechanical press (a Dove Rotation Machine) in grateful acknowledgment of the honorary degree they had conferred on him in July 1850. The four-year delay in their letter of thanks is inexplicable (see *BT*, 5:872).

84. Jean-Jacques-Gabriel de Lurieu and Adolphe Dupeuty, *Le Moulin à paroles, comédie-vaudeville* in one act (Paris, Théâtre des Variétés, 8 June 1847) [Wicks 11544].

85. *La Fille de Dominique, comédie-vaudeville* in one act (Villeneuve & Charles de Livry; Paris, Théâtre du Palais Royal, 22 June 1833 [Wicks 9310].

86. Josefa Vargas and a troupe of Spanish dancers appeared at the Théâtre du Palais-Royal in Paris on 7 June 1854 (Ivor Guest, *The Ballet of the Second Empire* [1953; reprint, London: Pitman Publishing; Middletown, Conn.: Wesleyan University Press, 1976], p. 265).

87. Mendelssohn, Overture to Victor Hugo's play, *Ruy Blas*, op. 95 (1839).

88. Théodore Letellier (d. 1878) was director of the Monnaie from 1852 to 1858, and was subsequently reappointed.

89. Tgb. *montieren.*

90. Fr. "no performance."

91. See 10 November 1849.

92. The soprano Mathilde Marlow had been part of the Darmstadt Court Opera, where she had sung the mezzo role of Fidès in the first performance there of *Le Prophète* on 1 April 1850.

93. The Wilhelma Palace, to the northwest of the Ehmannstrasse in Stuttgart, was designed in the Moorish style by L. W. Zanth for King Wilhelm I, and built between 1842 and 1853. It is famous for its botanical gardens, also laid out in Moorish patterns, with the largest magnolia grove in Europe, camellias, and azaleas. The complex now also contains a zoological garden.

94. Prince Karl Friedrich Alexander (1823–91), the only son of Wilhelm I, became king himself in June 1864.

95. Grand Duchess Olga Nikolaevna, later queen of Württemberg.

96. Peter II (Peter Nikolaus Friedrich), grand duke of Oldenburg, prince of Lübeck and of Birkenfeld (1827–99), had succeeded his father, August Paul Friedrich, in February 1853.

97. Sophia Frederica Mathilda, princess of Württemberg and queen of the Netherlands (1818–77), youngest daughter of Wilhelm I, king of Württemberg, and Catherine Pavlovna, grand duchess of Russia. She married Prince Willem, later King Willem III of the Netherlands, on 18 June 1839. "Zij was een schoone, geestige, hoog begaafde vrouw, letterkundig en artistiek zeer ontwikkeld" [she was a beautiful, spirited, highly gifted woman,

literate and artistically cultivated] (P. C. Molhuysen and P. J. Blok, eds., *Nieuw Nederlandsch Biografisch Woordenboek* [Leiden: A. W. Sijthofs-Uitgevers Maatschappij, 1911], 1:1478).

98. Marie Elisabeth Margarete Therese, princess of Württemberg.

99. Edwin Franz Ludwig Bernhard Ernst, Graf von Neipperg (1813–97), was a military man *(Feldmarschall-Leutnant)*.

100. Karl Alexander, grand duke of Saxe-Weimar-Eisenach (1818–1901), son of grand duke Karl Friedrich and the grand duchess Maria Pavlovna, had succeeded his father in July 1853. He was to reestablish Weimar as one of the cultural capitals of Germany.

101. This was the actress Amalie von Staubenrauch (1800–1876).

102. See 4 June 1812.

103. Cannstadt is properly the vast Schlossgarten, laid out with fountains and cafés. It is divided from the main railway station by the Cannstatterstrasse.

104. Meyerbeer never utilized this privilege.

105. Cruvelli had been scheduled to make her comeback as Alice in *Robert le Diable*. She refused this role, however, and was given Valentine instead.

106. Gevaert, *Le Billet de Marguerite, opéra comique* in three acts (De Leuven & Brunswick; Paris, Théâtre Lyrique National, 7 October 1854), with forty-one performances until 1855. The opera marked the début of the Belgian singer Mme. Deligne-Lauters.

107. Boulanger, *Les Sabots de la Marquise, opéra comique* in one act (Barbier & Carré; Paris, Opéra Comique, 29 September 1854). It was performed Paris until 1866, and revived there in 1899.

108. Eugène Nyon (1812–70), a writer, novelist, and dramatist.

109. Gounod, *La Nonne sanglante*, opera in five acts (Scribe & Delavigne, after Matthew Gregory Lewis's *The Monk* [1796]; Paris, Opéra, 18 October 1854). This was Gounod's second opera, a failure that was never revived.

110. See the appointment in the *Taschenkalender* for 20 February 1849. There is no record of any other meeting between the composers. They might have met at, or around, the première of *L'Étoile du Nord,* which Verdi attended, but it is most unlike Meyerbeer not to have noted such an encounter. Verdi was in Paris preparing for *Les Vêpres siciliennes.*

111. Marie Recio was the stage name of Marie Geneviève Martin, a singer, whom Berlioz met in 1841. See 5 April 1843 for Meyerbeer's first mention of her.

112. Fr. "dissatisfaction."

113. Dorn had known Wagner in Riga, but their friendship had turned to hostility over Wagner's dismissal. He anticipated Wagner by composing *Die Niebelungen, grosse romantische Oper* in five acts (E. Gerber, after the medieval saga; Weimar, Court Opera, 22 January 1854) to a text that had been rejected by Mendelssohn. The opera competes with Wagner, not only in the use of the *Niebelungenlied,* but also musically. Its scheme of reminiscence motifs could have been influenced by Liszt, who conducted the première in Weimar.

114. This was perhaps the actor and man of the theater Ludwig Cramolini (1805–84).

115. Sophie Förster (1831–99), German soprano.

116. This was Jean-François Sudre (1787–1862), French musician and inventor (see Marie-Fernande Alphandéry, *Dictionnaire des inventeurs français* [Paris: Seghers, 1963]). Telegraphy sends electrical impulses along a conducting wire; telephony converts sounds into electrical impulses which are transmitted along a conducting wire and reconverted into sounds at the receiving end of the wire. The transmitter is usually a carbon microphone, while the receiver is an iron diaphragm that vibrates as the impulses affect an electromagnet, between the poles of which the impulses pass round a solenoid.

117. Josephine Hugot is later mentioned as appearing in Paris (*Revue et gazette musicale*, July 1855).

118. Ernst Otto Timotheus Lindner (1820–67) was a music scholar and journalist. He edited the *Vossische Zeitung* and had written a critique of *Le Prophète* in 1850 ("Meyerbeers 'Prophet' als Kunstwerk beurteilt"). The work in question, *Die erste stehende deutsche Oper*, was actually published only in 1855.

119. *Signora Petipa, mein Name ist Meyer*, farce in one act (Rudolf Hahn; Hamburg, 1856) [Richel 58].

120. Charlotte (Löttschen) Moscheles (née Embden) (d. 1889) later wrote an account of her husband's life, *Aus Moscheles' Leben,* 2 vols. (Leipzig, 1872), published in English translation in London, 1873.

121. Kalisch and Weirauch, *Die Bummler von Berlin*, a *Lokalstück*. The latter term denotes a play intended for a popular audience, set in the urban or rural environment of the audience, and using dialect, either in authentic or modified form.

122. Dr. Bernhard Rudolph Konrad Langenbeck (1810–87) was professor and director of the Royal Surgical Clinic in Berlin from 1847.

123. This was Johann Michael Bach (1648–94).

124. Schubert, *Psalm 23* for female quartet with piano (words from the Bible, translated by M. Mendelssohn), D. 706 (1820).

125. Cherubini, Requiem Mass no. 2 in D Minor, for male chorus and orchestra (1836).

126. Mendelssohn, *Lauda Sion*, cantata for chorus and orchestra, op. 73 (1846).

127. Schubert, "Ständchen" (words by Ludwig Rellstab), no. 4 from the song cycle *Schwanengesang*, D. 957 (1828).

128. King Georg V (reg. 1851–66). The fact that the king was blind from a childhood accident may well have had something to do with his apparent coldness.

129. Beethoven, *Die Ruinen von Athen* (incidental music to Kotzebue's play): no. 4 ("Du hast in deines Ärmels Falten") (Chorus of Dervishes) and no. 5 Turkish March.

130. Rossini, *Le Comte Ory*, no. 19a ("Dans ce séjour calme et tranquille").

131. Rossini, *Le Siège de Corinthe*, no. 20a ("L'heure fatale approche") and no. 20b ("Juste ciel ah, ta clémence est ma seul espérance"). This scene of preparation for imminent death is a sublime prayer introduced by a long horn solo.

132. Marschner, *Der Templar und die Jüdin*, opera in three acts (W. A. Wolbrück, after Sir Walter Scott's novel *Ivanhoe* [1820]; Leipzig, 22 December 1822). This opera reflects the elevated manner of *Euryanthe*, and looks forward to *Tannhäuser* and *Lohengrin*, both in its functional use of the orchestra and in the character of Bois-Guilbert, with his complex mixture of good and evil motives. Meyerbeer was very sympathetic to Marschner's music, and the influence of French *grand opéra* is evident in the latter's *Kaiser Adolf von Nassau*. On 27 March 1845 Marschner had approached Meyerbeer with a view to having this work performed in Berlin; Meyerbeer replied on 2 April 1845. See Georg Münzer, "Brief Heinrich Marschners an Meyerbeer," *Die Musik* 1 (1902). The facsimile is reproduced facing p. 2,112, with notes on p. 2,100.

133. August Bournonville met Jenny Lind at this time, and provides a succinct picture of the changes in her life and attitudes: "I had an especially pleasant meeting with our Nordic goddess of song, Jenny Lind, now a wife and mother under the name of Madame Goldschmidt. She was the same cordial and unpretentious Jenny she had been at the time I had her as a guest in my humble home. I visited her family circle often, came to know and respect her husband, and attended two of her brilliant concerts. We had many a heated conversation about how wrong she was to turn her back on the stage forever, and thus

bury the rich talent that had once been the delight and edification of so many; but I always received the reply that she had now learnt that the theatre was nothing else but lies and delusions!" (*My Theatre Life* [*Mit Theaterliv*], translated from the Danish by Patricia N. McAndrew [Middleton, Conn.: Wesleyan University Press; London: Adam & Charles Black, 1979], p. 214).

134. Birch-Pfeiffer, *Die Waise von Lowood*, drama in four acts (published with first performances in Berlin and Vienna, 1853) [Richel 18]. This was based on Charlotte Brontë's novel *Jane Eyre* (1847), and was probably the most famous of Birch-Pfeiffer's seventy-four plays, which are predominantly adaptations of novels.

135. Wages was the pseudonym of August Wilhelm Hesse. The title is actually *s'Lorle, oder Der Berliner im Schwarzwald*, farce in one act from the French (first produced in Hamburg, 1851) [Richel 156].

136. Angely, *List und Pflegma*, vaudeville in one act, adapted from the French, and first produced in Berlin in 1827 [Richel 4].

137. Eugène Mirecourt (pseud. of Charles-Jean-Baptiste Jacquot) (1812–80), a writer and journalist, had just published a biography of the composer (*Meyerbeer* [Brussels, 1854]).

138. By imperial decree of 30 June 1854, the emperor ended the Opéra's status as *entreprise privée*, and placed the director under the orders of the *ministre d'État et de la Maison,* with the institution to be regulated by the civil list. Nestor Roqueplan was nominated as administrator and continued as director for some months, but realizing how unprofitable and frustrating the new regulations would be, he tended his resignation. He was replaced by François Crosnier, a self-educated man, briefly director of the Opéra Comique, and a deputy from the Loire-et-Cher. He assumed full responsibility only on 11 November 1855. (See Fulcher, *The Nation's Image* [Cambridge: Cambridge University Press, 1987], p. 169.)

139. Mendelssohn, *Veni Domine (Hear my prayer)*, from Three Motets for female chorus and organ, op. 39, no. 1 (1830).

140. Stadler, *Psalm 23* from *24 Psalmen Davids* for treble voice and pianoforte (trans. M. Mendelssohn) (1815–c. 17).

141. Nicolai, *Psalm 31* (31 in the Vulgate; 32 in the Hebrew Psalter) for eight voices, from *Psalmen* (ed. E. Naumann [Berlin, 1855]).

142. Fr. "agent for French artists."

143. See Meyerbeer to Bonard (Berlin, 22 December 1854), cited in Becker, *Giacomo Meyerbeer: A Life in Letters*, pp. 152.

144. This was John Henry Loftus, third marquis of Ely (1814–57), a Member of Parliament.

145. *L'Étoile du Nord*, no. 1bis A. *Récitatif et Scène* ("Eh quoi! tu serais donc, comme moi, Moscovite") and B. *Polonaise* ("Un bon soldat, plein d'ardeur et de cœur"). This scene is not in the full score, but appears in both the Brandus and Novello vocal scores.

146. *L'Étoile du Nord*, no. 18bis *Arioso de Danilowitz* ("Quel trouble affreux régne en son cœur!").

147. *Der Fechter von Ravenna*, tragedy in five acts [Richel 58]. The play had just been produced in Vienna (Burgtheater, 18 October 1854). It was by Friedrich Halm* (pseud. of E. F. J. von Münch-Bellinghausen), and tells the story of the captivity of the German queen Thesnulda by the Emperor Caligula in ancient Rome. It became a great stage success, and a cause célèbre, when authorship was claimed by a Bavarian schoolmaster, Bacherl. The noisy controversy that ensued was ended only with a public declaration of authorship by Halm (27 March 1856).

1855

Monday 1 January. God bless the beginning of the new year: may it be happy and joyful in all circumstances for my beloved wife, Minna, my three beloved children Blanca, Caecilia, and Cornelie, and for me. May he bless my artistic endeavors: may all my musical creations be successful, as well as those I have still to write. May he restore health to my beloved Minna, and grant my dearest Blanca a noble, kind husband, who will bring her happiness all her life long. May he help me and my loved ones to lead dignified, conscientious lives, worthy of his mercy and his blessings. Amen.

Letter from Count Lanckoronski. Wrote to Baron Gall in Stuttgart, to Count Lanckoronski, to Director Cornet. Called on Redern, and Alexander von Humboldt. In the evening wrote out the *cantabile* in act 3 for Tichatschek.

Tuesday 2 January. Letters from Bonard in London, from Gouin, from Roger. Letters to the king of Bavaria, Dingelstedt, Bonard. In the evening, I prepared the instrumentation of the *cantabile* in act 3, and finished it. Conference with Grünbaum about appropriate words, since I composed it without a text.

Wednesday 3 January. In order to consider the singer Demoiselle Geisthardt as a possible replacement of Catherine for Demoiselle Wildauer in Vienna (Roger thinks she is very capable), I traveled to Hanover (leaving at 7:30 in the morning, arriving at 3). Roger is singing here as guest artist in *Die Huguenotten*. Demoiselle Geisthardt was the Queen: good coloratura, relatively lovely voice, small, plump figure. Even though she has sufficient liveliness and acting ability for the role of Catherine, I am not able to judge properly on the basis of this role. Madame Nottes was Valentine: she has a dramatic talent, noble delivery in singing and acting, a strong but beautifully tailored voice, even though the high notes are often essayed with difficulty; a respectable talent, but, I believe, not sufficient for Vienna and Berlin. Demoiselle Janda was the Page: actually a contralto, she has a curious appearance, and even though her singing is rather odd, her voice and coloratura are good.[1] Herr Schott as Marcel was passable. The orchestra was excellent, and the chorus possesses really good and substantial vocal talent, but they had been badly rehearsed. The *tempi* were unbelievably violated, the cuts unintelligible, the *mise en scène* faulty, although not without a certain splendor.[2]

Thursday 4 January. At two o'clock by rail to Berlin. Letters from Gouin, Cornet, Bonard, Hofrat Teichmann, and Prof. Dehn.

Friday 5 January. Conferred with Grünbaum about the verses for the *cantabile*.

Saturday 6 January. Gave the score of *L'Étoile du Nord* and a letter for the king of Bavaria to the secretary of the Bavarian delegation, Count Baumgarten. Called on Dehn.

Sunday 7 January. Wrote to Count Lanckoronski in Vienna, to Hofrat Dingelstedt in Munich, to Cornet about the small F-clarinets.

Monday 8 January. Wrote to Brandus, to Dautresme in Elboeuf, and to Lutz, a member of the chorus in Frankfurt-am-Main. Letter from the Festival Committee in Birmingham. Called on Count Redern to inform him of my departure. To Schlesinger, to Dr. Lindner.

Tuesday 9 January. Letter from Herr von Gall. Wrote to Count Lanckoronski, and to Cornet. Preparations for departure. I was going to leave at two o'clock for Dresden, to direct the rehearsals of the *Étoile*, but when I arrived at the station I found the train just leaving, and had to return home for the day. Saw the cyclorama at Kroll's with the children.[3] This is a moving picture that gradually unfolds all the important events in the war currently being waged in the [Near] East[4] and on the Black Sea.[5]

Wednesday 10 January. Left at seven o'clock in the morning by express train for Dresden, where I arrived at 12:30. Visit from the pianist Schulhoff.[6] Letter from Tichatschek: he no longer wants to undertake his role.[7] [Attended] *Der Fechter von Ravenna*.

Thursday 11 January. Went through some of the choruses with the chorus master. Studied some of Demoiselle Ney's role with her. Called on Tichatschek: I hoped to persuade him to sing his role. In the Opera House: Auber's *Die Stumme von Portici*. The choruses were performed outstandingly.

Friday 12 January. Letters from Louis Brandus, from Bonard. Wrote out the two pieces especially composed for Tichatschek. Went through all of Mitterwurzer's role with him.

Saturday 13 January. I took Tichatschek the two pieces that I had composed especially for him, both of which pleased him. Went through the roles of the Camp Followers with Mesdames Kriete and Bredo. With Karl Kaskel to the critic Banck: Kaskel has effected a reconciliation between us. Bellini's *Die Nachtwandlerin*; Demoiselle Ney sang Amina outstandingly.

Sunday 14 January. Letter from Count Lanckoronski. To Tichatschek. Studied the role of Catherine with Demoiselle Ney. Called on Jenny Lind. The singer Mlle. Achilles came to see me. [Attended] *Uriel Acosta*, tragedy by Gutzkow, excellently acted.[8]

Monday 15 January. Letters from Dr. Bacher and Cornet. Called on Banck. Held a piano rehearsal—for the first time with the singers. Concert by the Männergesangverein: "Orpheus"; *Frau Musica*, a cantata by Reissiger; "An den Wasserflussen Babylons," a setting of Psalm 84 by Kapellmeister Möhring (really lovely); "Inclina Domine" by Cherubini.[9] Busied myself with the arrangement of the textbooks. In the theater: C. M. von Weber's *Euryanthe*. *L'Étoile du Nord* has been given in Lille, and apparently enjoyed great success.

Tuesday 16 January. Congratulated Tichatschek on his twenty-fifth theater anniversary.[10] Gave the chorus master Fischer the first revised libretto.[11] Concert by Jenny Lind. *Droits d'auteur* for the month of December: 3,011 fr.

Wednesday 17 January. Conferred with the ballet master, with the organizer of the military music and the bells. Called on the concert masters, Lipinski and Schubert, as well as Demoiselle Bunke. Worked on the revision of the printed textbook.

Thursday 18 January. Letter from Bonard. Completed the revision of the shortened textbook, and gave it to the regisseur Fischer. Second visit from Banck.

Friday 19 January. Held a rehearsal with the chorus. Studied Tichatschek's role with him. Went through the military music with the conductor. Called on Gutzkow. Began scoring the *cantabile*.

Saturday 20 January. First performance of *Lenz und Söhne*, a comedy by Gutzkow: it has only moderate appeal.[12]

Sunday 21 January. Finished scoring the *cantabile*. Called on Auerbach. [Attended] Otto von Nicolai's *Die lustigen Weiber von Windsor*.

Monday 22 January. Wrote the vocal line of the polonaise into the full score.

Tuesday 23 January. Combined chorus and soloists at the piano. Continued with the scoring of the polonaise. Letter from Louis Brandus, together with a proposal for power of attorney for Beale.

Wednesday 24 January. [No entry.]

Thursday 25 January. First quartet rehearsal with the collective string instruments, without singers; it lasted from 10 until 2:30, and yet we completed only two acts. In the afternoon rehearsed with the two flutes and Demoiselle Ney. For the first time saw Shakespeare's tragedy *Othello.*[13] Dawison[14] and Demoiselle Bayer-Bürck[15] played the roles of Othello and Desdemona unforgettably.

Friday 26 January. Second quartet rehearsal without singers; this time we completed all three acts.

Saturday 27 January. Letter from the Bavarian ambassador, Count Montgelas, containing the thanks of the king of Bavaria for the score of *L'Étoile du Nord.* Correction rehearsal for the whole orchestra without singers.

Sunday 28 January. Visits from Banck and Hofrat Winkler. Called on Dr. Carus and Geheimrat von Lüttichau.

Monday 29 January. Letter from Smith, director of Drury Lane Theatre. Note from Karl Banck. Correction rehearsal for the orchestra, without singers. *Mise en scène* rehearsal of act 1. In the evening studied the *mise en scène*; wrote to Winkler and Banck.

Tuesday 30 January. Letter from Gye, director of Covent Garden. First orchestral rehearsal with singing. On account of her wedding, Demoiselle Ney was not present, so we could rehearse only those pieces in which she does not appear. Afterward to the marriage and wedding reception of Demoiselle Ney and the actor Bürde.

Wednesday 31 January. Mise en scène rehearsal, but without Demoiselle Ney. Revised the textbook, put it in order as far as act 3, and gave it to the regisseur Fischer. In the evening with Banck to hear the singer Conia.

February 1855

Thursday 1 February. Letters from the music dealer Guidi in Florence, from Marquis Martellini, and from Karl Formes in London. *Mise en scène* rehearsal of parts of acts 1, 2, and 3. Called on Schladebach. Wrote to Gye.

Friday 2 February. Orchestral rehearsal, with singing, of acts 1 and 2 with *mise en scène*. In the theater: Lessing's *Emilia Galotti*, an outstanding production.[16]

Saturday 3 February. Orchestral rehearsal with singing of act 3, then a scene rehearsal of act 3.

Sunday 4 February. Small *mise en scène* rehearsal of the Tent Scene. Letter from Gouin. Wrote to Gouin about Perrin and Drury Lane Theatre. In the theater: Shakespeare's *Richard III*.[17]

Monday 5 February. First dress rehearsal of all three acts. Called on Auerbach. Visit from Banck.

Tuesday 6 February. Second dress rehearsal of all three acts. Called on Gutzkow. I had the news, through his son-in-law Fanna,[18] of the death in Verona of my old friend, the poet Gaetano Rossi, aged sixty years.[19]

Wednesday 7 February. Today was a purely costume rehearsal. Called on Banck. Visit from Gutzkow. Letter from the music dealer Glöggl in Vienna: wants to publish a "Wiegenlied" of mine, which I apparently composed,[20] for the confinement of the empress of Austria.[21] Letter from the music publisher Diabelli in Vienna about the same matter.

Thursday 8 February. Last dress rehearsal of the *Nordstern*: on the whole it went well. Until now there had been no sign of enthusiasm, from either the orchestra, chorus, or singers. To the theater for *Die Wiener in Paris*: Dawison as Bonjour was excellent.[22]

Friday 9 February. In the evening (from six until ten o'clock) the first performance of the *Nordstern*, which appeared to be a great success. Demoiselle Ney was called out after the Gypsy Roundelay, after act 1, and at the conclusion of the opera, Mitterwurzer after acts 2 and 3. Both the new pieces that I wrote for Tichatschek appealed greatly. The king summoned me to his box after act 1, and paid me many compliments. The chorus and orchestra were both very good. Demoiselle Bunke (Prascovia) and her two duets were the only pieces that did not make a good impression.

Saturday 10 February. Called on the singers and other people. Herr von Lüttichau presented to me, on behalf of the king, and as a sign of his regard, the Commander's Cross of the Albrecht's Order. The critique in the *Dresdener Zeitung* by my formerly bitter enemy, Karl Banck is, therefore, from this point of view, to be regarded as a good thing.

Sunday 11 February. Letter from Madame Zellner, wife of the editor of the new *Wiener Musikzeitung.* The sudden death of the duke of Genoa, son-in-law of the king, has meant an immediate assumption of profound court mourning: all the boxes and seats reserved for the diplomatic corps and other prominent people for today's (second) performance of the *Nordstern* were thus returned, and there were consequently many empty places. Otherwise this performance, and its reception, went as well as the first.

Monday 12 February. Conference about cuts for the third performance. Departed for Berlin at 4:15. *En route* I composed a second version of the opening chorus of *Le Chercheur des trésors.*[23]

Tuesday 13 February. Wrote to Kaskel, Kapellmeister Krebs, the chorus master Fischer.

Wednesday 14 February. Read in the papers of the death of the clarinetist Iwan Müller, whom I knew as far back as 1811, at Abbé Vogler's.[24] Wrote to Herr von Hülsen, and returned the manuscript *Daniel et Susanne.* Revised the copy of the two pieces composed for Tichatschek for the typesetter. To the rehearsal for the concert performance of Bernhard Klein's opera *Dido.*[25]

Thursday 15 February. Today I really want to begin serious composition of the *Chercheur.* Wrote out almost all the vocal parts of the first chorus. Letters from Dr. Bacher and Kaskel. Wrote to Madame Zellner, Diabelli, and Glöggl, all in Vienna. Today saw the death of our dear friend, Minister Ladenburg.

Friday 16 February. Letters from Schladebach, from Kaskel. *Droits d'auteur* for January: 2,679 fr. All letters, newspapers, and oral encounters for the last three days, have been unpleasant and disheartening for me as an artist. In the evening I believe I found a happy conclusion for the first chorus, and wrote out the whole piece. Today saw the 100th performance of *L'Étoile du Nord* (receipts 3,045 fr.).

Saturday 17 February. Wrote to Schladebach, enclosing thirty thalers. Concert by the Domchor: Menegalli's *Ave regina* for male voices (lovely),[26] Jomelli's *Lux aeterna* (wonderful).[27]

Sunday 18 February. Wanted to read through the poem of the *Chercheur* again, but could not get down to it. In the evening I wrote out the strophe for the Pâtre, thereby bringing the introduction to a conclusion; then wrote a long letter to Gouin.

Monday 19 February. Letter from Herr von Humboldt. Composed in general on the *Chercheur*, and read through the whole manuscript again.

Tuesday 20 February. Worked very little.

Wednesday 21 February. Unfortunately worked only a little. Vivier spent some time with us.

Thursday 22 February. Worked a little on the overture. *Des Adlers Horst,* romantic opera by Gläser.[28]

Friday 23 February. Worked for two hours on the overture to the *Chercheur,* but without particular success. With Dr. Lindner to Herr von Humboldt. To the English pianist, Arabella Goddard*. [Sent] two volumes of Handel arias and eight volumes of the collected Prince de la Moskowa to Karl Banck in Dresden.[29]

Saturday 24 February. The *Nordstern* has been performed in the German Theater in Amsterdam, with great success.[30] Worked on the overture without achieving much.

Sunday 25 February. Before breakfast at last found some inspiration again for the overture. Read through the scenario *La Tour des aigles,* by Jules Lecomte.

Monday 26 February. Worked on the overture before breakfast. Worked the whole evening, and nearly completed the whole of Corentin's *chanson* ("Dieu nous donne à chacun en partage").[31] I was very industrious today.

Tuesday 27 February. Letter from Hauptmann Wittich in Düsseldorf, together with an opera libretto, *Jatria.* Wrote to Hauptmann Wittich, returning the libretto. Altered and wrote out Corentin's *couplets.* Soirée at Madame Decker's, where the *Vogel-Cantate* by Madame Mockel (Kinkel*) was sung, a lovely piece of music that would be suitable for use in a Court Concert.

Wednesday 28 February. Letter from Herr von Holtzendorff: renewed request for the hand of my daughter Blanca. Dined at Prince Karl's. Afterward called on the singer Mme. Tedesco, who has arrived here from St. Petersburg. I have caught cold again.

March 1855

Thursday 1 March. Wrote to Herr von Holtzendorff: refused his proposal of marriage. In the evening wrote out the vocal line and sketches for the accompaniment of Corentin's *couplets.* On 26 February *L'Étoile du Nord* was performed at the Drury Lane Theatre in London in English: it was apparently a bad performance.

Friday 2 March. Visit from Gye, the director of the Italian Opera at Covent Garden in London, who wants to give *L'Étoile du Nord* in the forthcoming season. He stayed with me for three hours, conferring about the details.

Saturday 3 March. Conference with Gye. Wrote to the Comité des Auteurs et Compositeurs Dramatiques, requesting indefinite extension of my leave.

Sunday 4 March. So out of sorts for the whole morning that I could not work. Dined with the duchess of Sagan. In the evening worked on the overture. *L'Étoile du Nord* has been given in Strasbourg with success.

Monday 5 March. Worked a little on the overture. Called on Roger.

Tuesday 6 March. Wrote to Jules Lecomte, returning the scenario of *La Tour des aigles*. Improvised a little on the overture. Concert by the English pianist, Arabella Goddard. Demoiselle Burg sang my "Mailied."

Wednesday 7 March. Worked during the day on the operetta in general, but without particular success. Called on Madame Birch-Pfeiffer. In the evening in the theater: Auber's *Fra Diavolo*. Roger sang Fra Diavolo elegantly, but without sufficient gaiety.

Thursday 8 March. Coughed badly. Wrote to the director of the Grand Opéra, Crosnier. Concert by the Sternscher Gesangverein. At the end of February the *Nordstern* was produced in Erfurt with great success.

Friday 9 March. Stayed in bed all day. *L'Étoile du Nord* has been performed in Ghent, with great success.

Saturday 10 March. [No entry.]

Sunday 11 March. Drew up the contract with Gye for the production of the *Étoile* in the Covent Garden Theatre in London. English lesson with Lloyd.

Monday 12 March. Worked on the overture in the evening.

Tuesday 13 March. Worked on the overture, and composed the final Chorus of the Procession that occurs in it. Wieprecht demonstrated to me his newly invented wind instrument, the *Klaviercontrafagott,* which is intended to fulfill the same function for the wind instruments that the contrabass does for the strings.[32]

Wednesday 14 March. Worked a little on the overture and on Corentin's first aria.

Thursday 15 March. Worked on Corentin's first aria, in both the morning and evening. Composed the bagpipe piece for Corentin's entry.[33]

Friday 16 March. Wrote to Guidi: promised him the recitatives [for *L'Étoile du Nord*] by the month of May. Worked only a little on Corentin's aria.

Saturday 17 March. [Worked] on Corentin's aria. Symphony-Soirée: a new Symphony in C Minor by Taubert, to which he had invited me; Mendelssohn's overture *Meeresstille und glückliche Fahrt;*[34] Beethoven's Symphony no. 7 in A Major.

Sunday 18 March. Wrote to Gemmy Brandus, with permission for him to publish the Polonaise and Arioso, and sent him the full score. Wrote to Tichatschek, enclosing the pieces of music dedicated to him (piano score). Finished composing Corentin's aria.

Monday 19 March. An unworthy, mendacious article about me has appeared in *Die Feuerspritze*, ostensibly from the *Revue parisienne*, entitled "Das Loch in der Prunke im Feldlager" [The puncture in the Feldlager pomp].

Tuesday 20 March. Gluck's *Iphigenie in Aulis.*

Wednesday 21 March. In the evening began to orchestrate the Air de la Cornemeuse, and completed it.

Thursday 22 March. For one hour before breakfast began writing out Corentin's aria. Began composing Margaridd's first *romanza.*[35] In the evening wrote out Corentin's aria. Wrote to the father of the late Kapellmeister Nicolai (twenty thalers support).

Friday 23 March. Droits d'auteur for the month of February: 1,613 fr. 35 c. In the Opera House: Gläser's *Des Adlers Horst.*

Saturday 24 March. Finished writing out Corentin's aria. The first performance of Taglioni's four-act ballet *Ballanda*, music by Hertel*: lovely details, piquant décor, with the sea represented by a mirror. *L'Étoile du Nord* has been produced in Metz and Rennes.

Sunday 25 March. Worked on the overture; only the necessary consideration of the closing theme continues to hamper the progress of the composition.

Monday 26 March. In the Domkirche: Graun's *Der Tod Jesu.*

Tuesday 27 March. In the Opera House: Flotow's *Alessandro Stradella.* The *Nordstern* was given on 25 March in Darmstadt, with great success. Letter from Kapellmeister Schindelmeisser.

Wednesday 28 March. Worked for one hour before breakfast on the overture, with fairly good success. To the librarian Dehn about an English music dictionary. Concert by Tschirch, in which he performed his tone painting *Die Sankt Hubertus-Jagd,* for wind instruments.

Thursday 29 March. Dorn's *Die Niebelungen.*

Friday 30 March. Visit from the music dealer Dufour,[36] the associate of Brandus, who is going to St. Petersburg. Worked on the overture in the evening without success because of a headache. My composition "Der Wanderer und die Geister am Grabe Beethovens" was performed in Vienna, in a concert of the Akademie der Tonkunst.

Saturday 31 March. Worked on the overture, without particular success.

April 1855

Sunday 1 April. Worked a little on the overture. Gave the manuscript of *Le Chercheur des trésors* to Madame Birch-Pfeiffer to read. Letter from Gouin, enclosing the contract signed by Gye.

Monday 2 April. Worked on the overture. To Birch-Pfeiffer, to consult her advice about the libretto of *Le Chercheur des trésors.*

Tuesday 3 April. Visit from Dr. Bamberg from Paris. In the Opera: Weber's *Euryanthe. L'Étoile du Nord* was given in Bordeaux, with success.

Wednesday 4 April. Worked for an hour before breakfast on the overture. In the evening did not compose because of a headache.

Thursday 5 April. Composed for one hour before breakfast, working on the overture. Letter from Gemmy Brandus enclosing the translation of the two pieces from the *Étoile.* Since I was not at all in the mood for composing, I learnt English phrases by heart in the evening.

Friday 6 April. Wrote to Gemmy Brandus before breakfast, enclosing my observations on the French translations of my two new pieces for the *Étoile* (by

Mornais). Corrected my male-voice quartet, "Freundschaft," for Schlesinger.[37] Wrote to Witting*, returning the manuscript of his symphony.

Saturday 7 April. In the morning left at 9:15 by rail for Gotha, where I have been invited by the duke to hear a performance of his opera *Santa Chiara.* On my arrival in Gotha, the duke's intendant, von Wangenheim, met me in a court carriage to convey me to the ducal palace, where the duke has insisted I should stay. The duke himself then came to me to conduct me to the rehearsal of his opera. In the interval the duke took me on stage and introduced me to the kapellmeister and the court singers. On my entering the theater, the orchestra received me with applause.

Sunday 8 April. Visit from Herr von Lüttichau, who is also here to hear the duke's opera. Called on the theater intendant, von Wangenheim. The duke had me come at 12 to meet the duchess, born a princess of Baden. A big gala dinner given by the duke in his conservatory or winter garden: a charming place. Afterwards the duke took me to a box in the theater where I, seated between the ducal couple, heard his opera *Santa Chiara,* with words by Madame Birch-Pfeiffer. Act 2 of this opera has great musical beauties in a noble, dramatic style. Madame Bockholz-Falconi (the prima donna), Herr Beer (the tenor), and Abt (the bass) all have good voices, and sing well. In the morning I called on my old acquaintances, Kapellmeister Drouet and the concert master Lampert.[38]

Monday 9 April. The duke came to me before my departure and, with many kind words, presented the Commander's Cross of the Order of the Ernestine House (first class with star). At twelve o'clock I left by train for Weimar in order to attend the first performance there of Robert Schumann's opera *Genoveva.*[39] I waited four hours in Erfurt in order not to arrive there too early: I wanted to remain incognito, so as not to have to call on Liszt. But this precaution did not help at all, since the young Cornelius recognized me in the theater and told Liszt, who came to greet me during the interval, as did the intendant, Baron Beaulieu. I had to go with Liszt to the box of his beloved, the Princess Wittgenstein.[40] So the opera was Robert Schumann's *Genoveva:* totally without melodies, badly written for the voices, unclear and ponderous; and yet with many interesting harmonic and orchestral details, and occasional flashes of genial conception. A letter from the conductor Eugène Momas in Nîmes: *L'Étoile du Nord* has been performed there with great success.

Tuesday 10 April. Arrived back in Berlin at 10:45 in the evening.

Wednesday 11 April. [No entry.]

Thursday 12 April. Visits from the singer Mlle. Wildauer and from Gutzkow. I read through the libretto yet again, on account of the changes that Mme. Birch is to make in the *Chercheur*.[41] In the Opera: Gluck's *Orpheus*. Demoiselle Wagner was Orpheus, an outstanding achievement.

Friday 13 April. Before breakfast wrote down further observations about the *Chercheur*. Visit from the old violoncellist, Schäncken from Munich, who in 1813 played in my opera *Jephtha* in Munich.[42]

Saturday 14 April. Completed my observations about the *Chercheur* for Madame Birch. *Droits d'auteur* for the month of March: 1,093 fr. 30 c.

Sunday 15 April. Agreed with Birch-Pfeiffer that I will give her 140 louis d'or in return for her attending to any changes that I might want in the *Chercheur*. In the theater: *Ballanda*, a ballet by Taglioni. It contains a lovely new effect in the décor, whereby the sea is represented by a big mirror that lies *sur un plan incliné*,[43] and that reflects all the characters who appear on the raised seashore positioned behind the sea.

Monday 16 April. Count Redern took me to hear his overture played by a military band. Read through the Italian recitatives of the *Étoile*.

Tuesday 17 April. Wrote to Tichatschek, enclosing the full score of the Arioso and Polonaise. Dined with Count Redern, where Count Rossi, the husband of the famous singer Sontag, was also present with his two daughters.

Wednesday 18 April. Today I began working on the Italian recitatives for *L'Étoile du Nord* needed for the production in London.[44] Composed three-quarters of the first scene. I had to attend a performance of military music as the prize judge in a competition established by Bock. Called on Gutzkow. An unfriendly article by Berlioz in *Le Journal des débats* concerning the reprise of *Le Prophète* with Stoltz, has hurt me deeply.[45]

Thursday 19 April. Worked for an hour before breakfast on the recitatives, and finished composing and writing out the first scene. Continued adjudicating the military marches as prize judge. Visit from the Jewish cantor Ketter, from Posen, with his seven-year-old son, a very promising musical talent. In the evening composed and wrote out the small monologue for Peter, which follows on the first scene.

Friday 20 April. Worked for one hour before breakfast on the recitatives, and composed the fifth scene, but have still to write it out. Worked for another hour before lunch on the recitatives .

Saturday 21 April. Worked for one and a quarter hours before breakfast on the recitatives. Read through the new French translation of the Arioso and Polonaise. From 11 until 1:30 worked on the recitatives. I hosted a dinner in honor of Gutzkow. In the evening still worked for another hour on the recitatives.

Sunday 22 April. Worked on the recitatives.

Monday 23 April. Worked on the recitatives. Conferred with Birch-Pfeiffer about changes to the *Chercheur.*

Tuesday 24 April. Worked on the recitatives.

Wednesday 25 April. Letter from the poet Berlyn in Freiburg in Westphalia, enclosing his poems.[46] Worked on the recitatives and completed virtually the whole of act 1.

Thursday 26 April. Worked on the recitatives, completed the first act, and began to score them.

Friday 27 April. I finished the instrumentation of the recitatives of act 1 today. Conference with Rellstab about additions for the role of Lablache (Gritzenko) in the recitatives. Received from Nîmes, from an unknown hand, four numbers of the local paper, *L'Opinion du Midi,* which contains a very favorable letter about the performance of *L'Étoile du Nord* there. On 10 April *Der Nordstern* was performed for the first time in Mainz, but appears to have been unpopular.

Saturday 28 April. Read through the text of the recitatives of act 3 in order to shorten them. To Herr von Humboldt, and to Madame Birch-Pfeiffer to confer with her on the changes in the *Chercheur.* I have heard, through Tichatschek and Mitterwurzer, that *Tannhäuser* will be performed tomorrow in Hamburg, and since I have not yet heard this opera, I am going there by the afternoon train.

Sunday 29 April. Hamburg: I took a two-hour walk through the city and the harbor. In the theater: Richard Wagner's *Tannhäuser.* It was a so-called specimen performance,[47] i.e., singers came from various theaters, and each role was played by a visiting artist. The opera itself is incontestably a musical-artistic manifestation of the highest interest. There is indeed a great dearth of melody, an unclarity, and a formlessness, but nonetheless great flashes of genius in conception, in orchestral coloring, and in purely musical respects, particularly in the instrumental passages. I had hoped to remain incognito in Hamburg, but the director Cornet, who called on me, told me that everyone in the theater had known I was there.

Monday 30 April. At 7:30 in the morning I set off back to Berlin. Director Cornet spent some of the journey in my carriage. In the evening began composing the recitatives of act 3. Letter from the committee of the music festival in Düsseldorf, inviting me to attend.

May 1855

Tuesday 1 May. I sought out an Italian translator for the verses added to Gritzenko's recitatives by Rellstab. Worked at the recitatives, and finished the *Buffo* Trio. *L'Étoile du Nord* has been given in Grenoble with success.

Wednesday 2 May. Called on Rellstab and Schlesinger. Worked on the recitatives. *L'Étoile du Nord* has been performed in New Orleans, with great success.

Thursday 3 May. Visit from the singer Roger. Worked at the recitatives.

Friday 4 May. Called on Professor Schnackenburg, who is to translate the *couplets* for the role of Gritzenko into Italian. Worked on the recitatives: completed the composition of act 3, and began their instrumentation. Letter from Herr von Stückradt: requests the hand of my daughter Blanca.

Saturday 5 May. Finished scoring the recitatives of act 3.

Sunday 6 May. Studied the text of the Italian recitatives in act 2 before breakfast and made abridgments. To Professor Schnackenburg: he gave me his Italian translation of the comic verses that Rellstab wrote for the recitatives in the role of Gritzenko.

Monday 7 May. Worked a little on the recitatives this morning, and spent a lot of time on them in the afternoon, so that I could give my manuscript of act 2 to the copyist and explain it to him. Devoted the whole evening to reading through and correcting his copy of the recitatives in act 1.

Tuesday 8 May. Worked on the recitatives in act 3. Wrote to Gye in London, at the same time sending him the recitatives of act 1.

Wednesday 9 May. Worked for seven and a half hours on the recitatives.

Thursday 10 May. Worked for eight and a half hours on the recitatives. Called on Hofrat Hackländer.

Friday 11 May. Worked for six and a half hours on the recitatives. Wrote to Cornet in Vienna, enclosing the two new pieces for the role of Danilowitz.

Saturday 12 May. Wrote to Gye, and sent him the recitatives of act 2. Worked on the recitatives morning, afternoon, and evening, until midnight. Only for an hour in the evening did I go out, to a musical soirée at Madame Zimmermann's, where the trio from the *Crociato* was sung. Visit from Herr von Küstner. *L'Étoile du Nord* was performed in Avignon in the course of the winter.

Sunday 13 May. Worked for seven and a half hours on the recitatives.

Monday 14 May. Virtually completed the recitatives. In the Opera House: Rossini's *Die Belagerung von Corinth*.

Tuesday 15 May. Worked for two hours on the recitatives of act 2, completely finished them, and sent this last part of act 2 to the copyist Patschke. May Almighty God bless this work. Spent the evening revising the copy of the score of act 2, and dispatched it to Gye in the London post.

Wednesday 16 May. Early in the morning at Count Redern's, to hear his overture and march performed by military band. Wrote to Lieutenant Bernard von Stückradt in Stettin.

Thursday 17 May. I have a cold. In the evening examined the changes that Madame Birch has made in the *Chercheur*.

Friday 18 May. Visit from the critic Hanslick*, from Vienna. Returned his call.

Saturday 19 May. In the afternoon a long conference with Birch-Pfeiffer about the changes in the *Chercheur*.

Sunday 20 May. In the evening, for the first time in a month since starting the recitatives, I began working on the overture to the *Chercheur* again.

Monday 21 May. Answered the committee of the Lower Rhine music festival in Düsseldorf. With the critic Hanslick to a rehearsal of the Domchor.

Tuesday 22 May. In the Singakademie: Rungenhagen's cantata *La Morte di Abele*, a work composed with much understanding, in a clear, noble style, the recitatives molded with aesthetic beauty, the arias lyrical and resonant. While the whole hardly represents a radical development, it is nonetheless a noble, euphonious work that I would not have credited to the personality of this composer.

Wednesday 23 May. Took Burguis pieces of the *Chercheur* for translation.[48] *Droits d'auteur* for the month of April: 1,949 fr. 20 c.

Thursday 24 May. Conference with Louis Brandus. In Liège *L'Étoile du Nord* has been performed with great success.

Friday 25 May. Wrote to Gye about the Air de Danse and recitatives. In the theater: Auber's *Der Feensee* [*Le Lac des fées*].

Saturday 26 May. Ordered the text of the recitatives for Gye. *Matinée musicale* at the princess of Prussia's, where Hans von Bülow played the piano. Conferred with Brandus about his trip to London. In the evening a small soirée at Madame Birch-Pfeiffer's, where her daughter declaimed scenes from tragedies and plays.

Sunday 27 May. Worked on the overture, but without success. In Amsterdam the German Opera Society has performed *Der Nordstern* nineteen times recently, and twice in Utrecht.

Monday 28 May. [No entry.]

Tuesday 29 May. *Le Prophète* was performed on 23 May at the Teatro alla Scala in Milan for the first time.[49] I read about it in a letter from the singer Zezi.

Wednesday 30 May. Went through the copy of the recitatives with the new copyist Meinhard. In the evening worked on the overture.

Thursday 31 May. The *Crociato* has been performed in Rovereto to great enthusiasm.

June 1855

Friday 1 June. Called on Count Redern. Visit from the singer Mlle. Tietjens from Vienna, and from the Dresden music director Schladebach, who asked me for twenty thalers and received it.

Saturday 2 June. [Attended] *Der Goldschmied von Ulm*, drama by Mosenthal, which is derived from de la Motte Fouqué's novella *Das Galgenmädchen*.[50]

Sunday 3 June. Worked a little on the overture. In the theater: Mozart's *Don Juan*. Demoiselle Tietjens sang Donna Anna: a wonderfully beautiful soprano voice, with an evenness and lovely tone through two octaves, and an aptitude for coloratura, even if it is not fully developed; line and musical conception are not yet perfected, although the potential is all there.

Monday 4 June. Wrote to Lady Westmorland in Vienna, asking if she would give me testimonials for England. Visits from Herr von Bülow, from the singer Sieber who, in 1821, sang in my *L'Esule di Granata* at La Scala.[51] Called on Demoiselle Tietjens. In the evening read through the copy of the recitatives for act 2.

Tuesday 5 June. In the theater: a performance of Haydn's *Die Jahreszeiten.*[52] Afterwards to Madame Birch-Pfeiffer, to whom I paid forty friedrichs d'or for her verses for the *Chercheur.*

Wednesday 6 June. Flotow's *Martha* (Demoiselle Tietjens). Visit from Dufour, who is returning from St. Petersburg. Wrote ostensibly to Gouin, but actually for Perrin, concerning Madame Ugalde. *L'Étoile du Nord* has been performed in Nancy.

Thursday 7 June. In the morning and the evening wrote conducting directions in my score of the *Étoile.*

Friday 8 June. Entered conducting directions into my score.

Saturday 9 June. Did the same. Letters from Lady Westmorland, and from Gye. In the theater: Shakespeare's *Hamlet.* The famous actor Dawison played Hamlet.

Sunday 10 June. Wrote to the two daughters of the late poet Gaetano Rossi in Verona, and sent 100 fr. to each of them. In the evening finished revising the recitatives, and arranged the Prayer and Barcarolle at the end of act 1 of the *Étoile* in G-flat (instead of G) for Madame Ugalde.

Monday 11 June. Wrote to Brandus, to Gye: I will come to London if Gye promises to give the opera on 7 July. In the theater: Goethe's *Clavigo;*[53] Herr Dawison played Don Carlos; Holtei's *Die Wiener in Paris*: Herr Dawison was Bonjour.

Tuesday 12 June. Entered conducting directions into the score.

Wednesday 13 June. Read a libretto sent to me from Dresden by Herr Gottwald, *Der Graf von Provence*: a commonplace, worn-out subject.[54]

Thursday 14 June. In the evening left at ten o'clock by rail for Cologne.

Friday 15 June. In the afternoon at four o'clock we arrived in Cologne. After a three-hour rest, I took the railway train for Aachen.

Saturday 16 June. At 9:30 by railway train to Brussels, where we arrived at 3.

Sunday 17 June. Because the letter from Brandus in London had not yet arrived, informing me whether Gye has accepted my proposal (to give the *Étoile* only on 10 July, my condition for traveling to London), I must therefore wait here for an answer. At four o'clock in the afternoon letters finally arrived from Brandus and Gye, acceding to my request. *Droits d'auteur* for the month of May: 1,766 fr. 20 c.

Monday 18 June. At 7:15 in the morning left by railway train to go via Iubize, Tournai, and Lille to Calais. We arrived at 1:30 and left at 3:00 by steamship for Dover. I had seasickness to such an extent that it was impossible to travel on from Dover. The passage from Calais to Dover lasted about two and a half hours.

Tuesday 19 June. At eight o'clock left by train for London, where we arrived at 10:30. I have a *salon*, bedroom and servant's room, for which I pay eighteen shillings daily, with two shillings and six pence for service. Since I was very tired, I stayed in my rooms all day, and received only Gye's call. In the evening at Covent Garden, to the Italian Opera for Verdi's *Il Trovatore*.[55] Madame Ney, Madame Viardot, Tamberlik, and Graziani sang.

Wednesday 20 June. Rehearsed the *Étoile* with the chorus and act 2 with the singers. Called on Davison[56] and Grüneisen.[57]

Thursday 21 June. Rehearsed act 1 with the singers. Visits from Grüneisen and Viardot. Called on Beale, Berlioz,[58] Benedict, George Smart*. Bellini's *Norma*, Rossini's *Il Barbiere di Siviglia*.

Friday 22 June. Rehearsed act 2 with the singers. In the evening practice with Formes in my rooms.

Saturday 23 June. Prince Albert summoned me, and received me with great friendliness. Rehearsal of act 3 with the singers. In the Italian Opera: Verdi's *Il Trovatore*.

Sunday 24 June. The singer Mlle. Krall from Vienna sang for me. Called on Benedict, Dickens, Hogarth.[59] At the latter's I encountered Richard Wagner. We acknowledged each other coldly, without speaking.[60] Made a number of visits with Grüneisen.

Monday 25 June. Rehearsal with the chorus. Rehearsed acts 2 and 3 with the singers. Called on Madame Ney. Haymarket Theater: *Guy Mannering*, play with songs by Bishop.[61] The famous English tenor Sims Reeves*, who has a lovely voice, sang,[62] and Demoiselle Cushman, a famous actress, played the role of the Gypsy Meg Merrilies.[63] The music contains some attractive things, especially a Gypsy song for several voices.

Tuesday 26 June. Called on Madame Viardot. Went through the role of Prascovia with Demoiselle Maray. Held a rehearsal of the military music with Costa. Attended Ella's quartet matinée.[64] The public greeted me with applause on my entry. In the evening, in the small Surrey Theater, they performed Balfe's opera *The Bohemian Girl,* which is also known in Germany.[65] The singers had very good voices and to some extent passable delivery; the orchestra, however, was terrible. Then on to the Italian Opera in Covent Garden, for act 2 of Donizetti's *opera buffa, L'Elisir d'Amore.* There I made the acquaintance of Herr Glover*, who is known both as a composer and as a journalist.

Wednesday 27 June. Today it is a year since my precious, beloved mother died. May Almighty God grant the dear departed eternal blessedness. Amen: may it be so. Visit from the music publisher Beale. Rehearsal with the singers. Since Madame Bosio did not come, and Lablache had a rehearsal of *Don Pasquale,* the practice was entirely unsuccessful. Called on Berlioz.

Thursday 28 June. Rehearsal of the singers and chorus on stage. In the Opera: Donizetti's *Don Pasquale.*

Friday 29 June. Rehearsal with the singers. In the Opera: *Il Trovatore.*

Saturday 30 June. Rehearsal of all three acts with the singers. I felt very unwell during the rehearsal. Dined with the composer and writer Glover.[66]

July 1855

Sunday 1 July. Wrote nothing.

Monday 2 July. Rehearsal with the singers. Big dinner at Gye's.

Tuesday 3 July. Rehearsal with the singers. Today they performed *Les Huguenots* at Covent Garden. I did not attend, and busied myself with preparations for conducting. The Westminster Club has elected me an honorary member.

Wednesday 4 July. First *mise en scène* rehearsal of act 1 with the singers. Rehearsal with the flutes. Delivered the letters of the countess of Westmorland. Concert of the New Philharmonic Society: a new Scottish cantata by Glover,[67] very picturesque and interesting; Mendelssohn's Symphony no. 1 in C Minor,[68] not among his more outstanding compositions; Berlioz's *Childe Harold* Symphony.[69]

Thursday 5 July. The composer Benedict hosted a dinner in my honor, and a musical soirée in which only my compositions were sung; but apart from the

"Sonntagslied," sung by Mme. Novello, they elicited little reaction. At table I made the acquaintance of the charming author Dickens.

Friday 6 July. On account of Mr. Anderson's concert in the Theater, there was no rehearsal today. Worked on my annotations for conducting. Dinner and soirée that the writer and critic Chorley gave in my honor. I made the acquaintance there of many interesting personalities, like Lady Hastings.[70]

Saturday 7 July. Mise en scène rehearsal of act 2. Dined with the minister Lord John Russell*, for whom I had a letter from Humboldt.

Sunday 8 July. Busy all day long with annotations for conducting.

Monday 9 July. First orchestral rehearsal (of act 1). The orchestra received me with great applause. I thanked the orchestra in a little English speech. Dined with the Prussian ambassador, Count Bernstorff. *Droits d'auteur* for the month of June: 1,907 fr.

Tuesday 10 July. Annotations for conducting. *Mise en scène* rehearsal of act 3. Called on Princess Czartoryska and Lord Westmorland. Dinner that the old Beale gave in my honor.

Wednesday 11 July. Second orchestral rehearsal: act 2 and half of act 3. It lasted almost five hours, did not go very well, and did not seem to elicit any favorable reaction from the orchestra. To the Drury Lane Theatre, where they gave *Il Barbiere di Siviglia* for the benefit of the Spanish singer Mlle. Garsier.

Thursday 12 July. Mise en scène rehearsal. Busied myself with annotations for conducting.

Friday 13 July. Third orchestral rehearsal: tried the whole of act 3, the Chœur des Conjurés, and the act 2 finale. The orchestra, which had been very cold at the previous session, began to show its appreciation. Called on the composer Macfarren* and on Henry Smart. In the evening worked on the annotations for conducting.

Saturday 14 July. No rehearsal. Worked on my annotations for conducting. Davison, his brother, Vivier, and Brandus dined with me.

Sunday 15 July. Busied myself with notations for conducting. Visit from Dr. Schlesinger. Called on the marchioness of Hastings and Reagen, editor of the *Musical World.* In the evening concerned myself with annotations for conducting, and with abridgments.

Monday 16 July. Fourth orchestral rehearsal: act 1 and 2 with *mise en scène*, which went badly. Verdi and the two Escudier brothers arrived in London today. Busy with abridgments in the evening.

Tuesday 17 July. Fifth orchestral rehearsal: act 3, which also did not go well. Soirée at the marquis of Ely's.[71]

Wednesday 18 July. Last rehearsal, in which for the first time all three acts were played. It went well. Dined at Costa's, then in the evening visited Dr. Schlesinger.

Thursday 19 July. Called on Formes and Tedesco. Wrote down what I have to attend to this evening on stage, both musically and in respect of the *mise en scène*. First performance of *L'Étoile du Nord.*[72] The overture and the Duo des Vivandières were demanded *da capo*. After the Gypsy Roundelay, Madame Bosio was called out, also after act 1; Formes was called after act 2; everyone after act 3. I was likewise called twice after act 2 and again after act 3, and finally showered with flowers and garlands. On the whole the impression and reception were not warm. The only pieces that were fervently applauded were the overture, Bosio's Gypsy Roundelay, the duet for Catherine and Prascovia, the conclusion of act 1, Lablache's *Couplets de l'infanterie,* the *adagio* of the sextet, the act 2 finale, Gardoni's arioso in act 3, the *Buffo* Trio, and the Flute Piece. I allowed Costa to conduct.[73]

Friday 20 July. All the London papers are full of praise for the *Étoile*, Chorley least of all, but nonetheless not bad.[74] I hosted a so-called turtle-dinner, in which turtle in all shapes and sizes is the dominant motif. The guests were old Davison, Davison's two sons, Glover, Kenny (from the *Times*), and Brandus. To Costa.

Saturday 21 July. Second performance of the *Étoile* in Covent Garden. It was again very full: the reception was a little cooler than the first time; nevertheless, I was again called out after acts 2 and 3. Today nothing was requested *da capo*.

Sunday 22 July. Studied the role of Catherine with Jenny Bauer. Benedict gave a fish dinner in my honor.

Monday 23 July. With Davison to the Princess Theater, where for the last three months they have been performing Shakespeare's *Henry VIII*[75] to crowded houses: wonderful *mise en scène*, particularly Cardinal Wolsey's banquet and the mourning for Queen Catherine.

Tuesday 24 July. To Grüneisen, to Dr. Max Schlesinger, to Gye. The third performance of *L'Étoile du Nord*: very full, and the reception warmer than at the second performance. I was again called out after act 2.

Wednesday 25 July. To Davison (100 pounds sterling).[76] *Déjeuner* with Chorley. At the wish of the *Illustrated London News* I allowed myself to be photographed.[77]

Thursday 26 July. After I had completed the many preparations for departure (farewell visits, tickets, autographs, visiting cards etc.), I departed at 1:30 by train for Dover, where we arrived at four o'clock. At 5 we left by steamship for Calais, and arrived at 7. The weather was so mild, the sea so calm, that I experienced no seasickness. In Calais I went to the theater, where the singer, Demoiselle Borghese (a contralto), and a violinist gave a concert. I thought myself unrecognized, but that could not have been the case, since at midnight the theater orchestra serenaded me, playing the overture to *Emma di Resburgo.*[78]

Friday 27 July. At 8:45 left Calais by rail for Paris, where we arrived at five o'clock in the evening. I dined with my friend Gouin.

Saturday 28 July. Wrote to General Gedeonoff in St. Petersburg, director of the Italian Opera there, to recommend the engagement of Formes for the production of the *Étoile,* which is to take place soon. Since I am here entirely incognito, I received the calls of Dr. Bacher and the Brothers Brandus, who are the only ones who know of my presence. *Le Prophète* was apparently performed on 11 July in Venice to great enthusiasm.[79]

Sunday 29 July. Left at seven o'clock by train for Brussels, and arrived just after 3; then immediately by train for Spa, which we reached at 7:30 in the evening. Earlier this year railway lines were laid from Pepinstère to Spa, so that it is now no longer necessary to travel to Spa by carriage.

Monday 30 July. Visit from Hermann, brother of the famous violinist. Called on Davelouis and Jules Janin. The local wind band serenaded me.

Tuesday 31 July. [No entry.]

August 1855

Wednesday 1 August. Began working on the *Chercheur* again, in a very small way. In the theater: Auber's *Haydée.* Herr Barbot has a very pleasant tenor voice.[80]

Thursday 2 August. [No entry.]

Friday 3 August. At the wish of the Belgian artillery captain Deppe,[81] I listened to a quartet for piano and wind instruments by the late Martin-Joseph Mengal* from

Ghent: clear, flowing, lyrical in the manner of Hummel, but still rather too naive and fragmentary. In the evening worked a little on the *Chercheur*.

Saturday 4 August. Wrote out the text of the *Chercheur*, with the German additions. Spent a few moments at the fancy dress ball, *pour examiner la composition de la société*,[82] in case my daughter Blanca should want to come to this ball.

Sunday 5 August. Read Milanese and Neapolitan newspapers, which speak of the great success of *Le Prophète* in Venice, and also of the fervent polemic stirred up by it. In the theater: Auber's *La Part du Diable*.

Monday 6 August. I wrote a letter, ostensibly for Davison, but actually for publication in the *Musical World*, as a vindication of Costa, who has been attacked in the *Messager des théâtres* for hindering me from conducting the *Étoile* at the first London performance.[83] Today my beloved daughter Blanca arrived in Spa, with Antoinette Montalban, to keep me company.

Tuesday 7 August. Letter from Generalintendant von Hülsen. In the theater: Boieldieu's *La Dame blanche*.

Wednesday 8 August. In the evening to the ball with Blanca. None of the young men dancing presented themselves to my daughter, which rather upset us both.

Thursday 9 August to Friday 10 August. [No entries.]

Saturday 11 August. Captain Deppe and four musicians of the wind band played me two quintets by Reicha* for flute, oboe, clarinet, horn, and bassoon; I still find the one in B (op. 88) very lovely.[84]

Sunday 12 August. I have such dizziness that I am not able to work.

Monday 13 August. [No entry.]

Tuesday 14 August. Wrote a letter of thanks to the Singakademie in Berlin; they had congratulated me on the fiftieth anniversary (15 July [1805]) of my entrance into the Academy. Wrote to Herr von Hülsen.

Wednesday 15 August. *Droits d'auteur* for the month of July: 3,662 fr. 95 c.

Thursday 16 August. Concert by the excellent violinist Léonard, where my overture to *Romilda e Costanza* was played by the orchestra.[85]

Friday 17 August to Monday 20 August. [No entries.]

Tuesday 21 August. Wrote to Oliver Mason in Birmingham that I will not be able to come to the music festival.

Wednesday 22 August. [No entry.]

Thursday 23 August. In the evening, with the violinist Hermann,[86] played through the pieces by Pillet-Will that I have promised to orchestrate for him.[87] In Cassel *L'Étoile du Nord* has been performed with good success for the birthday of the elector.

Friday 24 August. [No entry.]

Saturday 25 August. Der Nordstern has been performed in Wiesbaden, with what success I do not know.

Sunday 26 August. Herr von Elssner took Blanca and me to a small soirée at the house of an English lady, Miss Cartwright, who had wanted to make my acquaintance. This lady writes poetry, composes music, and plays the piano very nicely.[88]

Monday 27 August. [No entry.]

Tuesday 28 August. Today at last, after long hesitation, wrote an answer to the theater agent Sachse in Hamburg about producing *L'Étoile du Nord* in the Hamburg Theater;[89] also wrote to Heinrich Schlesinger.

Wednesday 29 August. Wrote to Gemmy Brandus; to Roger, that unfortunately I cannot give him *L'Africaine.*

Thursday 30 August. [No entry.]

Friday 31 August. In the evening worked on the *canzonetta* that I am writing for the young princess of Capua, at the wish of her father (the brother of the king of Naples).[90]

September 1855

Saturday 1 September. I took the *canzonetta* to the prince of Capua.

Sunday 2 September. [No entry.]

Monday 3 September. At ten o'clock by train from Spa for Cologne, in order to accompany my daughter Blanca and Antoinette Montalban there. We arrived at three o'clock.

Tuesday 4 September. [No entry.]

Wednesday 5 September. My sixty-fourth birthday. May God preserve me so that in this year of my life I may compose a striking dramatic work, which could attain a brilliant success in performance and secure my name an honorable immortality. Resolutions: (1) to compose something everyday, whatever it may be; (2) to set aside one day in the week for answering the letters received; (3) always to be reading a classic book; (4) to concern myself with the theatrical and aesthetic aspects of music; (5) even if I do not compose, at least to improvise at the piano once a day.

At 8:45 I parted from my beloved daughter Blanca, who is returning with Antoinette to Minna in Kissingen. I went by train to Brussels, where I arrived at three o'clock. In the provisional Théâtre du Cirque, which is very big and attractive, Halévy's *La Juive*: Mlle. Vanderhaute (Rachel) mediocre, Depoitier (the Cardinal) the same, Nobanti (Eleazar) bad. The best of all was the *tenor léger* Anjac (Leopold).

Thursday 6 September. Early, at six o'clock, departed by express train from Brussels for Paris, where I arrived at five o'clock. My old friend Gouin was waiting for me on the station. I went to the Italian Theater, where Madame Ristori* is currently provoking so much interest, even eclipsing Rachel. They were performing Maffei's *Maria Stuarda*, a literal translation of Schiller's tragedy. Ristori enchanted me: noble, passionate, and yet measured, a splendid voice, plastic movements and posture—in sum, a great artist.[91] Today I did not keep to any of my resolutions.

Friday 7 September. The day passed in unpacking, in acquiring a pianoforte, and in other concerns. In the Théâtre Lyrique: Halévy's new opera *Jaguarita l'Indienne*.[92]

Saturday 8 September. Diarrhea, so stayed in bed.

Sunday 9 September. I also stayed in bed today, apart from a few hours.

Monday 10 September. General debility. I therefore could also not work today; only drafted a letter to Alexander von Humboldt, for his eighty-fifth birthday on 14 September, which Burguis will deliver to him, together with his favorite cake [*Braunkuchen*]. Le Roi from the Opéra came to see me.

Tuesday 11 September. On the whole I feel better. Visit from the Spanish singer Carion, who has been engaged by the Italian Opera.[93] In the Théâtre Lyrique: Halévy's *Jaguarita*. The music appealed to me more this time than on the first occasion: it has much that is beautiful and thematic, even if this is brought out mainly in the declamation of the verses.

Wednesday 12 September. I am feeling much better. Called on Perrin and Véron. My first fleeting visit to the Exhibition: a wonder of the world.[94] In the Opéra Comique: *L'Étoile du Nord* (142nd performance, receipts 6,173 fr.). Madame Ugalde sang Catherine. In the Tent Scene, she surpassed Madame Duprez in energy and vocal effect, but in everything else, and in intellectual grasp, Demoiselle Duprez takes the lead. *Droits d'auteur* for the month of August: 4,301 fr. 15 c.

Thursday 13 September. [No entry.]

Friday 14 September. Called on Auber. Visit from the music dealer Bock in Berlin. *Séance du Comité des auteurs et compositeurs dramatiques.*[95] Théâtre du Gymnase: *Le Demi-Monde* by Alexandre Dumas *(fils)*.[96]

Saturday 15 September. Visit from the director of the Grand Opéra, Crosnier. Called on Nestor Roqueplan. At the Opéra: Verdi's *Les Vêpres siciliennes*.[97]

Sunday 16 September. Visits from Perrin and Perrot, the owner of *L'Indépendance belge*, also from Berlioz, Julius [Beer], Halévy. In the evening wrote a little of the *Chercheur* (the German text).

Monday 17 September. Visit from Stephen Heller, who played me several very interesting piano compositions. Called on Roger and Madame Tedesco. *Le Prophète* (189th performance, receipts 10,752 fr. 93 c.). Alboni has lost much of her vocal flexibility and dramatic power, but, on the other hand, sings and acts with greater feeling and animation.

Tuesday 18 September. Opéra Comique: *Le Chien du jardinier* in one act by Grisar: a charming comedy for four characters, beautifully acted.[98] Conference with Scribe about *L'Africaine*.

Wednesday 19 September. Sniffling; so, on the advice of Dr. Ostenburg, stayed in bed all day.

Thursday 20 September. Stayed at home all day. Visit from the poet Carré.

Friday 21 September. Called on Fiorentino (see cash book). In the evening wrote out the German textual changes to the *Chercheur*.

Saturday 22 September. Visits from Jules Lecomte and Duponchel. In the evening wrote out the German changes to the *Chercheur*. Perrin came to see me.

Sunday 23 September. Called on Crosnier. In the evening wrote out the German changes to the *Chercheur*.

Monday 24 September. Dined at Véron's house, where the singer Madame Cabel was also present. Midday concert by the Kölner Gesangverein: choral songs for male voices, without accompaniment. The best pieces were Silcher's* "Die drei Röslein,"[99] Becker's* "Das Kirchlein," Reichardt's "Spanische Kanzonette,"[100] the dance chorus from J. Otto's* "Gesellenfahrten." The minister Fould invited me to his box during the concert to speak to me about *L'Africaine*.

Tuesday 25 September. The singer Scott from Rouen came to see me; he will perform the part of Danilowitz in Rouen, and I sang him the new arioso. Visit from Fiorentino, with Madame Pleyel and her daughter, so that I could hear the latter sing.

Wednesday 26 September. Called on the instrument-maker Gautrot in order to examine his new invention of a chromatic drum. Conferred with Duesberg, in Gemmy Brandus's presence, about the translation of the German words added to the *Chercheur*. Called on Rossini[101] and on Princess Wittgenstein. Made the acquaintance of the musical writer Professor Friedrich Christian Bischoff from Bonn. Concert by the Kölner Gesangverein: almost the same pieces as in the first concert.

Thursday 27 September. Conference with Carré about the *Chercheur*. Tried working on the *Chercheur* again, but without success. In the Grand Opéra: the first performance of *Santa Chiara* by the duke of Saxe-Coburg-Gotha.

Friday 28 September. Called on the duke of Saxe-Gotha. In the evening a severe bout of convulsive coughing. Later to the Théâtre des Variétés: *La Fille de l'avare*, vaudeville by Bayard and Duport.[102]

Saturday 29 September. Letter from Scribe. To Scribe. Visit from Count Pillet-Will. In the evening began writing out Carré's changes to the *Chercheur*.

Sunday 30 September. Théâtre des Variétés: Cormon's *Furnished Apartment*,[103] Blum's *Une Femme qui mord*,[104] Cormon's *Le Théâtre des Zouaves*.[105]

October 1855

Monday 1 October. Conference with Scribe about *L'Africaine*. Called on Chorley and on Rossini. Théâtre Lyrique: Halévy's *Jaguarita*.

Tuesday 2 October. Opéra Comique: Grisar's *L'Eau merveilleuse*[106] and the cantata *Victoria* by Adam.

Wednesday 3 October. Conference with Carré and Barbier about the *Chercheur*. In the evening wrote out the translation of the German verses of the *Chercheur*.

Thursday 4 October. Italian Opera: Rossini's *Mosè* (the new one).[107] The tenor Carion was very good, the bass Angelini and the baritone Evrardi very good, but not outstanding.[108]

Friday 5 October. Letter from the Spanish theater director Olonna about the role of foreign composers in Spain. *Séance des Comité des auteurs et compositeurs dramatiques*. In the morning and evening I composed a ballad, "La Lavandière," text by Carré, which was requested of me by Louis Desnoyer for *Le Messager des dames et desmoiselles*.[109] I began and finished the composition today, although I have not written it out yet.

Saturday 6 October. Wrote out nearly all of the ballad "La Lavandière." Visit from Dautresme. In the evening attended a concert of the Kölner Männergesangverein for the third time. The prominent pieces today were: "Türkisches Schenkenlied" and "Wanderlied," both by Mendelssohn;[110] Weber's "Schlummerlied";[111] and Kücken's "Im Walde."[112]

Sunday 7 October. Wrote out a clean copy of my new ballad "La Lavandière," and took it to Louis Desnoyer, who will publish it in *Le Messager des desmoiselles*.

Monday 8 October. Wrote out some of the German changes to the *Chercheur*. In the Grand Opéra: Verdi's *Les Vêpres siciliennes*. Visit from Scribe, who declared himself prepared to allow me more time to prepare my grand opera [*L'Africaine*], on condition that I do not first give the comic opera [*Le Chercheur des trésors*].

Tuesday 9 October. I feel myself catching cold again.

Wednesday 10 October. Wrote out the variants and translation of the German verses for the *Chercheur*. Conference with Scribe, who has come out against the idea that I should produce an *opéra comique* before completing either of the two *grand opéra* libretti I have from him. I pacified him, and he stopped protesting. I promised, in my turn, to first produce *Judith* rather than *L'Africaine* at the Grand Opéra. Corrected the proofs of my new ballad "La Lavandière." Opéra Comique: Montfort's *Deucalion et Pyrrha*, a mediocre work.[113]

Thursday 11 October. Conferred with Brandus about the receipt that Duesberg should receive for his translation of the German verses for the *Chercheur* (I paid him 300 fr. for this). Called on Madame Tedesco. Tested the *timbales chromatiques*[114] at the instrument-maker Gautrot's. Wrote out the translation of the German verses for the *Chercheur*. To the new theater Bouffes Parisiens, opened by the violoncellist Offenbach,[115] where they played one-act *comédies à ariettes* for only two or three characters: Offenbach's *Les Deux Aveugles*,[116] *Madame Papillon*,[117] *Le Violoneux*.[118]

Friday 12 October. Conference with the director of the Opéra, Crosnier. Conference with Duesberg, in the presence of Gemmy Brandus. Grand Opéra: *Les Vêpres siciliennes*.

Saturday 13 October. Conference with Carré and Barbier about the *Chercheur*. Audience with the minister Fould, as part of the Comité des Auteurs et Compositeurs Dramatiques, about the relation of the censor to the artist. In the Opéra Italien: Rossini's *La Cenerentola*. The *buffo* Zucchini and the baritone Evrardi were very good; Madame Borghi-Mamo* (Cenerentola) was also very good, but sometimes the voice was not even enough.

Sunday 14 October. Renewed resolutions: I want to compose every day, and if I cannot, then at least to improvise; to attend to my correspondence regularly; to read interesting books regularly. *L'Étoile du Nord* has been performed in Leipzig, but without any special success. Wrote out the translation of the German verses for the *Chercheur*. Visits from Perrin, from Bergson, from Galeotti, *agent des théâtres*, who wants the score of the *Étoile* for Lisbon and St. Petersburg. To the Opéra Comique: took Madame Ugalde through the abridgments that I have made in the role of Catherine, because of her indisposition. Studied the role of Fidès with the singer Mlle. Elmire, who will make her début in the Opéra in this part.[119] In the evening improvised on the *berceuse*[120] for two hours.

Monday 15 October. Composed some of the *berceuse*. In the Theater heard *Les Vêpres siciliennes* from Crosnier's box. Called on Demoiselle Cruvelli.

Tuesday 16 October. Finished composing the *berceuse*.

Wednesday 17 October. Began writing out the *berceuse*. Conference with Michel

Carré and Jules Barbier about the *Chercheur*. Opéra Comique: the first performance of Adam's *Le Houzard de Berchini*,[121] a moderate success; Montfort's
Deucalion et Pyrrha.

Thursday 18 October. Attended the funeral of the composer Batton* whom I knew
for thirty years, since the Italian days.[122] In the evening wrote out a little of the
berceuse. Letter from Ferdinand Hiller in Cologne.

Friday 19 October. Three unpleasant pieces of news so depressed me that I could
no longer work. In an article on Heine by Berlioz, I believe I have found malicious allusions to myself.[123] Then Gemmy Brandus told me that a new book on
opera by Castil-Blaze contains some nasty attacks on me.[124] Finally Madame
Viardot mentioned to me that Madame Bosio does not want to sing *L'Étoile du
Nord* this season in St. Petersburg. *Droits d'auteur* for the month of September:
5,116 fr.

Saturday 20 October. Called on Buloz, Scudo, Édouard Bertin, Jules Lecomte
(600 fr.), Count Pillet-Will. Personal indisposition, and unhappiness over Heine
and Berlioz's attacks, made it impossible for me to work.[125] In the evening at the
Opéra Comique attended act 2 of *L'Étoile du Nord*, in order to hear Faure singing
the role of Peter; he has a wonderfully beautiful voice, sings very well, but drags
out[126] the *tempi* and is not much of an actor. In short, I prefer Bataille.

Sunday 21 October. Called on Carré, and on Berlioz. Wrote to Cornet. Visit from
the sister of Demoiselle Cruvelli, who wants to make her début as Fidès at the
Opéra and sang the role to me. Visits from my nephew Julius and Édouard
Monnais.

Monday 22 October. Opéra: *Les Vêpres siciliennes*. Letter from the Comité de
l'Association des Musiciens Français, who have nominated me *président
honoraire*.[127]

Tuesday 23 October. Preparations for my journey. Wrote to the Comité des Auteurs
et Compositeurs Dramatiques, asking for leave of three months. Wrote to Corghi,
poet de l'Opéra Italien, returning his opera libretto, *Il Barbiere di Gheldria;*[128] to
Najac also, returning his libretto.[129]

Wednesday 24 October. Spent all day on preparations for my departure to Vienna,
where I am going to direct the rehearsals of the *Étoile* in the Kärntnertor-Theater.
Opéra Comique: Massé's *Miss Fauvette*.[130]

Thursday 25 October. Departed at nine o'clock by rail for Cologne, using the new route via St. Quentin, Charleroi, Namur, and Liège, whereby Brussels is bypassed, and which takes about twelve hours. We arrived in Cologne at ten o'clock in the evening.

Friday 26 October. Left at 6:30 by train for Leipzig, where we arrived at 9:15 at night.

Sunday 27 October. Left early at six o'clock for Dresden, where we arrived at 9. I wanted to stay until 12:15, when the train leaves for Prague, in order to visit my beloved wife and children, who are living here until the cholera has died down in Berlin. I found my dearest daughter Caecilie in such an emaciated condition that I hardly recognized her, something that has filled me with anxiety. May Almighty God prove these fears groundless. Through a misunderstanding on the part of the coachman, I arrived at the departure time, but on the wrong platform, and therefore could leave only in the evening, at 9:30. We arrived at Bodenbach at 11:30 later that night.

Sunday 28 October. We reached Prague early in the morning, at 4:45. The same train leaves at 6 for Vienna, where we arrived at 7:30 in the evening. Dr. Bacher was waiting to meet me at the station, as usual. This time I am lodging at the Erzherzog Karl,[131] in the Kärntnerstrasse, on the first floor: three lovely rooms for five gulden daily.

Monday 29 October. Visit from the director of the Court Opera, Cornet, who informed me that the baritone Beck,[132] who was to have sung the role of Peter in the *Nordstern*, has become seriously ill, and that the opera must therefore be postponed. The theater directorate had telegraphed me this news on Thursday in Paris, because this development makes my trip to Vienna pointless. Since I left Paris on Thursday, I did not, alas, receive this cable. Called on the *Oberstkammerherr*, Count Lanckoronski, and on Hofrat Raymond. Visit from my old friend Castelli and from Kapellmeister Eckert. In the Kärntnertor-Theater: Auber's *Die Stumme von Portici*. The tarantella in act 3 was wonderfully staged, much more effectively than in Paris.

Tuesday 30 October. Letter from the wife of the journalist L. A. Zellner, who asks for a loan of 2,000 gulden.

Wednesday 31 October. Kärntnertor-Theater: Auber's *Fra Diavolo*.

November 1855

Thursday 1 November. Wrote to Madame Zellner: agreed to a loan of 600 gulden.

Called on Count Lanckoronski, Kapellmeister Eckert, and a young singer, Mlle. Brandt, who has a lovely voice and talent, and on Saphir. In the Kärntnertor-Theater: the ballet *Die verwandelten Weiber (Le Diable à quatre),* music by Adam.

Friday 2 November. Called on Castelli and on Zellner. In the evening to the Kärntnertor-Theater for Flotow's *Martha.*

Saturday 3 November. Visit from Zellner. He offered to dedicate his magazine to the defense of my music. Kärntnertor-Theater: *Der Prophet,* in parts a really good performance; Herr Ander (the Prophet) very good; Madame Hermann-Csillagh (Fidès), who has a very beautiful voice of more than two octaves, sings with fire and understanding, also acts convincingly.[133]

Sunday 4 November. In the evening I stayed at home, and composed almost the whole of Castelli's ballad "Nein," since he asked me to set it to music.

Monday 5 November. In the morning and evening finished writing out all the stanzas of the ballad "Nein." Auditioned four different ladies for the roles of the Vivandières. Kärntnertor-Theater: Auber's *Der Maurer* [*Le Maçon*].

Tuesday 6 November. Letter from Hofrat Dingelstedt, theater intendant in Munich. Big rehearsal, with the whole chorus, of act 1. Rehearsed with Demoiselle Liebhardt, who is singing the role of Prascovia.[134] To Castelli, to play him the ballad I have set to music. In the Kärntnertor-Theater: Flotow's *Stradella.* After the theater worked on the abridgments and cuts in the recitatives of *L'Étoile du Nord.*

Wednesday 7 November. Studied their roles with Wildauer and Ander. Burgtheater: Shakespeare's *Coriolanus,*[135] in Gutzkow's adaptation.[136]

Thursday 8 November. Went through Wildauer's role with her. Called on Count Moritz Dietrichstein. Completed the abridgment of the recitatives in act 1, and handed them over to Kapellmeister Proch for translation. Visit from the *Waldhorn* player Levy, and from Kapellmeister Eckert. Wrote a long letter to Gouin. Kärntnertor-Theater: Nicolai's *Die lustigen Weiber von Windsor.*

Friday 9 November. Played act 2 to the chorus master, Weinkopf. Kärntnertor-Theater: Grisar's *Guten Abend, Herr Pantalon.*

Saturday 10 November. First piano rehearsal of *L'Étoile du Nord.* In the evening to an open session of the Männergesangverein.

Sunday 11 November. Second piano rehearsal. Called on the singer Csillagh. In the evening wrote out the recitatives for acts 2 and 3, and prepared them for the translator.

Monday 12 November. Wrote, ostensibly to Gouin, about the singer Csillagh, but actually for Crosnier. Third piano rehearsal. Visits from Professor Finkhof and from Tichy. Kärntnertor-Theater: Balfe's *Die Zigeunerin.*

Tuesday 13 November. Fourth piano rehearsal. In the evening went through the role of Catherine with Demoiselle Wildauer. Called on Castelli.

Wednesday 14 November. Fifth piano rehearsal, but without Beck and Ander. Rehearsed the military music. Kärntnertor-Theater: Donizetti's *Dom Sebastian.*

Thursday 15 November. Because of St. Leopold's Day (the patron of Austria),[137] no rehearsal could take place today. I have a bad cold, so stayed in bed all day.

Friday 16 November. Sixth piano rehearsal. Leopoldstädter Theater: *Die Schicksale der Familie Maxenpfutsch,* parody by Nestroy; bad.[138]

Saturday 17 November. Seventh piano rehearsal. Tried the recitatives of act 1 for the first time. Kärntnertor-Theater: Donizetti's *Lucia di Lammermoor.* A débutante, Fräulein Brenner, sang a mediocre Lucia, and Herr Steger a similarly mediocre Edgardo.[139] After the theater checked the full score of the recitatives for the copyist.

Sunday 18 November. Eighth piano rehearsal. Checked the German translation of the recitatives of act 2 with Kapellmeister Proch. Kärntnertor-Theater: Weber's *Der Freischütz.* Demoiselle Kesch, a young singer from Hamburg, sang Agathe as her début. After the theater, checked the recitatives for the copyist.

Monday 19 November. Because of the orchestral rehearsals of *Joconde,* there were no rehearsals of *L'Étoile du Nord* today. Kärntnertor-Theater: Nicolò Isouard's *Joconde.* After the theater, I worked for one hour on the *Chercheur* (duet Corentin-Hoël) for the first time in a long while.[140]

Tuesday 20 November. Ninth piano rehearsal. In the evening, at Cornet's wish, held a rehearsal with the singer, Mlle. Kesch, who is to make her début in *Les Huguenots.*

Wednesday 21 November. Tenth piano rehearsal. Since I have a cold, I stayed at home in the evening, and prepared the recitatives for the copyist. *Droits d'auteur* for October: 3,731 fr. 31 c.

Thursday 22 November. Eleventh piano rehearsal. Began the recitatives of act 2. Theater an der Wien: Baron Klesheim's *Geschichten und Märchen* in *tableaux vivants*,[141] and other presentations by children. This spectacle, which is very popular in Vienna, bored me totally.

Friday 23 November. Rehearsal with the chorus, then twelfth piano rehearsal. In the evening composed the big recitative in act 3 which is to replace the *Buffo* Trio [in *L'Étoile du Nord*],[142] but did not write it out.

Saturday 24 November. Thirteenth piano rehearsal. In the evening wrote out the new recitative in act 3. Called on Schlesinger.

Sunday 25 November. No rehearsal. Called on the Hanoverian ambassador Herr von Stockhausen, Vesque von Püttlingen, and Hanslick.

Monday 26 November. Fourteenth piano rehearsal: tried only the recitatives in all three acts. In the evening to the Kärntnertor-Theater: Halévy's *Die Jüdin*. The soirée last night, at Count Edmund Tichy's, has encouraged me to hear the music of the Hungarian Gypsies. Count and Countess Nako came from Schönau to Vienna expressly to let me hear the Gypsy band in their employ. It is made up of violins, cellos, a small clarinet, and dulcimer (this last is played with astonishing virtuosity).[143] These Gypsy airs, part plaintive *adagios*, part bacchanalian dance rhythms, are of unbelievable originality, boldness, expressiveness, and *entrainement;*[144] they resemble no other European music.[145]

Tuesday 27 November. Fifteenth piano rehearsal. In the evening composed more of the *Chercheur*.

Wednesday 28 November. Sixteenth piano rehearsal. First Viennese performance of the ballet *Ballanda*, music by Hertel.

Thursday 29 November. First *mise en scène* rehearsal, but only in the rehearsal room. In the evening wrote the newly composed recitative for act 3 into the full score.

Friday 30 November. Visits from Georg Hellmesberger and Haslinger. Chorus and singers were united for the first time. The rehearsal did not go well. In the evening scored the new recitative.

December 1855

Saturday 1 December. First correction rehearsal with the orchestra, without singing. The copies were so unbelievably full of errors that in three hours we could rehearse only up to the Women's Duet. It was a very bad rehearsal. Then tried the theater music with the *banda*, which went very well. Burgtheater: *Das letzte Abenteuer*, comedy by Bauernfeld,[146] was outstandingly acted, especially by Demoiselle Neumann* and Herr A. Fichtner*.

Sunday 2 December. No rehearsal. Concert by the Musikverein: Mendelssohn's overture *Melusine*,[147] and his finale to the *Loreley*; Mozart's Piano Concerto in D Minor,[148] and his Symphony in C Major with the fugue.[149]

Monday 3 December. From 9 until 1, a second correction rehearsal, without singing. We completed the Women's Duet, the act 1 finale, and the whole of act 2. There were fewer errors than in the copy of act 1, since these had been checked, but still far too many. The orchestra was obedient, but bad-tempered.

Tuesday 4 December. Third correction rehearsal, with the orchestra, of act 3, which had been copied much better. The orchestra was impatient because of the cold, and the rehearsal short and irritable. Evening soirée at the poet Tauber's; he arranged this in my honor, and had gathered the principal spokesmen of the press in order to solicit my help.[150] The press is angry with the director of theaters, Count Lanckoronski, because, most insensitively, he has withdrawn their free entry passes. I promised the gentlemen to ask the *Oberstkämmerer* to rescind this regulation. They sang a song by me, declaimed several poems addressed to me, drank my health, etc.

Wednesday 5 December. Today should have been the correction rehearsal of the recitatives, but the copies were not ready, and the orchestra had to return home without having accomplished anything. Again a day lost. Today, six-sixty years ago, the greatest musician of all time, the divine Mozart, died. To consecrate the day, they performed *Don Juan* —but not at all well.

Thursday 6 December. Fourth correction rehearsal, in which we tried the recitatives of all three acts and Danilowitz's arioso, all without singing. In the evening worked on the preparations for conducting.

Friday 7 December. *Mise en scène* rehearsal of act 2. In the Theater: the ballet *Satanella*, music by Pugni and Hertel.

Saturday 8 December. Asked Cornet for forty reserved economy seats, which he granted. Tried the bells in the Burgtheater. Prepared the printed recitatives for conducting. In the Burgtheater: Goethe's *Götz von Berlichingen* (with Demoiselle Seebach).[151]

Sunday 9 December. Called on Bauernfeld and Zang (owner of *Die Presse*). I confided to the latter that (in accordance with the undertaking I had made to him, to Heine, and to Landsheimer at Tauber's soirée) I had explained to Raymond that I would not be able to conduct my opera if the withdrawal of the free tickets to the whole press corps (instructed by Oberstkämmerer von Lanckoronski) was not rescinded. In the Kärntnertor-Theater: *Les Huguenots.* Arranged the collected recitatives of *L'Étoile du Nord*, as they are to be performed in productions here, and appended the conducting indications.

Monday 10 December. Orchestral rehearsal with the singers of act 1.

Tuesday 11 December. Mise en scène rehearsal of act 2.

From Wednesday 12 December to Tuesday 18 December. I was taken ill with influenza and feverish symptoms, complicated by two attacks of stomach cramps. I had to stay in bed for six days.

Wednesday 19 December. Droits d'auteur for the month of November: 2,369 fr. 65 c. I returned to the rehearsals again. It was an orchestral rehearsal of acts 1 and 3. Because the whole opera could not be completed in this rehearsal, and it is still necessary to rehearse all three acts twice, the projected production for the day after tomorrow (21 December) is now impossible. Added to this is that, from the twenty-second onwards, the theaters are all closed for Advent, so that the production must be postponed until after Christmas.

Thursday 20 December. Orchestral rehearsal with scenery of acts 1 and 2.

Friday 21 December. Orchestral rehearsal with scenery of acts 1 and 2, and the act 3 finale. Visit from Bauernfeld.

Saturday 22 December. Big rehearsal of all three acts, but again unproductive, because Beck was ill and his pieces were played only by the orchestra. Visit from the writer Dr. Weidmann.[152]

Sunday 23 December. Severe attack of coughing. Unwell all day.

Monday 24 December. Called on Saphir. Louis Brandus from Paris came to see me.

Tuesday 25 December. Suffered gastric and head pains and dizziness.

Wednesday 26 December. Coughed severely in the night.

Thursday 27 December. Since the four Advent and Christmas holidays are now over, there was an orchestral rehearsal at which the *Oberstkämmerer* was present.

Friday 28 December. Last dress rehearsal. Called on Seifried, editor of *Der Wandrer* (forty gulden). Letter from Gouin, containing a scandalously defamatory article in *Le Figaro*, which maintains that I hindered Massé from using a chorus in the overture to his opera *Les Saisons* because I intend to use a similar effect in my own new comic opera. Visit from Vesque von Püttlingen.

Saturday 29 December. First production of *L'Étoile du Nord*. It was much applauded. I was called out in act 1 after the chorus "Finnland soll leben," after the Women's Duet, and three times at the end of act 1. After both act 2 and act 3, I was called out three times. The singers were also called out often. Nevertheless, it appears to me that the work was not really crowded. The orchestra and chorus were outstanding, the singers sufficient without being exceptional.

Sunday 30 December. Communication from the *Oberstkämmerer*, Count Lanckoronski, in which, on behalf of the emperor, he sends me a *tabatier*[153] set in precious stones. This hurt me deeply because after *Le Prophète* the emperor had awarded me the Franz Joseph Order. I therefore went to Raymond to see whether he could influence the matter in another direction. On this occasion, I thought of leaving his wife a keepsake, and passed on to him a gift of money for this purpose. He accepted it, but sent it back to me an hour later, together with a letter. Today's second performance of *L'Étoile du Nord* saw a much warmer response on the part of the public and the artists. I was called out even more often than yesterday. The emperor, the empress, and the whole court were again present.

Monday 31 December. Called on Raymond, Saphir. The critiques of *L'Étoile du Nord* in the *Wandrer*, *Wiener Zeitung*, *Fremdenblatt*, and *Morgenpost* were very favorable. In the evening to the Burgtheater. May God bless the close of the old year. Amen.[154]

NOTES

1. Theresa Janda (Jander) became Heinrich Marschner's fourth wife on 10 June 1855. Her second husband was Otto Bach. Meyerbeer's comments on her "curious" appearance are borne out by others. "She had 'an imposing stature, black glittering hair, and a face that no one forgot once he had seen it.' . . . Though she was only 28 and he 59, she fell in love with him [Marschner] and gave up an offer of marriage from a duke to become his wife. . . . Theresa was the daughter of J. C. Jander in Vienna and had been born on 30 September 1826." See Dean Allen Palmer, "Heinrich August Marschener (1795–1861) and his Stage Works" (diss., University of California at Los Angeles, 1978), pp. 279–80, quot-

ing from Georg Münzer, *Heinrich Marschner*, Berühmte Musiker 12 (Berlin: Harmonie, 1901), p. 77.

2. This occasion marked a deterioration in relations between Meyerbeer and Marschner, who was conductor at the Hoftheater. Marschner was told of the Meyerbeer's dissatisfaction with the musical direction of his opera (see 18 December 1861).

3. A cyclorama is a circular panorama, a curved wall or cloth, usually at the rear of a stage, especially used to represent the sky.

4. Apart from Anglo-French activities in the Baltic, secondary operations in the Crimean War also took place in the Sea of Azov and the Caucasus in order to cut off the Russian supply routes to Sebastopol.

5. At this stage of the Crimean War, the year-long siege of Sebastopol (September 1854–September 1855) was at its halfway mark, after the bloody engagements at Alma, Balaklava, and Inkerman. On 26 January 1855 Piedmont-Sardinia entered the war on the side of the Allies, with 10,000 troops. This conflict was a record of futility and mismanagement; a disproportionate number of the 250,000 men who died were lost to disease. The political implications of the war, however, were momentous: Russia began a process of modernization, and Austria, having lost Russian support in central European affairs, became dependent on Britain and France. Their failure to support the Habsburg State resulted in the Austrian defeats of 1859 and 1866, which, in their turn, were to lead directly to the unifications of both Italy and Germany, and the establishment of the Dual Monarchy of Austria-Hungary.

6. Julius Schulhoff, a Prague-born pianist, made his debut in Dresden in 1843. See 8 April 1854.

7. Given Meyerbeer's admiration of Tichatschek, which had led him to write two special numbers for the latter, the singer's ambiguous attitude to the composer, and his later dismissive reports to Richard Wagner, make for unedifying reading: "For sixteen days now we have been busy with rehearsals for *Nordstern* for five to six hours a day—first performance on the 9th. You know my profession of faith—dealers in fancy goods must do business too" (Letter of 5 February 1855, to Wagner in Switzerland, *Letters of Richard Wagner: The Burrell Collection*, ed. John Burk [New York: Macmillan, 1951], p. 153).

8. Gutzkow, *Uriel Acosta, Trauerspiel* in five acts (first produced in Dresden, December 1846 and a year later in Berlin) [Richel 56]. The subject matter echoes Lessing's *Nathan der Weise*, dealing with a freethinking individual beset by the intolerance and bigotry of orthodox religion, in this case Judaism. He is eventually driven to suicide.

9. Cherubini, "Inclina Domine," introit for four voices and orchestra (no date) from *Three Pieces for the Royal Chapel* (1823).

10. Tichatschek had lessons in Vienna with Ciccimarra while studying medicine. He joined the chorus of the Kärntnertor-Theater in 1830, and made his solo début there in 1835, singing Raimbaud in *Robert le Diable*.

11. Wilhelm Fischer (b. 1790) was the stage manager and chorus master of the Court Opera in Dresden. He began his career as a bass singer and chorus master in Leipzig; his connection with Dresden dated from 1831.

12. Gutzkow, *Lenz und Söhne*, comedy in five acts (produced and published in 1856) [Richel 56].

13. Meyerbeer seems to have forgotten the performance of *Othello* with Kean he saw in London on 11 December 1815.

14. This was the celebrated virtuoso Polish actor Bogumil Dawison (1818–72), whose career was spent mainly in the German theater as a member of the Burgtheater (1849–52)

and of the Dresden Court Theater (1852–64). He was noted for his unpolished, even aggressive, interpretations of Shakespearian and other roles. In this he was a bitter rival of Emil Devrient, and his acting regarded as the antithesis of the "Weimar style" embodied by the former. He performed all over Europe, and was one of the first German actors to tour America.

15. The actress Marie Katharina Bayer-Bürck (1820–1910) was first engaged in Dresden in 1840, where she worked for fifty years at the Hoftheater, winning especial renown in roles by Shakespeare, Goethe, Schiller, and Grillparzer.

16. Lessing, *Emilia Galotti*, first produced in 1772, was important for its establishment of the middle-class tragedy as a distinct genre, and for its anticipation of the social criticism of the *Sturm und Drang*.

17. Shakespeare's *Richard III* was first produced in London in 1592[?], and published in a quarto in 1597 and in the First Folio (1623). The play completes the historical tetralogy describing the struggle for power between the houses of Lancaster and York. The first three parts are made up of the *Henry VI* plays.

18. Fanna was a brother of the Venetian pianist and composer Antonio Fanna (1792–1846) who undertook several concert tours.

19. Gaetano Rossi died on 25 January 1855.

20. Perhaps this is the song "An den Neugeborenen" (1846)?

21. The Empress Elisabeth gave birth to her first child, the Archduchess Sophie, on 5 March 1855.

22. *Die Wiener in Paris, oder Der 12. Februar*, drama in two acts by Holtei (published 1839, first performed in Berlin 1855) [Richel 70].

23. *Dinorah*, no. 1 *Chœur villageois* ("Le jour radieux").

24. See 11 December 1815.

25. Klein, *Dido*, opera in three acts (Rellstab; Berlin, 15 October 1823). This was the only staged opera of the conductor; it had been earlier performed in concert at Hofrat Parthey's on 9 April 1821.

26. There are no biographical details available for Menegali (mid eighteenth to early nineteenth century). His *Ave regina coelorum* for male voices was published in volume 59 of the *Institut für Kirchenmusik in Breslau und Berliner Singakademie* (Robert Eitner, *Biographisch-Bibliographisches Quellen-Lexikon der Musiker und Musikgelehrten der Christlichen Zeitrechnung bis zur Mitte des 19. Jahrhunderts*, 10 vols. (Leipzig: Breitkopf & Härtel, 1899–1904), 6:435).

27. Niccolò Jommeli, *Lux aeterna*, motet for four voices.

28. Gläser, *Des Adlers Horst* (K. von Holtei, after a story by Johanna Schopenhauer; Berlin, Königstädter-Theater, 29 December 1832). This opera was once in all German repertories, and was known to Wagner. It contains several features now thought prefigurative of the latter, like an apostrophe to the sun and the use of insistently repeated short figures to create dramatic tension (see John Warrack and Ewan West, *The Oxford Dictionary of Opera* [Oxford and New York: Oxford University Press, 1992], p. 282). According to Loewenberg (col. 747), the text was originally written for Meyerbeer.

29. In all Prince de la Moskowa's Société de la Musique Vocale, Religieuse, et Classique (founded in 1843) published eleven volumes of works from the sixteenth and seventeenth centuries under the title *Recueil des morceaux de musique ancienne*.

30. *L'Étoile du Nord* was performed in Amsterdam on 20 February 1855 in Ludwig Rellstab's translation.

31. *Dinorah*, no. 5 *Couplets de Corentin*.

32. Wieprecht had already achieved fame as a trombonist in Dresden and Leipzig before moving to Berlin in 1824, where he became director-general of all the Prussian military bands. But he was also famous as an inventor, and produced the bass tuba (1835, with Moritz), the bathyphon, a sort of bass clarinet (1839, with Skorra), the *piangendo* for use on bass instruments with pistons, and the improved contrabass bassoon (1855).

33. *Dinorah*, no. 2bis *Air de la Cornemeuse*.

34. Mendelssohn, Overture *Meeresstille und glückliche Fahrt*, op. 27 (1828).

35. *Dinorah*, no. 2 *Récitatif et Berceuse de Dinorah* ("Bella! ma chèvre chérie!"). Margaridd was the Breton name originally chosen for the heroine.

36. After helping Gemmy Brandus back to solvency, Sélim-François Dufour had become his business partner. From September 1854 the publishing house was known as "G. Brandus & Cie" or "G. Brandus & S. Dufour" until the death of Louis Brandus in 1887.

37. See 17 January 1842.

38. Ernst Lampert, *Hofkapellmeister* of the ducal orchestra in Gotha, had arranged and orchestrated Duke Ernst II's opera *Casilda* in 1851.

39. *Genoveva*, opera in four acts by Schumann (Robert Reinick, altered by the composer, after Tieck's tragedy *Das Leben und Tod der heiligen Genoveva* [1799] and Hebbel's tragedy *Genoveva* [1843]; Leipzig, 25 June 1850). The composer's only opera was never successful, but was nonetheless produced on many German stages throughout the late nineteenth century, and revived at intervals up to the present. It was also given in London (1893), Paris (1894), and St. Petersburg (1896).

40. Princess Jeanne Elisabeth Carolyne of Sayn-Wittgenstein (1819–87), the daughter of a great Polish landowner, Peter von Iwanovski, and the wife of Prince Nicholas of Sayn-Wittgenstein (a millionaire and adjutant to the tsar) from whom she was separated on grounds of incompatibility. Her decision to leave her husband (1847) and take up residence with Liszt in Weimar (1848–59), brought about momentous changes in the latter's artistic life, and confirmed his resolution to abandon the career of a virtuoso, and devote himself to composition in the larger forms. See Sacheverell Sitwell, *Liszt* (1955; reprint, New York: Dover, 1967), pp. 143–48.

41. Charlotte Birch-Pfeiffer, in working on *Dinorah* and *L'Africaine*, was to take over the role Émile Deschamps had fulfilled for Meyerbeer in altering Scribe's libretti of *Les Huguenots* and *Le Prophète* to the composer's satisfaction.

42. *Jephtha* was performed on 23 and 29 December 1812.

43. Fr. "at a tilted angle."

44. The recitatives for *L'Étoile du Nord* were published in those versions of the Brandus score *contenant les récitatifs et les morceaux ajoutés par l'Auteur* (containing the recitatives and the pieces added by the author), and also in the Novello and Ricordi scores.

45. See the feuilleton of the *Journal des débats* (17 April 1855) where Berlioz's contemptuously satirical attitude to aspects of Meyerbeer's dramaturgy is unmistakable: "tandis que les noirs anabaptistes du *Prophète*, reparaissant toujours quand on se croit délivrer d'eux, exaspèrent l'auditeur et finiraient, si l'ouvrage avait un sixième acte, par donner des attaques de nerfs aux hommes les plus robustes" [whereas the dark Anabaptists, always popping up when one hopes to have seen the last of them, exasperate the listener to such an extent that if the work had six acts, even the strongest of men might be driven to an attack of nerves].

46. Gustav Berlyn (1822–90), a merchant and poet.

47. Tgb. *Mustervorstellung*.

48. Burguis was to translate the new words by Charlotte Birch-Pfeiffer.

49. *Le Prophète* was first performed at La Scala on 23 May 1855 (as *Il Profeta* in the Italian translation revised by L. Fortis) with Dell'Armi (Giovanni di Leida), Giulia Sanchioli (Fede), and Fanny Gordosa (Berta).

50. Mosenthal, *Der Goldschmied von Ulm, Volksstück* in three acts (first performance in Berlin, 1855; in Dresden, 1 January 1856). This antedates Richel [107], who has the first Berlin performance in 1856. Marschner wrote incidental music for the Dresden performance.

51. The première of *L'Esule di Granata* (*melodramma serio*) was in Milan's La Scala on 12 March 1822. Carlo Sieber created the small role of Ali.

52. Haydn, *Die Jahreszeiten,* secular oratorio, HobXXI/3 (words by Gottfried van Swieten, after James Thomson's *The Seasons* [1726–30]; Vienna, 24 April 1801).

53. *Clavigo,* drama written in 1774 and first performed in Goethe's presence in Mannheim (1779), is a domestic tragedy in the vein of Lessing's *Emilia Galotti.*

54. Eduard Gottwald (1808–71), writer and archivist, was a minor playwright remembered for his four-act comedy *Die Universalerben* (first performed in Dresden, 1848) [Richel 52].

55. See 10 January 1856 for the details of this opera.

56. James William Davison, whom Meyerbeer had met in Paris in 1849, was musical critic of the *Times* and editor of the *Musical World.* He was regarded as the doyen of the London critical establishment. "The range of his musical or general intelligence was on the whole no wider than that of Chorley, though he wrote with a blustering cocksure belief in himself and knockabout comedian's gusto in his journalism that attracted to him a larger public than Chorley's. He was undoubtedly on terms of greater intimacy with numbers of composers and performers than it was wise for any critic to be . . ." (Ernest Newman, *The Life of Richard Wagner,* vol. 2, *1848–1860* [1933; reprint, Cambridge: Cambridge University Press, 1976], p. 464).

57. Charles L. Grüneisen was editor of the *Morning Chronicle,* and had written a very positive account of the composer: *A Memoir of Meyerbeer, with Notices Historical and Critical of his Celebrated Operas, "Les Huguenots," "Robert le Diable," "Il Crociato in Egitto" Compiled from Various Sources and Edited by C. L. Grüneisen* (London, 1848). He had met Meyerbeer in Paris in 1849, and asserted that he had always been "an enthusiastic admirer of Meyerbeer's great compositions, with which a long residence in the French capital had rendered me familiar, having for many years as a musical critic, ardently maintained the supremacy of his musical genius, and having enjoyed the advantage and pleasure of the composer's personal acquaintance" (*Memoir,* pt. 2, p. 3).

58. Berlioz and Wagner were both in London at the time, conducting the Philharmonic Society in the same season: Wagner was the master of rubato, Berlioz strict and precise in the French classical tradition. See Robert Gutman, *Richard Wagner: The Man, His Mind, and His Music* (Harmondsworth: Penguin, 1971), p. 250 for a discussion of their respective characteristics.

59. Charles Dickens* was George Hogarth's* son-in-law.

60. See Richard Wagner, *Mein Leben,* ed. Wilhelm Altmann (Leipzig, n.d.): 2:1045–47): "Hogarth, who felt sure that we were acquainted, was greatly astonished: and when I was leaving he asked me if I did not know Herr Meyerbeer. I replied that he had better ask Meyerbeer himself about me. When I met Hogarth again that evening he assured me that Meyerbeer had spoken of me in terms of the warmest appreciation. Thereupon I suggested that he read certain numbers of the Paris *Gazette musicale* in which Fétis, some time be-

fore, had given a less favourable account of Meyerbeer's views about me. Hogarth shook his head, and could not understand 'how two such great composers could meet in so strange a manner'."

61. Sir Henry Rowley Bishop (with Attwood and Whitaker), *Guy Mannering, or The Gypsey's Prophecy*, melodrama after Sir Walter Scott's novel (1815) (London, Covent Garden, 1816). The work was revived at the Oxford Street Theatre in 1845.

62. Sim Reeves had actually made his English début in *Guy Mannering* (Newcastle, 1838).

63. Charlotte Saunders Cushman (1816–76) was an American actress born in Boston. She made her stage debut in 1835, and became famous for her highly emotional portrayals, as in *Fazio* (London, 1845). She first appeared in *Guy Mannering* in 1837, and was particularly renowned in Shakespearian roles like Lady Macbeth and Bianca, as well as in male assumptions, like Hamlet and Cardinal Wolsey.

64. Ella had established The Musical Union in 1845 for the presentation of morning concerts of chamber music. He was its director until 1880.

65. Meyerbeer attended performances of *Die Zigeunerin* in Vienna on 14 December 1846 and 28 January 1848.

66. Berlioz wrote to Theodore Ritter on 3 July 1855. The tone of his letter reveals a malicious, if not contemptuous, attitude to Meyerbeer. He begins with a reference to one of the rehearsals in the Exeter Hall: "[T]he cornets . . . couldn't come because of the military bandwagon of *L'Étoile du Nord* . . . always *L'Étoile du Nord*, evening party at Glover's to which Meyerbeer was supposed to come, excuses from the great man saying he had a terrible colic, . . . then Meyerbeer finally arriving when everybody had stopped bemoaning his absence, congratulations on the end of his colic . . ." (*Hector Berlioz: A Selection from His Letters*, trans. Humphrey Searle [New York: Vienna House, 1973], pp. 140–41).

67. This was Glover's *Tam O'Shanter*, after Robert Burns's narrative poem (1791), conducted by Berlioz.

68. Mendelssohn, Symphony no. 1 in C Minor, op. 11 (1824).

69. Berlioz, *Harold in Italy*, symphony for viola and orchestra after Byron's poem "Childe Harold's Pilgrimage" (1812), op. 16 (1834).

70. Lady Sophia Frederica Christina Rawdon Hastings (afterwards Crichton-Stuart, marchioness of Bute) (1809–59), a benefactress and editor, sister of George Augustus Francis Rawdon Hastings, second marquis of Hastings.

71. John Henry Loftus, third marquis of Ely, had written to Meyerbeer on 24 December 1854.

72. *L'Étoile du Nord* was performed in Italian as *La Stella del Nord*. Queen Victoria stayed in London expressly to hear the performance.

73. Meyerbeer's account of the event reads somewhat disingenuously in the light of the public perception of his great success. It is described by Harold Rosenthal in his *Two Hundred Years of Opera at Covent Garden* (London: Putman and Company, 1958), p. 109: "Meyerbeer, who was present, was called to the stage and accorded a tremendous reception. He was so overcome that when he went backstage at the end of the evening to greet the orchestra he completely forgot the set speech he had prepared in English, and all he could say was: 'Gentlemen, the heart is so full, that the words are nowhere'."

74. See Chorley, *Thirty Years' Musical Recollections* (1862; reprint, London and New York: Alfred A. Knopf, 1926), pp. 346–49. "*L'Étoile du Nord* has been justly styled by that acute critic, M. Berlioz, as the most-highly finished example of M. Meyerbeer's peculiar

manner which that master of combination has given to the world. . . . the score of *L'Étoile* contains pages full of pure, original ideas, as clearly designed as they are sharply wrought out" (p. 346).

75. *Henry VIII* was first produced in London 1612, and published in the First Folio (1623). Shakespeare had retired to Stratford in 1611, but collaborated with John Fletcher on this spectacular chronicle-play.

76. This entry raises the old question of Meyerbeer's alleged bribery of the press. According to Charles Stuart, "Davison himself, his friends insisted, was never a bribe-taker. About Meyerbeer he had no illusions. He used to say that the composer of *Les Huguenots*, notwithstanding his brilliant position, would grovel in the dust before a representative of the smallest and most insignificant journal" (*The Decca Book of Opera* [London: Werner Laurie, 1956], p. 260). But the situation would seem to have been more complicated than this. "Berlioz often flattered Davison for diplomatic reasons, even going so far as to dedicate the *Corsaire* overture to him. Such trifling tokens of disinterested regard as snuff-boxes, diamond pins, shirt-studs and so on, frequently came his way. Meyerbeer in particular had an exquisitely sensitive perception of Davison's unique abilities as a critic—at any rate as a critic of Meyerbeer's operas. . . . Perhaps, after all, Davison had not been entirely uninfluenced, in his public utterances about Meyerbeer, by the latter's dinners, flatteries and 'little souvenirs'" (see Newman, *Life of Richard Wagner*, 3:467). In 1848, during his sojourn in England, the tenor Gustav Roger had recorded Davison as saying about Meyerbeer and Halévy that they "are not musicians, that they cannot write correctly." Perhaps the experience of *Le Prophète* had changed Davison's opinion of Meyerbeer's ability. Certainly he maintained friendly relations with the composer thereafter.

77. An article on Meyerbeer, with a lithograph of the photograph by Claudet, appeared in the *Illustrated London News* on 11 August 1855, 173–74.

78. The overture to *Emma di Resburgo* (1819) is fairly elaborate, and gives evidence of Meyerbeer's thorough German training—as in the contrapuntal combination of the two principal themes in the middle section. At the same time the musical ideas of this work "show a composer who is mastering the techniques of Italian opera, without always knowing how to develop them in an individual manner. . . , [and] amply document Meyerbeer's growing compositional assurance and justify the success *Emma* was to have both in Italy and Germany" (Philip Gossett, introduction to *Giacomo Meyerbeer: Excerpts from the Early Italian Operas (1817–1822)* [New York and London: Garland, 1991], p. [viii]).

79. *Il Profeta* was given at La Fenice on 11 July 1855 with Carlo Negrini (Giovanni di Leida), Giulia Sanchioli (Fede), and Carlotta Carrozzi Zucchi (Berta).

80. The tenor Joseph-Théodore-Désiré Barbot (1824–96) was engaged by the Opéra in 1848. In the 1850s he sang at the Opéra Comique, and in 1859 succeeded Guardi at the Théâtre Lyrique, where he created the title role in Gounod's *Faust* (19 March). In 1875 he succeeded Pauline Viardot as *professeur de chant* at the Paris Conservatoire.

81. Auguste-Michel Deppe (1814–59), Belgian army officer and military musician.

82. Fr. "to assess the social scene."

83. The text of Meyerbeer's letter about Costa is reprinted in the *Revue et gazette musicale* 34 (26 August 1855): 263.

84. Antoine-Joseph Reicha, Six Wind Quintets, op. 88 (1811–17). No. 5 is actually in B-flat major.

85. The overture, or *sinfonia*, to *Romilda e Costanza* (1817) "demonstrates Meyerbeer's good understanding of the Italian style, without abandoning himself to mimicry of every Rossinian gesture" (Gossett, introduction to *Giacomo Meyerbeer*, p. [iii]).

86. Constant Hermann ("le jeune et célèbre violiniste") had just given a concert at Trouville with Ponchard, where he played his fantasies on themes from *Robert le Diable* and *Lucrezia Borgia* (see *Revue et gazette musicale* 33 [19 August 1855]: 263).

87. See 14 April 1854.

88. This was probably Frances Dorothy Cartwright (1780–1863), a poet, biographer, and translator.

89. See 15 June 1852 and 10 April 1853 for other references to Dr. Sachse.

90. "Se per tutte ordisce amore" (words by Pietro Metastasio) (published in Florence, 1866).

91. Adelaide Ristori was threatening to eclipse Rachel, particularly in Alfieri's play *Myrrha*. A few months later Ristori ("a tall and noble figure of a woman") appeared in Vienna, where her performances were seen by the Danish choreographer August Bournonville. In his reminiscences, *My Theatre Life* (Middletown, Conn.: Wesleyan University Press, 1979), p. 230, he corroborates Meyerbeer's enthusiastic reactions: "Even if one did not understand a single word of Italian, Ristori's eloquence of eye and tone of voice alone would have been enough to interpret her feelings and emotions. I had seen Mlle. Rachel in the same role [Schiller's *Maria Stuart*] and shared the enthusiasm over her superb declamation, but with her I did not for a moment lose sight of the famous actress, whereas Ristori led me into the time and reality." See also Kenneth Richards: "Ristori's great strength lay in her combination of classical appearance, pose and deportment, and accurate physical realism" (Martin Benham, ed., *The Cambridge Guide to Theatre* [Cambridge: Cambridge University Press, 1995], p. 922).

92. Halévy, *Jaguarita l'Indienne*, *opéra comique* in three acts (Saint-Georges & De Leuven; Paris, Théâtre Lyrique, 14 May 1855). The work enjoyed considerable success, performed 124 times until 1862, and revived at the Opéra Comique in 1869. "It was one of Halévy's greatest successes for some time and the Théâtre-Lyrique's longest run since its foundation" (Ruth Jordan, *Fromental Halévy: His Life and Music, 1799–1862* [London: Kahn & Averill, 1994], p. 174). It was very popular in the French provincial theaters.

93. Emmanuel Carrion made his début at the Théâtre Italien in Rossini's *La Cenerentola* and then appeared in *Mosè*. The *Revue et gazette musicale* 22 (October 1855) commented that he had voice and talent, and sang with fire and energy.

94. The International Exhibition of Paris was the brainchild of Emperor Napoleon III, who was determined to go ahead with it despite difficulties and delays of every kind; he officially opened it on 15 May 1855. "The world could witness the achievement of France and its ruler in organizing an international exhibition in wartime. Neither the war nor the cold weather prevented the success of the Exhibition, though it was a wet and unduly cold summer. . . . The Exhibition was held in two great buildings—the industrial side in the Palais de l'Industrie in the Champs-Élysées, and the artistic side a little distance away in the Avenue Montaigne. The press proudly announced that the Exhibition covered an area of 115,000 square yards, had 20,839 exhibitors, and cost 11 million francs . . . ; but the 5,162,330 people who visited the Exhibition before it closed on 15 November fell short of the 6,039,195 visitors to the London Exhibition [of 1851]. There were exhibitors from Britain, Austria, Prussia, Bavaria, the Kingdom of Naples, the Papal States, the United States, Peru, from more than twenty states in all, including Russia, whose traders were given a safe-conduct to visit Paris for the occasion . . ." (Jasper Ridley, *Napoleon and Eugènie* [London: Constable, 1979], pp. 382–83).

95. Fr. "sitting of the Committee of Authors and Dramatic Composers."

96. Alexandre Dumas *(fils)*, *Le Demi-Monde*, prose *comédie* in five acts (Paris, Théâtre du Gymnase Dramatique, 20 March 1855) [Wicks 16223].

97. Verdi, *Les Vêpres siciliennes, grand opéra* in five acts (Scribe & Duveyrier; Paris, Opéra, 13 June 1855). Apart from *Jérusalem* (an adaptation of *I Lombardi*), Verdi's first foray into French *grand opéra*. It was given in Paris sixty-two times until 1865, performed all over the world in the nineteenth century, and frequently revived in the twentieth.

98. This was the première of Grisar's *Le Chien du jardinier*, text by Lockroy & Cormon. "La pièce est amusante, fine et spirituelle" [the work is amusing, refined, and witty] (Clément & Larousse, 1:233).

99. Silcher composed 250 songs modeled after Mozart, Weber, and Mendelssohn, but folklike in style.

100. Reichardt, "Spanische Canzonette," from *VI Canzonette con Pianoforte* (Leipzig: Peters, n.d.) (see Eitner, *Biographisch-Bibliographisches Quellen-Lexikon der Musik und Musikgelehrten*, 8:167).

101. After an absence of many years, Rossini returned to Paris on 25 May 1855: "Rossini was never to see Italy again. But after some further delay, occasioned by continuing bad health, the nearly fourteen years of his final apotheosis were about to begin." See Herbert Weinstock, *Rossini: A Bibliography* (New York: Alfred A. Knopf, 1968), p. 259.

102. Bayard and Duport, *La Fille de l'avare*. This was a revival of the *comédie-vaudeville* in two acts (Paris, Théâtre du Gymnase Dramatique, 7 January 1835) [Wicks 9315].

103. Cormon, *Furnished Apartment, comédie-vaudeville* in one act (with Eugène Grangé; Paris, Théâtre des Variétés, 7 June 1855) [Wicks 17612].

104. Blum, *Une Femme qui mord, comédie* in one act (Paris, Théâtre des Variétés, 7 August 1855) [Wicks 17200].

105. Cormon, *Le Théâtre des Zouaves, tableau militaire* (with Grangé; Paris, Théâtre des Variétés, 1 September 1855) [Wicks 21851].

106. Grisar, *L'Eau merveilleuse, opéra comique* in two acts (Sauvage; Paris, Théâtre de la Renaissance, 30 January 1839). This was Grisar's first greater success; some of the music had been commissioned by Flotow. It was transferred to the Opéra Comique on 1 November 1842, and performed there until 1858.

107. This was the Italian translation (by Calisto Bassi) of the French version of *Mosè in Egitto* (1818), *Moïse et Pharaon, ou Le Passage de la Mer Rouge* (1827). The first performance of this second version (with Italian text) was at Perugia (4 February 1829). Thereafter the opera was performed on Italian stages in either the first (*Mosè in Egitto*) or second versions (*Mosè Nuovo* or *Mosè e Faraone* or simply *Mosè*).

108. Bournonville calls this Belgian singer "the superb coloratura-baritone Evrardi" (*My Theatre Life*, p. 215).

109. The ballad "La Lavandière" was published on 15 October 1855.

110. Mendelssohn, "Türkisches Schenckenlied" (words by Goethe), no. 1 from *Sechs Lieder*, op. 50 (1842); "Wanderlied" (words by Eichendorff), no. 6 from *Sechs Lieder*, op. 57 (1843).

111. Weber, "Schlummerlied" for four male voices (words Ignaz Castelli), from *Two Partsongs*, J. 284–85 (1822).

112. Kücken's reputation as a composer rests on his songs, where he captured the mood of the text in the accompaniments, revealing a penchant for folklike settings, subtle harmonies, and melodic simplicity.

113. Monfort, *Deucalion et Pyrrha, opéra comique* in one act (Barbier & Carré; Paris, Opéra Comique, 8 October 1855).

114. Fr. "chromatic kettledrums."

115. The Bouffes Parisiens was at the Salle Lacaze, Carré Marigny.

116. Offenbach, *Les Deux Aveugles, bouffonnerie musicale* in one act (Moinaux; Paris, Bouffes Parisiens, 5 July 1855). This was the first of Offenbach's works to spread all over Europe, and indeed the world (the first opera to be performed in Saigon, in 1864).

117. Offenbach, *Madame Papillon*, operetta in one act (Servières [Léon Halévy]; 3 October 1855).

118. Offenbach, *Le Violoneux, légende bretonne* in one act (E. Mestépès & E. Chevalet; Paris, Bouffes Parisiens, 31 August 1855).

119. Mlle. Elmire was to sing Madeleine in the Brussels première of *Rigoletto* in 1858, and in the first French language performance of this opera in France (Marseille, 13 May 1860).

120. *Dinorah*, no. 2b *Berceuse de Dinorah* ("Dors petite, dors tranquille").

121. Adam, *Le Houzard de Berchini, opéra comique* in two acts (E. Rosier). This was not one of Adam's more popular works.

122. Désiré-Alexandre Batton died in Versailles on 15 October 1855.

123. See the *feuilleton* of the *Journal des débats* (19 Oct. 1855), "Henri Heine," in which Berlioz discusses the ravages of Heine's wasting illness ("c'est un cerveau vivant sur un corps mort" [a brain living in a dead body]) and the poet's critical interest in music. Berlioz mentions Heine's love for Mozart and Beethoven, his admiration for Spontini, Mendelssohn, Heller, and various virtuosi (Vieuxtemps, Ernst, Bériot, Thalberg, Doehler). Meyerbeer, the most famous living opera composer, a fellow Gèrman and friend of Heine, is pointedly not mentioned. Perhaps Meyerbeer rightly felt he was the unspoken subject of Berlioz's maliciously ambiguous observation concerning an unnamed third party, open discussion of whom would be politically awkward; Heine had in fact opened his eyes to this person's monstrousness: "Je lui dois beaucoup aussi pour avoir fait de quelqu'un de ma connaissance une sorte de cyclope à peu près nécessairement dépouvru de sentiments humains. . . . Mais quand il vient nous dire. . . que. . . O triple poëte! vous le voyez, je serais entraîné jusqu'aux antipodes par une telle discussion. . . 'Soyons prudent! — Taisons nous! — Laissons faire au temps'" [I also owe him much for having shown that someone I know is a sort of Cyclops, more or less by necessity devoid of human feelings. . . . But when it comes to our speaking . . . of. . . . O poet thrice-over! you can see that I would be dragged to the antipodes by such a discussion. . . . Let's be prudent . . . let's be quiet. . . . Time will tell].

124. See François Castil-Blaze, *Théâtres lyriques de Paris: L'Académie Royale de Musique (1645–1847)*, 2 vols. (Paris: Morris & Cie, 1855–56).

125. If anything, Heine's attitude to Meyerbeer had sharpened in its satirical cruelty during his last years of life. "Paralysis of the body . . . did not mean paralysis of the intellect; most of Heine's visitors testified, on the contrary, to the most unimpaired liveliness of his mind and the enhanced trenchancy of his (often self-lacerating) wit. Nor did it mean a drying up of the well-springs of poetry" (S. Prawer, *Heine: The Tragic Satirist* [Cambridge: Cambridge University Press, 1961], p. 145).

126. Tgb. *trainiert.*

127. Fr. "honorary president of the Association of French Musicians."

128. Carlo Corghi, theater poet of the Théâtre Italien, produced his only significant work with *L'Assedio di Firenze*, written for the famous double-bass virtuoso Giovanni Bottesini (1821–89), and produced at the Italiens on 21 February 1856.

129. Émile-Fernand, comte de Najac (1828–89), French dramatist, wrote comedies, vaudevilles and libretti (sometimes using the pseudonym E. Fernand), including a libretto for Grisar (*Les Bégaiements d'amour*, 1864). In addition to the Théâtre Lyriqe, his works were performed at the Opéra Comique, Bouffes-Parisiens, Folies-Marigny, and Variétés.

130. Massé, *Miss Fauvette, opéra comique* in one act (Barbier & Carré; Paris, Opéra Comique, 13 February 1855).

131. "The Archduke Charles."

132. Johann Nepomuck Beck, Austrian baritone.

133. See 18 February 1851. August Bournonville, who was working in Vienna in 1855, commented on the excellent standards of the Kärntnertor-Theater: "[T]he Opera offered superb productions and excellent singing talents. I will only mention the tenors Ander and Steger, the basses Drachsler and Beck, the sopranos Tietjens, La Grua, and Wildauer, together with the altos Hermann-Czillag and Schwartz, in order to give my readers some idea of the ensemble, which was further heightened by the finest chorus I have ever heard" (*My Theatre Life*, p. 220).

134. See 3 April 1852.

135. Shakespeare's *Coriolanus* was first produced in London between 1607 and 1610, and is in the First Folio (1623). The play explores self-destructive pride and arrogance, in the context of political and military power.

136. Bournonville commented also on the high standard of the spoken theater in Vienna. Of the Burgtheater he observes, ". . . I noticed a rather varied repertoire, partly classical, but above all handled with the greatest care: for both newer and older authors and foreign as well German dramatic literature were represented there in tasteful selection. One could go to the drama every evening for several weeks in succession without seeing the same piece twice; and along with the finest new works of the day, was always certain to find Shakespeare, Goethe and Schiller; indeed, even Lessing, Iffland, and Kotzebue emerged from time to time in order to maintain certain stock character roles, which were performed with great talent. The famous actor Korn had recently passed away, but there still shone Anschütz, Löwe, Laroche, the superb Fichtner, and the comedians Bechmann and Meissner—all of them older men. . . . The female personnel were excellent. Mmes. Rettich, Hebbel, and Haitzinger; Mlles. Louise Neumann and Marie Seebach (both unmarried at the time) maintained the large repertoire, and the talented Frau Bayer-Bürch from Dresden appeared as guest. Unfortunately, I did not get to see the famous Dawison . . ." (*My Theatre Life*, p. 215).

137. St. Leopold of Austria (1073–1136; canonized 1485). Little is known about Leopold III, margrave of Austria from 1095, other than that he was a capable and generous ruler, beloved of the people and munificent in benefaction. Three of his religious foundations still exist: Marienzell, Heiligenkreuz, and Klosterneuburg. He was free of personal ambition, and refused to be nominated as a candidate for the imperial crown (1125).

138. Nestroy, *Nagerl und Handschuh; oder, Die Schicksale der Familie Maxenpfutsch*, from a libretto by C.-G. Étienne (Vienna, Theater an der Wien, 1832).

139. Steger was a member of the ensemble at the Kärntnertor-Theater. August Bournonville tells of the problems he encountered in the title role of *Robert le Diable*, in the famous Ballet of the Nuns, where "he had been laughed to scorn because of his clumsiness" and his subsequent altercation with the director Cornet. "The dispute was now settled by mediation, but Steger had sworn that hereafter during the scene in question he would not budge from his spot. And he kept his word with a brutality that could take place only at a German theatre" (*My Theatre Life*, p. 222).

140. *Dinorah*, no. 7 *Duo bouffe d'Hoël et de Corentin* ("Un trésor! bois encore!").

141. Anton von Klesheim (1809/1812/1816?–84), a popular Austrian dramatist.

142. *L'Étoile du Nord*, no. 16 *Scène* ("Moi, Majesté, je voudrais"), published in the Brandus vocal score.

143. The dulcimer is a musical instrument with strings of graduated length over a sounding board or box struck with hammers, the prototype of the pianoforte.

144. Fr. "vivacity."

145. Meyerbeer is in fact describing the *verbunkos* tradition in Hungarian folk music. From the Magyar for "recruiting music," it has a peculiar scale, with a double augmented second, and a snapped rhythmic figure known as the choriamb. "*Verbunkos* implies melodic invention, principles of form and methods of orchestration. Its melodic characteristics are dotted rhythm, certain typical patterns and regular musical periods of broad melodic lines. It has a three-part structure, slow-fast-faster. (In the course of its development, it became simply a slow-fast form.) Orchestration of the *verbunkos* was dominated by the tonal colors of the Gypsy bands that popularized it, with the primary emphasis upon the strings, especially the violin" (see Péter Várnai, introduction to *Bánk bán: Opera három felvonàsban,* by Ferenc Erkel [Budapest: Qualiton, n.d.], p. 8).

146. Bauernfeld, *Das letzte Abenteuer.* This was a revival of the five-act comedy that had its first performance in Vienna in 1832, and in Berlin in 1834 [Richel 10].

147. Mendelssohn, *Die schöne Melusine*, overture after Grillparzer, op. 32 (1833).

148. Mozart, Piano Concerto no. 20 in D Minor, K. 466 (1785).

149. Mozart, Symphony no. 41 in C Major *(The Jupiter)*, K. 551 (1788).

150. Meyerbeer first made the acquaintance of Tauber, a poet and journalist, in Berlin (see 10 and 11 June 1847), and had been in intermittent correspondence with him since (see 7 and 13 April, and 23 May 1853).

151. This was Marie Niemann-Seebach (1830–97), actress and writer.

152. Paul Weidmann was a theater poet.

153. Fr. "snuffbox."

154. Bournonville left a vivid account of Meyerbeer's visit: "It was extremely interesting for me to renew my acquaintance with the famous composer, whom I had met in Paris thirty years earlier. He was now an old and rather feeble man, with a demeanour like that of the finest diplomat, exquisitely polite, gentle, pleasant, but unshakeable in his convictions. He had the most extensive authority, and it was a pleasure to see how he crushed the teeth-gnashing Cornet to the ground with 'iron hand in velvet glove'. In order to speed up the work, the Director had a series of singing rehearsals held before the maestro's arrival. But the latter immediately said with the most charming smile: 'My dear ladies and gentlemen! Here it is not a question of good or bad, for it is obvious that you do not yet know my music at all.' Only now began a purgatory of rehearsals, lessons and corrective rehearsals that often lasted far into the night. The personnel rivalled the Director in wishing 'the Jew' down in the deepest abyss, and it became a saying to be doomed to 'three months Meyerbeer'. But 'Emperor's command' kept the unruly elements under control and the maestro did not allow himself to be disconcerted.

Although often ill and miserable, he appeared every morning at the piano and at the podium, always with a smile on his face, drilled the singers and the chorus until his work was performed to the letter as it had been some months before in Paris. At the same time he did not wish to neglect the help which a large *corps de ballet* could give the scenic effects and for this reason conferred with me, played all the dance melodies himself, indicated tempi, and denoted the places that he wanted 'filled out' with dancing and military manoeuvres. A large camp scene was to be represented, with *cantinières*, infantry men and hussars. Of necessity these last arms had to be represented by women! My objections were fruitless. 'You are perfectly right, my dear Bournonville,' said the old professional, 'but the public is fond of such things and I dare not oppose the prevailing tendency.' The recruiting of the above-mentioned corps was in and of itself no easy matter; for after the maestro had chosen the most voluptuous *figurantes* for the hussars and the prettiest girls from the chorus and the ballet for the *cantinières*, there were no recruits left for the infantry but corpulent old matrons whom I was now to instruct in manual exercises, the execution of countermarches, etc. It was truly a Herculean task. In light of the circumstances, I succeeded in working wonders with these troops, and Meyerbeer was ecstatic over my arrangement.

Everything was done to place *L'Étoile du Nord* at the pinnacle of the firmament; every possible stage effect was employed, and in order to secure the support of the press, Meyerbeer was not the man to disdain paying his respects to the most obscure critic in the highest garret in the most remote suburb, and, if it were necessary, accompanying his affable expressions with irresistible arguments. World famous and a millionaire, he still had an inordinate desire to dazzle his contemporaries with a praise which, in the end, he might even disdain—what a doctrine!

The new opera went over brilliantly. Everybody wanted to see and hear it but no one was fully satisfied with this adaptation of *Vielka*, which they already knew from Jenny Lind's debuts at the Theater an der Wien. They found the music lovely but far less original than Meyerbeer's earlier composition [a view, incidentally, supported by Hanslick]. In an agitated frame of mind, he now hastened to depart for Milan, where they awaited him with splendid ovations but where his *Étoile du Nord* met with a cold reception." (See *My Theatre Life*, pp. 228–30.)

Portrait of Meyerbeer seated. Photograph by Pierre Petit (Paris, c. 1856–57)

1856

Tuesday 1 January. May God bless the new year. May He make it a blessed year for all mankind, but particularly for my beloved family—and for me myself. May the Almighty restore to Minna and Caecilie their lost health; may he grant my beloved Blanca an outstanding, noble, virtuous, and affectionate husband, who will love her devotedly all her life long, and whom she in her turn will make happy. May he allow my beloved Cornelie to bloom and flourish, and preserve her for a hundred years in virtue, contentment, happiness, and peace. May the Almighty also protect and bless me; may he grant me enduring health, genial musical inspiration and brilliant successes. May he preserve the prosperity with which he has blessed me. Amen.

Called to convey my New Year's greetings to, among others, Oberstkämmerer Count Lanckoronski. Since he began to speak to me about the snuffbox, I spoke my mind openly to the effect that I do not regard this as an appropriate acknowledgment, and told him what other monarchs had done for me in similar circumstances, but all in the friendliest manner. I also went to Landsheimer and asked him to withdraw the article intended for his paper, *Die Morgenpost*, against the *Oberstkämmerer* for taking the theater seats away from me. He promised to do this.

Yesterday in the Burgtheater I saw three small plays all translated from the French: *Die Partie piquant,*[1] *Das Grüsschen von Buchnau*[2] and *Der Hut des Uhrmachers.*[3] Today in the Burgtheater I saw Goethe's *Egmont*, with Beethoven's music. Demoiselle Seebach by no means fulfilled the expectations raised by her great reputation: a toneless voice and immobile features generated no sparks. Anschütz (Orange) and La Roche (Schreiber Vansen), by contrast, were outstanding.

Wednesday 2 January. Rehearsed the *coupure*[4] in the act 3 duet with the orchestra. Visits from Glöggl (100 gulden annual subscription to his paper), Weinkopf, Landgutsritter Licat. Attended to preparations for departure. Sent old Sina 200 fr. Sent Brandus (1) the German recitatives for Schlesinger, (2) the printed Italian recitatives for Dufour.

Thursday 3 January. Preparations for departure. Visits. Raymond has given me to understand that the dissatisfaction with the snuffbox, which I expressed to the *Oberstkämmerer*, has prompted the latter to approach the emperor about a decoration for me. Third performance of *L'Étoile du Nord* to a crowded house; the reaction was far cooler than at the second. I was not called out at all during the performance, but three times after each act. The applause was generally much more restrained, and the execution not so rounded. *L'Étoile du Nord* has been performed in Amiens, with much success; it has also been given in Stettin, but apparently did not appeal much there.

Friday 4 January. Visit from the husband of the singer Holoschi, from Pest.[5] The whole troupe of the Hungarian Opera in Pest wants to come to Vienna so that I can hold a rehearsal of *L'Étoile du Nord* with them, because it is to be performed there in the Hungarian Theater. However, I definitely have to leave on Sunday, since my physician Dr. Seeburger is urging me to hurry away to the warmer climate of Venice in order to fight the cough. Visit from the singer Mlle. Huber.

Saturday 5 January. Wrote to Dingelstedt.[6] Visits from Tauber, Stullner, Count Dietrichstein, Cornet, and Count Lanckoronski. The Hungarian singer Holoschi and the bass from the Hungarian Theater[7] came expressly from Pest so that I could rehearse with them the roles (of Catherine and Peter) that they are to sing there. I held this rehearsal with them and, in order to have another rehearsal, postponed my departure to Venice until the day after tomorrow.

Sunday 6 January. Studied the role of Catherine with the Hungarian singer Holoschi. In the evening I did not attend *L'Étoile du Nord*, so that I could write letters (a note of thanks to Ander).[8] Kapellmeister Eckert and Dr. Bacher came to me after the performance, and reported many good things about the execution and reception of the work.

Monday 7 January. Began my journey to Venice. At 8:45 in the morning I departed by rail for Laibach.[9] We arrived there at 9:30 in the evening. During today's journey, I worked on the overture to the *Chercheur*, which I have not yet written out, and which has almost completely vanished from my memory. I brought it all back into recollection and altered, polished, and improved much in it.

Tuesday 8 January. Worked on the overture and the *Buffo* Duet. I took for myself one of the so-called private express coaches[10]—that is, the supplementary post—without having to book my own coach. This excellent arrangement applies only in Austria: a private post coach is placed at one's disposal, and one can travel to one's chosen destination in as long or short a time as desired. One pays all at once for the whole affair—the coach, the horses, the tips for the postillions—and then has nothing further to worry about. I took the post coach to Casarra, where the railway line starts again, four hours from Venice. I left at 8:30 and arrived at 7:30 in the evening (in torrential rain, and in an appalling coach) at Wippach, where I stayed overnight in a bad inn.

Wednesday 9 January. At seven o'clock departed from Wippach, in order to arrive at five o'clock in the evening in Casarra. Since the train leaves at only six o'clock, I could have left but for the fact that my trunk, which was too big for the coach, and which the postmaster in Laibach had promised to send on directly by express coach, had not yet arrived, and I wanted to wait for it. I spent the whole day composing Hoël's romance in act 3,[11] completed it, and also wrote it down. *Le Prophète*, which had already been performed at the Canobbiana in Milan last summer,[12] is now being produced at La Scala, with Demoiselle Masson singing Fidès.[13]

Thursday 10 January. Since the trunk had still not appeared, I left early, at 8:10, by train for Venice, and arrived there at eleven o'clock.[14] I am staying at the Hotel Europa (three lovely rooms, the middle one of which looks onto the Grand Canal, second floor, twelve fr. per day, five fr. for dinner in my room). In the evening to the Teatro La Fenice, where the *Crociato* was premièred thirty-two years ago,[15] and which, in my opinion, is the most beautiful theater in the world:[16] Verdi's *Il Trovatore*.[17] Donna Lewnieska [Lesniewska], a Pole, has a lovely voice, but only in supported passages: it breaks in dramatic moments; fairly good delivery; a small, plump figure; certainly no outstanding talent.[18] The tenor Pancani has a lovely, mellifluous voice, even if it is sometimes a little dissonant. His delivery is fairly good; he appears to be the most popular of the troupe.[19] The big ballet *La Giocoliera* is insignificant.[20] Demoiselle Plunkett, from the Paris Opéra, was the principal dancer.[21] To my surprise, the rumor of my arrival had spread, and all the lorgnettes in the theater were directed at me, all very embarrassing. The *presidenza* of the theater, Count Mocenigo[22] and Tornielli,[23] offered me their box, and when I did not accept it, they sent me an invitation for tomorrow to the dress rehearsal of *La Traviata*.[24] My old acquaintances Perucchini[25] and Tropeani[26] looked me up, as did Armand Baschet from Paris.[27]

Friday 11 January. As an acknowledgment of the kindness shown me last evening by the *presidenza*, I called on them, and was amazed to recognize in Count Mocenigo an acquaintance of thirty years standing, whom I knew in Recoaro and then later in Berlin, where he became the secretary to the Austrian Legation. The directors informed me they had intended giving *Les Huguenots* in the coming season, but that the opera will be mounted next month in the small Teatro Apollo,[28] with bad singers and a bad orchestra, and because of this they will not undertake a production. It saddens me that this is to happen during my stay in Venice, and I begged the gentlemen to prevent it if they could. In the evening to the dress rehearsal of Verdi's opera *La Traviata*. When the orchestra heard that I was in the theater, they cheered me with great applause. *La Traviata* is, from a musical perspective, much more melodic, simpler, and less noisy than Verdi's other operas, with the exception of *Il Trovatore*. It contains many melodic traits, with the melody always being brought forward by a rhythmic invention that is often highly interesting. The principal singer in this opera, Madame Cortesi, has much feeling and passion in delivery, also a lovely voice; the voice, however, is very fatigued.[29]

Saturday 12 January. Began composing a little of Hoël's act 1 aria ("O puissante magie").[30] In the evening to the Fenice: *La Traviata*. The performance had little appeal, largely the fault of Madame Cortesi.

Sunday 13 January. Worked on Hoël's aria. Teatro La Fenice: *La Traviata*. *L'Étoile du Nord* has been performed in Perpignan.

Monday 14 January. Worked on Hoël's first aria. In the evening to the Teatro San Samuele, where comedy is performed:[31] *La coscienza publica*, a bad play in two acts, and Goldoni's *Il campiello*, a neat little comedy in Venetian dialect.[32]

Tuesday 15 January. Letter from Madame Jagds-Rote in Wiesbaden: she would like *L'Étoile du Nord* for her benefit concert in Basel. The Wiesbaden Theater does not want to lend her the score unless I give my permission—which I did. Before and after breakfast worked very diligently and with good success on Hoël's aria. In the Teatro Apollo: Rossini's *L'Assedio di Corinto*. Madame de Roissy, from the Grand Opéra in Paris: a thin, toneless voice, with some volume only in the high passages; quite a lot of coloratura (she could sing the Queen in *Les Huguenots* fairly well), but, on the whole, insignificant.[33] The baritone Ottaviani has a lovely, soft voice, also with good coloratura, but completely cold and without a trace of acting talent.[34] The tenor Dell'Armi is unimportant.[35] The orchestra and chorus were barely average. And they want to give *Les Huguenots* in this theater? *Orrore!*[36]

Wednesday 16 January. Worked on Hoël's aria. Visits from the singers Lesniewska, *prima donna* of the Fenice, and from Demoiselle de Roissy. In the Fenice: *Il Trovatore*.

Thursday 17 January. Worked on Hoël's aria and almost finished composing it; also began writing it out. Teatro La Fenice: Donizetti's *Don Sebastiano*.

Friday 18 January. Even though Hoël's aria is actually fully composed, I nonetheless polished and altered it. I could only work a little on it, since I wrote letters (to Guidi, to Gouin about *Le Figaro* and Perrin, to Dr. Bacher about Zellner and Bach), and paid some calls. Concert by the pianist Fumagalli* in the Teatro San Benedetto. He belongs to the pianists of the very first order: extraordinary fluency, a very beautiful touch, noble, tender delivery. He played a fantasy on *Le Prophète*, a second on *Robert* entirely with the left hand, quite astounding. After the latter a voice from the *parterre*[37] shouted, "Evviva anche il maestro Meyerbeer,"[38] and the public began clapping with such enthusiasm and so persistently that I had to bow three times from my seat in the stalls.

Saturday 19 January. Worked just a little on Hoël's aria. Teatro La Fenice: *La Traviata*.

Sunday 20 January. Worked for one and a half hours before breakfast on Hoël's aria, also on writing it out, the same for an hour after breakfast. In the evening wrote out Hoël's aria. A headache somewhat hampered my activity.

Monday 21 January. Worked on Hoël's aria for an hour before and after breakfast. In the evening finished writing out Hoël's aria.

Tuesday 22 January. Before breakfast worked a little on the duet for Hoël and Corentin. After breakfast, and also in the afternoon, worked on the ensemble of this duet with good success. Teatro La Fenice: *Il Trovatore*.

Wednesday 23 January. Worked successfully for two hours before breakfast on the duet. Auguste Villemot, in *Le Figaro* of 10 January, has publicly withdrawn the slander alleging that it was through my agency that Massé had to suppress the chorus in his overture to *Les Saisons*.[39]

Thursday 24 January. Worked for two hours before breakfast on the duet, with good success. In the evening worked for three hours, and wrote out the duet up to the ensemble.

Friday 25 January. Worked for three hours on the ensemble of the duet. Letter from Maestro Mazzucato, director of the Teatro alla Scala:[40] he wants *L'Étoile du Nord* for the spring.

Saturday 26 January. In order to acquaint myself with the singers and productions of today's Italian opera theaters, I have decided to visit several Italian cities.[41] I therefore left at 11:15 by train for Verona (arrived in four hours). In the big Teatro Filarmonico:[42] *Il Trovatore*. Madame Albertini, an Englishwoman, must once have had a really fine voice, in the mode of Cruvelli; the middle and lower registers are still lovely, but the higher, while still strongly resonant, is already

strained. Even with such great strength, she has a lovely piano and fire in delivery; an attractive physiognomy. Whether or not she has coloratura, or is an actress, is not something one can deduce from this role. In any case, she is a significant talent.[43] Her husband, Baucardé, has a strong but worn voice, sings from the
chest, has no high notes, no acting.[44] The baritone Bencich is not bad,[45] but
Guicciardi is much better.[46] A new ballet, *Le educande di Arragona,* is unimportant, but the young dancer called Baratte revealed such admirably fluent footwork
and brilliant execution that I am sure she could please in Paris.[47] Corti, the former
director of the Italian Opera in Paris, recognized me in the theater.[48]

Sunday 27 January. At 12:15 by train to Mantua in one hour. The brother of the
Venetian impresario Marzi, who runs the theater *impresa*[49] these days, called on
me, and took me to his box.[50] They were giving Verdi's *La Traviata,* with thoroughly unmemorable singers. The prima donna, Madame Dolgosa, sang Berthe
in *Le Prophète* in Milan last summer; she has fire and considerable *éclat* in the
higher register, but bungles a good deal.[51] Rota's* ballet *Il Giocatore* (after
Ducange's famous drama)[52] is very popular.[53] This choreographer is attracting much
attention with this work. I found much that is special in it.[54] The different members of the *presidenza,* Maestro Appiani, and the director of the orchestra, came
to my box to greet me. The public, who in the meantime had learned of my presence, called out my name after act 1 with such enthusiasm, and applauded so
loudly and persistently, that I had to leave my box at least ten times to bow to
them. Today, 27 January, is the hundredth anniversary of Mozart's birth, which is
being celebrated in all the cities of Germany.

Monday 28 January. Traveled by diligence from Mantua to Parma in nine hours.

Tuesday 29 January. Yesterday in the coach, today while walking, continued
composing the second part of the duet, but without satisfying results. Went to
see: (1) the great Teatro Farnese which is unfortunately now quite decayed;[55]
(2) the glorious picture gallery—with its many Correggios, a Raphael, and many
Parmigianinos;[56] (3) the old Chiesa alla Madonna; (4) the *giardino publico*; and
(5) the promenade around the city. In the theater, which is very beautiful, big, and
elegant:[57] *Maria di Rohan,* one of Donizetti's weakest operas. Cresci, the baritone, has a mellow, lovely voice (even if it is not particularly strong), and deliv-
ers with much feeling, and good acting.[58] The tenor, Giulini, who sang Raoul in
Les Huguenots in Milan, likewise has a very attractive, mellow, vibrant voice although not very strong, a tender, rounded delivery, little acting ability, but not
annoyingly so.[59] Demoiselle Goldberg, the prima donna,[60] is the sister of the once
famous singer.[61] This is only her second theatrical engagement. She sings with
fire and understanding, but the voice is uneven in the middle register. She will no
doubt make great progress in the future. The orchestra, long famous, belongs to

the very best in Italy, as does the orchestra director, De Giovanni.[62] Even though in Parma no one calls and no one visits, news of my arrival had spread, most probably because of my passport, which had to be shown to the police. A gentleman came to my stall seat to invite me, on behalf of the *presidenza*, to accept their box, but I declined. The public, which in the meantime appeared to have been apprised of my presence, applauded so fervently in the interval, calling out my name (mixed with *evviva* and *bravo*) so loudly, that I had to stand up in my place at least ten times and bow. During the ballet I had to give in to the urgings of the *presidenza* and go to their box, where I received many visits, and all the singers were presented to me.

Wednesday 30 January. Since all the places in the diligence were already booked up, I had to take a *vetturino*[63] to Mantua. We took nine hours to reach Mantua, so I could take the train for Verona in the same evening.

Thursday 31 January. By train to Brescia in two and a half hours. To the theater, which is big, but old and badly decorated:[64] *I Masnadieri*, one of Verdi's weakest operas, which he composed for Jenny Lind in London.[65] The prima donna Rapazzini,[66] the tenor Massini,[67] and the baritone De Giorgi were all hardly even mediocre, the orchestra and chorus as well. The ballet *Il paggio della regina* was also only average. This ballet is derived from a vaudeville, *Le Capitaine Charlotte*, which could be made into a nice little comic opera.[68] I thought myself unrecognized in the theater today, but a former *souffleur*[69] from the Italian Opera in Berlin, Profendo, recognized me, and when I reached home I found the director of the theater orchestra, Conti, who begged me to allow the theater orchestra to show a sign of their homage by serenading me; I could hardly refuse, since the orchestra, already accompanied by torches, was arranged in the courtyard. When, at the end of the serenade, I went into the courtyard to thank them, I was received with enthusiastic *applaudissement*[70] by both orchestra and the many spectators.

February 1856

Friday 1 February. Returned to Venice by train in six and a half hours. Unfortunately, my lovely rooms in the Hôtel de l'Europe had been rented out. During the whole journey I concerned myself with the composition of the second part of the duet,[71] but have not been able to bring it to a satisfying conclusion.

Saturday 2 February. In the Teatro Apollo: *Rigoletto*, one of Verdi's most popular operas, which also contains lovely pieces and many interesting details. The libretto has powerful situations.[72]

Sunday 3 February. Answered the maestro Mazzucato in Milan: he had requested my authorization for the production of *L'Étoile du Nord*, and I want to know beforehand the names of the singers. Today finished composing the duet.

Monday 4 February. Wrote out the duet to within a few bars. In the Fenice *Il Trovatore*: the *presidenza* had prepared a joint surprise for me. After act 2, the orchestra and the *banda* played the march from *Le Prophète*; this was demanded *da capo* with great applause by the public, who continued to cheer for so long that I had to stand up in my seat several times and bow.

Tuesday 5 February. The last day of Carnival. Wrote out the whole of the duet. During an evening stroll through the market bustle in St. Mark's Square, an idea came to me for the *terzettino* with goat bells,[73] which seems good to me. I wrote it down immediately.

Wednesday 6 February. I have a cold. Worked on the *terzettino*.

Thursday 7 February. The streaming cold continues. Worked for one and a half hours before breakfast on the *terzettino*. In the evening wrote one sheet of the vocal parts of the duet into the full score. On 1 February, in the Hungarian Theater in Pest, *L'Étoile du Nord* was performed to great enthusiasm, according to Doppler, who has written to me.[74] On 27 January in St. Petersburg *L'Étoile du Nord* was performed for the benefit of Demoiselle Maray.

Friday 8 February. The cold and digestive indisposition persist. I therefore could not work at all. Walked *sulle* Sattere[75] for the first time; one is always discovering new, interesting, and overwhelming sections of the city in Venice. Visit from the artist Astolfoni,[76] who painted a life-size portrait of my late, blessed father thirty years ago, which, he says, I paid him for but was never collected. He asked if I would take it away with me, which I would like to do. The writer Servadio from Florence came to see me; he has written very favorable articles on *Le Prophète* in the Florentine journal *L'Arte*.[77] He brought me a letter of introduction from Sabatier-Ungher in Pisa, but did not find me in. At the beginning of February *Der Nordstern* was performed in Munich for the first time.

Saturday 9 February. Worked for one and a half hours on the *terzettino*. Only a good conclusion is now wanting: I have been trying in vain to compose it over the last few days. This conclusion also constitutes the finale of act 1, and is therefore very important. Visit from the music director of the Teatro Apollo, Borsolotti, who wanted to question me about the abridgments in *Les Huguenots* and the *tempi*, since this little theater unfortunately persists in wanting to stage the opera. Visit from the writer Servadio. Teatro San Samuele: *Le baruffe chiozzote*, Venetian comedy by Goldoni.[78] In Barcelona *Les Huguenots* is currently being performed at the Teatro del Liceo by an Italian opera troupe, with great success.[79] Madame Julien-Dejan is singing Valentine.[80] *L'Étoile du Nord* has been produced in Brest and Antwerp, to great enthusiasm.

Sunday 10 February. Letter from the music dealer Bernard in St. Petersburg: he asks me for a march for the forthcoming coronation of the Emperor Alexander.[81] Conferred with Borsolotti for two hours about abridgments in *Les Huguenots*. For the first time visited the Campo di Marte, a vast drill-ground on which people also ride, on the seashore close to the Sattere. My old friend, the famous castrato Velluti (for whom I composed *Il Crociato* in 1824 here in Venice) has arrived, and I called on him. In the evening worked for two and a half hours on the trio, and finished composing it. All that remains is the introduction.

Monday 11 February. Worked for two and a half hours before breakfast on the *terzettino*. I destroyed the conclusion that I composed yesterday and devised a new one, the definitive one I hope, and began writing out the whole piece. Visits from Velluti and Perucchini, Galli (impresario of the Teatro Apollo), and Demoiselle Goddard, the pianist from London.

Tuesday 12 February. Worked for two hours before breakfast on writing out the *terzettino*. Went through the *tempi* in act 4 of *Les Huguenots* with the director of the Teatro Apollo. Gave directions to the *décorateur* about the scenery of act 5. Teatro La Fenice: *Norma*, with a new tenor, Masoleni [Mazzoleni], who was very bad, and laughed off the stage.[82] Mme. Cortesi also sang badly. A count from Siebenbürgen (he is called Betschlafen, I believe)[83] presented himself to me in the theater, and told me *L'Étoile du Nord* has had great success in Pest. The singer Cruvelli from the Grand Opéra, who has married Baron Vigier and left the stage, is here with her husband;[84] I went to see them in their box.

Wednesday 13 February. Wrote out the trio for two hours before breakfast. Went through the *tempi* in act 3 of *Les Huguenots* with the music director of the Teatro Apollo. A censorious article has appeared in the *Allgemeine Zeitung* about *Der Nordstern* in Munich. It does not appear to have been very successful.[85] Teatro San Samuele: *La putta onorata*, a charming comedy by Goldoni.[86]

Thursday 14 February. Wrote out the trio for two hours before breakfast. Played the ballet master of the Teatro Apollo the *tempi* of the ballet music in *Les Huguenots*. Visit from the doctor Benvenuti, whose eighteen-year-old son has composed an opera that reveals a considerable talent, especially in many new and piquant harmonic modulations and details; the lyrical, melodic side, however, is weaker. Letter from Marchese Martellini in Florence, enclosing the Italian translation of *Struensee*.

Friday 15 February. Wrote out the trio for two and a quarter hours before break-fast. Concluded the study of the *tempi* in *Les Huguenots* with the director of the Teatro Apollo. Visit from the impresario of the Fenice, Marzi; he wants me to recommend the engagement of the tenor Giulini to the *presidenza*.[87] To the dress rehearsal of Verdi's *Les Vêpres siciliennes*, which the censor in Italy has refash-ioned into a Portuguese fable called *Maria di Guzman*.[88]

Saturday 16 February. Finished writing out the trio in the two hours before break-fast, and also found just the right means of linking the duet with the trio. Visit from the composer and writer Alberto Mazzucato from Milan, who currently leads the *impresa* of the Teatro alla Scala; he would like to give *L'Étoile du Nord* there this coming spring, and wants my authorization for it. In the Fenice the first per-formance of Verdi's opera *Maria di Guzman*: it succeeded.[89] The production was, from the musical and scenic point of view, just as good as the Parisian one; only the prima donna, Lesniewska—even though she was not bad—was far below Cruvelli's standard.

Sunday 17 February. Visit from Mazzucato. I have allowed him my score *L'Étoile du Nord* for Milan. In the Fenice heard act 4 of *Maria di Guzman*.

Monday 18 February. Went to the Giudecca for the first time, and explored its whole length.[90] A headache prevented me from working.

Tuesday 19 February. Letter from Kapellmeister Erkel* in Pest.[91] Unfortunately, I did nothing all day, other than write two different *canzonette* into the albums of Princess Clary[92] and Perruchino, as well as write a small piano piece from my notebook into Fumagalli's album.

Wednesday 20 February. Preparations for departure, which I am hastening in or-der to avoid the first performance of *Les Huguenots* in the Teatro Apollo, which is scheduled for this Saturday.

Thursday 21 February. Farewell visits. Bad attack of colic with diarrhea. The *maestro concertatore* for the musical *mise en scène* in the Teatro Apollo is called Torresilla, and is admirable in his job.

Friday 22 February. Worked in the evening on the ensemble in the finale.

Saturday 23 February. There has been a very brilliant reprise of *Der Nordstern* in Dresden, where the opera had not been performed for the last six months. Left for Verona at 12:15 by train in order to arrive there at 4:15. From a theater journal I have learned that Heinrich Heine died on 17 February: peace to his ashes. I forgive him from my heart for his ingratitude and many wickednesses against me in his later writings.[93] In the Teatro Filarmonico I heard Donizetti's *Lucrezia Borgia*. Mme. Alberti sang the last scene of act 3 wonderfully. The public had learned, to my amazement, that I was in the theater, even though, in order to remain incognito, I had taken a box. They called "Viva Meyerbeer" and applauded for so long that I had had to bow from my box several times. My old friend Giulio Nicolini, whom I had not seen for thirty years, visited me in my box,[94] as did Maestro Pedrotti*, the composer of *Fiorina*.[95]

Sunday 24 February. In Munich blessed Michael's *Struensee*, with my music, has again been newly mounted (with success). In Béziers *Le Prophète* has been performed for the first time, to great enthusiasm. Maestro Pedrotti came to me to ask about performance cuts in *Le Prophète*, since this opera is to be produced in Verona in the spring. At five o'clock by train for Mantua, in order to leave for Florence from there.

Monday 25 February. By diligence to Parma. Yesterday and today I composed a *canzonetta,* "Venezia," the words by the late son of the Consigliere Beltrame.[96] The father asked this of me.[97] I finished composing it up to the last strophe. *Droits d'auteur* for the month of January: 778 fr. 45 c.

Tuesday 26 February. By diligence from Parma to Bologna. We left at four o'clock in the morning and were in Bologna by three o'clock in the afternoon.

Wednesday 27 February. At four o'clock in the morning by diligence from Bologna to Florence. We arrived only at 8:30 in the evening, even though we had made excellent progress.

Thursday 28 February. Improvised in the morning and evening on the act 1 finale. Today I received the news that my poor brother-in-law, Hermann Eberty, has died, after long suffering from dropsy of the chest.[98]

Friday 29 February. Worked for a little before breakfast on the act 1 finale. Visit from Guidi, the Italian publisher of *L'Étoile du Nord*, with the editor of his musical journal, *L'Armonia*. In the Teatro della Pergola:[99] *Rigoletto*, music by Verdi. The opera is called *Viscerdello* here. The tenor Negrini*, who has had such great success as the Prophet in Venice and Trieste, has a very powerful, resonant voice, and sings with fire, but has absolutely no mellowness, no color in the voice; everything is sung *fortissimo*. He further has no coloratura. One cannot asses his acting ability from this role [the Duke of Mantua].[100] The baritone Varesi*, once a great celebrity, now has a completely worn-out, toneless voice.[101] The prima donna,

Madame Dolgosa [Gordosa], whom I had already heard in Mantua, is almost insignificant.

March 1856

Saturday 1 March. Yesterday's north wind has given me a cold. Called on Marquis Martellini and Madame Ungher-Sabatier.

Sunday 2 March. I had wanted to leave at 7:30 in the morning for Siena by rail, in order to hear the singer Piccolomini*, who is becoming so famous, singing in *La Traviata*. However, since my passport had not been stamped with a visa by the police, I could not travel until this formality had been attended to. I worked diligently in the morning on the finale. At 4:30 left by train for Siena, where I arrived at eight o'clock in the evening. In the theater:[102] Verdi's *La Traviata*. Piccolomini is, without doubt, a very significant talent. Not a big voice, no great singing style, little by way of top notes, but spirit, grace, elegance, fire, important acting ability, peculiarly genial perception of detail; in short, she pleased me very much. The tenor Prudenza has several lovely resonant high notes—A, B, B-flat *di petto*[103]— but the voice is uneven; sometimes individual notes are blurred, and he also sings crudely and without taste.[104] The baritone [Sebastiano] Ronconi sings with refinement and good style, but has little voice; he is a brother of the famous [Giorgio] Ronconi.

Monday 3 March. My cold is getting better. Viewed the city. Returned to Florence by train. In Florence to the Teatro della Pergola: Verdi's *I due Foscari*. The public must have heard that I was in the theater (again I just do not know how), and after act 2 there was such a general clapping and cheering and calling of my name that a man from the *presidenza* came into my box (which I had taken expressly to remain unrecognized) to ask me to show myself to the public. I went to the front of the box and indicated my thanks; three times I drew back and three times I had to appear again, the applause lasted so long. Mme. Gordosa, who in Mantua seemed bad to me in *La Traviata*, today revealed a lovely voice in *Rigoletto*, particularly her lower register; she has much fire and expression. She could well be a good Valentine in *Les Huguenots*. Negrini also sang and acted better in *Rigoletto*. Wrote to Locatelli, the editor of the Venetian newspaper, who sent me his article about *Les Huguenots*.[105]

Tuesday 4 March. Because I want to go to Genoa, I left for Pisa by rail, stayed there overnight, and called on Madame Ungher-Sabbatier and Nina Viganò, who always spend the winter there. I took two places in Bertolani's diligence, which travels to Genoa in thirty hours.

Wednesday 5 March. Departed at six o'clock in the morning for Genoa in a really good diligence. The route is enchantingly beautiful, particularly from Massa to Carrara, and then again from the Golfo di Spezia, where the road mostly twists along the edge of the sea. We traveled through the night.

Thursday 6 March. We arrived in Genoa at eleven o'clock in the morning. I was last here in 1816 when my beloved parents, accompanied by Heinrich and Michael, came to Genoa, and Wilhelm and I came up from Sicily to meet them. All of them have since then been called to heaven, the precious darlings. May God grant them eternal peace, eternal blessedness. Amen. I have just remembered that I did come to Genoa again, in 1835, when I went to Nice with Minna and Blanca. To the big Teatro Carlo Felice,[106] which is as spacious as the Fenice (even to having six rows of boxes) for Verdi's *Macbeth*. The prima donna was Bendazzi, who is among the most famous in Italy: she has a very strong, vibrant, true soprano voice, but without mellowness or nuance, and further sings without style; she appears to have no acting talent, and she is also not attractive.[107] The baritone Ferri, or Ferrari, likewise has a powerful, resonant voice, but again without mellowness, and his singing is rough.[108] The tenor part in this opera is so small that they chose someone very insignificant. The ballet *Il Giocatore*, which I had already seen in Mantua, has been staged here even more brilliantly. Rota himself played the Giocatore, but impressed me little as a mime. The orchestra was crude, with the string instruments sounding tired. *L'Étoile du Nord* has been performed in Antwerp and Amiens, with great success.

Friday 7 March. Began to write out some of the "Canzonette Venezia." I have a bad cold. To the Teatro Andrea Doria, a new, large theater, very pretty, if not nearly as big as the Carlo Felice. They gave the *opera buffa Pipelè*, music by Serafino Amedeo de Ferrari.[109] This opera has proved popular in Rome and here. I did not like it at all; it is a flat imitation of Verdi without a spark of humor, without a trace of thematic invention.[110] The singers were very mediocre. The libretto is based on the episode of the porter Pipelé in Sue's *Les Mystères de Paris*.[111] In Magdeburg the late, blessed Michael's *Struensee*, with my music, has been revived in a new production.

Saturday 8 March. My general indisposition has so intensified that I went to bed at two o'clock in the afternoon.

Sunday 9 March. Unexpectedly met the song composer Gustav Pressel from Stuttgart.[112] In the Teatro Carlo Felice I heard act 1 of *La Traviata* and act 2 of *Nabucco* by Verdi. My opinions of Bendazzi and Ferri have been confirmed.

Monday 10 March. Early in the morning at six o'clock by train for Novara, and from there by the diligence already booked in Genoa (which is called *Corriere* and is pitifully bad) to Milan. We arrived there at five o'clock. In the Teatro Carcano:[113] *La Rediviva, opera seria* in four acts, music by Maestro Carrer.[114] It has been successful here, and shows a certain skill in the instrumentation; the harmonic modulations and disposition of form are, however, totally in the Verdian mode and perception, without a single bar of originality.[115] The singers were collectively mediocre. The prima donna Donati screeches, without voice and with dubious intonation. The tenor was the Swabian Stigelli, who even twelve years ago in Germany had too little voice, even though he sings with relative clarity.[116] Both baritones, Antonucci and Spellini, are very average.

Tuesday 11 March. My dear friend of forty years, Count Pachta, whom I knew in Vienna in 1813, is living here in the same guest house as I am, and has asked me to visit him, since for the last five months he has been lying paralyzed in bed.[117] Called on Maestro Mazzucato who, as *capo dell'impresa della Scala*,[118] came to me in Venice to ask for *L'Étoile du Nord* for the Teatro Canobbiana in Milan.[119] In the evening he took me to his box *alla Scala*[120] where they gave the first Milanese performance of *Marino Faliero*, one of Donizetti's weakest operas.[121] The public whistled and hissed the singers continually. The tenor Liverani was bad,[122] the baritone Corsi, who is well-known, and is to sing Peter in *L'Étoile du Nord*, appears to have a weak voice; I could not assess his talent in this ungrateful role [Marino Faliero].[123] The other baritone, Giraldoni, is not bad, but certainly not excellent.[124] The prima donna Barbieri-Nini, formerly such a celebrity, has a very lovely voice, but is short of breath, and cannot, even with *slancio*,[125] negotiate a strong orchestral accompaniment without noticeable gaps and weaknesses appearing in the voice. Only in a single *adagio* did she sing attractively.[126] Mazzucato, Zezi,[127] Ricordi, Raboni,[128] Demoiselle Masson—all called on me in my box.

At one o'clock in the morning, I was awakened from the deepest sleep by music: the orchestra and chorus of the Teatro alla Scala were serenading me with the Chœur d'Introduction and the Appel aux Armes from *Le Prophète*, as well as the ballet music from act 3. The numerous audience who had gathered, and the orchestra itself, applauded so tumultuously after each piece, calling out my name, that I had to get out of bed and go into the *cortile*, even though it was raining. When I appeared, I was received with the greatest enthusiasm. I embraced Cavallini, the orchestral director of La Scala, and spoke a few words.[129]

L'Étoile du Nord has been performed in Cologne and Versailles. *Le Prophète* has been performed in Boston by the Italian Company (Madame Lagrange, Herr Salviari, etc.), to great enthusiasm. On 21 February in Karlsruhe *Le Prophète* was performed for the first time. In Bonn *Le Prophète* was performed for the benefit of the tenor Rademacher.[130] Letter from Eduard Devrient. Letter of invitation, in the name of the duke of Gotha, to become a member of the Committee of the Mozart Society.

Wednesday 12 March. Early in the morning, at eight o'clock, by train for Venice. From Treviglio to Cocaglia, however, one must travel for four hours by diligence. The coughing and sniffling unfortunately continue uninterruptedly.

Thursday 13 March. Alas, did nothing all day. Teatro La Fenice: *Norma.* Madame Boccherini sang Norma as her guest role. She is the same one who sang Valentine in *Les Huguenots* in Milan, a Hungarian who has italianized her name. She has a fine theatrical presence, good physiognomy, acts very well, sings with expression and great clarity, with coloratura, and with a good style; only the middle voice is not suitable for a big orchestra.[131] Rota's ballet *Il Fallo*, which is very popular in Italy, struck me as rather ordinary.[132]

Friday 14 March. Worked for a little, but indisposition has dulled my spirit of invention. Today's Milanese newspaper contains a very flattering article about my serenade from the chorus and orchestra of La Scala. Teatro La Fenice: individual scenes from several operas for the benefit of a poor family. I gave twenty fr. The baritone Cresci, who sang today, has good delivery and a rather good voice, although Guicciardi surpasses him on both counts. Cresci is the same baritone whom I heard in Parma in *Maria di Rohan.*

Saturday 15 March. Began writing out the "Canzonette Venezia." In the Fenice the last performance of the season of Verdi's *Maria di Guzman*, and Rota's ballet *Il Fallo.*

Sunday 16 March. Severe coughing. I spent the whole day in bed.

Monday 17 March. I stayed in bed again today.

Tuesday 18 March. Towards midday the doctor allowed me to get up, even though my condition has only improved a little.

Wednesday 19 March. Today I was again in no condition to work. Letter from the Società Filarmonica Apollinea in Venice, naming me an honorary member.

Thursday 20 March. After five days, went out again for the first time, but felt bad.

Friday 21 March. Hardly worked at all. *Droits d'auteur* for the month of February: 544 fr. 50 c.

Saturday 22 March. Worked a little on the finale.

Sunday 23 March. Improvised on the opera reluctantly.

Monday 24 March. Worked diligently on the act 3 intermezzo.[133] Teatro San Benedetto[134] (the same theater where *Emma di Resburgo* was premièred in 1819):[135] Verdi's *Nabucco*. Madame Gordosa, a Spaniard, the same one I heard in Mantua and Florence, was full of exaggeration and *vibrato*, sang with false intonation some of the time, and with the most inaccurate coloratura. The baritone Bencich, whom I heard in Verona, has a powerful voice, often great expression, but shouts, often sings falsely, and always crudely. Velluti is in Venice again.[136]

Tuesday 25 March. Finished composing the *Chanson du Faucheur*[137] before breakfast. In the morning and evening wrote out the *Chanson du Faucheur*.

Wednesday 26 March. Wrote out the *Chant du Faucheur*. Teatro San Samuele: Donizetti's *Don Pasquale*. This is a third-class opera company: the prima donna Madame Pollack (a Jewess) has a certain *éclat* in her voice, fire, and a good trill, but sings falsely and inaccurately much of the time, and is a laughable actress; the *buffo* Finetti is cold, without comedy. *Le Prophète* has been produced in Dijon and Perpignan, also in St. Quentin and Béziers.

Thursday 27 March. Worked for two hours before breakfast on the *Chant du Braconnier*[138] with happy inspiration. In the evening finished composing the *Chant du Braconnier*, and wrote out half of it.

Friday 28 March. Finished writing out the *Chant du Braconnier*.

Saturday 29 March. At 12:30 left by train for Mantua. Arrived at 5:15. In the theater:[139] Donizetti's *Poliuto*. This is the opera that he later transformed into *Les Martyrs* for the French Grand Opéra in Paris. Insofar as I can remember,[140] I think the latter contains more interesting pieces, and maintains a more consistent style, than this original *Poliuto*. The overture, for example, is entirely missing from the original. Demoiselle Piccolomini appealed to me far less in this opera than in Siena, where I heard her in *La Traviata*. The high notes, from G upwards, appear to sour; she slurs them both up and down, and is often false [in intonation]. Her tone is simply not adequate for a big theater, but she does have many genial moments. The tenor Negrini's voice and delivery suit this role [Poliuto] very well. The baritone Giraldoni was also very good During the railway journey, composed without success on a new version of the *Chant du Pâtre*,[141] since the one I wrote a few days ago no longer pleases me.

Sunday 30 March. Worked with considerable success on the *Chant du Pâtre*. In the theater heard *Poliuto* for the second time. The act 2 finale, and the Dungeon Duet in the last act, are two beautiful pieces. On the whole *Poliuto*, in the Italian version at least, is not one of Donizetti's best works. *L'Étoile du Nord* has been produced in Nantes.

Monday 31 March. At 10:30 to Verona. At 3:45 by train to Venice. Arrived at 10:30. On the journey worked diligently on the *Chant du Pâtre* and the three-voice ensemble.[142]

April 1856

Tuesday 1 April. After breakfast, felt happily inspired, and finished composing the *Chant du Pâtre* and the three-voice ensemble. Worked for another two and a half hours before lunch and wrote out the whole of the three-voice movement. In the evening composed the *ventre des Intermède.*[143]

Wednesday 2 April. Composed for a while before breakfast. During the day, and in the evening, wrote out the *Chant des Pâtres* up to the last few bars. Went through the *tempi* of *Les Huguenots* with the orchestral director of the Fenice, Bossola [Busoni], since the opera is to be produced at the Fenice in the coming summer.

Thursday 3 April. Finished writing out the *Chant des Pâtres* (which I want to call *Villanelle*) and prepared it for instrumentation. Teatro San Samuele: Pacini's *Saffo.*[144] For the last twelve or fifteen years, this has been one of Italy's favorite operas. The production was so bad, that I cannot pass an opinion on the work. The orchestra and chorus were abysmal. The prima donna was Sanazzaro: no voice, no enunciation, no acting, sings inaccurately, and yet was much applauded. The first contralto was Boraldi, with little voice, who sings fairly accurately, but coldly. The tenor, Biendi, and the bass, Colombo, were both bad.

Friday 4 April. Worked on the link between the *Villanelle* and the three-voice ensemble, and finished writing it out. Teatro Apollo: Dondini's troupe of comedians, one of the best in Italy,[145] gave Goldoni's *Il bugiardo.*[146] I found the performance very mediocre. Went through the *tempi* of the last three acts of *Les Huguenots* with the orchestral director of the Fenice, Bossola [Bosoni]. For the first time in my life read through the New Testament (Luther's translation).

Saturday 5 April. Worked for one and a half hours before breakfast. Partially altered the body of the three-voice ensemble and prepared it for instrumentation. The entire intermezzo is now completed, including the entr'acte. Teatro San Samuele: Pacini's *Saffo.*

Sunday 6 April. Worked without success on the opera. Teatro San Benedetto: Verdi's *Nabucco.*

Monday 7 April. Worked on the last finale[147] both before and after breakfast, without much success. Also worked in the evening for an hour. Teatro Apollo, where

Dondini's comedy troupe gave *La forza dell'amore*, a drama by Bayard, a conventional French tearjerker.[148] Madame Cassola and Herr Salvini* are fine actors.

Tuesday 8 April. Worked for two hours before breakfast on the finale. Devised what I think is a lovely idea for the phrase "à l'ombre d'un noyer." Teatro San Samuele: Verdi's *Nabucco*.

Wednesday 9 April. In the morning made some alterations to the *canzonette* "Venezia," and worked on the duo-finale. Teatro Apollo: Pacini's *Saffo*.

Thursday 10 April. Began writing out the duo-finale, which I have finished composing up to the big *a due* in A-flat major. Worked on this for three to four hours. Dined with the Belgian prince d'Aremberg.[149] During the dinner, the so-called Compagnia dei Pittori sang their male-voice *canzonette* in several parts. These are fifteen *gondolieri* and workers from the Arsenal,[150] none of whom know a single note of music, all under the direction of a house painter of this district (who distinguishes himself as a *pittore*), who likewise does not know a note of music, and yet is the composer of all these songs. Among them are the most delightful, unusual, original *canzone*, quite unlike any other music, often crude and unpalatable. On the whole, though, for me it was a very interesting musical manifestation, rather like the Gypsy music that Count Nako arranged for me to hear in Vienna.

Friday 11 April. Wrote out the duo-finale for one and a quarter hours before breakfast, and for three hours afterward. In the Teatro Apollo I saw the Dondini acting troupe in *La Zaïra, tragedia di* Voltaire:[151] it was well performed throughout. Salvini was particularly outstanding as Orosman. His voice sounds like the loveliest music, is full of modulation, and capable of both extreme tenderness and the greatest power. Letter of invitation from the committee of the music festival in Düsseldorf.

Sunday 12 April. Worked for one hour before breakfast writing out the duo-finale. Improvised generally and wrote down a few things. Gondolier songs, floating up from the nearby Riva all evening, prevented me from working. *Le Prophète* has been performed in Reval for the first time, and successfully, under the title *Die Belagerung von Gent*.[152]

Sunday 13 April. Composed and wrote out the duo-finale for two and a half hours before breakfast. Afterward, I continued writing it out for another two and a half hours, but made little progress. Teatro San Samuele: Pacini's *Saffo*. After a break of many years, the *Feldlager* has been performed again in Berlin.

Monday 14 April. Worked for one hour before breakfast on the duo-finale. On account of the stormy weather, I did not go out, and worked very diligently. Margaridd's cabaletta "je venais, je respire" emerged from my improvisation, very happily I think. Did not work in the evening, only polished away at the new cabaletta. In the latest German opera season in Vienna, I am the most frequently performed composer. Of the one hundred seventy-three opera performances that took place there, forty-five were of my operas: *Nordstern* fifteen times, *Prophet* twelve times, *Hugenotten* eleven times, *Robert* seven times.

Tuesday 15 April. Wrote out the new cabaletta. Soirée at Princess Clary's, where a group of dilettantes performed Scribe's *Bataille de dames*—and very well too.[153]

Wednesday 16 April. In the Teatro Apollo: *Cuore e Arte*, drama in seven acts by Fortis, a Jewish writer from Padua.[154] This play is very popular in Italy at the moment. It is written in the Gutzkow mode, with many philosophical reflections in every role, animated dialogue, but no naturalness, no true dramatic life.[155] I saw only four and a half of the seven acts, since it had already passed midnight. *L'Étoile du Nord* has been performed with much success in Algiers.[156]

Thursday 17 April. Improvised happily, but did not work on the opera. In my improvisation a phrase emerged that will serve as the opening of the refrain "O madonne, douce et bonne" in the romance of Margaridd, part of her big scene.[157] In the evening I composed the full refrain, and could do no more because I was disturbed by a big serenade provided by the military bands for Field Marshal Wallmoden.[158]

Friday 18 April. Worked for three and a half hours, with success. I concerned myself for the first time with the romance, the refrain of which I composed yesterday. I finished composing it and wrote it down so as not to forget it, even if it is only a sketch. Teatro San Benedetto: the American circus riders and acrobats of the famous Miss Eller. They did not live up to the expectations of the public.

Saturday 19 April. Took up the romance again, altered many details, and fully wrote it out, with indications of the instrumentation. In the evening began writing down the *canzona* "Venezia" that I had composed earlier.

Sunday 20 April. Finished writing out the *canzonetta* "Venezia" in the two hours before breakfast. In the evening to the concert of Demoiselle Goddard, then began working on the abridgments in *Les Huguenots* for the Teatro La Fenice.

Monday 21 April. Spent the whole day making the cuts in *Les Huguenots*, writing them down, and translating the earlier observations about the *mise en scène* into Italian for Music Director Bosoni.

Tuesday 22 April. Wrote to Cavaliere Tornielli, president of the Teatro La Fenice,[159] and at the same time sent him the observations about the musical and scenic details for *Les Huguenots*. This took up one and a half hours before breakfast. Studied the abridgments and scenic arrangements for *Les Huguenots* with Bosoni, the musical director of La Fenice. In the Teatro Apollo: *Saul*, tragedy by Alfieri.[160] Before the performance, I read through this play, which contains many poetic beauties of a high order, in order the better to understand it. Salvini, in his acting, costumes, and declamation, was movingly beautiful as Saul. Indeed, it seems to me that Salvini is the greatest of all living tragedians.[161]

Wednesday 23 April. Composed the duo-finale to its *a due* conclusion in A-flat, and wrote it out. Composed a small piano piece for Demoiselle Goddard's album, and wrote it out. *Droits d'auteur* for March: 913 fr. 45 c.

Thursday 24 April. Finished composing the duo-finale up to the entry of the chorus, and wrote it out. Dress rehearsal of *L'Ebreo*, opera by Apolloni.[162] The singer Galetti has a lovely, mellow, wide-ranging soprano voice, naturalness and good delivery. She promises much for the future.

Friday 25 April. Wrote to the Comité des Association des Auteurs et Compositeurs Dramatiques: I sent my *démission*[163] as a member of the committee. Today is the Feast of St. Mark, patron saint of Venice.[164] In the Teatro San Benedetto: Apolloni's *L'Ebreo*, a complete imitation of Verdi, with everlasting trumpet flourishes accompanying the singers, but nonetheless a few lovely pieces.

Saturday 26 April. At 8:45 by train for Casarra, in order to begin my return to Berlin. We arrived there at 11:30, and I left for Laibach by so-called private express coach. In Görz I stopped for an hour to eat, and arrived at 10:30 in the evening at Wippach, where I stayed overnight. I tried to work on the *Chercheur*, but without success.

Sunday 27 April. Left Wippach at eight o'clock. Arrived in Laibach at six o'clock. I was not lucky in composition today. *Le Prophète* has been performed in Meiningen.

Monday 28 April. [Left] early, at 4:45, by train for Vienna. My excellent friend Dr. Bacher met me at the station. In the Burgtheater: *Ella Rosa, oder Die Rechte des Herzens*, a new drama by Gutzkow that is enjoying great currency in Germany.[165] Demoiselle Seebach, Herren Fichtner, and Wagner played the principal parts. *L'Étoile du Nord* has been produced in Verviers with great success.

Tuesday 29 April. Received many letters, including, unfortunately, very unpleasant news. Lumley is not going to produce the *Étoile* in his theater, while Gye is also neglecting it on account of the limited [stage] space.[166] The health of my dear friend Gouin, my staff and my protector in Paris, is deteriorating, and he is becoming weaker by the day. Burguis has obtained a position in Berlin that no longer allows him to function as my secretary. Called on the singer Medori, who has been engaged as of September by the Parisian Grand Opéra.[167] In the Italian Opera: a striking performance of *Don Juan*.

Wednesday 30 April. At 8:30 in the morning I started by rail to Berlin; the director Cornet was my traveling companion for part of the way. In the evening I began composing the act 3 recitatives. Letter from the Music Festival in Düsseldorf, with an invitation to attend.

May 1856

Thursday 1 May. In the Burgtheater: Schiller's *Kabale und Liebe*, a very good production.[168] Madame Bayer-Bürck from Dresden made a guest appearance as Lady Milford. Demoiselle Seebach pleased me for the first time today (as Luise).

Friday 2 May. In the Italian Opera: Rossini's *Mosè*. Angelini as Moses was very good.

Saturday 3 May. Since Medori, whom I wanted to hear in one of her better roles, was unwell yesterday and is singing only today, I had to postpone my departure for Berlin. Italian Opera: Verdi's *Ernani*. Medori did not fully live up to my expectations. Her higher register is extraordinarily strong and resonant, but not the lower. She has fire, but no correct execution, while her coloratura is curtailed and compromised. Her build is stocky, and she has an expressionless face, although she is not ugly. *L'Étoile du Nord* has been performed in Milan, but (according to Zezi's letter) does not appear to have pleased very much.[169]

Sunday 4 May. [Left] at seven o'clock in the morning by train from Vienna for Prague, where we arrived at eight in the evening. During the journey I had no inspiration for composition. The theater director, Stöger,[170] sent his secretary to me on the train to apologize that he could not give *Lohengrin* today. Dr. Bacher had telegraphed him that I wished to see this opera in Prague.[171]

Monday 5 May. Early at 8:15 by rail to Dresden, where we arrived at 2:30. Called on my cousin Sophie Brandenstein, and on Karl Kaskel. The former told me about a letter she had received from Jenny Lind, in which she wrote most hurtfully about me.

Tuesday 6 May. Departed by train for Berlin. May God bless my return. May he allow me to find my beloved wife and dear children well and contented, and let me have only good news. Arrived in Berlin at three o'clock. I found my dear ones well, except for my daughter Caecilie, who has still not recovered. There was also depressing news about the state of health of my dear friend Gouin.

Wednesday 7 May. Wrote to Gouin and Madame Célérier.[172] I begged him to allow me to rent a house with grounds in St. Germain to help in the restoration of his health.

Thursday 8 May. In the theater: Mozart's *Die Zauberflöte*. The Swedish singer Michal was the Queen of the Night. She is the same singer whom I heard years ago in Paris and tried to have engaged for the Parisian Opéra.[173] She has a small voice, a lovely high register, poor middle notes, fairly good coloratura, no animation, no acting.

Friday 9 May. Called on Count Redern. Answered Daniel's letter from Karlsruhe. I was deeply depressed by the Milanese *Gazzetta dei Teatri*, which gloats over the fiasco of *L'Étoile du Nord* in the colorful language.

Saturday 10 May. Letter from the Société des Auteurs et Compositeurs Dramatiques: they do not want to accept my resignation, and grant me any leave I need. Letter from Zezi in Milan indicating that in the following performances *L'Étoile du Nord* found a much better reception. Concert by the Gustav Adolf Society: Mendelssohn's *Elijah*. Visit from Kapellmeister Kücken from Stuttgart.

Sunday 11 May. Worked without success in the evening on the overture.

Monday 12 May. Worked on the overture without especial success.

Tuesday 13 May. Worked on the overture: found another, and I think better, second theme for the first part of the overture. Communications from Mazzucato and Philippi in Milan: the subsequent performances of *L'Étoile du Nord* were much more successful, but the papers have continued to judge the work very inimically.

Wednesday 14 May. Worked on the overture both before and after breakfast. With Count Redern, attended the rehearsal of the Domchor, where several of the count's compositions were sung, including an *Agnus Dei* that exerts a noble, beautiful effect. There I made the acquaintance of Quien, a director of church music from Baden, who has been sent here by his court in order to organize a similar choir for Karlsruhe. In *L'Armonia*, a Florentine musical journal issued by Guidi (the

Italian publisher of *L'Étoile du Nord*), there is an interesting article about all the efforts made in Milan to wreck the *Étoile*, and yet how the work has nonetheless succeeded in the subsequent performances. In the Schauspielhaus: *Narciss*, a tragedy by Brachvogel*: this has been very popular here and is well acted. It is about Rameau's nephew, Narciss, and his dealings with Madame de Pompadour.[174]

Thursday 15 May. My servant Karl, who has been with me four or five years, gave notice today, since he wishes to settle down.[175] This is very unpleasant for me, since I have grown accustomed to him. In the theater: Donizetti's *Der Liebestrank*. Demoiselle Bianchi sang Adina: a really vibrant soprano voice, especially in the higher register, innate fluency and feeling, but amateurish, inaccurate singing.[176]

Friday 16 May. The composer Münchheimer, from Warsaw, came to see me. Called on Herr von Humboldt and presented him with the photographs that the prince of Aremberg gave me in Venice. Humboldt had written to me earlier, gently chiding me for not having visited him since my return. Tried in vain to compose. Late in the evening I had a happy inspiration for the *buffo* duet[177] in act 2. *Droits d'auteur* for April: 965 fr. 80 c.

Saturday 17 May. Worked on the *buffo* duet. Returned to Grünbaum the two opera libretti that he had sent for my inspection: *Ein Tag in Russland* (after *La Lune de miel*) will be set by Dorn, and the *Todeslos* [The lottery of death] (after *La Courte Paille*) by Flotow.[178] Both are mediocre libretti, with little poetry in the verses. In the evening worked on the *buffo* duet.

Sunday 18 May. Worked only a little on the *buffo* duet. Schönlein examined the condition of my chest and lungs with a stethoscope, and found no internal disorder.

Monday 19 May. Worked on the *buffo* duet.

Tuesday 20 May. Finished composing the *buffo* duet. In the Opera House: Mozart's *Figaros Hochzeit*.

Wednesday 21 May. New resolutions to compose diligently. Wrote down the *buffo* duet for one hour before breakfast. Commercial transactions tired me a good deal, so that I could work for only one and a half hours in the evening. Therefore I did not fulfill my musical resolutions today. Letter from the secretary of the Royal Theater in Naples, inviting me to rehearse *Robert le Diable* there.

Thursday 22 May. Wrote out the *buffo* duet for one hour before breakfast. Visit from the music teacher Oswald; she wants to propagate a new system of music instruction that she has invented. Wrote the *buffo* duet for one hour. Dined with Count Redern. In the Opera House: Dorn's *Die Niebelungen*. Again did not fulfill my work resolutions.

Friday 23 May. Wrote out the *buffo* duet. Wrote to Perrin that I will be able to determine only at the end of August whether I can give him my comic opera. Opera House: Auber's *Der Feensee* [*Le Lac des fées*]. Worked for three and a half hours. Fulfilled my work resolutions most imperfectly.

Saturday 24 May. Finished writing out the *buffo* duet one hour before breakfast, and prepared it for instrumentation. At Count Redern's the military band played several of his own compositions, among which *Allemande* and *Elfenreizen* are really graceful and impressive pieces of music. Sitting of the senate of the Academy. There I paged through an anonymous aesthetic-musical brochure in which I am judged very unfavorably. Visit from the contrabassist Mehmel, from St. Petersburg, who told me that *L'Étoile du Nord* has had a fairly cold reception in St. Petersburg,[179] a situation he ascribes to the subject matter, in that the sight of a drunken Peter the Great has shocked[180] Russian patriotism. In all worked for only three and a half hours.

Sunday 25 May. Letter from the husband of the singer Medori in Vienna. Composed Corentin's *couplets*[181] for an hour before breakfast. Worked for one and a half hours on writing out the *couplets*. Opera House: Richard Wagner's *Tannhäuser*.[182]

Monday 26 May. Did not fulfill my work resolutions. Wrote out the *couplets* for one hour before breakfast, and for one and a half hours in the evening. Visits from the singer Parisotti, from the musician Hartmann.[183] Wrote to the singer Medori in Vienna, enclosing the act 4 romance from *Les Huguenots*.

Tuesday 27 May. Worked for an hour before breakfast on the *couplets*. Visit from Hermann Wichmann and from the violinist Laub*. In spite of the physical indisposition brought on by diarrhea, worked for nearly three hours on the *couplets*, finished writing them out, and prepared them for instrumentation.

Wednesday 28 May. Felt so exhausted that I could not work all day. Again returned the call of Lieutenant Baron Korff.[184]

Thursday 29 May. Count Redern came to see me about a possible Court Concert during the stay of the emperor of Russia.[185] Called on the singer Johanna Wagner. During the whole day I could not find any happy inspiration for the passage "De l'oiseau dans le bocage" in the trio, but in the evening it came.[186]

Friday 30 May. Diarrhea. Geheimrat Schönlein ordered me to stay in bed all day.

Saturday 31 May. Invitation from the committee of the Magdeburg music festival. Watched the big parade held in honor of the visiting emperor of Russia.[187] In the evening began composing the act 2 trio. Gala performance for the emperor of Russia: the overture and act 2 of my *Feldlager*, and the ballet *Paul und Virginie*, music by Gährich.[188]

June 1856

Sunday 1 June. Worked in the morning and evening on the trio for a couple of hours. To the theater, where they performed Schiller's *Wilhelm Tell*, in order to hear Bernhard Anselm Weber's music for the overture and Fisherman's Song, before returning home.[189]

Monday 2 June. Worked on the trio for half an hour before breakfast. Went through and corrected the Italian edition of the *Étoile*. Worked on the trio for two and a half hours in the evening.

Tuesday 3 June. Composed a little on the trio. Wrote a number of letters to princes and other authorities in my capacity as codirector of the Mozart Society.

Wednesday 4 June. Sent the music director Markull in Danzig the circulating newsletters of the Mozart Society.[190] Worked on the trio before and after breakfast for two hours, and in the evening for three hours.

Thursday 5 June. Composed and wrote out the trio for two and a half hours in the evening.

Friday 6 June. Composed and wrote out the trio for one hour before and two hours after breakfast. Visit from the Spanish singer Fortuni.[191] Wrote out the trio for an hour after lunch. In the Opera House: Mozart's *Don Juan*. Demoiselle Lehmann, from the German Theater in Amsterdam, was Donna Anna: only average.

Saturday 7 June. Composed and wrote out the trio for an hour before breakfast, then the singer Fortuni sang me several pieces from *Les Huguenots*, *L'Étoile du Nord,* and *Lucia*; brilliant coloratura, but a small head voice and cold delivery. Composed and wrote out the trio for only one hour in the evening.

Sunday 8 June. Conference with Intendant-General von Hülsen about the arrangements for a welfare institution for old actors. Composed and wrote out the trio for one hour before breakfast and for only an hour in the evening.

Monday 9 June. Today my beloved wife, Minna, and my two dear children, Caecilie and Cornelie, left for Aachen, where Caecilie will take the sulfurous waters.[192] May God grant them a safe journey; may the Almighty bless the cure with positive results. Visit from Rellstab. Composed and wrote out the trio. Attended a few acts of Goethe's *Faust*[193] in the theater. *L'Étoile du Nord* has been performed with great success in Montpellier.

Tuesday 10 June. Composed and wrote out the trio for two hours after breakfast. *La France musicale* has devoted two issues to what it calls the "fiasco" of *L'Étoile du Nord* in Milan. Composed and wrote out the trio for one and three-quarter hours in the evening. *L'Étoile du Nord* has been performed with great success in Geneva.[194]

Wednesday 11 June. Composed and wrote out the trio for an hour before breakfast. Worked for another two hours on the trio in the evening: finished composing this to within a few bars and also finished writing it out.

Thursday 12 June. Worked a little on the trio, and composed the conclusion. In the evening again began composing and writing out the overture.

Friday 13 June. Visit from the music publisher Dufour from Paris: he gave me the sad news that my dear, cherished friend Gouin has had another dangerous attack. This information so shook me that I was unable to work all day. Called on the Russian composer Glinka.[195]

Saturday 14 June. Worked a little on the overture. In the evening worked on the overture.

Sunday 15 June. Worked on the overture in the evening.

Monday 16 June. Worked on the overture. In the Schauspielhaus: *Der Goldschmied von Ulm*, a dramatic fairy tale in three acts by Mosenthal.[196] It is an adaptation of de la Motte Fouqué's novella *Das Galgenmännchen*.[197]

Tuesday 17 June. Today could eventually work on the overture only in the evening. *Le Prophète* has been produced in Livorno, with great success. The overture to *L'Étoile du Nord* has been performed at the Magdeburg Music Festival to great enthusiasm.

Wednesday 18 June. In the course of the morning, and in the evening, worked a little on the overture.

Thursday 19 June. In the Opera House the Spanish singer Fortuni sang several arias; then the ballet *Giselle*, music by Adam.[198]

Friday 20 June. In the Opera House heard the first two acts of *Tannhäuser*. Demoiselle Storck from the Brunswick Theater sang Elisabeth. Her upper register is resonant, but the middle and low notes are without tone; on the whole mediocre.[199] *Droits d'auteur* for the month of May: 505 fr. 60 c.

Saturday 21 June. In the evening worked a little on the overture.

Sunday 22 June. I have to compose a choral song for an album that the Berlin composers want to present to the daughter [Luise] of the princess of Prussia. Rellstab had produced two different texts for this purpose for me to choose from. I selected the "Brautreigen" and composed it in a couple of days, but I was not happy with what I had written. So today I looked at the second poem, "Holdes Liebespaar," and immediately felt so inspired by it that I wrote down the first strophe (for four male voices).[200]

Monday 23 June. Visit from the lieutenant of Dragoons, Baron Korff. Wrote the second strophe of the choral song (for four female voices). Employed a new servant (Franz Kaufmann), beginning on 1 September. In the evening worked on the third strophe of the choral song (which is going to be for four female voices).

Tuesday 24 June. Finished composing the third strophe of the choral song. In the evening completely revised and concluded the choral song.

Wednesday 25 June. Unfortunately, did not work at all.

Thursday 26 June. In the Viennese press there have been foolish and mendacious stories about my purported activities in Baden-Baden (where I have never been in years!). Worked for two hours on the overture, but without any success.

Friday 27 June. An article in *L'Assemblée nationale*, about Weber's *Pintos* (and presumably by Henri Blaze), makes unpleasant reference to me. Worked on the overture for an hour, but without success. For the last six days I have been stuck in the storm section of the overture and, having reached a certain point,

Example 3. Theme from the overture to *Le Pardon de Ploërmel*

cannot move further to the entry of the organ. In the same way, I have not been able to weave the theme of the chorus into the *cantabile* of the coda, something that I regard as necessary for the logic of the piece. This evening I was fortunate enough to find solutions to both problems.

Saturday 28 June. The proposal by Herr von Korff for the hand of my daughter, and the manner in which Blanca responded to this news, preoccupied me to such an extent that I was incapable of any musical work.

Sunday 29 June. In the evening worked only a little on the overture, because of a headache.

Monday 30 June. Called on Gubitz to thank him for his outstanding article on my beloved mother in *Die Vossische Zeitung* last year, and took him a portrait of my mother as a souvenir.[201] To Rellstab. Worked a little on the overture.

July 1856

Tuesday 1 July. Today I sent my beloved daughter Blanca, accompanied by Antoinette Montalban, by rail to Minna in Aachen. Called on Count Redern. Wrote to Zellner: promised him a song for his journal within the month; sent him a subscription of 100 gulden (for July until January 1857); refused to give him unpublished pieces of my music for his projected concert.

Wednesday 2 July. Worked a little on the overture, also in the evening. I finished writing out the overture.

Thursday 3 July. Revised the overture several times in the evening.

Friday 4 July. After dining, to the Odeon, where Wieprecht gave a concert for military band. I heard the introduction and chorus from act 3 of Wagner's *Lohengrin*, beautiful pieces,[202] and Liszt's *Vom Fels zum Meer*,[203] very lively music, not bad. My *Fackeltanz* no. 3 was also played, but I did not hear it. Alas, did not compose at all today.

Saturday 5 July. In the evening wrote a part of the *Chorlied* for the wedding of the young princess Luise of Prussia into the appropriate album.

Sunday 6 July. Copied my *Chorlied* into the album. Opera House: the ballet *Das hübsche Mädchen von Gent*, music by Adam.

Monday 7 July. Finished inscribing my *Chorlied* into the festive album, and took it to Kapellmeister Dorn, who is in change of the whole procedure. Visit from the poetess Elise Schmidt, who wants music from me for her recital of Greek drama.

Tuesday 8 July. [No entry.]

Wednesday 9 July. In the evening corrected the Italian vocal score of *L'Étoile du Nord*.

Thursday 10 July. To Herr von Herzberg, second director of the Domchor,[204] to play him the *Chorlied*, so that he can rehearse it with the choir. Wrote a long letter to Gemmy Brandus, which he is to show to the new director of the Opéra, Alphonse Royer.[205]

Friday 11 July. Worked on the *berceuse*.[206] To Gustav Vaëz, who has been sent expressly to Berlin by the new director of the Grand Opéra in Paris (Royer) to invite me to give my *Africaine*. In the evening worked on the *berceuse*.

Saturday 12 July. I hosted a small dinner for Herr Vaëz at Mäder's, because I do not want to give him a definite answer for the director of the Opéra. I also invited [Paul] Taglioni. It cost me fifteen thalers for three people.

Sunday 13 July. Dictated a long letter, ostensibly to Gemmy Brandus but actually for Perrin. Worked on the *berceuse* in the evening.

Monday 14 July. Worked on the *berceuse* in the evening.

Tuesday 15 July. Visits from Count Redern and from the Danish singer Fossum, who has been recommended by Kapellmeister Gläser.[207] She has a very beautiful voice, especially in the lower register, fluency, a trill, and much fire, but often bad comprehension; nonetheless a most remarkable manifestation.

Wednesday 16 July. Attended to my packing, and in the evening worked for two and a half hours on the *berceuse*. I finished writing it down, and began working on the preceding recitative.[208]

Thursday 17 July. Composed and wrote out the *ritornello* and the recitative that precede the *berceuse*. The piece is now completed. Departed for the water cure in Spa. In order not to meet my family in Aachen on a Friday, I left today only at 5:30 in the evening, and stayed overnight in Magdeburg.

Friday 18 July. Visited the famous Magdeburg Cathedral;[209] instead of relics, one sees Tilly's boots, his helmet, his sword, etc.;[210] then on the Prince's Wall, from which one has a lovely view of the River Elbe.[211] The Breiter Weg is the only pleasant street in this city. Departed by train at 10:30; we arrived in Cologne at 10:30 in the evening. Tried in vain to compose today. Visit from Wieprecht.

Saturday 19 July. At 8:15 to Aachen, where we arrived at eleven o'clock. I hurried to the Hôtel du Grand Monarque, where my beloved wife is living with my lovely children, in the interests of Caecilie's cure. Unfortunately I found, by all appearances, no improvement in her condition. In the afternoon the military band of the infantry regiment garrisoned in Aachen serenaded me, playing four of my compositions: (1) the overture to *L'Étoile du Nord*; (2) the Benediction of the Daggers from *Les Huguenots*; (3) the act 2 duet for Raoul and the Queen from *Les Huguenots*; (4) my *Fackeltanz* no.1 in B Major. In the evening the local choral society wanted to serenade me, but I asked them, through Minna's doctor who advised me thus, to refrain on account of my great tiredness, and instead went off to their usual meeting place. They sang extraordinarily well (with the finest nuancing), and have a solo tenor of the most wonderful mellowness. The singers greeted me, on my entry and departure, with fervent applause. Visit from the pianist Georg Aloys Schmitt from Frankfurt-am-Main, son of my old acquaintance Aloys Schmitt.[212]

Sunday 20 July. At 10:45 by train to Spa, where we arrived at 1. Letter from Madame Célérier: my dear, cherished friend Gouin is deteriorating all the time. *Droits d'auteur* for June: 1,041 fr. 70 c.

Monday 21 July. Having composed Hoël's romance in act 3 in two different versions, today I began a third version of this piece. In *Le Revue et gazette musicale* is a letter by Offenbach about comic opera that, to say the least, is not well disposed to me.[213] Furthermore, Castil-Blaze has again written a book in which he appears to attack me strongly, as I understand the analysis in *La Gazette des théâtres*.[214] Annoyance and insults continue to pull me down.

Tuesday 22 July. Letter from Gemmy Brandus: Fould does not want to sanction the début of Borghi-Mamo.[215] Tried to work on Hoël's romance for a couple of hours, but without any results. In the evening began writing the vocal line of the romance into the full score.

Wednesday 23 July. Finished writing the vocal line of the romance into the full score. Wrote to Gemmy Brandus about *Emma di Resburgo* and Borghi-Mamo.

Thursday 24 July. Worked on Hoël's romance.

Friday 25 July. In the evening again began composing a new version of Hoël's romance.

Saturday 26 July. In the evening wrote out the greater portion of Hoël's romance.

Sunday 27 July. Finished composing and writing out the romance, and prepared it for instrumentation. In the evening composed a new prelude to Hoël's romance.

Monday 28 July. In the evening continued preparing Hoël's romance for instrumentation.

Tuesday 29 July. Letter from the music dealer Hellberg in Stuttgart: invitation to provide contributions to the new periodical *Das Pianoforte*. Letter from the singer Borghi-Mamo in Paris. Did not work in the evening: the long afternoon walks and donkey rides tire me too much.

Thursday 31 July. Count Wielhorsky had the local orchestra perform several highly interesting and effective pieces by Glinka: a fantasy on Russian folk songs, *Kamarinskaya*,[216] and a mazurka and a polonaise.[217] In the evening to a small soirée at Count Wielhorsky's, where he played several cello pieces by Romberg very pleasantly.[218]

August 1856

Friday 1 August. In the evening read through all the sketches of my opera *Le Chercheur*.

Saturday 2 August. Composed a little of Margaridd's aria. In the evening wrote the vocal line of Hoël's romance into the full score, and began scoring it.

Sunday 3 August. In the evening scored the romance for a while.

Monday 4 August. In the morning scored the romance for a while. Colic made it impossible for me to work. A very interesting book called *L'Oiseau*, by [Jules] Michelet*, contains descriptions of the lives and habits of all types of birds, and is as poetic as it is instructive.[219]

Tuesday 5 August. For the first time in many years I read through the vocal score of my old opera *Emma di Resburgo*.[220]

Wednesday 6 August. Scored the romance in the morning.

Thursday 7 August. Today I finished scoring Hoël's romance. In the evening I began to score the *berceuse* a little.

Caricature of Meyerbeer taking one of his famous donkey rides during his summer sojourns in Spa (mid-1850s). Etching by G. Gernay. (From Albin Body, *Meyerbeer aux eaux de Spa* [Brussels, 1885].)

Friday 8 August. News that my beloved wife and the dear children have arrived at the waters in Heinrichsbad in the Swiss canton of Appenzell,[221] where Caecelie is to take the whey cure.[222]

Saturday 9 August. Scored the *berceuse* in the evening.

Sunday 10 August. Scored the *berceuse* for two hours in the morning and for two hours in the evening.

Monday 11 August. Finished scoring the *berceuse* and the preceding recitative.

Tuesday 12 August. Revised the orchestration of the *berceuse*. In the evening, from 8 until 10:30, began writing the vocal part of Hoël's big act 1 aria into the full score: two and a half sheets.

Wednesday 13 August. Finished writing the vocal line of Hoël's aria into the full score. Concert by the singer van der Maessen:[223] weak, sharp voice, inaccurate singing. Wrote three autographs for Count Wielhorsky's daughter, Madame Wanewitino.[224] Once more enjoyed reading Goethe's *Wilhelm Meister*.[225]

Thursday 14 August. In the evening scored four sides of Hoël's aria (two and a half hours).

Friday 15 August. Scored Hoël's aria both in the morning and in afternoon: seven pages.

Saturday 16 August. Called on Fétis. Letter from Dr. Bacher: he tells me that Madame Medori has unfortunately had no success as Valentine at La Fenice in Venice. The opera has obviously suffered because of the bad winter production in the Teatro Apollo, which robbed it of any credibility in Venice.[226] Captain Deppe arranged a performance of Hummel's Military Septet,[227] a very attractive, interesting, and extremely melodious piece of music, which I heard for the first time. In the evening scored three sides of Hoël's aria.

Sunday 17 August. Scored three sides of Hoël's aria in the morning, and another three in the evening.

Monday 18 August. Called on Fétis. In the evening finished scoring and revising Hoël's aria.

Tuesday 19 August. In both the morning and evening I entered eleven pages of the vocal parts of the act 1 *buffo* duet, for Hoël and Corentin, into the full score, and also worked on changes to this duet. The director of the Opéra Comique, Émile Perrin, has come to Spa expressly to inquire about my new comic opera. I told him that I will be able decide whether I can give my new opera this winter only after 15 October. This in turn depends on Caecilie's health, and whether she must spend the winter in a southern clime.

Wednesday 20 August. From 11:30 until 3 worked on changes in the *buffo* duet, and wrote the vocal parts into the full score. In the evening nearly completed writing the vocal parts of the *buffo* duet into the full score.

Thursday 21 August. Incapable of any activity.

Friday 22 August. Preparations for departure.

Saturday 23 August. Antoinette Montalban has come to visit Spa in order to discuss Korff's proposal.

Sunday 24 August. At 10:30 I left by train for Paris, where we arrived at 9:05 in the evening. Again to the Hôtel du Danube, rue Robespierre 11. May God bless my return to Paris, and grant success to the purpose of my being here—to help Borghi-Mamo learn the role of Fidès.

Monday 25 August. To my old friend Gouin, whom I found in bed but in good spirits. Called on the director of the Opéra, Alphonse Royer, and on Dufour. In the Opéra Comique: *Manon Lescaut*[228] Auber's music is still full of freshness and invention, melodious and witty, in spite of his advanced age. This opera afforded me much pleasure.

Tuesday 26 August. Went through the role of Fidès with Madame Borghi-Mamo, who is to make her début in this part. Opéra Comique: Grétry's *Richard Cœur de Lion*.[229] The new tenor Barbi sang Blondel stylishly, but has a mediocre voice.

Wednesday 27 August. Visit from the director of the Grand Opéra, Alphonse Royer, and Gustav Vaëz. I promised that, if I like Medori and Borghi-Mamo, I will start rehearsals of *L'Africaine* in July next year. To the Opéra Comique, where I heard *Manon Lescaut* for the second time.

Thursday 28 August. Held a piano rehearsal of *Le Prophète* in the Opéra. To Scribe. Conference with Perrin. Opéra Comique: Grétry's *Le Tableau parlant*,[230] Auber's *L'Ambassadrice*.

Friday 29 August. In the Grand Opéra: Rossini's *Guillaume Tell*.

Saturday 30 August. Improvised musically and wrote down a small piece. Opéra Comique: Grisar's *Les Porcherons;*[231] there are some pretty pieces in act 3, but otherwise it is insignificant.

Sunday 31 August. Conference with the poet Michel Carré. Called on Dr. Bamberg, together with 500 fr. Opéra Comique: *Manon Lescaut.*

September 1856

Monday 1 September. Rehearsal of *Le Prophète.* In the Grand Opéra: *Les Elfes*, a new ballet by Saint-Georges, music by Count Gabrielli.[232] This is a bad work with very ordinary music.[233] The new dancer Demoiselle Ferraris, an Italian, is very popular; she dances brilliantly, but has no musical talent.[234]

Tuesday 2 September. Called on Jules Lecomte, Pillet-Will, Berlioz. In the evening a rehearsal on stage.

Wednesday 3 September. Called on Girardin, Auber, Halévy. Dined with Véron.

Thursday 4 September. Letter from the musician Böhmer in Erfurt.[235] Théâtre Lyrique: Clapisson's *Fanchonette*,[236] this year's biggest success. It has a pretty libretto, and the music has much that is piquant and effective. Madame Miolan excels as a coloratura singer in this role, and also acts very charmingly.

Friday 5 September. Today Brandus paid the fourth of the eight parts of his debt, 3,375 fr. My birthday. May God bless this new year of my life. May he mercifully restore health to my beloved daughter Caecilie, and preserve her; may he grant an outstanding husband to my daughter Blanca who will make her happy all her life long; and may he restore good health to my beloved wife, Minna, and maintain her and my three darling children, Blanca, Caecilie, and Cornelie, in joy, health, virtue and contentment for a hundred years. Amen. May it be so. May God preserve my health and the prosperity with which he has blessed me in his mercy; may he grant me vivid musical inspirations and a brilliant, enduring success throughout the whole world for the new comic opera on which I am currently working.

Renewed resolution not to allow a day to go by without some kind of musical activity.

Studied the role of Catherine in *L'Étoile du Nord* with Madame Cabel. In the evening put in order the changes that I myself have made in the *Chercheur*, in order to present them to the librettists. *L'Étoile du Nord* has been performed to great enthusiasm at Cette (France),[237] as has *Robert* in Bergamo.

Saturday 6 September. Stage rehearsal of *Le Prophète*. Went through all the changes I myself have made in the *Chercheur* with the poet Carré.

Sunday 7 September. Conference with Scribe about *L'Africaine*. In the evening read through *L'Africaine* in order to be completely *au fait* with it.

Monday 8 September. In the evening to the Théâtre de la Porte-Saint-Martin for *Le Fils de la nuit*, a new melodrama by Séjour.[238] I went to see this solely because of the décor: a ship on the open sea, which is remarkably constructed and makes formal maneuvers. I did this because *L'Africaine* also has a ship scene.

Tuesday 9 September. Mise en scène rehearsal of *Le Prophète*. I hosted a dinner in the Café de Paris for eight people, which cost me 300 fr. The guests were Édouard Bertin, Vitet, Cousin, Janin, Berlioz, John Lemoine, Vicomte Daru. Afterwards in the Théâtre Lyrique I saw act 2 and part of act 3 of Clapisson's *Fanchonette*.

Wednesday 10 September. Visit from Lumley.

Thursday 11 September. Stage rehearsal of *Le Prophète*. Théâtre Lyrique: Clapisson's *Fanchonette*.

Friday 12 September. Sitting of the Comité des Auteurs et Compositeurs Dramatiques. In the evening read through the altered manuscript of the *Chercheur*. Corrected the copy of my *canzonetta* "A Venezia."

Saturday 13 September. Conference with the poet Carré about the *Chercheur*. In the evening to the Opéra for a complete dress rehearsal of *Le Prophète*. Borghi-Mamo sings the role of Fidès very beautifully, and also acts really well.

Sunday 14 September. Rehearsed the role of Catherine with Madame Cabel. Heard an act of *Manon Lescaut*.

Monday 15 September. On account of the indisposition of Poinsot, the reprise of *Le Prophète* could not take place today.[239] Letter from Bock, who wants to publish my new choral piece "Brautgesang." Bouffes-Parisiens: *La Rose de Saint-Flour*, with lovely music by Offenbach;[240] also Adam's *Les Pantins de Violette*.[241]

Tuesday 16 September. Opéra Comique: Hérold's *Zampa*.

Wednesday 17 September. Farewell visits to Borghi-Mamo and Véron. Bade goodbye to my dear, true friend Gouin with deep sorrow. His strength is ebbing away ever more, and I will not see him again on this earth. In the Opéra: the début of Borghi-Mamo as Fidès in *Le Prophète*. The success was not as great as I had expected from the rehearsals. Opinions were divided: many found her cold and her singing uneven. She has impressed me as a great artist, and the restraint of effect in singing and acting that makes her seem reserved to the French seems beneficial to me. Only after two or three performances will one be able to judge whether or not she has broken through to them.

Thursday 18 September. At nine o'clock I left by train for Cologne. Arrived at 9:30 in the evening.

Friday 19 September. At 6:30 I left for Berlin by train, but slept at Potsdam, since I did not want to arrive in Berlin on a Friday.

Saturday 20 September. Immediately upon my arrival in Berlin, I went to Count Redern. The program for the Court Concert had already been arranged by Herr von Hülsen, since both Count Redern and I arrived back in Berlin so late. I altered it slightly, because I will direct only the first part; Taubert has composed a *Festival Overture* for the second part, which one must reasonably let him conduct. Furthermore, a chorus from Wagner's *Lohengrin* will be performed, and I do not want to touch it. To the rehearsal of the Domchor, where they tried the new *Chorlied* that I have composed for the album of the young princess Luise of Prussia. It makes a really charming, gentle impression, but will, however, not be publicly performed, since, as Count Redern said, there are no free days left to the princess before her departure when the choir could be assembled. I was invited to the betrothal celebrations, but could not participate in the court festivities in the evening because of colic.

Sunday 21 September. To Count Redern, Herr von Humboldt, the singer Johanna Wagner. Went through the pieces of music that I am to conduct at the Court Concert.

Monday 22 September. To Count Redern. To the duke of Gotha to discuss his overture to *Zaire*, which I am to conduct at the Court Concert. To Herr von Humboldt. Orchestral rehearsal of the Court Concert. The orchestra received me with great applause and a flourish.

Tuesday 23 September. Studied the overture to *Santa Chiara* by the duke of Gotha, which I am now to conduct at the Court Concert instead of *Zaire*. Orchestral rehearsal. In the evening the Court Concert: I conducted the first part. The king came to me and said many friendly things about my return. The grand duke of Weimar and all the princes also came over to chat with me.

Wednesday 24 September. Today my acquaintance of many years, Hofrat Winkler, died at an advanced old age. As a writer he was known under the name of Theodor Hell.[242] In the Opera House: Spontini's *Ferdinand Cortez.* Demoiselle Storck from Brunswick was Amazili; she is very mediocre, if more effective in the broad passages, but even here she has a nasal quality. Herr Hoffmann, a newly engaged member of the company, was Cortez: good acting, good intonation, but the voice is worn and very baritonal.

Thursday 25 September. Began to prepare the *buffo* duet in act 1 for instrumentation, and scored a side. In the evening scored another three pages.

Friday 26 September. Scored the *buffo* duet for a while. Attended the rehearsals of a choral concert in the Singakademie. In the evening corrected the act 1 finale in the Italian edition of *L'Étoile du Nord*, expressly for the Schlesinger edition.

Saturday 27 September. Choral concert by the Singakademie: a sixteen-part Mass by Fasch.

Sunday 28 September. Scored a little of the *buffo* duet. Heard the first two acts of *Ferdinand Cortez.*

Monday 29 September. At Count Redern's, heard the different military marches competing for the prize advertised by Schlesinger. I am one of the adjudicators. Scored a little of the *buffo* duet. Heard the first two acts of Dorn's *Die Niebelungen.*

Tuesday 30 September. Improvised a little, but without any success. Friedrich-Wilhelmstädtisches-Theater: Gutzkow's *Der Königsleutnant.*[243] Herr Haase from Frankfurt-am-Main, who enjoys a certain reputation in Germany, played the King's Lieutenant.[244]

October 1856

Wednesday 1 October. In the evening began to compose a little of the duet for Margaridd and Corentin.[245]

Thursday 2 October. In the Opera House: Gläser's *Des Adlers Horst.* One's general mood does have an effect on any capacity to appreciate music. When I last heard this opera, it left me quite cold, with the exception of two numbers.[246] Today it struck me as thoroughly good throughout.

Friday 3 October. According to letters from Madame Célérier[247] and Louis Brandus, Madame Cabel has had great success as Catherine in *L'Étoile du Nord.*

Called on Professor Gubitz to thank him for his friendly mention of my blessed brother Michael's *Klytämnestra*[248] in his article on Tempeltey's play of the same name that appeared today.[249]

Saturday 4 October. In the evening an examination in the Stern Conservatory. Demoiselle Jenny Meyer, a sister-in-law of Stern, has a very beautiful, wide-ranging voice.[250]

Sunday 5 October. Letter from Breitkopf & Härtel: they want the publishing rights for my two new operas. In the Opera House: *Der Prophet.* The new tenor from Danzig, Hoffmann, was the Prophet, generally very good, bad in parts, but in any case better than Pfister. Demoiselle Wagner (Fidès) very good; Demoiselle Trietsch (Berthe) much better than before. Many curtain calls.

Monday 6 October. In the evening corrected the Italian *Étoile.*

Tuesday 7 October. In the Singakademie: fragments of the great Mass [in B minor] by Sebastian Bach.

Wednesday 8 October. I had the singer Jenny Bauer perform for Count Redern, with an eye to the Court Concert. Friedrich-Wilhelmstädtisches-Theater: *Die beiden Klingsberge,* comedy by Kotzebue;[251] *Ein Arzt,* comedy in one act from the French.[252] In the first play, Herr Haase played the old Klingsberg, in the second an Englishman; both roles were most inventively acted.

Thursday 9 October. Conference with the husband of the singer Bürde-Ney. In the Opera House: Gluck's *Orpheus.* The opera impressed me today more than ever, especially in passages that had previously left me cold, like Eurydice's aria in act 3 and the duet for Orpheus and Eurydice,[253] and in the second part of act 2, the scene in the Elysian Fields.[254]

Friday 10 October. Königstädter-Theater: *Der Aktienbudiker,* a local farce by Kalisch;[255] it has had great success for several months without, I think, deserving it.

Saturday 11 October. Letter from the Academy of Arts in Florence, indicating my nomination as a foreign member. Rehearsal by the Domchor of my "Brautgeleite," which is to be sung in the next Court Concert.

Sunday 12 October. Today my beloved wife, Minna, and my three dear children · arrived back in Berlin from their water cure.

Monday 13 October. L'Étoile du Nord has been performed with success at the

Italian Theater in New York; Madame Lagrange sang Catherine.[256] I have learned by telegram from Louis Brandus in Paris that my dear friend Gouin died early today, aged seventy-six. For twenty-five years he was a true, kind, sincere friend, my staff and my protector in all my artistic activities in Paris. His death is an irreplaceable loss for me.

Tuesday 14 October. I hosted a small dinner for the brothers Davison from London.[257]

Wednesday 15 October. To Davison: took him to the open sitting of the Academy of Arts, which was held to mark the birthday of the king today. A new *Hymne* by the music director August Wilhelm Bach was performed there, worthily conceived, but dry and without invention. With both Davisons to the Opera, to Mozart's *Titus*.[258] The trio in act 1 for Vitellia, Sextus and Publius,[259] the act 1 finale,[260] the chorus at the beginning of act 2, with the intercalated song of Titus,[261] and the two big arias of Vitellia and Sextus[262] are glorious, immortal pieces. The rest has aged a little.[263] Madame Köster was outstanding as Vitellia, but not as good as usual. Demoiselle Wagner sang Sextus.

Thursday 16 October. With Davison to Liebig's* symphony concert: they performed, among other things, Sterndale Bennett's* overture *The Bayadères*, a refined, elegant composition in the style of Mendelssohn.[264]

Friday 17 October. The first evening visit by Lieutenant Korff, who is courting Blanca.

Saturday 18 October. [No entry.]

Sunday 19 October. Correction of the "Brautgeleite." To the Opera with Davison: Auber's *Des Teufels Anteil* [*Le Part du Diable*].

Monday 20 October. Guest appearance in the Opera House of the famous Italian *tragédienne*, Madame Ristori, who performed (in Italian) with an Italian troupe: *Medea*, tragedy by Legouvé,[265] translated by Montanelli.[266]

Tuesday 21 October. Attended a Liebig Concert in the Tonhalle: Beethoven's Symphony [No.7] in A Major.

Wednesday 22 October. In the Opera: *Tannhäuser*.

Thursday 23 October. With Davison to the symphony-soirée: (1) Beethoven's overture *Weihe des Hauses;*[267] (2) Mendelssohn's Symphony [no. 4] in A Major;[268] (3)

Beethoven's Symphony [no. 8] in F Major. Wrote to Perrin that I cannot come to Paris to give him my new opera. *Droits d'auteur* for the month of September: 629 fr. 55 c.

Friday 24 October. Visits from the composer [Anton] Rubinstein, from the *chef d'orchestre* Pasdeloup*. To Davison, to Bock, and took from the latter the scores of my *Fackeltänze* for dispatch to Pasdeloup.

Saturday 25 October. Performance by the Italian acting company with Madame Ristori. They gave *Francesca da Rimini, tragedia di* Silvio Pellico,[269] and *I gelosi fortunati*, a small comedy by Giraud.[270]

Sunday 26 October. Today Josephy was buried. He was the leading figure of the *Spenersche Zeitung*, and for the last twenty-five years a sincere friend to my late, blessed mother, to my late, blessed brother Wilhelm, and to me as well. His attitude to me in his newspaper was always friendly, and often very helpful. His death is a real loss for me. Peace to his ashes.[271] Rubinstein played me the first part of his oratorio *Das verlorene Paradies*.[272] In the evening composed without success.

Monday 27 October. Visit from Stadtrat Friboes from Breslau, who wants to produce *L'Étoile du Nord* there. With Davison to the theater: *Essex*, a new tragedy by Laube, which is being widely performed in Germany.[273] *L'Étoile du Nord* has been produced in Rouen with success.

Tuesday 28 October. In the afternoon to the Singakademie, where I heard a rehearsal of Sebastian Bach's Mass in B Minor.[274] In the evening I was so tired that I could not work.

Wednesday 29 October. Italian production: *Pia de' Tolomei*, a *tragedia* by Cava.[275] Madame Ristori played Pia.

Thursday 30 October. In a concert of the Singakademie heard Sebastian Bach's Mass in B Minor for the first time: what a gigantic work! Rubinstein played me the second part of his oratorio *Das verlorene Paradies*.

Friday 31 October. I gave my consent to the engagement of my daughter Blanca to Lieutenant von Korff.

November 1856

Saturday 1 November. To Count Redern, who played me his composition for the ballet *Der Sturm*; then with him to an orchestral rehearsal in order to hear his

Elfenreigen. Symphony-soirée: (1) Schumann's overture *Genoveva*; (2) Mozart's Symphony [no. 40] in G Minor; (3) Beethoven's Symphony [no. 2] in D Major.

Sunday 2 November. In the Opera: *Tannhäuser.*

Monday 3 November. Studied the role of Isabelle [in *Robert le Diable*] with Madame Köster. In the Opera House: Bellini's *Die Nachtwandlerin.* Demoiselle Mandel, a young Jewish singer, sang Amina. The voice is brilliant in the upper register, but the middle and lower are weak; coloratura and trills are good, her vocal training and style, though, are bad.

Tuesday 4 November. In the evening to the Sternscher Musikverein where, before an invited audience, there was a musical commemoration for Felix Mendelssohn. They performed his *Psalm 95*[276] and *Die Walpurgisnacht*,[277] in my opinion two of Mendelssohn's weakest works, but then also his Violin Concerto,[278] a wonderfully beautiful composition, played outstandingly well by Laub.

Wednesday 5 November. Studied the role of Alice [in *Robert le Diable*] with Demoiselle Jenny Bauer. Stayed at home in the evening, but did not compose.

Thursday 6 November. Called on Rellstab: took him six friedrichs d'or as honorarium for his two poems "Brautgeleite aus der Heimat" and "An Mozarts Mauer." To a Liebig concert: (1) Beethoven's overture *Coriolan;* (2) Haydn's Symphony in D Major 3/4,[279] one of his weakest works; (3) Mendelssohn's overture *Die Hebriden*[280] (I have never been able to find coherence and a leading principal idea in this composition, in spite of its lovely moments); (4) Mozart's *Jupiter* Symphony in C Major.

Friday 7 November. Worked on the *Chercheur*, without particular success. In the Opera House: *Robert der Teufel.* Demoiselle Jenny Bauer sang Alice: the voice resonant, but weak for a big opera house; coupled with many treasurable qualities (as both singer and actress) are far too many overall immaturities and inaccuracies for her to be altogether satisfying. All the others—Pfister, Salomon, Madame Tuczek—were weak. On the whole, it was a very poor production. Even the public was not as numerous as usual at my operas.

Saturday 8 November. Liszt sent me his *Symphonische Dichtungen* through Herr von Bülow, but I was not at home when he called.[281] Worked without success. Soirée at the Portuguese ambassador, Baron de Santa Guiterie's, where the eleven-year-old pianist Arthur Napoleon played; he has great talent.[282]

Sunday 9 November. [No entry.]

Monday 10 November. Worked for two and a half hours preparing the overture for orchestration. Visit from the writer Schucht. Bock has suggested that he write an article on my musical style for his (Bock's) music journal. He asked for a loan of fifteen thalers, which I gave him.[283]

Tuesday 11 November. Quartet-soirée by the four sons of the concert master Müller from Brunswick: (1) Mendelssohn's Quintet in B-flat Major *(œuvre posthume)*.[284] (The first three movements, most especially a slow minuet with a rococo theme, contain great beauties; the finale is less successful.) (2) Beethoven's Quintet in C Major;[285] (3) Haydn's Quartet in D Major, with a wonderfully beautiful finale that is both brilliant and intricate.[286]

Wednesday 12 November. [No entry.]

Thursday 13 November. Prepared the overture for orchestration. Visit from the French quartet players Morin, Chevillard, etc.[287] Symphony-soirée: (1) Haydn's Symphony in D 6/8; this is not the one in D 3/4 that I heard recently at Liebig's,[288] but the one with the totally charming *andante [The Clock]*;[289] (2) Ehlert's overture to *Das Wintermärchen*; (3) Mendelssohn's overture *Ruy Blas*; (4) Beethoven's Symphony [no. 4] in B-flat.[290]

Friday 14 November. Visits from Kapellmeister Bott from Cassel,[291] from Wieprecht. Quartet-soirée by the Brothers Müller: (1) Mozart's Quartet [no. 19] in C Major;[292] (2) Schubert's Quintet in C Major with two violoncelli.[293] (I heard this work for the first time. It appears to me that his quartet with the variations is a better structured work, with a more unifying organization;[294] but this quintet nonetheless contains great beauties.) (3) Beethoven's Quartet [no. 14] in C-sharp Minor.[295] The introduction *(adagio),* the *allegro* and the *andante*, which together form an unbroken movement, still remain incomprehensible to me. I cannot find the leading thread, or grasp the organic structuring. The scherzo, on the other hand, delights me, a masterpiece of invention, humor, and beautiful control.

Saturday 15 November. With Count Redern to the Domchor to hear his new composition. Concert by the Sternscher Gesangverein: (1) Robert Schumann's Symphony [no. 3] in E-flat;[296] (2) Beethoven's Piano Concerto [no. 5] in E-flat,[297] played by von Bülow; (3) Franz Schubert's *Psalm 23* ("Gott ist mein Hirt") for female choir and orchestra;[298] (4) Mozart's *Ave Verum;*[299] (5) Mendelssohn's overture *Die schöne Melusine.*

Sunday 16 November. Matinée musicale at Bock's. The famous and totally outstanding Parisian string quartet of Chevillard, Morin, etc. played one of Beethoven's last quartets (the one in A Minor),[300] then the very brilliant one in C Major.[301]

Monday 17 November. [No entry.]

Tuesday 18 November. Coughing. I did absolutely nothing, and stayed at home all day.

Wednesday 19 November. Rehearsal in the morning for today's Court Concert: (1) a string quartet by the young Müller brothers (Haydn); (2) duet *Königin von Cypern* (Halévy);[302] (3) an eight-voice motet *Nunc Dimittis* (Count Redern), sung by the Domchor; (4) aria *Iphigenia in Tauris* (Gluck), Madame Bürde-Ney and chorus;[303] (5) duet *Huguenots* (Meyerbeer) sung by Bürde and Salomon;[304] (6) piano piece by Arthur Napoleon; (7) songs sung by Formes; (8) the choral song "Brautgeleite," which I composed for the marriage of the grand duke of Baden with our princess Luise of Prussia, sung by the Domchor; (9) a waltz by Venzano*, sung by Madame Bürde-Ney.[305] The king, the queen, and the queen of the Netherlands spoke to me in the friendliest way after the first part. As neither of my pieces had been performed at that stage, I do not know whether or not my new song pleased the king.

Thursday 20 November. In the evening began the instrumentation of the overture, but managed only a side.

Friday 21 November. In the evening again scored a little of the overture.

Saturday 22 November. Wrote to Zellner in Vienna, enclosing the manuscript of the song "Der Fischer."

Sunday 23 November. Coughing. Again I did not work much today, and scored only a side of the overture.

Monday 24 November. In the evening to the Opera for the last two acts of *Tannhäuser.*

Tuesday 25 November. Did not work. In the evening, with my daughter Caecilie, to the Friedrich-Wilhelmstädtisches-Theater to see Emil Devrient's guest appearance in Beaumont and Fletcher's *Stille Wasser sind tief,*[306] and Maltitz's* *Die Leibrente.*[307]

Wednesday 26 November. Today I decided, quite definitely, on the manner in which I will score the *Marcia religiosa* in the overture. To the Opera: Gluck's *Iphigenie in Tauris.* In the theater I spoke with the Russian composer Glinka.

Friday 28 November. Today again worked seriously, for the first time in a long while, for about four hours. Scored four sides of the overture.

Saturday 29 November. At Count Redern's request, I accompanied the French string quartet Chevillard to a rehearsal of the Domchor. They sang: (1) a *Sanctus* by Palestrina;[308] (2) a *Miserere* by Orlando di Lasso;[309] (3) *Vere languores* by Lotti, very beautiful;[310] (4) *Christus factus est* by Fioravanti, very interesting;[311] (5) a chorale, *Ich lug in tiefe Todesangst,* by Eccard*, songlike, gently melodious;[312] (6) the motet *Nun habe ich überwunden* by Michael Bach, lovely and intimate;[313] (7) an *Ave Maria* by Mendelssohn, for tenor and chorus, a beautiful, interesting piece of music.[314]

Monday 30 November. [No entry.]

December 1856

Monday 1 December. Did nothing.

Tuesday 2 December. Dined at Prince Karl's. The prince, the princess, Field Marshal Wrangel, and many others congratulated me in the friendliest way on the betrothal of my daughter Blanca with Korff. With my daughter to a session of the outstanding French string quartet of Morin, Chevillard, etc.: (1) Beethoven's Quartet [no. 13] in B-flat Major, op. 130; (2) Mozart's Quartet in D Major (dedicated to Friedrich Wilhelm II), a divine tone painting of great clarity, characterized by melodic sensuousness and masterly control;[315] (3) Beethoven's Quartet [no. 7] in F Major, op. 59 [no. 1].[316]

Wednesday 3 December. Renewed resolutions to diligence. Scored the overture for two hours before breakfast, and again for two heavy hours after lunch.

Thursday 4 December. Worked for five hours on the revision of those sections of the overture that have already been scored.

Friday 5 December. Worked on the overture for five hours.

Saturday 6 December. L'Étoile du Nord has been produced in Riga; the first two acts apparently did not appeal, but the last one very much so. Worked for three hours. Attended a concert of the Domchor, with old Korff.[317]

Sunday 7 December. Scored the overture for an hour before, and an hour after, breakfast. In the evening worked from 6:30 to 10:30 on setting a lithographed motto to music, conceived as a *terzettino* in canon, and developed for three voices. I want to send it to Holtei in Graz as a musical contribution for an album that he is publishing to help establish a Protestant churchyard.

Monday 8 December. Revised the canonic "Motto," which I composed yesterday. Spent a part of the morning, and the whole evening, on writing out this canon for three voices, together with its piano accompaniment. Wrote to Holtei. Corrected the German version of "Venezia" (which will be published by Schloss in Cologne).

Tuesday 9 December. Worked only a little on the overture. Concert by [Friedrich Wilhelm] Tschirch: (1) Méhul's overture *Adrien;*[318] (2) Mozart's Piano Sonatas in B-flat and F,[319] orchestrated by Streit; (3) Norman March and aria from the opera *Frithjof* by the late Ernst Tschirch.[320]

Wednesday 10 December. Scored five pages of the overture in all; worked for six hours.

Thursday 11 December. Scored the overture for three-quarters of an hour before, and for two hours after, breakfast. Symphony-soirée: (1) Spohr's Symphony in C Minor;[321] (2) Beethoven's Symphony No.1 [in C Major]; (3) Beethoven's overture *Egmont*; (4) Weber's overture *Euryanthe.*

Friday 12 December. Worked on the instrumentation of the overture for an hour before, and two hours after, breakfast, then again for three and a half hours in the evening.

Saturday 13 December. Scored the overture for three-quarters of an hour before breakfast and one hour after, as well as for one hour in the evening; thus worked only a little. Concert by the Sternscher Orchesterverein: (1) Robert Schumann's overture *Manfred;*[322] (2) Beethoven's concert aria "Ah perfido,"[323] sung by Demoiselle Jenny Meyer; (3) violin pieces played by Singer; (4) Mendelssohn's *Walpurgisnacht.*

Sunday 14 December. Letter from Holtei. For three-quarters of an hour before breakfast and one and a quarter hours after, revised what I have scored so far of the overture. Worked very little.

Monday 15 December. Wrote to Holtei. Scored for three-quarters of an hour before breakfast. Visit from the dance composer Strauss on his way back from St. Petersburg.[324] In the evening scored another two pages.

Tuesday 16 December. Worked on the overture for four and a half hours.

Wednesday 17 December. Worked for five hours on the instrumentation of the overture.

Thursday 18 December. Worked for six hours. In the evening to the cathedral for a *concert spirituel*, performed by the Domchor.

Friday 19 December. Did not work much: scored only a couple of pages of the overture. First performance of *Ein Tag in Russland* (after *La Lune de miel*), comic opera by Dorn; it pleases, without causing great enthusiasm.[325] Demoiselle Wagner was very good in a lighter role for once.

Saturday 20 December. Worked for only a couple of hours on the instrumentation of the overture. Symphony-soirée: (1) Haydn's Symphony in G Major, with the drumroll in the *andante;*[326] (2) Cherubini's overture *Faniska;* (3) Weber's *Freischütz* overture; (4) Beethoven's *Pastoral* Symphony.

Sunday 21 December. Scored the overture for one and a quarter hours before breakfast, and again during the course of the morning. In the evening I finished the orchestration of the overture, and even revised some of it.

Monday 22 December. Tried without success to compose the first duet for Margaridd and Corentin. By chance I came across the vocal score of Taubert's comic opera *Joggeli*, and read half of it with pleasure and interest. While depending on the style of Weigl's *Die Schweizerfamilie*, it has an independence of thought, which is German, genial, simple, and also arresting.[327]

Tuesday 23 December. Worked on the duet, but perfunctorily. I feel depressed, since it seems to me that my operas are losing *terrain*,[328] in France as well as in Germany. For example, Borghi-Mamo, who had only moderate appeal in *Le Prophète*, is causing a furore in Donizetti's *La Favorite*. Heard the second performance of *Ein Tag in Russland*. The house was empty. The opera does not seem to appeal particularly.

Wednesday 24 December. Worked on the duet, but I am so morally depressed that I am robbed of all artistic inspiration.

Thursday 25 December. Before breakfast I wrote the melodion accompaniment for the chorus in the overture, which I had forgotten to do. Scored a page of the act 1 duet for Corentin and Hoël; I have already scored eleven pages. In the Schauspielhaus: *Die Grille*, a new comedy by Birch-Pfeiffer,[329] after the novel *La Petite Fadette* by George Sand.[330] It is really beautifully and effectively done, and pleases very much.

Friday 26 December. Scored the duet for seven hours, a total of eight pages.

Saturday 27 December. Finished scoring and revising the whole duet.

Sunday 28 December. Visit from the Dresden writer Auerbach, who had called on me yesterday. In the evening to the big top for Benz's circus riders. Wrote to Zellner in Vienna, enclosing 100 fl. subscription, and to Madame Zellner, with 100 fl. support. *Le Prophète* has been performed for the first time in Rouen, to great enthusiasm.

Monday 29 December. [No entry.]

Tuesday 30 December. Schauspielhaus: *Adalbert vom Babenberge*, a new chivalric drama by Brachvogel, author of the popular drama *Narciss.*[331]

Wednesday 31 December. Letter from Kapellmeister Eckert in Vienna. The old year is drawing to a close. May God bless everything to do with my family and all our endeavors, most especially Blanca's engagement to Korff, and my new *opéra comique.* May God grant genuine, enduring success to everything I have composed and will still compose, and may it carry my name into posterity. May He grant me genial musical inspirations in the new year, and help me to use them properly. *Droits d'auteur* for December: 1,047 fr. 75 c.

NOTES

1. Actually *Eine Partie piquet*, comedy in one act by F. Denecke. This Viennese performance antedates the Berlin production (1865) listed by Richel [33]. The play is a translation of *La Partie de piquet*, *vaudeville* in one act (H. Meyer & N. Fournier; Paris, Théâtre du Gymnase Dramatique, 5 February 1854) [Wicks 20125].

2. *Das Grüsschen von Buchnau* is not listed in Richel.

3. *Der Hut des Uhrmachers* is not listed in Richel.

4. Fr. "cut."

5. Actually Hollósy, or Holozy. Kornélia Hollósy-Lonovics was the foremost Hungarian opera star of the times. She was later to create the role of Gertrudis in Ferenc Erkel's great nationalist opera *Bánk bán* (Budapest, National Theater, 9 March 1861).

6. See Meyerbeer to Franz Baron von Dingelstedt (Vienna, 5 January 1856) (Becker, *Giacomo Meyerbeer: A Life in Letters* [Portland, Ore.: Amadeus Press, 1989], pp. 155–56).

7. This was either the singer Udvarhelyi or the singer Havi.

8. See Meyerbeer to Aloys Ander, Vienna 6 January 1856: "Your making the modest role of Danilowitz a permanent part of your repertoire will transform it in the eyes of the public into a major operatic role" (Becker, *Giacomo Meyerbeer: A Life in Letters*, p. 157).

9. Laibach is the German name for Ljubljana, the capital of Slovenia.

10. Tgb. *Separat-Eilwagen.*

11. *Dinorah*, no. 20 *Romance d'Hoël* ("Ah! mon remonds te venge"). This was to be the first of five versions of the aria.

12. The first Milan performance of *Il Profeta* was on 23 May 1855.

13. Pauline Masson, a pupil of Duprez, sang at the Opéra Comique in the mid-1840s. She made her debut at the Opéra in 1847 in the role of Odette in Halévy's *Charles VI*, and later sang Catarina Cornaro in *La Reine de Chypre.* Auber describes her qualities in a letter to Scribe on 24 June 1847 (see Herbert Schneider, *Correspondance d'Eugène Scribe et de Daniel-François-Esprit Auber* [Sprimont, Belgium: Mardaga, 1998], p. 62).

14. Venice had been an Austrian city since 1798. Lombardi-Venezia was constituted a province of the Habsburg Empire in 1815 at the Congress of Vienna, and remained so until the 'liberation' of Lombardy (in 1859) and Venezia (in 1866), which marked the climax of the Italian Risorgimento, and would culminate in the unification of Italy, with its capital in Rome (1871). Alvise Zorzi, *Venezia Austriaca, 1798–1866* (Rome-Bari: Editori Laterza, 1985), provides a historical overview of these seventy years, and a wide-ranging survey of life and society in the city during this period. Of particular interest are chap. 7, "Scrittori, scolari, artisti" (pp. 313–42) and chap. 8, "Feste, piaceri, spettacoli, conversazioni" (pp. 343–72).

15. *Il Crociato in Egitto* was first performed at the Teatro La Fenice on 7 March 1824.

16. The Teatro La Fenice, Venice's most famous opera house, was opened in 1792 and saw the premières of works by Paisiello (*I giuochi d'Argentina*, 1792), Rossini (*Tancredi*, 1813; *Sigismondo*, 1814; *Semiramide*, 1823), Meyerbeer (*Il Crociato in Egitto*, 1824), Bellini (*I Capuleti e i Montecchi*, 1830; *Beatrice di Tenda*, 1833), and Donizetti (*Belisario*, 1836; *Maria di Rudenz*, 1838). It burned down in December 1836 and reopened on the same site, on the same ground plan as the original by Gianantonio Selva, in less than a year, on 26 December 1837. The auditorium seated 1,500, and with its dazzling chandelier, ninety-six boxes, and blue, cream, and gold decorations has indeed been "considered by many the most beautiful opera-house in the world" (John Warrack and Ewan West, *The Oxford Dictionary of Opera* [Oxford: Oxford University Press, 1992], p. 735).

17. Verdi, *Il Trovatore*, opera in four acts (Salvatore Cammerano & Leone Emanuele Bardare, after the drama *El trovador* [1836] by Gutiérrez; Rome, Teatro Apollo, 19 January 1853). Its sumptuous melodies, bold characterizations, and strong dramatic situations, as well the sustained melancholy of its coloring, made it one of the most popular operas in the world, an enduring success. With *Rigoletto* and *La Traviata*, it forms a unique trilogy, bringing the traditions of Italian romantic melodrama to a culminating high point, and initiating the subtle musico-dramatic achievements of Verdi's maturity.

18. The soprano Luigia Lesniewska was part of the company of La Fenice for the season 1855–56. In August 1859 she sang the title role in Donizetti's *Lucia di Lammermoor* at La Scala Milan. For the details of many minor figures of the operatic scene in Venice at this time, see Michele Girardi and Franco Rossi, *Il Teatro la Fenice: Cronologia degli spettacoli 1792–1936* (Venice: Albrizzi Editore, 1989).

19. The tenor Emilio Pancani (1830–98) was to create the title role in *Aroldo*, Verdi's adaptation of *Stiffelio* (Rimini, Teatro Nuovo, 16 August 1857).

20. *La Giuocaliera* [The juggler, or acrobat], *ballo romantico* in five parts (scenario after Ernst Ritter's play [Vienna, 1846]; choreography by Pasquale Borri [with additional *pas* and effects by Giuseppe Rota]; music by Paolo Giorza [Vienna, Theater Labarre, 2 August 1855, as *Die Gauklerin*; Venice, La Fenice, 27 December 1855]). This ballet was written for Adeline Plunkett, produced in Milan (La Scala, 7 March 1857), in Bologna

(1857) for Amalia Ferraris, and revised for the latter as *L'Étoile de Messine* in Paris (Opéra, 20 November 1861, with new scenario in two acts by Paul Foucher, and some new music by Count Nicolò Gabrielli). The Parisian version was more successful, with thirty-seven performances until 1863. Pasquale Borri (1820–84) was a Milanese dancer and choreographer, a pupil of Blasis and the husband of the dancer Carolina Pochini. He produced most of his ballets for the Kärntnertor-Theater in Vienna and La Scala in Milan, and was regarded as one of the most celebrated Italian choreographers of the day, with a special gift for handling crowd scenes and an innate grasp of design and color (see Ivor Guest, *The Ballet of the Second Empire* [London: Pitman Publishing, 1976], p. 174).

21. The Belgian Adeline Plunkett (1824–1910) made her début in Trieste (1841), and danced in London (1843), before becoming a principal ballerina at the Paris Opéra in 1845, where she created roles in *Ozaï, ou i'insulaire* (1847), *Nisida, ou les Amazones des Açores* (1848), and *Vert-Vert* (1851). In 1856 she was engaged by La Fenice, where she danced with Pasquale Borri in Giuseppe Rota's ballets. She left the Opéra in 1857, and appeared for some years in Rome before marrying Paul Dalloz, the proprietor of *Le Moniteur.*

22. Count Alvise Francesco ("Nanni") Mocenigo da San Samuele (b. 1808/1818?), member of a noble Venetian family and a patriot, was president *(presidente all'economia)* of the Teatro La Fenice during the 1840s and 1850s. He had dealt with Verdi over the production of *Ernani* (9 March 1844), persuading reluctant members of the company to pay the young composer the sum he had requested, and helping Francesco Maria Piave to draft the first libretto; he also sent Verdi Zacharias Werner's play *Attila* in 1845 to consider as material for a new opera (cf. Luca Zoppelli, "Venice" in the *New Grove Dictionary of Opera*, ed. Stanley Sadie [London and New York: Macmillan, 1992], 4:918). Mocenigo's civic role is discussed by Zorzi, *Venezia Austriaca*, esp. pp. 247–48.

23. Count Giovanni Battista Tornielli was *presidente anziano e agli spettacoli* (senior president in charge of productions) at the Teatro La Fenice. Also see the 22 April 1856 entry.

24. Verdi, *La Traviata*, opera in three acts (Francesco Maria Piave, after the drama *La Dame aux camélias* [1852] by Alexandre Dumas *(fils),* after his novel [1848], in turn based on his own experiences; Venice, La Fenice, 6 March 1853). This opera stands at the high point of Verdi's middle period and shows a new integration of operatic conventions in the achievement of an unprecedentedly sustained and subtle exploration of characterization. The initial failure of the work was vindicated in the revival a year later in the same theater on 6 May 1854, with a different cast. The first performances of five of Verdi's operas took place at La Fenice (*Ernani,* 1844; *Attila,* 1846; *Rigoletto,* 1851; *La Traviata,* 1853; and *Simone Boccanegra,* 1857), more than at any other theater apart from La Scala. Indeed, after the premiere of *Giovanna d'Arco* (15 February 1845) Verdi had broken with La Scala when he had been informed by Ricordi that Merelli was swindling him.

25. Giovanni Battista Perucchini (1782–1870) was a Venetian dilettante, a writer of ariettas and piano music. Meyerbeer mentions meeting Velluti in Perucchini's home (3 January 1818, see *DGM,* 1:347); Gaetano Rossi, writing to Meyerbeer from Bologna (25 October 1822) and Verona (28 November 1822), asks after him (see *BT,* 1:444, 450).

26. See Gaetano's Rossi's letter to Meyerbeer (Verona, 12 July 1829) (*BT,* 1:81), and Meyerbeer's reference to Troppeani in the diary for 1 August 1829 (*DGM,* 1:388) in which he asks for advice about the availability of singers in Trieste.

27. Armand Baschet (1829–86), a French historian.

28. The Teatro Apollo, the oldest theater in Venice, was built in 1661, and originally known as the Teatro San Salvatore. It was renamed in 1833, and again in 1875 when it

became the Teatro Goldoni, as it is to the present. Goldoni wrote over sixty plays for this house.

29. This is the soprano Adelaide Cortesi (1828–89).

30. *Dinorah*, no. 5 *Grand Air d'Hoël*.

31. The Teatro San Samuele was opened in 1655 for comedy, and from 1710 gave *opera buffa*. It was reconstructed after a fire in 1748, and continued to stage opera until 1894.

32. Goldoni, *Il campiello* (Venice, Teatro San Luca, 1756).

33. Mme. de Roissy [= Noema De Rossi?] had worked for the Paris Opéra since 1842 when she sang both Alice and Isabelle in *Robert le Diable*, and later Princess Eudoxie in *La Juive* (1846). The *Revue et gazette musicale* (October 1855) records that she sang Mathilde in Rossini's *Guillaume Tell* and Donizetti's Lucia at the Théâtre Italien, and comments on her "nervous voice." She pursued her career in Italy in the 1850s; an engagement at a secondary Italian house suggests a diminution in her vocal powers.

34. A. Ottaviani sang widely in Italian provincial theaters (e.g., Parma and Rovigo in 1855).

35. Perhaps A. Dell'Armi was unimportant, but he nevertheless had the ability to undertake the role of Giovanni di Leida at the Scala presentation of *Il Profeta* on 23 May 1855. He later sang Alfredo in *La Traviata* (Cremona, 16 September 1856).

36. It. "Horror!," what a horrifying thought.

37. Fr. "auditorium."

38. It. "Hurrah also for maestro Meyerbeer!"

39. See 28 December 1855. Auguste Villemot's retraction appeared in *Le Figaro* 94 (10 January 1856): 2. "Je ne veux pas entamer l'année 1856 sans liquider une sottise de l'année 1855. A propos de la représentation des *Saisons*, à l'Opéra Comique, j'ai raconté une histoire recueille dans un monde à moi bien cher, mais mal informé, où je faisais intervenir M. Meyerbeer rognant à M. Massé des choeurs que celui-ci a supprimés très spontanément.

M. Meyerbeer est à Vienne, occupé de bien autre chose, ma foi! Il a en perspective, à la vérité, un opéra comique. — Mais dont on reconnait une note, et on sait, du reste, que M. Meyerbeer n'est jamais bien pressé. — Au bout de tout cela, je ne crois pas avoir entamé la gloire de M. Meyerbeer; mais j'ai agi avec la légèreté d'un polisson de lettres" [I do not want to enter 1856 without sorting out a silliness dating from 1855. Regarding the presentation of the *Saisons* at the Opéra Comique, I related a story derived from a source dear to me, but badly informed, where I suggested that M. Meyerbeer had intervened to pare away the chorus which, in fact, M. Massé had spontaneously suppressed on his own. Well, M. Meyerbeer is in Vienna occupied with other matters. It is true that he has an *opéra comique* in view—but nobody knows so much as a note of this, and as one knows in any case, M. Meyerbeer can never be hurried. —After all that, I do not believe I have impugned M. Meyerbeer's glory: but I have acted with the irresponsibility of a naughty journalist].

40. Alberto Mazzucato (1813–77) was a violinist, composer, and writer on music. He wrote seven operas between 1834 and 1843 when Verdi's ascendance overshadowed him. From 1839 he taught singing at the Milan Conservatory, later composition, music history, aesthetics and instrumentation. He was principal from 1872 on. In 1856 became *direttore* of La Scala, and from 1859 to 1868 also covered the position of *maestro concertatore* of the orchestra there, preparing the way for the modern figure of the music director. As a journalist he was editor of the influential *Gazetta musicale di Milano* (1856–58).

41. Details of the productions in Italian provincial theaters are meticulously listed by Thomas G. Kaufman (with the research assistance of Marion Kaufman) in *Verdi and His Major Contemporaries: A Selected Chronology of Performances with Casts,* Garland Reference Library of the Humanities, 1016 (New York and London: Garland, 1990).

42. The Teatro Filarmonico in Verona, designed by Francesco Galli-Bibiena*, was built in 1732 and staged operas with leading singers and conductors until it was bombed in February 1945. The fourteen-year-old Mozart performed here on his first visit to Italy in 1770.

43. This is the soprano Augusta Albertini-Baucardé. She sang throughout Italy in the 1850s (e.g., Rome, 1850; Ferrara and Florence, 1851; Sinigaglia, 1852; Treviso, 1854; Bologna, 1855; Milan, 1855 and 1858).

44. Meyerbeer's negative opinion comes as a surprise, since the tenor Carlo Baucardé created the role of Manrico in *Il Trovatore* (Rome, Teatro Apollo, 19 January 1853). He was regarded as a star, and, according to Spike Hughes, introduced the famous, and subsequently traditional, high-C, in "Di quella pira" at performances of the work in Florence in 1855 (*Famous Verdi Operas* [London: Robert Hale, 1968], p. 155).

45. Giovanni Battista Bencich sang in the Italian provinces (e.g., Treviso, 1854; Livorno, 1855). He was part of the company of La Fenice in the season 1853–54 when he sang in Verdi's *Il Trovatore*, Rossini's *Otello* and Pacini's *La Punizione*. In 1854 he appeared at the Teatro Apollo in Rome.

46. The baritone Giovanni Guicciardi had also taken part in the première of *Il Trovatore* in Rome three years earlier when he created the role of Count di Luna.

47. Maria Baratte did indeed please in Paris. She joined the Opéra ballet where she became a *petit sujet* in the company. She attracted attention when her dress caught fire during a rehearsal of Marie Taglioni and Offenbach's *Le Papillon* (1860), and by her fine dancing in the *pas de quatre* in Saint-Léon and Pugni's *Diavolina* (1863). (See Guest, *Ballet of the Second Empire*, pp. 152, 187.)

48. See 21 October 1852 for Meyerbeer's last meeting with Corti.

49. This was the management of the Teatro Sociale (1822).

50. These were the brothers Ercole and Luciano Marzi.

51. This is Fanny Gordosa (b. 1830), whom Meyerbeer later heard in Florence (29 February and 3 March 1856) and in Venice (24 March). She had sung Berta in *Il Profeta* at La Scala Milan in 1855, and Giselda in Verdi's *I Lombardi* earlier in the same season.

52. Victor-Henri-Joseph Brahain Ducange (1783–1833), French novelist and playwright, author of novels like *Agathe* (1820), *Thélène* (1822), *Léonide* (1823), and melodramas like *Calas* (1819), *Trente ans* (1827), and *Le Jésuite* (1830). Rota's ballet, however, appears to have been based on a drama by Iffland.

53. *Il Giuocatore* [The gambler], *azione mimo-danzante* in four parts (scenario after August Wilhelm Iffland's five-act drama, *Der Spieler* [1800]; music by Paolo Giorza, in collaboration with L. Madaglio and G. Bajetti; Milan, Teatro Cannobiana, spring 1853; then at La Scala, 14 January 1854). This popular ballet was widely produced. It was at the performance in Turin's Teatro Carlo Felice in 1855 that the great dancer, ballet master, and teacher, Enrico Cecchetti (1850–1928), made his début aged only five years. The music of Giorza (1832–1914) "was marked by a popular vein 'full of spirit and of a lively dancing quality' [Monaldi, 1910]. The collaboration between Rota and Giorza, both fervent patriots, continued regularly until Rota's death" (Claudia Celi in *International Encyclopedia of Dance,* ed. Selma Jeanne Cohen [New York and Oxford: Oxford University Press, 1998], 5:409).

54. Meyerbeer's reactions to Giuseppe Rota (1822–65) recall his pleasure in the work of Salvatore Viganò and Gaetano Gioia in Italy in 1818. Rota was to reach the peak of his fame with *Cleopatra* (1859). He had begun his career as a dancer, but after a short professional apprenticeship emerged as a precocious choreographer and staged a number of ballets in various Italian towns—most especially in Milan, first in the Cannobiana, then at La Scala, and later at the Paris Opéra (*Le Maschera*, 1864). The ethos of his *azione mimo-danzante* has an affinity with the dramaturgical world of *grand opéra*. "In Rota's choreography the perfect balance of Carlo Blasis's ideal ballet was upset by the inflated emotions of that particular moment of Italian history just after the Risorgimento, which led to the positivist euphoria of Manzotti. Poised between two different epochs, Rota's productions were characterized by impressive mimed action and spectacularly grouped crowd scenes" (Carla Maria Casanova, *Phaidon Book of the Ballet* [Milan: Arnoldo Mondadori, 1980; London: Phaidon Press, 1981], p. 127). Rota is the link between Gaetano Gioia (1756–1828) and Luigi Manzotti (1835–1905): ". . . [Gioia's] use of large numbers of dancers and spectacular scenic effects gave audiences a taste for visual extravagance matched only when grand opera conquered Italian stages in the 1850s" (Kathleen Kuzmick Hansell, in Sadie, *New Grove Dictionary of Opera*, 2:424). For further comments on Rota, see Guest, *Ballet of the Second Empire*, p. 194.

55. The Teatro Farnese in Parma was abandoned in 1732, damaged by bombs in 1944, and rebuilt in the 1950s.

56. The Parma Galleria. Antonio Allegri Correggio (1489–1534) pioneered the use of light and balance, perspective and foreshortening, with a new softness of style; Raphael Sanzio (1483–1520), one of the greatest of Renaissance painters and architects, did his best paintings (famous for their harmonious groupings and serene coloring) in Florence and Rome; Francesco Parmigianino (1503–40) was the most sensitive and elegant of the early mannerists.

57. Parma's Teatro Regio was built during the reign of Marie-Louise (May 1829), designed after La Scala Milan, and decorated in white, gold, and red velvet.

58. Francesco Cresci was a member of the company of La Fenice for the season 1855–56.

59. Antonio Giuglini (1827–65) had studied with Cellini and made his début in Fermo. Meyerbeer heard him on the threshold of his greatest success, the period 1857–64 when he starred in London, at Her Majesty's Theatre, Drury Lane, and the Lyceum, particularly in Verdi roles: he was the first London Riccardo *(Un Ballo in maschera)*, Rudolfo *(Luisa Miller)*, and Arrigo *(Les Vêpres sicilliennes)*. In 1865, while in St. Petersburg, he showed signs of mental instability, and on his return to London had to be confined to an asylum. He was taken back to Italy in the autumn and died shortly afterwards in Pesaro (12 October 1865).

60. This is the singer Goldberg-Strossi, who sang Abigaille in Verdi's *Nabucco* during the 1855 season at La Scala.

61. Fanny Goldberg sang Adalgisa at La Scala, Milan, on 11 September 1838, and was part of the company at La Fenice, Venice, in the 1840s, where she performed roles in Pacini's operas (e.g., *Saffo* [26 December 1841], the première of *Il Duca d'Alba* [26 February 1842]).

62. N. De Giovanni, musical director of the Teatro Regio in Parma.

63. It., a private carriage and coachman.

64. Brescia's Teatro degli Erranti (1688) was rebuilt several times, and renamed the Teatro Grande (1811). The present auditorium was opened in 1863.

65. Verdi, *I Masnadieri*, opera in four acts (Andrea Maffei, after Schiller's drama

Die Räuber [1781], in turn based on C. F. D. Schubart's story [1777]; London, His Majesty's Theatre, 22 July 1847), a work "whose beautiful parts do not add up to an individual or satisfying whole" (Warrack and West, *Oxford Dictionary of Opera*, p. 737).

66. This was the soprano Carolina Rapazzini, who created the role of Medora in Verdi's opera *Il Corsaro* (Trieste, Teatro Grande, 25 October 1848).

67. This was presumably the father of the better-known tenor, Angelo Massini (1845–1926).

68. *Le Capitaine Charlotte, comédie-vaudeville* in two acts (J.-F.-A. Bayard & P.-F.-P. Dumanoir; Paris, Palais Royale, 3 December 1842) [Wicks 7301].

69. Fr. "prompter."

70. Fr. "applause."

71. *Dinorah*, no. 7, *Allegro con spirito* ("Sans nous étonner").

72. Verdi, *Rigoletto*, opera in three acts (Francesco Maria Piave, after Victor Hugo's drama *Le Roi s'amuse* [1832]; Venice, La Fenice, 11 March 1851). This is the first masterpiece of Verdi's middle period, with a fluent new handling of the conventions of Italian opera in the interests of the drama. The orchestra is put to more effective use in characterization and sustaining atmosphere.

73. *Dinorah*, no. 8 *Terzettino de la Clochette de Dinorah, Corentin et Hoël* ("Ce tintement que l'on entend").

74. Loeweberg gives the date of the first Budapest performance of *L'Étoile du Nord* as 31 January 1856. The Hungarian translation was by M. Havi (Loewenberg, col. 912). Albert Franz Doppler (1821–83) studied the flute with his father and was premier flautist at the Pest Opera Orchestra at this time. His opera *Grof Benjowsky* (with a Hungarian text by R. Köffinger, 29 September 1847) was well received in Budapest and had several revivals as *Afanasia*, as did his comic opera *Ilka* (29 December 1849). He was about to produce his Hungarian opera *Wanda* (T. Bakody; 16 December 1856), which enjoyed success across Germany until 1877. In 1858 he settled in Vienna as dance conductor at the Hofoper, where he wrote fifteen ballets.

75. For Sattere read Záttere. The Venetian Fondamento sulle Záttere is a series of quays lining the Canale della Giudecca. It is planted with trees and has fine views across to the Giudecca and the large ships bound for the port of Marghera.

76. This is the painter Gaetano Astolfoni, also known as Gaetano Astolfini (mentioned c. 1820).

77. This was Giacomo Servadio (d. 1875), a journalist, musician, and the deputy for Montepulciano.

78. *Le baruffe chiozzote*, one of Goldoni's most famous plays, was first produced in 1762 (Venice, Teatro San Luca), the year he left for Paris.

79. *Gli Ugonotti* was produced in Barcelona on 17 January 1856.

80. This is Eugenia Julienne-Dejean who worked at the Opéra from 1845, and after 1850 toured widely through Europe. She created the role of Amelia in Verdi's *Un Ballo in maschera* (Rome, Teatro Apollo, 17 February 1859).

81. Tsar Nicholas I died on 4 March 1855 and was succeeded by his thirty-six-year-old son as Alexander II. The latter became the emperor of Russia on 19 February 1856. For further commentary, see 29 May 1856.

82. Francesco Mazzoleni was engaged as one of the *primi tenori assoluti* at La Fenice for the season 1855–56.

83. The count was from the former Hungarian province of Banat, a region of the middle Danube now divided between Rumania and Serbia.

84. Cruvelli married Achille-Pierre-Félix, comte Vigier (1801–68), a French aristocrat and politician.

85. *L'Étoile du Nord* was produced in Munich on 2 February 1856.

86. Goldoni, *La putta onorata* (Venice, Teatro Sant'Angelo, 1749).

87. While the *presidenza* of La Fenice often managed the company directly, without the intervention of impresarios (as in 1823, 1831, 1843–44, 1847), most seasons were left to them, and often they were used simply as agents working on detailed instructions from the *presidente agli spettacoli* (Tornielli at the time).

88. *Les Vêpres siciliennes* was given in the Italian translation of A. Fusinato as *Giovanna de Guzman*.

89. Tgb. *reüssierte*.

90. La Giudecca is an area of Venice comprised of eight linked islands. It owes its present name to the fact that Jews established a colony there at the end of the eighth century. Later it became the site of aristocratic villas and pleasure gardens. The long *fondamenta*, along the length of the Giudecca Canal, commands magnificent views across to the city itself.

91. Ferenc Erkel (1810–93) had given up a promising career as a pianist on hearing Liszt, and turned increasingly to composition. He became musical director of the new Hungarian National Theater in Pest (1838), and achieved fame with *Hunyadi László* (Béni Egressy; 27 January 1844), the most successful of his operas, and the cornerstone of Hungarian national music. While using Viennese and Italian elements, it achieves a genuinely Magyar character by its Hungarian-inflected recitative, the incorporation of national dances, and the infusion of the *verbunkos* into the musical idiom. The final chorus of act 1 ("The intriguer is dead. . . . A new day breaks, o Hungary") became the song of the revolutionary movement in 1848, and over the next fifty years the opera was performed 270 times in Pest. This achievement was consolidated by Erkel's second great national opera, *Bánk bán* (Béni Egressy; 9 March 1861), which was given about three hundred times in Budapest until 1934.

92. The princes of Clary were and still are owners of the Palazzo Priuli-Bon on the Záttere (Zorzi, *Venezia Austriaca*, p. 364).

93. The best account of Heine's relentless and cruel satirical treatment of Meyerbeer is provided by Becker in *Der Fall Heine-Meyerbeer* (Berlin: De Gruyter, 1958); see especially the summation, "Dichter und Musiker," pp. 130–38. Heine the man was a complex and prickly subject; his work as a poet is an enduring achievement of the spirit. "Heine died in February 1856. His voyage . . . had ended in death, certainly, but it had ended also in a new world of poetry which he opened up not only for himself but for posterity and in which he will outlive all those changes of fashion that occasionally obscure his achievement" (S. Prawer, *Heine: The Tragic Satirist* [Cambridge: Cambridge University Press, 1961], p. 281). See 12 December 1851.

94. Giulio ("Giulietto") Nicolini is mentioned frequently in the letters of Gaetano Rossi addressed to Meyerbeer in late 1822 from Bologna, and in 1823 from Verona (30 March 1823, when the marriage of Nicolini to the "spiritosa figlia del General Polfranceschi" is reported; also on 12 August 1823 when there are greetings from Nicolini, who had been ill) (see *BT*, 1:443, 444, 445, 450, 461, 462, 517).

95. Carlo Pedrotti (1817–93) was a native of Verona. *Fiorina, ossia La Fanciulla di Glaris,* opera in two acts (L. Serenelli Honorati; Verona, 22 November 1851) was his first success: it was performed in Trieste (1852), Warsaw (1853), Paris (1855), Barcelona (1856), Rio de Janeiro (1857), Vienna (1859), Lisbon (1863), Malta (1863), and in Hungarian at

Budapest (1859). Having achieved some notice with his first opera *Lina* (Verona, 1840), Pedrotti became conductor of the Italian Opera in Amsterdam, where he wrote two operas before returning to Verona in 1845. Here he wrote *Fiorina* and his chief work, the fluent and graceful comedy *Tutti in maschera* (4 November 1856), which was widely produced in Italy as late as 1924 (Verona) and 1930 (Pesaro). In 1868 he settled in Turin as a teacher and conductor of popular concerts, but aware of his own limitations and deteriorating health, he eventually took his own life in the Adige River.

96. The *canzonetta* "A Venezia" is designated a *barcarolle* (Paris, 1856).

97. Giovanni Beltrame was a Venetian commissioner.

98. The correct medical term for this form of dropsy is "hydrothorax."

99. The Teatro della Pergola in Florence was built in 1656, and considerably altered by Antonio Galli-Bibiena* in 1738 and again in 1857. This theater saw the premières of Donizetti's *Parisina* (1833), Verdi's *Macbeth* (1847), Mascagni's *I Rantzau* (1892), and the first performances in Italy of Mozart's *Figaro* (1788), *Don Giovanni* (1792), and *Die Entführung aus dem Serail* (1935), as well as Meyerbeer's *Robert le Diable* (1840), *Les Huguenots* (1841), *Le Prophète* (1852), and *Dinorah* (1867).

100. Carlo Negrini was to create Gabriele Adorno in Verdi's *Simone Boccanegra* in the following year (La Fenice, 12 March 1857). His voice "was of the powerful, somewhat baritonic variety (Petrella was to write for him a characteristically barnstorming part in *Morosina*). His line is not a particularly high one" (Julian Budden, *The Operas of Verdi,* rev. ed. [Oxford: Clarendon Press, 1992], 2:252).

101. Felice Varesi created some of Verdi's greatest parts: the title roles in *Macbeth* (Florence, Pergola, 14 March 1847), *Rigoletto* (Venice, La Fenice, 11 March 1851), and Giorgio Germont in *La Traviata* (La Fenice, 6 March 1853). Meyerbeer's negative impression of his voice is borne out by general opinion of his declining vocal powers at this time. Indeed, the initial fiasco of *Traviata* was ascribed in large measure to his diminishing prowess: "[H]e was one of those dramatic baritones who concentrate exclusively on the upper part of their voice. When the tone begins to wear thin and the intonation to slip through lack of proper support they have no remedy except bluster. . . . In vain did Verdi in 1853 keep the baritone floating above the stave for bar after bar. Varesi's career was already coming to an end; indeed, it barely survived the year. He was to create no new roles. His last appearance was in 1857 in a revival of *Rigoletto* . . ." (Budden, *Operas of Verdi,* 2:124).

102. The Teatro dei Rinovati (1753) in Siena was adapted by Francesco Galli-Bibiena from the ancient hall of the Grand Council of the Republic.

103. It. "from the chest."

104. This was the tenor Antonio Prudenza (b. 1823/1826?).

105. Tommaso Locatelli was the moderate columnist of the *Gazzetta privilegiata Veneta*, then of the *Gazzetta di Venezia*.

106. Genoa had no opera house worthy of its prosperous status until the opening of the Teatro Carlo Felice on 7 April 1828. The architect was Carlo Barabino. Mariani was the music director there from 1852 to 1873, and it was the scene of the young Toscanini's early triumphs. The premières of Gomes's *Salvator Rosa* (1874) and Franchetti's *Cristoforo Colombo* (1892) took place here.

107. Luigia Bendazzi was to create the role of Amelia in *Simone Boccanegra* (Venice, Teatro La Fenice, 12 March 1857). According to Budden, she was "a fine singer in the somewhat robust tradition of Sofia Loewe. Verdi had written approvingly of her in a letter to Vigna . . ." (*Operas of Verdi,* 2:252).

108. This was the baritone Gaetano Ferri, who was to create the role of Egberto in Verdi's adaptation of *Stiffelio*, *Aroldo* (Rimini, Teatro Nuovo, 16 August 1857). Verdi regarded him as "excellent" (Budden, *Operas of Verdi*, 3:339).

109. Serafino Amedeo De Ferrari (1824–85) studied in Genoa and Milan, and appeared in public as a pianist, organist, and conductor. He was conductor in Amsterdam (1852), before becoming the director of singing at the Teatro Carlo Felice in Genoa and later at the Teatro Carignano in Turin. His operas *Pipelè* (1855) and *Il Menestrello* (1859) were performed throughout Italy and abroad. "[T]hese works, although elegantly written, charming and melodious, were not original enough to maintain their popularity" (Francesco Bussi, in Sadie, *New Grove Dictionary of Opera*, 1:1103).

110. De Ferrari, *Pipelè, ossia Il Portinaio di Parigi*, opera *buffa* in three acts (R. Berninzone, after Eugène Sue's *Les Mystères de Paris* [1842–43]; Venice, Teatro San Benedetto, 25 November 1855). Meyerbeer's opinion notwithstanding, this was De Ferrari's most successful opera, given in Italy until 1906 and performed all over the world (Rio de Janeiro, 1859; Santiago, 1866; New York, 1869; Sydney, 1871; Oporto, 1890).

111. Because he had been elected a Socialist deputy (1850), Eugène Sue lived in exile in Savoy after Louis Napoleon's coup d'état (1851). His later novels championed Socialism, and are set in the underworld of Paris, like *Les Mystères de Paris* (1842–43) and *Le Juif errant* (1844–45). His idealization of the poor has been seen as melodramatic, but his novels were nonetheless successful in their day and had a profound effect on Victor Hugo.

112. Gustav Adolf Pressel (1827–90), composer and writer on music.

113. The Milanese Teatro Carcano opened in September 1803. The premières of Donizetti's *Anna Bolena* (1830) and Bellini's *La Sonnambula* (1831) took place here, as well the first concert of Wagner's music in Milan (1883, under Faccio).

114. Pavlos Carrer (1829–96), the most important Greek composer of the nineteenth century before Spyridon Samaras, was noted for his operas on historical figures and events surrounding the revolt against Turkish rule. He studied in his native Zákinthos and in Milan (1850), where the first three of some eleven operas were produced before he returned to Greece in 1857 to produce his most famous work, *Marcos Botsaris* (Athens, 1858). His style was close to early Verdi, but he was "the most important of the older generation of Ionian composers who began, timidly, to abandon the Italian musical heritage and turn towards the cultural and historical background of the Hellenic mainland" (George Leotsakos, in Sadie, *New Grove Dictionary of Opera*, 1:744).

115. Carrer, *La Rediviva, tragedia lirica* in a prologue and three acts (I. Sapios; Milan, Teatro Carcano, February 1856). This opera is lost, but the libretto was published in Milan in the same year. The title refers to one who comes back to life.

116. This was Georgio Stigelli (Georg Stiegele), whom Meyerbeer met in Berlin (1 and 5 May 1844). He appeared regularly in Italy in the 1850s (e.g., Verona 1850).

117. Pachta worked in the Austrian civil service of Lombardy-Venetia, where he stayed for the rest of his life. Meyerbeer's only reference is to "Mr. le Comte de Pachta (secretaire intime du Gouverneur)" in a letter to Prosper Levasseur from Milan (11 July 1823) (see *BT*, 1:516). He visited Meyerbeer in Berlin in 1843, and the *Taschenkalendar* records meetings on 14, 16 and 19 April (see *BT*, 3:432–33; *DGM*, 2:75).

118. It. "head of the management at La Scala."

119. The Teatro della Canobbiana was built in 1779 on land given free to the city of Milan by the Empress Maria Theresa. It gave hospitality to La Scala (1807), and was regularly used for opera and ballet until the 1860s. The most famous première there was Donizetti's *L'Elisir d'amore*. It was finally demolished in 1894 and replaced by the Teatro Lirico.

120. The Teatro alla Scala was built by the architect Piermarini to replace the Royal Ducal Theater, which had burned down (1776). It opened on 3 August 1778, and was named after Regina della Scala who had founded a church there in the fourteenth century. Many great composers wrote for this theater, and it saw the premières of Rossini's *La Gazza ladra* (1817), Meyerbeer's *Margherita d'Anjou* (1820) and *L'Esule di Granata* (1822), Bellini's *Norma* (1831), Donizetti's *Lucrezia Borgia* (1833), Verdi's *Nabucco* (1842), *Otello* (1887), and *Falstaff* (1893), and Puccini's *Madama Butterfly* (1904) and *Turandot* (1926).

121. Donizetti, *Marino Faliero*, opera in three acts (E. Bidèra, after Casimir Delavigne's tragedy [1829] and also Byron's tragedy [1821]; Paris, Théâtre Italien 12 March 1835), was produced all over the world during the 1840s, and revived in Verona (1887), Leghorn (1888) and Florence (1892).

122. G. Liverani sang in the Italian provincial theaters. Later in 1856 he appeared in Lugo, and in 1857 at Ferrara. For specific details of the distribution of roles at La Scala, see Giampietro Tintori, *Cronologia opere-balletti-concerti, 1778–1977* (Bergamo: Grafica Gutenberg, 1979).

123. This is the baritone Giovanni Corsi, who sang several big baritone roles in the 1855–56 season at La Scala (Rigoletto, Don Alfonso in Donizetti's *Lucrezia Borgia*). He was superseded by Francesco Cresci, but resumed his position by 1859 when he again appeared as Rigoletto.

124. The baritone Leone Giraldoni (1824–97) was to create the title role in Verdi's *Simone Boccanegra* (Venice, La Fenice, 12 March 1857). He was "a sensitive, nervous high baritone, much prone to indisposition" according to Verdi (Budden, *Operas of Verdi*, 3:252).

125. It. "dash, impulse"; *pieno di slancio*, "full of go."

126. Marianna Barbieri-Nini, who created Lucrezia in *I due Foscari* (1844), Lady Macbeth in *Macbeth* (1847), and Gulnara in *Il Corsaro* (1848) for Verdi, in fact retired from singing later in 1856. Meyerbeer first heard her in October 1851.

127. Zezi, a singer. See 29 May 1855.

128. Pietro and Prospero Raboni were Italian patriots who had been imprisoned (1825, 1831) for their nationalistic activities.

129. Ernesto Cavallini, a friend of Verdi's student days, would later become first clari-netist at the St. Petersburg Opera.

130. See Meyerbeer's reactions to Rademacher on 17 April 1852.

131. Emilia Boccherini, together with Cortesi and Lesniewska, was counted among the *primi soprani assoluti* of the company of La Fenice for the season 1855–56.

132. Rota, *Il Fallo, o Il Fornaretto* [The mistake, or The little baker boy], *azione mimo-danzante* in five acts (scenario after the sentimental play *Il Fornaretto di Venezia* by Francesco Dall'Ongaro; music by Paolo Giorza in collaboration with A. Buzzi [Mussi?]; Milan, La Scala, 24 September 1853). The work was a success, and widely produced in Italy.

133. *Dinorah*, no. 16a *Entr'acte*.

134. The Venetian Teatro San Benedetto opened in 1755, was damaged by fire, and reopened in 1784. Two Rossini operas had their premières there (*L'Italiana in Algeri*, 1813; *Eduardo e Cristina*, 1819). In 1868 it was renamed the Teatro Rossini, and is a cinema today.

135. The première of *Emma di Resburgo* (*melodramma eroico* by Rossi) was on 26 June 1819.

136. Velluti invited Meyerbeer to visit his country estate during his stay in Venice.

The composer had postponed coming on the grounds of ill-health, and before leaving Venice wrote to apologize. "[L]et me take this opportunity to tell you how delighted I was to see you after so many years of separation . . . I am proud and honored to have your friendship. . . . As soon as I arrive in Berlin I will send you a lithograph of my poor, dear mother who so loved and admired you" (Meyerbeer to Giovanni Battista Velluti, Venice, 25 April 1856; Becker, *Giacomo Meyerbeer: A Life in Letters*, pp. 157–58).

137. *Dinorah*, no. 17 *Chanson du faucheur* [Song of the reaper] ("Les blés son bon à faucher").

138. *Dinorah*, no. 16b *Chant du chasseur* ("En chasse, piqueurs adroits!"). Meyerbeer originally called it the "Song of the Poacher," but changed this to 'Hunter' in the final version.

139. The Teatro Sociale in Mantua, designed by L. Cannonica, was opened in 1822.

140. See 28 April 1841.

141. *Dinorah*, no. 18 *Villanelle des deux pâtres* [Song of two herdsmen] ("Sous les génévriers").

142. *Dinorah*, no. 18a *Scène* ("Bonjour faucheur!").

143. Fr. "the body of the intermezzo."

144. Pacini, *Saffo*, *opera seria* in three acts (Salvatore Cammarano, based on Greek history/legend; Naples, San Carlo, 29 November 1840). This was the work with which Pacini staged his comeback after the retirement of Rossini and the death of Bellini. It was his masterpiece and most successful work, given throughout Europe and around the world (e.g., Buenos Aires, 1854; Sydney, 1871).

145. This was the famous Venetian actor, Ettore Dondini (1822–97).

146. Goldoni's *Il bugiardo* was first produced in Mantua (1750).

147. *Dinorah*, no. 21a *Récitatif et Duo de Dinorah et Hoël* ("Grand Dieu! son teint s'anime").

148. Tgb. *Rührstück*.

149. This was the Belgian aristocrat and cabinet secretary Pierre-d'Alcantera-Charles-Marie, prince de Aremberg [Arenberg] (1790–1877).

150. The Arsenal is a fortified dockyards, with two massive towers and crenellated walls that protect the entry to the lagoon. For centuries it was the symbol of the economic and military power of Venice.

151. *Zaïre* (1732) is one of Voltaire's most accomplished tragedies.

152. The Reval performance of *Le Prophète* took place during March 1856 (see Loewenberg, col. 874).

153. See 10 August 1851 for details of this play.

154. Leone Fortis (1828–96) was a journalist, critic, dramatist, and philologist. He was particularly noted for his direction of the politically moderate journal *Il Pungolo* [The stimulus, or spur].

155. *Cuore e Arte* was first performed at the Teatro Rè in Milan in 1853, and was Fortis's greatest success, an enduring triumph for the actor F. Sadowski.

156. Loewenberg gives only "Spring 1856" for the Algerian performance of *L'Étoile du Nord* (col. 912).

157. Originally part of no. 10 *Récitatif et Romance de Dinorah*, the refrain was later moved to no. 21b *Chœur de Pardon* ("Sainte Marie!").

158. This was probably Karl, Graf von Wallmoden-Gimborn (1792–1883). The Austrian military presence was strongly in evidence, because of Venice's naval importance and the tension surrounding the Risorgimento, especially after the troubles of 1848–49.

See Zorzi, *Venezia Austriaca, 1798–1866,* chap. 4, "L'imperiale e regia Veneta Marina" (pp. 223–38).

159. Count Tornielli, with fellow president of La Fenice Carlo Marzari, conducted the difficult negotiations with Verdi over *Rigoletto, La Traviata,* and *Simone Boccanegra.* After the treaty of Villafranca in 1859, which upheld the cession of the Veneto to Austria, he headed the company's decision to close the theater until the political situation had changed. It reopened only in October 1866, when the Veneto was reunited with Italy (cf. Sadie, *New Grove Dictionary of Opera,* 4:918).

160. *Saul* (published 1789) is one of Alfieri's best tragedies, and is dominated, like all his other plays, by the theme of tyranny and a romantic insistence on heroic willpower, whether toward good or evil.

161. Meyerbeer's opinion of Salvini reflects a general enthusiasm. He "was the most consummate 'star' actor of the century," becoming "the most internationally celebrated actor of his age, enjoying a triumphant histrionic progress from 1869 onwards to his retirement through North and South America, Western Europe and Russia. . . . Endowed with rich physical attributes—a powerful sonorous voice, striking and muscular figure, stage presence and perfect command of gesture and movement—he brought intelligence and perception to his preparation and execution of roles, on occasion retiring from the stage for months at a time in order to study a new piece" (Kenneth Richards, *The Cambridge Guide to Theatre* (Cambridge: Cambridge University Press, 1995], p. 922).

162. Apolloni, *L'Ebreo, melodramma tragico* in a prologue and three acts (A. Boni, after Bulwer-Lytton's novel *Leila;* Venice, La Fenice, 27 January 1855). The opera was performed in Barcelona and Malta; in Roma and Bologna it was given as *Lida di Granata* at the insistence of the censors. Giuseppe Apolloni (1822–89), the composer of six operas, was a native of Vicenza; his political involvement had led to a period of exile in Florence (1848–52). On his return he produced an opera, *Adelchi* (14 August 1852), and the success of *L'Ebreo* led the management of La Fenice to invite him to revise this earlier score for production in Venice (26 December 1856). See T. G. Kaufman, *Verdi and His Major Contemporaries,* pp. 1–10.

163. Fr. "resignation."

164. St. Mark is associated with the city of Venice because in 829 his supposed relics where taken there from Alexandria and enshrined in the original church of San Marco. His symbol of the winged lion was adopted as the emblem of the city. The basilica of St. Mark was completed in 1094.

165. Gutzkow, *Ella Rosa,* drama in five acts (first performance in Dresden, 1856) [Richel 56]. In this double tragedy an insignificant and rejected wife becomes a famous actress, is saved from suicide, and ostensibly is reconciled with her estranged husband.

166. Gye's neglect was compounded by the destruction of the theater later in the year. Chorley commented on the career of the *L'Étoile du Nord* in London: "How far its success might have justified the care and cost lavished on its production cannot be ascertained; for the fire at Covent Garden Theatre swept it away, —I can hardly fancy with much hope of its frequent return. The work is thoroughly Parisian, and not, like *Les Huguenots,* universal" (*Thirty Years' Musical Recollections* [1862; reprint, London and New York: Alfred A. Knopf, 1926], p. 349). Later London performances were at Drury Lane (17 April 1890) and the Kennington Theater (25 September 1901, in English).

167. The Belgian soprano Giuseppina Medori was to sing Valentine in *Les Huguenots* later in the year, both at La Fenice and at the Paris Opéra.

168. See 12 July 1812 for Meyerbeer's first encounter with Schiller's play.

169. *L'Étoile du Nord* was performed in the Teatro Canobbiana on 30 April 1856 in Italian (translated by E. Picchi), under the title *La Stella del Nord*.

170. Albert Stöger had succeeded Josef Tyl as director of the Prague Theater in 1851.

171. *Lohengrin* was first performed in Prague on 25 January 1856.

172. This was Thérèse Célérier, the daughter of Louis Gouin.

173. See 2, 7, 15, 17 September 1853.

174. Brachvogel, *Narciss*, tragedy in five acts (first produced in Berlin, 1856) [Richel 23].

175. Tgb. *etablieren*.

176. Valentina Bianchi sang at the Théâtre Italien in 1855.

177. *Dinorah*, no. 14 *Duo d'Hoël et de Corentin* ("Quand l'heure sonnera").

178. There is no record of Flotow having composed this opera (cf. John Towers, *Dictionary-Catalogue of Operas and Operettas* [1910; reprint, New York: Da Capo Press, 1967], 2:753; Sadie, *New Grove Dictionary of Opera*, 2:246–47).

179. *L'Étoile du Nord* was performed in St. Petersburg on 26 January 1856 (in Italian).

180. Tgb. *choquiert*.

181. *Dinorah*, no. 12 *Chanson de Corentin* ("Ah! que j'ai froid").

182. *Tannhäuser* was the first successful production of a Wagner opera in Berlin. The first performance had been on 7 January 1856, conducted by Heinrich Dorn. "The extent of public interest in Wagner at this time may be gauged from the fact that no fewer than 10,172 applications were received for seats for the first performance. Johanna Wagner, according to Liszt . . . was superb as Elisabeth; Theodore Formes seems to have been reasonably good as Tannhäuser. . . . All accounts agree as to the magnificence of the scenery and costumes, on which no expense had been spared . . ." (Ernest Newman, *The Life of Richard Wagner* [1933; reprint, Cambridge: Cambridge University Press, 1975], 2:488–89).

183. Johan Peter Emilius Hartmann (1805–1900), the Danish composer of operas (esp. *Little Kirsten*, 1846), ballets, symphonic poems, choral works, and orchestral works. He was a teacher at the Conservatory of Copenhagen (1827), and eventually director of the new Copenhagen Conservatoire (1867). With Gade he was the chief representative of the Danish romantic school.

184. Emanuel Freiherr Schmysingk von Korff (1826–1903), a member of the Prussian aristocracy, was to become Blanca Meyerbeer's husband. In later life he was promoted to major general, and was a frequent guest of Kaiser Wilhelm II.

185. The plump and amiable Alexander II (Aleksandr Nikolayevich) (1818–81) had succeeded his father, who died on 4 March 1855 at the height of the Crimean War. During 1855 the French and British generals slowly tightened their grip upon Sebastopol, and on 11 September the Russians abandoned the town. The new tsar was obliged to confront the magnitude of Russia's defeat. He signed the Treaty of Paris (30 March 1856), which terminated the war, neutralized the Black Sea, asserted the independence of the Ottoman Empire, and removed Wallachia and Moldavia from Russian protection. Alexander had strong reforming convictions, and emancipated the serfs in the empire (1861).

186. *Dinorah*, no. 15 *Grand Trio final* ("Taisez-vous! pauvre victime!").

187. The tsar, like his father, was married to a German princess—in this case, Marie (Maria Alexandrovna), daughter of grand duke Ludwig II of Hesse-Darmstadt. The imperial visit to Berlin was part of a friendly outreach in Russian foreign policy. "If Alexander

hoped to preserve the glory his predecessors had won for Russia, he must seek greatness in the less exalted arena of domestic affairs. Russia must modernize if she were still to compete with Europe's Great Powers" (W. Bruce Lincoln, *The Romanovs* [London: Weidenfeld & Nicholson, 1981], p. 575).

188. Meyerbeer first saw the ballet *Paul und Virginie* on 8 December 1850. Hoguet, the choreographer, retired in 1856. He had came to Berlin as premier *danseur* in 1817, and stayed there all his professional life, becoming second choreographer, director of the ballet school, and ballet master.

189. See 10 and 14 July 1812 for Meyerbeer's first contact with Schiller's drama.

190. Tgb. *die zirkulierenden Papiere vom Mozartverein.*

191. The soprano Fortuni sang Marguerite de Valois in *Les Huguenots* at the Paris Opéra in 1855.

192. Aachen (Aix-la-Chapelle) was the former residence of Charlemagne. Apart from its famous cathedral and Carolingian architecture, it is a notable spa, and known as such since Roman times, with thirty-eight chloride-sulfur springs. The suburb of Burtscheid boasts the hottest spring in Central Europe (76° C), in the center of a rich coal bed.

193. This would have been Goethe's *Faust. Eine Tragödie (Erster Teil)* [Part One] (published 1808) with its themes of cosmic questioning, titanic academic dissatisfaction, seduction and infanticide.

194. This predates the Geneva performance listed by Loewenberg (col. 912).

195. The last years of Glinka's life were spent in St. Petersburg, Paris, and Berlin. During his sojourn in Berlin he was to have close contact with Meyerbeer. See David Brown, *Mikhail Glinka: A Biographical and Critical Study* (London: Oxford University Press, 1974), chap. 13, "Last Years," pp. 278–99, esp. p. 279.

196. Mosenthal, *Der Goldschmied von Ulm, dramatisches Märchen* in three acts. This was the first performance of Mosenthal's folk play [Richel 107].

197. See 1829 and 2 June 1855 for earlier reference to Fouqué's *Das Galgenmännchen.*

198. Adam, *Giselle.* See 26 February 1846 for details of this most famous and enduring of romantic ballets.

199. Mlle. Storck sang Catherine in the first performance of *L'Étoile du Nord* in Brunswick on 15 October 1855.

200. *Brautgeleite aus der Heimat* for eight-voice mixed chorus, for the wedding of princess Luise of Prussia with the prince regent of Baden (published Berlin and Posen, 1856; French translation, Paris, 1857).

201. Friedrich Wilhelm Gubitz, "Gedenkblatt an Amalia Beer," *Die Vossische Zeitung* 27 (June 1855), *1. Beilage.*

202. Wagner, *Lohengrin*, no. 17 Prelude to act 3 and no. 18 Wedding March ("Treulich geführt").

203. Liszt, *Deutscher Siegesmarsch*, for piano, S. 229 (c. 1853–56). This was an arrangement for military band, probably by Wieprecht himself; the full orchestral version by Liszt appeared only in 1865.

204. Rudolph von Herzberg (1818–93) studied composition with Dehn. He became the teacher of the Berlin Hof- and Domchors, the director of the Domchor, and eventually its music director (1858).

205. Alphonse Royer replaced Crosnier as director of the Paris Opéra on 1 July 1856.

206. *Dinorah*, no. 2b *Berceuse* ("Dors petite, dors tranquille").

207. Gläser had worked in Copenhagen from 1842, and was appointed court conductor there in 1845.

208. *Dinorah*, no. 2a *Récitatif* ("Bellah! ma chèvre chérie").

209. Dom St. Mauritius und Katharina in Magdeburg is the oldest Gothic church in Germany (1209), with Gothic pews and alabaster figures. At the razing of Magdeburg during the Thirty Years' War (1618–48), only the great Gothic cathedral was left standing among the ruins. This destruction shocked Protestant Europe and caused Saxony to join the cause under King Gustavus Adolphus of Sweden.

210. Johann Tserklaes, count of Tilly* (1559–1632), general of the Catholic League, won the battle of Magdeburg and in the ensuing "Magdebürgscher Reigen" [Magdeburg round dance] (30 May 1631) allowed his troops to pillage the city in one of the worst atrocities of the Thirty Years' War. This monumental conflict devastated Germany, but the Treaties of Westphalia that concluded the war established the status quo that was more or less to prevail in Europe until the First World War (1914–18).

211. The walk along the embankment in Magdeburg from the Lukasturm provides good views of the town and the river.

212. See January 1833.

213. See Offenbach's article, "Concours pour une opérette en un acte," *Revue et gazette musicale* 29 (20 July 1856): 230–31. Offenbach saw in the establishment of the Bouffes-Parisiens an opportunity to restore the true traditions of *opéra comique* "which had been vitiated by the inflated ideas of modern composers." His announcement of a competition for a one-act operetta was virtually a manifesto declaring the artistic intentions of the new theater (see Alexander Faris, *Jacques Offenbach* [London and Boston: Faber & Faber, 1980], p. 55). "Mais dès l'instant qu'une partition de l'*Étoile du Nord* — un grand opéra tout à fait celui-là — atteint un chiffre de près de deux cents réprésentations, et dépasse en quelques mois les recettes encaissés depuis trente ans par la *Dame blanche*, il faut bien qu'un directeur éclairé suive le courant du succès et s'abandonne aux impulsions de son public, qui va de préférence aux grandes choses" [But from the moment that the score of *L'Étoile du Nord*— and there can be no doubt that this is a *grand opéra*—attains nearly two hundred performances, and surpasses in a few months the cash receipts earned by *La Dame blanche* over thirty years, the enlightened director must follow the current of success and give himself over to the preferences of his public—who always prefer big shows]. Offenbach was undoubtedly exercising his caustic wit at Meyerbeer's expense, and ironically blaming him for the huge popularity of his *opéra comique*. Offenbach's artistic philosophy of 'small is beautiful' may seem superficially accurate in the light of his triumphs in the realm of *opéra bouffe*, but his attitude was perhaps based on a subliminal jealousy of Meyerbeer, and his real desire to write a grand romantic opera (see his attempts in the abortive *Die Rheinnixen* [1864] and *Robinson Crusoe* [1867], and final posthumous triumph with *Les Contes d'Hoffmann* [1881]). Alexander Faris again has a very interesting perspective on this issue: "His distaste for the pretentious and grandiose was genuine, but was there in his mockery of this kind of music, a secret envy? Did Offenbach's pilloring of Meyerbeer derive partly from a callow lack of confidence in his own ability to compose music on a large scale? Had he a reluctant admiration for the old master's magic?" (p. 155).

214. François Castil-Blaze, *Théâtres lyriques de Paris: L'Opéra-Italien de 1548 à 1856* (Paris: Castil-Blaze, 1856). Blaze quoted gleefully from Heine's viciously satirical *Lutitia (Lutèce)*, accusing Meyerbeer of manipulation (pp. 408–9).

215. Borghi-Mamo was to make her début as Fidès in *Le Prophète* later in the year.

216. The disappointment with his second opera and the disaster of his marriage had sent Glinka on his travels, including a prolonged visit to Spain. The creative outcome had

been a series of works originally entitled *Fantasies pittoresques*. The second of these, *Kamarinskaya* (1848), presents two Russian folk tunes that are elaborated: a wedding song of comfortable speed, and an alert dance song, both prefaced by a short introduction. This very personal and brilliant work was to exercise a great influence on the development of the Russian symphonic tradition, and corresponded perfectly to Glinka's own ideas: "I think it would be possible to unite the requirements of art and the demands of the public . . . to compose works which could satisfy both the connoisseur and the ordinary listener." (Cited by John S. Weissmann, "Glinka" [New York: Vox Productions, 1958], n.p.) Tchaikovsky was to liken it to the acorn from which grew the oak tree of Russian orchestral music.

217. These dances are from the ballet in act 2 of Glinka's *A Life for the Tsar*: no. 5 Polonaise and no. 8a Mazurka.

218. This was Count Matvey [Matthieu] Yurievich Wielhorsky, the famous cellist. His 1856 sojourn in Spa and his passionate devotion to the violoncello, are documented in contemporary accounts given by Albin Body in *Meyerbeer aux eaux de Spa* [Brussels: Veuve J. Rozez, 1885], pp. 123–25). The concert at the Hôtel d'Irlande was reported in the *Guide musical* (7 août 1856): "Là, au milieu de plusieurs Russes de distinction, se trouvait un auditeur rare, un fin connaisseur, un musicien. . . devant qui tous les fronts s'inclinent: Meyerbeer. L'illustre maestro a beaucoup applaudi. En dépit de ses 72 ans, M. le comte Wielhorski tire de son violoncelle des sons aussi pur, aussi moelleux, aussi fermes. . . . Meyerbeer a surtout admiré la musique d'air varié de la composition de M. le comte Michel Wielhorski, le frère de Matthieu. Cet air d'une simplicité charmante, a été rendu avec une piété fraternelle qui a touché tous les cœurs" [There, among many Russians of distinction, he found a very special audience, a refined connoisseur, a musician . . . respected by all: Meyerbeer. The illustrious maestro applauded a great deal. In spite of his seventy-two years, Count Wielhorsky drew the purest tones from his violoncello, now mellow, now firm. . . . Meyerbeer especially admired an air with variations composed by Count Michael Wielhorsky, brother of Matthew. This air of charming simplicity was played with a touching fraternal devotion]. The melody in question was probably Mikhail Wielhorsky's romance, "Autrefois," later transcribed by Franz Liszt (1885).

219. *L'Oiseau* had just been published. Jules Michelet (1798–1874) was the first and the greatest of the nationalist and romantic historians of France. He was head of the historical section of the National Archives (1831–52), and professor at the Collège de France (1831–52). His wife Adèle-Athénaïs Mialaret (1826–99) was also a writer and collaborated with her husband in a series of natural studies: *L'Oiseau* (1856), *L'Insecte* (1858) and *La Mer* (1872).

220. The vocal score of *Emma di Resburgo* (1819) was published in Berlin (as *Emma di Leicester*, 1820).

221. Appenzell, the mountainous German-speaking canton in northeastern Switzerland, is divided into a northern Protestant area, Ausser Rhoden, around Herisau, and a southern, largely Catholic area, Inner Rhoden, with Appenzell the capital. Heinrichsbad is in Herisau, and was a resort centered around its thermal springs. It subsequently changed ownership and purpose on several occasions (becoming, for example, a culinary school and a refugee center). (This information was kindly supplied by Beatrice and Roland Marthaler of Vufflens-le-Chateau, Switzerland.)

222. This is a diet of whey and whey products. The whey is the watery part of milk left when curds have formed and separated.

223. Presumably Léontine de Maësen (1835–1906), who was engaged by Carvalho for the Théâtre Lyrique from 1863 to 1865, where she created the role of Leïla in Bizet's

Les Pêcheurs de perles (30 September 1863). She had a younger sister, Camille, who later sang at the Opéra (see T. J. Walsh, *Second Empire Opera* [London: John Calder, 1981], p. 164).

224. Body designates her Mme. Wenevitinoff, and calls her Wielhorsky's niece (*Meyerbeer aux eaux de Spa*, p. 124).

225. See 6 October 1841 for Meyerbeer's first reading of Goethe's famous *Bildungsroman*.

226. *Gli Ugonotti* was given at La Fenice on 10 July 1856 with Medori as Valentine and Pancani as Raoul.

227. Hummel, Septet in C Major *(Septet militaire)* for flute, clarinet, trumpet, violin, violoncello, double bass, and pianoforte, op. 114 (1829).

228. Auber, *Manon Lescaut, opéra comique* in three acts (Scribe, after the Abbé Prévost's novel *Manon Lescaut* [1731]; Paris, Opéra Comique, 23 February 1856). This was only moderately successful by Auber's standards, with sixty-five performances. Revived in Paris in 1882. Admired by Charles Malherbe for Manon's death scene, unusual in Auber, and full of "simple grandeur et réelle émotion" [simple grandeur and real emotion] (Malherbe, *Auber: Biographie critique* [Paris: Librarie Renouard, 1911], p. 54).

229. Grétry, *Richard Cœur de Lion, opéra comique* in three acts (Sedaine, after a thirteenth-century fable; Paris, Opéra Comique, 21 October 1784). This was Grétry's masterpiece and most enduring work, performed on French stages throughout the nineteenth century, and also popular in English, German, and Swedish. It was revived into the twentieth century (Paris, 1910 and 1918; Liège, 1930; and Brussels, 1933), and is famous for the use of a recurrent melody to unify story and music.

230. Grétry, *Le Tableau parlant, opéra comique* (L. Anseaume; Paris, Comédie-Italienne, 20 September 1769). This work was very popular on French stages, given in Paris until 1865 and revived in 1895 and 1910. It was also performed in German, Spanish, Danish, Russian, Polish, Swedish, and Dutch.

231. Grisar, *Les Porcherons, opéra comique* in three acts (T. Sauvage & J. Gabriel; Paris, Opéra Comique, 12 January 1850), performed in Belgium, and revived in Paris in 1855 and 1865.

232. Gabrielli, *Les Elfes*, ballet in three acts (scenario Saint-Georges, choreography Mazilier; Paris, Opéra, 11 August 1856). Modestly successful, it was performed thirty-seven times until 1861.

233. "The ballet was long, Gabrielli's score being colourless and Mazilier's choreography at times lacking in originality. . . . But these shortcomings were almost forgotten in the light of Ferraris's personal triumph. . . . At the end of the ballet she was nearly smothered by the shower of bouquets" (Guest, *Ballet of the Second Empire*, pp. 106–7).

234. Amalia Ferraris (1830–1904) made her début in Turin, where she studied with the legendary teacher Carlo Blasis (1797–1878). She worked in London (1849) before going to the Opéra (1856), and to Russia in 1858. She created many roles in ballets by Mazilier, L. Petipa, Borri, and Montplaisir before her retirement in 1868, and was regarded as a supreme technician.

235. This was perhaps the violinist Carl Hermann Ehrfried Böhmer.

236. Clapisson, *Fanchonette, opéra comique* in three acts (De Leuven & Saint-Georges; Paris, Théâtre Lyrique, 1 March 1856). This was Clapisson's best work, and a considerable success, performed 192 times in Paris until 1868, revived in 1873 and 1880. Outside France it was not popular, and given only a few times in Belgium and Germany.

237. Cette = Sète, on the Gulf of Lions, near Montpellier.

238. Séjour, *Le Fils de la nuit, drame* in five acts; this was the première [Wicks 17416].

239. Mlle. Poinsot was singing the role of Berthe. See October 1851.

240. Offenbach, *La Rose de Saint-Flour, opérette* in one act (Carré; Paris, Bouffes-Parisiens, 18 June 1856).

241. Adam, *Les Pantins de Violette, opérette* in one act (L. Battu; Paris, Bouffes-Parisiens, 29 April 1856). This was Adam's last work: he died on 3 May, only four days after the première. This little opera was also given in German, Croatian, Czech, and Slovenian.

242. Winkler, whom Meyerbeer had known intimately, died on 24 September 1856. For Meyerbeer's first contact with him, as the playwright Theodor Hell, see the very beginning of his diary, in April 1812 (*BT*, 1:159; *DGM*, 1:257).

243. Guztkow, *Der Königsleutnant*, comedy in four acts, an occasional play written for the Goethe centenary in 1849 (published 1852) [Richel 56].

244. This is the famous German actor, Friedrich Ludwig Heinrich Haase (b.1826).

245. *Dinorah*, no. 4 *Duo de Dinorah et de Corentin* ("Encor, encor, encor!").

246. See 22 February 1855.

247. Gouin's daughter had taken over some of his functions for Meyerbeer.

248. The four-act tragedy *Klytämnestra* was the third and least successful of Michael Beer's plays. It was first performed in Berlin in 1819 and in Vienna the following year. Publication followed in 1823 [Richel 12].

249. Tempeltey's five-act tragedy *Klytämnestra* was performed in Berlin, Dresden, and Vienna in 1856, and published in 1857 [Richel 146].

250. This was the soprano Jenny Meyer (b. 1837).

251. Kotzebue, *Die beiden Klingsberge*, comedy in four acts (Vienna, Burgtheater 1799, and first published in 1801) [Richel 84].

252. *Ein Arzt*, an adaptation by August Wilhelm Hesse [pseud. J. C. H. Wages], was first produced in Berlin in 1847 and Vienna in 1851 (published 1869) [Richel 66].

253. Gluck, *Orfeo e Euridice*, no. 41 *Aria e Duetto* ("Che fiero momento!...Avvezza al contento").

254. The scene in the Elysian Fields in act 2 of *Orfeo e Euridice* is made up of a sequence of ballets, arias, and choruses (nos. 29–37).

255. Kalisch, *Der Aktienbudiker, Lokalposse* in three acts (first performed in Hamburg 1856) [Richel 78].

256. *La Stella del Nord* was given in New York on 24 September 1856.

257. The brothers were the publisher William Duncan Davison and the critic James William Davison.

258. Meyerbeer last saw *La Clemenza di Tito* in March 1813, during his months in Vienna. For a description of the opera see *DGM*, 1:362.

259. Mozart, *La Clemenza di Tito*. The trio no. 11 ("Vengo, aspettate") is "dramatically, the finest piece in the score . . . in which Annio and Publio, who sing together throughout the trio, mistake for joy the anguish expressed by Vitellia in her fierce *allegro*" (see Charles Osborne, *The Complete Operas of Mozart: A Critical Guide* [1978; reprint, London: Indigo, 1997], p. 307).

260. The act 1 finale no. 12b ("Deh! conservate, o dei!"), after the Capitol has been set on fire by Sextus, is the most notable part of the score of *La Clemenza di Tito*. "An agitated crowd off stage adds to the terror of the characters on stage, and Mozart builds up the whole ensemble to imposing dimensions" (see *Kobbé's Complete Opera Book*, ed. and rev. by the earl of Harewood [London: Putnam & Co., 1978], p. 129).

261. It is actually the opening of act 2, sc. 2, when the chorus thank Fate for sparing Titus (no. 15, "Ah, grazie si rendano"). The middle section of this ironically serene *andante* is a solo passage for Titus in which he thanks them for their loyalty.

262. These are the arias no. 10 ("Parto, parto") for Sextus (with clarinet obbligato) and no. 22b ("Non più di fiori") for Vitellia (with basset horn obbligato). Mozart wrote both instrumental parts especially for the famous woodwind player Anton Stadler.

263. For many years after Mozart's death, *La Clemenza di Tito* remained one of his most popular operas. "Now, critical and popular opinion places it decidedly below the three great operas which precede it . . ." (Osborne, *Complete Operas of Mozart*, p. 308).

264. The piece was actually *The Naiads* (1836), the most famous of Sterndale Bennett's five concert overtures, long in the popular repertory.

265. Legouvé, *Médée*, verse *tragédie* in three acts (Paris, Théâtre des Jeunes Artistes, 1854) [Wicks 19116].

266. Giuseppe Montanelli (1813–62) was the Italian poet and politician who founded the nationalist newspaper *L'Italia* (1847). He also formed the ministry in the revolutionary Tuscan republic (1849), for which he was sentenced in absentia to hard labor for life. During the 1850s he lived in exile in Paris, was a combatant in the war of independence in 1859, and was later a deputy to the Italian parliament (1861–62). He cooperated with Verdi in providing additions to Piave's libretto *Simone Boccanegra*

267. Beethoven, *Die Weihe des Hauses*, overture to Meisl's play, op. 124 (1822), written for the opening of the Theater-in-der-Josefstadt in Vienna.

268. Mendelssohn, Symphony no. 4 in A Major *(The Italian),* op. 90 (1833).

269. Silvio Pellico (1789–1854) was a writer and Italian patriot. He founded and edited the liberal nationalist journal *Il Conciliatore* (1818–19), endured eight years of imprisonment (1822–31), and from 1834 lived as librarian to the Marchesa di Barolo. As a writer he was known especially for the memoirs of his imprisonment (*Le mie prigioni*, 1832), but he was also the author of plays (like the tragedy *Francesca da Rimini*, 1815; translated by Byron), as well as mystic and religious poetry *(Cantiche).*

270. Giraud's *I gelosi fortunati* was written between 1815 and 1824.

271. Siegfried Julius Josephy died on 22 October 1856. He was principally a book dealer, being the owner of the Haude and Spenersche Buchhandlung.

272. Anton Rubinstein, *Das verlorene Paradies*, sacred oratorio (text after John Milton), op. 54.

273. Laube, *Graf Essex*, tragedy in five acts in blank verse and prose (Vienna, Burgtheater February 1856, published in the same year) [Richel 95]. This was Laube's greatest success, dealing with the well-known story of the rebellion by the earl of Essex and the opportunity to save him by the ring entrusted to Lady Nottingham.

274. Johann Sebastian Bach, Mass in B Minor, BWV 232 (1733).

275. The story of Pia can ultimately be traced to the conclusion of canto 5 of Dante's *Purgatorio*. It was used by Bartolomeo Sestini for his novella *Pia de' Tolomei*, the source of Salvatore Cammarano's libretto for Donizetti (February 1837).

276. Mendelssohn, *Psalm 95*, op. 46 (1839).

277. Mendelssohn, *Die erste Walpurgisnacht*, cantata for chorus and orchestra (words by J. W. von Goethe), op. 60 (1832).

278. Mendelssohn, Concerto for Violin and Orchestra in E Minor, op. 64 (1844).

279. Haydn, Symphony no. 96 in D Major *(The Miracle)* (1791).

280. Mendelssohn, *The Hebrides (Fingal's Cave)* overture, op. 26 (1830, rev. 1832).

281. By 1856 Liszt had completed six of his thirteen symphonic poems: *Prometheus*

(1850), *Orpheus* (1854–56), *Hungaria* (1856), *Hunnenschlacht* (1856), *Les Préludes* (1856), *Tasso–Lamento e Trionfo* (1856).

282. This was Arturo Napoleone (Artur Napoleão dos Santos) (1843–1925), a Brazilian pianist, composer and teacher. He made his first concert appearance at the age of seven in Lisbon (1850), and then began touring Europe (1852): London, Paris, Berlin, and Weimar. After concert tours in Brazil and the United States, he settled in Rio de Janeiro (1868) as a performer, businessman, and teacher, established the Sociedade de Concertos Classicos, founded a publishing house (1878), and composed an opera, songs, orchestral works, and piano pieces. Napoleon was thirteen, not eleven, when he played in Berlin. Meyerbeer's record puts in question the dates given in Sadie, *New Grove Dictionary of Music,* 13:32) for the child pianist's visit to Berlin (1854) and for the commencement of his concert tour to Brazil (1855).

283. Jean F. Schucht was eventually to write a survey of the composer's life and work, *Meyerbeers Leben und Bildungsgang, seine Stellung als Operkomponist im Vergleich zu den Tondichtern der Neuzeit* (Leipzig: H. Mattes, 1869), which is regarded as unreliable in detail.

284. Mendelssohn, String Quintet no. 2 in B-flat Major, op. 87 (1845).

285. Beethoven, String Quintet in C Major, op. 29 (1801).

286. Haydn, String Quartet in D Major *(The Lark),* op. 64, no. 5 (1790).

287. The Chevillard Quartet had been touring various German cities during 1855–56. See 22 December 1852.

288. See 6 November 1856.

289. Haydn, Symphony no. 101 in D Major *(The Clock)* (1794).

290. Beethoven, Symphony no. 4 in B-flat Major, op. 60 (1806).

291. Jean Joseph Bott (1826–95) a violinist and conductor, was a native of Kassel. He studied with his father and the court musician A. Bott, and later with M. Hauptmann and L. Spohr. He became court conductor at Meiningen (1852–57) and Hanover (1865), retired in 1878, and settled in New York (1885). He wrote two operas, a symphony, overtures, violin concertos, and piano music.

292. Mozart, String Quartet no. 19 in C major *(Dissonance),* K. 465 (1785).

293. Schubert, String Quintet in C Major, D. 956 (1828).

294. Schubert, String Quartet no. 14 in D Minor *(Death and the Maiden),* D. 810 (1824).

295. Beethoven, String Quartet no. 14 in C-sharp Minor, op. 131 (1826).

296. Schumann, Symphony no. 3 in E-flat Major *(The Rhenish),* op. 97 (1850).

297. Beethoven, Concerto for Piano and Orchestra no. 5 in E-flat Major *(The Emperor),* op. 73 (1809).

298. Schubert, *Psalm 23* for female quartet with piano (words from the Bible, trans. M. Mendelssohn), D. 706 (1820).

299. Mozart, *Ave verum corpus,* motet in D Major for chorus, strings and organ, K. 618 (1791).

300. Beethoven, String Quartet no. 15 in A Minor, op. 132 (1825).

301. Beethoven, String Quartet no. 9 in C Major *(Rasumovsky),* op. 59, no. 3 (1805–6).

302. This is without doubt no. 14, the *Duo final* for tenor and baritone, "Vous qui de la chevalrie," one of the best moments in Halévy's *La Reine de Chypre.* Clément & Larousse comment: "Le grand duo. . . dans lequel se trouve la romance: *Triste exilé,* est, jusqu'à l'allégro, un des plus beaux morceaux du répertoire; interprété par Duprez et Baroilhet, il électrisait l'auditoire" [the big duet . . . which interpolates the romance "Triste exilé," and including the *allegro,* is one of the great pieces in the repertoire; interpreted by Duprez

and Baroilhet, it electrified the audience] (2:934). The piece was chosen for the tenor Theodore Formes, who was engaged by the Court Opera in Berlin in 1851, and the bass Heinrich Rudolf Salomon, who was contracted in 1850.

303. Gluck, *Iphigénie en Tauride, Introduction et chœur* ("Grands Dieux! soyez-nous secourables") for Iphigénie and a chorus of priestesses.

304. This is *Les Huguenots,* no. 18, the pivotal act 3 duet for soprano and bass ("Dans la nuit"), the cathartic moral encounter between Valentine and Marcel, in which integrity, compassion, and loving-kindness win a decisive victory over religious prejudice, class, and sexual determinants.

305. Venzano's famous *Valzer cantabile* was often included in the Lesson Scene of *The Barber of Seville.*

306. Richel [138] cites the play *Stille Wasser sind tief,* adapted from the English by Friedrich Ludwig Schröder (1744–1816), and published in 1804, even though the first performance in Berlin was in 1795. Beaumont and Fletcher, whether alone or in collaboration, did not write a play of this name. It could possibly be a translation of *Still Waters Run Deep* by Tom Taylor (1817–80), which had just been produced at the Olympic Theatre in London (1855).

307. Maltitz, *Die Leibrente,* comedy in one act (first performed in Dresden, 1835; in Berlin, 1836; and published 1838) [Richel 103].

308. This was probably the *Sanctus* from Palestrina's *Missa Papae Marcelli* for six voices (published 1567).

309. Roland de Lassus, "Misere mei Deus," no. 4 from the *Psalmi Davidis poenitentiales* for five voices (published 1584).

310. This is from Lotti's *Duette, terzetti e madrigali* (1705).

311. Fioravanti's church music was written in his capacity as *maestro di cappella* at St. Peter's in Rome from 1816.

312. This is from Eccard's *Neue geistliche und weltliche Lieder mit 4 und 5 Stimmen* (1589; ed. in score by R. Eitner, in *Publikationen älterer Musik*, vol. 25).

313. Johann Michael Bach (1648–94). Some of his motets were published in *Denkmäler deutscher Tonkunst* (vols. 49–50).

314. Mendelssohn, *Ave Maria,* no. 2 from *Three Sacred Pieces* for tenor, chorus, and organ, op. 23 (1830).

315. Mozart, String Quartet no. 21 in D Major *(Prussian),* K.575 (1789).

316. This is the first of Beethoven's *Rasumovsky* Quartets (1806). See 16 November 1856.

317. This was the father of Meyerbeer's future son-in-law, Emanuel.

318. Méhul, *Adrien,* opera in three acts (F. B. Hoffman, after Metastasio's *Adriano in Siria*; Paris, Opéra, 4 June 1799). It had been written in 1792, but production was not permitted then, and it was not performed in Paris until 1803. The overture was taken from an earlier work, *Horatius Coclès.*

319. Mozart, Piano Sonatas no. 3 in B-flat Major, K. 281 (1775) and no. 12 in F Major, K. 332 (1783), respectively.

320. Ernst Tschirch had died in Berlin on 26 December 1856. His opera *Frithjof* was first produced in Stettin (1852). See 7 December 1851 for Meyerbeer's thoughts about this family of musicians.

321. Spohr, Symphony no. 5 in C Minor, op. 102 (1837).

322. Schumann, *Manfred,* incidental music to the play by Byron (1817), op. 115 (1849).

323. Beethoven, "Ah! perfido," scene and aria (words from Metastasio's *Achille in Sciro*), op. 65 (1795–96).

324. Johann Strauss *(Sohn)* had begun a highly successful series of annual concerts in the Russian capital in 1853.

325. Dorn, *Ein Tag in Russland, komische Oper* in three acts (J. C. Grünbaum, after Scribe; Berlin, Court Opera, 19 December 1856). The works embodies Dorn's penchant for sentimentality and light humor.

326. Haydn, Symphony no. 94 in G Major *(The Surprise)* (1791). The drum roll *("mit dem Paukenschlag")* in the slow movement helped to make this "Haydn's most celebrated piece of music" for at least a century and a half (H. C. Robbins Landon, *Notes on Symphonies 93–104 "London Symphonies"* [London: Decca, 1976, p. 15).

327. Taubert, *Joggeli*, comic opera (Köster, after Gotthelf's *Novelle* [1848]; Berlin, 1 October 1853). "C'est une gracieuse idylle, traitée avec goût par le musicien" [this is a gracious idyll, handled with taste by the composer] (Clément & Larousse, 1:614).

328. Fr. "ground."

329. Birch-Pfeiffer, *Die Grille*, drama in one act (this was the Berlin première; the first Viennese performance followed a year later) [Richel 17].

330. *La Petite Fadette* was another of George Sand's idyllic romances of country life (1848). In it an ungovernable termagant is transformed by the miraculous alchemy of love from a village brat into a sweet, affectionate, and hardworking young woman—a "juvenile version of *The Taming of the Shrew*, to which Vladimir Kerénine later compared it" (Curtis Cate, *George Sand: A Biography* [New York: Avon Books, 1975], p. 606).

331. Brachvogel, *Adalbert vom Babenberge*, tragedy in five acts [Richel 23].

Index of Names

Names in brackets give the authentic or original form. Names in parentheses provide additional or supplementary information. An asterisk identifies an entry in the Register of Names (vol. 1, pp. 86–251). Numbers in parentheses indicate references in the endnotes.

Abt, bass in Gotha, 316
Achard, Pierre-Frédéric, actor, 56, (79)
Achilles, Mademoiselle, singer in Dresden, 308
Adam*, Adolphe-Charles, composer, 52, 54, 59, (76), 94, 99, 143, 158, 179, 180, 183–84, 186, 187, 190, (205), (206), (207), 209, 210, 213, 232, 239, 242, 243, 245, 250, (256), (257), (258), 275, 290, (297), 333, 335, 337, (351), 382, 383, 391, (417)
Aeschylus*, Greek tragedian, 147, 171, (192)
Agoult, Marie-Cathérine-Sophie, comtesse d', 189
Aguado, Marquis, dilettante photographer, 210
Aigoin, Marie-Charles-Louis, writer, 239, 241, (257)
Aland, student on Rügen, 55
Alary*, Jules-Eugène-Abraham [Giulio Eugenio Abramo], composer, 151, (193)
Albert, Ferdinand-François, choreographer, (81)
Albert Franz August Karl Emanuel*, prince consort of England, 12, (192), 323
Alberti, Madame, singer in Venice, 366
Albertini-Baucardé, Augusta, soprano in Verona, 360–61, (407)
Alboize de Pujol, Jules-Edouard, librettist, (78)
Alboni*, Marietta [Maria Anna Marzia],

singer, 37, 40, 53, 54, 55, 57, 116, 118, 124, (136), 268, 331
Albrecht* (Friedrich Heinrich), prince of Prussia, 86, 141, 145
Albrecht, Princess, of Meiningen. *See* Charlotte, princess of Saxe-Meiningen
Albrecht*, crown prince and then king of Saxony, 24
Alexander II, emperor of Russia, 364, 379, 380, (409), (416–17)
Alexandra Feodorovna*, empress of Russia, sister of King Friedrich Wilhelm IV of Prussia, 158, 164, (195)
Alexandre*, Jacob, organ-maker, 188, (206), 246
Alfieri*, Vittorio, Conte, dramatist, (349), 375, (415)
Allary, Raoul, instrument-maker, 275
Ander*, Aloys, tenor, 25, 26, 27, 28, 29, 32, 38, 39, 40, 41, 281, 337, 338, (352), 357, (403)
Anderson, musician in London, 325
Andlaw-Birseck*, Franz Xaver, Reichsfreiherr von, Baden ambassador, 28
Andral, Gabriel, Dr., physician in Paris, 116, (135), 172, 271
André [Andrée], baron d', French diplomat, 23, 24, 146,
Anelli, Angelo, librettist,
Angelini, bass in Paris and Vienna, 333, 376
Angely*, Louis, dramatist, 294, (305)

426

Index of Scholars

(Biography, Criticism, History, Geography)

Alphandéry, Marie-Fernande, 303
Altmann, Wilhelm, 71, 346

Becker, Gudrun, 18
Becker, Heinz, 18, 301, 410
Becker, Heinz and Gudrun, 18, 128, 132, 136, 192, 297–98, 305, 403, 414
Benham, Martin, 349
Berlioz, Hector, 317
Body, Albin, 76, 419, 420
Bournonville, August, 304–5, 349, 350, 352, 353–54
Briefwechsel und Tagebücher (BT): I (405, 410, 412, 421); III (412); IV (67, 253, 299); V (63, 65, 66, 67, 68, 69, 70, 72, 78, 81, 82, 125, 126, 127, 128, 130, 134, 137, 138, 139, 140, 194, 195, 199, 200, 204, 302)
Brown, David, 417
Bruce Lincoln, W., 417
Budden, Julian, 411, 412, 413
Burk, John, 343
Bussi, Francesco, 412

Cairns, David, 196
Casanova, Carla Maria, (408)
Castil-Blaze, François, 351, 418
Cate, Curtis, 425
Celi, Claudia, 407
Charlton, David, 298
Cherpas, Teresa, 297
Chorley, Henry Fothergill, 77, 252, 257, 346, 347–48, 415
Clément, Félix and Pierre Larousse, 18, 78, 130, 196, 203, 205, 206, 251, 252, 254, 255, 257, 259, 301, 350, 423, 425

Cohen, Selma Jeanne, 407
Conati, Marcello, 192
Corghi, Azio, 196

Diaries of Giacomo Meyerbeer, The (DGM): I (299, 405, 412, 421)
Döhring, Sieghard, 130
Dole, Nathan Haskell, 67, 132, 297, 298, 301

Eitner, Robert, 344, 350, 424
Ella, John, 202

Faris, Alexander, 418
Fétis, François, 299, 300
Figaro, Le 406
Forbes, Elizabeth, 67, 192
Fulcher, Jane, 257–58, 305

Galland, Marthe, 255
Girardi, Michele, and Franco Rossi, 404
Gold, Mick, 297
Gossett, Philip, 348
Grüneisen, Charles L., 346
Guest, Ivor, 302, 405, 407, 420
Guide to Belgium and Holland, 75
Gumbel, Andrew, 137
Gutman, Robert, 138, 346

Harewood, earl of, 421
Hansell, Kathleen Kuzmick, 408
Hensel, Sebastian, 134
Henze-Döhring, Sabine, 18, 196
Hughes, Spike, 407

Illustrated London News, The, 348

Index of Stage Works

Title, genre, dramatist/librettist/choreographer, and composer are listed